KU-744-327

Business Information Systems

A PROBLEM-SOLVING APPROACH

Kenneth C. Laudon
NEW YORK UNIVERSITY

Jane Price Laudon
AZIMUTH CORPORATION

THE DRYDEN PRESS

Chicago Fort Worth San Francisco Philadelphia Montreal Toronto London Sydney Tokyo

Acquisitions Editor: DeVilla Williams
Developmental Editor: Mary Beth Nelligan
Project Editors: Teresa Chartos, Paula Dempsey
Production Manager: Barb Bahnsen
Permissions Editors: Doris Milligan, Cindy Lombardo
Director of Editing, Design, and Production: Jane Perkins

Text and Cover Designer: Rebecca Lemna
Copy Editor: Pat Lewis
Indexer: Leoni McVey
Compositor: Weimer Typesetting Company, Inc.
Text Type: 10/12 Stempel Garamond

Library of Congress Cataloging-in-Publication Data

Laudon, Kenneth C., 1944-
Business information systems: a problem solving approach /
Kenneth C. Laudon, Jane Price Laudon.
p. cm.
Includes bibliographical references and index.
ISBN 0-03-030453-9
1. Management information systems. I. Laudon, Jane Price.
II. Title.
T58.6.L375 1991
658.4'038—dc20 90-37599
CIP

Printed in the United States of America
12-041-98765432

Address orders:
The Dryden Press
Orlando, FL 32887

Address editorial correspondence:
The Dryden Press
908 N. Elm St.
Hinsdale, IL 60521

The Dryden Press
Holt, Rinehart and Winston
Saunders College Publishing

Cover Source: © Herb Comess.
Photo Researcher: Mary E. Goljenboom, Ferret Research, Inc.

The Dryden Press Series in Information Systems

ARTHUR ANDERSEN & Co., BOYNTON AND SHANK
Foundations of Business Systems: Projects and Cases

ARTHUR ANDERSEN & Co., FLAATTEN, McCUBBREY, O'RIORDAN, AND BURGESS
Foundations of Business Systems

BRADLEY
Case Studies in Business Data Bases

BRADLEY
Introduction to Data Base Management

BRADLEY
Introduction to Data Base Management in Business
Second Edition

BURSTEIN AND MARTIN
Computer Information Systems

GOLDSTEIN SOFTWARE, INC.
Joe Spreadsheet Statistical

GOLDSTEIN SOFTWARE, INC.
Joe Spreadsheet Statistical, Macintosh Version

GRAY, KING, WATSON, AND McLEAN
Management of Information Systems

HARRINGTON
Making Database Management Work

HARRINGTON
Microsoft® Works: A Window to Computing

HARRINGTON
Relational Database Management for Microcomputers: Design and Implementation

LAUDON AND LAUDON
Business Information Systems: A Problem-Solving Approach

LAUDON, LAUDON, AND WEILL
The Integrated Solution

LIEBOWITZ
The Dynamics of Decision Support Systems and Expert Systems

MARTIN AND BURSTEIN
Computer Systems Fundamentals

PARKER
Computers and Their Applications
Second Edition

PARKER
Computers and Their Applications
Second Edition
With Productivity Software Tools

PARKER
Microcomputers: Concepts and Applications

PARKER
Productivity Software Guide
Third Edition

PARKER
Understanding Computers and Information Processing: Today and Tomorrow
Third Edition

PRICE
Microcomputer Applications

PRICE
Microcomputer Applications Workbook

ROCHE
Telecommunications and Business Strategy

About the Authors

KENNETH C. LAUDON is Professor of Information Systems at New York University's Stern Graduate School of Business. At Stern he is the MIS Course Coordinator and the MBA Information Systems Curriculum Coordinator. He has played an important role in defining new teaching materials, content, and techniques for business students throughout the United States. Ken holds a B.A. in economics and philosophy from Stanford University and a Ph.D. from Columbia University.

Ken has written five books and numerous articles in academic journals about the organizational and societal impacts of information technology. He has testified before Congress on many occasions, and has worked as a consultant to the Office of Technology Assessment (United States Congress), the Office of the President, several executive branch agencies, and congressional committees.

Ken's current research deals with the planning and management of very large-scale systems for the 1990s. This research is funded by the National Science Foundation and private corporations.

JANE PRICE LAUDON is a management consultant in the information systems area and a professional writer. She has written six books. Her special interests include systems analysis and design, software evaluation, and teaching business professionals how to design and use information systems. She has taught at the New York University Stern Graduate School of Business and at Columbia University. She received her B.A. from Barnard College, M.A. from Harvard University, and Ph.D. from Columbia University. For the past eight years, Jane has been an information systems consultant for leading *Fortune* 500 companies. She and her husband, Ken, have two daughters, Erica and Elisabeth.

Business Information Systems: A Problem-Solving Approach is the second book the Laudons have written together. It reflects the Laudons' personal belief that undergraduate information systems texts must include a multidimensional perspective involving people, technology, and organizations and that such books must be, above all, readable, enjoyable, and informative.

Preface

This book is based on the premise that virtually all college graduates in the 1990s will be employed in computerized organizations. Regardless of their occupation, college graduates will be expected by employers to understand, use, and possibly design computer-based information systems.

Accordingly, we wrote this book for nontechnical undergraduate students in finance, accounting, management, information systems, and the liberal arts who will find a knowledge of information systems and technology vital for professional success. This book also provides a broad foundation and understanding for students who will become MIS majors.

This text presents the introductory information systems course from a business and problem-solving perspective. Traditionally, the introductory information systems course has had a technology or computer hardware orientation. Much of the course was devoted to the computer input, output, and processing equipment, with a secondary focus on introductory programming concepts.

Increasingly, many colleges, universities, and business employers are finding that students cannot apply computer technology effectively unless they understand more about business—important features of business organizations, business processes, and how businesses use information and information systems. They realize that students cannot appreciate the full potential of information technology unless they can see how it is used in real-world business settings. Moreover, information technology has been changing so rapidly that using computer hardware and software effectively requires considerably less technical knowledge than in the past. Both businesses and educators are finding that the major stumbling block to using computers effectively is not insufficient knowledge of the nuts and bolts of computers but the need for greater understanding of the role of information technology in business and how it can be applied effectively to solve business problems.

Unique Thrusts of the Book

Our text departs from previous texts by treating information systems as more than just computers. Instead, we see information systems as composed of information technologies, business organizations, and people. We emphasize the broader concepts of information systems rather than computer systems and information systems literacy rather than computer literacy. By information systems literacy, we mean a full understanding of business organizations and individuals from a behavioral perspective combined with knowledge of information technology. In this view, a firm's procedures, values, and plans, as well as the training it provides for its employees, are just as important as information technology.

One solid discovery of the last five years is that information technology alone is not sufficient to bring about changes in business productivity or personal effectiveness. We need to redesign business organizations, create new roles for people, and develop new ideas about how to use information technology wisely to achieve higher levels of productivity.

In the systems environment of the 1990s, the computer is just one of many technical elements in a network of devices that may include "smart" printers, facsimile machines, plotters, modems, and a host of other devices. "Data Processing" is just one of many functions that such networks perform. A host of new functions have appeared: image processing, graphics, desktop publishing, communications, and group support, to name only a few. Therefore, this book will shift from a singular focus on the "computer in the box" toward an understanding of the many information technologies used in computer-based networks.

Our textbook further departs from the past by avoiding a simple "hands-on" approach to undergraduate education. Instead, the approach taken emphasizes teaching critical thinking and problem-solving skills and showing how information systems fit into the broader context of business organizations. We will be exploring how businesses and individuals design and use information systems to solve business problems.

Without a broader understanding of the business and organizational setting of systems, mere computer literacy, or hands-on training, will not suffice as the basis of an enduring professional education. Knowing how to hit keys on the keyboard is insufficient preparation for the 1990s. It is more important to know why and how an information system might solve a business problem, how to evaluate software and hardware, and what organizational changes are required to make systems work for a business. Knowing the difference between an organizational problem, a people problem, and a technology problem is central to this understanding.

How This Book Prepares You for the 1990s

During this decade, the success of a business—whether it becomes the market leader in design and quality, the low-cost producer, or a successful innovator—will increasingly depend on the quality of its information systems and technologies. In turn, the quality of a business's systems and technologies will depend largely on you—the professionals who work in the firm. You will be expected to perform the following functions: suggest new uses for information systems; participate in the design of systems; purchase information systems equipment; solve business problems using information technology; and understand the limitations of information technology. These new roles and expectations for business professionals require a much deeper understanding of information and information systems than ever before.

As a business owner or employee, you will be expected to assimilate a dizzying array of new hardware, software, and telecommunications developments. To keep up with the rapid pace of change tomorrow, you will need a firm foundation today. All of your reading, analysis, writing, and problem-solving skills will be required.

To prepare you for this world of the mid-to-late 1990s, this book aims to accomplish three goals:

- Show you how to envision, design, and evaluate computer-based solutions to typical business problems
- Teach you how to use contemporary and emerging hardware and software tools
- Provide enduring concepts for understanding information systems that you can apply in your future careers or information systems courses

The various features of the book accomplish these objectives in a variety of ways.

Providing Critical Thinking and Problem-Solving Skills

Computers cannot solve problems unless people can first understand the problem, describe it, and then design a solution. Accordingly, Part 3 of this book (Problem Solving with Information Systems) is devoted to this topic. Earlier chapters introduce problem solving by providing a framework for analyzing business problems in terms of people, organizational, and technological dimensions.

How we define a problem fundamentally shapes the solutions we devise. Some problems can be solved by changing organizational structure, management, or procedures. Others require a solution that changes the way an existing information system works or provides an entirely new one. Thus, problem solving in the information systems world requires a methodology that considers technology, people, and organizations. This methodology, accompanied by real-world case studies depicting alternative solutions, is presented in two core chapters of the text. It appears in many of the other chapters as well.

Using Business Information Technologies

This book offers an unparalleled package of both internal and supplementary hands-on materials that make it relatively easy to learn how to use contemporary technology to solve business problems.

Parts 2 and 4—Foundations of Information Technologies and Overview of Business Information Systems—provide an overview and in-depth understanding of business information technologies using real-world examples from the business world. Because personal computers are important tools for individual workers, entrepreneurs, and large corporations, many examples of personal computer hardware, software, and applications are included. Yet, mainframes, minicomputers, long-distance telecommunications networks, and large corporate information systems also receive full discussion. The focus of the text is the entire array of contemporary information technologies.

Internal software case studies in key chapters provide the opportunity to use spreadsheet and database software to solve real business problems. These cases are "generic" in the sense that they can be used with any available software on your campus or in your home.

Hands-on software exercises have played an important role in introductory information systems courses because they have enormous potential for teaching information systems concepts. In competing texts, the primary emphasis has been on learning commands and keystrokes to gain facility with various software packages. In this text, software exercises are problem driven. The emphasis is placed on developing concepts and skills for applying software to problem solving. In both the text and the supplemental software package, students are first presented with problems and then are taught how to use software to solve them.

Providing an Enduring Sense of Understanding

Most of the hardware and software you see now is at least five years old. Much of it will be gone in five to ten years, replaced by better hardware and software. Hence some of what you learn today will no longer be relevant five years after graduation. What will be relevant?

We believe critical thinking and problem-solving skills will last a lifetime. In addition, many underlying principles of business information systems—the structure of computing hardware and software and ways of using this technology intelligently—will not change.

For instance, the basic principles of how computer hardware and software work will not have changed a great deal by the year 2000. Some radically new principles of computing may be discovered, but full implementation of totally new computing concepts usually takes a long time. Similarly, the basic professional, financial, accounting, and management knowledge base will change slowly over the years. The basic skills that enable you first to understand a problem and then to solve it will not change.

In addition to enhancing your knowledge of contemporary information systems, this text develops a more fundamental understanding of technology, business organizations, and human beings. We believe this understanding is necessary to cope with a rapidly changing technological base.

Overview of the Book

Part 1 describes the major themes of the book and introduces the role of information systems in contemporary businesses. These chapters are especially important for describing the major challenges that we all face in applying information technology effectively. This part raises several major questions: What is an information system? What is a business? How much do I need to know about information systems and why?

Part 2 provides the technical foundation for understanding information and telecommunications technologies. It answers two questions: How do information technologies work? How are they likely to change in the near future? Students with no prior background in computing will find Part 2 very helpful because it provides a basic foundation for computing and systems literacy. More advanced students will find that these chapters considerably extend and update their knowledge of contemporary systems. Chapter 7 is entirely devoted to new telecommunications technologies, and Chapter 8 describes current leading-edge business uses of expert systems.

Part 3 describes how to use the knowledge gained in Parts 1 and 2 to analyze and design solutions to business problems. This part focuses on the question, How can information systems be used to solve a business problem? Two entire chapters in Part 3 are devoted to critical thinking and problem solving. Chapter 9 describes an overall methodology for analyzing business problems. Chapter 10 puts this methodology to work. The emphasis throughout is on a broad understanding of how organizations, technologies, and people must work together. Chapter 11 examines various ways of building systems using basic problem-solving methods and alternative systems development methodologies.

Part 4 provides a more extensive introduction to real-world information systems in business. It answers two major questions: How do contemporary businesses use information systems? What broader social and organizational concerns are raised by information systems in business? The emphasis here is on real-world examples of information systems and how these systems fit into the larger world of business organizations. Chapters 13 and 14 are noteworthy for their description of an entirely new class of systems—knowledge-based systems for office automation and professional work.

Some of the new themes covered in this book are given complete chapter-length treatment. Among these unique chapters are Systems for Knowledge Work, Problem Solving and Critical Thinking Skills, and Designing Information Systems Solutions.

Book Design Features

This book makes several large stylistic departures from previous works. These design features reflect the authors' concern for providing a comprehensive understanding of issues and a highly readable text that students and professors will appreciate.

Focus On Boxes · In each chapter you will find examples of the four highlighted Focus On boxes. The purpose of these boxes is to present contemporary examples of the conceptual foundation, design, use, and management of information technology and systems. Focus On box themes are:

- **Technology:** Hardware, software, telecommunications, and data and information storage.

- **Organizations:** Histories, activities, and plans of business organizations using information systems.
- **People:** Careers and experiences of individuals working with systems.
- **Problem solving:** Examples of successful and unsuccessful business solutions and their consequences.

Real-World Examples · Only real-world examples are used throughout the text for cases and Focus On boxes. More than 200 American and foreign corporations are discussed (see the Organization Index).

Problem-Solving Exercises · Each chapter concludes with exercises or projects based on the material covered in the chapter. All of these exercises are designed to sharpen problem-solving skills and can be used with any available software or paper and pencil.

Chapter Cases · Thirty-two real-world business cases are included in the text, one at the beginning and one at the end of each chapter. The chapter-opening cases introduce or illustrate the major theme of each chapter. Typically, they focus on how a real-world business organization uses a technology (or fails to use it properly) to solve a problem. The chapter-ending cases, called "Problem-Solving Cases," help students review the material covered in each chapter and apply this new knowledge to specific problems.

Leading-Edge Application Section · Many chapters conclude with an illustration of an information systems application related to chapter topics that uses leading-edge information technology.

Chapter Format

We have made every effort to ensure that each chapter is lively, informative, and often provocative of further debate, discussion, and thought. Each chapter uses the following format:

- A detailed outline at the beginning to provide an overview of chapter contents
- A list of chapter learning objectives
- A one-page chapter-opening case
- A summary that identifies key themes, terms, and topics introduced in the chapter
- A list of key terms for students to review
- A set of review questions for student use in reading
- A set of discussion questions for the instructor and students to use in class discussion or individual study
- Problem-solving exercises at the end
- A problem-solving case at the end

- A list of references at the end to provide students with guidance for additional research or term papers

Instructional Support Materials

Many additional resources available with this text will assist students in learning more about information systems.

Software

In our experience teaching this course, we have found that a strong computer-based learning package is vital to strengthen student understanding. The support package for this text includes a software problem case package called *The Integrated Solution. The Integrated Solution* consists of 21 business problem-solving cases in a book with accompanying computer diskettes. These cases provide students with a truly unique opportunity to learn how software is actually used in business settings. They are based on real-world problems and solutions from American businesses. The cases are solved using spreadsheet, database, and word processing software. *The Integrated Solution* includes documentation on how to use WordPerfect, Lotus 1-2-3, and dBASE III PLUS (and most of their clone products). If software is not available, *The Integrated Solution* can be purchased with academic versions of WordPerfect 4.2, dBase III PLUS, and VP Planner Plus. In addition, a tutorial lab manual, *Productivity Software Guide* by Charles S. Parker, provides complete proficiency-base software instructions and abundant exercises. The *Productivity Software Guide* introduces students to MS DOS, WordPerfect 4.2, 5.0, and 5.1, dBase III PLUS, as well as Lotus 1-2-3 and Joe Spreadsheet. The *Productivity Software Guide* is also available in individual modules (including one covering dBase IV), allowing you to select the modules that best fit your course. The guide can also be purchased with academic versions of WordPerfect 4.2, dBase III PLUS, and a full-featured version of Joe Spreadsheet.

Instructor's Resource Manual

The *Instructor's Resource Manual,* written by Jane and Ken Laudon, provides additional material to support your classroom preparation and lecture presentation. For each of the 16 chapters of the text, the *Instructor's Resource Manual* includes a chapter summary, learning objectives, key terms, lecture outline, answers to review questions, answers to discussion questions, answers to case questions, and transparency masters.

Student Study Guide

The *Student Study Guide,* written by Marilyn Moore of Purdue University—Calumet, offers students an innovative and active approach to the study of information systems. The guide begins by having students assess their understanding of textual concepts, and then initiates further exploration of focus topics and problem-solving techniques. The guide features a tutorial walk-through summary, keyed to the learning objectives; chapter terminology review; questions on the focus boxes and vignettes; short-answer questions; additional resources section; and assignments with software applications.

Test Bank

The *Test Bank,* written by Milan Kaldenberg of Northwest Nazarene College, contains more than 2,100 test items, including multiple choice, true/false, matching, vocabulary application, short-answer questions, and problem-solving applications. Questions are keyed to the chapter learning objectives and include an answer key noting the question level and cognitive type.

The *Test Bank* is also available on the ExaMaster Computerized Test Bank in IBM 5¼", 3½", and Macintosh versions. The electronic versions allow instructors to easily preview, edit, or delete questions as well as add their own questions, print scrambled forms of tests, and print answer keys.

Transparency Acetates

A set of approximately 100 full-color transparency acetates is available to illustrate and explain key concepts. The acetates feature both selected text diagrams and new pieces of art. Teaching notes for each transparency are included.

Videotapes

A growing collection of videotapes from Dryden's new Information Processing Video Library is available to adopters of *Business Information Systems: A Problem-Solving Approach.* Videos focus on applications and cutting-edge technology involving computers, and illustrate concepts such as hardware, software, and systems; database management; graphics; and telecommunications. Adopters will have immediate access to professional quality videotapes, which explore such landmarks of technology as the electrical digital computer, the laser, and communications satellites. Other topics include information theory, the role of computers at Florida's Sea World theme parks, and a demonstration of active problem-solving techniques.

Acknowledgments

This book was developed over an eight-year period of teaching information systems courses at the Leonard N. Stern School of Business, New York University. We want to thank the more than 1,500 students who have helped us learn how to teach this material in an engaging manner. We would also like to thank colleagues at NYU for encouraging us to rethink the curriculum in information systems. At current rates of technological change, this appears to be a biannual process.

Many persons were very helpful in shaping the content and style of this book. We are especially grateful for the comments and insights provided by William H. Starbuck of the Stern School of Business, New York University; Edward Roche of the University of Arizona; Jiri Rodovsky; and Russell Polo. The following persons provided in-depth reviews of early drafts and made extensive critical remarks:

- Gary Armstrong, *Shippensburg University*
- Thomas Case, *Georgia Southern University*
- Sergio Davalos, *Pima Community College*
- James Divoky, *University of Akron*
- David Farwell, *Metropolitan State College*
- Dan Flynn, *Shoreline Community College*
- Carroll Frenzel, *University of Colorado*
- Tom Harris, *Ball State University*
- Bill Harrison, *Oregon State University*
- Al Kagan, *North Dakota State University*
- Milan Kaldenberg, *Northwest Nazarene College*
- David Letcher, *Trenton State University*
- Ian McKillop, *Wilfrid Laurier University*
- John Melrose, *University of Wisconsin—Eau Claire*
- Marilyn Moore, *Purdue University—Calumet*
- Jim Payne, *Kellogg Community College*
- Shailendra Palvia, *Babson College*
- Eugene Rathswohl, *University of San Diego*
- Arline Sachs, *Northern Virginia Community College*
- Ronald Schwartz, *Wayne State University*
- Irmtraud Seeborg, *Ball State University*
- Shashi Shah, *Seton Hall University*
- Charles Snyder, *Auburn University*
- Mohan Tanniru, *Syracuse University*
- David Van Over, *University of Georgia*
- Ronald Vaughn, *Western Illinois University*
- Randy Weinberg, *St. Cloud State University*

We would also like to acknowledge the following people who made special contributions to the text:

- Patricia Ayers, *Arapahoe Community College*
- David Bryant, *Pepperdine University*
- Eli Boyd Cohen, *Bradley University*
- Mark Dishaw, *Boston University*
- John King, *University of California—Irvine*
- Ken Kraemer, *University of California—Irvine*
- Joseph Morrell, *Metropolitan State University*
- Ted Surynt, *Stetson University*

- G. Torkzadeh, *University of Toledo*
- Alan F. Westin, *Columbia University*
- Sue Wynick, *Kirkwood Community College*

Edward G. Martin, Kingsborough Community College, and Karen Schenkenfelder were closely involved in finalizing the Focus On boxes. Paul Ransdell also contributed ideas for boxed items. Alice Fugate assisted in developing the art program, and Mary E. Goljenboom made a significant contribution to the selection of photos.

Special thanks to Marilyn Moore and Milan Kaldenberg for their splendid work on the *Student Study Guide* and *Test Bank,* and to Paul Konigstein for his assistance with the *Instructor's Resource Manual.*

Thanks to Elizabeth Evans, Grace A. Evans, and Elaine Gilleran at Wells Fargo; Steve Heit and Kathy Shovlin at UPS; and Michael R. Hudson and Dorothy A. Waite at Andersen Consulting for supplying information and photos for the illustrated vignettes.

We also want to thank our editors at The Dryden Press for insisting on a high-quality text, and for encouraging first-rate design and graphics. Special thanks to DeVilla Williams who initiated the project with such great enthusiasm; Mary Beth Nelligan, developmental editor, and Teresa Chartos and Paula Dempsey, project editors, for superb project development, management, and coordination; Becky Lemna for excellent design and artwork; and Doris Milligan and Cindy Lombardo for securing permissions. We want to acknowledge several behind-the-scenes people at Dryden whose contributions significantly improved *Business Information Systems*: Jan Huskisson, Aimeé Gosse, Jennifer Lloyd, Barb Bahnsen, and Jane Perkins. Special thanks to Bill Schoof who fosters a creative environment for The Dryden Press.

Finally, we want to dedicate this book to our children—Erica and Elisabeth—and to our families for putting up with a couple of writers through yet another project.

Kenneth C. Laudon
Jane Price Laudon

January 1991

Contents in Brief

PART ONE — The World of Information Systems 1

CHAPTER ONE — Introduction to Information Systems in the 1990s 2

CHAPTER TWO — How Business Firms Use Information Systems 32

PART TWO — Foundations of Information Technologies 71

CHAPTER THREE — Computer Processing Technology 72

CHAPTER FOUR — Storage, Input, and Output Technologies 106

CHAPTER FIVE — Information Systems Software for Problem Solving 138

CHAPTER SIX — Organizing Information: Files and Databases 178

CHAPTER SEVEN — Telecommunications 214

CHAPTER EIGHT — Artificial Intelligence in Business 252

PART THREE — Problem Solving with Information Systems 291

CHAPTER NINE — Business Problem Analysis: Critical Thinking Skills 292

CHAPTER TEN — Designing Information System Solutions 334

CHAPTER ELEVEN — Alternative Approaches to Information System Solutions 384

PART FOUR — Overview of Business Information Systems 421

CHAPTER TWELVE — Basic Business Systems 422

CHAPTER THIRTEEN — Knowledge and Information Work: Office Automation 454

CHAPTER FOURTEEN — Knowledge and Information Work: Professional Work Systems 490

CHAPTER FIFTEEN — Management Support Systems 512

CHAPTER SIXTEEN — Social and Organizational Impacts of Computers 550

Contents

PART ONE | The World of Information Systems 1

CHAPTER ONE | Introduction to Information Systems in the 1990s 2

Introduction 4
Approaches to Studying Information Systems 12
Purpose of Studying Information Systems 16
The Challenges Ahead 19
Organizing Concepts of the Book 26
Summary 27

PROBLEM-SOLVING CASE | Customers at the Drawing Board 30
FOCUS ON PEOPLE | Computer Conversations 11
FOCUS ON ORGANIZATIONS | Dun and Brad: America's Oldest Information Company? 16
FOCUS ON TECHNOLOGY | Technology Transforms the Supermarket Business 23
FOCUS ON PROBLEM SOLVING | Wheels for the Mind 26

CHAPTER TWO | How Business Firms Use Information Systems 32

Components of Business 34
Placement of Information Systems in a Business 40
Examples of Business Information Systems 44
How Businesses Use Information Systems for Competitive Advantage 55
Summary 61

PROBLEM-SOLVING CASE | Tying in the Sales Force 63
FOCUS ON PROBLEM SOLVING | The Liability of Newness 38
FOCUS ON ORGANIZATIONS | Quaker Oats Copes with Europe 1992 41
FOCUS ON TECHNOLOGY | Computer Builds the Stealth Bomber 48
FOCUS ON PEOPLE | Wanted: The Everything Person 60

PART ONE | Illustrated Vignette: *Information Technology Gives Wells Fargo an Edge* 65

PART TWO Foundations of Information Technologies 71

CHAPTER THREE Computer Processing Technology 72

Introduction: A Variety of Information Technologies 74
Computer Concepts and Components 76
The Microcomputer Revolution 89
Information Technology Trends 97
Summary 100

PROBLEM-SOLVING CASE Downsizing Halves Borg Warner's Information Systems Budget 103
FOCUS ON PEOPLE Viewing Data without the Filters 75
FOCUS ON ORGANIZATIONS Cray Stands Alone 89
FOCUS ON PROBLEM SOLVING Laptops Keep Workers in Touch 91
FOCUS ON TECHNOLOGY Chips for the Year 2000 100

CHAPTER FOUR Storage, Input, and Output Technologies 106

Introduction 108
Information Storage Technology 108
Input Technology 118
Output Technology 125
Leading-Edge Technology: The NeXT Computer 129
Summary 132

PROBLEM-SOLVING CASE Selecting Printers: Caution Advised 134
FOCUS ON PEOPLE Workers Get a Feel for Touch Screens 120
FOCUS ON ORGANIZATIONS If a Laser Printer Ran Backwards 124
FOCUS ON TECHNOLOGY Are VDTs Safe? 128
FOCUS ON PROBLEM SOLVING Why Can't Computers Talk? 130

CHAPTER FIVE Information Systems Software for Problem Solving 138

Introduction 140
Systems Software 144
Programming Languages 153
Application Software 165
Leading-Edge Application: Maps that Can Read People's Minds 169
Summary 173

PROBLEM-SOLVING CASE UNIX Solves Publishing Problems at Kaiser Electronics 175
FOCUS ON ORGANIZATIONS Johnsonizing Software 142
FOCUS ON PEOPLE Profiles in Angst 151
FOCUS ON PROBLEM SOLVING A Promise Fulfilled 170
FOCUS ON TECHNOLOGY Stewart Alsop's All-Time Vaporware List 172

CHAPTER SIX Organizing Information: Files and Databases 178

Introduction 180
The Traditional File Environment 183
The Database Vision 188
Applying Database Concepts to Problem Solving 197
Distributing Information: Distributed and On-Line Databases 202
Leading-Edge Application: HyperCard 206
Summary 209

PROBLEM-SOLVING CASE Cutting Electricity Bills at Ontario Hydro 211
FOCUS ON PEOPLE A Farm Journal for Every Farmer 193
FOCUS ON ORGANIZATIONS A New Weapon for Car Insurers 202
FOCUS ON PROBLEM SOLVING Why the Fuss over SQL? 204
FOCUS ON TECHNOLOGY Mapping out Database Information 208

CHAPTER SEVEN Telecommunications 214

Introduction 216
Telecommunications Technology 220
Telecommunications Networks 227
Applying Telecommunications to Business Problems 237
Leading-Edge Application: New Networks Speed Airline Travel 244
Summary 247

PROBLEM-SOLVING CASE Tying in Acquisitions at First Union Bank 250
FOCUS ON ORGANIZATIONS Holiday Inns Uses Satellite Network to Maintain Lead in Customer Service 227
FOCUS ON TECHNOLOGY PBXs Get Smarter 231
FOCUS ON PROBLEM SOLVING GE Bases Global Net Strategy on Video Teleconferencing 241
FOCUS ON PEOPLE Electronic Bulletin Board Speeds Catalog Preparation 245

CHAPTER EIGHT Artificial Intelligence in Business 252

Introduction 254
Expert Systems 263
Other Intelligent Techniques 274
Summary 282

PROBLEM-SOLVING CASE Taking Care of Sick Robots at Ford Motor Company 284
FOCUS ON TECHNOLOGY Coping with Information Overload: Let Machines Do It 257
FOCUS ON PEOPLE The Chess Grandmaster Is a Machine 262
FOCUS ON ORGANIZATIONS Where Lisp Slipped 274
FOCUS ON PROBLEM SOLVING Smart Sam? 281

PART TWO Illustrated Vignette: *Slaying the Paper Dragon* 286

PART THREE — Problem Solving with Information Systems 291

CHAPTER NINE — Business Problem Analysis: Critical Thinking Skills 292

Introduction: Concepts 294
A Five-Step Model of Problem Solving 301
Typical Business Problems: Analysis and Understanding 303
Problem Solving: Making Decisions 317
Problem Solving: Designing Solutions 321
Problem Solving: Implementing Solutions 325
Summary 328

PROBLEM-SOLVING CASE — Clouds at Sun Microsystems, Inc. 331
FOCUS ON PEOPLE — The "Electric Army" Battles Support Problems 309
FOCUS ON ORGANIZATIONS — A Not-So-Feasible Solution 320
FOCUS ON PROBLEM SOLVING — U.S. Defense Department Software Standards Put Requirements First 322
FOCUS ON TECHNOLOGY — Today's Leaders Look to Tomorrow 326

CHAPTER TEN — Designing Information System Solutions 334

Introduction 336
Problem Solving in Action: New Technology 339
Problem Solving in Action: Management and Procedures 343
Problem Solving in Action: Database Application 349
Problem Solving in Action: Spreadsheet Application 353
Problem Solving in Action: Mainframe Application 358
Systems-Building Tools and Methodologies 364
Summary 377

PROBLEM-SOLVING CASE — Solution Design Projects 379
FOCUS ON ORGANIZATIONS — Justice Aims Database at Gun Sales 353
FOCUS ON PROBLEM SOLVING — Not Just Another Spreadsheet 360
FOCUS ON TECHNOLOGY — OOPS: Object-Oriented Programming Software 373
FOCUS ON PEOPLE — CASE Training Must Begin before Tools Are Installed 376

CHAPTER ELEVEN — Alternative Approaches to Information System Solutions 384

Introduction 386
The Traditional Systems Life Cycle 386
The Prototyping Alternative 392
Developing Solutions with Software Packages 396
Fourth-Generation Development 401
Leading-Edge Application: On-Demand Mortgage Reports for Merrill Lynch Brokers 409
Summary 410

PROBLEM-SOLVING CASE — A Management System to Track Coast Guard Personnel 413

FOCUS ON PEOPLE — Consumers, Legislators, and Publishers Consider Rules to Cover Programmers 391

FOCUS ON PROBLEM SOLVING — Government Agencies Seek Package Solutions 397

FOCUS ON TECHNOLOGY — "Customizable" Software from McCormack & Dodge 400

FOCUS ON ORGANIZATIONS — Publicizing Productivity Tools 407

PART THREE — Illustrated Vignette: *Automated Solutions Computer-Aided with Software Engineering* 416

PART FOUR — Overview of Business Information Systems 421

CHAPTER TWELVE — Basic Business Systems 422

Introduction: Basic Business Systems 424
Features of Basic Business Systems 425
Examples of Basic Business Systems 429
The Challenges of Building Basic Business Systems 446
Summary 448

PROBLEM-SOLVING CASE — Doing Away with Checks 451

FOCUS ON ORGANIZATIONS — Computerized Reservation Processing Is a Formidable Competitive Weapon 427

FOCUS ON TECHNOLOGY — No Bad ATMs 429

FOCUS ON PROBLEM SOLVING — Brodart Decentralizes Corporate Accounting Applications 439

FOCUS ON PEOPLE — Wanted: Skilled Transaction Processing Specialists 447

CHAPTER THIRTEEN — Knowledge and Information Work: Office Automation 454

Introduction: The Information and Knowledge Economy 457
The New Information and Knowledge Workers 459
Office Automation: Automating Information Work 464
Leading-Edge Application: Staying in the Fast Lane at BMW 479
Summary 483

PROBLEM-SOLVING CASE — Unions Seek a Say in Office Automation Decisions 486

FOCUS ON ORGANIZATIONS — Northrop Builds the First Paperless Airplane 470

FOCUS ON TECHNOLOGY — Some Alternatives to Laser Printers 473

FOCUS ON PROBLEM SOLVING — Project Manager for the Olympics 476

FOCUS ON PEOPLE — Computerized Meetings 480

CHAPTER FOURTEEN **Knowledge and Information Work: Professional Work Systems** 490

Introduction 492
Knowledge Work Systems 496
Leading-Edge Applications: Knowledge Work Systems 500
Challenges of Building Knowledge and Information Work Systems 505
Summary 507

PROBLEM-SOLVING CASE Walking through a Factory before It Is Built 509
FOCUS ON PROBLEM SOLVING 3D Data Shed Light on Surgery 498
FOCUS ON TECHNOLOGY IBM Introduces Line of Workstations 500
FOCUS ON ORGANIZATIONS Merging Art and Engineering 505
FOCUS ON PEOPLE Architects Resist Computer-Aided Rendering 506

CHAPTER FIFTEEN **Management Support Systems** 512

Introduction: Management Support Systems 514
What Managers Do 516
Management Information Systems 526
Decision Support Systems 530
Executive Support Systems 536
The Challenge of Building Management Support Systems 541
Summary 543

PROBLEM-SOLVING CASE Day in the Life of Tomorrow's Manager 546
FOCUS ON PEOPLE How Two PC Managers Traveled the Decade of Change 518
FOCUS ON ORGANIZATIONS Hustle and Vision as the Plan 524
FOCUS ON PROBLEM SOLVING The Shape of Things to Come 538
FOCUS ON TECHNOLOGY American Cyanamid Uses an ESS to Track Competitors 541

CHAPTER SIXTEEN **Social and Organizational Impacts of Computers** 550

Introduction: The Social and Organizational Impacts of Computers 552
General Social Impacts of Computers 555
Organizational Impacts 563
Computer Crime and Other Threats 569
Safeguarding Information Systems: Approaches and Techniques 576
Leading-Edge Application: Digital Envelopes for Networks 587
Summary 588

PROBLEM-SOLVING CASE Electronic Vaults for Banks 592
FOCUS ON ORGANIZATIONS Problems in Your Credit Record? 558
FOCUS ON TECHNOLOGY Death by Software: Malfunction Error Code 54 562
FOCUS ON PEOPLE Computer Felon Plants a Time Bomb 575
FOCUS ON PROBLEM SOLVING Forbes Fire Destroyed PCs but Not Data 581

PART FOUR Illustrated Vignette: *UPS Delivers with Personal Computers* 594

Glossary 598
Name Index 613
Organization Index 617
Subject Index 621

PART · ONE

The World of Information Systems

CHAPTER · ONE

Introduction to Information Systems in the 1990*s*

Chapter Outline

1.1 Introduction
- Information Systems in Business
- Components of Business Information Systems

1.2 Approaches to Studying Information Systems
- Differences between Computers and Information Systems
- Computer Literacy
- Information Systems Literacy
- Differences among Knowledge, Information, and Data
- A Sociotechnical Perspective on Information Systems

1.3 Purpose of Studying Information Systems
- Intersecting Skills
- Career Paths and Crucial Skills
- Related Courses

1.4 The Challenges Ahead
- Technology Challenge
- Productivity Challenge
- Strategic Business Challenge
- People Challenge

1.5 Organizing Concepts of the Book
- Knowledge and Information versus Data
- Analysis and Problem Solving versus Technology
- A Sociotechnical Perspective
- Systems are Networks of Information Technologies

Learning Objectives

After reading and studying this chapter, you will:

1. Be able to define an information system.
2. Understand the basic components of information systems: organizations, people, and technology.
3. Know how knowledge, information, and data differ.
4. Know what skills are required for information systems literacy.
5. Be aware of the information system challenges ahead of you.

Communicating Electronically

The managers of the not-so-distant past sent and received a great deal of information through letters. In a typical interchange, one manager would dictate a letter to his or her secretary, who would type it up and mail it. The recipient would respond by dictating another letter, which also had to be typed and mailed. Even when an overseas transmission was speeded up by telex, such an exchange could take days.

Especially at large companies, today's managers are increasingly able to speed up this process by communicating electronically. For example, Westinghouse Electric Corporation created its own computer system for electronic mail, known as E-Mail for short. Westinghouse's system now connects 6,000 personal computers, which are used by 10,700 of the company's managers and 1,000 of its customers. The E-Mail user types a message directly into the computer, which immediately makes it available to the receiver. Thus, the sender of the original message can receive a reply within 24 hours, even from someone on another continent. Westinghouse's president, Paul E. Lego, uses E-Mail for round-the-clock communications about company activities in 37 countries.

Convenience is one attraction of communicating electronically. The Discovery Channel, which acquires and delivers 200 television programs to 34 million homes in the United States each month, benefits from this advantage of its electronic mail system. Ruth Otte, the company's president, uses elec-

tronic mail to send more than 100 messages a day. Because she can send messages from a portable laptop computer, she can reach managers from wherever she happens to be, as long as a telephone jack is available.

Similarly, Clifton E. Haley, president of Budget Rent A Car Corporation, can be in touch with managers 24 hours a day, no matter what city he is in. With his cellular phone, Haley can arrange telephone conference calls, and he can use a facsimile machine to send documents from any location that has a telephone connection.

As these examples illustrate, business communications have been reshaped by such technological innovations as cellular telephones, facsimile machines, laptop computers, and dial-in electronic data services. Managers no longer have to choose between being tied to their desks or out of touch with their colleagues.

These developments are likely to continue throughout the 1990s. Telephone lines may be able to transmit moving pictures as well as documents, words, and data. As physical proximity becomes less important to the transmission of information, corporations may leave urban areas, and individual employees may be able to work from the location of their—or their company's—choice.

Source: Geoff Lewis, "The Portable Executive," *Business Week,* October 10, 1988.

The opening vignette and the photographs in this chapter illustrate the kind of information-intense environment you are likely to face as a professional businessperson in the 1990s. This text is designed to prepare you for this future world in which you will need to use information systems effectively.

1.1 Introduction

Why should you be concerned about information systems? Isn't that the job of technical people? After all, no one asks that you take a course on the "telephone system." The examples of Westinghouse, Budget Rent A Car, and the Discovery Channel above provide at least three reasons why you should understand how information systems work.

As a society, we are engaged in a global economic competition for resources, markets, and incomes with other nations in both Europe and Asia. For Adam Smith, the eighteenth-century Scottish economist who initiated the modern study of economics with his book *The Wealth of Nations,* the income of a nation depended on how well that society organized production in its domestic factories. Now, in the 1990s, it is clear that our society will have to organize global markets, international corporations, and multinational work forces if we are to maintain and enhance our standard of living. We will need information systems to do this effectively and successfully.

Second, we will need a thorough understanding of information systems to achieve higher levels of productivity and effectiveness within our domestic factories and offices. Without higher levels of productivity in domestic businesses, we will lose the international competition for incomes and resources. This translates directly into lower real incomes for us all. It simply will be impossible to operate even a small business efficiently without significant systems investments in the 1990s. Those of you who want to become entrepreneurs should note that almost half of all new businesses in the 1990s will involve a computer-based service or product.

But perhaps the most important reason that you personally should understand information systems is that your effectiveness as a business professional or entrepreneur, indeed your career and income in the 1990s, will in part depend on how well you apply yourself to the task of understanding information systems. Whether you want to be a graphic artist, professional musician, lawyer, business manager, or small business owner, you will be working with and through information systems in the 1990s. The conclusion is inescapable: in the 1990s you will have to be information systems literate.

Before we explore the growing role of information systems in business, we must first define an information system and its basic components.

Information Systems in Business

An **information system** (IS) can be defined as a set of interrelated components working together to collect, retrieve, process, store, and disseminate information for the purpose of facilitating planning, control, coordination, and decision making in businesses and other organizations (see Figure 1.1). Information systems contain information on significant people, places, and things in a business organization's surrounding environment and within the business itself. Information systems essentially transform information into a form usable for coordinating the flow of work in a firm, helping employees or managers make decisions, and solving other kinds of problems. Information systems accomplish this through a cycle of three basic activities: input, processing, and output.

Input entails capturing or collecting raw data resources from within the business or from its external environment. **Processing** entails converting this raw input into a more appropriate and useful form. **Output** entails transferring the processed information to the people or business activities that will use it. Information systems also store information, in various forms of completeness, until it is needed for processing or output. **Feedback** is

Information system
A set of interrelated components working together to collect, retrieve, process, store, and disseminate information for the purpose of facilitating planning, control, coordination, and decision making in businesses and other organizations.

Input
The capture or collection of raw data resources from within a business or from its external environment.

Processing
The conversion of raw input into a more appropriate and useful form.

Output
The transfer of processed information to the people or business activities that will use it.

Feedback
Output that is returned to appropriate members of the organization to help them refine or correct the input phase.

Figure 1.1

Activities of Information Systems: Input, Processing, and Output

An information system operates in cycles of three steps each. In the first step, input, the system collects data from within the organization or from the organization's environment. The next step, processing, involves converting the raw input data into a form that is more useful and understandable. Finally, the output information is transferred to people or business activities that can use it. Feedback is output that is "fed back" to appropriate people or activities; it can be used to evaluate and refine the input stage.

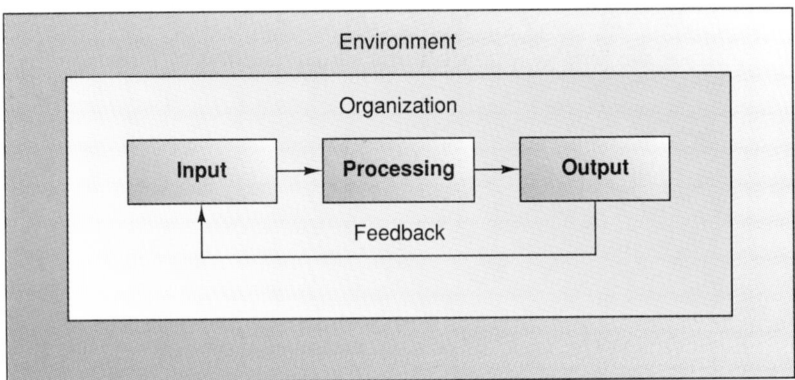

output that is returned to appropriate members of the organization to help them refine or correct the input phase.

Computerized information systems capture data from either inside or outside a business firm by recording them on paper forms or by entering them directly into a computer system using a keyboard or other device. Input activities, such as recording, coding, classifying, and editing, focus on ensuring that the required data are correct and complete. During processing, the data are organized, analyzed, and manipulated through calculations, comparisons, summarization, and sorting into a more meaningful and useful form. Output activities transmit the results of processing to where they will be used for decision making, coordination, or control. The output of information systems takes various forms—printed reports, graphic displays, video displays, sound, or data to feed other information systems. The information system must also store data and information in an organized fashion so that they can be easily accessed for processing or for output.

For example, the Hilton Hotel chain uses an information system called Answer*Net to book and keep track of travel reservations for group bookings and conventions. Approximately 600 Hilton salespeople enter client data into the system using desktop computer workstations (input). The data are transmitted to a large computer center in Texas for updating Hilton's reservation and client records (processing) and for storage. The system produces bookings forms, market reports, and forecasts (output). Figure 1.2 illustrates the input, processing, output, and feedback functions of this system.

We need to clarify our definition further by saying that we are concerned exclusively in this book with formal, organizational, computer-based

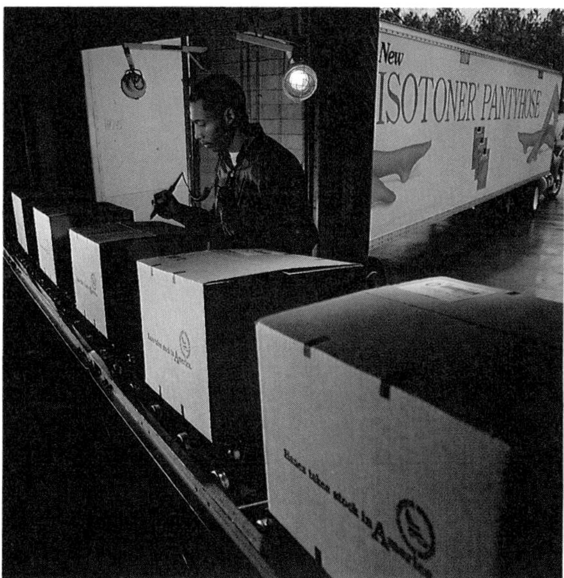

With a hand-held wand, a Hanes warehouse employee enters stock information into order and inventory systems. This information is processed into forms useful for decision making, coordination, and control of Hanes products.

Source: Courtesy of Ameritech.

information systems (CBIS). Each of these words deserves some comment. The CBIS we describe in this book are **formal systems,** which rely on mutually accepted and relatively fixed definitions of data and procedures for collecting, storing, processing, and disseminating information. For instance, a manual file of customer names and addresses, or an alphabetical card catalog in a library, is a formal information system because it is established by an organization and conforms to organizational rules and procedures; this means that each entry in the system has the same format of information and the same content.

Formal systems
Information systems that rely on mutually accepted and relatively fixed definitions of data and procedures for collecting, storing, processing, and disseminating information.

Informal systems, by contrast, do not have these features. For instance, students inevitably form small groups of friends, and these groups usually have information systems. In these informal information systems, there is no agreement on what is information, how it will be stored, and what will be stored or processed. Like office gossip networks, groups of friends freely share information on a large and constantly changing set of objects, topics, and personalities. These open, informal systems are very important—indeed, they are very powerful and flexible—but they are not the direct subject of this book.

CBIS are built for the purpose of solving significant business problems as they are perceived in organizations. This insight—that systems exist to solve business problems—will be used often throughout this book. We can use this insight to understand not only the systems that exist now (and why) but also the way to build systems in the future and the skills you will need to have.

Figure 1.2

Input/Processing/Output Model Applied to the Hilton Answer*Net System

This diagram of the Hilton Answer*Net reservations system illustrates the input, processing, and output functions of a typical information system. About 600 Hilton salespeople from all over the United States enter raw data into the system via desktop computer workstations. The central computer center in Texas processes the data by updating records and storing necessary information. The output includes numerous forms such as bookings, market reports, and market forecasts. These are sent to appropriate staff members, whose feedback can have an impact on how future input data are collected.

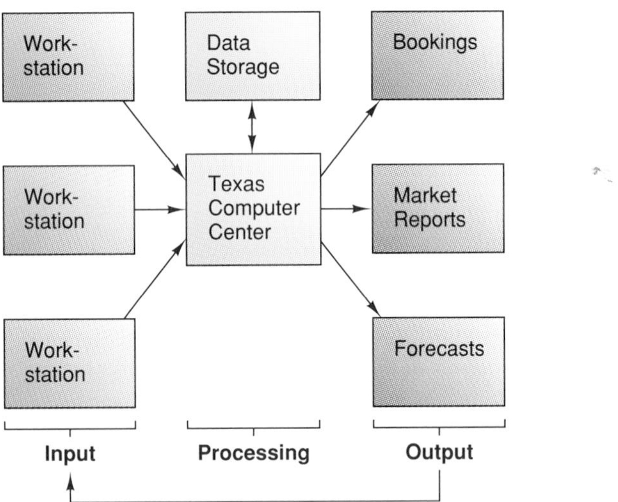

Source: Michael Puttre, "New IS Checks in to Hilton," *InformationWEEK,* July 31, 1989. Reprinted by permission of InformationWEEK Magazine, a CMP Publication, Manhasset, NY.

Components of Business Information Systems

Computer-based information systems utilize computer technology to perform some portions of the processing functions of an information system and some of the input and output functions as well. It would be a mistake, however, to describe an information system in terms of the computer alone. An information system is an integral part of an organization and is a product of three components: technology, organizations, and people (see Figure 1.3). One cannot understand or use information systems effectively in business without knowledge of their organizational and people dimensions as well as their technical dimensions.

Organizations · Organizations shape information systems in several obvious ways. Business firms are formal organizations. They consist of specialized units with a clear-cut division of labor and experts employed and trained for different business functions such as sales, manufacturing, human resources, and finance. Organizations are hierarchial and structured. Employees in a business firm are arranged in rising levels of authority in which each person is accountable to someone above him or her. The upper levels of the hierarchy consist of management, and the lower levels consist of

Figure 1.3

An Information System: Not Just a Computer

Throughout this book we emphasize a sociotechnical approach to information systems. A successful system has organizational and people dimensions in addition to technical components. It exists to answer organizational needs. The organization, in turn, is shaped by its external environment, which includes political, demographic, economic, and social trends.

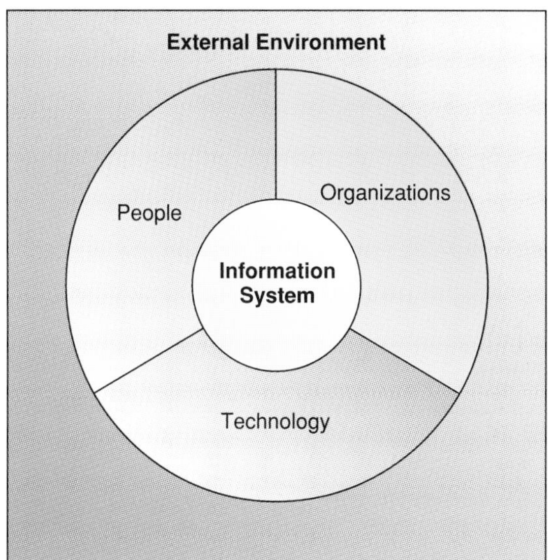

nonmanagerial employees. Formal procedures, or rules for accomplishing tasks, are used to coordinate specialized groups in the firm so they will complete their work in an acceptable manner. Some of these procedures, such as how to write up a purchase order or how to correct an erroneous bill, are incorporated into information systems. Each organization has a unique culture, or bedrock assumptions, values, and ways of doing things that have been accepted by most members of the firm.

Different levels and different specialties in an organization in turn create different interests in the organization and different points of view, which often conflict. Out of these conflicts, politics, and eventual compromises come information systems. Organizations need to build these systems to solve problems created both by these internal factors and by external environmental factors, such as changes in government regulations or market conditions.

People · People use information from computer-based systems in their jobs, integrating it into the business environment. People are required to input data into the system, either by entering data into the system themselves or by putting the data on a medium that can be read by a computer.

Employees require special training to perform their jobs or to use information systems effectively. Their attitudes about their jobs, employers, or computer technology can have a powerful effect on their ability to use information systems productively. Ergonomics refers to the interaction of

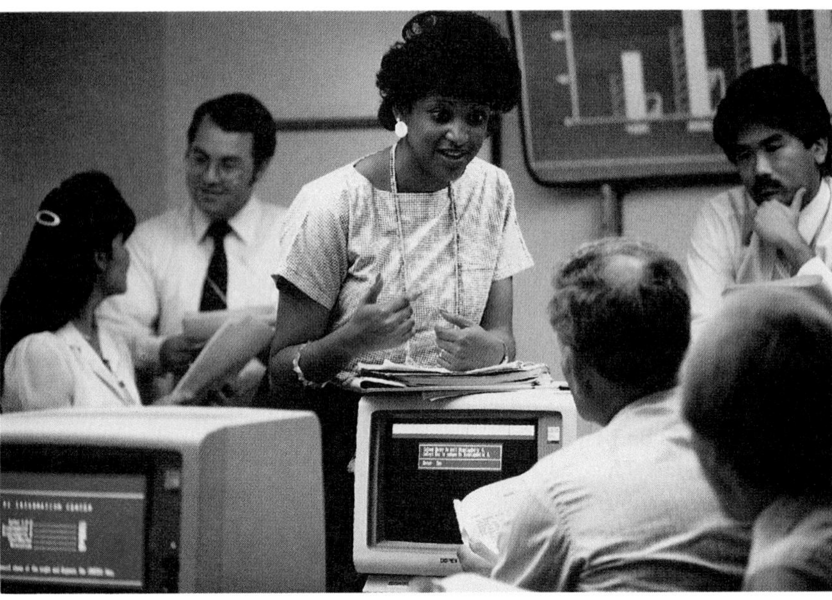

Personal computer training classes take place at Rockwell International's Newport Beach, California, plant. In all companies, proper training is essential to the effective use of information systems.

Source: Courtesy of Rockwell International.

humans and machines in the work environment; it includes the design of jobs, health issues, and the way in which people interact with information systems, and it has a strong bearing on employees' morale, productivity, and receptiveness to information systems. The user interface, or portions of an information system that business professionals must interact with, such as reports or video displays, also has a strong bearing on employees' efficiency and productivity.

The Focus on People shows how advances in information systems have opened up new ways for people to communicate, creating friendships and work groups that transcend traditional geographic barriers.

Manual system
An information system that uses only paper and pencil technology and does not rely on computers.

Technology · The technology is the means by which data are transformed and organized for business use. An information system can be an entirely **manual system,** using only paper and pencil technology. (An example would be a professor's file folder containing course records and grades.) Computers, however, have replaced manual technology for processing large volumes of data or for complex processing work. Computers can execute millions and even hundreds of millions of instructions per second. A processing task that might take years to perform manually can be performed by a computer in a matter of seconds. Computers can also perform consistently and reliably over a longer period of time than a human being can. The information systems described in this text are computer based; that is, they rely on some form of computer technology for input, output, processing, and storage.

FOCUS ON *People*

Computer Conversations

Brian Dear and Patricia Gemmell "met" when Patricia responded to a friendly message that appeared on her computer screen one day. The message was sent on a computer network linking Patricia's computer with many others. Although Patricia and Brian were on different campuses at the University of Maryland, they conversed electronically for weeks before they finally met in person. Two years later they were married.

Exchanges over computer networks, known as "electronic bulletin boards," "computer conferences," or "electronic mail," permit a group of people to converse by typing in messages that can be read by other members of the network. Participants can get acquainted, trade anecdotes, or exchange ideas.

The Microsoft Corporation is run largely through a computer network that can be used by most of the software maker's 5,200 employees. Decisions on issues such as new product plans or changing vacation policy are announced on the network, and any employee is free to send a message to Microsoft's chairman William Gates. Santa Monica, California, started a computer network to let citizens use their home or office computers to send comments about local council meetings.

Among the users of computer networks are groups as diverse as the International Business Machines Corporation, Chinese students protesting the Beijing government crackdown on the pro-democracy movement, and fans of the Grateful Dead rock band. Thousands of specialized networks have sprung up to cater to cooks, travelers, sports fans, recovering alcoholics, retirees, Go players, and those with other diverse interests.

Robert Lucky, executive director of research at Bell Laboratories, believes that computer networks create "electronic communities" that can create the feeling of a small village among people living thousands of miles apart. Many experts believe the proliferation of computer networks has changed the way millions of Americans find friends, work, and even govern themselves.

Source: John Markoff, "Computer Conversation Is Changing Human Contact," *The New York Times*, May 13, 1990.

Computer hardware is the physical equipment used for the input, processing, and output work in an information system. It consists of the computer processing unit itself and various input, output, and storage devices plus physical media to link these devices together.

Computer hardware
The physical equipment used for the input, processing, and output work in an information system.

Input hardware collects data and converts them into a form that the computer can process. The most common computer input device is the computer keyboard, but others will be described in subsequent chapters. Processing hardware transforms input to output based on instructions supplied to the computer through software. A special processing unit in the computer itself, called the central processing unit, is primarily responsible for this task. Output hardware delivers the output of an information system to its user and commonly consists of printers or video display terminals. Chapters 3 and 4 discuss computer hardware in greater detail.

Computer software consists of preprogrammed instructions that coordinate the work of computer hardware components to perform the busi-

Computer software
Preprogrammed instructions that coordinate the work of computer hardware components to perform the business processes required by each business information system.

ness processes required by each business information system. Without software, computer hardware would not know what to do and how and when to do it. Software consists of related programs, each of which is a group of instructions for performing specific processing tasks. Chapter 5 treats computer software in more detail.

Storage technology
Physical media for storing data (e.g., magnetic disks or tapes) and the software governing the organization of data on these media.

Telecommunications technology
Physical media and software that support communication by electronic means, usually over some distance.

The storage technology for organizing and storing the data used by a business is a powerful determinant of the data's usefulness and availability. **Storage technology** includes both the physical media for storing data, such as magnetic disk or tape, and also the software governing the organization of data on these physical media. Storage media are discussed in Chapter 4, and data organization and access methods are treated in Chapter 6.

Telecommunications technology is used to link different pieces of hardware and to transfer data from one location to another. Telecommunications involve both physical media and software that support communication by electronic means, usually over some distance. Chapter 7 covers telecommunications.

Let's return to the Hilton Answer*Net reservation system and see where each of these components fits in. The technology consists of a large central computer linked via telecommunications to desktop workstations and technology for storing reservation and client data. By using a computer, Answer*Net can process hundreds of thousands, even millions, of reservation requests each day. The people component requires training the sales staff to enter and receive bookings and to use the workstations, as well as designing an appropriate user interface for these tasks. The organization component anchors the Answer*Net system in Hilton's sales and marketing function; it identifies specific procedures for booking reservations (i.e., obtaining customer identification, confirming the reservation, securing the reservation with a deposit or credit card number) and provides reports and forecasts for higher levels of management.

The remaining chapters in this text provide a more detailed look at the organization, people, and technology components of information systems as they exist in real-world businesses.

1.2 Approaches to Studying Information Systems

You have probably already gathered that our emphasis in this book will be on how information systems work, not just on computers. Most people think that computers and information systems are the same thing. They also think that computer literacy and information systems literacy are identical. Although this may have been true in the early days of computing and systems, it is no longer true today.

Differences between Computers and Information Systems

We will draw a sharp distinction in this text between a computer, a computer program, and an information system. Computers—and other information technologies—are the technical foundations or the tools of information systems. Computers and telecommunications equipment store, process, disseminate, and communicate information. Computer programs, or software, are the sets of instructions that direct computer processing.

Information systems are much broader in scope. They encompass the technologies, business procedures, practices, and policies that generate information as well as the people who work with that information.

Computer Literacy

Computer literacy means knowing how to use information technology equipment. It involves a knowledge of hardware, software, telecommunications, and information storage techniques. In general, computer literacy focuses on what goes on inside the box called a computer—how disk drives work, how a random access memory works, and so forth. Computer literacy is an important part of designing solutions to business problems, but it is just the first step.

Computer literacy
Knowledge about the use of information technology equipment; it involves knowing about hardware, software, telecommunications, and information storage techniques.

Information Systems Literacy

As we saw earlier, an information system involves not just technology, but people and organizations as well. Thus, in order to develop information systems literacy, you need more than just computer literacy. You also need to understand the nature of business problems: Where do they come from? How can systems be designed to solve them? Who else is involved in building system solutions? How can the work be coordinated? These issues involve design, organization, and people.

Thus **information systems literacy** consists of three elements:

- A knowledge and hands-on facility with information technologies.
- A broadly based understanding of business organizations and individuals from a behavioral perspective.
- A broadly based understanding of how to analyze and solve business problems.

Information systems literacy
Knowledge and hands-on facility with information technologies, a broadly based understanding of business organizations and individuals from a behavioral perspective, and a similar understanding of how to analyze and solve business problems.

Figure 1.4 illustrates the three components of information systems literacy. Generally, students who major in information systems take courses in these three areas.

A house provides a good analogy for the difference between computer literacy and information systems literacy. Houses are built with nails, hammers, wood, and plaster. But these alone do not make a house. Also involved in a good house are design, location, setting, landscaping, and hundreds of other features. These other considerations are crucial to the essential problem: putting a roof over one's head.

So it is with information systems; information technologies are the tools—the hammers, nails, and materials. But to understand the systems, you need to understand the problems they were designed to solve, the proposed architectural and aesthetic solutions, and the business process that leads to systems.

Figure 1.4

Information Systems Literacy: More Than Just Using a Computer

Because an information system involves people and organizations as well as technology, it follows that information systems literacy is more than just knowing how to program. To be information literate in the 1990s, you must develop skills in analyzing and solving problems and in dealing effectively with people at both the individual and organizational levels. Think of this course as the center of this diagram, with the three skill areas comprising the major themes of the course. This also gives you an idea of what you will study if you major in Information Systems. Generally, an IS major will take classes in all three skill areas.

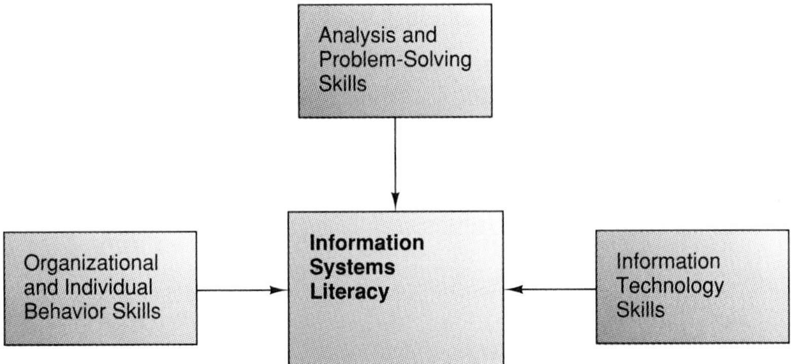

Differences among Knowledge, Information, and Data

Data
Raw facts that can be shaped and formed to create information.

Information
Data that have been shaped or formed by humans into a meaningful and useful form.

Knowledge
The stock of conceptual tools and categories used by humans to create, collect, store, and share information.

Philosophers have for centuries been struggling to define knowledge, information, and data or facts. A small library could easily be filled with their results. To arrive at some operational definitions, we can start with Plato (c. 428–348 B.C.), an ancient Greek philosopher whom you will no doubt read while in college. For Plato, pure data were a shadowy reflection on a wall of all the things going on in the world.[1] Thus **data** can be considered the raw facts, the infinite stream of things that are happening now and have happened in the past.

Information comes from the Latin word *informare,* meaning "to give form or shape." Most philosophers believe that it is the human mind that gives shape and form to data in order to create meaningful "information" and knowledge. Plato, and other Greek philosophers, originated this concept of a world of meaning, intention, and knowledge created by human beings. These ideas are at the heart of Western culture.

We will define **information** as data that have been given shape and form by human beings to make them meaningful and useful. **Knowledge** is the stock of conceptual tools and categories used by humans to create, collect, store, and share information. Knowledge can be stored as an artifact in a library—as a book, for instance—or in a computer program as a set of instructions that gives shape to otherwise meaningless streams of data. The Focus on Organizations examines a company that makes billions of dollars every year by transforming data into information.

Human beings have a long history of developing systems for the purpose of giving shape to data, as well as recording, storing, and sharing information and knowledge. Libraries, tabloids, writing, language, art, and mathematics are all examples of information systems. The focus of this text,

The Cleveland Public Library, like libraries throughout the world, is a traditional information system, collecting, storing, and sharing data, information, and knowledge. Modern information systems—computers—combined with the telephone offer users great speed and convenience in accessing many types of information and knowledge held in libraries.
Source: © Mike Steinberg.

and much of the course, will be on how computer-based information systems store, collect, and share information and knowledge in business organizations.

A Sociotechnical Perspective on Information Systems

The view we adopt in this book is that information systems and information technologies are sociotechnical systems that involve the coordination of technology, organizations, and people. The information architecture of the firm—the computers, networks, and software—rests on these three pillars.

In the past the study of information systems was regarded as a technical subject, of interest primarily to computer science students. By the 1970s, however, there was a growing recognition that a purely technical approach to information technology failed to take into account organizational and individual factors. The most advanced computing technology is essentially worthless unless businesses can make use of the technology and unless individuals feel comfortable using it.

Sociotechnical perspective
An approach to information systems that involves the coordination of technology, organizations, and people; in this approach, information technology, organizations, and individuals go through a process of mutual adjustment and discovery as systems are developed.

In the **sociotechnical perspective,** information technology, organizations, and individuals go through a process of mutual adjustment and dis-

FOCUS ON *Organizations*

Dun and Brad: America's Oldest Information Company?

Banks, insurance companies, and airlines all claim to be in the information business and regard themselves as leaders in the information age. But for 150 years—since 1841—the Dun and Bradstreet Corporation has been transforming countless streams of data into meaningful information. In the process it has made a whopping amount of money—in the billions of dollars. Current revenues are $3.3 billion annually, with a 20 percent return on investment!

Dun and Brad claims to embody the information age, which it says started in the nineteenth century. It owns some of the flagship information products of all time: D&B Credit Report—the key to business financing; Moody's Investor Services—bond and stock analysis; A. C. Nielsen—the television rating service; and over a hundred other information products. As one of the country's oldest corporations, it is a rarity in an age of short-lived conglomerates, sold-off fragments, and has-been start-ups.

Dun and Brad has adopted the nuclear accelerator theory of data: gather as much as possible and whoosh it through tunnels of computer circuits and communications wires, where it collides, combines, and splits into new pieces of data; then whoosh it back out to the customers, where the data, transformed into information, are a valuable commodity.

Actually, the process of turning data into information is not quite as random as a nuclear chain reaction. Hundreds of focus groups, surveys, and interviews are conducted each year to find out what the customer wants, what kinds of information are needed, and how much the client will pay. Once this is understood, the company looks for technology that can deliver the products.

The lifeblood of Dun and Bradstreet is computer-based information systems. It takes 3,000 D&B reporters following 2.5 million companies to keep the computers filled with useful information. The biggest problem management faces is keeping the technology up to speed with customer expectations. Now, more than 75 percent of credit reports are delivered directly to customer computers, often on a desktop. In 1980, all credit reports went through the mail or via phone.

Source: "Information Merchandisers," *Information Week*, October 31, 1988.

covery as systems are developed. Figure 1.5 illustrates what happens over time, as information systems are built. In many instances, the technology must be altered to fit the unique needs of each business. Almost always, organizational changes must be invented and then implemented. And, of course, a considerable amount of retraining of employees must take place to develop a successful, useful system.

1.3 Purpose of Studying Information Systems

You don't have to know how a car engine works in order to drive a car, so you shouldn't have to learn about how information systems or computers work if all you want to do is use them.

Figure 1.5

A Sociotechnical View of Information Systems

In a system, technology, organizations, and people must cooperate and support one another to optimize the performance of the entire system. The three elements adjust as they move from planning to actual operation and continue to change over time, not always improving but sometimes degrading until they must be corrected or entirely replaced.

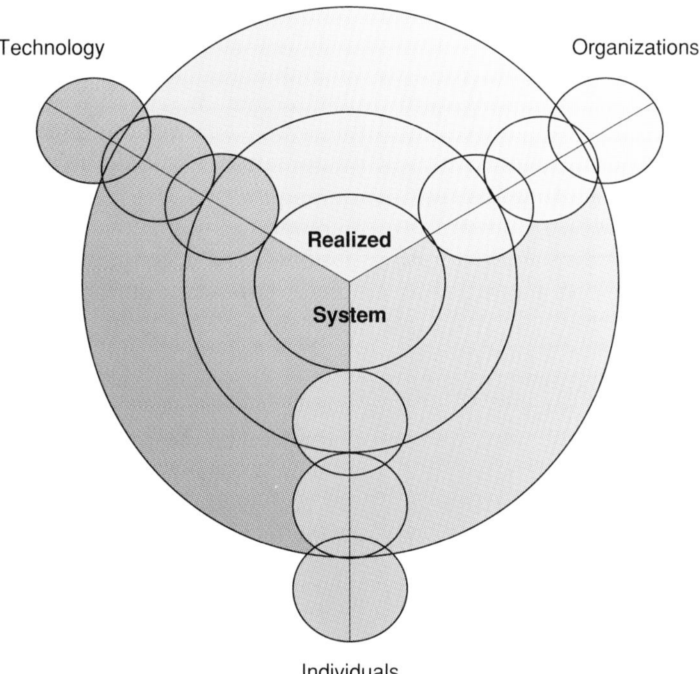

There is some truth to this statement, but it has clear limitations as well. If you want to buy a car, especially a used car, you might want to know something about how a car engine works—at least what a healthy engine sounds like. If you want to fix a car, you surely will need to know something about cars. When you are stranded on the highway in a rain storm, you might wish you knew a little more about your own car engine. Certainly, if someone told you to go out and put a car together in order to save the business (or your job), you would really need to know something about how a car works.

As we pointed out earlier, in the 1990s the chances are very high that your employer will in fact ask you to go out and find some sort of system solution to a business problem. The intent of this book is to prepare you for that eventuality.

But what do you really need to know about computers and information systems to succeed in the job markets of the 1990s? Do you have to know how a computer processes bits of data, how to program a computer in some esoteric language, how to wire together a microcomputer workstation and a printer, how electrons behave on the surface of a chip, how a disk drive works, or how a business uses information systems for competitive advantage? Do you have to know everything about computers? These are difficult questions with which educators themselves struggle.

Intersecting Skills

Given the broad sociotechnical perspective on systems described above, it is clear that no one person has all the expertise needed to put together successful information systems that can solve business problems. Even technical professionals acknowledge that no one person has a complete technical understanding of all there is to know about, say, an IBM or an Apple Macintosh microcomputer. As it turns out, information systems are inherently a group effort involving different people with different technical, business, and analytic skills.

So one answer to how much you need to know is that there are three skills to consider: technical, organizational, and analytic/problem-solving abilities. Some people will excel in one or two areas; most people will not excel in all three.

Career Paths and Crucial Skills

Some of you will want to pursue a career in the information systems profession either as a technical person or as a manager of projects and systems. Others will choose a career path outside information systems, either in a technical area like engineering or biology or in a business field such as management, marketing, accounting, finance, or sales. But life and careers are unpredictable. Many current managers of information systems divisions, even entire computer companies, had little or no background in computers or systems. Hence, you will have to be prepared for several possible futures.

Depending on what kind of career path you want to pursue, you can obtain some idea of the skills you will need from Figure 1.6. There we have ranked the importance of specific skills on a scale from 1 to 5 with 1 indicating that no knowledge is required and 5 indicating that extensive training is needed.

Related Courses

Figure 1.7 lists specific interpersonal and on-the-job abilities that are part of these skills. It also shows courses in related disciplines that will help you develop these crucial skills. You can use this table to plan your undergraduate career and to see the relationships between diverse courses. You might wonder, for instance, what possible relevance a philosophy course has to information systems. Philosophy courses teach you about the difference between data, information, and knowledge, and they can help you understand how to conceptualize systems and how to proceed with problem solving. Psychology classes can help you understand the dynamics of individual change, interpersonal conflict, and learning. Sociology courses are useful for understanding organizational structure, change, and decision making, while economics courses provide you with the concepts needed to evaluate the return on investment in information systems and productivity.

Figure 1.6

The Importance of Sociotechnical Skills in Your Career

Whether you're interested in a technical or nontechnical career, sociotechnical skills are crucial. Note that analysis and problem solving are important abilities for all four of the career paths shown. Managers—whether in IS or some other business function—need to develop their behavior and communications skills, and technical skills are important even for non-IS professionals. As the graph shows, all of these career paths demand at least some expertise in all three skill areas.

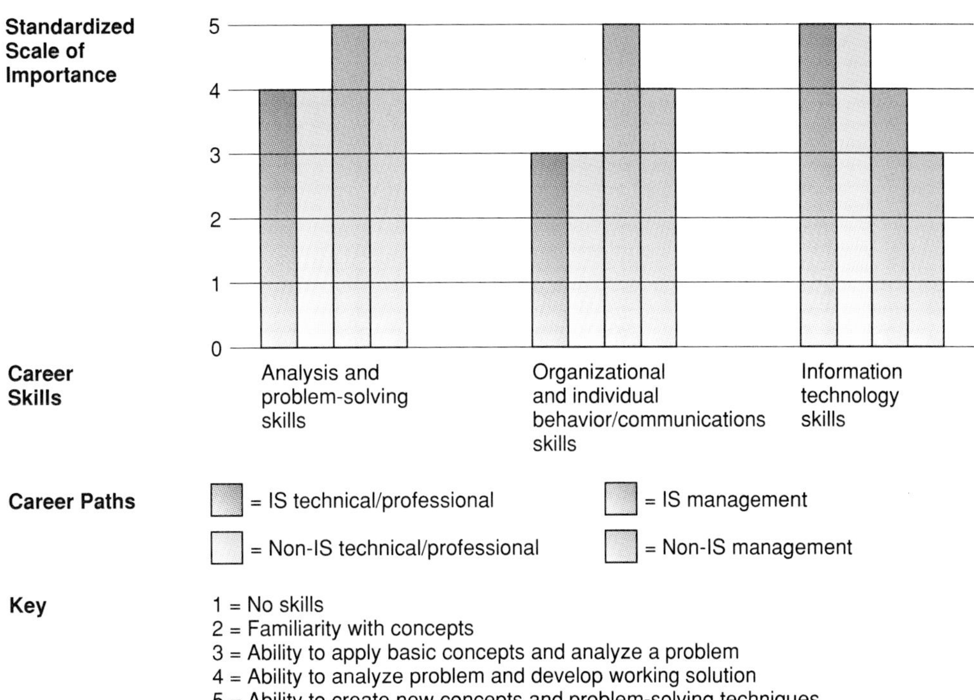

As these figures show, information systems are no longer islands isolated from the mainstream of the corporation, staffed by technical experts. A person must have a very broad background in the liberal arts, behavioral sciences, and technology areas to really excel in an information systems world. Communication skills—being able to read, write, speak, and think clearly—will be more important in the information economy of the 1990s than at any time in history. Therefore, you should see this course in relation to others in your college career and plan accordingly.

1.4 The Challenges Ahead

You might think from listening to advertisements or reading the newspaper that most of the significant problems with computers and information systems have been solved and that all we have to do is rely on cheaper, more powerful technology to solve our pressing productivity, quality, national wealth, and competitive problems in world markets. Nothing could be fur-

Figure 1.7

Courses That Will Help You Develop Important Career Skills

Each of the skill areas shown in Figure 1.6 involves an ability to perform specific organizational tasks. Here we break down each skill area into some of the particular skills that it includes. The third row lists relevant courses that will help you develop your abilities in this area. Note that even nontechnical courses are important for developing information systems literacy.

Career Skill	Analysis/Problem Solving	Behavior and Communication Skills	Technology Skills
Specific Skills	Analytic framework Functional requirements Physical design Implementation Systems development	Organizational strategy Structure Culture Making decisions Business procedures and functions	Hardware Software Telecommunications Database
Relevant Courses	Philosophy English literature History Behavioral sciences Mathematics	Psychology Sociology Economics English literature Languages Speech	MIS Database Telecommunications Advanced software

ther from the truth. In fact, we are just beginning to learn how to use the currently available technology wisely, not to mention the new technology being tested in the lab.

Every technology has a development path, and it often takes almost two generations (30–40 years) before the full potential of a technology even begins to be exploited. For example, most experts would agree that although automobiles were invented in 1890, it was not until the 1920s, or even the 1930s, that the modern, mass-produced, consciously engineered automobile appeared. For a considerable period, the auto was simply a "horseless carriage" with a tiller rather than a steering wheel.

With computers and information systems we are still facing many difficult challenges. Here are four challenges for you to think about as you read this book. You might want to discuss and debate these challenges with your classmates or professor.

Technology challenge
The gap that has developed between the rapid advances in computer hardware and our ability to write useful software for it; also the gap between the changes in both hardware and software and businesses' ability to understand and apply them.

Technology Challenge

Briefly stated, the **technology challenge** involves two related problems: (1) computing hardware is advancing far more rapidly than our ability to write useful software, and (2) both are changing much faster than the ability

Figure 1.8

The Productivity Challenge: Why Can't We Get Better Faster?

Since 1950 the power of software has steadily improved; it doubles approximately every eight years. The power of hardware has soared; it grows by a factor of ten every five years. Meanwhile, the average rate at which people (and organizations) learn and apply new information and knowledge in the workplace grows very slowly—an average increase in productivity of 2 percent per year. As we move into the twenty-first century, the United States must learn how to become more productive in order to compete economically with other countries.

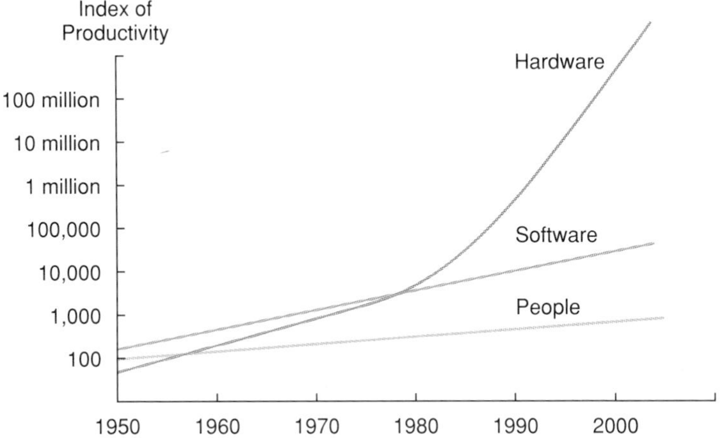

of our businesses to understand and apply the hardware and software (see Figure 1.8). Moreover, information systems must not only perform the well-defined tasks for which they have traditionally been used, but they must also provide resources that will enable people to do their jobs more efficiently and effectively.

An appropriate analogy might be your college library. Once the library has installed and mastered the card index system, and students have learned the mechanics of working with card catalogs, the college dean, president, and professors must answer a more challenging question: What else is needed at the library to raise the quality of student research, thinking, and education? This is a far more complex problem than the mere mechanics of storing and accessing information. Similarly, information technology must address the broader concern of changing the way people work and think so that they will be able to take full advantage of the technology.

As we will discuss in greater detail in Chapters 3–5, while computing hardware is growing exponentially in power, and prices are falling about as fast, software—the set of instructions that controls information systems—is growing in power linearly. In contrast, the rate at which people learn is relatively constant, and the rate of change in the absorption and application of new knowledge in factories and offices is no greater than the annual rate of productivity increase (about 2 percent a year).

No one wants (or knows how) to slow down the growth of technology because potentially it is so beneficial. Therefore, we must find a way to increase the rate of growth in the power of software and reduce its cost.

And we must also increase the rate at which individuals absorb and understand information technology knowledge.

One possibility is to make writing software applications as simple as, say, using pen and ink to write an essay. In Chapter 5 we talk about new developments in programming and applications development that might make this possible.

But how can we increase the rate at which individuals in business firms increase their stock of knowledge and learn new technologies and techniques? What do we do about senior and middle managers who do not want to learn? What about other employees?

Productivity Challenge

Productivity challenge The need to increase U.S. productivity and bring it into line with the growth in computing power.

Although the United States has invested more in computers than any other country, we still face a **productivity challenge** in that there is an enormous—and still expanding—gap between the growth in computing power and the annual increase in productivity in the United States (see Figure 1.7 for an illustration). Why is this so? How can the power of hardware grow so fast, while software and ultimate productivity in offices and factories grow so slowly? One central challenge of this course will be to learn how to bend the productivity curve upward so it will be more in line with the growing power of the technology.

Finding a solution to this problem is essential because the United States is losing the competition for economic resources, and indeed wealth itself, to economies that not only save and invest more but also apply information technology more wisely. The United States saves much less than other countries, it invests in new businesses and technology at a lower rate, and, consequently, its productivity suffers. Japan (our major competitor) and most other industrialized countries save much more. Higher savings translate into higher investment, which leads to higher productivity. It is not surprising, then, that since 1950, Japan and other countries have been growing at up to twice the rate of the United States. This gap may continue unless the United States can find a way to use the growth in computing power to increase productivity.

Strategic Business Challenge

Strategic business challenge The need for businesses to develop the ability to change quickly in response to changes in the external environment, technology, or markets.

As you learn more about business organizations in Chapter 2, you will discover that successful businesses become very good at doing certain things relentlessly, repetitively, and routinely, which permits them to make a great deal of money. The **strategic business challenge** arises when a major change occurs in a firm's external environments, such as a change in technology or markets. How fast can a business change to take advantage of the new technology (before its competitors do)? How fast can a business change its routine procedures to make new products or deliver new services?

Many expert observers believe we must redesign, rethink, and reconceptualize how we produce and deliver products and services in order to achieve breakthroughs in productivity. As the Focus on Technology explains, this is how the California-based Vons supermarket chain has used information technology to gain a competitive edge.

FOCUS ON *Technology*

Technology Transforms the Supermarket Business

The Vons Companies, a $3.9 billion supermarket chain based in El Monte, California, is considered one of the country's most innovative supermarket chains in a highly competitive business that is difficult to automate. In the retail food business supermarkets earn between two and four cents on every pretax dollar, which places a high premium on efficiency and productivity.

Time spent in the checkout lane is a critical service factor. Like many other supermarket chains, Vons has switched to checkout scanners. But it has further boosted throughput at the checkout counter by automating payments. Customers using a plastic bank card with a magnetic strip to debit their bank accounts can pay for groceries in 14 seconds compared with the 25 to 35 seconds required to write a check. This has raised the cashier throughput from 15 items per minute in manual checkout to 28 items a minute.

Vons also found that hardly anyone clips coupons anymore and that it was expensive to run ads in the newspaper. Instead, it set up a Valueplus Coupon Club. Members receive a plastic card that a checker passes through a machine. Discounts are automatically deducted for items on special.

Vons is experimenting with special sensor-equipped Videocarts from International Resources in Chicago. Each cart is outfitted with a sensor and a 6-inch square video terminal. As a shopper pushes this cart down the aisles, a corresponding sensor will activate vendor commercials and store specials on the video screen.

Source: Helen Pike, "Check Out This Supermarket," *Computerworld Focus on Integration,* November 6, 1989.

People Challenge

Yet another problem we face is the **people challenge,** which involves the interrelationship of technology and humans. It refers both to the need for individuals and businesses to adjust to rapid changes in technology and to the need to design systems individuals can control and understand. The estimated half-life of information systems knowledge is about five years. That means that roughly half of what you learn in this book will be outdated in five years! This is true of most other technical fields as well. Therefore, to stay current, individuals will have to invest more of their own time in retraining themselves. Obviously, business firms will have to contribute, facilitate, and even lead in this process. How much retraining a firm should undertake and how much it should invest in this process are critical questions raised throughout this book.

People challenge
The problems posed by the interrelationship of technology and humans; refers both to the problems rapid changes in technology present for individuals and businesses and to the need to design systems individuals can control and understand.

For example, chocolate maker L. S. Heath and Sons found out the hard way that information technology is advancing somewhat faster than the ability of people to understand it.[2] Heath filed suit against AT&T alleging that an AT&T sales representative promised to deliver a fully interactive computer system in which people could communicate directly with the computer. But this was not the system delivered. Heath claimed that AT&T's sales staff does not understand the huge product line that AT&T

sells. As a result, its salespersons overpromise what AT&T systems can do. Other critics contend that AT&T should divide its product line so that people who sell voice equipment do not also try to sell computers that they do not understand. Obviously, the critics point out, AT&T's sales staff needs to be continually retrained.

The second part of the people challenge involves the need to design appropriate interfaces between human beings and machines. Somehow, we must learn to design information systems—and other control systems—that permit and encourage humans to control the process and that function according to design and intentions. To understand the difficulties in designing systems that individuals can control and understand, consider the situation of the USS *Vincennes* on July 3, 1988, when it mistakenly shot down an Iranian civilian airliner on a routine flight.

On July 3, 1988, at 6:47ZULU (Greenwich mean time), Iran Air Flight 655 took off from Bandar Abbas Joint Military Civilian Airport destined for Dubai.[3] Flight 655 was a routine, on-time, international air flight using commercial airway Amber 59. At the same moment, the USS *Vincennes,* cruising 47 miles offshore, picked up Flight 655 on AEGIS, the world's most sophisticated air combat control system. The AEGIS display system consists of four screens, each 42 inches square, which display the tactical information contained in the command and decision computers that keep track of all air and surface combatants.

At 3 minutes and 20 seconds after takeoff, Flight 655 was identified by the *Vincennes*'s officers as a "potential threat." At 6:54 A.M., 7 minutes

Systems made by Honeywell, Inc. control key functions of Domtar Canada's automated pulp-and-paper mill and power plant. Companies take great care in designing the apparatus with which people interact to ensure that human beings control and understand the information from these systems.

Source: Courtesy of Honeywell, Inc.

and 8 seconds after takeoff, the ship's captain turned the firing key, and two SM-2 Blk II missiles left the launch rails and destroyed Flight 655 at a range of eight miles and an altitude of 13,500 feet. Two hundred and ninety civilians died in the Airbus 300 plane.

Subsequent investigations by the Joint Chiefs of Staff and Department of Defense concluded that the AEGIS system worked perfectly, and that neither the captain nor the crew were at fault or made material mistakes. The investigation showed that the AEGIS system accurately reported the bearing and location of Flight 655. Unfortunately, however, system operators mistakenly perceived the plane to be descending, in an attack mode, against the *Vincennes.* These mistaken perceptions occurred despite the fact that Flight 655 was continuously transmitting a civilian aircraft radio signal.

In the last three minutes, AEGIS operators sent numerous messages to what they believed was a plane at 7,000 feet. Flight 655 was at 13,500 feet, and the plane's captain had no reason to respond to signals that appeared to be directed to some other plane, perhaps a military plane. Hence Flight 655 did not respond to any messages sent by the *Vincennes.*

Navy psychiatrists and psychologists were called in to explain how a well-trained crew could misinterpret the AEGIS output, which was completely correct. They concluded that "stress, task fixation, and unconscious distortion of data may have played a major role in this incident."

Both the tactical information coordinator (TIC) and the identification supervisor (IS) became convinced that Flight 655 was a hostile Iranian F-14 when the IS received a report that the plane was squawking a military identification signal. The IS had momentarily forgotten to move the electronic marker for Flight 655 from Bandar Abbas airport to its current location. This 90-second error may have permitted an Iranian military jet issuing a military identification signal from Bandar Abbas to become confused on the TIC's screen with Flight 655. This mistake may have been critical.

In any event, once the mistaken identification of Flight 655 occurred, "the TIC appears to have distorted data flow in an unconscious attempt to make available evidence fit a preconceived scenario ('scenario fulfillment')."

In briefings that followed, Defense Secretary Carlucci and the Chairman of the Joint Chiefs of Staff, Admiral William J. Crowe, Jr., concluded that given the heat of battle, the large number of things that the captain had to keep track of, the time compression, and the setting, no one was at fault.

In a separate report on crew training for the AEGIS system, the General Accounting Office—a congressional watchdog agency that monitors government spending and performance—concluded that neither ships nor crew using AEGIS were trained in settings that even approached combat conditions.

Control rooms where controls do not work, where people do not understand and are not trained to understand the system, where instruments give false signals, where time is compressed, and where mistakes are costly, perhaps deadly, are all invitations to disaster in the computer age. Every day we rely more and more on semiautomated activities, which, if they fail or are poorly operated, have extremely harmful consequences. The Focus on Problem Solving examines some of the advantages of computers, but also reminds us that there are some things computers alone cannot do.

FOCUS ON *Problem Solving*

Wheels for the Mind

What fascinates me about computers is not that they're humanlike, but that they're complementary: they are good at what we are bad at. They're precise, accurate, reliable, and predictable—and boring, unemotional, dry, and uncaring. They can reason, but only with rules and facts, not with intuition and wisdom. They can handle uncertainty as a percentage, but not as a concept.

Much as I love computers, I have come to love them only in their place, which is working for us, not replacing us. I love them for their differences from us, not for their similarities (that is, people are infinitely better at being people than computers could ever be).

Consider a brief history of modern computers. They began as big batch machines. You submitted "jobs" to them on punch cards; they clanked and creaked and returned results as long fanfolded printouts. These computers did heavy industrial work: accounting, record keeping, and managing massive amounts of not very complex data. The earliest computers knew only yes, no, and sequence.

Over the years, computers have become easier for people like me to deal with. They are now small and quick and can handle complex data: graphics, text, and rich structures such as outlines, org charts, and project schematics.

Some years ago Apple used the slogan (attributed to Steve Jobs) "wheels for the mind," handing out T-shirts showing a person riding a bicycle. The analogy is apt. Just as we have both trains and bicycles, so we have both mainframes and PCs. Trains enable us to go farther, but bicycles give us individual freedom. In the same way, mainframes can run bigger businesses, but PCs help us in our individual tasks.

The computer has the power—and gives you the power—to manipulate things that would otherwise be tedious. You can create outlines and rearrange them; you can make your software automatically restructure a mass of information by person, by project, by urgency, or by any other criteria you define. You can give a computer data and watch it create recognizable patterns or pick out the anomalies in mostly boring information.

The computer can take down and display your thoughts, but it can't help you think them. The meaning still resides in the mind of the beholder.

Source: Esther Dyson, column, reprinted with permission from *PC/Computing,* August 1988, p. 27. Copyright © 1988, Ziff Communications Company.

These challenges of technology, productivity, business organization, and people—while daunting—also suggest that there are great opportunities for applying information technology in new and powerful ways that have not yet been discovered.

1.5 Organizing Concepts of the Book

There are four key organizing concepts in this book that are reflected in each chapter. We have already alluded to these concepts earlier in the chapter, but we want to emphasize them here before you go further. In general, if you understand these four concepts and their implications, you will have mastered the book. We briefly review each concept below.

Knowledge and Information versus Data

Our focus in this book is on how to deliver information and knowledge to business professionals who are engaged in business problem solving and analysis. This is not a data processing book focused primarily on how data are input and output by computers or on the growing power of information processing technology. Although we do cover this technical material, it is always with an eye to what difference it will make to the success (or failure) of the business, or to your success as a business professional.

Analysis and Problem Solving versus Technology

Some people think choosing the right technology for a system is a difficult problem. Actually, the most difficult part of designing an effective information system is understanding the problem it is intended to solve. Information systems and technologies are useful tools only when they are used wisely.

Therefore we start with the strategic needs of the business, the needs of work groups, and the needs of individual business professionals. Once we have developed a broadly based analysis of a business situation, we can begin to talk about how to solve problems. Only then can we begin to talk about technology.

A Sociotechnical Perspective

Our approach throughout is to think of information systems as composed of three mutually adjusting entities: technologies, organizations, and people. A broadly based set of skills is required to understand systems; the subject is inherently multidisciplinary, involving teams of people working together.

Systems Are Networks of Information Technologies

The technical foundations of information systems today are much broader than in the past. Whereas most attention in the past focused on the computer itself, our focus will be on a wide variety of information technologies that share some principles but are very different. We will be considering telecommunications and networking technology, printing and facsimile transmission, and various software issues.

Summary

- An information system is a set of interrelated components designed to collect, process, store, and disseminate information.

• Input, processing, and output are the three basic activities of an information system; through these activities, raw data are transformed into useful information.

• The purpose of building information systems is to solve a variety of business problems. This insight can be used to describe existing systems and to develop new systems.

• An information system consists of three components: organizations, people, and technology.

• The people dimension of information systems involves issues such as training, job attitudes, ergonomics, and the user interface.

• The technology dimension of information systems consists of computer hardware, software, storage, and telecommunications technology.

• The organization dimension of information systems involves issues such as the organization's hierarchy, functional specialties, business procedures, culture, and political interest groups.

• Computers and information systems and computer literacy and information systems literacy are different. Information systems literacy involves understanding the people and organizational dimensions of information systems as well as information technology.

• Knowledge, information, and data are different. Information is created from streams of data through the application of knowledge. The purpose of information systems is to create and disseminate useful information and knowledge in a manner designed to solve some business problem.

• A sociotechnical approach to information systems combines three areas of study: information technology, organizational and individual behavior, and analytic problem-solving skills.

• You do not need to know everything about information systems to know a great deal, perhaps enough. Skills in three areas are important: technical skills, business and organizational skills, and analytic problem-solving skills. Many courses in your college—both information systems courses and liberal arts and math courses—can be helpful. The specific mix of skills you need depends on what you want to become.

• This book raises four challenges, which reflect the realistic situation of systems today. The technology is changing very rapidly, faster than software or people. Productivity—at least in the United States—has not yet responded to massive investments in information technology. Business organizations do not change easily, even though they must do so to make optimal use of new technology. And people often must work with awkward systems, under duress, in situations that have not been anticipated or tested by designers.

Key Terms

Information system
Input
Processing
Output
Feedback
Formal systems
Manual system
Computer hardware

Computer software
Storage technology
Telecommunications technology
Computer literacy
Information systems literacy
Data
Information
Knowledge
Sociotechnical perspective
Technology challenge
Productivity challenge
Strategic business challenge
People challenge

Review Questions

1. Define an information system.
2. How do an information system, a computer program, and a computer differ?
3. What are the three basic activities of information systems?
4. What role is played by feedback in an information system?
5. What are the three components of an information system? Describe each of them.
6. What role does the surrounding environment play in shaping a business organization's information systems?
7. What is the basic flow of information in an information system?
8. What is the organizational basis of information systems?
9. Distinguish between computer literacy and information systems literacy.
10. How do knowledge, information, and data differ?
11. What are the major reasons why you should study information systems?
12. What challenges are posed by information systems?

Discussion Questions

1. Some people argue that information systems should be designed and built by technical specialists, persons trained in computer science and engineering. Discuss and comment.

2. With faster and better computers, most of the problems we are currently experiencing with information systems will simply disappear. Comment and discuss.

Problem-Solving Exercises

1. The Yamaha Motor Corporation, one of the world's largest motorcycle manufacturers, uses a computer-based information system for supplying its dealers with parts. The system stores data about the quantity, price, and location of the parts in Yamaha's inventory. Each dealer has a terminal connected to Yamaha's central computer in Atlanta. When a part is needed, the dealer uses a menu on the terminal screen to select the correct parts, specifying each part with a 12-digit part number. At the end of the order,

a shipping/packing list is transmitted back to the dealer and prints out on the dealer's own printer. The shipping/packing list states where each part will come from and indicates back-ordered parts, retail and dealer value, and preferred freight route. Describe the inputs, outputs, and processes of this information system and its people, organizational, and technical components.

2. Find a description of a business information system in a business or computer magazine. Describe the system in terms of its inputs, processes, and outputs. What are the people components of the system? The technical components? The organizational components?

References

Ralph Landau, "U.S. Economic Growth," *Scientific American,* June 1988.

Stephen S. Roach, "White Collar Productivity: A Glimmer of Hope?" Special Economic Study, Morgan Stanley, September 16, 1988.

Notes

1. Plato, *The Republic.*
2. "Keeping the Sales Force Up to Date at AT&T," *Information Week,* October 10, 1988.
3. "Formal Investigation into the Circumstances Surrounding the Downing of Iran Air Flight 655 on 3 July 1988," Department of Defense, July 28, 1988.

Problem-Solving Case

Customers at the Drawing Board

One way firms are boosting profits is by using information systems that customers can interact with to design products directly to their individual specifications. Weyerhaeuser, in Seattle, Washington, faced sluggish sales from its retail lumber operations. Home improvement centers affiliated with Weyerhaeuser complained that there was little to distinguish them from competitors. Weyerhaeuser responded with a computer-aided Design Center.

The Weyerhaeuser Design Center consists of specialized hardware and software housed in a kiosk on the showroom floor. Using three-dimensional imagery, the center presents the customer with various construction plans and helps compile a materials list and cost estimates for building a backyard deck. Sales staff can thus design a deck to the customer's requirements. The touch of a button prints out a color blueprint and an itemized list of what the homeowner needs to build the customized deck.

Weyerhaeuser claims the Design Center has increased sales of lumber and related materials, set it apart from competitors in consumers' minds, and strengthened its business relationship with affiliated home improvement centers.

Second Skin Swimwear, Inc. in Riviera Beach, Florida, has also profited from using information systems to involve customers in product design. The firm uses a system called Digifit to combat the "flab and sag" factor. A cus-

tomer tries on one of Second Skin's ten basic tops, bottoms, or one-piece suits in a dressing booth. A video camera connected to a desktop-sized personal computer digitizes her image into a form that can be accepted by the computer.

The customer then reviews her image on the computer with a company designer, using the system to alter the swimsuit design to fit her needs. She can add a higher bodice, a less plunging back, a skirt, or elegant bows and ribbons, and she can choose the swimsuit fabric from 300 fabric swatches. The entire process takes 20 to 45 minutes. The system then generates and prints a customized pattern and passes it to a cutter who begins the manufacturing process. The custom-designed swimsuit is finished within several days. With Digifit, Second Skin Swimwear can manufacture 20 suits a day, compared to 2 per day if the suits were entirely handmade.

Depending on the design, Second Skin's creations are priced from $60 to $100, which is comparable to the cost of handmade swimsuits. Second Skin, however, provides the customer with speedier delivery of merchandise and greater design variety.

Digifit was recently upgraded to allow a full-color image display on the screen and more pattern manipulation. The new version of the system has halved labor costs and manufacturing time. A swimsuit that previously took 30 minutes to craft now takes just 15.

Source: Helen Pike, "Close to the Customer," *Computerworld Focus on Integration*, October 2, 1989.

Case Study Questions

1. What are the people components of these systems? The organizational components? The technology components?
2. What people, technology, and strategic business challenges did these systems deal with?
3. Analyze one of these systems in terms of inputs, processing, and outputs.

CHAPTER · TWO

How Business Firms Use Information Systems

Chapter Outline

2.1 Components of Business
- Organizing a Business
- Major Business Functions and Structure
- Levels in a Business Organization
- The Business Environment

2.2 Placement of Information Systems in a Business
- Purposes of Information Systems
- Functional Business Systems

2.3 Examples of Business Information Systems
- Manufacturing and Production Systems
- Sales and Marketing Systems
- Finance and Accounting Systems
- Human Resources Systems

2.4 How Businesses Use Information Systems for Competitive Advantage
- Examples of Strategic Impact Systems
- Strategic People

Learning Objectives

After reading and studying this chapter, you will:

1. Be able to define a business organization.
2. Understand the major functions performed by businesses.
3. Know why business organizations need information systems.
4. Understand how the core business information systems support the manufacturing and production, finance and accounting, sales and marketing, and human resources functions.
5. Know how businesses use information systems for competitive advantage.

Bringing Information Technology and Business Together at New York Life Insurance Company

After 12 years at New York Life, Jim Bain finally discovered what his company's business is. Bain spent 11 years in the Data Processing Division before he was reassigned to a major product division, the Agency Department. This profit center supplies insurance services to thousands of agencies across the nation. In his new job, Bain advises the senior manager of the Agency Department about how to bring new technology into the division to better serve customers.

New York Life is the fifth-largest insurance company in the United States, with revenues of $40 billion, 9,000 employees, and 10,000 agents. From the beginning it was organized along hierarchical, functional lines: the major divisions were marketing, human resources, agent services, and operations (which included information systems and services). New York Life was an early investor in information systems, beginning in the 1950s. Throughout the 1960s and 1970s it continued to develop a large central information systems group like those of most insurance companies.

By the 1980s this method of organization was no longer satisfactory, because the insurance industry and the company's needs were changing. It couldn't move quickly to accommodate change because it was hampered by large, inflexible systems. The company fell behind in integrating new information technology. The company's hierarchical structure, which emphasized

specialized areas of competence like human resources, information systems, and finance, failed to provide cross-fertilization. People needed to experience different areas in order to understand the company as a whole. The company needed to put more businesspeople into the systems group; the computer types were directing businesspeople, rather than the reverse.

To compensate for this familiar pattern, New York Life appointed a corporate lawyer, Michael J. McLaughlin, to head up the Information Systems and Services Department. McLaughlin was given the task of changing the direction of information systems from technology centered to business driven. His first act was to initiate Project Steer, a $150 million, five-year effort to update and change systems from an orientation that sought to lower costs to a customer orientation that emphasizes sales and service.

McLaughlin's second major effort was the Business Analyst program. Attempting to overcome the isolation of information systems people from the business, McLaughlin reassigns mid-level information systems personnel like Jim Bain to work in the major product and service areas. The hope is that business managers will learn directly how information technology can be used to increase sales and serve customers better.

Source: Nell Margolis, "Business Gets the Upper Hand at New York Life," *Computerworld*, September 12, 1988.

The problems faced by New York Life illustrate the changing relationship between business organizations, information technology, and people. Briefly, business people need to become more aware of the potential offered by information systems, and computer and information technology experts need to become more aware of the business environment in which they work. This chapter explains what businesses are and how they use information systems.

2.1 Components of Business

Business organization
A complex, formal organization established for the purpose of producing products or services for a profit.

A **business organization** is a complex, formal organization whose aim is to produce products or services for a profit—that is, to sell products at a price greater than the cost of producing the product. Customers are willing to pay a price greater than the cost of production because they believe they receive a value equal to or greater than the sale price. Of course, there are nonprofit firms (the Society for the Blind produces goods but does not aim to make a profit), nonprofit organizations (like churches and public interest groups), and government agencies, all of which are complex formal organizations but do not operate to produce a profit. In general, the information systems found in nonprofit organizations are remarkably similar to those found in private industry.[1]

Organizing a Business

Imagine that you wanted to set up your own business. Just deciding to go into business, of course, would be the most important decision, but next would come the question of what product or service you would produce. The decision of what product or service to produce is called a strategic choice because it will determine the kinds of employees you need, the production methods, the marketing themes, and a host of other factors.

Once you answer these questions, what kind of an organization would you need? First, you would have to design some sort of production division—an arrangement of people, machines, and procedures to be followed to produce the product (which could be a service). Second, you would need a sales and marketing group or division whose principal job would be to sell the product or service at a profitable price. Third, you would need a finance

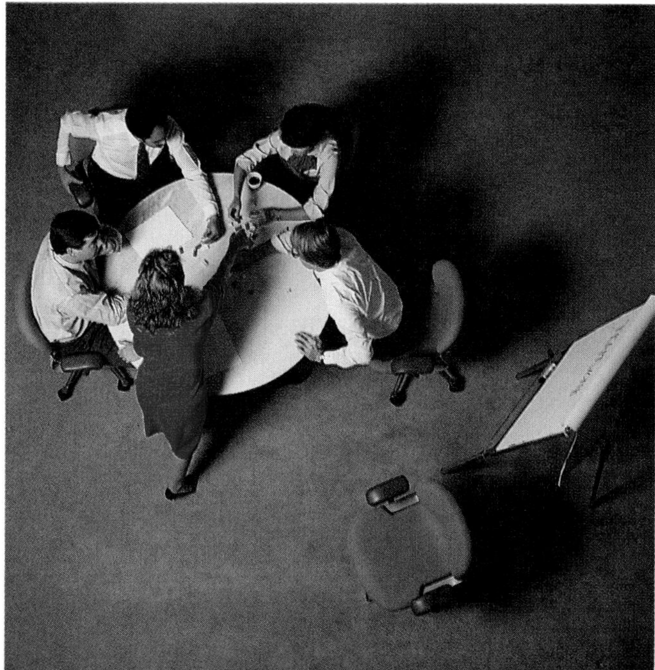

The human resources group at The Travelers Corporation conducts training sessions for employees, encouraging them to share ideas and expertise. In organizing a business, vital functions like human resources cannot be neglected.

Source: © R. J. Muna.

and accounting group. These people would seek out sources of credit or funds (loans from friends?) and would also keep track of current financial transactions such as orders, purchases, disbursements, payroll, and the like. Finally, you would want a group of people to focus on recruiting, hiring, training, and retaining people to work for you. In other words, you would want a human resources group (see Figure 2.1).

Of course, if your business was very small with only a few employees, you would not need, nor would you have the resources, to create specialized groups or divisions to perform these tasks. You would be doing all the work yourself with the assistance of one or two others. But your business would still entail the **business functions** of production, marketing, finance and accounting, and human resources activities.

Business functions
The various tasks performed in a business organization—for example, manufacturing and production, sales and marketing, finance and accounting, and human resources activities.

How would you go about actually organizing a business? Most organizations go through several stages. First, work is divided among a large number of employees, which permits **specialization:** each employee focuses on a specific task and in short order becomes very good at it. Next, a **hierarchy** of reporting and authority relationships is developed to assure that the work is completed. Over time, an **informal structure** emerges in a formal organization as people get to know one another. Birthday parties, births, new hires, and retirements are all occasions for informal relationships to build and for a culture to emerge. An organization needs both informal relationships and culture to help coordinate work and to provide meaning to work. In general, organizing is never completed but is instead an ongoing process driven by constant environmental change and changing perceptions within the organization.

Specialization
The division of work in a business organization so that each employee focuses on a specific task.

Hierarchy
The arrangement of persons in a business organization according to rank and authority; persons at the bottom of the hierarchy report to those on the next level who have more authority, these persons in turn report to the next level, and so on, up to senior management.

Informal structure
A network of personal relationships within a formal business organization.

Figure 2.1

The Four Major Functions of a Business

Every business, regardless of its size, must perform these four functions in order to succeed. It must *produce* something, whether a physical product or a service, and it must *market and sell* the product. The firm must perform *finance and accounting* tasks in order to manage its financial assets and fund flows, and it must also focus on *human resources* issues. In large corporations these functions are split into separate divisions or departments; in a one-person company the business owner must perform all these tasks.

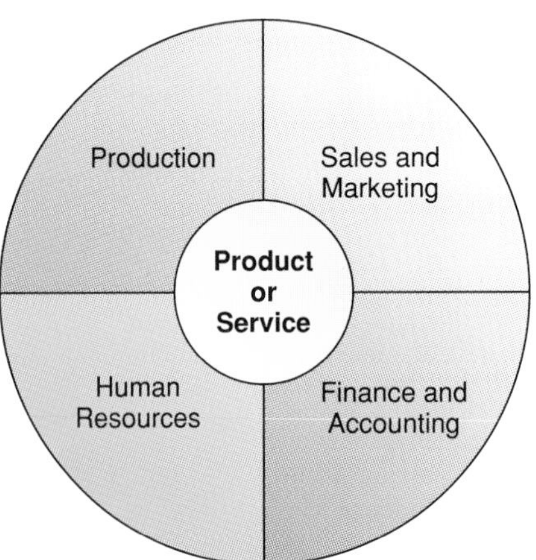

Major Business Functions and Structure

Like your hypothetical business, most business organizations typically perform four specific functions. A specialized department or division is usually created for each function shown in Figure 2.1 (e.g., the Marketing Department, the Production Division, and so on).

Levels in a Business Organization

Like all organizations, business firms coordinate the work of employees through a hierarchy in which authority is concentrated in the top. The hierarchy is typically composed of a **senior management** group, which makes long-range decisions about what products and services to produce; a general or **middle management** group organized into specialized divisions, which carries out the programs and plans of senior management by supervising employees; a group we call **knowledge and data workers,** who design the product or service (such as engineers) and administer the paper work associated with a business (such as clerical workers); and, finally, **production** or service **workers,** who actually produce the products or services of the firm (see Figure 2.2).

Organizations differ in terms of how much authority is concentrated in each layer. Some organizations are "flat" with a small group of senior managers and a single layer of middle management, followed immediately

Senior management
The persons at the top of the hierarchy in a business organization; they have the most authority and make long-range decisions for the organization.

Middle management
The persons in the middle of the hierarchy in a business organization; they carry out the programs and plans of senior management by supervising employees.

Knowledge and data workers
The employees in a business organization who create and/or use knowledge (e.g., engineers) or data (e.g., clerical workers) to solve business problems.

Production workers
The employees in a business organization who actually produce the firm's products or services.

Figure 2.2

The Organizational Pyramid: Levels in a Firm

All business organizations are hierarchies consisting of four principal levels: senior management, general or middle management, knowledge and data workers, and production and service workers. Each level of employees specializes in carrying out an important organizational role. Senior managers make long-term decisions about the future of the firm; middle managers implement these plans and programs. Knowledge and data workers design the firm's product or service and do much of the paperwork that running a business involves. Production and service workers are responsible for producing what the firm sells—be it a tangible product or an intangible service.

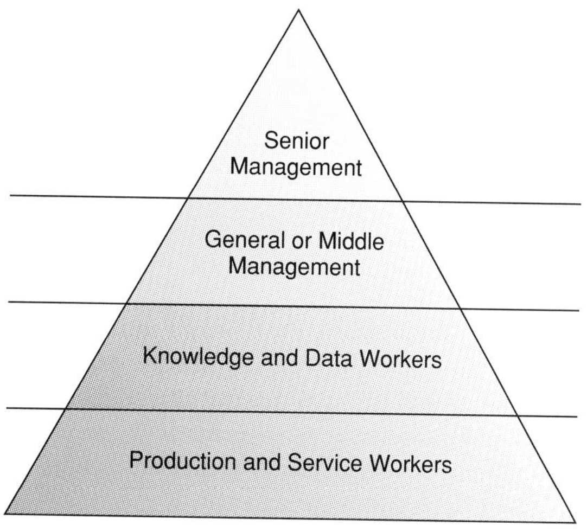

FOCUS ON *Problem Solving*

The Liability of Newness

If you were an entrepreneur just starting out with little money, you would not have the resources to hire many people, so you would have to perform most of the business functions yourself. How likely do you think it is that one person, or even a small group, could perform all these tasks really well? Now you can see why 74 percent of all new businesses fail within five years of starting out. This is called the liability of newness. How would you organize a small business to avoid these problems?

Obviously, the difficulties of organizing a new business properly are significant, but remember that 26 percent of new businesses survive more than five years. Furthermore, 260,000 new businesses are formed each year, an indication that many people believe the rewards of success are great.

Source: William H. Starbuck, "Why Organizations Run into Crises and Sometimes Survive Them," in Kenneth C. Laudon and Jon Turner, eds., *Information Technology and Strategic Management* (Englewood Cliffs, N.J.: Prentice-Hall, 1989).

by production workers. Other organizations are much more bureaucratic and may have as many as 7 to 15 layers of management between the senior group and the production worker. Never, however, is all authority concentrated at the top. Indeed, production workers can often stop production entirely; hence what they do and feel is quite important to the firm. Perhaps the most important strategic business decision employees make every day is the decision to come to work.

As you can see, a business firm is a complicated entity that requires many different kinds of skills and people, who must be organized rather tightly to enable the firm to operate efficiently and make a profit. Imagine, then, how difficult it is to start a new business. The Focus on Problem Solving examines some other aspects of this "liability of newness."

Business environment
The aggregate conditions in which a business organization operates; the general environment includes government regulations, economic and political conditions, and ~~t~~echnological developments, while ~~the t~~ask environment includes ~~other~~ ~~o~~r entities with which the ~~firm a~~re directly involved, such ~~as customer~~s, suppliers, and

The Business Environment

So far we have talked about business firms as if they existed in a vacuum. Actually, organizations depend heavily on their surrounding **business environment** to supply resources like capital and labor, to supply symbolic support or legitimacy (which helps in getting capital and labor), to provide protection, and, usually, to provide new technology, techniques, and learning. Most important, the environment provides customers to the business, for without customers the business would fail.

Figure 2.3

The Complex Environment of a Business

The environment of a business firm has two elements: a general environment and a task environment. The task environment involves specific groups with which the business must deal directly, such as customers, suppliers, and competitors. Beyond this is the broader general environment: socioeconomic trends, political conditions, technological innovations, and global events. To be successful, an organization must constantly monitor and respond to—or even anticipate—developments in both arenas.

The business environment can be broken down into two components: a general environment and a specific task environment (see Figure 2.3). The general environment encompasses the political, economic, and technological conditions within which the business must operate. To stay in business, organizations must keep track of changes in their general environment. A business, for instance, must comply with government directives and laws, respond to changing economic and political conditions, and continually watch for new technologies. In addition to having this broad view, businesses must also keep track of important groups with which they are directly involved. This is the task environment, which includes customers, suppliers, competitors, regulators, and stockholders.

Environments are always changing and fluid: new technology, economic trends, political developments, or regulations that affect businesses

Companies must respond to continually changing conditions in order to stay in business. To assist Vietnamese and other employees, the McCord Winn division of Textron Inc. sponsors in-house mathematics and English language classes at its Winchester, Massachusetts, plant.

Source: Courtesy of Textron, Inc.

are constantly emerging. When capital and labor can move freely, competitors are always present to take away customers. In general, when businesses fail, it is because they failed to respond adequately to their changing environments.

2.2 Placement of Information Systems in a Business

Up to now we have not mentioned information systems or described their place in the organizational structure because we wanted to introduce the traditional business organization, structure, and environment. Now, let's bring systems into the picture.

Purposes of Information Systems

All businesses face two generic problems: how to manage the internal forces and groups that produce their products and services and how to deal with customers, government agencies, competitors, and general socioeconomic trends in their surrounding environment. The most powerful explanation of why businesses build systems, then, is to solve organizational problems and to respond to a changing environment.

FOCUS ON *Organizations*

Quaker Oats Copes with Europe 1992

In 1992, Europe, that constellation of small countries, will become a single united market called the European Community. Trade barriers and tariffs will disappear, and new common standards will be established. As a result, the European market of 320 million consumers with a $4 trillion combined economy will replace the United States as the largest single market in the world. Although 1992 promises an economic boom for Europe, both European and American companies are finding that vast changes in their information systems will be required.

Historically, Quaker Oats, the Chicago-based food products company, marketed products only in country markets. The products had country-specific names, but all used the Quaker Oats logo. Because each country had different products and brand names, Quaker Oats organized its information systems around each European country and the unique products in that country. Now with a single Europe, this will change. Because of the promised integration of Europe, Quaker Oats is developing more transnational products like Gatorade, which is marketed in Italy, Canada, and Germany. With more transnational products, it makes sense to restructure operations and systems into unified organizations that serve large economic blocks. For Quaker Oats, 1992 is both a challenge and an opportunity: the company will have to rebuild its systems to support common products sold to large geographic regions, but it may also find that the potential for profits has increased.

Source: "Planning an IS Eurostrategy," *Information Week*, January 9, 1989.

Businesses build systems to respond to competitors, customers, suppliers, and vendors in a dynamic and fluid environment. As external forces and organizational problems change, new systems are required and old systems must be modified. Consider, for example, the impact that the unification of Europe into a single economic trading zone in 1992 is having on the information systems of multinational firms. The Focus on Organizations looks at how one company is responding to this challenge.

Fortunately, not all environmental changes are as massive as the creation of new trading communities the size of Europe. Moreover, no single system governs all the activities of an entire business. Businesses have different kinds of information systems that address different levels of problems and different business functions. Since a firm's information systems tend to be specialized, changes in one area do not always spill over into other areas.

Businesses also build systems to track materials, people, and activities inside the firm and to manage their internal problems, such as the production of goods and services or the tracking of parts, inventories, and employees. Some information systems deal with purely internal problems, some with purely external issues, and some with both internal and external phenomena. Typically, systems are categorized by the functional specialty they serve and by the type of business problem they address.

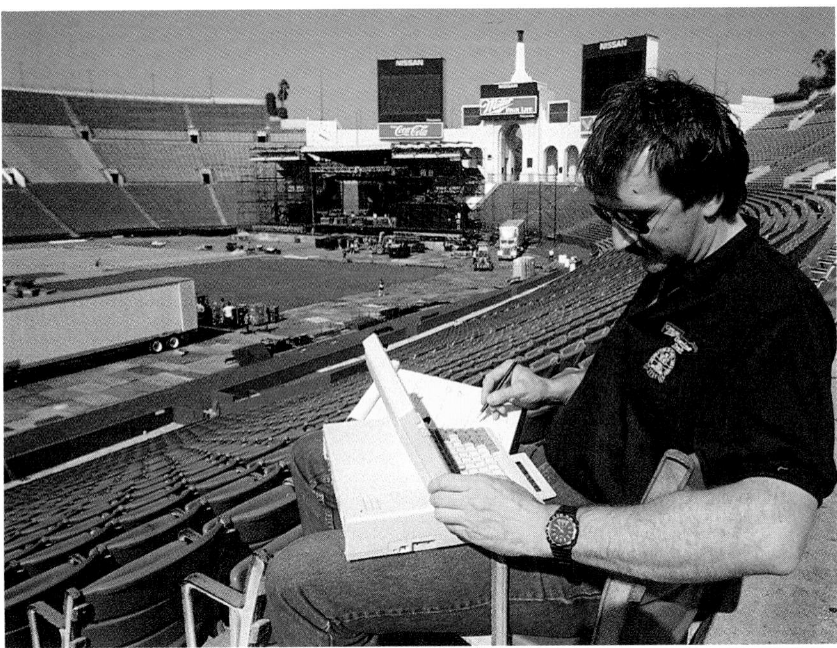

Businesses large and small use information systems to solve organizational problems and respond to a changing environment. The tour production manager for The Who's 1989 tour, Mick Double, used a Toshiba laptop computer to oversee 200 full-time crew, 11 trucks, and five tour buses; coordinate stage, sound, light, and video rentals at over 40 locations; and confirm all band and crew travel arrangements and timetables.

Source: © Ken Chen.

Functional Business Systems

Figure 2.4 provides a single integrated view of the role of information systems in business firms. Here you can see that business firms do not have one huge system but, instead, many different specialized systems. Each functional area of a firm develops systems: there are manufacturing and production systems, finance and accounting systems, sales and marketing systems, and human resources systems. The systems also serve different levels: strategic-level systems help senior managers plan; middle management systems help control an organization's day-to-day activities; knowledge systems assist engineers and office workers; and operational systems are used in manufacturing and service delivery.

Systems can be classified according to the type of organizational problem they solve. This usually corresponds to the level in the corporation that the system serves. For instance, some problems are clearly strategic because they involve questions of organizational goals, products, services, and long-term survival. Such problems in organizations are typically handled by senior management, and often **strategic-level systems** and applications are developed. Strategic-level systems might be used in deciding whether to introduce new products, invest in new technology, or move to a new location. Other problems in an organization are clearly tactical because they involve questions of how to achieve goals and how to control and evaluate the process of achieving goals. These problems are the province of middle

Strategic-level systems
Information systems used in solving a business organization's long-range, or strategic, problems.

Figure 2.4

An Integrated View of the Role of Information Systems within a Firm

Information systems can perform different functional specialties, depending on the organizational level that uses them. Strategic-level systems help senior managers plan the firm's long-term course of action. Tactical systems help middle managers supervise and coordinate day-to-day business activities. Knowledge and data workers use knowledge systems to design products, streamline services, and cope with paperwork, while operational systems deal with day-to-day production and service activities.

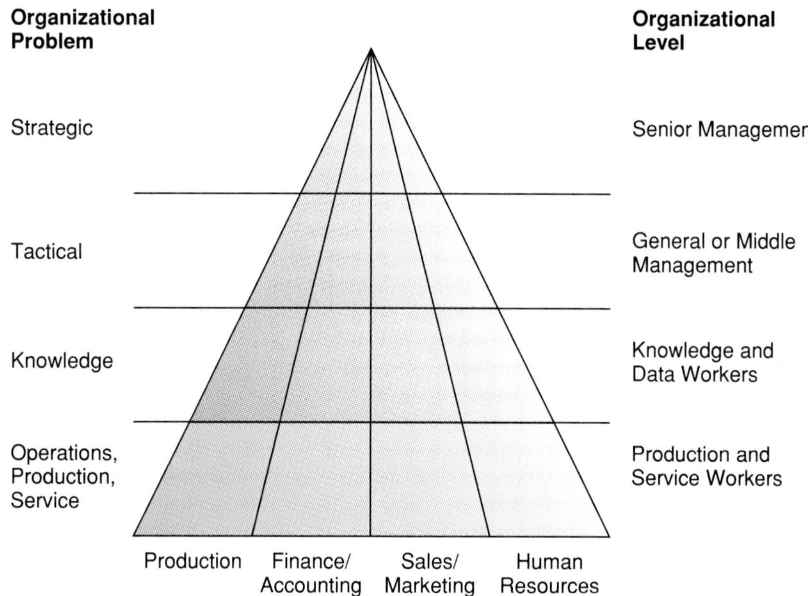

management and typically involve the development of **tactical,** or management support, **systems.** Tactical systems might be used in such applications as monitoring sales to see if annual or quarterly targets were met or reviewing departmental budgets to make sure the firm is not wasting its resources.

Tactical systems
Information systems used in solving a business organization's short-term, or tactical, problems, such as how to achieve goals and how to evaluate the process of achieving goals.

A very different set of newly recognized problems faced by organizations involves questions of knowledge and technical expertise. Knowledge problems encompass a very wide range of questions, such as: What is the optimal production mix? Where should factories be located? How should a bolt assembly be designed? How should training be performed? and What kind of information technologies should be employed? Knowledge problems are the province of knowledge and data workers, who create, distribute, and use knowledge and information on behalf of the firm. **Knowledge systems** are used in applications that serve these groups and solve this class of problems. In general, knowledge workers hold formal university degrees and often are members of a profession such as engineers, doctors, lawyers, scientists, and the like. (Data workers have primarily clerical skills and backgrounds.)

Knowledge systems
Information systems used by knowledge workers in business organizations to solve questions requiring knowledge and technical expertise.

Finally, **operational systems** are used to solve problems related to operations, services, and production: How fast should machines be operated? How should today's letters be produced? How many orders were

Operational systems
Information systems used in monitoring the day-to-day activities of a business organization.

shipped out today? How can an angry queue of customers best be handled? These problems are the province of technical, production, service, and operations workers and involve monitoring the day-to-day activities of the firm.

2.3 Examples of Business Information Systems

Below we discuss how organizations use information systems (from a functional perspective) to solve problems in specific functional areas. The examples of systems in this chapter provide an overview. More detail on how various types of information systems in the firm deal specifically with operational, tactical, knowledge, and strategic problems can be found in Chapters 12–15.

Manufacturing and Production Systems

Manufacturing and production function The division of a business organization that produces the firm's goods or services.

Goods-producing organizations typically develop a **manufacturing and production function,** with a division or department of manufacturing that specializes in the production of the goods or services that the firm produces for the environment (customers). In service industries these departments are called "operations" or "production" functions rather than "manufacturing."

The typical production process can be divided into three stages: inbound logistics, production, and outbound logistics. Each of these can be conceived as part of a long value chain, where each part contributes some economic value (see Figure 2.5).

At Marathon Oil's North Brae platform in the North Sea off Scotland, computerized systems facilitate natural gas and oil production. In the North Brae control room, workers watch computer screens to monitor the process and utility systems aboard the platform.

Source: Courtesy of USX Corporation.

Figure 2.5

Stages of the Production Process

The manufacturing or production process typically has three stages: in-bound logistics, production, and out-bound logistics.

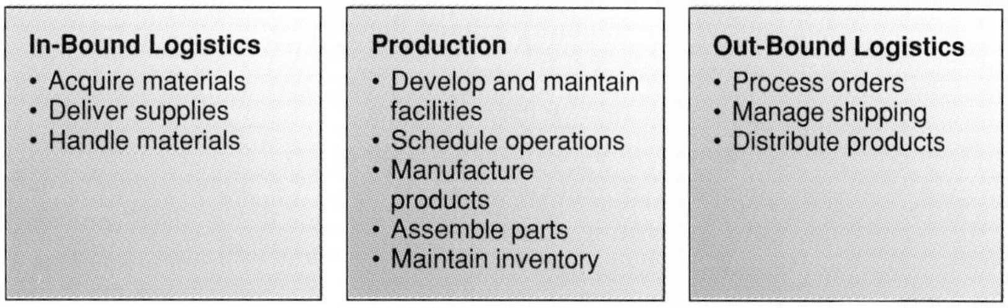

In-Bound Logistics	Production	Out-Bound Logistics
• Acquire materials • Deliver supplies • Handle materials	• Develop and maintain facilities • Schedule operations • Manufacture products • Assemble parts • Maintain inventory	• Process orders • Manage shipping • Distribute products

To support this production process, a number of key strategic, management, knowledge, and operational systems are required. Manufacturing and production systems deal with the planning, development, and maintenance of production facilities; the establishment of production goals; the acquisition, storage, and availability of production materials; and the scheduling of equipment, facilities, materials, and labor required to fashion finished products.

Manufacturing and production systems help provide answers to the following questions: What production technology will be used? What production plan will produce the required quantity of products and services within the required time frame and budget? How will parts and operations be designed and tested? How will the flow of production be controlled?

Table 2.1 shows some typical manufacturing and production information systems arranged by the organizational level of problem. Strategic-level manufacturing systems deal with the firm's long-term manufacturing goals, such as where to locate new plants or whether to invest in new manufacturing technology. Tactical manufacturing and production systems deal with the management and control of manufacturing and production costs and resources. Knowledge manufacturing and production systems create and distribute design knowledge or expertise to drive the production process, and operational manufacturing and production systems deal with the status of production tasks.

An example of a manufacturing and production system would be a bill-of-materials system, which is typically found in most factories today (see Figure 2.6). A bill-of-materials system provides managers and factory supervisors with a list of all the manufactured items that require a specific part—in this case a six-foot power cord used in home and industrial air fan assemblies. The list can be "hard copy" (on paper) or on a computer screen.

Table 2.1

Manufacturing and Production Information Systems

Strategic-Level Systems	Knowledge Systems
Production technology scanning applications	Computer-aided design systems (CAD)
Facilities location applications	Computer-aided manufacturing systems (CAM)
Competitor scanning and intelligence	Engineering workstations
Tactical Systems	Numerically controlled machine tools
Manufacturing resource planning	Robotics
Computer-integrated manufacturing	*Operational Systems*
Inventory control systems	Purchase/receiving systems
Cost accounting systems	Shipping systems
Capacity planning	Labor-costing systems
Labor-costing systems	Materials systems
Production scheduling	Equipment maintenance systems
	Quality control systems

As the figure indicates, the system itself is quite simple. Key data elements (pieces of information) in the system include the component description, cost, unit, and component part number. The system must also keep track of the item code of the end product that uses the part, a description of the end product, the quantity needed for each product produced, and the extended cost (unit times cost).

The component in the report shown is the "Triple S power cord," which is a three-conductor, six-foot long, grounded cable with a plug at one end and soldered lugs at the other and which attaches to the fan motor. This component costs $0.47 a foot and is used in three different fans, each of which requires a single unit (quantity = 1.0), with an extended cost of $2.82.

To build the B-2 bomber, Northrop Corporation developed and implemented a three-dimensional computer database that contained every detail of the B-2's design plus engineering, manufacturing, and support specifications. Because such sophisticated manufacturing systems provide high levels of design, manufacturing, and testing precision and efficiency, many companies will be investing in them.

Source: Courtesy of Northrop Corporation.

Figure 2.6

A Bill-of-Materials System

A common example of a manufacturing/production system is the bill-of-materials system, which helps staff keep track of all products that require a particular part. One output from this particular system is a report on a Triple S power cord, which is readable both on paper (hard copy) and on a computer screen. A bill-of-materials system is useful for determining costs, coordinating orders, and managing inventory.

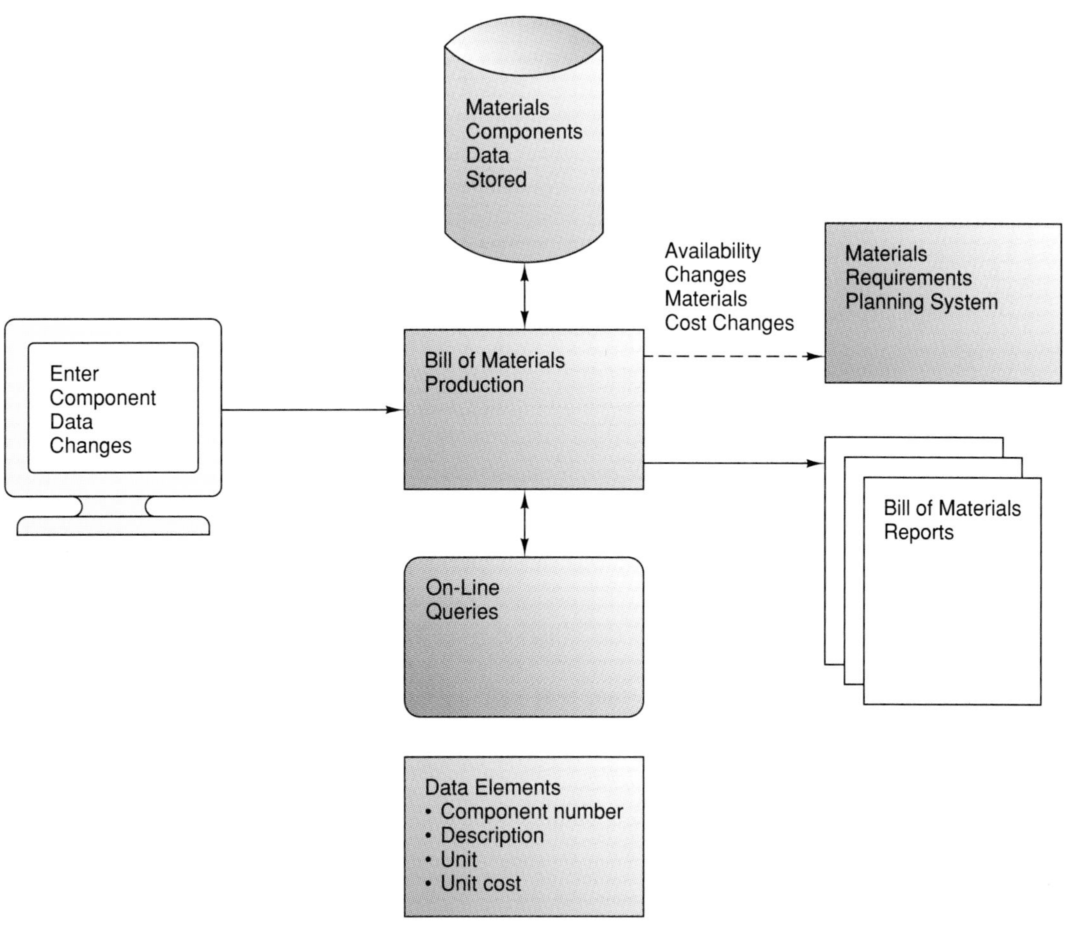

Hard-Copy Report

Week No.: 11 Where Used Bill of Material Report Date: 7/9/91

COMPONENT: Triple S Power Cord COST: $0.47 PART NO.: 2085
UNIT: 6ft.

ITEM CODE	DESCRIPTION	QUANTITY	EXTENDED COST
662	Double window fan	1.0	$2.82
175	12" utility fan	1.0	$2.82
227	15" utility fan	1.0	$2.82

FOCUS ON *Technology*

Computer Builds the Stealth Bomber

It would be an understatement to say that designing and building the B-2 bomber, commonly known as the Stealth bomber, posed a challenge for Northrop Corporation. This airplane was meant to represent the cutting edge of aircraft technology. To make the plane invisible to enemy radar, Northrop used nonmetallic materials, smooth surfaces, and a sleek swept-wing design.

To handle the many design and manufacturing challenges, Northrop applied computers on a grand scale. Design engineers used computer-aided design to simulate three-dimensional images of each component on their computer screens. In addition, the computer used advanced simulation techniques to test the consequences of design decisions before the company began fabricating components.

To build the aircraft, Northrop relied on what its officials call a "computerized central nervous system" to control all facets of production, from polishing joints to replacing screws. Supporting this system, robotic machine tools cut materials into complex shapes. A vast pool of computerized data provides visual information about the bomber's plan to engineers, production workers, and others involved in the manufacturing process.

The system more closely links design and manufacturing engineers. Traditionally, design engineers have drafted plans, then handed them over to experts in manufacturing. But at Northrop, the system automatically sets up the robotic machine tools used to fabricate structures, then runs simulations early in the design phase so that design engineers can look for manufacturing problems.

According to Northrop, the computer system enables the company to react to design changes two to five times faster than if the company had relied on conventional drafting techniques. For example, if a maintenance expert wants to determine whether a part can be easily removed from a machine for repairs, he or she can review the computerized image of the part's design, then suggest changes.

Source: John H. Cushman, Jr., "Stealth Bomber Built by Computer at Northrop," *The New York Times,* September 22, 1988.

A bill-of-materials system has several uses. In the event of a part shortage or failure, factory supervisors can look on the screen to see immediately which ultimate end products may be affected and change delivery schedules accordingly. Perhaps most important, the bill-of-materials system can feed directly into the firm's tactical systems that coordinate orders, available parts, cost, and delivery dates.

Many firms are trying to create a seamless manufacturing process by integrating the various types of automated manufacturing systems. Northrop Corporation's experience building the Stealth bomber, which is described in the Focus on Technology, is a leading-edge example of the high level of sophistication that computerized manufacturing systems are starting to achieve.

Although we will be describing some of these systems in greater detail in later chapters, you should also be aware that production systems and problems are discussed in courses on Operations Management, or Production Management, in most business schools. If you are interested in a more detailed view of production systems, you should be sure to take one of these courses.[2]

Sales and Marketing Systems

The basic purpose of the **sales and marketing function** is to sell the product or service to customers willing to pay the asking price. While this sounds simple enough, to accomplish these goals, you will have to identify who the customers are, what their needs are, how to create awareness and need for your product, how to contact the customers, what channels of distribution to use, how to record and track sales, how to physically distribute the product, how to finance marketing, and how to evaluate the results (see Figure 2.7).

Sales and marketing function
The division of a business organization that sells the firm's product or service.

Information systems are used in marketing in a number of ways. Strategic-level sales and marketing systems monitor trends affecting new products and sales opportunities, support planning for new products and services and monitor the performance of competitors. Tactical-level sales and marketing systems support market research, advertising and promotional campaigns, and pricing decisions and analyze sales performance and the performance of the sales staff. Knowledge-level sales and marketing systems support marketing analysis workstations, and operational-level sales and marketing systems assist in locating and contacting prospective custom-

Figure 2.7

The Sales and Marketing Process

There are three basic steps involved in sales and marketing: identify and create a market, develop it, and maintain it. This can be more difficult than it sounds. Identifying market needs, locating potential customers, and satisfying those customers requires a great deal of information that must be effectively analyzed and applied. Table 2.2 lists several ways in which information systems help firms become more effective marketers.

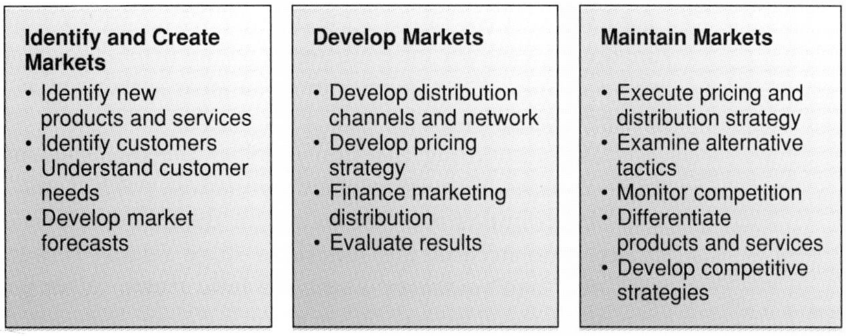

Identify and Create Markets
- Identify new products and services
- Identify customers
- Understand customer needs
- Develop market forecasts

Develop Markets
- Develop distribution channels and network
- Develop pricing strategy
- Finance marketing distribution
- Evaluate results

Maintain Markets
- Execute pricing and distribution strategy
- Examine alternative tactics
- Monitor competition
- Differentiate products and services
- Develop competitive strategies

Table 2.2

Sales and Marketing Information Systems

Strategic-Level Systems	*Knowledge Systems*
Demographic market forecasting systems	Marketing workstations
Economic forecasts	*Operational Systems*
Competitor scanning applications	Salesperson support systems
Tactical Systems	Order entry systems
Sales management systems	Point-of-sale systems (POS)
Pricing strategy decision support systems	Telemarketing systems
Sales personnel management systems	Credit information systems
Marketing data analysis	

ers, tracking sales, processing orders, and providing customer service (see Table 2.2).

One straightforward example of a sales information system (see Figure 2.8) is used by business firms like Benetton, The Gap, and many other retailers. In this Sales Analysis and Reporting System, data are captured from point-of-sale devices (typically hand-held scanners), which record each sale by item and item identification code. This sales information is recorded immediately in some systems, permitting precise and timely analysis of inventory levels, market trends, advertising effectiveness ("Did the television campaign really work?"), and sales targets.

Finance and Accounting Systems

In most firms, finance and accounting are a single division even though they are relatively distinct functions (see Figure 2.9). Finance involves the proper management of a firm's financial assets: cash on hand, securities, stocks, bonds, and the like. The purpose of finance is to maximize the return on the firm's financial assets and to manage the capitalization of the firm (find new financial assets in stocks, bonds, or other forms of debt). In many large manufacturing concerns, these financial assets are so large that the financial function is a significant contributor to the firm's profits. Hence finance has grown in importance from a mere support activity to a "primary" activity in many firms.

The accounting function involves the management of financial records—receipts, disbursements, depreciation, payroll, and so forth. The purpose of accounting is to "account" for the flow of funds in a firm. Both the **finance and accounting functions** share related problems: how to keep track of a firm's financial assets and fund flows. What is the current inventory of financial assets? What records do we have for disbursements, receipts, payroll, and other fund flows?

Finance and accounting function
The division of a business organization that manages the firm's financial assets (finance) and maintains the firm's financial records (accounting).

The finance function must obtain a considerable amount of information from sources external to the business. Finance ultimately must answer

Figure 2.8

A Sales Information System

A sales information system can capture data about sales by having people key these data into the computer or by using point-of-sale devices such as cash registers or hand-held scanners, which capture sales data for the computer at the moment the sale takes place. The report displayed here compares sales figures for various items with the figures for the same items one week or one year ago as a means of pinpointing sales trends and identifying popular and unpopular items.

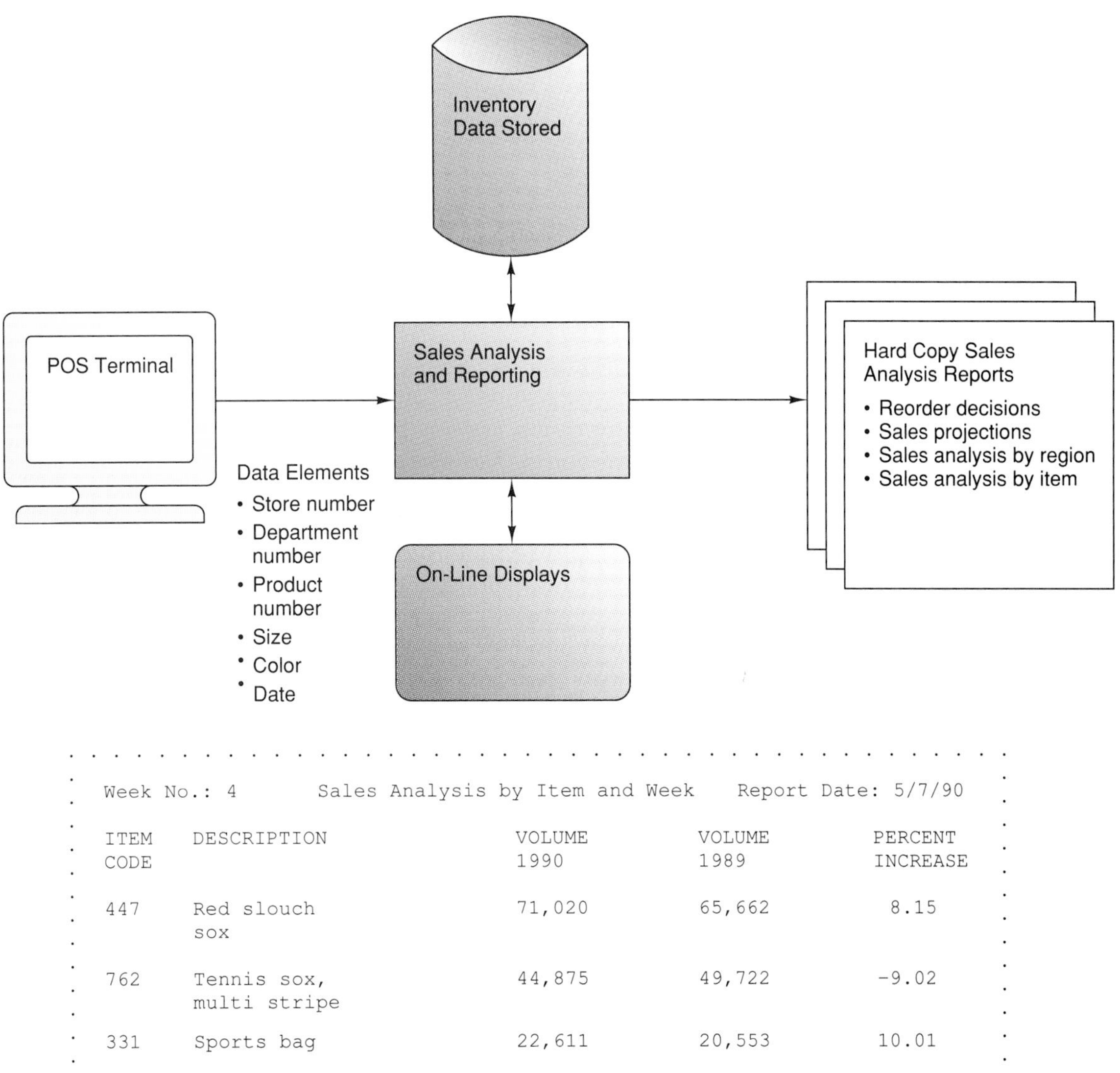

Week No.: 4 Sales Analysis by Item and Week Report Date: 5/7/90

ITEM CODE	DESCRIPTION	VOLUME 1990	VOLUME 1989	PERCENT INCREASE
447	Red slouch sox	71,020	65,662	8.15
762	Tennis sox, multi stripe	44,875	49,722	-9.02
331	Sports bag	22,611	20,553	10.01

the question, "Are we getting the best return on our investments?" This can only be answered by obtaining a steady flow of daily financial information from outside the firm.

Table 2.3 shows some of the leading finance and accounting systems found in a typical large organization. Strategic-level systems for the finance

Figure 2.9

The Finance and Accounting Process

Many firms place finance and accounting in the same department, although they are actually separate processes. Finance is the function of managing a firm's financial assets; the accounting process manages financial records. While these can often be supported by separate systems, a great deal of information flows between the two.

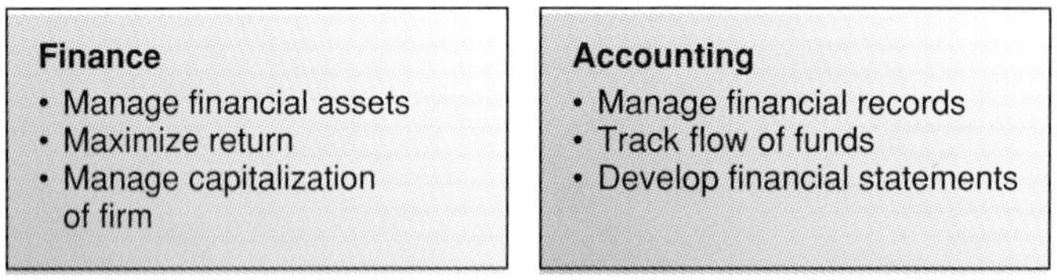

and accounting function establish long-term investment goals for the firm and provide long-range forecasts of the firm's financial performance. Tactical financial information systems help managers oversee and control the firm's financial resources. Knowledge systems support finance and accounting by providing analytical tools and workstations for evaluating the firm's financial performance. Operational systems in finance and accounting track the flow of funds in the firm through transactions such as paychecks, payments to vendors, stock reports, and receipts.

A simple but powerful example of a finance and accounting system that is found in all businesses is an accounts receivable system (see Figure 2.10). An accounts receivable system keeps track of every customer invoice: each invoice generates an "account receivable"—that is, the customer owes the firm money. Some customers pay immediately in cash, and others are granted credit. As the business owner, you must decide if you wish to grant credit (some people really don't pay their bills).

Table 2.3

Finance and Accounting Information Systems

Strategic-Level Systems
Financial and securities market data analysis
Economic and demographic forecasting systems
Budget forecasting systems

Tactical Systems
Fixed assets accounting
Cost accounting systems
Budgeting systems

Knowledge Systems
Financial management workstations
Portfolio analysis systems
Security analysis systems
Trader workstations

Operational Systems
Accounts payable/receivable
General ledger
Payroll

Figure 2.10

An Accounts Receivable System

Every organization that collects payment from customers has an accounts receivable system. The system tracks and stores important customer data such as payment history, credit rating, and billing history. Input to the system includes payment and invoice data; answers and information can arrive both on paper and on a screen. As with all other accounting systems within a firm, the accounts receivable system is linked to the general ledger system, which tracks all of the firm's cash flows.

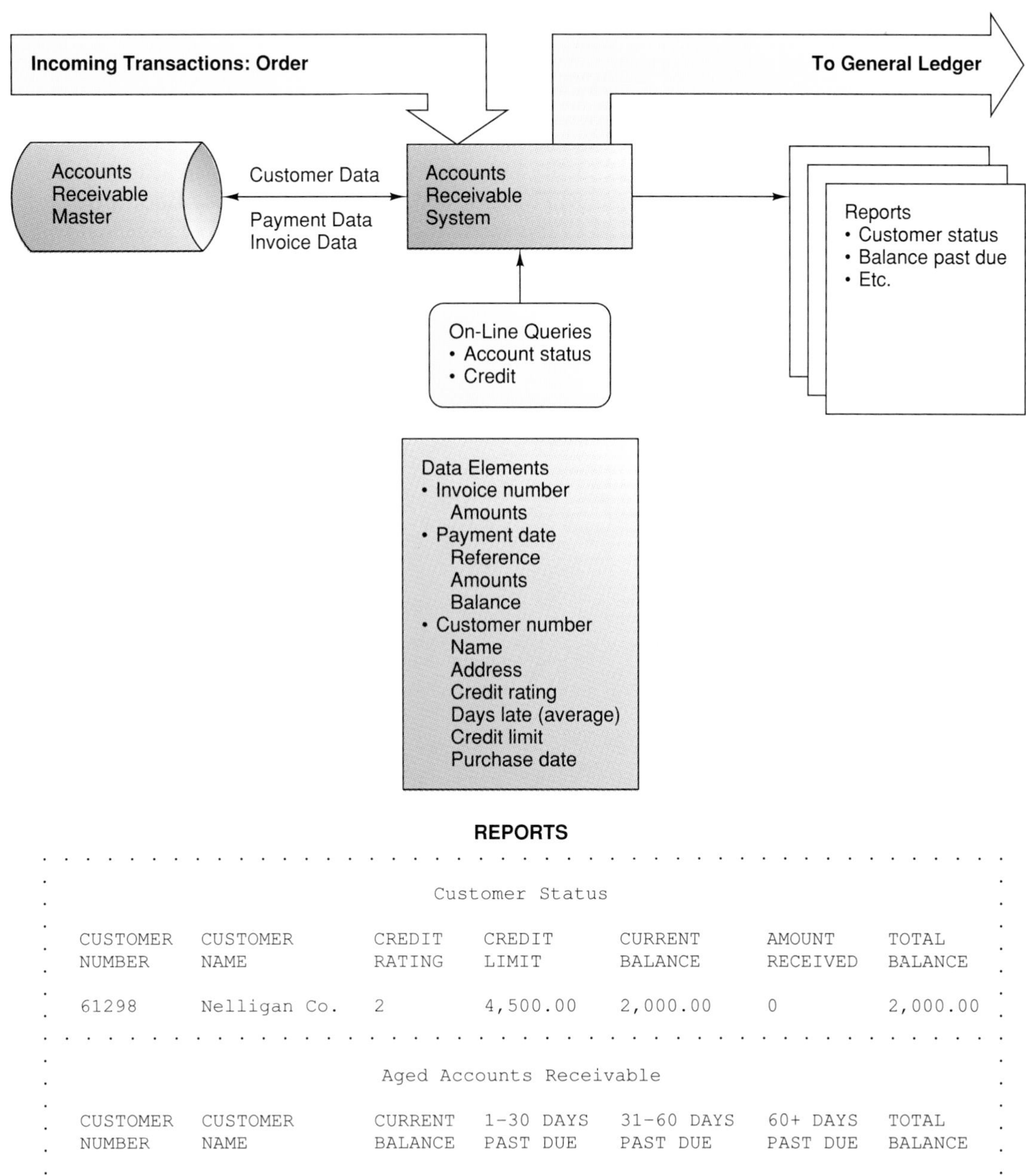

REPORTS

Customer Status

CUSTOMER NUMBER	CUSTOMER NAME	CREDIT RATING	CREDIT LIMIT	CURRENT BALANCE	AMOUNT RECEIVED	TOTAL BALANCE
61298	Nelligan Co.	2	4,500.00	2,000.00	0	2,000.00

Aged Accounts Receivable

CUSTOMER NUMBER	CUSTOMER NAME	CURRENT BALANCE	1-30 DAYS PAST DUE	31-60 DAYS PAST DUE	60+ DAYS PAST DUE	TOTAL BALANCE
61298	Nelligan Co.	0		2,000.00		2,000.00

The accounts receivable system records each invoice in a master file that also contains information on each customer, including credit rating. As the business goes on day after day, the system also keeps track of all the bills outstanding and can produce a variety of output reports, both on paper and on computer screens, to help the business collect bills. The system also answers queries regarding a customer's payment history and credit rating.

Note, however, that although this system is important on its own, it is connected directly to the general ledger system, which tracks all cash flows of the firm. We describe more extensive financial systems in later chapters.

Human Resources Systems

Human resources function
The division of a business organization that concentrates on attracting and maintaining a stable work force for the firm; it identifies potential employees, maintains records on existing employees, and creates training programs.

The purpose of the **human resources function** is to attract, develop, and maintain a stable, effective, and appropriately trained labor force (see Figure 2.11). Crucial to this mission are the identification of potential employees, the maintenance of complete records on existing employees, and the creation of training programs.

Human resources managers use many types of human resources systems in solving problems. In some cases these "systems" are specific applications that can run on a small desktop computer (for instance, a small desktop-based system can help managers plan for the succession of key managers). In other instances, such as employee compensation and benefits, a major commitment of organizational resources is required to build very large systems.

As we have done for the other organizational functions, let's examine some human resources information systems by type and level. Strategic-

Figure 2.11

The Human Resources Process

The role of the firm's human resources function is to attract, develop, and maintain an effective labor force. This includes locating and hiring new employees, measuring and improving the performance of current employees, and maintaining an appropriate and competitive staff over time.

Attract Labor Force
- Forecast labor needs
- Identify potential employees
- Analyze jobs
- Recruit employees

Develop Labor Force
- Forecast future needs
- Appraise performance
- Compensate employees
- Plan career paths
- Manage labor relations
- Train employees

Maintain Labor Force
- Provide competitive compensation/benefits
- Maintain records
- Meet legal and safety requirements

Table 2.4

Human Resources Information Systems

Strategic-Level Systems	*Knowledge Systems*
Human resources planning	Career path systems
Labor force forecasting systems	Training systems
Demographic analyses	Human resources workstations
Succession planning systems	*Operational Systems*
Tactical Systems	Personnel record keeping
Labor force budgeting systems	Applicant tracking
Positions control systems	Benefit systems
Compensation and job analysis systems	Training and skills inventory systems
Contract cost and labor relations systems	Positions tracking
Equal employment opportunity (EEO) compliance systems	

level human resources systems identify the manpower requirements (skills, educational level, types of positions, number of positions, and cost) for meeting the firm's long-term business plans. At the tactical level, human resources systems help managers monitor and analyze the recruitment, allocation, and compensation of employees. Knowledge systems for human resources support analysis activities related to job design, training, and the modeling of employee career paths and reporting relationships. Human resources operational systems track the recruitment and placement of the firm's employees (see Table 2.4).

A typical human resources system for personnel record keeping maintains basic employee data, such as the employee's name, age, sex, marital status, address, educational background, citizenship, salary, job title, date of hire, and date of termination (see Figure 2.12). The screen in the figure shows a report on newly hired and recently terminated employees. Another output of the system might be a "profile" of data on each individual employee, such as that illustrated in Figure 11.3 in Chapter 11.

2.4 How Businesses Use Information Systems for Competitive Advantage

To stay in business, many firms must worry about their competitive advantage—that is, their ability to compete with other firms. In general, a business can pursue four competitive strategies:[3]

- Low-cost leadership: produce products and services at a lower price than competitors.
- Focus on market niche: create new market niches.
- Product differentiation: develop unique new products.

Figure 2.12

A Typical Personnel Record-Keeping System

All businesses need to keep records of their employees to satisfy government regulations as well as their own internal requirements. A typical personnel record-keeping system maintains data on the firm's employees, identifying those who have been newly hired or terminated. Human resources specialists can view employee data directly on their terminal screens or they can obtain hard copy reports such as the sample report displayed here.

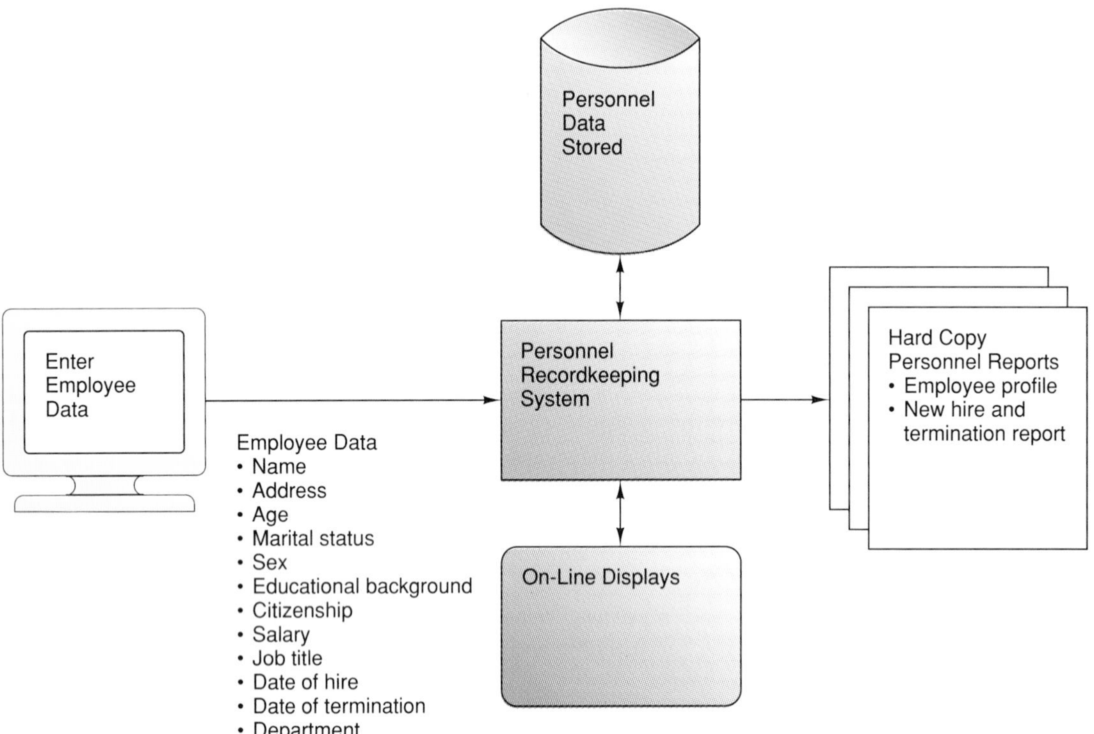

New Hires and Terminations — Report Date: 11/3/91

NEW HIRES

DATE	NAME	DEPARTMENT	JOB
10/29/91	Stevens, Fred	Accounts Payable	Accounts Payable Manager
10/30/91	Ellison, Maria	Shipping	Warehouse Packer

TERMINATIONS

DATE	NAME	DEPARTMENT	JOB	REASON
10/27/91	Forsythe, Pat	Information Systems	Programmer	Retired
10/28/91	Beale, Bruce	Buildings/Grounds	Janitor	Excess Absenteeism
10/28/91	Duffy, Carole	Payroll	Payroll Clerk	Position Eliminated

- Develop tight linkages to customers and suppliers that "lock" them into the firm's products.

These strategies are summarized in Table 2.5.

A new role for information systems has been their application to problems concerning the firm's competitive advantage. Such systems are said to have a strategic impact on the business because they focus on solving problems related to the firm's long-term prosperity and survival. Such problems may entail creating new products and services, forging new relationships with customers and suppliers, or finding more efficient and effective ways of managing the firm's internal activities. The objective of such systems is to provide solutions that will enable firms to defeat and frustrate their competition.

Although any information system application is "important" in the sense that it solves some important business problem, a **strategic impact system** is one that places the firm at a competitive advantage. Strategic impact systems are far-reaching and deeply rooted; they fundamentally change the firm's goals, products, services, or internal and external relationships.

Strategic impact systems Information systems that focus on solving problems related to the firm's long-term prosperity and survival; in particular, they are used to help a firm maintain its competitive advantage.

Examples of Strategic Impact Systems

Firms can use information systems to support each of the four competitive strategies. Information systems can create unique products or services that

Table 2.5

Four Basic Competitive Strategies

Strategy	Problem to be Solved	Solution
1. Low-cost leadership	Competition from firms with comparable products and services at the same cost is taking away customers.	Produce products and services at a lower price than competitors without sacrificing quality and level of service.
2. Focus on market niche	Multiple firms are competing for the same market.	Identify a specific focal point for a product or service. The firm can serve this narrow target area better than competitors and attract a specific buyer group more easily.
3. Product differentiation	Customers have no brand loyalty, and competitors can lure them away with lower prices.	Create brand loyalty by developing unique new products that are distinct from competitors' products.
4. Linkage	Customers can easily switch to another firm. Suppliers deliver late or at unfavorable prices.	"Lock in" customers and suppliers, making it difficult for customers to switch and tying suppliers into a price structure and delivery timetable shaped by the firm.

cannot easily be duplicated so that competitors cannot respond. Information systems can also target marketing campaigns more precisely or "lock in" customers and suppliers, making switching to competitors too costly and inconvenient to be worthwhile. Finally, information systems can have a strategic impact if they enable firms to do what they have been doing in a more efficient, cost-effective manner and to offer their goods and services at higher quality or lower prices than competitors. The following examples illustrate how leading U.S. and foreign firms have used strategic impact systems for competitive advantage.

New Marketing Strategies · Powerful new sales and marketing information systems enable firms to "mine" existing information as a resource to increase profitability and market penetration. Firms can use this information to identify and target products for a particular market or product niche, or they may use it to determine ways to serve specific market segments more effectively.

The Avon Corporation, whose order distribution facility in Newark, Delaware, is one of the most automated in the country, mines its invoices for marketing information. Avon is one of the nation's largest publishers, issuing 15 million product brochures every two weeks. The brochures are the firm's only instrument for direct sales. Avon's sales campaign management group utilizes information captured from the invoices to lay out the brochures. Invoice information is also employed to link the special offers in the brochures—for example, a necklace offered for $6.99 when accompanied by a perfume purchase. Avon thus can link its promotions more effectively to a range of objectives—profitability, movement of inventory, or giveaways to boost customer service.

New Products and Services · Information systems have been used to create appealing new products and services that cannot easily be replicated by competitors. Many of these new products and services have been created for the financial industry.

For example, Fannie Mae, the Federal National Mortgage Association, devised a desktop computer–based Loan Stratification Service to analyze its customers' loan portfolios. The system is based on the belief that once the loans are analyzed, customers will want to deal with Fannie Mae rather than someone else in the secondary mortgage market.

Based on assets of $112 billion, Fannie Mae has a federal charter to provide products and services that increase the availability and affordability of housing for low- and moderate-income families. It buys mortgages for its investment portfolio and guarantees mortgage-backed securities. The Loan Stratification Service was a response to the explosive growth in adjustable-rate mortgages, which combined with new government regulations to make it more attractive for lenders to convert their adjustable-rate mortgages to mortgage-backed securities. Mortgage-backed securities are guaranteed by Fannie Mae and represent a more liquid asset than a mortgage. By guaranteeing mortgage-backed securities, Fannie Mae earns a guarantee fee and fulfills its charter to provide liquidity and stability in the home mortgage market.

Stratification of adjustable-rate mortgage portfolios is very laborious because a portfolio may contain several thousand loans, each with a different interest rate, adjustment data, and other variable factors to consider. Fannie Mae offers its Loan Stratification Service to banks, thrift institutions, and mortgage companies that originate complex, adjustable-rate mortgages. Using a small desktop computer and loan data furnished by the mortgage lender, the system analyzes the lender's portfolio of mortgages to determine the best strategy for pooling certain loans together for trading in the secondary market. The lender thus gains a better idea of which loans are eligible to swap or sell. The Fannie Mae Loan Stratification Service takes only one day and allows comparison of up to 36 different pooling scenarios, whereas conventional loan stratification services performed by Wall Street brokerage houses take one to two weeks. Third-party stratification services charge $5,000–$10,000 to evaluate a portfolio, whereas the Fannie Mae service entails no cost to the lender.

New Relationships with Customers and Suppliers · Information systems have also been used to "lock in" customers, making it costly or inconvenient for customers to switch to a competitor. For instance, Little Company of Mary Hospital (LCM) in Evergreen Park, Illinois, is a 376-bed non-profit Catholic hospital. To build the loyalty of physicians and encourage them to choose its beds over two competing area hospitals, LCM developed a comprehensive information system that "moved into" physicians' offices, producing $4 million in additional annual revenue.

A computer-linking system designed by Annson Systems Division of Baxter Healthcare Corporation in Northbrook, Illinois, enables 100 physicians to access the hospital's comprehensive information system from their 50 different offices to obtain data about their patients. LCM supplies physicians' offices with desktop computers and software that enables them to obtain patient data from LCM's information system, using a special access code. A coordinator from LCM also trains the physicians' staff in computer use and publishes a newsletter illustrating how to use the system effectively and how changing reimbursement patterns affect physicians' practices.

Physicians' office managers reported that the system increased revenues from their practices. A study by Baxter's Management Services Division found that between 1984 and 1986, the physicians linked to the hospital had 14 percent higher revenue than nonlinked physicians. Ninety-two percent of the physicians also reported that they were more likely to send patients to LCM; 90 percent said their offices had been made more productive; and 81 percent believed the system improved the quality of patient care.

Information systems can also create new relationships with suppliers that maximize the firm's purchasing power. For example, the Chrysler Corporation and all of the major U.S. auto companies have established electronic links with major suppliers. The Budd Company of Rochester, Michigan, a leading supplier of sheet metal parts, wheel products, and frames, extracts manufacturing releases from Chrysler terminals installed in all of its work areas. Chrysler achieves savings from strict delivery requirements that specify parts to be supplied on the day they are needed.

FOCUS ON People

Wanted: The Everything Person

If you listen to corporate recruiters and read the want ads, you sometimes might think that employers want the impossible person: "under 25, ten years experience in programming, with strong demonstrated management skills."

According to a recent survey, corporations are especially interested in the growth of desktop computing, networking across departments, and the strategic use of information technology. Organizations not only want technical prowess in new employees but business and management savvy as well. Businesses are beginning to look beyond the typical computer science and data processing major. They want more students with liberal arts or financing, marketing, and human resources skills. And they want technical skills as well—in the same person.

Given this emphasis on broad backgrounds, employees are spending up to 25 percent of their time retraining and learning new skills. The message is: change with the times. Not all experts believe that all these different skills can be found in one person. They recommend two career ladders in organizations: one ladder for technical people and one ladder for general managers.

Source: "Wanted: Business Savvy Staff," *Computerworld Focus on Integration,* February 6, 1989.

Improved Operations and Internal Management · Companies can also gain competitive advantage by doing the basic nuts-and-bolts business tasks better, improving productivity, reducing costs, or enhancing the quality of products or service. Basic business systems (such as those described in Chapter 12) that cut administrative costs, reduce costs from excess inventory, or speed production can be strategic if they help a firm become the low-cost leader in its field. For example, L'eggs Brands, Inc., a major hosiery company, developed a Focused Manufacturing and Inventory Control system in 1988 to reduce inventory and cut manufacturing costs by closely coordinating inventory and production requirements. The L'eggs sales force collects sales data from stores and transmits them to a central computer in Winston-Salem, North Carolina. Production control then accesses the central computer to obtain the week's orders and conveys them to the plant floor. Previously, L'eggs had problems shipping the right goods to the right place. By coordinating production plans tightly with sales, L'eggs was able to eliminate inventory in warehouses and distribution centers.

Strategic People

Clearly, information technology does not automatically lead to competitive advantages. It takes insightful people who know both the business and how information technology works. These are just the kinds of people that business is looking for, as the Focus on People illustrates. During the 1990s most business firms will have to make significant changes—some may even have to rebuild themselves completely—just to stay in business. To an important degree, the success of the rebuilding process will depend on highly trained people like you.

Summary

- To understand business systems, you need to know what a business is and how business firms operate.
- A business firm is a formal, complex organization that seeks to maximize profits.
- The major business functions are manufacturing and production, sales and marketing, finance and accounting, and human resources.
- Business organizations are arranged hierarchically in levels composed of senior management, middle management, knowledge and data workers, and production workers.
- Businesses develop information systems to deal with internal organizational problems and to ensure their survival in a changing external environment.
- Information systems can usefully be seen in two perspectives. First, information systems serve specific functional areas of the firm. Second, different kinds of systems are designed to solve different kinds of problems at different levels of the business.
- Manufacturing and production systems solve problems related to production technology, planning for production, design of products and operations, and controlling the flow of production.
- Sales and marketing systems help businesses promote products, contact customers, physically distribute products, and track sales.
- Finance and accounting systems keep track of the firm's financial assets and fund flows.
- Human resources systems develop staffing requirements; identify potential employees; maintain records of the firm's employees; track employee training, skills, and job performance; and help managers devise appropriate plans for compensating employees and developing career paths.
- Information systems can be used to gain a strategic competitive advantage over other firms. Information systems can be used to develop new market niches, lock in customers and suppliers, differentiate products, and lower production and distribution costs.

Key Terms

Business organization
Business functions
Specialization
Hierarchy
Informal structure
Senior management
Middle management
Knowledge and data workers
Production workers
Business environment

Strategic-level systems
Tactical systems
Knowledge systems
Operational systems
Manufacturing and production function
Sales and marketing function
Finance and accounting function
Human resources function
Strategic impact systems

Review Questions

1. How would you define a business organization?
2. What are the major steps you would go through in organizing a business?
3. What are the major business functions typically found in all business firms?
4. What are the levels of a business firm?
5. Why are external environments important for understanding a business?
6. Why do business organizations develop information systems?
7. What are the major functional information systems of businesses? Give some examples of each.
8. What are the different levels of information systems in a firm? Give some examples of each.
9. What are the four competitive strategies a firm can follow?
10. Give examples of how information systems can support each of the four competitive strategies.

Discussion Questions

1. Some people argue that computers will reduce the need for managers in an organization. They believe fewer managers will be required because employees using computers will supervise themselves. The results of their work will be monitored by computer and passed directly to senior management without the need for middle managers. Discuss and comment.

2. How would the framework for describing business information systems introduced in this chapter have to be adjusted for a small business such as a drug store consisting of an owner and several sales clerks?

Problem-Solving Exercises

1. Obtain an annual report of a business or find an article describing a business in *Business Week, Fortune,* or another publication. Use the information provided to describe the kinds of information systems you might find in that business.

2. Describe an operational process that you think can be radically improved by the introduction of information systems. You could focus on your college or university bookstore, cafeteria, or registrar's office or a local delicatessen.

Notes

1. Kenneth C. Laudon, "Information Technology and Non-Profit Organizations: A Concepts Paper" (Teaneck, N.J.: Reference Point Incorporated, an online public information utility for the nonprofit sector, 1989).
2. An excellent text, likely to be found in most university libraries, is Roger G. Schroeder, *Operations Management: Decision Making in the Operations Function* (New York: McGraw-Hill, 1985). In this text, as well as in others, you will find useful descriptions of the manufacturing and operations process as well as many examples of where information systems are and could be used.
3. Michael Porter, *Competitive Strategy* (New York: Free Press, 1985). See also Kenneth C. Laudon and Jon Turner, eds., *Information Technology and Management Strategy* (Englewood Cliffs, N.J.: Prentice-Hall, 1989).

Problem-Solving Case

Tying in the Sales Force

The distilled spirits industry has fallen on hard times. Due to the aging of the U.S. population and changing consumer tastes, liquor sales declined 3 to 4 percent in 1988. The Seagram Company, Ltd. is struggling to keep its number-two position in the declining spirits industry. It acquired new products, such as Tropicana orange juice and Martell cognac, and sold off 25 of its less profitable brands. It also embarked on an ambitious campaign to automate its sales force.

Seagram's sales force has many duties. In addition to making sales, it is responsible for compiling detailed information on product movement, liquor store inventory levels, store displays, and merchandising suggestions. It also records the shelf position of competitors.

Beginning in 1986, Seagram armed its sales force with laptop computers that could be linked to a central computer. Seagram's sales information system has capabilities for territory management, electronic mail, and electronic report distribution. It can compile detailed daily information on local retail accounts by various criteria, such as state, sales zone, zip code, and type of account. The system tracks sales activities such as store display setups and product movement, as well as comments from sales representatives. Seagram's district and state managers can review these data.

Seagram's sales representatives transmit information nightly to the company's central computer. The central computer then consolidates and compiles this information into forms and reports for distribution to Seagram's sales managers, who can use it to review sales figures and the progress of individual accounts. They can also determine how quickly products are being sold and the effectiveness of various promotional and pricing schemes. Seagram's regional sales managers, in turn, can transmit new promotional information to the sales staff with a couple of keystrokes.

In Florida, for example, Seagram's three supervisors manage 23 sales representatives handling retail liquor store accounts. Pat Sanders, the statewide sales manager who oversees the supervisors, can retrieve information from everyone using the desktop computer in his office. Sanders observed that he was no longer weighted down by all kinds of books and reports. If he is going to work a market, he can pull up that information on his computer

terminal and see what goals have been set. Before the system was installed, he had to deal with reams of information and a book for the whole state. Sanders can also compute the highest, lowest, and most frequent price of a single brand across the 1,000 accounts he monitors, a process that takes only 10 minutes.

Statewide sales managers can also use the system to communicate more easily with their far-flung sales force. Instead of writing 26 letters or promotional announcements to all of his salespeople, Sanders writes only one, and the system transmits a copy to each sales representative. Sales managers have also used the system to send messages instructing the sales force to discount discontinued products so they do not pile up in the warehouse. When the salespeople turn their computers on in the morning, they receive a message to sell a given item that day. Previously, it took weeks or months to send out such instructions.

Julie Hardesty, a Seagram's sales representative to retail liquor stores, estimates that a detailed sales call might take her 15 to 20 minutes to write up by hand but a maximum of 5 minutes to enter on her laptop computer. The sales information system gives her time to make several extra calls per day. Hardesty also uses the information system to complete her monthly sales reports. Her list of objectives becomes a page of the report. Salespeople want to prove to their bosses that they are working, and the information system provides the information and detail to do this.

Industry analysts estimate that as much as 50 percent of a sales force may resent computerized information systems because they are perceived as a threat to their independence. Yet salespeople are often hampered by inefficient or out-of-date information, especially if they are selling a complex product or if product prices fluctuate constantly. Salespeople can benefit from up-to-date facts and hard information to present to their retail clients. Automating a sales force can be costly, however—a *Harvard Business Review* survey found that the cost of sales force automation could reach $7,000 per salesperson.

The firm also might have to do some reorganizing to incorporate new sales information systems effectively. For example, sales representatives can immediately transmit orders to be processed and shipped out the same day. Orders taken by pen and pad might have taken between four days and two weeks before they were shipped, provided the product was in stock. In addition, sales projections and trend analyses can be more precise.

Source: Jason Forsythe, "Seagram Soaks up Technology," *Information Week*, February 6, 1989.

Case Study Questions

1. What aspects of the sales and marketing function does Seagram's sales system support? What problems does it solve?
2. What level or levels of the business (operational, knowledge, tactical, strategic) are supported by Seagram's sales system?
3. What kinds of changes in a business's external environment would increase the need for sales support systems?

Information Technology Gives Wells Fargo an Edge

Wells Fargo, the nation's 11th-largest bank, has a reputation for using technology. In the 19th century, Wells Fargo was an avid user and financial supporter of the telegraph, the pony express, and transcontinental stagecoach companies. In recent years, Wells Fargo has applied computer technology to a number of business information systems that give the bank a subtle strategic advantage.

The advantage of Wells Fargo's applications is not their technical novelty. Rather than seek out the leading edge, the company has invested in a number of basic business systems. It successfully applies this technology to cut costs, acquire new companies, offer new services, and make management more effective.

The biggest challenge at Wells Fargo has been to use the technology in ways that effectively support its business strategy. Like most big banks, it had to move into new areas of banking where it could tap new markets. Wells Fargo has traditionally focused on retail banking—serving consumers and small to medium-sized businesses. But throughout the 1970s and 1980s the bank expanded into commercial banking, offering major construction loans and leveraged buyouts. In addition, the bank has begun to use money management as a way to retain these large customers. Last, Wells Fargo moved into the information business: it now sells money management services and provides information about the location and uses of their deposits instead of just taking deposits and making loans.

WEBS: Wells Electronic Banking System

To support its 490 retail branches, Wells Fargo centralized retail customer information such as loan processing, check verification, and account balance information into a centralized system called the Wells Electronic Banking System (WEBS). Now clerks at the branches can perform over 100 separate operations on WEBS, from verifying a customer's balance and opening accounts to answering questions about safe-deposit boxes (see the accompanying table). Formerly, to find answers to customer questions, clerks would have to phone other branches or central headquarters.

WEBS has enabled Wells Fargo to cut costs without cutting its level of service. For example, fewer employees are needed to staff

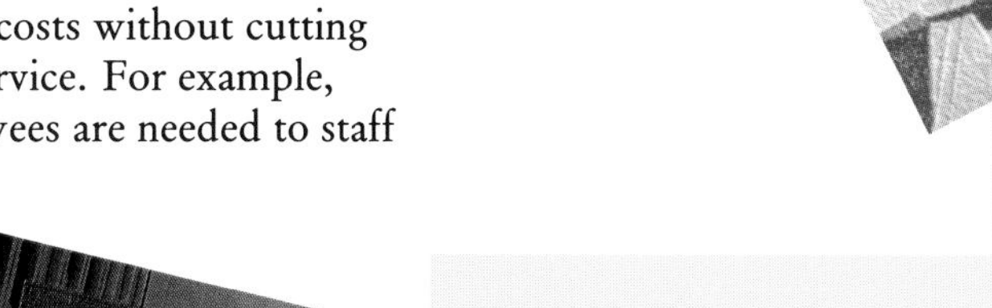

The entrance to Wells Fargo & Company in San Francisco features an award-winning museum displaying the company's past.

Source: Photo by David Wakely.

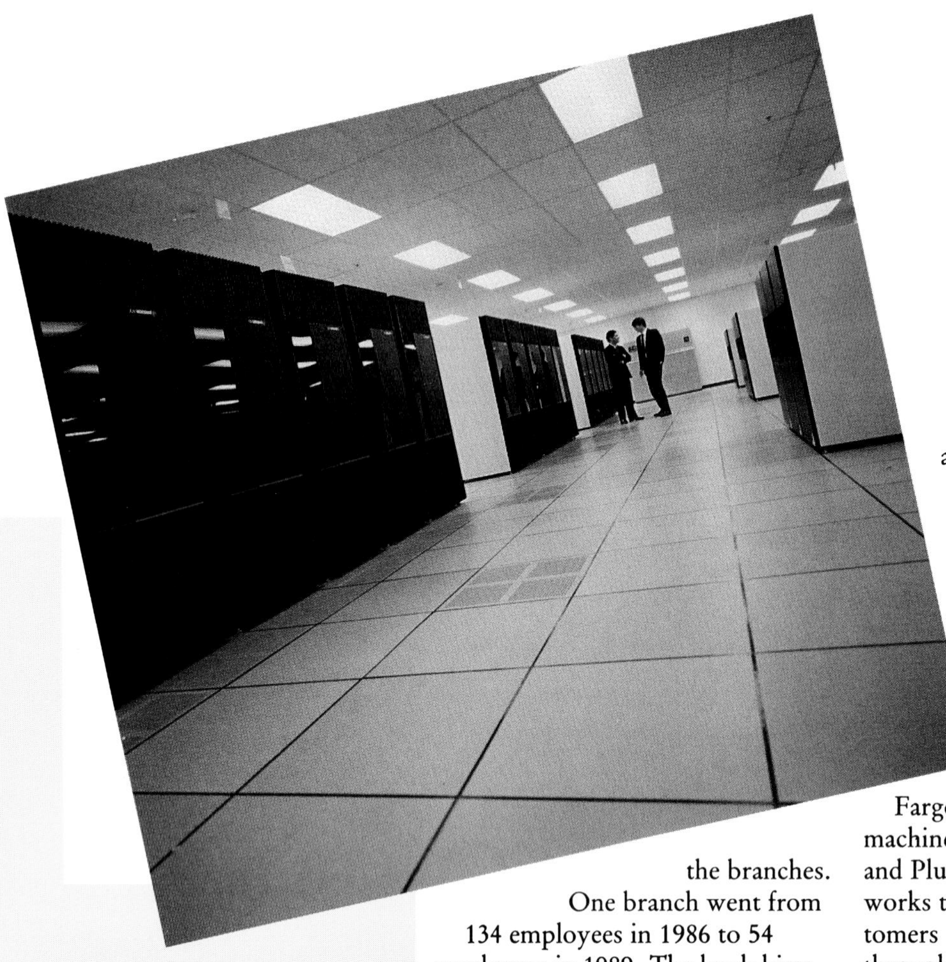

A Wells Fargo data center makes possible the Bank's 24-hour person-to-person service.

Source: Courtesy Wells Fargo Bank.

the branches.

One branch went from 134 employees in 1986 to 54 employees in 1989. The bank hires part-time workers based on computer projections and management rules specifying that customers should wait less than five minutes for service. WEBS also made it cost-effective for the bank to extend its hours to 6:00 P.M. on weekdays and to open all day on Saturday. According to Wells Fargo officials, the bank's operations are now so lean that competitors have difficulty matching its moves.

The bank also runs a central Tandem based system that operates and maintains Wells Fargo's 1,246 automatic teller machines. These connect to Star and Plus, two regional ATM networks that permit the bank's customers to use 25,000 other ATMs throughout the western United States. Almost three-quarters of the bank's checking customers use ATM machines—the highest rate for any bank in the country.

WEBS also allows customers to call into the bank around the clock to find out about bank services or accounts. Through Wells Fargo's telebanking services, five sites are open 24 hours a day for phone inquiries. Students and people seeking second jobs staff the night shifts, answering calls by looking up information on WEBS. Now three million callers a month request information from the bank.

Customers find 24-hour ATMs such as this Wells Fargo Express Stop™ indispensable.

Source: Courtesy Wells Fargo Bank.

Still another system, Info Express, has supported Wells Fargo's aggressive efforts to attract corporate banking. A corporate equivalent to home banking gives corporate treasurers direct access to information about their companies' accounts. Treasurers can see exactly where the money is and can move money from one account to another at will. Some corporations, including Hilton Hotels, have connected their computers directly to the Info Express system. In the middle of the night, Hilton's information systems start inquiring about overnight balances and account activity. By morning, Hilton executives have reports on their computer screens showing the exact financial position of the company.

Moving into New Roles: Information Clearinghouse

For corporate customers, a hot new development is electronic data interchange (EDI), a system that allows businesses to make payments electronically. Instead of paying a bill with a check, a company sends an electronic message to its bank to transfer funds electronically to the account of the business it owes money to. The bank acts as a clearinghouse for such electronic transfers.

Companies that use EDI can slash their administrative costs. According to major consulting firms, every bill received by a company is handled by five different employees and costs on an average about $40 to process. With millions of bills to pay each year, large corporations spend enormous sums just tracking and handling pieces of paper called bills, invoices, and purchase orders.

Wells Fargo is involved in an experiment with Citibank, Philadelphia National Bank, Chevron, Shell Oil, and Amoco to use EDI to settle accounts for an oil field the two oil companies operate in partnership with Chevron.

The Growth of Wells Fargo's Computer Systems

Retail Banking: Wells Electronic Banking System

Year	Total Functions	Some of the Functions Added	Terminals
1986	50	Opening accounts; issuing A.T.M. cards; obtaining interest rates; immediate notice of overdrafts	2,300
1987	96	Establishing links to credit bureaus for credit-card authorization; deposit account history	6,892
1988	104	Faster account transfers; enhanced security; cross-referencing for accounts acquired with purchase of Barclay's Bank of California	7,024
1989 (1st Qtr.)	122	Reporting large currency transactions; credit-card payments by phone	7,300

Commercial Banking: Wholesale Integrated Network (WIN)

Year	Total Functions	Some of the Functions Added	Users
1984	2	Word processing; electronic mail	40
1985	8	Tracking delinquent loans; analyzing financial data	180
1986	10	Reports from credit bureaus and news wires	290
1987	22	Electronic reminders to check whether loan requirements (such as insurance) are being observed by customers	1,000
1988	28	Pricing loans to maximize bank income while meeting customers' needs	1,320
1989 (1st Qtr.)	40	Commodity price projections; attaching personal data, like CEO birthdays, to customer data base	1,400

Wholesale Integrated Network (WIN)

Commercial banking at Wells Fargo involves working with corporations to purchase other corporations, providing financing for real estate development, and providing cash management service to corporations. For these operations, Wells Fargo developed the Wholesale Integrated Network (WIN). As shown in the preceding table, WIN now performs over 40 different functions and has 1,400 users within the bank.

The Supply Requisition System (SRS) supports Wells Fargo's own inventory control. The bank used to have over 150 suppliers for the more than 2,000 forms and 5,000 office supply items it needed. No more. Using SRS to track inventory and generate electronic orders, Wells Fargo now has seven suppliers and writes only a handful of checks. Most of the money is paid out electronically to supplier accounts. As a result, the purchasing staff has shrunk from 40 to 10 persons.

Perhaps one of the most utilized accesses of WIN—at least in terms of popularity—is electronic mail, by which employees use their computer terminals to send each other messages. Sending messages electronically helps avoid telephone tag: trying to reach people who are not in the office or cannot come to the phone. Furthermore, according to Elizabeth Evans, Wells Fargo's senior vice president in charge of the Information Services Division, electronic mail (known as E-mail) is breaking down barriers at the bank. In Evans's view, E-mail encourages communication with a wider group of employees than traditional corporate memos.

Currently 7,000 Wells Fargo employees use the E-mail system to send 20,000 messages each day. One result of the system has been that secretaries spend far less time typing memos and reports and do more real administrative work. Managers tend to do more communicating and to propose more new ideas in an informal way, to a larger number of colleagues.

The move to electronic communications has, however, complicated the life of corporate historian Andy Anderson. "E-mail doesn't leave the kind of paper trail that would have existed prior to 1984," Anderson said, so "we have to do more oral interviews to document how things happened around here."

Source: Barnaby J. Feder, "Getting the Electronics Just Right," *The New York Times*, June 4, 1989.

Wells Fargo's headquarters is located in southern California—the region responsible for the company's longevity and growth.

Source: Courtesy of Maguire Thomas Partners.

PART · TWO

2

Foundations of Information Technologies

CHAPTER · THREE

Computer Processing Technology

Chapter Outline

3.1 Introduction: A Variety of Information Technologies

3.2 Computer Concepts and Components
- The CPU and Its Components
- Measuring Time, Size, and Processing Power
- How Computers Represent Data
- Generations of Computer Hardware
- Mainframes, Minicomputers, Microcomputers, and Supercomputers

3.3 The Microcomputer Revolution
- Mainframes on a Desk Top—Powerhouse Micros
- Microprocessor Technology: The Chips behind the Machines
- Workstations
- Standard-Setting Machines: IBM and Apple

3.4 Information Technology Trends
- The Future of the Mainframe
- A Fifth Generation
- Superchips
- Reduced Instruction Set Computing

Learning Objectives

After reading and studying this chapter, you will:

1. Know the components of a computer and how they work.
2. Understand how a computer represents and processes data.
3. Be able to distinguish between mainframes, minicomputers, and microcomputers.
4. Know how to measure computer speed, storage capacity, and processing power.
5. Be aware of past and future information technology trends.

Obsolete Computers Heighten Air Traffic Anxiety

On a busy Friday afternoon in October 1989, air traffic controllers' screens at the Dallas–Fort Worth Airport went blank for 16 minutes. According to a U.S. General Accounting Office (GAO) report, events like this occur at nearly 70 percent of the nation's 63 largest airports during peak hours, increasing the risk of midair collisions. The blank or flickering screens or slow response times are indicative of overloaded computer systems. According to the GAO report, "Existing computer capacity shortfalls at some large, busy Tracons [Terminal Radar Approach Control facilities] are impairing controllers' ability to maintain safe separation of aircraft." The Tracon facilities use 15-year-old Univac 8303 processors.

The GAO sharply criticized the Federal Aviation Administration (FAA) for not anticipating computer capacity problems years ago. The FAA has responded to the capacity shortfall by reducing training sessions for controllers and streamlining the software. But the GAO report claimed these measures created additional safety hazards rather than solving the problem. Instead, the GAO faulted the FAA managers who knew the problem existed years ago but did nothing to develop a computer capacity management program.

Unfortunately, the capacity problem is likely to worsen because the FAA ordered 44,000 small planes, as of July 1, 1989, to transmit flight information

to airport Tracon facilities. To boost their capacity, the FAA has ordered memory upgrades for the existing equipment and an additional three hundred 8303 computers. The FAA has concluded that it cannot purchase newer and faster computer hardware because the existing software would have to be completely rewritten to run on the new processors. Instead, the FAA has chosen to stay with the old processors, hoping that with more of them it will be able to handle the processing load.

Sources: J. A. Savage, "Anxiety Grows as Traffic Systems Age," *Computerworld,* March 5, 1990; Mitch Betts, "Busy Airline Systems Blank Out Screens," *Computerworld,* July 24, 1989.

The air traffic control problem described above illustrates both our dependence on computer hardware and our need to manage that hardware to solve problems that directly affect human lives. Computers cannot be deployed successfully unless their capabilities, as well as their limitations, are clearly understood.

3.1 Introduction: A Variety of Information Technologies

Traditionally, information systems courses have treated the computer as the central actor in a business firm's technological response to its environment. To some extent this is no longer appropriate. The problem-solving business technologies of the 1990s range far beyond the computer alone and include telecommunications networks, fax machines, "smart" printers and copiers, workstations, and video communications. Increasingly, problems will be solved not by an isolated mainframe or personal computer but by an array of digital devices networked together.

Likewise, the problems solved by this array of information technologies will no longer be limited to data processing. Image processing, graphics, desktop publishing, communications, and group support are some of the new kinds of problems information technologies can solve. Therefore, instead of focusing exclusively on the computer, all of today's information technologies must work together.

Nevertheless, the electronic computer remains at the core of this digital revolution. And to understand today's array of information technologies and the way they can work together, you must still understand how a computer represents and processes information. As the Focus on People explains, high-ranking business executives in a variety of industries are discovering that they must learn something about computers. Hence, this chapter focuses primarily on computer processing, and the following chap-

FOCUS ON People

Viewing Data without the Filters

Philip B. Fletcher, president of Conagra, Inc., would not think of hitting the road without his laptop computer. "I carry it with me when I travel and do my electronic mail from my hotel room each night so it doesn't get ahead of me," says Fletcher, chief operating officer of the Omaha-based conglomerate whose activities span the food chain from fertilizer to frozen TV dinners.

Even at corporate headquarters, Fletcher is seldom far from his keyboard. Although he and Conagra Chairman Charles M. (Mike) Harper sit in adjoining offices, many of their most productive conversations take place via computer.

This kind of regular contact with computers is still the exception among senior executives, however.

One of the most fervent and tireless advocates of executive computing is Robert G. Wallace, the recently retired president of Phillips 66 Company and executive vice-president of its parent, Phillips Petroleum Company, both in Bartlesville, Oklahoma.

To a certain extent, Wallace's introduction to the computer as an executive tool was forced upon him. His decision to commission the development of an executive business system at Phillips 66 four years ago was an economic necessity.

If the company was going to keep operating in an efficient and informed manner, it had no choice: executives would have to learn to fend for themselves.

What started as a make-do proposition has turned into something of a crusade for Wallace, who now spends much of his time talking with individuals and management groups about spearheading the development of what he calls an "integrated business system." What he discovered in working with the Phillips 66 system, which was based on IBM's Professional Office System, he says, is that an information-rich computing system is a must in the executive suite. "Executives can no longer hide behind the statement that they didn't know and were not informed," he says.

Since many people are reluctant to use a keyboard, many executive systems use a mouse or touch screen, but sooner or later, the executive who wants to communicate electronically or go beyond seeing what other people think he or she wants to see will have to do some typing.

Conagra's Fletcher did not exactly rush to embrace the new technology. "It took about a year before I really realized the value of staying current by using the computer myself," he says. "I had been accustomed to having a secretary take the correspondence and respond to it, and I felt she would be so much faster than I would be [at] typing. That was the rationale I used to avoid it. Now, I find it very helpful."

Source: Mickey Williamson, "Viewing Data without the Filters," *Computerworld,* December 4, 1988, pp. 79–86.

ter deals with computer input, output, and storage devices. Other chapters in this section treat related information technologies—software, telecommunications, files and databases, and artificial intelligence and expert systems. Throughout, the emphasis is on how all of these technologies interact and work together.

3.2 Computer Concepts and Components

Computer
Physical device that takes data as an input, transforms these data by executing a stored program, and outputs information to a number of devices.

Central processing unit (CPU)
A hardware component of a computer system, consisting of primary storage and a main processor; it processes raw data and controls other parts of the computer system.

At the most general level, a computer is any device that takes an input from its environment, processes this input in some logical or mathematical manner, and produces a resulting output to the environment. More specifically, a modern **computer** is a physical device that takes data as an input, transforms these data by executing a stored program, and outputs information to a number of devices. Key words here are *input, process, output,* and, of course, *stored program* or *software.* The speed, capacity, and processing features of computers determine the role they can play in problem solving.

As Figure 3.1 illustrates, a contemporary computer system has several physical hardware components: a central processing unit, input devices, output devices, secondary storage devices, and communications devices. The **central processing unit (CPU)** manipulates raw data into another form and controls the other parts of the computer system. Input devices such as keyboards, optical scanners, and computer "mice" convert data into electronic form for input into the computer. Output devices, such as printers

Figure 3.1

Hardware Components of a Computer System

A contemporary computer system includes a CPU (central processing unit), which processes the data and manages the entire system; secondary storage, which holds additional data and instructions until the CPU needs them; and devices for input, output, and communications.

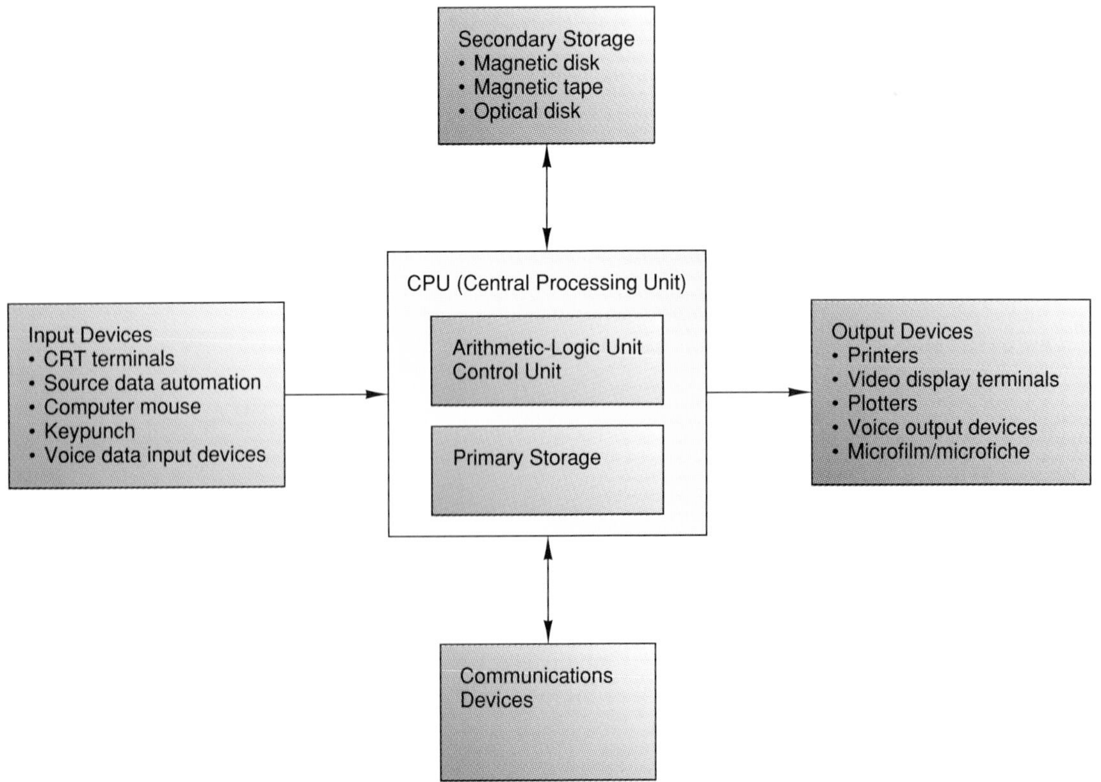

and video display units, convert electronic data produced by the CPU into a form intelligible to humans. Secondary storage devices store data and program instructions when the CPU is not using them in processing. Communications devices help control communication between the CPU, input and output devices, and business specialists.

The CPU and Its Components

The heart of the computer is the CPU. This is the part of the computer system where the manipulation of symbols, letters, and numbers occurs. The nature of the CPU largely determines a computer's speed and capacity for solving problems. As Figure 3.2 shows, a CPU has two components: (1) primary storage and (2) a main processor containing an arithmetic-logic unit and a control unit. The main processor is located on an individual **semiconductor chip** (a silicon chip upon which hundreds of thousands of circuit elements can be etched) with semiconductor chips for primary storage located nearby.

Semiconductor chip
A silicon chip upon which hundreds of thousands of circuit elements can be etched.

Primary Storage · **Primary storage** (also called main memory or primary memory) is the portion of the CPU that stores program instructions and the data being used by those instructions. Data and programs are placed in primary storage before processing, between processing steps, and after processing has terminated, prior to being released as output. Once the computer is finished with specific pieces of data and program instructions, they are removed from primary storage, released as output or returned to secondary storage where they will remain until the CPU needs them again, and replaced by others.

Primary storage
The component of the CPU that temporarily stores program instructions and the data being used by these instructions..

Figure 3.2

Closeup of the CPU

The CPU has two components: primary storage and a main processor (which includes the control unit and the arithmetic-logic unit, or ALU). Primary storage temporarily stores data, instructions, intermediate results, and output. Each piece of data in primary storage has a unique address. The arithmetic-logic unit performs calculations and logical operations on data. The control unit coordinates the transfer of data between primary storage and the main processor, and between the CPU and input/output devices.

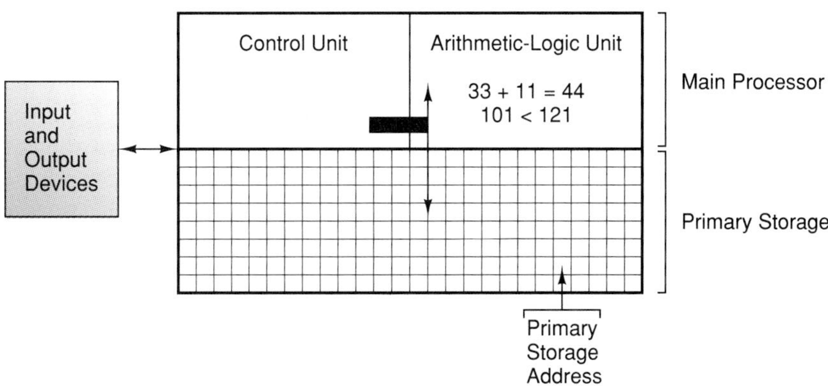

Address
The particular location in primary storage where data or program instructions are stored.

Byte
A single character of data made up of a combination of bits that a computer processes or stores as a unit; the unit in which computer storage capacity is measured.

Arithmetic-logic unit (ALU)
The component of the main processor that performs arithmetic and logical operations on data.

Control unit
The component of the main processor that controls and coordinates the other components of the computer.

Machine cycle
The series of operations involved in executing a single instruction.

Instruction cycle
The portion of a machine cycle in which an instruction is retrieved from primary storage and decoded.

Execution cycle
The portion of a machine cycle in which the required data are located, the instruction is executed, and the results are stored.

Register
A storage location in the ALU or control unit; it may be an instruction register, an address register, or a storage register, depending on what is stored in it.

Whenever data or program instructions are placed in primary storage, they are assigned a unique **address,** so they can be located when they are needed. The address functions like a mailbox. In many computers, this "mailbox" only stores a single character of data, or one **byte.** As Figure 3.2 shows, primary storage contains many such storage addresses.

Primary storage capacity has a profound impact on a computer's problem-solving capability. The earliest electronic computers, which relied on vacuum tubes, had very limited primary storage. Only a very small number of instructions and pieces of data could be placed in primary storage at one time. Later machines used transistors, followed by semiconductor chips, which have vastly increased primary storage capacity while reducing its cost.

The Arithmetic-Logic Unit · The **arithmetic-logic unit (ALU)** performs arithmetic and logical operations on data. It adds, subtracts, multiplies, divides, and determines whether a number is positive, negative, or zero. The ALU can make logical comparisons of two numbers to determine whether one is greater than, less than, or equal to the other. The ALU can also perform logical operations on letters or words.

The Control Unit · The **control unit** controls and coordinates the other components of the computer. It reads stored program instructions one at a time, and based on what the program tells it to do, the control unit directs other components of the computer system to perform the required tasks. For example, it might specify which data should be placed into primary storage, which operation the ALU should perform on the data, and where the results should be stored. It might also direct the result to an appropriate output device, such as a printer. After each instruction is executed, the control unit proceeds to the next instruction.

The Basic Machine Cycle · The control unit is a key element in the most basic and fundamental CPU operation, called a **machine cycle.** As you will see, a machine cycle has two parts. One part is called the **instruction cycle (I-cycle),** in which an instruction is retrieved from primary storage and decoded. A second part is called the **execution cycle (E-cycle),** in which the required data are located, the instruction executed, and the results stored.

Figure 3.3 shows in greater detail how the machine cycle works. The control unit fetches an instruction from the program stored in primary storage, decodes the instruction, and places it in a special instruction **register.** Registers are special storage locations in the ALU and the control unit that act like high-speed staging areas. There are several different kinds of registers. The control unit breaks each instruction into two parts. The part of the instruction telling the ALU what to do next is placed into an instruction register. The part of the instruction specifying the address of the data to be used in the operation is moved to an address register. A storage register is used to store any data that have been retrieved from primary storage. Last, an accumulator is used to store results of an operation.

In this manner, the modern digital computer methodically reads through a computer program and executes the program one instruction at a time, in sequential order. There may be millions, or hundreds of millions, of such machine cycles to perform in a program. However, because the

Figure 3.3

A Machine Cycle

Each machine cycle consists of two smaller cycles: the instruction cycle (I-cycle) and the execution cycle (E-cycle). These involve a series of steps in which instructions are retrieved from a software program, decoded, and performed. Running even a simple software program involves thousands of machine cycles.

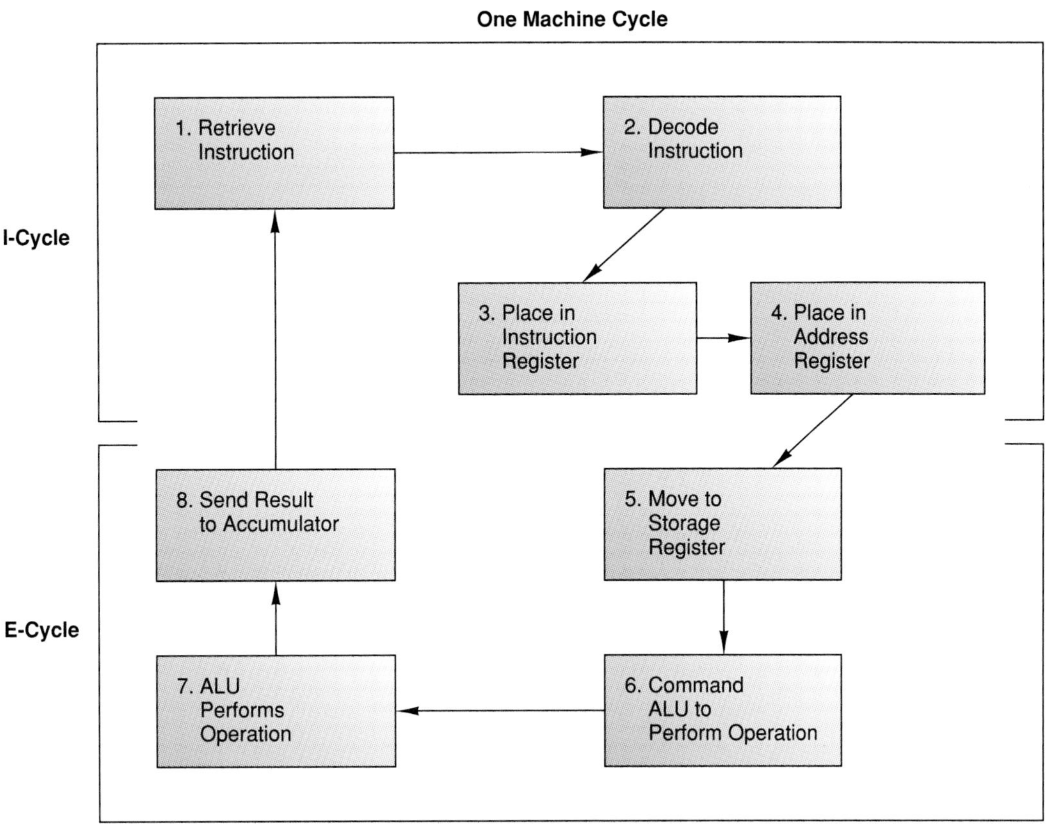

machine works very fast—millions of instructions per second—extremely large programs can be executed in a few moments.

Memory Devices · There are several different kinds of semiconductor memory chips used in primary storage. Each serves a different purpose. **RAM,** or random-access memory, is used for short-term storage of data or program instructions. RAM is located in RAM chips physically close to the CPU. The sole purpose of these chips is to store digital data. The contents of RAM can be read and changed when required. RAM is **volatile:** this means that if the computer's electric supply is disrupted or the computer is turned off, its contents will be lost.

Another kind of memory found in a computer is **ROM,** or read-only memory, which stores important program instructions permanently. For example, in the IBM Personal System/2 microcomputer workstation, ROM permanently stores instructions concerning the display screen, keyboard,

RAM
A memory device used for the short-term storage of data or program instructions; stands for random-access memory.

Volatile
Property of memory that means that its contents will be lost if electric power is disrupted or the computer is turned off.

ROM
A memory device used for the permanent storage of program instructions; stands for read-only memory.

Nonvolatile
Property of memory that means that its contents will not be lost if electric power is disrupted or the computer is turned off.

PROM
A memory device in which the memory chips can only be programmed once and are used to store instructions entered by the purchaser; stands for programmable read-only memory.

EPROM
A memory device in which the memory chips can be erased and reprogrammed with new instructions; stands for erasable programmable read-only memory.

and printer. ROM is **nonvolatile,** meaning that its contents will not be lost if electric power is disrupted or the computer is turned off. Nor can it be destroyed if someone tries to write over the instructions.

There are several other categories of nonvolatile memory chips. **PROM,** or programmable read-only memory, is similar to ROM in that it can only be read from and cannot be changed once the chips have been programmed. Initially, however, PROM chips contain no program instructions. These are entered by the purchaser, usually a manufacturer, who programs the chips and implants them in manufactured products where they serve as control devices. For example, instead of fabricating a specialized chip to control small motors, a manufacturer can program a PROM chip with the control instructions. **EPROM,** or erasable programmable read-only memory, chips are also nonvolatile. Unlike PROM chips, however, EPROM chips can be erased and reprogrammed. Consequently, they are used in robots and other devices where the program may have to be changed periodically.

Measuring Time, Size, and Processing Power

How can we determine whether a given computer will help us with problem solving? How can we determine which model or size of computer to use?

Robots are part of Lockheed Corporation's advanced circuit board production facility, in which all aspects of production—from design to completed assemblies—are electronically integrated by computer systems. Industrial robots often use erasable programmable read-only memory chips because, when required, their instructions can be changed.

Source: Courtesy of Lockheed Missiles & Space Company.

Assuming the problem lends itself to automation (see Chapters 9–11), we need to know how fast a computer can work, how much data it can store, and whether it can store the data required to solve our problem. Therefore, knowing the measures of computer speed and capacity is essential.

Slower computers will measure machine cycle times in **milliseconds** (thousandths of a second). More powerful machines will use measures of **microseconds** (millionths of a second) or **nanoseconds** (billionths of a second). A few very powerful computers measure machine cycles in **picoseconds** (trillionths of a second). The largest business computers (such as IBM mainframes in the 3090 series) have a machine cycle time of less than 20 nanoseconds. Thus such computers can execute 20 to 100 million instructions per second. MIPS, or millions of instructions per second, is a common benchmark for measuring the speed of larger computers.

Computer storage capacity is measured in terms of bytes. A thousand bytes (actually 1,024 or 2^{10} storage positions) are termed a **kilobyte.** The kilobyte is the typical measure of microcomputer storage capacity. Thus, when someone speaks of a microcomputer with a 640K memory, this means that the machine has an internal RAM capacity of 640 kilobytes. Larger machines have storage capacities in the **megabyte** (over 1 million bytes) or **gigabyte** (over 1 billion bytes) range. Table 3.1 summarizes the key measures of computer time and storage capacity.

Millisecond
A measure of machine cycle time; equals one one-thousandth of a second.

Microsecond
A measure of machine cycle time; equals one one-millionth of a second.

Nanosecond
A measure of machine cycle time; equals one one-billionth of a second.

Picosecond
A measure of machine cycle time; equals one one-trillionth of a second.

Kilobyte
The usual measure of microcomputer storage capacity; approximately 1,000 bytes.

Megabyte
A measure of computer storage capacity; approximately 1 million bytes.

Gigabyte
A measure of computer storage capacity; approximately 1 billion bytes.

Bit
A binary digit that can have only one of two states, representing zero or one.

How Computers Represent Data

A computer represents data by reducing all symbols, pictures, or words into a string of binary digits. Binary means having two states, and each binary digit can have only one of two states or conditions, based on the presence or absence of electronic or magnetic signals. A conducting state in a semiconductor circuit represents a one; a nonconducting state represents a zero. In magnetic media, a magnetized spot represents a one when a magnetic field is in one direction and represents a zero when the magnetism is in the other direction.

A binary digit is called a **bit** and represents either a zero or a one. The binary number system, or base 2 system, can express all numbers as groups of zeros and ones. As in the decimal (base 10) system, which we ordinarily

Table 3.1

Key Measures of Computer Time and Storage Capacity

Time		*Storage Capacity*	
Millisecond	1/1000 second	Kilobyte	1,000 (1,024) storage positions
Microsecond	1/1,000,000 second	Megabyte	1,000,000 (1,048,576) storage positions
Nanosecond	1/1,000,000,000 second	Gigabyte	1,000,000,000 (1,073,741,824) storage positions
Picosecond	1/1,000,000,000,000 second		

use, the value of each number depends on the place of each digit in a string of digits. Figure 3.4 illustrates how the decimal system works. Each digit has been broken down according to its place value to show how numbers are created. In Figure 3.5 we apply the same approach to show how to convert a binary number to its decimal equivalent. Any number in the decimal system can be expressed as a binary number and vice versa. For example, the decimal number 25 would be represented as 11001 in the binary system; the decimal number 27 would be the binary number 11011.

Figure 3.4

Converting a Decimal Number to Its Decimal Components

The value of a number depends on the place of each digit within a series of digits. In the decimal (or base 10) number system, each number can be expressed as a power of the number 10.

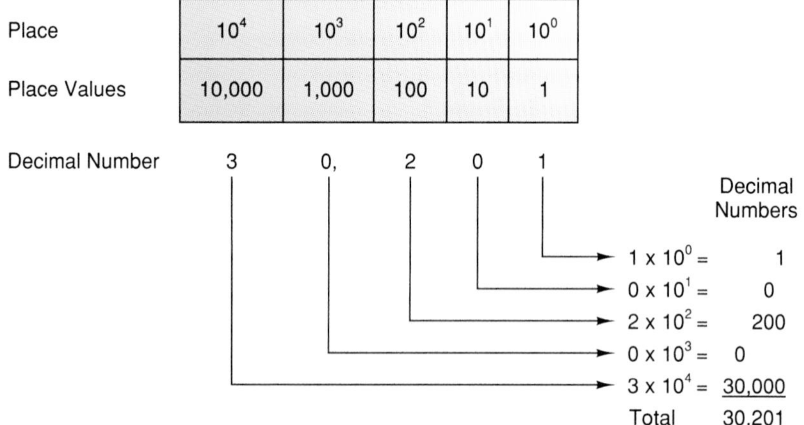

Figure 3.5

Converting a Binary Number to Its Decimal Equivalent

In the binary, or base 2, number system, each number can be expressed as a power of the number 2.

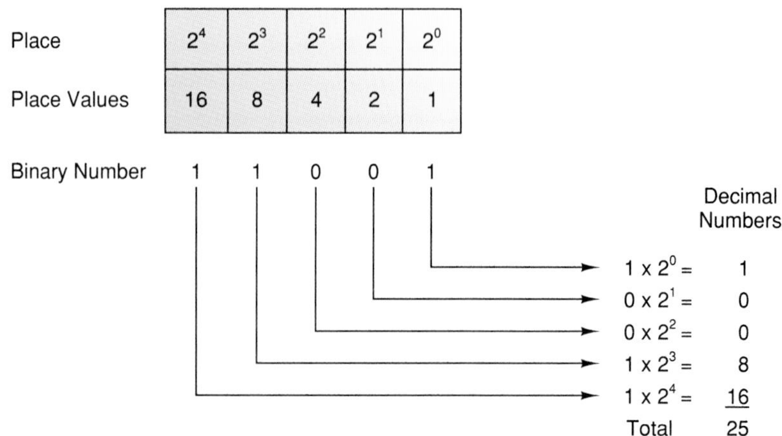

What about letters and symbols such as $ and &? These can also be represented in binary form using special coding schemes. The two most popular binary coding schemes are EBCDIC (Extended Binary Coded Decimal Interchange Code) and ASCII (American Standard Code for Information Interchange). **EBCDIC** (pronounced ib-si-dick) was developed by IBM in the 1950s and is used in IBM and other mainframe computers. **ASCII** was developed by the American National Standards Institute (ANSI) as a standard code that could be used by many different computer manufacturers to make their machines compatible. ASCII is used in data transmission, in microcomputers, and in some larger computers.

EBCDIC
An 8-bit binary coding scheme used in IBM and other mainframe computers; stands for Extended Binary Coded Decimal Interchange Code.

ASCII
A 7- or 8-bit binary coding scheme used in data transmission, microcomputers, and some larger computers; stands for American Standard Code for Information Interchange.

EBCDIC is an 8-bit coding scheme; that is, 8 bits are grouped together to form a byte. Each byte represents a single letter, symbol, or number and consists of a unique combination of bits. For example, the decimal digit 8 is represented by the EBCDIC code as 11111000. An A is represented in EBCDIC as 11000001. ASCII was originally designed as a 7-bit code, but most computers use 8-bit versions of ASCII. Table 3.2 compares the EBCDIC and ASCII 8-bit coding schemes.

EBCDIC and ASCII also contain an extra bit position called a parity bit. This bit is automatically set to zero or one to make all the bits in a byte add up to an even or odd number. Computers are constructed to have either even or odd parity. An even parity machine expects the number of "on" bits in a byte to add up to an even number. An odd parity machine expects the number of "on" bits in a byte to be odd. If the number of "on" bits in a byte is even in an odd parity machine, the parity bit will be turned on to make the total number of "on" bits odd. Figure 3.6 shows both valid and invalid representations of a character in an odd parity computer. Parity bits are used to detect errors caused by environmental disturbances or garbled data transmission.

Generations of Computer Hardware

Computer hardware has undergone a series of transitions, each of which has widened the range of problems computers can solve. Each stage, or generation, in the history of computing has used a different technology for the computer's logic elements, the electronic components used in the computer's processing work. Each new logic element has dramatically boosted computer processing power and storage capabilities while lowering costs. Generational changes in computer hardware have been accompanied by generational changes in computer software (see Chapter 5). From an exclusive and esoteric toy of a handful of scientists and researchers, computers have become a major tool for solving problems in the business and commercial world.

Vacuum tubes permitted computers such as the IBM 701 to calculate thousands of times faster than did their electromechanical forerunners. Despite their enormous physical size, these computers had less processing power than today's IBM PCs.

Source: Courtesy of International Business Machines Corporation.

The First Generation (1951–1958): Vacuum-Tube Technology · The first generation of computers used vacuum tubes to store and process information. These tubes were not very satisfactory: they consumed large quantities of electric power, generated a great deal of heat, and had short lives. First-generation computers were colossal in size, yet they had very limited memories and processing capacity. The maximum memory size was only about 2 kilobytes, with speed of 10 kilo instructions per second. Rotating

Table 3.2

EBCDIC and ASCII Coding Systems

Character	EBCDIC Binary	ASCII-8 Binary
A	1100 0001	1010 0001
B	1100 0010	1010 0010
C	1100 0011	1010 0011
D	1100 0100	1010 0100
E	1100 0101	1010 0101
F	1100 0110	1010 0110
G	1100 0111	1010 0111
H	1100 1000	1010 1000
I	1100 1001	1010 1001
J	1101 0001	1010 1010
K	1101 0010	1010 1011
L	1101 0011	1010 1100
M	1101 0100	1010 1101
N	1101 0101	1010 1110
O	1101 0110	1010 1111
P	1101 0111	1011 0000
Q	1101 1000	1011 0001
R	1101 1001	1011 0010
S	1110 0010	1011 0011
T	1110 0011	1011 0100
U	1110 0100	1011 0101
V	1110 0101	1011 0110
W	1110 0110	1011 0111
X	1110 0111	1011 1000
Y	1110 1000	1011 1001
Z	1110 1001	1011 1010
0	1111 0000	0101 0000
1	1111 0001	0101 0001
2	1111 0010	0101 0010
3	1111 0011	0101 0011
4	1111 0100	0101 0100
5	1111 0101	0101 0101
6	1111 0110	0101 0110
7	1111 0111	0101 0111
8	1111 1000	0101 1000
9	1111 1001	0101 1001

magnetic drums were used for internal storage, and punched cards were used for external storage. Jobs such as running programs or printing output had to be coordinated manually.

All in all, first-generation computers were so costly, unwieldy, and difficult to program that their problem-solving capabilities were very re-

Figure 3.6

Detecting Errors with a Parity Check, Using Odd Parity

With odd parity, the correct representation will involve an odd number of "on" bits. If there is an even number of "on" bits, this alerts the computer that an error has occurred.

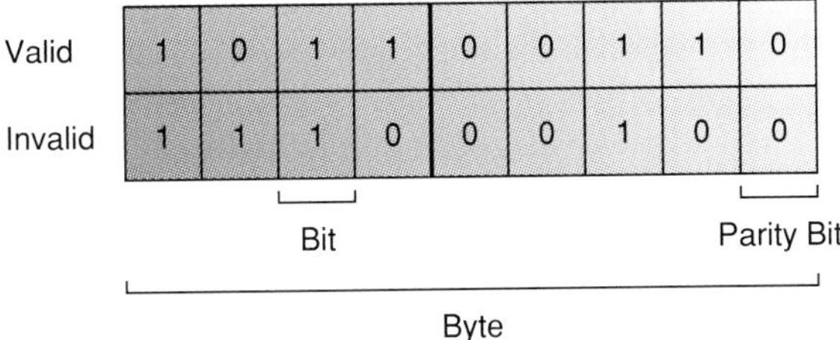

stricted. Consequently, these machines were used primarily for very limited scientific and engineering problems.

The Second Generation (1959–1963): Transistor Technology · Second-generation computers were based on transistor technology, with individual transistors wired into printed circuit boards. Not only were transistors smaller, cheaper, and more reliable than vacuum tubes, but they also generated far less heat and consumed less power. Memory size expanded to 32 kilobytes of RAM, and speeds reached 200,000–300,000 instructions per second. Internal storage utilized magnetic cores (small doughnut-shaped devices strung together on racks within the computer, which have much faster access speeds than magnetic drums). Magnetic tape and disks started to be used for external storage.

Second-generation computers saw more widespread use for scientific and business problems because of their greatly increased processing power, which supported easier-to-use software. Businesses started using computers to automate accounting and clerical tasks such as payroll and billing.

The Third Generation (1964–1979): Integrated Circuit Technology · Third-generation computers relied on integrated circuits, which printed thousands of tiny transistors onto small silicon chips. Computers thus could expand to 2 megabytes of RAM and accelerate processing speed to as much as 5 MIPS. Third-generation machines also supported software that was even closer to the English language and easier to use. This meant that persons without a technical background could start using these machines and associated software personally without having to rely on specialists.

Increased capacity and processing power made it possible to use sophisticated operating systems—special software that automated the running of programs and communication between the CPU, printers, and other devices. Moreover, these operating systems could work on several programs or tasks simultaneously, whereas first- and second-generation computers could only handle one program at a time. Section 2.0 of Chapter 5 treats operating systems in detail.

The Fourth Generation (1979–Present): Very-Large-Scale Integrated Circuit Technology · Fourth-generation computers use very-large-scale integrated circuits (VLSIC), which contain from 200,000 to over 1 million circuits per chip. More circuits can be packed into increasingly less space, so hundreds of thousands of circuits can be accommodated on a silicon chip the size of a fingernail. Fourth-generation technology has enabled conventional mainframes to achieve memory sizes over 500 megabytes and speeds over 100 MIPS. Supercomputers exceed these capacities and speeds.

Microprocessor
A silicon chip containing an entire CPU; used in microcomputers.

Another feature of fourth-generation hardware is the **microprocessor.** A microprocessor actually consists of an entire CPU on a single silicon chip. Microcomputers and "intelligent" features in automobiles, watches, toys, and other items are based on microprocessor technology. Microminiaturization has produced computers that are so small, fast, and cheap that they have become ubiquitous in daily life. Software for such computers is becoming increasingly easy to use, so nontechnical specialists can use microcomputers to solve problems on their own.

A chip begins with a wafer of silicon. A layer of high-quality, single-crystal silicon is deposited on the wafer's surface. Circuit structures are defined by a mask of photosensitive materials. Etching removes unwanted portions of the deposited layers not covered by the mask. Conductive and insulating materials are layered on the wafer in a process called chemical vapor deposition (CVD). In the implant process, electrically charged impurities are bombarded into the silicon wafer to increase electrical conductivity in selected regions on the circuit.

Source: Jacobs/Fulton Design Group; Paper Sculpture by Pat Allen, © Applied Materials, Inc.

A silicon wafer

A side view of an etched wafer

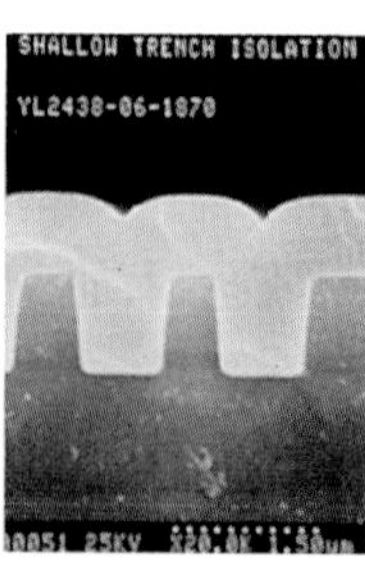

CVD over an etched wafer

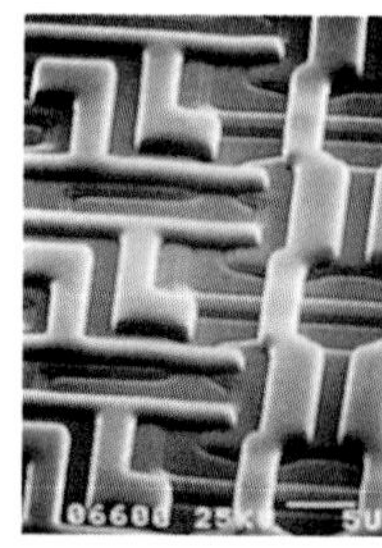

A top view of a wafer after multi-layer processing

Patterned wafer following fabrication process

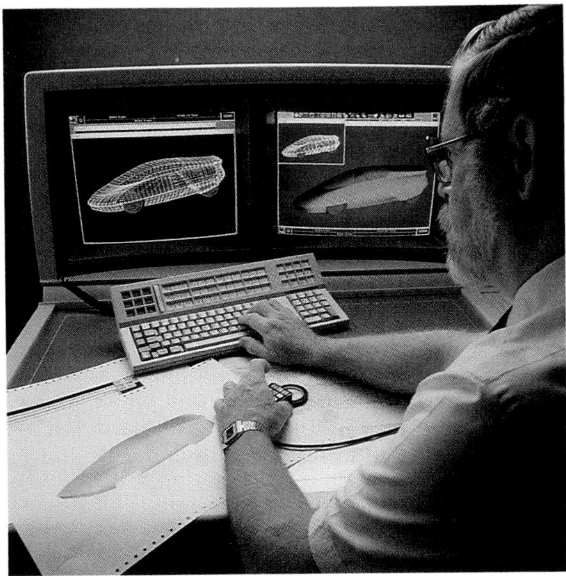

Microprocessors are used not only in the tools that design automobiles but in the autos themselves. Here, a Ford Motor Company designer works on an advanced vehicle. Microprocessors are used in various Ford products to control performance and fuel economy in the engine control module, to prevent wheel lock-up in the anti-lock braking system, and to smooth the ride in the air suspension system.
Source: Courtesy of Ford Motor Company.

Mainframes, Minicomputers, Microcomputers, and Supercomputers

Computers are typically classified as mainframes, minicomputers, or microcomputers. Generally speaking, a **mainframe** is the largest computer, a big powerhouse of a machine with huge memory and extremely rapid processing power. Mainframes are typically used for solving very large commercial, scientific, or military problems where a computer must handle massive amounts of data or many complicated processes. A **minicomputer** is a midrange computer, about the size of an office desk; minicomputers are often used in universities, factories, or research laboratories. A **microcomputer** is small enough that it can be placed on a desk top or carried from room to room. Organizations use microcomputers for solving problems, but they are also widely used as personal machines (they were originally designed for nontechnical specialists).

Mainframe
A large computer, generally having 50 to 500 or more megabytes of RAM.

Minicomputer
A medium-sized computer, generally having 10 to 100 megabytes of RAM.

Microcomputer
A small, desktop or portable computer, generally having 256 kilobytes to 16 megabytes of RAM.

Generally, mainframes can be classified as having 50 to over 500 megabytes of RAM; minicomputers, 10 to 100 megabytes of RAM; and microcomputers, 256 kilobytes to 16 megabytes of RAM. These distinctions are becoming less meaningful, however, because the capacity of computer hardware is constantly changing. The microcomputers of the early 1980s had as much memory (64K) as an IBM System 360 mainframe in 1965. And the computing power of micros continues to soar. With memories of up to 16 megabytes and processing speeds of 5 MIPS, micros today can handle as much work as the big mainframes of the 1970s.

Supercomputer
A very sophisticated and powerful computer that can perform complex computations very rapidly.

A **supercomputer** is an especially sophisticated and powerful computer used for problems requiring extremely rapid and complex computations with hundreds or thousands of variable factors. Because supercomputers are extremely expensive, they have been used mainly for military and scientific applications, although they are starting to be adopted by business firms. For example, Dow Jones & Company uses two supercomputers to handle its customer information requests and extra database services. Typically, however, supercomputers are used for highly classified weapons research, weather forecasting, and petroleum and engineering applications, which involve complex mathematical models and simulations.

Parallel processing
A type of processing in which more than one instruction is processed at a time; used in supercomputers.

Supercomputers can perform complex and massive computations much faster than conventional computers because they can process up to 64 bits in a machine cycle as small as 4 nanoseconds—five times faster than the largest mainframes. Supercomputers do not process one instruction at a time but instead rely on **parallel processing.** Figure 3.7 illustrates parallel processing for a hypothetical problem involving four parts (A–D). Multiple processing units (CPUs) break down the problem into smaller parts and

Figure 3.7

Parallel Processing: An Important Ingredient in Supercomputers

Supercomputers can perform complex calculations much faster than even a mainframe can. This is possible in part due to parallel processing, in which multiple CPUs break down a problem into smaller portions and work on them simultaneously.

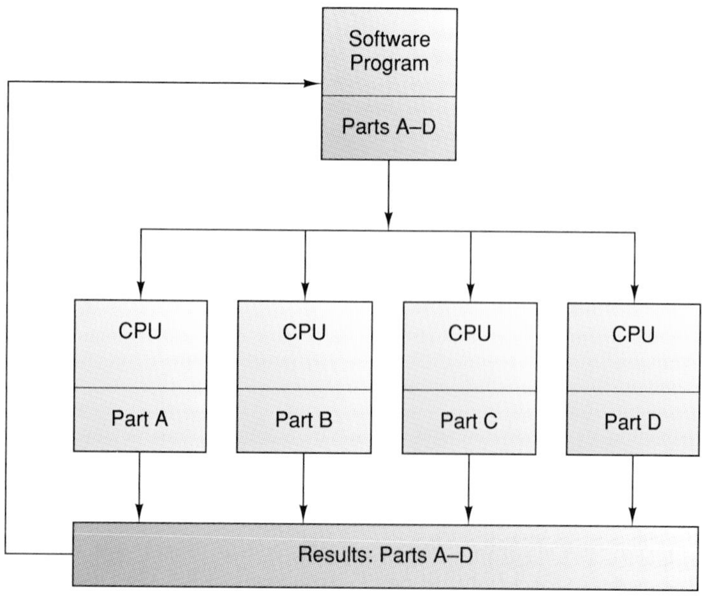

FOCUS ON *Organizations*

Cray Stands Alone

In the supercomputer industry, Cray Research is the only American manufacturer since Minneapolis-based Control Data Corporation bowed out in the spring of 1989. Control Data left the field after it lost money in the six years it attempted to market supercomputers.

Cray is not only the sole U.S. maker of supercomputers, it is also the industry's leader in a growing marketplace for the sophisticated hardware. Supercomputers are increasingly popular because they can handle enormous masses of data—an ability useful in a variety of fields, including oil exploration and the development of new drugs.

Cray may have more domestic competition before long. Among the U.S. companies that have expressed interest in developing their own supercomputers is IBM. In late 1987, IBM entered into a joint venture with Steve Chen, formerly a designer at Cray, to develop a line of advanced supercomputers. According to Allan Weis, a vice-president in the Data Systems Division at IBM, "We're very serious about the supercomputer market. The Japanese are formidable competitors, but IBM and Cray are very formidable, too."

In the meantime, Cray's main competition comes from Japan. The result may be an aggravation of trade disagreements between Japan and the United States. In 1987 the two nations signed an accord in which Japan agreed to eliminate discrimination by Japanese government agencies and universities against U.S. supercomputer makers. Nevertheless, in the two years following the signing of the accord, the Japanese government has not bought a single U.S. supercomputer. Cray and IBM will have to scramble to change that track record.

Source: Michael Quinn, "And Then There Was One," *Time,* May 1, 1989, pp. 56–57.

work on it simultaneously. Some experimental supercomputers use as many as 64,000 processors.

The leading U.S. supercomputer manufacturer is Cray Research. Its supercomputers, which cost between $5 and $20 million, can process up to 16 gigaflops, a billion floating-point operations, per second. (A floating-point operation is a basic computer arithmetic operation, such as addition.) Although the world market for supercomputers is growing, as the Focus on Organizations points out, Cray and other U.S. supercomputer makers are facing increased competition from the Japanese.

3.3 The Microcomputer Revolution

The microcomputer has emerged as one of the most powerful problem-solving tools in use today. The term *microcomputer* is sometimes used synonymously with *personal computer,* since micros originally were intended as primarily single-user problem-solving tools. Microcomputers have become so powerful, however, that they are no longer confined to personal

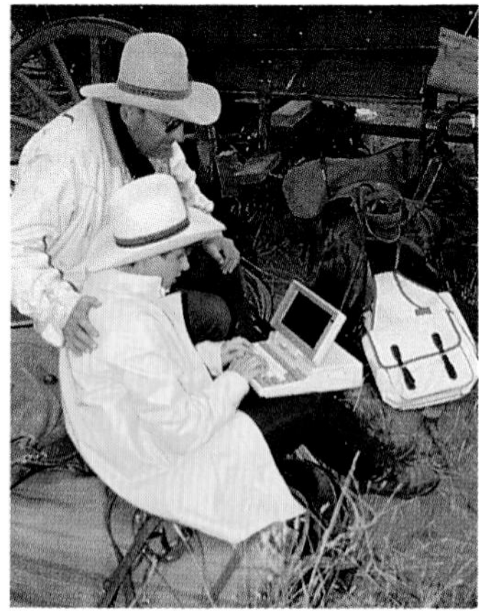

Powerful laptop computers allow flexibility in locations where work can take place. During the six-day trip, organizers for the Great Montana Centennial Cattle Drive used Toshiba computers to keep track of 3,500 horses, 2,500 riders, 2,700 head of cattle, 188 covered wagons, 1,200 tons of hay and oats, 1 million gallons of water, participant registration information, permits, and insurance forms.

Source: © McKain.

information systems. Indeed, the micros of the 1990s have the same computing power as the mainframes of the 1970s plus new graphic and interactive capabilities. Microcomputers can also be applied to group and organization-wide problem solving, performing tasks that previously were reserved for minicomputers and mainframes.

Mainframes on a Desk Top—Powerhouse Micros

Micros range in size from desktop units to lightweight portable "laptops" weighing several pounds. Their popularity is growing as advances in computer hardware have packed more computing power into increasingly smaller space at increasingly lower prices.

Micros can be used either as individual stand-alone machines with their own processing power, stored data, and software or as part of a departmental or company-wide network. As stand-alone processing devices, micros have turned desk tops into powerful personal workstations. Lightweight, portable laptop micros make it possible to use computers in many locations—at home, on the train, or on an airplane. No longer must business problem solving take place within the physical confines of the office. The Focus on Problem Solving examines this trend.

Micros can be linked together in networks with other micros, printers, "intelligent" copy machines, and telephones; this enables the micros to

With a laptop computer, a cellular telephone, and Ameritech's Mobile Access Data Service, sales representatives and other business people can access data stored in any computer in the United States reachable through a local or 800 telephone number.

Source: Courtesy of Ameritech.

FOCUS ON *Problem Solving*

Laptops Keep Workers in Touch

Users of microcomputers are increasingly choosing the portable variety of that hardware. Much of the attraction of these so-called laptop computers is their advanced technology, which enables the computers to handle ever more data and to display the data on screens with improved resolution.

However, hardware alone has not fueled the drive to using portable computers. Attractive applications also have become available. Particularly important has been the combination of portable computers with communications technology that links the computers to sources of information. Specifically, modems allow laptop users to link their computers to their office or home computer.

For example, agents of the Farm Credit Administration—a federal regulatory agency with headquarters in McLean, Virginia—conduct on-site examinations of the financial records of banks participating in the agency's Farm Credit Program. These duties keep agents away from the office about five out of every six weeks. To take computer power with them, the agents use Zenith Z-181 laptop computers.

Each of these computers is loaded with Lotus 1-2-3 spreadsheet software for analyzing numbers, as well as software for word processing and communications. While the FCA agents are visiting banks, the laptops can print out reports or documents on inexpensive, two-pound printers; at the home office, the computers can be hooked up to more sophisticated printers.

In similar ways, other traveling professionals, such as salespeople and auditors, have found that portable computers are useful problem-solving tools on the road.

Source: Richard Dalton, "Porting More Than Computers," *Personal Computing,* May 1988, pp. 99–100.

provide intelligence and processing power to coordinate the flow of documents and work without having to rely on mainframes. Such networks are discussed in Chapter 7. Micros can also be linked to minicomputers and mainframes, forming company-wide information networks that share hardware, software, and data resources. The use of multiple computers connected by a communication network for processing is called **distributed processing.** Instead of relying exclusively on a large central mainframe computer or several independent computers, processing work is distributed

Distributed processing
The distribution of processing among multiple computers linked by a communications network.

Figure 3.8

Distributed Processing Linking a Computer Network

The network can include various combinations of mainframes, minicomputers, and microcomputers.

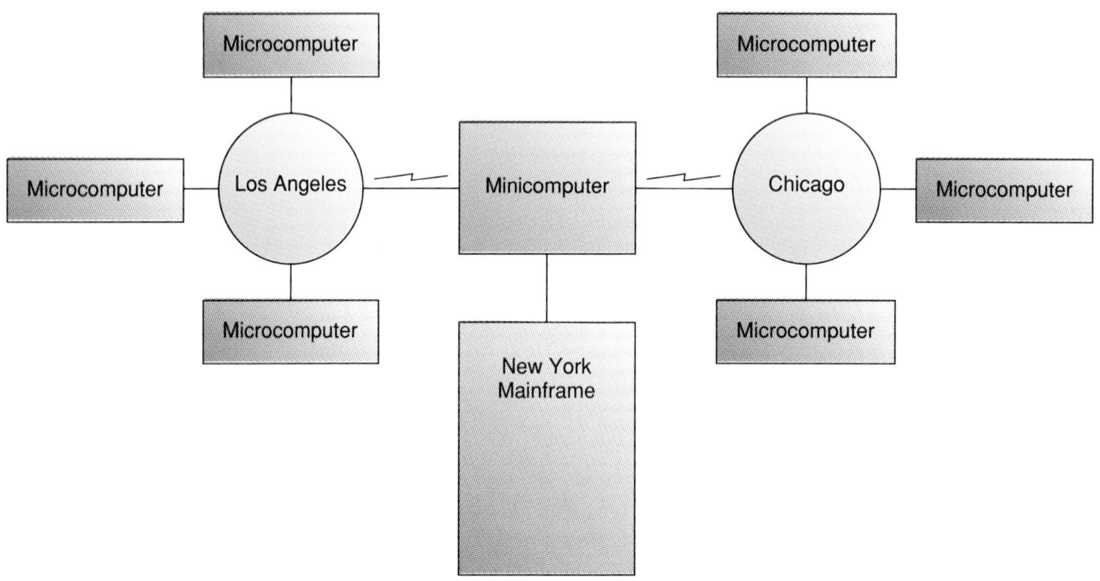

among the various microcomputers, minicomputers, and mainframes linked together. The network can be simple, as shown in Figure 3.8, or it can involve hundreds or thousands of separate computers.

Microcomputers can be linked to mainframes in a variety of relationships. Special software can make microcomputers emulate ordinary mainframe terminals. Such terminals are called "dumb terminals" because they do not make use of their internal processing capacity. Special file-transfer software can be used to extract data from mainframes, reformat it, and place it in the microcomputer. This is called **downloading.** A typical problem solved by downloading might involve extracting corporate data from a mainframe system and downloading them to a microcomputer where they can be manipulated by spreadsheet software for next year's budget projections (see Section 5.4 of Chapter 5 on spreadsheets).

Downloading
The process of extracting data from mainframes, reformatting them, and placing them in a microcomputer.

Downsizing · Microcomputers can now perform many problem-solving tasks that were formerly reserved for much larger machines. As a result, many business organizations are **downsizing,** or shifting problem-solving applications from large computers to smaller ones. Indeed, computer industry reports show a fundamental shift in purchasing patterns away from giant mainframes toward lower-cost desktop machines. Some analysts predict that as much as 80 percent of corporate computing power will be on desktop systems by the mid-1990s.

Downsizing
The process of moving business software applications from large computers, such as mainframes or minicomputers, to smaller computers, such as microcomputers.

Firms have actually scaled down their hardware, replacing mainframes and minicomputers with microcomputers. Often microcomputers are networked together so that they can share data and communicate with each other (see Chapter 7).

Downsizing can lead to substantial cost savings for firms. According to a 1988 International Data Corporation report, it costs about $120,000 per MIPS on a mainframe, compared to $1,000 on a microcomputer. A megabyte of primary memory on a mainframe costs $3,000 to $5,000, ten times the cost of equivalent memory on a micro.[1] Mainframe disk storage costs twice as much as for a micro. Echlin, Inc., a $1.3 billion automotive parts manufacturer headquartered in Branford, Connecticut, saved $800,000 per year by scrapping its IBM 4341 mainframe in favor of 65 networked personal computers.[2]

Cooperative Processing · Another computing pattern divides processing work for a particular application between mainframes and personal computers. They communicate with each other, with each assigned the functions it performs best. For example, the personal computer might be used for data entry and validation, while the mainframe would be responsible for processing the input data and handling data stored by the system. This division of labor is called **cooperative processing.** Personal computers are utilized because they can provide the same processing power much more cheaply than a mainframe.

Cooperative processing
The division of processing work for applications among mainframes and personal computers.

Microprocessor Technology: The Chips behind the Machines

The computing power of microcomputers depends heavily on the speed and performance of the microprocessor on which they are based. This can be measured in several ways.

Microcomputers are typically labeled as 8-bit, 16-bit, or 32-bit machines, according to their **dataword length.** A dataword is the number of bits that may be processed together as a unit. An 8-bit chip can retrieve or process 8 bits in a single machine cycle, a 32-bit machine, 32 bits. Thus, the bigger the dataword size, the more data and instructions the computer can handle at one time and the greater its speed. A 32-bit chip can process four 8-bit bytes at once.

Dataword length
The number of bits that a computer can process or store together as a unit.

Another factor affecting speed is the **input/output (I/O) bus width.** The bus, which acts as a highway between the CPU and other devices, determines how much data can be moved at one time. The 8088 chip used in the original IBM Personal Computer, for example, has a 16-bit data word length but only an 8-bit I/O bus width. This means that data are transferred within the CPU chip itself in 16-bit chunks but can only be moved 8 bits at a time from the CPU to external devices. On the other hand, the 80386 chip, used in the most powerful IBM Personal System/2 machines, and the Motorola 68030 chip, used in the Macintosh microcomputers, have both a 32-bit data word length and a 32-bit I/O bus width.

Input/output bus width
The number of bits that can be moved at one time between the CPU and the other devices of a computer.

Cycle speed also affects speed and performance. An internal clock in the control unit sets the pace for sequencing events in the computer by emitting millions of electronic pulses per second. This clock speed is measured in **megahertz (MHz)**, or millions of cycles per second. For example, the Intel 8088 microprocessor, which was the foundation for the early IBM Personal Computers, operates at 4.7 megahertz, or 4.7 million cycles per

Megahertz
A measure of clock speed, or the pacing of events in a computer; stands for one million cycles per second.

second. In the more recent IBM Personal System/2 Model 70 microcomputer, the Intel 80386 microprocessor operates at 25 megahertz.

Intel's 80486 chip and the Motorola 68040 are 32-bit chips that are three times faster than their predecessors. In fact, Intel's 80486 chip, which contains more than 1 million transistors on a thumbtack-sized silicon sliver, has been described as a "veritable mainframe-on-a-chip." With the number-crunching power of a low-end IBM 3090 mainframe, the 80486 chip and others like it will inaugurate an era of "personal mainframes" in desktop computing. While personal computers based on Intel's 80386 chip can perform a handful of tasks simultaneously, the 80486 can perform dozens, each much larger and more sophisticated than anything being done now.[3] Table 3.3 compares the capabilities of the most popular microcomputer chips.

Workstations

Workstation
A desktop computer with powerful graphics and mathematical processing capabilities as well as the ability to perform several tasks at once.

Workstations are desktop machines with very powerful graphics and mathematical processing capabilities plus the ability to perform several tasks at once. They are typically used by scientists, engineers, designers, and other knowledge workers. With very powerful graphics and CPU capacity, they can present fully rendered, multiple views of a physical object, such as an airplane wing; rotate the object three dimensionally; give its physical parameters, such as dimensions and weight; and provide its design history and cost factors. Workstations can easily integrate text and graphics, displaying

Table 3.3

Generations of Microprocessors

Microprocessor Chip	Manufacturer	Data Word Length	I/O Bus Width	Clock Speed (MH_z)	Microcomputers Used in
6502	MOS Technology	8	8	4	Apple IIe Commodore 64 Atari 800
8088	Intel	16	8	8	IBM PC and XT COMPAQ Portable
80286	Intel	16	16	8–28	IBM AT AT&T PC 6300 Plus
68000	Motorola	32	16	12.5	Macintosh Plus Macintosh SE Model 16B
80386	Intel	32	32	16–32	IBM Personal System/2 Models 60-80 COMPAQ 386
68020	Motorola	32	32	12.5–32	Macintosh II
68030	Motorola	32	32	25	Macintosh IIx, IIcx Sun workstations Apollo workstations
80486	Intel	32	32	25	High-end IBM Personal System/2 and future workstations Model 70 A21
68040	Motorola	32	32	—	Future workstations

At Loma Linda University, Autographix graphics workstations create over 36,000 slides each year for medical lectures and instruction. Unlike many desktop personal computers, workstations combine text and graphics and simultaneously display data, applications, and tools.

Source: Courtesy of Autographix and photographer, Duane R. Miller, Loma Linda University, Department of Media Services.

multiple tools, applications, and types of data simultaneously. They are spreading to the financial industry, where powerhouse desktop machines simultaneously provide financial data and news services, analyze portfolios, and process securities and commodities trades.

Chapter 14 describes the SPARC station 1, a compact workstation with the power of a minicomputer, manufactured by Sun Microsystems, the leading technical and engineering workstation manufacturer. Yet, for all its power, a SPARC station costs less than $5,000—about the same as IBM's most powerful personal computer. This raises the question of how workstations can be differentiated from personal computers.

Indeed, workstations and personal computers are becoming harder to distinguish. Some of the more sophisticated personal computers have workstation-like features, and as personal computers become ever more powerful and graphics oriented, the distinction is likely to blur further. Distinctions based on price (a workstation typically costs $20,000 or more; a personal computer $10,000 or less) are also evaporating. Until personal computers and workstations become one and the same, however, a workstation can be distinguished by the following characteristics:[4]

1. A powerful 32-bit microprocessor.
2. Networking capabilities.
3. Capabilities for multitasking, or performing two different tasks simultaneously.

4. Used primarily to solve scientific, engineering, or other technical problems such as CAD/CAM.
5. Heavy graphics orientation, fostering a visual, multidimensional approach to problem solving.

Standard-Setting Machines: IBM and Apple

Not only have the IBM Personal Computer and Apple Macintosh been market leaders, they have set the standards for what a microcomputer should be. Each embodies a distinct computing philosophy and approach to problem solving.

The IBM PC · The IBM Personal Computer (PC) was introduced in 1981 and immediately became the standard-setting machine for the business world. The PC legitimized desktop computing in business by popularizing spreadsheet, database, and word processing applications (see Chapter 5). It also created a standard platform for a wide variety of hardware and software tools.

The original IBM PC model of computing can be distinguished by the following characteristics:

- Information is presented mainly in textual format.
- Humans interact with the computer by issuing text-based commands.
- The computing environment treats problems by dividing them into discrete applications—word processing, spreadsheets, databases, and so forth. Problem solvers are constrained to using one tool at a time rather than combining data from many sources and looking at many facets of a problem simultaneously.

Typical IBM PC applications are primarily text oriented. Until the advent of the IBM Personal System/2 series, the machine produced relatively low-quality, low-resolution graphics and did not integrate graphics and text well, nor did it easily combine information from different sources and diverse applications. It could only handle one processing task at a time.

The original IBM PC embodies an older computing philosophy derived from the mainframe computer tradition. As such, it was designed more for technical specialists or sophisticated users than for nontechnical users, and it required a more formal "learning" of commands and files.

The Personal System/2 series, especially the models at the upper end, were designed to overcome these limitations. The PS/2 models 70 and 80 have the computing power for more sophisticated graphics with 32-bit 80386 chips and larger memories. The machines can handle several processing tasks at once and present the user with graphic symbols as options to traditional commands.

The original IBM PC was designed as a stand-alone machine. IBM's new Personal System/2 line envisions the microcomputer as one component in an interconnected array of mainframes, minicomputers, microcomputers, and storage media.

The Apple Macintosh · Apple Computer Corporation introduced the Macintosh in 1984 as an alternative microcomputing standard for business as well as personal use. Most companies adopted the Macintosh as a graphics or desktop publishing machine. Increasingly, Apple Computer is focusing on business applications like spreadsheets, databases, and word processing applications. Apple Computer and the Digital Equipment Corporation (DEC) agreed to use a single communications standard so that Macs could easily be linked with DEC Vax minicomputers, making Apple and DEC competitive with IBM in technologies for larger networks.

The Macintosh supports a vision of "workstation computing" that has a primarily visual or graphical orientation. The Macintosh is best known for its user interface, which uses graphic symbols. With a graphical user interface like Macintosh, menus, icons, computer "mice," and other devices eliminate the need for learning textual commands and focus the problem solver on the problem itself rather than the solution technology. The primary method of accessing information or making selections is to "point and click." Text can be displayed graphically on high-resolution monitors, appearing as "printed" pages that are typographically composed.

The Macintosh II machines have many workstation-like features, including integrated text and graphics and some ability to perform more than one processing task simultaneously. They also have more computing power, with memory of up to 8 megabytes and speeds up to 25 megahertz.

The IBM PC and the Macintosh had very different origins, reflecting different models of computing, but they are moving toward a common model that combines elements of both. The latest IBM PCs are equal to the Macintosh in sheer graphics power, and they have a large established base in the business community because they can use a very large number of business software applications. Macintosh, in turn, has broken out of its traditional desktop publishing and graphics artist base and is moving aggressively to develop more business applications.

3.4 Information Technology Trends

For the past 30 years, each decade has seen computing power increase by a factor of 100, while costs have dropped by a factor of 10. Advances in science, technology, and manufacturing will enable this momentum to continue. The future will see even more "intelligence" built into everyday devices, with mainframe-like computing power packed into a device the size of a shirt pocket or notebook.

Computers on a chip will guide automobiles, military weaponry, robots, and everyday household items. By 1995 organizations will be able to put the power of a fax machine, a 4-megabyte RAM personal computer, and a cellular telephone in an "office in a briefcase." Computers and related information technologies will be able to blend data, images, and sound and send them coursing through vast networks that can process all of them with equal ease. Supercomputers will be capable of at least 100 billion complex calculations per second—ten times more than today.

The Future of the Mainframe

Will computers on a chip turn mainframes into technological dinosaurs? This is unlikely. The remaining chapters of this book may help explain why. Firms have invested too much effort and expense in mainframes to shift to desktop technology to "solve" all of their problems. Building information systems is just too complex and costly for firms to redesign for smaller machines, at least in the short run of three to five years. Moreover, some functions in a business are best handled by a centralized mainframe installation. For instance, business firms in the year 2000 will still have to consolidate the operating incomes of all their divisions and subsidiaries. The information may be collected and transmitted by microcomputers, but chances are it will be consolidated and stored on a central mainframe. Mainframes are also necessary when thousands of users must work with the same machine.

What is likely to happen is that desktop machines will be the technology of choice for solving new problems that arise in the next decade, not only because of their low cost but because desktop technology has proved easier to use and more innovative. Moreover, the role of the mainframe will change from being the focal point of corporate computing to being one element in an intelligent network.

How important will the mainframe be? Will it be merely another machine connected to micros, minicomputers, workstations, and communications devices? Mainframe manufacturers such as IBM are hoping it will be the central hub that anchors the entire network, storing all the firm's data in one repository and then parceling the data out for processing on smaller machines. Microcomputer manufacturers claim, on the other hand, that new, more powerful desktop machines will accomplish most jobs in the future, while the mainframe is relegated to a central library where it will simply store and switch information at the behest of microcomputers.

A Fifth Generation

Conventional computers are based on what is called the Von Neuman architecture, which processes information serially, one instruction at a time. This name derives from John Von Neuman, an influential mathematician at Princeton University who sketched out the design elements of digital computers in the early 1940s. The Von Neuman design in which a computer works through a list of instructions, one at a time, has been the basis for virtually all conventional digital computing.

In the future, more computers will use parallel and vector processing (described below) to work on many parts of a problem at the same time, producing solutions 10 to 100 times faster than the most powerful sequential processors. (Parallel processing was introduced in Section 3.2.)

Vector processing
Processing technique that breaks a complex problem down into vectors, or groups of similar operations, and assigns each operation to a specially designed processor that can operate in tandem with others, enabling it to process the calculations hundreds of times faster than an ordinary computer chip.

"Fifth-generation computers" are supercomputers designed to function like the human brain in the sense that they carry out multiple streams of activity at once. Using a technique called **vector processing,** supercomputer software breaks a complex problem down into vectors, or groups of similar operations, such as additions, subtractions, square roots, and so forth. Each operation is assigned to a specially designed processor that can operate in tandem with the others. Then, at a single command, each processor churns through the entire string of calculations assigned to it. Because each processor does one simple task (e.g., adding two integers), it can process the calculations hundreds of times faster than an ordinary computer chip. In the end, the separate results are amalgamated into a single solution. Using artificial intelligence and intricate mathematical models, this new wave of computers will be able to blend voice, images, and massive pools of data from diverse sources.

Superchips

Much of the progress in information technology will continue to be based on advances in semiconductor chips, which soon will contain well over a million transistors on a tiny wafer. Such microprocessors will foster desktop supercomputing.

The dream of a supercomputer on a chip may be brought to fruition with Intel Corporation's i860 microprocessor (see photo). With more than 1 million transistors, this chip handles 64-bit-long instructions and can perform nearly 80 million calculations per second.[5] The i860 has three parallel processors. It can perform scientific calculations faster than the processors in Cray supercomputers. The head of Intel's microprocessor group believes the i860 "is like putting Cray on a chip." The i860 is expected to find applications in workstations and supercomputers. Even faster chips are anticipated for the year 2000, as the Focus on Technology explains.

Reduced Instruction Set Computing

The newest microprocessors utilize reduced instruction set computing (RISC), which drastically simplifies computer design. The speed of RISC chips is increasing as much as 70 percent annually. Conventional chips,

The Intel i860™ microprocessor contains more than one million transistors and has supercomputer processing capabilities. Powerful chips will continue to advance information technology.

Source: Courtesy Intel Corporation.

FOCUS ON *Technology*

Chips for the Year 2000

Twenty-five years ago, Robert Noyce and Gordon Moore, co-founders of the Intel Corporation, a major U.S. producer of microprocessors, found that the number of transistors that could be placed on an integrated circuit doubled every 18 months. Noyce predicted this trend would continue and probably accelerate in the 1990s.

Intel's Micro 2000 display at the annual PC Expo show in New York in June 1990 described what microchips would be like if these predictions held true until the year 2000. The Micro 2000 chip would have one hundred million transistors on a one-inch square die, taking up as much space as a single transistor did when Noyce invented the integrated circuit in the late 1950s. Laboratory researchers have already experimented with chips with features as small as one-tenth of a micron. (A micron is equivalent to one-millionth of a meter.) Transistors and other components packed close together increase speed, since the electrons that move through the chip don't have to travel as far.

The Micro 2000 chip would have a speed of 250 megahertz and could handle 2 billion instructions per second because up to four CPUs would be integrated on a single chip. A single central processing unit would be able to execute 700 million instructions per second, with three to five instructions executed per clock cycle. To make the chip compatible with existing computer software, the equivalent of today's 80486 microprocessor would be built into a tiny corner of the Micro 2000 chip.

Source: Peter H. Lewis, "Chips for the Year 2000," *The New York Times,* June 19, 1990.

which are based on complex instruction set computing, have many internal instructions built into their circuitry and take several clock cycles to execute an instruction. However, only 20 percent of these instructions are needed for 80 percent of the computer's tasks. The most frequently used instructions are the simple operations that can be performed at peak efficiency.

RISC chips, on the other hand, have only the most frequently used instructions embedded in them. With pared-down circuit design, a RISC CPU can execute most of its instructions in one cycle and, with a technique called pipelining, can actually execute many instructions at the same time. RISC is most appropriate for scientific and workstation computing.

Summary

- The physical hardware components of a contemporary computer system are a central processing unit, secondary storage devices, input devices, output devices, and communications devices.
- The central processing unit, where the computer manipulates symbols, letters, and numbers, consists of primary storage and a main processor with an arithmetic-logic unit and a control unit.
- Primary storage stores program instructions and data being used by those instructions. The arithmetic-logic unit performs the arithmetic and

logical operations on data. The control unit controls and coordinates the other components of a computer.

• Primary storage includes RAM (random-access memory) for short-term storage of data and program instructions and ROM (read-only memory) for permanent storage of important instructions. Other memory devices include PROM (programmable read-only memory) and EPROM (erasable programmable read-only memory).

• A computer represents data as a string of binary digits. Two popular binary coding standards are ASCII and EBCDIC.

• The generations of computer hardware evolution can be classified by the technology used for the computer's processing work. First-generation computers used vacuum-tube technology; second generation, transistor technology; third-generation, integrated circuit technology; and fourth-generation, very-large-scale integrated circuit technology.

• Contemporary computers rely on very-large-scale integrated circuits and microprocessors that can accommodate an entire CPU on a single silicon chip.

• Computers can be classified as mainframes, minicomputers, and microcomputers, with special distinctions made for supercomputers and workstations.

• The capabilities of microcomputers depend on the nature of their specific microprocessors and can be gauged by their dataword length, input/output bus width, and cycle speed.

• Microcomputers perform much of the work formerly limited to mainframes as firms switch to downsizing and cooperative processing.

• The IBM Personal Computer and the Macintosh computer represent two different computing standards and approaches to problem solving.

• Advances in microprocessor design and parallel processing technology will produce desktop microcomputers, workstations, and supercomputers that will eclipse today's mainframes in the near future.

Key Terms

Computer
Central processing unit (CPU)
Semiconductor chip
Primary storage
Address
Byte
Arithmetic-logic unit
Control unit
Machine cycle
Instruction cycle
Execution cycle
Register
RAM
Volatile
ROM
Nonvolatile
PROM
EPROM
Millisecond
Microsecond
Nanosecond
Picosecond
Kilobyte
Megabyte
Gigabyte
Bit

EBCDIC
ASCII
Microprocessor
Mainframe
Minicomputer
Microcomputer
Supercomputer
Parallel processing
Distributed processing
Downloading
Downsizing
Cooperative processing
Dataword length
Input/output bus width
Megahertz
Workstation
Vector processing

Review Questions

1. Name the components of a contemporary computer system and describe the function of each.
2. Name the major components of the CPU and the function of each.
3. What is the difference between RAM, ROM, PROM, and EPROM?
4. What takes place during a machine cycle?
5. Name and define the principal measures of computer time and storage capacity.
6. How are data represented in a computer?
7. Distinguish between a bit and a byte.
8. Define ASCII and EBCDIC. Why are they used?
9. List the major generations of computers and the characteristics of each.
10. Define downloading, cooperative processing, and downsizing.
11. Name and describe the factors affecting the speed and performance of a microprocessor.
12. Distinguish between serial and parallel processing.
13. Name and describe three information technology trends.

Discussion Questions

1. What is the difference between a mainframe, a minicomputer, and a microcomputer? Between a mainframe and a supercomputer? Between a microcomputer and a workstation? Are these distinctions disappearing?

2. Why do the Macintosh and the IBM Personal Computer represent two different computing standards?

Problem-Solving Exercises

1. Find a writeup or review of an IBM Personal System/2 workstation or of one of the models of the Macintosh computer. Using the information in that article, write a description of its features and analyze its computing capabilities.

2. You have been given enough money to purchase either an IBM Personal System/2 workstation or a Macintosh computer to use for your college

work. Write an analysis of which brand of microcomputer you would choose and why.

Notes

1. Alan Radding, "There Is More to Downsizing than Bargain Prices," *Computerworld,* June 12, 1989.
2. *Computerworld,* June 12, 1989.
3. Richard Brandt, Otis Port, and Robert D. Hof, "Intel: The Next Revolution," *Business Week,* September 26, 1988.
4. "Workstations: Do They Have a Future?" *A Guide to the Personal Computer,* supplement to *The New York Times,* May 21, 1989.
5. Charles Pelton, "MIS Finds Intel Chip Overpowering," *Information Week,* March 6, 1989; "Intel's New N-10: A Supercomputer-on-a-Chip," *Business Week,* March 6, 1989.

Problem-Solving Case:

Downsizing Halves Borg Warner's Information Systems Budget

In July 1987, Borg Warner Corporation was the object of a takeover attempt. As a protective strategy, the firm went private in a leveraged buyout, selling four of its six businesses so it could manage the resulting $4.5 billion debt load. It was left with only two operating groups, Borg Warner Automotive, a half-century-old automotive parts business, and Borg Warner Protective Services, the largest armored car and security guard operation in the United States.

Pared down in size, Borg Warner had to make drastic cuts in staff and budget. Its Chicago corporate headquarters staff shrank from 235 people in 1984 to just under 100 in 1989. Among those let go were the management information systems director and two of his four managers. The controller issued a stern directive to the remaining information systems managers: Cut the information systems budget, historically around $1.5 million per year, to $500,000.

The cost savings were accomplished by dismantling the firm's IBM 4341 (a small mainframe) at Borg Warner's Des Plaines, Illinois, computing center, which was linked to 90 terminals at headquarters on Chicago's Michigan Avenue.

The firm's IBM sales representative recommended an IBM System/38 minicomputer as an alternative. However, this solution option required installing new terminals. It was also unclear if the firm's mainframe information systems could be easily transported to System/38 hardware because of software incompatibilities (see Chapter 5). The main question was whether an alternative hardware solution could run the same business information systems that ran on Borg Warner's mainframe.

Leonard Murrell, manager of systems and programming, and Steve Derry, manager of technical support, had replaced electric typewriters in corporate headquarters with IBM Personal Computer XTs using software that enabled them to emulate dumb terminals and linked them to the firm's computer center. They replaced the 4341 machine with a personal computer–based network, allocating $260,000 for the job.

The principal clients were the accounting department and the human resources department. The human resources department had used the mainframe for processing a corporatewide investment plan for 401K (a before-tax savings plan) that tracked pension plans and other data for Borg Warner's 70,000 employees. Borg Warner's information systems staff, which prepared the tax forms and managed the people database, found software that could do the same thing on a microcomputer.

All software to run the applications on the personal computers is up and running, with a cautious, small-scale test underway. The accounting department has appreciated the ease of use of its new general ledger system. The automotive and protective services divisions, headquartered in Troy, Michigan, and Parsippany, New Jersey, respectively, had always been microcomputer based. They can use the same software as before to make their personal computers emulate dumb terminals.

Murrell and Derry noted that they could no longer count on support from their IBM representative, because IBM was primarily interested in servicing mainframe customers, and that downsizing had pushed their microcomputers to the limit.

Source: Ellis Booker, "From Mainframe to PC," *Computerworld*, May 22, 1989.

Case Study Questions

1. What was the problem at Borg Warner? What were the causes of the problem?
2. Why was downsizing an appropriate solution alternative?
3. Describe the factors that must be considered when downsizing computer hardware.
4. Why were microcomputers a more attractive solution option than using an IBM System/38?
5. Can you see any disadvantages to downsizing to microcomputers?

CHAPTER · FOUR

Storage, Input, and Output Technologies

Chapter Outline

4.1 Introduction

4.2 Information Storage Technology
- Characteristics of Secondary Storage
- Magnetic Tape
- Magnetic Disk
- Optical Disk Technology

4.3 Input Technology
- Batch versus On-Line Input and Processing
- Traditional Data Entry
- Touch Screens
- Light Pens
- The Computer Mouse
- Source Data Automation

4.4 Output Technology
- Printers
- Plotters
- Video Display Terminals
- Microfilm and Microfiche
- Voice Output Devices

4.5 Leading-Edge Technology: The NeXT Computer

Learning Objectives

After reading and studying this chapter, you will:

1. Know the major secondary storage technologies and be able to describe how they work.
2. Be familiar with how the major input technologies work.
3. Understand how the major output technologies work.
4. Know which storage, input, and output technology is best suited to solve certain types of problems.

Benetton Sets the Pace in Fashion and Technology

Benetton, the 15-year-old Italian clothing manufacturer and retailer, is a world leader in both fashion merchandising and the use of information technology. Benetton's 5,000 shops in 79 countries now sell a total of 50 million pieces of clothing each year. With so many stores and so much volume, Benetton has had to devise a system that keeps inventory and costs down.

When the clothing is manufactured, a bar code is placed on each item. The bar code carries information about the item's size, style, color, destination, and price in the currency of the country where it will be sold. The clothing with these bar codes is prepackaged and sent to the firm's highly automated warehouse in Castrette, Italy, where it is placed on a conveyor belt. There the bar codes are scanned and their data are passed to a Digital Equipment (DEC) PDP11/44 minicomputer that randomly chooses where each package will be stored in the warehouse. Only the minicomputer knows where each package is located.

The information entered into the DEC minicomputer via bar-code scanning is eventually transferred to Benetton's central mainframe in Treviso, Italy. When a package is ready to be shipped, the DEC minicomputer queries the central mainframe for the package's location. Then robot arms find the bar-coded package and convey it to one of 15 loading bays. More than 20,000

packages are handled this way each day. This system eliminates the need for peripheral warehouses and creates a direct link between Benetton's production and retail outlets. As a result, the time required to complete a last-minute order has dropped from 28 to 7 working days.

Source: John P. McPartlin, "At Benetton, It Is Always in Fashion," *Information Week*, February 12, 1990.

Benetton's use of bar coding and scanning for data input illustrates how business efficiencies and advantage over competitors can be enhanced by the proper input technology. Storage and output technology can play a similar role in improving business efficiency.

4.1 Introduction

Input and output devices make it possible for human beings to interact with computers. Input devices convert data, programs, or images into a form that can be processed by a computer. After the computer processes this input, output devices convert the resulting data into a form that humans can understand and use. Consequently, the speed, capacity, and ease of use of input and output devices have a direct bearing on the computer's usefulness in problem solving.

The speed and capacity of the CPU differ enormously from that of the input or output devices. For instance, the CPU operates at the microsecond and nanosecond level, whereas some printers may only be able to output 40 characters per second. This means the CPU is thousands of times faster than the printer. Since the CPU processes information much faster than it can be printed out, the flow of information must be arranged in stages to make the best use of the CPU. (See the discussion of operating systems in Chapter 5.) Additional memory and storage devices must be placed between the CPU and the output media so that the CPU is not held back.

Storage technology is likewise important because it affects how quickly and flexibly data can be accessed and utilized by the CPU. Although the manner in which information is organized on storage devices will be discussed in Chapter 6, this chapter examines the major computer storage technologies themselves.

4.2 Information Storage Technology

Section 3.2 in Chapter 3 introduced the concept of primary storage, where data and program instructions are stored for immediate processing. Even in the biggest mainframes, however, the amount of data that can be kept in primary storage is very limited, and the cost of storing information there is high. Moreover, data stored in primary storage can easily be lost or destroyed if the electric power is disrupted. Therefore, unless information is needed at this very instant, it usually is stored outside primary storage.

Characteristics of Secondary Storage

Secondary storage refers to the relatively long-term storage of data outside the CPU. Secondary storage is nonvolatile; that is, it will retain data even if the electric power is turned off. Secondary storage is slower than primary storage because it uses a number of electromechanical components, whereas primary storage is electronic and occurs nearly at the speed of light. Nevertheless, secondary storage media must still be able to transfer large bodies of data rapidly to the CPU. The principal secondary storage technologies are magnetic tape, magnetic disk, and optical disk.

Secondary storage
The relatively long-term storage of data outside the CPU.

Magnetic Tape

Magnetic tape is the oldest of the secondary storage technologies and one of the least expensive. It is used primarily in older computer systems or when large amounts of data must be stored at very low cost. A magnetic tape is much like a tape cassette for storing music, in that records are stored in sequential order, from beginning to end.

Magnetic tape
A secondary storage medium in which data are stored by means of magnetized and nonmagnetized spots on tape; it is inexpensive and relatively stable but also is relatively slow and can only store information sequentially.

Magnetic tape comes in 14-inch reels that are approximately one-half inch wide and up to 2,400 feet long. Figure 4.1 shows how the number 6 is represented on magnetic tape using the EBCDIC coding scheme. Each byte of data utilizes one column on the tape. Each column consists of 8 bits plus a parity bit. Magnetic tapes have a range of densities for storing data, measured in bytes per inch (bpi). A low-density tape has 1,600 bpi, and a high-density tape has 6,250 bpi.

The principal advantages of magnetic tape are that it is very low in cost and is a relatively stable storage medium (although the tape can age and crack over time and the environment where it is stored must be carefully controlled). Magnetic tape is also reusable; its contents can be erased so that it can be used for storing new information. Magnetic tape is most appropriate for storage of large amounts of data in a relatively stable form, and when a large number of records must be processed in sequential order. It is often used as a "backup" storage medium for data in more volatile and expensive storage media like hard disks.

The disadvantages of magnetic tape are that it can only store information sequentially and that it is relatively slow. To find an individual record on magnetic tape, such as your Social Security earnings history, the tape must be read from beginning to end, one record at a time, until the desired record has been located. Magnetic tape is also very labor-intensive to mount and dismount. If a problem requires frequent access to only a few records (as opposed to accessing all or most of the records on a tape reel) and continual mounting and dismounting of tapes, it may be more cost-effective and more efficient to store information another way, such as on magnetic disk. For example, before converting to disk technology, the Social Security Administration had 50 full-time employees who did nothing but mount and

Figure 4.1

How a Magnetic Tape Stores Data

The number "6" is stored on magnetic tape using a unique combination of magnetized and nonmagnetized spots. Each magnetized area represents a "one" bit (a "1" in EBCDIC binary code); nonmagnetized areas correspond to zeros in binary representation. There is an additional parity track, containing a parity bit, for checking transmission errors.

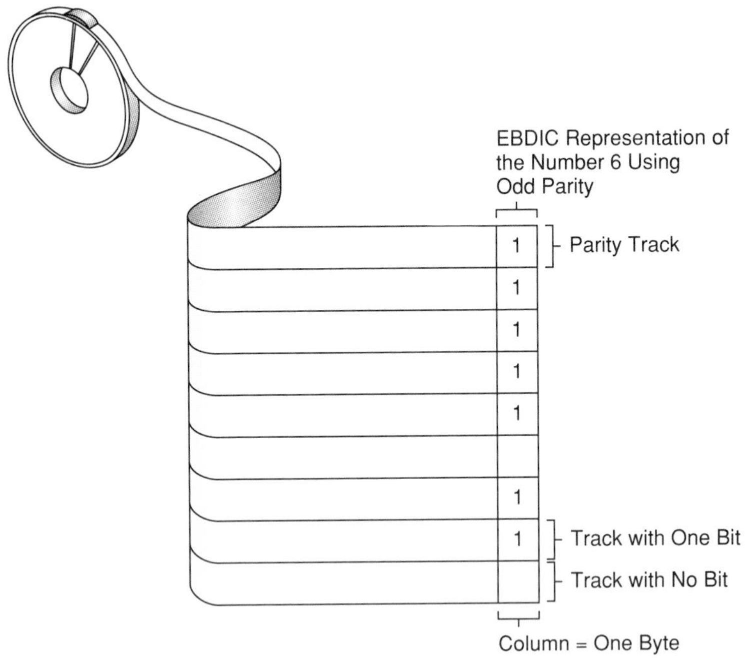

dismount more than 500,000 reels of tape. Much of the time, only a few pieces of information were accessed from each tape reel because much of the agency's work consisted of answering individual citizens' questions about their accounts. Firms such as Arco Oil and Gas Corporation have developed tape management strategies to deal with this problem.[1] The computer operations department of Arco Oil and Gas Corporation used to take ten minutes to mount three reel-to-reel tapes. By changing the way it manages tape operations, the same job has been cut down to three minutes, and two tape librarians can handle the work instead of the former six.

Under the old procedure, the computer would alert the tape librarians as to which tapes were needed for the next processing job. Then the librarians would pull the tapes from their storage racks and stage them by stacking them in order near the tape drive area. This was a time-consuming process. Jobs had to be put on hold while librarians tracked down the required tapes, and appreciable delays resulted when jobs required several tapes that were located in racks throughout the storage area. Further delays were caused by tapes not being returned to the right rack.

The computer operations manager found he could shorten the tape-mounting process by several minutes by changing the procedures for finding and staging the tapes. The tape drives had been located in one section of the computer operations room and the racks of tapes in another. The staff rearranged the racks in a horseshoe pattern and moved the tape drives to the center of the horseshoe.

The horseshoe is partitioned into three areas, each designated by a different color. The tapes are color-coded to correspond to the area where they are stored. Each area has 12 tape drives to which only the tapes in that area can be assigned. Now when a computer job asks for tapes to be loaded in a blue drive, the corresponding blue-coded tapes are no more than 15 feet away. As a result, tapes can not only be found quickly but can also be easily returned to their proper racks.

Magnetic tape clearly is inappropriate for problems, such as booking airline reservations, that call for rapid access to data and an immediate response. Since information systems increasingly require immediate and direct access to data, and other mass storage alternatives have become available, tape storage is becoming a fading technology.

Microcomputers, which rely on floppy and hard disks as their principal secondary storage medium, use magnetic tape primarily to back up large volumes of data. Magnetic tape for micros comes in small cassettes similar to home recording cassettes, and the drive units (called "streaming tape" systems) can be mounted either internally or externally.

Magnetic Disk

The most popular and important secondary storage medium today is the **magnetic disk.** Disk technology permits direct and immediate access to data. The computer can proceed immediately to a specific record or piece of data on the disk instead of reading through records one by one. For this reason, disk technology is often referred to as **direct-access storage devices (DASD).** There are two kinds of magnetic disks: hard disks and floppy disks.

Hard Disks · Magnetic **hard disks** are thin steel platters—large ones are about the size of phonograph records—with an iron oxide coating. Several disks may be mounted together on a vertical shaft, where they rotate at speeds of approximately 3,500 revolutions per minute. Electromagnetic **read/write heads** are mounted on access arms. The heads fly over the spinning disks and read or write data on concentric circles called **tracks.** Data are recorded on tracks as tiny magnetized spots forming binary digits. Each track can store thousands of bytes. In most disk systems each track contains the same number of bytes with the data packed together more closely on the inner tracks. The read/write head never actually touches the disk but hovers a few thousandths or millionths of an inch above it. A smoke particle or human hair on the disk surface would cause the head to crash into the disk.

Disk storage capacity depends on the type, quantity, and arrangement of disks in a unit. Individual disk packs or fixed disk drives may have storage capacities ranging from several megabytes to several gigabytes. Microcomputer hard disks can store up to 300 megabytes, but the most common sizes are 40- and 80-megabyte units.

Magnetic disk
The most popular secondary storage medium; data are stored by means of magnetized spots on hard or floppy disks.

Direct-access storage device (DASD)
Magnetic disks, including both hard and floppy disks; called *direct access* because in this technology the computer can proceed immediately to a specific record without having to read all the preceding records.

Hard disk
Type of magnetic disk resembling a thin steel platter about the size of a phonograph record with an iron oxide coating; generally several are mounted together on a vertical shaft.

Read/write head
An electromagnetic device that reads or writes the data stored on magnetic disks.

Track
A concentric circle on a hard disk on which data are stored as magnetized spots; each track can store thousands of bytes.

The read/write head of a hard disk flies over the spinning disk, never touching it.

Source: Courtesy of Amdahl Corporation.

Removable-pack disk system
Hard disks stacked into an indivisible unit called a pack that can be mounted and removed as a unit.

Cylinder
Represents circular tracks on the same vertical line within a disk pack.

Winchester disk system
A hermetically sealed unit of hard disks that cannot be removed from the disk drive.

Disk access time
The speed at which data can be located on magnetic disks and loaded into primary storage or written onto a disk device.

Two popular kinds of hard disk systems are removable-pack disk systems, used with larger computers, and Winchester disk systems, used with both small and large computers.

Removable-pack disk systems consist of hard disks stacked into a pack or indivisible unit that can be mounted and removed as a unit. They are typically found on mainframe and minicomputer systems, but some smaller units are available for microcomputers as well. A typical commercial removable disk pack has 11 disks, each with 2 surfaces (see Figure 4.2). Only 20 surfaces on the disk pack can be used for recording data, however, because the top and bottom surfaces are not used for this purpose. Each surface area, in turn, is divided into tracks, where data are recorded. A **cylinder** consists of 20 circular tracks located at one position of the read/write access arms; they are on the same vertical line, one above the other. Read/write heads are directed to a specific record using a disk address consisting of the cylinder number, the recording surface number, and the data record number.

Winchester disk systems do not differ in principle from removable-pack disk systems. The primary difference is that Winchester disks are hermetically sealed units that cannot be removed from the disk drive. They are typically used in microcomputers and come in sizes of 20, 40, 80, 130, and 300 megabytes. Because they are hermetically sealed from dust in the environment, Winchester disks can achieve very high rotation speeds and smaller distances between the disks and the read/write heads. These advantages translate into high-speed access times: many Winchester disk units can retrieve information in 15 to 25 milliseconds (thousandths of a second). At the same time, because they are sealed, Winchester disks cannot be replaced with an empty disk once they are full. Instead, the user must transfer the information to some other storage device, like a backup tape or floppy disk, or write over the existing disk.

Disk access time refers to the speed at which data can be located on the disks and loaded into primary storage or written onto a disk device. It is determined by three factors: (1) the access motion time, which is the time required to position the read/write head on the cylinder where the required data are stored; (2) the rotational delay, which is the time required for the disk to rotate so that the read/write head is positioned where the required data are stored; and (3) the data transfer rate, which is the time needed to read the data from the disk and transfer them to primary storage (or transfer them from the computer to the disk). Sophisticated commercial disks have access times of 1.5–10 milliseconds, but typical microcomputer hard disks require 20–40 milliseconds. The data transfer rate ranges from 200,000 to 4 million bytes per second, depending on the speed of the disk and other factors.

Magnetic disks offer several advantages. Individual records can be accessed directly in 20–60 milliseconds because they have a precise disk address. Thus disk technology permits solutions to problems requiring immediate access to data, such as airline reservation systems or customer information systems. Moreover, as will be discussed in Chapter 6, disk storage permits records and pieces of related data to be organized and combined easily.

Figure 4.2

Side and Top Views of a Removable-Pack Disk System

Currently the most popular secondary storage medium, magnetic disks are an important direct access storage device (DASD). A typical removable-pack system contains 11 two-sided disks. (There are actually only 20 surfaces in the pack on which data can be recorded, however; the top and bottom surfaces are not used since they can be damaged more easily.) Each disk contains concentric tracks; the 20 tracks located on the same vertical line form a cylinder. Data are stored in records, each of which has a unique location, or address, which references the specific cylinder, recording surface, and data record number.

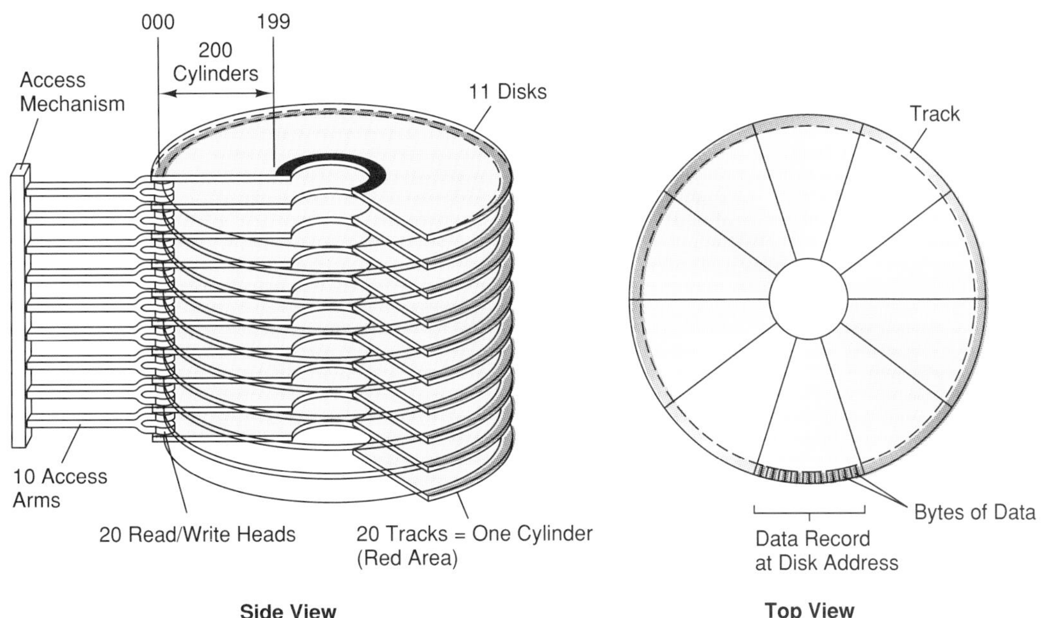

The principal drawbacks of disk technology are the need for backup, susceptibility to environmental disturbances, and cost. In disk technology there is only one copy of the information because the old record on the disk is written over if the record is changed. In contrast, record or file changes on magnetic tape are made on a different reel of tape, so the old version of the tape can be retained (and recovered). Disk technology also requires a pure and stable environment, since smoke or other particles can cause a disk pack to "crash." Technical advances have boosted disk storage capacity while reducing costs, but it is still much more expensive than magnetic tape.

Floppy Disks · **Floppy disks** are used primarily with microcomputers. These disks, which are round, flexible, and very inexpensive, are an ideal medium for storing data and programs that are not in constant use or for transporting data and programs. Floppy disks are available in different sizes: 8 inches, 5¼ inches, and 3½ inches (see Figure 4.3). The 5¼-inch diskette has been the most popular since the early 1980s, but the 3½-inch disk will soon become the standard, since it has been adopted by the Apple Macintosh and the IBM Personal System/2 microcomputer lines.

Floppy disks
Flexible, inexpensive magnetic disks used as a secondary storage medium; primarily used with microcomputers.

Figure 4.3

5¼-Inch and 3½-Inch Floppy Disks

Floppy disks (so called because they are flexible) are most often used with microcomputers. Each disk is encased in a protective plastic jacket pierced by an opening. The computer's read/write head "reads" the data on the disk through this opening. The 5¼-inch size is still common, but it will soon be replaced by its 3½-inch counterpart. The smaller disks can actually store more information (see Table 4.1), and their more durable construction protects the data better.

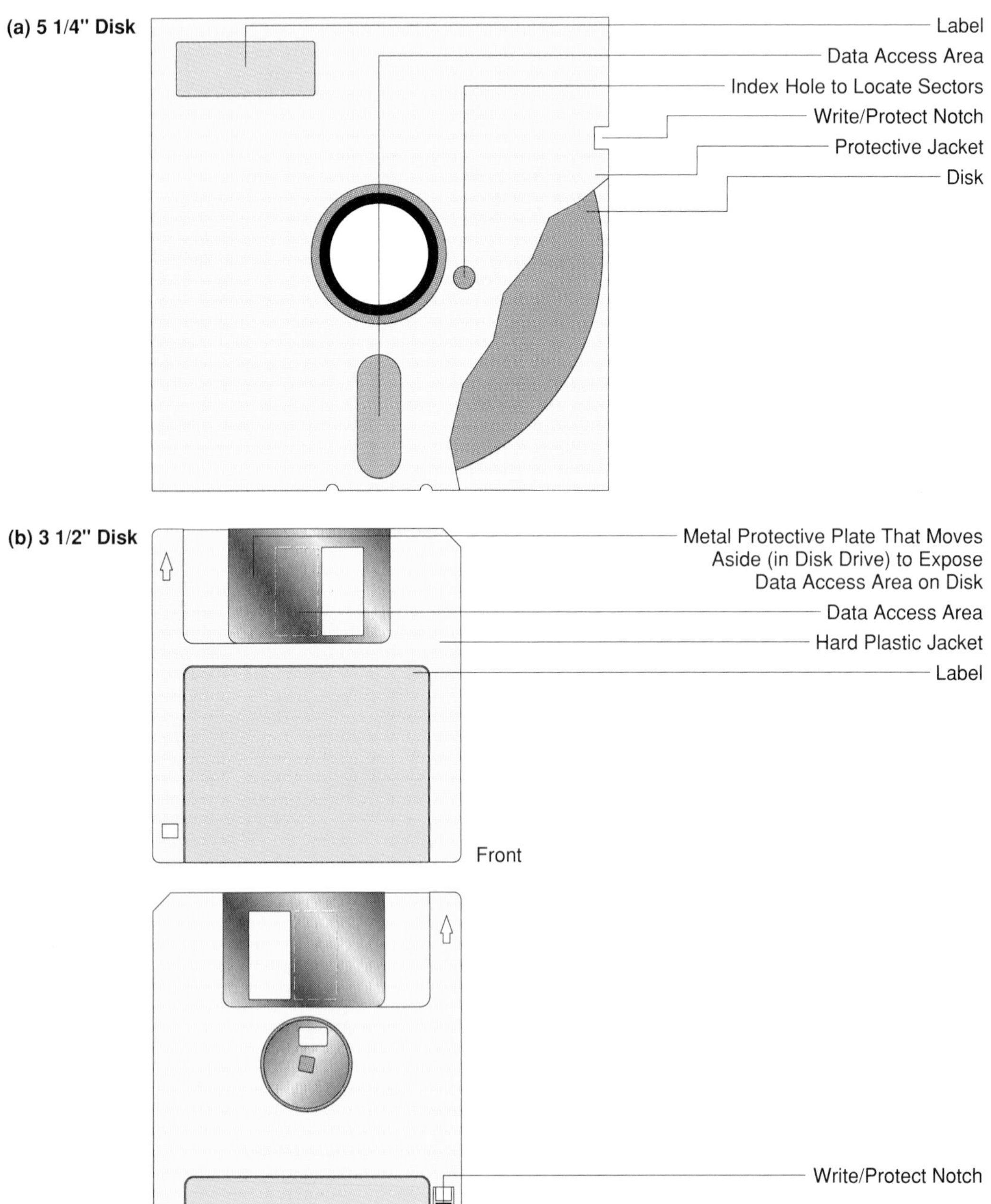

Figure 4.4

The Sector Method: How a Floppy Disk Stores Data

Like hard disks, floppy disks contain concentric tracks where data are stored as magnetized bits. In addition, the disk surface is divided into triangular sectors, each of which has a unique number. Data can be accessed directly by using an address that includes the sector and data record number. Some manufacturers divide disks into nine sectors, as shown here; others divide them into eight.

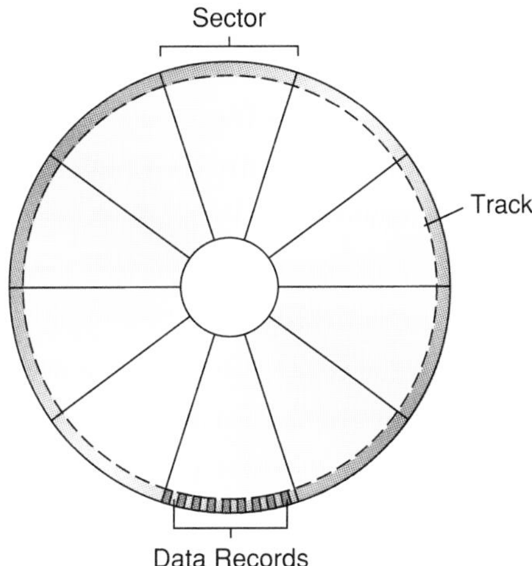

Floppy disks use a **sector method for storing data.** The disk surface is divided into eight or nine wedges like a pie; the actual number depends on the disk system used (see Figure 4.4). In most disks, each sector has the same storage capacity, since data are recorded more densely on the inner disk tracks. Each sector is assigned a unique number. Data can be located using an address consisting of the sector number and an individual data record number.

The Apple Macintosh disk system is a newer approach that varies the number of sectors on a single disk by adding sectors to the outer tracks so that all sectors take up the same space over the entire disk surface. This has increased the storage capacity on Apple's 3½-inch floppy disk by over 40 percent, compared to earlier Macintosh disks.

Floppy disk storage capacities vary, depending on whether the disk stores data on only one side (these are called **single-sided disks**) or on both sides **(double-sided disks),** the disk's data-recording density, the track density, and whether the disk drive has read/write heads for the top and bottom surfaces of the disk. **Recording density** refers to the number of bits per inch that can be written on the surface of the disk; disks are characterized as single density, double density, and quad-density. The 3½-inch disk, for example, can store more data than the 5¼-inch disk and is more portable and durable. Table 4.1 shows the range of storage capacities for the various floppy disk sizes.

Sector method for storing data

A method of storing data on floppy disks in which the disk is divided into pie-shaped pieces, or sectors; each sector has a unique number that becomes part of the address.

Single-sided disk

A floppy disk on which data can be stored on only one side.

Double-sided disk

A floppy disk on which data can be stored on both sides.

Recording density

The number of bits per inch that can be written on the surface of a magnetic disk.

Table 4.1
Floppy Disk Storage Capacities

Disk Size	Storage Capacity
3½ inch	720K to 1.44 megabytes
5¼ inch	360K to 1.2 megabytes
8 inch	1 to 2.5 megabytes

Optical disk
A disk on which data are recorded and read by laser beams rather than by magnetic means; such disks can store data at densities much greater than magnetic disks.

CD-ROM
An optical disk system used with microcomputers; it is a form of read-only storage in that data can only be read from it, not written to it; stands for Compact Disk/Read-Only Memory.

WORM
An optical disk system in which data can only be recorded once on the disk by users and cannot be erased; stands for Write Once, Read Many.

Using CD-ROM technology, The Reynolds and Reynolds Company developed the PartsVision electronic parts cataloging system for auto manufacturers/importers and their dealers. This image-based system is replacing the traditional methods of updating and maintaining parts information for GM, Chrysler, Honda/Acura, Volvo, Mercedes-Benz, and Nissan dealers.

Source: Courtesy of The Reynolds and Reynolds Company.

Optical Disk Technology

Using a laser device that records data by burning microscopic pits in a spiral track, **optical disks** (also called compact disks or laser optical disks) store data at densities much greater than those of magnetic disks. There are two basic ways in which information is placed on an optical disk. The most common way is by using a small laser to burn permanent pits into the surface of the plastic optical disk (called an ablative technique). The resulting pattern of pits and clear surface is used to define a single bit of information. A pit can be defined as a "0" and a clear area as a "1." A small reading laser is used to read the pattern of bits. (See Figure 4.5.)

Massive quantities of data can be stored in a highly compact form. For example, a 5¼-inch optical disk can store over 250,000 pages of text, equivalent to the storage capacity of fifteen hundred 360K 5¼-inch floppy disks. Consequently, optical disks are most appropriate for problems requiring enormous quantities of data to be stored compactly for easy retrieval.

The second technique, used for rewritable optical disks, employs a laser and a magnetic field to melt and magnetize tiny areas on the surface of an optical disk. The magneto-optical disk consists of layers of magnetic film deposited on a rotating disk substrate. A strong laser beam strikes the disk as it rotates, heating a microscopic spot and causing atoms in the recording layer of the disk to form into a magnetized zone representing one bit of data. The size of each spot determines whether it represents a 0 or a 1. To read the disk, a weak laser beam scans the magnetized spots. This beam is reflected to a photodetector that converts the variations in spot size into binary data.

The optical disk system most often used with microcomputers is called **CD-ROM (Compact Disk/Read-Only Memory).** CD-ROM is read-only storage, which means that no new data can be written to it; it can only be read. CD-ROM has been most widely used for reference materials with massive amounts of data, such as encyclopedias, directories, and on-line databases. For example, financial databases from Quotron, Dun & Bradstreet, and Dow Jones are available on CD-ROM. Microsoft's Bookshelf places ten reference books, including the *American Heritage Dictionary, Bartlett's Familiar Quotations,* and the *U.S. ZIP Code Directory,* on one CD-ROM. CD-ROM is also becoming popular for storing images (described in later chapters) because of its large capacity.

WORM (Write Once, Read Many) optical disk systems allow users to record data only once on an optical disk. Once written, the data cannot

Figure 4.5

How a WORM Drive Works

To write data on a Write Once Read Many (WORM) optical disk drive, a high-power laser beam (panel a) heats the disk substrate, leaving a permanent pit on its surface for a binary 0 and leaving the disk surface smooth and reflective for a binary 1. A low-power laser (panel b) is used to read the data. The laser reflects from areas with no pits to read a binary 1. The pits diffuse the laser, creating no reflection, to read a binary 0.

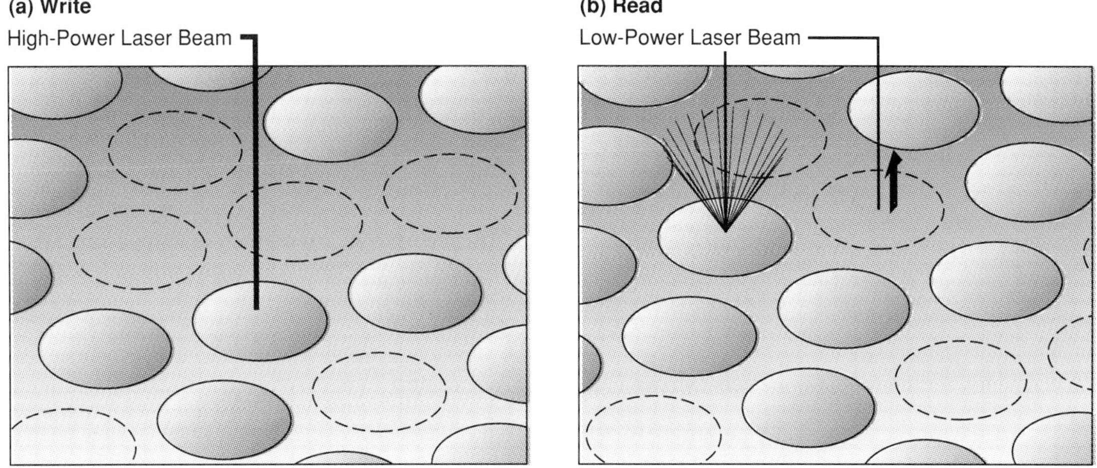

Source: Macworld, July 1989, p. 120.

be erased, but they can be read indefinitely. WORM has been used as an alternative to microfilm for archiving digitized document images. For instance, California's Department of Motor Vehicles used WORM media attached to an IBM 9370 computer to store pictures, signatures, and fingerprints so that no one could tamper with permanent information.

Rewritable optical disk storage (see the discussion of the NeXT Computer in Section 4.5) is becoming faster and cheaper than tape storage. Fast rewritable magneto-optical disks have an access time of 48 milliseconds, and slow WORM optical disk drives operate at around 200 milliseconds; both are much faster than the 60 seconds required for a person to mount a tape and up to 30 minutes to read a whole tape.

Through special software with electronic search features and techniques for organizing data on CD-ROM, individual pieces of information become easy to retrieve (see the discussion of files and databases in Chapter 6). Herein lies another advantage of optical disk technology: it makes information more accessible for problem solving. In seconds, one can wade through vast amounts of data to find the right quotation or zip code or the correct meaning of a term.

For example, Cummins Engine Company, a diesel engine manufacturer in Columbus, Indiana, found that its master price book could be more easily searched on CD-ROM than on paper or microfilm. The Cummins master price book, which contains over 60,000 pages of text and graphics, is used as a reference by the company's field staff of engine repairpersons. In the pilot program to put the master price book on CD-ROM, personal computers were utilized because the firm did not want to convert its 8,500 mainframe terminals for graphics work. According to project manager William Seltzer, the advantage to using CD-ROM is that "you can find things without wading through 800 film cards."[2] Cummins still publishes the master price book on paper and microfilm, but CD-ROM has significantly reduced the number of printed copies in circulation.

4.3 Input Technology

As the opening vignette of this chapter illustrates, the nature of input technology affects processing and the way an entire information system can perform. The input technologies discussed here support several alternative approaches to data input. In selecting an input technology, a business must decide not only how it wants to capture data for input but when and how it wants to process and use the data it has entered.

Batch versus On-Line Input and Processing

Batch input and processing
An approach to input and processing in which data are grouped together as source documents before being input; once they are input, they are stored as a transaction file before processing, which occurs some time later.

On-line input
An input approach in which data are input into the computer as they become available rather than being grouped as source documents.

On-line real-time processing
A type of processing in which data are processed as soon as they are input into the system rather than being stored for later processing.

The manner in which data are collected for input is closely tied to processing. In **batch input and processing,** data are collected in the form of source documents such as orders or payroll time cards; these are accumulated and stored for a period of time in groups called batches. Then the batches of documents are keyed into the computer and stored in computer-usable form as a transaction file until they are needed for processing; that may be a few hours or a few weeks or even months later. Finally, the batch is processed as a group in a computer job (see Figure 4.6). The output is created only when new batches are processed. This was the earliest approach to input and processing and is still used today for processing payrolls and utility bills.

In contrast, with **on-line input,** data are immediately captured for computer processing instead of being collected and stored on source documents. In **on-line real-time processing,** the data are processed immediately upon input into the system. There is no waiting, and output and information stored by the system is always up-to-date. Airline reservation systems, which must respond immediately to new data, require an on-line real-time approach.

In on-line input with delayed processing, data are directly translated into computer-usable form, but they are not processed immediately. Instead, the data are held in temporary storage until scheduled processing occurs. For instance, some merchandise catalog sales firms input orders directly into terminals as the orders are taken over the telephone. The computer holds the orders in a transaction file until the end of the day, when they are all processed together.

Traditional Data Entry

Keypunch
An early form of inputting data in which data were coded onto 80-column cards, with each location on the card representing a character.

Traditionally, data have been input through a keyboard. In the past, data entry clerks used a **keypunch** machine to code their data onto 80-column punched cards; each character was identified by a unique punch in a specific

Figure 4.6

Three Different Approaches to Input and Processing

When choosing an input technology, a firm must also decide how it wants to process the input data and how up-to-date the output and data stored in the system must be. The oldest approach is batch processing, in which source documents are collected and entered into the computer as a batch, or group. There they are stored in a transaction file, and eventually the entire batch will be processed together. Thus the system is only updated when each batch is completed. With another option, on-line real-time processing, data are processed immediately as they are entered, so the system is constantly updated. A third approach combines the first two: data are entered immediately but are stored temporarily in a transaction file. At scheduled intervals the computer processes the new input.

(a) Batch Processing

Storage

Terminal

Transaction File

CPU

Output

Group source documents into batches.

Input batch into computer system.

Store data from batch in transaction file.

Process entire batch as a group. Output and data stored in the system are updated with each batch processing.

(b) On-Line Real-Time Processing

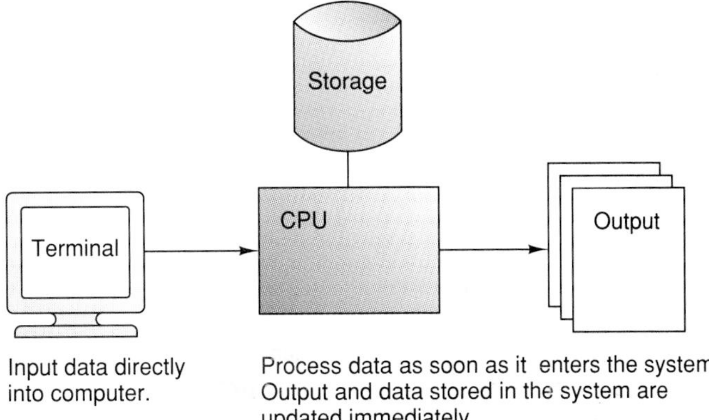

Input data directly into computer.

Process data as soon as it enters the system. Output and data stored in the system are updated immediately.

(c) On-Line Input with Delayed Processing

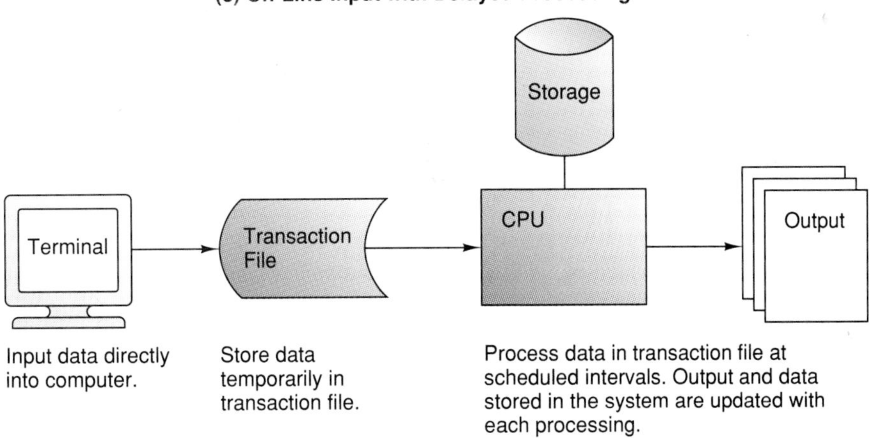

Input data directly into computer.

Store data temporarily in transaction file.

Process data in transaction file at scheduled intervals. Output and data stored in the system are updated with each processing.

FOCUS ON *People*

Workers Get a Feel for Touch Screens

Once ridiculed as cumbersome and imprecise, touch computer screens are making a minor comeback. Although they are being used mainly in stores, restaurants, and industrial sites, where workers are more likely to be uncomfortable or unfamiliar with keyboards, some offices are adopting them as well.

Princeton University, for instance, is testing an electronic mail system that has a touch screen at its heart. The screen displays pictures of a dozen mailboxes, one for each worker in the department. When a worker receives a message, his or her mailbox displays a letter. As soon as the worker touches the letter, the message appears. "Even when people have a computer on their desk, they don't use electronic mail," says Howard Jay Strauss, manager of advanced computer applications at the university. "We're finding much more interest this way."

Touch screens are a tiny part of the computer-display market, but demand is growing. Stanford Resources, Inc., a market researcher based in San Jose, California, reports worldwide shipments of touch screens increased 24 percent to 226,000 last year. The market researcher predicts shipments will grow to 2.8 million in 1995.

Source: Adapted from Zachary G. Pascal, "Technology," *The Wall Street Journal,* February 26, 1990, p. B1. Adapted by permission of The Wall Street Journal,

Key-to-tape
A form of inputting in which data are keyed directly onto magnetic tape.

Key-to-disk
A form of inputting in which data are keyed directly onto magnetic disks.

Touch screen
A sensitized video display screen that allows data to be input by touching the screen surface with a finger or pointer.

location on the card. Another alternative was a **key-to-tape** or **key-to-disk** machine that allowed data to be keyed directly onto a magnetic tape or magnetic disk for computer processing. Such methods are being discarded in favor of more direct methods of entering data. Data can now be entered directly into a computer system using a keyboard and computer terminal or by using new interactive tools such as those described below.

Touch Screens

Touch screens allow limited amounts of data to be entered by touching the surface of a sensitized video display monitor with a finger or a pointer. The operator makes selections by touching specified parts of the screen. Although the applications of touch screens are limited at present, they are easy to use and appeal to persons who are not familiar with a keyboard. Stores, restaurants, and some offices are using them, as the Focus on People explains.

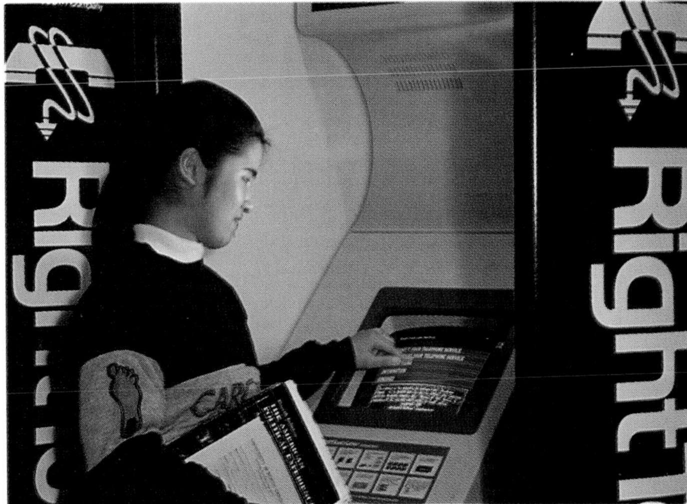

Students at the University of North Carolina order telephone service using a touch screen at a BellSouth Right Touch Center. Customers make choices by touching specified parts of the screen.

Source: © 1989 Chipp Jamison for BellSouth Corporation. Reprinted with permission.

Light Pens

Frequently used for graphics work, **light pens** have tips with light-sensitive photoelectric cells that enable the operator to "write" on a video display device. When the tip of the pen is placed near a video display screen, it signals its position to the computer.

Light pen
An input device with light-sensitive photoelectric cells in its tip that is used to input data by "writing" on a video display device; usually used for graphics.

The Computer Mouse

The **computer mouse** is a hand-held device connected to the computer by a cable; the mouse can be moved around on a desk top to control the position of the cursor on a video display screen. Once the cursor is in the desired location, the operator can push a button on the mouse to make a selection. The mouse can also be used to "draw" images on the graphics display screen. The "point and click" capability of the electric mouse is an alternative to keyboard and text-based commands.

A computer track ball is an inverted mouse that performs the same function as a mouse. A track ball unit has a small ball in a housing over which the user's palm can move. As the ball rotates in any direction, the screen cursor follows. The user selects elements on the screen by pushing a button or, on some units, depressing the track ball slightly.

Computer mouse
A hand-held device that can be moved on a desk top to control the position of the cursor on a video display screen.

Source Data Automation

Traditional data input methods involve multiple steps, human intervention, and the handling of data as they are converted from one form to another. Not only can transcription errors occur at several points, but all of the extra handling and duplicate effort adds to costs. The most advanced data input technology focuses on **source data automation,** in which machine-readable data are generated at their point of origin.

Source data automation
Advanced forms of data input technology that generate machine-readable data at their point of origin; includes optical character recognition, magnetic ink character recognition, digitizers, and voice input.

The leading source data automation technologies—magnetic ink character recognition, optical character recognition, digitizers, and voice input—are more rapid and accurate than traditional input methods because they collect machine-readable data at the time the data are created. Such technologies eliminate the need for special data entry staff and are more accurate than keying in data. The error rate for bar code scanners, for example, is less than 1 in 10,000 transactions (keypunchers make up to 1 error per 1,000 keystrokes).

Magnetic ink character recognition (MICR)
A form of source data automation in which an MICR reader identifies characters written in magnetic ink; used primarily for check processing.

Optical character recognition (OCR)
A form of source data automation in which optical scanning devices read specially designed data off source documents and translate the data into digital form for the computer; bar codes are an example of OCR technology.

Magnetic ink character recognition (MICR) technology is used primarily by the banking industry for processing massive numbers of checks. The characters in the lower left portion of the check in Figure 4.7 are preprinted in special magnetic ink to indicate the bank identification number, the checking account number, and the check number. After the check has been cashed and sent to the bank for processing, a MICR reader senses the MICR characters on the check and feeds them into the computer. The amount of the check, which is written in ordinary ink, must be keyed in by hand.

Optical character recognition (OCR) devices read marks, characters, and codes and translate them into digital form for the computer. Optical character reading devices reflect light off characters on source documents and convert them into digital patterns that the computer can recognize.

Figure 4.7

Checks: A Common Application for Magnetic Ink Character Recognition (MICR)

MICR is a common method of source data automation; it creates machine-readable data directly on the document. Banks, for instance, use checks with characters preprinted in magnetic ink that identify the bank and checking account number. A MICR reader "reads" the characters by identifying their shapes. This and other methods of source data automation eliminate the error-prone step of keying data into a computer.

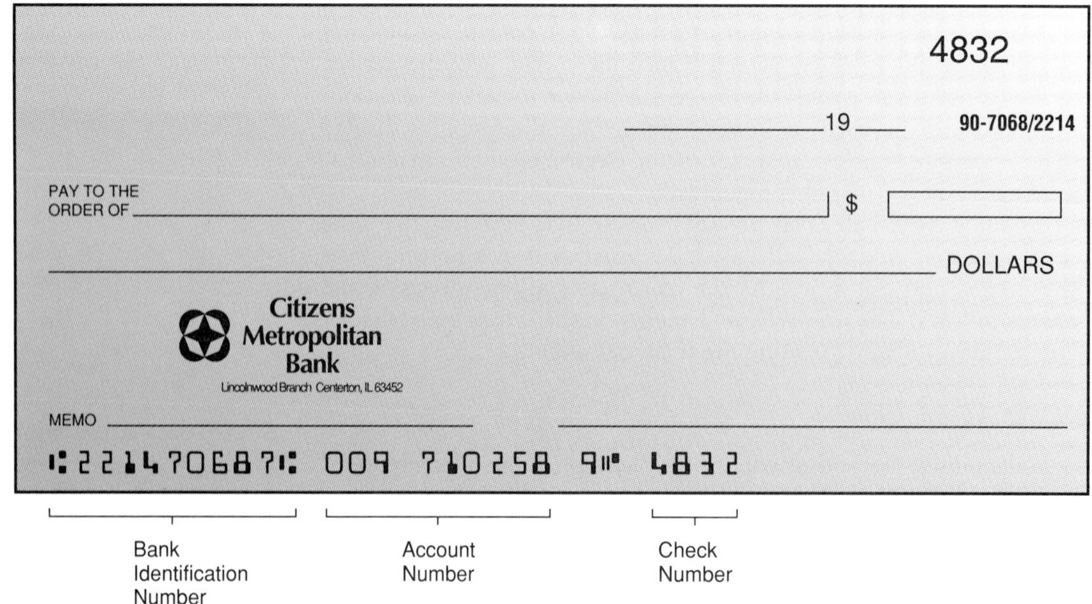

Only characters printed using special fonts can be read, however. For example, the optical reader will read only the optical characters on a charge account bill, not the characters in regular type. As the reader optically scans the data on the bill, it passes them immediately to the computer. The number of fonts that can be optically scanned has been increasing as OCR technology grows more sophisticated. For example, the Discover 7320 Model 30 scanner, a personal computer–based system by Kurzweil Computer Products, Inc., can automatically recognize multiple-column documents and several thousand fonts and type styles.

The most widely used optical code is the **bar code,** which can be found on supermarket items, clothing price tags, and other items. Scanning devices built into countertops or hand-held wands are employed to read the bar codes. Bar codes frequently utilize a **Universal Product Code** that records data based on the width of the bars and the space between them. The codes include manufacturer and product identification numbers (see Figure 4.8). Some point-of-sale systems, such as those found at Shoprite supermarket checkout counters, capture bar-coded data and use them to obtain the item's price from the firm's computer system. These data can also immediately update the firm's sales and inventory records.

Bar code
Specially designed bar characters that can be read by OCR scanning devices; used primarily on price tags and supermarket items.

Universal Product Code
A coding scheme in which bars and the width of space between them represent data that can be read by OCR scanning devices; frequently used in bar codes.

Bar codes are used not only in supermarkets and warehouses but also in hospitals, libraries, military operations, transportation facilities, and every kind of manufacturing operation. For example, bar codes are used for the 2,500 items stocked by the pharmacy at Detroit's Henry Ford Hospital. Because bar codes can contain other useful pieces of information, such as time, date, and location data in addition to identification data, they can be used to track an item, analyze its movement, and calculate what has happened to it during production or other processes.

Figure 4.8

Bar Codes: The Most Commonly Used Optical Code

You are no doubt familiar with the bar code, which is used to identify merchandise ranging from designer clothing to dog food. Optical codes consist of special fonts, or shapes, that are converted into digital form by optical character recognition (OCR) devices. Here we see a common type of bar code, the Universal Product Code, which identifies each product with a unique code based on the width of the bars and the spaces between them. The codes include manufacturer and product identification numbers.

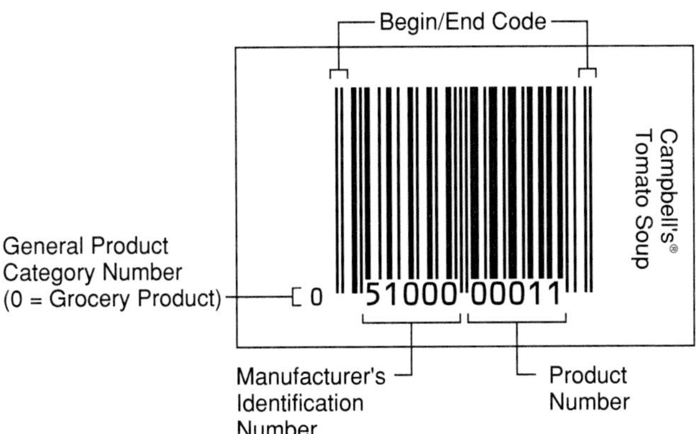

FOCUS ON *Organizations*

If a Laser Printer Ran Backwards

The Caere Corporation, which two years ago created the first optical character recognition system for personal computers, is preparing to introduce a $10,995 computer that is said to recognize printed words at a rate of 2,500 a minute and convert them to electronic form with a high level of accuracy.

The Caere Parallel Page Reader attaches to a computer network with relative ease and functions as a sort of laser printer in reverse. That is, the user feeds the printed documents into a scanner, and the Parallel Page Reader converts them into word processing or database files.

The new machine is expected to appeal to government agencies, large law offices, insurance companies, aerospace companies, and other computer-intensive businesses that must deal with a large volume of paper. In fact, the Parallel Page Reader was developed as part of a special project for the Securities and Exchange Commission. The commission, which receives about 40 million paper pages of official filings a year, was looking for an inexpensive way to convert those pages into electronic form for speedy retrieval and efficient archiving. If the Parallel Page Reader performs as predicted, one reader could equal the output of 25 secretaries, each typing 100 words a minute.

The Parallel Page Reader breaks ground in another way as well. It is one of the first commercial desktop applications of parallel processing, a technique that has been the domain of advanced computer researchers and supercomputer companies. In parallel processing, several individual microprocessors work in tandem on a single problem. Some parallel machines comprise 16, 64, 128, or even more processors, using personal computer–level chips to yield supercomputer performance at a fraction of the cost.

Source: Adapted from Peter H. Lewis, "If a Laser Printer Ran Backwards," *The New York Times,* March 4, 1990.

Another recent development in source data automation is Caere Corporation's Parallel Page Reader. Unlike MICR technology, which requires the characters to be printed in magnetic ink, and OCR technology, in which special fonts are required, the Parallel Page Reader can scan and input documents printed in ordinary ink in standard typefaces (see the Focus on Organizations).

Image Processing and Digitized Images · Image processing is the use of computers and related equipment like digital scanners and high-resolution printers to enter, store, process, and distribute images such as pictures or documents. Image processing requires that an image be digitized or transformed into a series of digital bits so it can be processed by a computer. A scanner is a device that digitizes an image.

Voice input devices convert spoken words into digital form. Special voice recognition software (see Chapter 5) compares the electrical patterns produced by the speaker's voice to a set of prerecorded patterns. If the patterns match, the input is accepted. This technology is still in its infancy. Most voice systems have limited "vocabularies" of several hundred to a thousand words and can accept only very simple commands. It is hoped that the technology will mature so that one day it can automate office correspondence.

4.4 Output Technology

When computers were in their infancy and performed only batch processing, printers were the primary output medium. Today, there are many more options for displaying computer output, such as video display terminals, color graphics, and voice output. The sophisticated array of output media allows us to further customize information technology to meet specific problem-solving requirements.

Printers

Printers are still the medium of choice when permanent, hard-copy output is required. For example, bank statements and bills are still printed out. Printer output consists of characters, symbols, and occasionally graphics. A wide range of printer options is available, based on their speed and the way they print. The speed, cost, and quality of printer output are important considerations in selecting the right printer. Choosing the appropriate printer can be a crucial decision for a firm (see the Problem-Solving Case at the end of the chapter).

Character printers, which print one character at a time, are quite slow, outputting 40 to 200 characters per second. **Line printers** print an entire line at a time, reaching speeds of 3,000 lines per minute. **Page printers** print an entire page at a time, with speeds surpassing 20,000 lines per minute. High-speed line and page printers are typically found in large corporate computer centers.

Impact printers, such as a daisy-wheel printer or a dot-matrix printer, form characters by pressing a typeface device such as a print wheel or cylinder against paper and inked ribbon. **Letter-quality printers,** such as the daisy-wheel printer, produce a high-quality print image by pressing the image of a fully formed character against the ribbon. **Dot-matrix printers** use a print head composed of a series of tiny print hammers that look like pins. The print hammers strike the ribbon as the print mechanism moves across the print line from right to left and from left to right. Depending on the character to be printed, different pins are activated.

Dot-matrix printers tend to be faster than letter-quality printers and produce lower-quality output. Many dot-matrix printers can also produce graphical or color output. Letter-quality printers are most appropriate for important business letters or reports, whereas dot-matrix printers are used for drafts of documents, large-volume output, or graphics.

Nonimpact printers do not strike characters between ribbon and paper and are usually less noisy than impact printers. The main categories of nonimpact printers are laser printers, ink-jet printers, and thermal-transfer printers.

The Focus on Technology in Chapter 13 describes additional printer technologies: laser, light-emitting diode (LED), and liquid crystal shutter

Character printer
A printer that prints one character at a time; such printers are very slow, outputting 40 to 200 characters per second.

Line printer
A printer that prints an entire line at a time; can reach speeds of 3,000 lines per minute.

Page printer
A printer that can print an entire page at a time; can reach speeds of more than 20,000 lines per minute.

Impact printer
A printer that forms characters by pressing a typeface device, such as a print wheel or cylinder, against paper and inked ribbon.

Letter-quality printer
An impact printer that produces a high-quality image by pressing the image of a fully formed character against inked ribbon.

Dot-matrix printer
An impact printer that uses a print head composed of many small hammers or pins that strike an inked ribbon as the print mechanism moves from side to side; such printers are usually faster than letter-quality printers but produce lower-quality output.

Nonimpact printer
A printer, such as a laser, ink-jet, or thermal-transfer printer, that does not form characters by pressing a typeface device against ribbon and paper.

Laser printer
A printer that produces an image by scanning a laser beam across a light-sensitive drum; the toner that adheres to the charged portions of the drum is then pulled off onto the paper.

Ink-jet printer
A printer that produces an image by spraying electrically charged ink particles against paper through holes in the printhead.

Thermal-transfer printer
A printer that produces high-quality images by transferring ink from a wax-based ribbon onto chemically treated paper.

(LCS) printers. **Laser printers,** perhaps the most familiar of the three, scan a laser beam across a light-sensitive drum, turning the beam on and off to produce dots that form an image. As the drum turns, it picks up toner. Toner particles adhere to the charged parts of the drum and are pulled off by paper as it passes by. Laser printers can generate from six pages per minute for personal computer models to over a hundred pages per minute for high-volume work in large commercial and corporate data centers. These printers have become increasingly popular because they are relatively fast and can produce relatively high-quality graphic images and text, although their output is inferior to many letter-quality printers.

Ink-jet printers spray tiny electrically charged ink particles against paper through tiny nozzles, forming high-quality characters at speeds of over 200 characters per second. Since many models hold multiple color cartridges, they can be used for color output. **Thermal-transfer printers** transfer ink from a wax-based ribbon onto chemically treated paper, producing very high quality character and graphic output (see Figure 4.9).

Some processing and storage capacity is being built into printers and other input and output devices to reduce the load on the main computer. Almost all microcomputer printers, for instance, have at least 2K (2,000

Figure 4.9

How Ink-Jet and Thermal-Transfer Printers Work

(a) Inside an ink-jet printer, a rotating drum spins a sheet of paper. As the paper spins, the printer shoots electrically charged particles of ink from four tiny nozzles. The nozzles move parallel with the drum, producing lines of color until the image is complete. There are four bottles of ink (cyan [blue], magenta, yellow, and black). The nozzles create additional colors by superimposing inks. **(b)** A thermal-transfer printer uses ribbons made of a thin Mylar film with a waxy coating of color pigment. The ribbons have alternating page-sized blocks of yellow, magenta, cyan, and black. The printer lines up an area of colored ribbon with the sheet of paper, and a thermal head scans the page to selectively melt color onto the paper in small dots. The printer repeats these steps for each color.

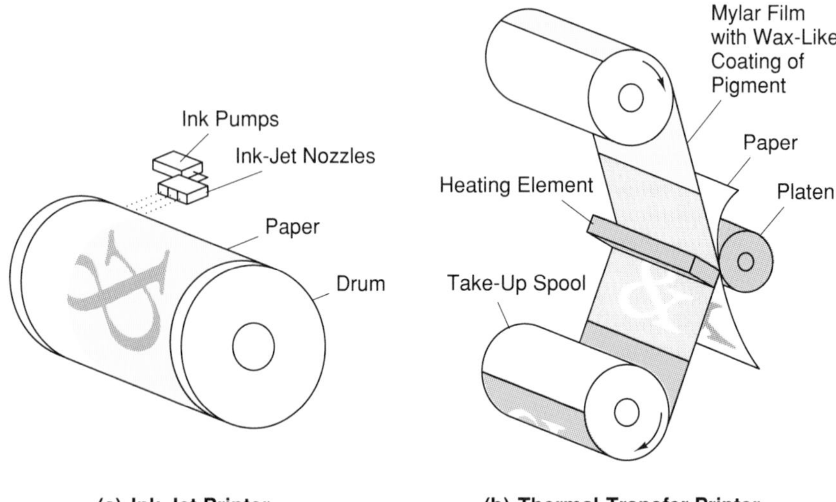

Source: Ron Risley, "Printing a Rainbow," *Macworld,* January 1989, p. 136. Reprinted with permission.

bytes) of memory, called a buffer, that can store several sentences, and some printers have up to 8 megabytes to store fonts and characters. The Xerox Corporation's intelligent printing systems can be programmed to produce complex documents on their own so that CPU resources will not be tied up in the printing process. The printers can store forms, page-formatting instructions, logos, and signatures, thus eliminating the need for preprinted stocks. Using various professional-quality type fonts and half-tones, they can merge text with graphics and forms. Microcomputer printers such as the Hewlett Packard Laserjet Plus or the Apple LaserWriter are programmed to store graphic elements and various type fonts that can be used selectively by different pieces of software.

Plotters

Plotters are special devices for outputting high-quality graphics, such as maps, charts, drawings, and graphs. They are commonly used by engineers and architects. A pen plotter is programmed to move in various directions to produce a series of straight lines; it draws curves as a series of very short lines. Electrostatic plotters produce images from tiny dots on treated paper using electrostatic charges.

Plotter
A device that is used for outputting high-quality graphics; pen plotters move in various directions to produce straight lines, whereas electrostatic plotters use electrostatic charges to produce images from tiny dots on treated paper.

Video Display Terminals

Displaying output on a **video display terminal** is appropriate when there is no need for a permanent paper record or when an immediate response is

Video display terminal
A screen on which output can be displayed; varieties include monochrome or color and text or text/graphics.

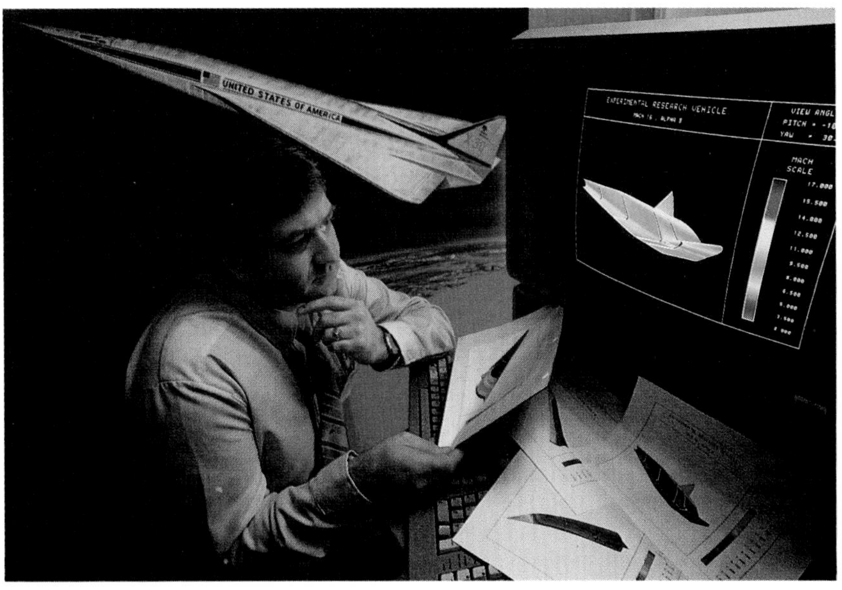

An engineer works on the preliminary design of the national aerospace plane's airframe at Rockwell International. Workstations with multiple output technologies—high-resolution color monitors, printers, and plotters—allow designers flexibility for displaying their work.

Source: Courtesy of Rockwell International.

FOCUS ON *Technology*

Are VDTs Safe?

Are data entry workers and programmers who stare into video display terminals (VDTs) for eight hours a day being exposed to harmful radiation; eye strain; neck, back, and wrist injuries; and, if they are pregnant, danger to their unborn children? This question is being raised more and more frequently.

Reports of workers who have developed irreversible eye strain or damage or repetitive strain injury (RSI)—keyboard-related wrist and hand injuries—are becoming more common. The people most seriously affected are those who sit and work at terminals for more than half the work day—data entry personnel, programmers, telephone operators, and journalists. In Denver, Colorado, for example, 183 of 500 telephone operators were diagnosed as having carpal tunnel syndrome, one type of repetitive strain injury. A Department of Labor study noted that repetitive motion disorders accounted for 48 percent of all workplace illness in 1988, up 10 percent from the previous year.

VDTs emit electric and magnetic fields in very low frequency and extra low frequency ranges. These fields contain nonionizing radiation, which must be distinguished from the ionizing radiation emitted in gamma rays and X-rays. Does the radiation from VDTs affect cell membranes or chromosomes? Does it cause high stress, depression, and disorientation? Can it be linked to cancer? Is it hazardous to pregnancy? Several studies have examined the effects of low levels of radiation emitted from VDTs, but none have been conclusive.

State and local legislators are considering restrictions on VDTs. For instance, the California Occupational Safety and Health Administration cited owners of the newspaper *Fresno Bee* in September 1989 for certain ergonomic infractions. The *Bee* was ordered to provide more ergonomic workstations, training programs, and rest breaks for employees who used VDTs more than one hour per day. A third of the paper's workers had been diagnosed as having repetitive strain injuries.

But is legislation the best way to protect workers from VDT health risks? Many companies believe they should be allowed to devise their own plans for protecting workers' health. Beyond educating workers about VDT risks, employers can pay more attention to ergonomics. The optimal VDT work environment includes lower levels of light that reduce glare on the VDT screen, easily adjustable furniture and lighting, and brief, frequent rest breaks. Employers can also reduce the number of VDT work hours for pregnant employees or give pregnant employees the option to transfer.

Sources: John P. McPartlin, "Are VDTs Safe?" *Information Week,* February 12, 1990; David Kirkpatrick, "How Safe Are Video Terminals?" *Fortune,* August 29, 1988.

CRT
An electronic tube that shoots a beam of electrons that illuminate pixels, or tiny dots, on a video display screen; stands for cathode ray tube.

required. Video display terminals can be classified in terms of whether they are monochrome or color and whether they can display text only or text and graphics. The traditional technology for displaying output on a terminal screen is the cathode ray tube, or **CRT.** CRTs work much like television picture tubes, in that an electronic "gun" shoots a beam of electrons that illuminate tiny dots, called pixels, on the screen. The more pixels (a contraction of the phrase *picture element*) per screen, the higher the resolution, or sharpness of the screen image.

Display devices for graphics often utilize **bit mapping,** which allows each pixel on the screen to be addressed and manipulated by the computer (as opposed to blocks of pixels in character addressable displays). This requires more computer memory, but it permits finer detail and the ability to produce any kind of image on the display screen.

Flat panel display devices use charged chemicals or gases sandwiched between panes of glass. Because they are compact, lightweight, and consume minimal power, they are used in portable computers. The two leading flat panel technologies are plasma and liquid crystal.

As the Focus on Technology explains, controversy has arisen over the safety of video display terminals (VDTs). Since the late 1970s suspicions have arisen that working long hours in front of these terminals can be hazardous to one's health.

Bit mapping
A technology often used for displaying graphics on a video display terminal; it allows each pixel on the screen to be addressed and manipulated by the computer.

Flat panel display
A technology that uses charged chemicals or gases sandwiched between panes of glass to display output on a screen; used in lightweight, portable computers.

Microfilm and microfiche
Media that record output as microscopic filmed images that can be stored compactly.

Voice output
Output that emerges as spoken words rather than as a visual display.

Microfilm and Microfiche

Microfilm and microfiche have been used to record output as microscopic filmed images, which can be stored compactly for future use. These media are cumbersome to search through, however, and are gradually being replaced by optical disk technology.

Voice Output Devices

Voice output devices convert digital data into speechlike form. When you call for information on the telephone, for example, a computer "voice" may respond with the telephone number you requested. Sounds needed to process inquiries are prerecorded, coded, and stored on disk, to be translated back as spoken words. Voice output is gaining popularity in toys, automobiles, and games as well as in situations in which visual output is not appropriate.

The expansion of voice output technology is limited, in part, by the same problems that limit the use of computer translators. As the Focus on Problem Solving explains, the nuances of English and other languages are still beyond available computer programs.

Matthew Chao, who is totally blind, installs the speech synthesis card into his Toshiba laptop computer. This voice output device, together with a "screen reader program," allows Matthew to hear what is visible on screen.

Source: Courtesy of Phil Rounsville for Talking Computer Systems, Watertown, Mass.

4.5 Leading-Edge Technology: The NeXT Computer

Will the NeXT Computer play the same role in shaping information technology as the Apple? Housed in a sleek black magnesium cube, the NeXT Computer, designed by Apple Computer co-founder Steven Jobs, has been touted as "the first computer of the 1990s." NeXT's producers claim it will "revolutionize higher education" and perhaps the entire computer industry by combining the power of an engineering workstation with the friendliness of a personal computer.

What makes the NeXT Computer System so innovative and leading edge? First, it has a highly efficient design. The computer is built around a

FOCUS ON *Problem Solving*

Why Can't Computers Talk?

Long before the spreadsheet program or desktop publishing was even dreamed of, scientists seized on automated translation as a technology of the future. Beginning in the 1960s, when some computers still ran on vacuum tubes, the U.S. Air Force began pouring millions of dollars into machine translation. The notion was that, within a few years, computers would automatically translate Russian scientific journals into English.

By the mid-1960s, however, the scientists realized that translation involves more than lexicons and parsing. In the output of a computer translator, "out of sight, out of mind" became the equivalent of "blind idiot" in Russian; "heavy duty truck" became "truck with a grave responsibility" in Vietnamese. In a 1966 report the National Science Foundation conceded that the effort had not been successful, and government funding for the project declined.

Now, with computers vastly more powerful and cheaper than they were a generation ago, the dream of machine translation is being revived. Certainly, a successful computer translator could have enormous market potential. Worldwide, businesses and governments spend $20 billion a year translating, according to Future Technology Surveys in Madison, Georgia. To date, however, the dream of machine translation has not been realized.

The problem is that language translation is far subtler than simply substituting words from a dictionary. To translate, a machine must understand; to understand, it must have not just a dictionary and rules of syntax, but also common sense. "The green house on the hill" would be clear to most speakers of English, but a computer might wonder whether the house is green in color or inexperienced. That's why the best of the computer programs can furnish only crude translations, very much in need of polishing by a human. Currently, then, we have, at best, machine-assisted translating—not machine translating.

Source: Adapted from Diana Fong, "Why Can't Computers Talk?" *Forbes,* May 1, 1989, p. 130. Adapted by permission of Forbes Magazine.

single circuit board, whereas most personal computers use several. The board's two custom chips are designed to make the machine very fast—it is faster than machines costing three times as much. NeXT has a large storage capacity. Instead of regular disk drives, it uses an erasable optical disk that can store 256 megabytes—roughly 100,000 typed pages. Students will be able to create digital libraries of reference works, musical scores, or photographic-quality images.

NeXT is also unusually versatile. A special digital signal processor chip lets it produce compact disk–quality music, including an entire orchestra, or send and receive voice mail. The 17-inch monitor screen is of photographic-quality resolution, supporting fine detail work such as molecular modeling. Its laser printer can produce desktop publishing–quality output at much lower cost (only $2,000) because the software that controls laser printing is built into the computer itself. NeXT does not make a breakthrough in microprocessor technology, but it does combine many leading-

NeXT computer's efficient internal and external design and its versatility make it one of the most innovative computers on the market.

Source: Courtesy of NeXT, Inc.

edge technologies into an appealing, affordable package. All in all, NeXT's main features can be summarized as follows:[3]

- **Microprocessor:** Motorola 68030 (32-bit).
- **Primary memory:** 8 megabytes of RAM.
- **Secondary storage:** 256-megabyte erasable optical disk drive (no floppy disk available).
- **Monitor:** 17-inch black and white with 1 million pixels for high resolution to display photographic-quality images.
- **Printer:** 400-dots-per-inch laser printer.
- **Price:** $6,500 for computer, $2,000 for printer.
- **Software included:** text retrieval software, desktop publishing software, equation-solving software, electronic mail software, word processing software, database software, network access software, music kit, sound kit, dictionary and thesaurus, Oxford's *Dictionary of Quotations,* and Oxford's *Complete Works of Shakespeare.*

Will NeXT set the standard for computing in the 1990s? It's still too early to tell. NeXT's primary target is university computing. Although it provides many revolutionary features at bargain prices, the machine carries a $6,500 price tag, much higher than the $3,000 students are accustomed to spending.

Another challenge is providing software to make the NeXT truly useful. The machine comes equipped with a proprietary word processing program called Write Now; mathematical equation-solving software; database software from Sybase Corporation; Jot, a personal memo-taking program; and Lisp, a programming language used for artificial intelligence applications. The optical disk houses a library that includes Webster's *Ninth Col-*

legiate Dictionary and Thesaurus, the *Oxford Dictionary of Quotations,* the complete works of William Shakespeare, and other reference materials.

NeXT also contains programming tools that should make it easy to write software to solve new kinds of problems. The machine is equipped with a starter set of 30 software objects, or prewritten chunks of software, that can be used as the foundations for new software programs. It can run much of the scientific and technical software that runs on Sun, Apollo, and other UNIX-based workstations. Nevertheless, it remains to be seen whether NeXT will revolutionize computing.

Summary

- The principal secondary storage devices are magnetic tape, magnetic disk, and optical disk.
- Magnetic tape is most useful for storing large volumes of data at a relatively low price. The disadvantages of magnetic tape are its slow access speed and the fact that it can only store data sequentially.
- Magnetic disk technology permits direct access to data, but it is more expensive than magnetic tape, is vulnerable to environmental disturbances, and needs to be backed up.
- There are two kinds of magnetic disks: hard disks and floppy disks. Removable-pack hard disk systems are used with larger computers, and Winchester hard disk systems are used with both small and large computers. Floppy disks are used in microcomputers; the most popular sizes are 3½ inches and 5¼ inches.
- The cylinder method and the sector method are two ways of storing data on magnetic disks.
- Optical disks use laser technology to store vast amounts of data in a compact space. CD-ROM disk systems can only be read from. WORM optical disk systems can only write data supplied by the user once. Rewritable optical disks are starting to be developed.
- There are several approaches to input and processing: a batch approach, an on-line real-time approach, and on-line input with delayed processing.
- The principal input devices are keyboards, touch screens, computer mice, magnetic and optical character recognition, and voice input.
- The most advanced data input technology is source data automation, in which computer-readable data are generated at the point of origin.
- The principal output devices are printers, plotters, video display terminals, microfilm and microfiche, and voice output devices.
- Printers can be classified in terms of speed, as character printers, line printers, or page printers; and in terms of the way they print, as impact or nonimpact printers.
- Impact printers can be classified as letter-quality printers with a solid font mechanism or as dot-matrix printers with a dot-matrix mechanism.

• The main types of nonimpact printers are laser printers, ink-jet printers, and thermal-transfer printers.

• Video display terminals can be classified according to whether they are monochrome or color and whether they can display text only or text and graphics.

Key Terms

Secondary storage
Magnetic tape
Magnetic disk
Direct-access storage device (DASD)
Hard disk
Read/write head
Track
Removable-pack disk system
Cylinder
Winchester disk system
Disk access time
Floppy disks
Sector
Single-sided disk
Double-sided disk
Recording density
Optical disk
CD-ROM
WORM
Batch input and processing
On-line input
On-line real-time processing
Keypunch
Key-to-tape
Key-to-disk
Touch screen
Light pen
Computer mouse
Source data automation
Magnetic ink character recognition (MICR)
Optical character recognition (OCR)
Bar code
Universal Product Code
Character printer
Line printer
Page printer
Impact printer
Letter-quality printer
Dot-matrix printer
Nonimpact printer
Laser printer
Ink-jet printer
Thermal-transfer printer
Plotter
Video display terminal
CRT
Bit mapping
Flat panel display
Microfilm and microfiche
Voice output

Review Questions

1. What is the difference between primary and secondary storage?
2. What are the advantages and disadvantages of magnetic tape storage?
3. What are the two kinds of magnetic disks? In what situations is each useful?
4. What are the various ways of physically storing data on magnetic disk?
5. What is an optical disk? In what situations are optical disks useful?

6. What is the difference between CD-ROM and WORM?
7. Distinguish among the following: batch input and processing; on-line input and real-time processing; on-line input with delayed processing.
8. What are the traditional data input devices?
9. What is source data automation?
10. Name and describe each of the leading source data automation technologies.
11. List and describe the major output devices.
12. Describe the various classifications of printers.
13. How can video display terminals be classified?

Discussion Questions

1. Why is source data automation becoming more widespread?

2. How do input, output, and storage technologies affect the design and performance of an information system?

Problem-Solving Exercises

1. Using magazine articles and research materials available in your library, prepare a report on VDT safety. What are your conclusions about VDT hazards? If you used VDTs in your business, what would you do?

2. The Bancroft Chemical Corporation is required by law to store information on its employees' medical histories for 25 years. Currently, employee medical claim forms are stored in document retention centers, where they are very difficult to access. Write an analysis of how you could use information technologies to help Bancroft fulfill its legal requirements.

Notes

1. Rosemary Hamilton, "Color Codes Tame Unruly Tapes," *Computerworld,* March 13, 1989.
2. Doug Iles, "CD-ROM Enters Mainstream IS," *Computerworld,* June 5, 1989; Daniel Gross, "Rock 'n ROM," *Computerworld,* June 1, 1988.
3. "How the NeXT Computer Stacks Up against Its Rivals," *The Wall Street Journal,* October 13, 1988; Andrew Pollack, "The Return of a Computer Star," *The New York Times,* October 13, 1988.

Problem-Solving Case

Selecting Printers: Caution Advised

Companies are finding that selecting a printer and plotters is no longer a simple matter. Previously, information systems managers focused on the cost and speed of the printer and the maintenance record of the manufacturer.

Now, the options are almost overwhelming. Printers appropriate for a firm's computer center have speeds ranging from 60–70 pages per minute to 200 and even 400 pages per minute. Practical color capability is on the horizon.

With such a rich array of choices come new responsibilities. Selecting a computer now entails close attention to print quality, consumption of paper, and software requirements as well as volume and cost. Some experts claim the wrong choice of printer can create a multimillion-dollar monster for the firm.

The question of the merits of impact versus nonimpact technology is often raised when a printer is being selected. Impact printers are very cost-effective and essential for multipart forms, but firms like the flexibility of laser technology. Moreover, lasers are starting to handle forms-generation tasks previously monopolized by impact printers. Since the laser printer generates a form electronically as it prints data, alterations are easy to make. Laser printers reduce handling and waste when preprinted forms become obsolete. Preprinted forms are still required when color is used, however.

The Vancouver Stock Exchange in British Columbia recently switched from impact to laser printer. It previously employed seven IBM impact printers to generate 100 million lines per month, consuming 30 tons of paper. Altogether the stock exchange used 68 impact printer forms. This created a very labor-intensive and unpleasant working environment with many report distribution errors.

After studying the matter, the stock exchange's information systems department replaced the impact printers with five IBM laser printers that could output 90 pages per minute. It hoped this equipment change would lower costs by reducing labor requirements, reducing physical space requirements, and improving paper and forms management by using plain paper in a standardized size. The new printers were also expected to provide superior print quality and more responsiveness to business document distribution deadlines. As a result of the change, the stock exchange was able to save $25,000 per month by standardizing paper size, finding different methods of paper storage, and making major improvements in computer room operations.

Another issue in printer selection is the question of single-sheet versus continuous-feed paper. New printers have paper-handling features such as multiple paper feeds and giant paper rolls that reduce the amount of attention the printer requires. Still, the paper must be handled manually at the outgoing end, and it jams periodically.

Buyers need to analyze their projected volume of printer output to determine how large a printer they need. In addition to total number of pages, the number and variety of jobs and periods of peak demand must be considered. Would-be purchasers must also think about software issues, which were never a problem when printers only turned out line format text. Experts note that the worst printer purchasing mistakes are software related.

Nonimpact printers employ special software for storing type fonts and graphic elements, storing forms, and formatting documents. Purchasers of this type of printer must be able to understand and work with this software. Most business software cannot be sent to any printer in the firm. Instead, instructions for sending output to the printer vary according to the particular make of printer. If the business changes its printers, all of the printer-related

instructions in all of its business software must be changed. Blue Cross/Blue Shield of Massachusetts decided to use only Xerox Corporation printers for this reason.

Case Study Questions

1. Analysts have observed that printers have an effect on the profitability of a business. Why?
2. What aspects of a business are affected by printers?
3. If you were choosing printers for your business, what criteria would you use?

C H A P T E R · F I V E

Information Systems Software for Problem Solving

Chapter Outline

5.1 Introduction
- Software Programs
- Major Types of Software
- Generations of Software

5.2 Systems Software
- The Operating System
- Language Translators and Utility Programs
- How to Choose a Microcomputer Operating System

5.3 Programming Languages
- Major Programming Languages
- Fourth-Generation Languages
- Selecting a Programming Language

5.4 Applications Software
- Software Packages
- Popular Microcomputer Applications Packages

5.5 Leading-Edge Application: Maps that Can Read People's Minds

Learning Objectives

After reading and studying this chapter, you will:

1. Understand the roles systems software and applications software play in information systems.
2. Be familiar with the generations of computer software.
3. Know how the operating system functions.
4. Understand the strengths and limitations of the major programming languages.
5. Be able to select appropriate software for business applications.

The Software Crunch

A computer is only as good as its software—the instructions that tell the computer what to do. Therefore, organizations depend on the producers of software to make today's wide variety of computer applications possible. Unfortunately, the buyers of software are increasingly finding that the supply cannot keep pace with their demand.

The U.S. Department of Defense, for example, reported in 1987 that it could not obtain enough reliable software fast enough or at a low enough cost to meet the needs of the designers and users of weapons systems. The Defense Department predicted that, if its demand for software continued to grow at a constant rate, about 60 million software workers would be needed to meet that demand. That enormous number of workers represents almost half of today's entire labor force.

Today significant defense projects are being held back because of the software shortage. In March 1988, the House Armed Services Committee had to cut all funding for procurement related to an advanced-warning radar system with a range beyond that of existing radars. According to the committee, there was no sense in building the sophisticated hardware when the necessary software was unavailable.

In the private sector, the Bank of America canceled a $20 million, three-year project. The reason: it could not find a supplier that could deliver the necessary software on time.

One reason for the software crunch is that software production uses low-tech methods. Software is written by programmers working one line at a time. A programmer can typically produce 15 or 20 lines of tested code per day. The supply of programmers is growing at a rate of about 4 percent a year, whereas the length of programs is growing at a 25 percent rate, and the overall demand for software is increasing at about 12 percent a year.

Source: Otis Port, "The Software Trap: Automate—or Else," *Business Week*, May 19, 1988.

The plight of the Defense Department and the Bank of America reflects problems throughout the information systems world. Without software, computer hardware is useless.

5.1 Introduction

Software refers to the detailed instructions that control the operation of computer hardware. Without the instructions provided by software, computer hardware is unable to perform any of the tasks we associate with computers. Software has three principal functions: (1) it develops the tools for applying computer hardware to problem solving; (2) it enables the firm to manage its computer resources; and (3) it serves as an intermediary between the firm and its stored information.

Software Programs

Program
A series of statements or instructions to the computer.

A software **program** is a series of statements or instructions to the computer. The process of writing or coding the program is called programming, and the individual who performs this task is called a programmer.

In order to execute, or have its instructions performed by the computer, a program must be stored in the computer's primary storage along with the required data. This is called the **stored-program concept.** Once a program has finished executing, the computer hardware can be used for another task by loading a new program into primary storage.

Stored-program concept
The concept that a program cannot be executed unless it is stored in the computer's primary storage along with the required data.

Major Types of Software

There are two major types of software: systems software and applications software. Each handles a different set of problems.

GTE telephone company combines applications software with NCR computers to prevent service interruptions. The system collects information from GTE's testing network. When patterns of trouble arise, technicians can locate and fix problems before customers notice a problem.
Source: Courtesy of NCR and GTE Corporations.

Systems software consists of generalized programs that manage computer resources such as the central processing unit (CPU), printers, terminals, communications links, and peripheral equipment. In other words, systems software serves as the intermediary between the software used by business specialists and the computer itself.

Systems software
Generalized software that manages computer resources such as the CPU, printers, terminals, communications links, and peripheral equipment.

Applications software consists of programs designed for applying the computer to solve a specific problem. Payroll processing programs or sales order entry programs are examples of applications software. Systems software provides the platform on which applications software runs. The relationships among people, the two different kinds of software, and computer hardware are illustrated in Figure 5.1. As the figure shows, people send instructions to the applications software, which "translates" the instructions for the systems software, which in turn forwards them to the hardware. Information flows in two directions: from the person using the computer to the hardware and back again.

Applications software
Programs designed to handle the processing for a particular computer application.

The Focus on Organizations points out that the users of software are primarily business people with no technical background. Software itself has little value unless these users feel comfortable using it and the software truly meets their business needs.

Generations of Software

The sophistication and range of problems that can be addressed by programming languages can be attributed to the increased capacity of computer hardware. Just as computer hardware evolved over time, software has developed over several generations.

FOCUS ON *Organizations*

Johnsonizing Software

For the S. C. Johnson & Son Corporation, the term "johnsonification" represents the kind of singlemindedness that Samuel Curtis Johnson exhibited when he created the first can of Johnson's Prepared Paste Wax over a hundred years ago. The Johnson company is still family-owned and is still trying to "johnsonize" the 46 companies it owns throughout the world.

Milton C. Habeck, Johnson's controller for the Americas, is responsible for "johnsonizing" the software used in Johnson manufacturing facilities in Venezuela, Chile, Mexico, and other Latin American countries. The people who use the software typically do not have data processing backgrounds; they come from within manufacturing, distribution, or finance.

Habeck works with these business specialists to show them the software. He claims it satisfies 88 percent of their needs, and he is working to fine-tune software that could meet over 90 percent of these needs. To ease its Latin American employees' concerns, Johnson adopted Spanish-language versions of the software.

Johnson looks for software that can be adjusted to different countries' commercial and business practices. A bill of materials can be as simple as one with only two components, or it can be one with pages of specifications. Manufacturing processes can consist of mixing and filling only or encompass the activities of hundreds of work centers. Some facilities need only a few suppliers of manufacturing materials, whereas others depend on thousands of vendors. In Latin America, as well as other areas of the world, government regulations can put additional strain on the manufacturing process, hindering the ability of manufacturers to know when materials will arrive.

Source: Robert Knight, "Data Converging on Factory Floor," *Software Magazine,* March 1989.

Machine language
The programming language used in the first generation of computer software; consists of strings of binary digits (0 and 1).

High-level language
A programming language that consists of statements that, to some degree, resemble a natural language, such as English.

Assembly language
A programming language used for second-generation software; it consists of natural language–like acronyms and words such as add, sub(tract), and load and is considered a symbolic language.

The first generation of computer software was **machine language.** Machine language, consisting of strings of the binary digits 0 and 1, was the only way to communicate with the primitive computers of the 1940s. It took highly trained, specialized programmers to understand, think, and work directly with the machine language of a particular computer. Machine language instructions must specify the storage location for every instruction and data item used. Consequently, writing software in this language was excruciatingly slow and labor-intensive; very few problems could be addressed this way.

Machine language is no longer used to develop software, having been replaced by symbolic and high-level languages. Symbolic languages, or assembly languages, use symbols and alphabetic abbreviations in place of the 0's and 1's of machine language for representing operation codes, storage locations, and data elements. **High-level languages** consist of statements that, to varying degrees, resemble natural languages (e.g., English). Both symbolic and high-level languages must be translated into machine language for execution by the computer, however (Section 5.2 discusses language translators).

The second generation of software, which began in the early 1950s, consisted of **assembly language.** Assembly language is considered a sym-

Figure 5.1

The Relationship between Hardware, Systems Software, Applications Software, and the User

Software serves as the intermediary between people and computer hardware. Most of the software that business professionals use directly is applications software: computer programs that "apply" the computer to perform a specific business function, such as calculating payroll checks or amount of sales. Systems software coordinates the various parts of the computer system and transforms instructions from applications software into instructions that will operate the hardware. Information flows both ways; the results of the hardware's operations travel through the systems software, and the applications programs transform them into results that people can use.

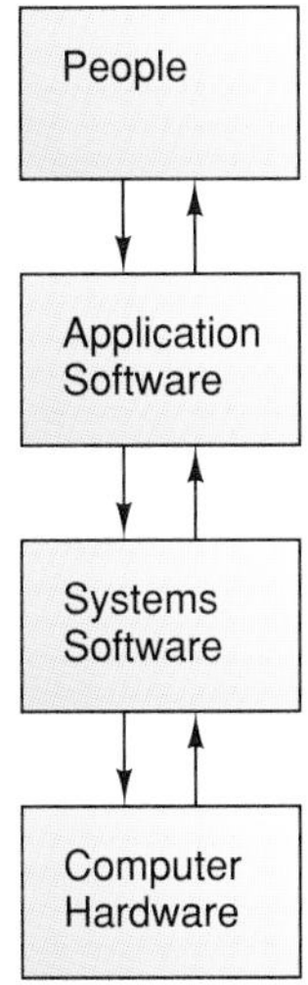

bolic language because it consists of language-like acronyms and words such as add, sub (subtract), and load. The programs that translate assembly language into machine code are called **assemblers.** Today assembly language has limited use for problems that require maximum execution efficiency or highly intricate manipulations.

Assembler
A program that translates assembly language into machine code so it can be used by the computer.

Third-generation computer software, which prevailed from the late 1950s to the 1970s, featured high-level languages that were more sophisticated, easier to use, and directed toward specialized classes of problems. High-level languages also are less machine dependent and often can be used on more than one type of computer. Popular third-generation languages include FORTRAN (FORmula TRANslator) for scientific and mathematical problems, COBOL (COmmon Business-Oriented Language) for business problems entailing extensive file manipulation and large lists, and BASIC (Beginner's All-purpose Symbolic Instruction Code), a generalized programming language popular for microcomputers. Third-generation software is still in wide use today.

Fourth-generation software was developed in the late 1970s and is used widely for business application development today. Fourth-generation software consists of query software, report generators, graphics software, application generators, and other tools (discussed later in this chapter) that dramatically reduce programming time and make some software tasks easy enough to be performed by nontechnical specialists.

The first three generations of software languages were procedural. Program instructions had to detail a sequence of steps, or procedures, telling the computer what to do and how to do it. In contrast, fourth-generation software has nonprocedural features. Program instructions need only specify *what* has to be accomplished rather than provide details about how to carry out the task. Consequently, the same process can be accomplished with fewer program steps and lines of program code than with third-generation languages.

Some fourth-generation software has natural-language features, meaning that commands are expressed in English-language form. Offices and factories are starting to take advantage of voice recognition software, in which users communicate with computers through spoken commands. For example, Burlington Industries in Greensboro, North Carolina, has equipped its quality control inspectors with Texas Instruments Voice Boards. As lengths of cloth pass, the inspectors describe the defects into microphones connected to their computers, while a yardage meter automatically reports the defect's location to the computer. Defects have dropped 20 percent since the voice recognition system was adopted. Previously, inspectors wasted much time switching back and forth between their notepads and repair tools.[1] The next wave of software will feature more prominent use of such natural-language tools, as well as graphic interfaces, touch screens, and other features that will make it easier for nontechnical specialists to use.

5.2 Systems Software

Operating system
The systems software that manages and controls the activities of the computer.

Systems software consists of programs that coordinate the various parts of a computer system and mediate between application software and computer hardware. The **operating system** is the systems software that manages and controls the activities of the computer. It supervises the operation of the CPU; controls input, output, and storage activities; and provides various support services. Other vital services, such as computer language translation facilities and utility programs for common processing tasks, are provided by language translators and utility programs (discussed later in this chapter).

The Operating System

The operating system can be visualized as the chief manager of the computer system. Like a human manager in a firm, the operating system determines which computer resources will be used for solving which problems and the order in which they will be used. As shown in Figure 5.2, it has three principal functions:

- Allocating and assigning system resources
- Scheduling the use of resources and computer jobs
- Monitoring computer system activities

Figure 5.2

The Tasks of the Operating System

The operating system is the systems software that manages the computer's operations. It has three major roles: it allocates hardware resources as needed; it schedules the various functions, such as input and output; and it monitors the functioning of the system.

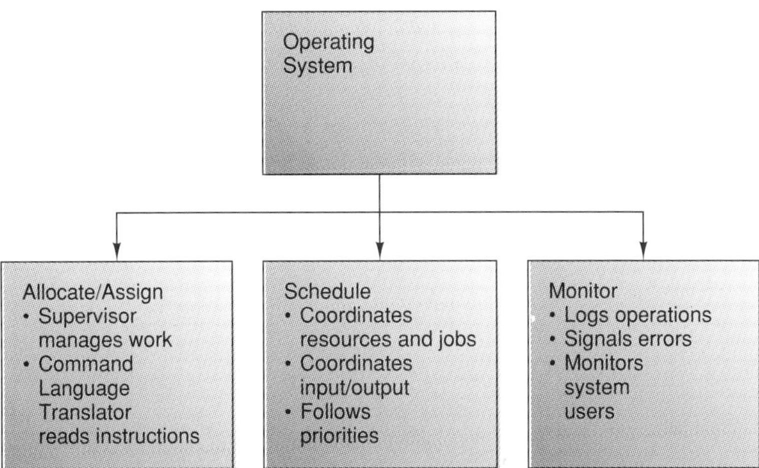

Allocation and Assignment · A master control program called a supervisor, executive, or monitor oversees computer operations and coordinates all of the computer's work. The supervisor, which remains in primary storage, brings other programs from secondary storage to primary storage when they are needed. As each program is activated, the supervisor cedes control to that program. Once that program ends, control returns to the supervisor.

A command language translator controls the assignment of system resources. The command language translator reads special instructions to the operating system, which contain specifications for retrieving, saving, deleting, copying, or moving files; selecting input/output devices; selecting programming languages and application programs; and performing other processing requirements for a particular application. These instructions are called command language. The commands you use with your personal computer to format a disk or copy a file are examples of command language for microcomputer operating systems.

Scheduling · Thousands of pieces of work can be going on in a computer at the same time. The operating system decides when to schedule them, since computer jobs are not necessarily performed in the order they are submitted. For example, payroll or on-line order processing may have a higher priority than other kinds of work. Other processing jobs, such as software program testing, would have to wait until these jobs were finished or left enough computer resources free to accommodate them.

The operating system coordinates scheduling in various areas of the computer so that different parts of different jobs can be worked on simultaneously. For example, while some programs are executing, the operating system is also scheduling the use of input and output devices.

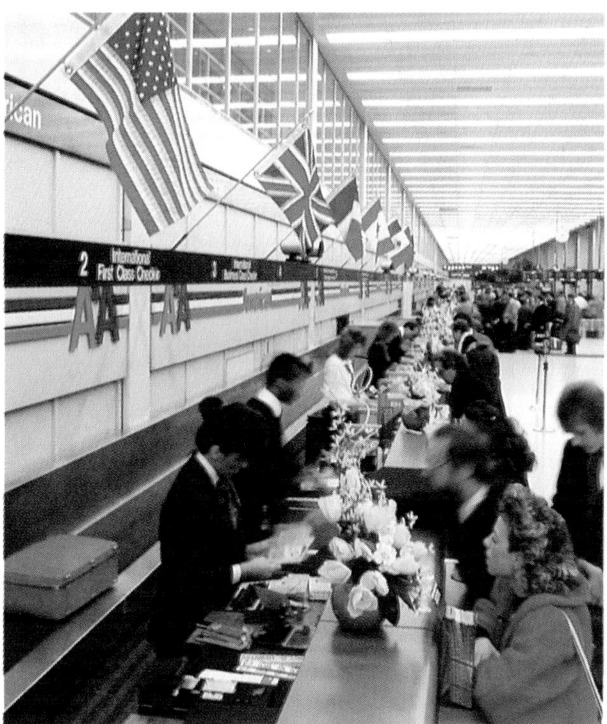

Ticket agents at American Airlines' international ticket counter at Chicago's O'Hare Field confirm reservations and seat assignments. Hundreds of ticket agents and reservation clerks can use an information system simultaneously because of the multiprogramming, multiprocessing, and time-sharing capabilities of operating systems software.

Source: Courtesy of American Airlines.

Monitoring · The operating system is also responsible for keeping track of the activities in the computer system. It maintains logs of job operations, notifying end-users or computer operators of any abnormal terminations or error conditions. It terminates programs that run longer than the maximum time allowed.

Operating system software may also contain security monitoring features, such as recording who has logged onto and off the system, what programs they have run, and any unauthorized attempts to access the system. Security issues are explored in greater detail in Chapter 16.

If a computer can execute only one instruction from one program at a time, how can thousands of American Airlines reservation clerks use the computer simultaneously to book flights? How can American Airlines run its on-line reservation software 24 hours a day and still use its computers for accounting and other activities? Operating system software has special capabilities for these purposes.

Multiprogramming
The concurrent use of a computer by several programs; one program uses the CPU while the others use other components such as input and output devices.

Multiprogramming · **Multiprogramming** allows multiple programs to use the computer's resources at the same time through concurrent use of the CPU. Only one program actually uses the CPU at any given moment, but at this same instant the other programs can use the computer for other

Figure 5.3

Multiprogramming Uses the CPU More Efficiently

Early computers could execute only one software program at a time. This meant that the CPU had to stop all processing until the program it had just processed finished outputting. This wasted a great deal of valuable CPU time that could have been more profitably spent in processing other programs. Multiprogramming means that the systems software allows the CPU to work on several programs simultaneously (see panel b). Even though the computer can still *process* only one program at a time, it can simultaneously perform input and output functions on other programs. This dramatically cuts down on the amount of idle time between CPU tasks.

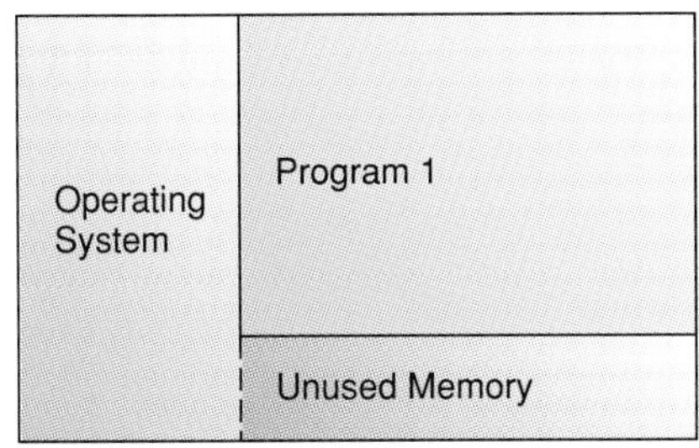

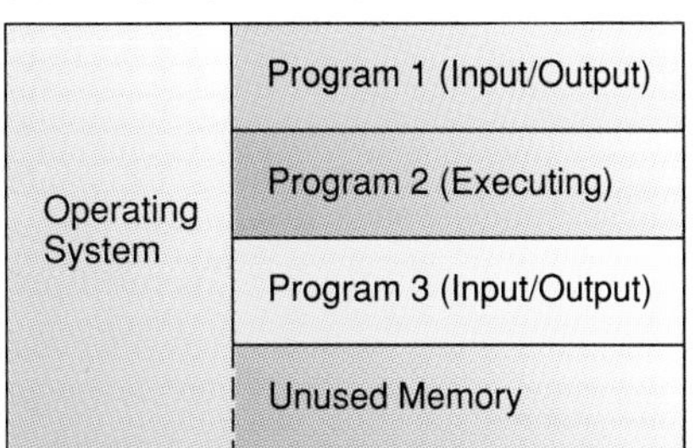

needs, such as input and output. Thus a number of programs can be active in the computer at the same time, but they do not use the same computer resources simultaneously.

Figure 5.3 shows three programs (1, 2, and 3) stored in primary storage. The first program (1) uses the CPU to execute until it comes to an input/output event (in this case, output). The CPU then moves to the second incoming program and directs a communications channel (a small processor limited to input/output processing functions) to read the input and move the output to a printer or other output device. The CPU executes the second program until an input/output statement occurs. It then switches to program 3, moving back and forth between all three programs until they have finished executing.

The advantage of multiprogramming is that it enables computers to be used much more efficiently. Before multiprogramming, computers were a single-program environment; only one program could be executed at a time. The CPU had to stop and wait whenever a program had to read input or write output. With multiprogramming, more problems can be solved at the same time using a single computer.

Multitasking · **Multitasking** refers to multiprogramming capability on single-user operating systems such as those for microcomputers. It enables one person to run two or more programs concurrently on a single computer. For example, a stockbroker could write a letter to clients with a word processing program while simultaneously using another program to record and update client account information. Multitasking allows the broker to display both programs on the computer screen and work with them at the same time, instead of having to terminate the session with the word processing program, return to the operating system, and then initiate a session with the program handling client account information.

Multitasking
The multiprogramming capability of single-user operating systems such as those for microcomputers; it enables the user to run two or more programs at once on a single computer.

Multiprocessing
The simultaneous use of two or more CPUs under common control to execute different instructions for the same program or multiple programs.

Multiprocessing · The use of two or more CPUs linked together to work in parallel is **multiprocessing.** Two CPUs may be assigned to execute different instructions from the same program simultaneously so that they can be accomplished more rapidly than on a single machine, or instructions from more than one program can be processed simultaneously. The operating system is responsible for scheduling and coordinating the tasks of the various processors. The two CPUs can "communicate," or exchange information, in order to execute programs more efficiently.

Time-sharing
A technique in which many users share computer resources simultaneously (e.g., one CPU with many terminals); the computer spends a fixed amount of time on each user's program before proceeding to the next.

Time-Sharing · A technique that enables many users to share computer resources simultaneously is **time-sharing.** It differs from multiprogramming in that the computer spends a fixed amount of time on one program before proceeding to another. Each user is allocated a tiny slice of time (say, two milliseconds). The computer performs whatever operations it can for that user in the allocated time and then releases two milliseconds to the next user. (In multiprogramming, the computer works on one program until it reaches a logical stopping point, such as an input/output event. Then the computer starts processing another program.)

In a typical time-sharing environment, a CPU is connected to thousands of users at terminals. Many people can be connected to the same CPU simultaneously, with each receiving a tiny amount of CPU time. Since computers now operate at the nanosecond level, the CPU can actually do a great deal of processing in two milliseconds.

Virtual storage
A way of dividing programs into small fixed- or variable-length portions with only a small portion stored in primary memory at one time so that programs can be used more efficiently by the computer.

Virtual Storage · **Virtual storage** is a way of splitting up programs so that they can be managed more efficiently by the operating system. Before virtual storage was developed in the early 1970s, only a few programs could be loaded into primary storage. A certain portion of primary storage usually remained underutilized because the programs did not take up the total amount of space available. In addition, very large programs could not be accommodated in their entirety in primary storage. Programmers had to split up such programs to find portions that would fit into limited memory space.

Virtual storage is based on the realization that only a few program statements can actually be utilized in the computer at any one time. Virtual storage divides programs into fixed-length portions called pages (each page is approximately 2–4 kilobytes) or into variable-length portions called segments. The actual breakpoint in the program can be determined by the programmer or the operating system.

A page is read into the CPU when needed and sent back to secondary storage, or disk, when it is no longer required. The CPU executes the instructions from each page, then moves on, either to the next page of the program or to a page from a different program (see Figure 5.4). Therefore, many portions of programs, broken down into pages, can reside in primary storage at once. All other program pages are stored in a secondary storage peripheral disk unit until they are required for execution.

Virtual storage has several advantages. Not only does it promote fuller utilization of the CPU, but programmers no longer have to worry about program size because any program can be broken down into pages or segments. In addition, large programs do not need large machines to run; they can be executed on smaller computers.

Figure 5.4

Virtual Storage Expands the Computer's Memory

Virtual storage is a feature of operating systems that expands the potential memory of the CPU. Software programs are split into portions called pages (fixed-length, as shown here) or segments (variable-length). The pages are stored in secondary storage and shuttled into and out of main memory as needed for processing. Thus the CPU can process pieces of many programs almost simultaneously.

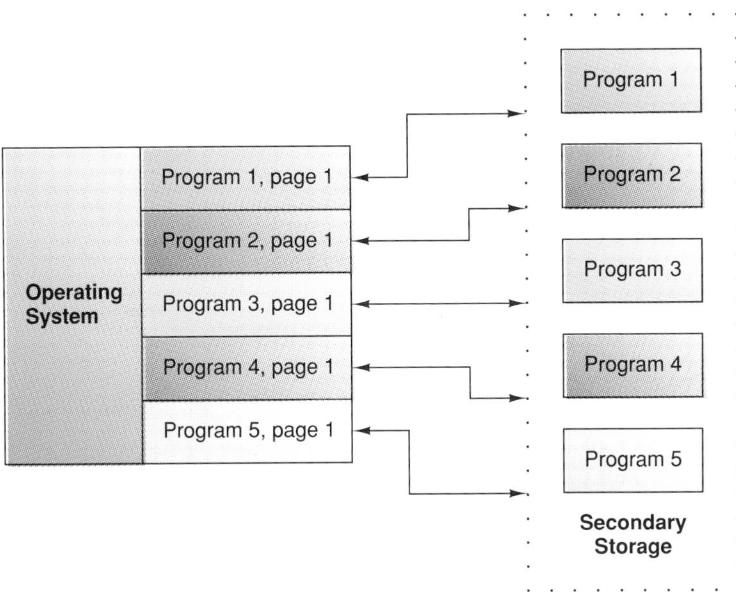

Language Translators and Utility Programs

Another important function of operating system software is to translate high-level language programs into machine language so that they can be executed by the computer. The high-level language is called **source code,** and the machine-language version is called **object code.** Before actually being executed by the computer, object code modules normally are joined together with other object code modules in a process called linkage editing. The result, called the load module, is what is executed by the computer.

There are three kinds of language translator programs: compilers, interpreters, and assemblers. A **compiler** translates an entire high-level language program into machine language. An **interpreter** translates each source code statement one at a time into machine code and executes it. Consequently, interpreted programs run more slowly than compiled programs. Many versions of BASIC use interpreters. An assembler is similar to a compiler but is used only for assembly languages. (See Section 5.3.) Figure 5.5 illustrates the language translation process for a compiler, the most common type.

Source code
The high-level language translated by operating system software into machine language so that the high-level programs can be executed by the computer.

Object code
The machine-language version of source code after it has been translated into a form usable by the computer.

Compiler
A language translator program that translates an entire high-level language program into machine language.

Interpreter
A language translator program that translates a high-level language program into machine code by translating one statement at a time and executing it.

Utility Programs · Systems software typically includes utility programs for common, routine, repetitive tasks, such as sorting records or copying

Figure 5.5

Language Translation

A compiler is a type of operating system software that serves as a language translator: it "translates" software that people use into instructions that the computer can use. As shown here, the compiler transforms high-level language instructions (called source code) into their machine language equivalent (object code). A linkage editor combines modules of object code with those from other incoming programs into a load module, the group of instructions that the computer follows.

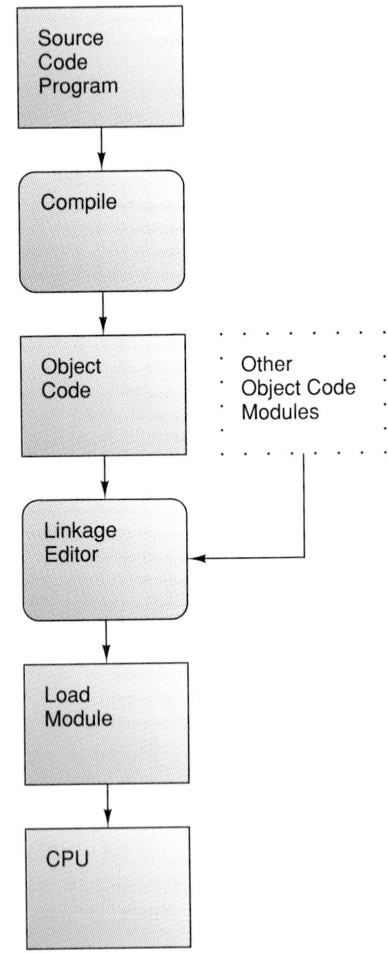

programs from tape to disk. Utility programs are stored in libraries where they can be shared by all users of a computer system. Utility programs are very important. The Focus on People describes what can happen if utility programs are not operating properly.

How to Choose a Microcomputer Operating System

Microcomputer software is based on specific operating systems and machines. A software package written for one microcomputer operating system

FOCUS ON *People*

Profiles in Angst

Michael Brown, president of Central Point Software in Portland, Oregon, had finished shipping version 3.2 of PC Tools just two days before and was finally taking a well-deserved holiday in Europe when the phone rang. A distraught employee in Oregon delivered the bad news: the just-shipped program had a lethal bug that could, under certain circumstances, trash the file allocation table (and the data) on a user's hard disk.

Like a field commander mobilizing his troops, Brown issued orders that every employee, from accounting to sales, start contacting the approximately 2,000 users who had received copies of the upgraded program. Central Point contacted as many customers as it could by phone, then turned to Federal Express to help with a mass mailing. "We must have had every Federal Express worker in Portland out there that afternoon," says Brown. By 4:30 P.M., over 1,000 Federal Express packages were ready for Saturday morning delivery.

The bill was steep. Brown estimates that Central Point spent at least $50,000 total contacting users. "We may have lost every penny on that update, but we had to do it," says Brown. "In retrospect, it was the best business decision I ever made."

Source: Judy Getts, "Garlands and Glitches," *PC World*, January 1988, p. 160.

cannot run on another. Operating systems themselves have distinctive features, such as whether they support multitasking or graphics work, that make them conducive to specific classes of problems. Therefore, in order to use microcomputers effectively, one must understand the capabilities of their operating system software.

Table 5.1 compares the leading microcomputer operating systems—DOS, OS/2, UNIX, CP/M, and the Macintosh operating system. CP/M was the most popular operating system for 8-bit microcomputers. The most popular operating system for 16-bit microcomputers is **DOS.** There are two versions of DOS: PC-DOS, which is used exclusively with the IBM Personal Computer, and MS-DOS, which is used with other 16-bit microcomputers that function like the IBM PC. **OS/2 (Operating System/2)** is a powerful operating system that can support multitasking and is used with the new 32-bit IBM Personal System/2 line of microcomputers.

UNIX, which was developed at Bell Laboratories in 1969 to link different types of computers together, is an interactive, multiuser, multitasking operating system that is highly supportive of communications and networking. Many people can use UNIX simultaneously, or one user can run many tasks on UNIX concurrently. UNIX was initially designed for minicomputers, but now there are versions for microcomputers and mainframes. At present, UNIX is primarily used for workstations, minicomputers, and inexpensive multiuser environments in small businesses, but its use in large businesses is growing because of its machine independence. Applications software that runs under UNIX can be transported from one computer to another with little modification.

DOS
An operating system for 16-bit microcomputers; PC-DOS is used with the IBM Personal Computer; MS-DOS is used with other 16-bit microcomputers that function like the IBM PC.

OS/2
An operating system that supports multitasking and is used with the 32-bit IBM Personal System/2 microcomputer.

UNIX
A machine-independent operating system for microcomputers, minicomputers, and mainframes; it is interactive and supports multiuser processing, multitasking, and networking.

Table 5.1

Microcomputer Operating Systems: A Comparison

Operating System	Features
PC-DOS	Operating system for the IBM Personal Computer. Limits use of memory to 640K.
MS-DOS	Features similar to *PC-DOS* but is the operating system for IBM PC clones (microcomputers that function like the IBM Personal Computer).
OS/2 (Operating System/2)®	Operating system for the IBM Personal System/2 line of microcomputers. Can take advantage of the 32-bit microprocessor. Supports multitasking and can run large programs that require more than 640K of memory.
UNIX (XENIX)	Used for AT&T microcomputers, other powerful microcomputers, and minicomputers. Supports multitasking, multiuser processing, and networking. Is portable to different models of computer hardware.
MultiFinder	Operating system for the Macintosh computer. Supports multitasking and has powerful graphics capabilities.
CP/M	An older system widely used for 8-bit microcomputers.

MultiFinder, the new operating system for the Macintosh computer, supports multitasking and spooling of documents as well as powerful graphics capabilities and a mouse-driven graphical user interface. Spooling is the storage of documents in a temporary memory called a spooler. The main processor can perform other tasks once it sends documents to the spooler. The spooled documents are then printed by the printer.

Graphical user interface
The feature of a microcomputer operating system that uses graphical symbols, or icons; rather than typing in commands, the user moves the cursor to the appropriate icon by rolling a mouse on a desk top.

The **graphical user interface** is becoming the dominant model for the "look and feel" of microcomputer operating systems. OS/2 for the IBM Personal System/2 computers has its own version of a graphical user interface called Presentation Manager.™ Sun Microsystems' version is called Open Look.

How does a graphical user interface impact problem solving? Older microcomputer operating systems, such as PC-DOS or MS-DOS, are command driven. The user must type in commands such as DELETE FILEA to perform tasks such as deleting a file named FILEA. A graphical user interface, in contrast, makes extensive use of icons to perform the same task. For example, the MultiFinder operating system for the Macintosh computer uses graphical symbols called icons to depict programs, files, and activities. Commands can be activated by rolling a mouse to move a cursor about the screen and clicking a button on the mouse to make a selection. A file can be deleted by moving the cursor to the "Trash" icon.

Proponents of graphical user interfaces claim that they are easier for computing novices to master. A complex series of commands can be issued simply by linking icons. Commands are standardized from one program to the next, so new programs can often be used without additional training or studying reference manuals. For example, the steps involved in printing a letter created by a word processing program or a financial statement generated by a spreadsheet program should be the same. Graphical user interfaces also encourage solutions communicated through graphics.

As this brief survey suggests, the various microcomputer operating systems offer various features as well as advantages and disadvantages. Therefore, when selecting a microcomputer operating system, one should ask several key questions:

- What kind of computer hardware is required?
- What kinds of applications software does it support?
- How easy is it to learn and use?
- How quickly does it run?
- Are many problems anticipated that would best be solved in a multitasking environment?
- Is the operating system primarily designed for single users or for networking?
- How much technical and support assistance is available?

5.3 Programming Languages

Each of the major kinds of software consists of programs written in specific programming languages. Each programming language was designed to solve a particular class of problems. It is important to understand the strengths and limitations of each of these languages in order to select appropriate software.

Major Programming Languages

Assembly Language · As we explained in Section 5.1, assembly language was developed to overcome some of the difficulties of machine language. Mnemonic (easy to remember) codes and symbols are used to represent operations (such as adding or moving) and storage locations. For example, A stands for "Add" and L stands for "Load." Assembly language is very machine oriented, because assembly-language instructions correspond closely to the machine-language instructions for a specific computer and specific microprocessor. Each assembly-language instruction corresponds to a single machine-language instruction (see Figure 5.6).

Assembly language emphasizes efficient use of computer resources. Minimal memory and CPU activity are required for processing with assembly language. Therefore, execution of assembly-language programs is extremely rapid and efficient.

Although assembly language is easier to use than pure machine language, it is still extremely difficult to learn and requires highly skilled pro-

Figure 5.6

Examples of Machine Language Code and Assembly Language Code to Add the Value of B to A

Assembly language is primarily used today for writing software for operating systems. As you can see, it is very different from English and much closer to machine language in its commands. Although this can make it inefficient for humans to learn, it is very efficient for computers to execute.

```
Machine Code

11111010010100101001000000000000100100000000110 0

Assembly Code

AP TOTALA,   VALUEB
```

Source: Figure 4–15, "Examples of machine language code and assembly language code to add the value of B to A (A = A + B)," from *Computer Information Systems* by Jerome S. Burstein and Edward G. Martin, p. 113, copyright © 1989 by The Dryden Press, a division of Holt, Rinehart and Winston, Inc. Reprinted by permission of the publisher.

grammers. Assembly language is used primarily for writing operating systems software, when highly detailed programs that are sensitive to a specific computer's machine language must be designed.

FORTRAN
A programming language developed in 1954 for scientific, mathematical, and engineering applications; stands for FORmula TRANslator.

FORTRAN · **FORTRAN** (which stands for FORmula TRANslator) was developed in 1954 to facilitate writing of scientific, mathematical, and engineering software. Although business applications can be written in FORTRAN, the language is most appropriate for scientific, engineering, and mathematical problems that use complicated formulas. A FORTRAN program is shown in Figure 5.7. It reads a list of students and their grade point averages (GPAs) on a scale of 0 to 4. From the list shown below, the program selects those students with a GPA of 3.5 or more and prints their names and GPAs for the honor roll.

Student	GPA
Mary Smith	3.75
Robert Lopez	2.95
Christine Jones	2.85
Tom Toshiba	3.95
Janis Roberts	3.49
Ralph Brown	3.20
Ronald Chang	3.00
Susan O'Malley	3.50
Cathy Schwartz	3.00
Michael Ramirez	3.65

FORTRAN's great strength lies in its facilities for mathematical computations. It does not have strong facilities for input/output activities or for working with lists. Thus it would not be appropriate for business problems that involve reading massive amounts of records and producing reports. On the other hand, for business problems requiring sophisticated computations, such as forecasting and modeling, FORTRAN has been used successfully.

Figure 5.7

The Honor-Roll Program in FORTRAN

FORTRAN is a relatively old computer language (created in 1954), but it is still in common use today. It is generally used for scientific, mathematical, and engineering calculations rather than for business.

```
      PROGRAM HONORF(INPUT,OUTPUT,SCOREF,TAPE60=INPUT,TAPE61=SCOREF)
C   THIS PROGRAM EXTRACTS THE NAMES OF THOSE STUDENTS WHO
C   HAVE A GRADE-POINT AVERAGE (GPA) GREATER THAN OR EQUAL
C   TO 3.50.   THE NAME AND GPA OF EACH QUALIFYING STUDENT, AND
C   THE TOTAL NUMBER OF THE QUALIFYING STUDENTS IS PRINTED OUT.
      CHARACTER * 20 NAME(10)
      REAL GPA(10)
      INTEGER COUNT
      COUNT = 0
         PRINT *,'    OAKRIVER UNIVERSITY HONOR ROLL REPORT'
         PRINT *,' '
         PRINT *,'          THE HONOR ROLL STUDENTS'
         PRINT *,' '
         PRINT *,'    STUDENT NAME                     GPA'
         PRINT *,' '
      DO 70 I = 1, 10
         READ(61,40) NAME(I), GPA(I)
   40    FORMAT(A20,F4.2)
       IF (GPA(I) .GE. 3.5) THEN
          PRINT 50, NAME(I), GPA(I)
   50     FORMAT(5X,A20,10X,F4.2)          IF THEN ELSE
          COUNT = COUNT + 1
       END IF
   70 CONTINUE
      PRINT 80, COUNT
   80 FORMAT(//,5X,'THE NUMBER OF HONOR ROLL STUDENTS IS:', I3)
      END

RUN

      OAKRIVER UNIVERSITY HONOR ROLL REPORT

            THE HONOR ROLL STUDENTS

      STUDENT NAME                    GPA

      MARY SMITH                      3.75
      TOM TOSHIBA                     3.95
      SUSAN O'MALLEY                  3.50
      MICHAEL RAMIREZ                 3.65


      THE NUMBER OF HONOR STUDENTS IS:  4
```

Source: Figure 15–8, "The honor roll problem in FORTRAN," from *Computer Information Systems* by Jerome S. Burstein and Edward G. Martin, p. 516, copyright © 1989 by The Dryden Press, a division of Holt, Rinehart and Winston, Inc. Reprinted by permission of the publisher.

COBOL · **COBOL** (which comes from COmmon Business-Oriented Language) was introduced in the early 1960s and remains the predominant language for business problems. It was designed to process large data files with alphanumeric characters (mixed alphabetic and numeric data), which are characteristic of business problems. COBOL can read, write, and manipulate records very effectively. Business specialists also find it easier to learn than most other programming languages. It uses relatively English-like statements, is easily readable, and supports well-structured programs.

COBOL
A programming language with English-like statements designed for processing large data files with alphanumeric characters; the predominant programming language for business applications; stands for COmmon Business Oriented Language.

Figure 5.8

The Honor-Roll Program in COBOL

As you can see, COBOL commands are much closer to English sentences than either FORTRAN or assembly language. Created to process large data files such as those used in business (payroll and accounting, for example), COBOL is still the most common computer language in business programming.

```
IDENTIFICATION DIVISION.

PROGRAM-ID.               PROGRAM-SCORE.
AUTHOR.                   TOM LEE.
INSTALLATION.             ORISC.
DATE-WRITTEN.             JANUARY-12, 1990.

ENVIRONMENT DIVISION.

CONFIGURATION SECTION.
SOURCE-COMPUTER.   CYBER-174.
OBJECT-COMPUTER.   CYBER-174.
INPUT-OUTPUT SECTION.
FILE-CONTROL.
    SELECT RECORDS-IN ASSIGN TO SCORES, USE "RT=Z".
    SELECT PRINT-OUT ASSIGN TO OUTPUT.

DATA DIVISION.

FILE SECTION.
FD  RECORDS-IN
    LABEL RECORDS ARE OMITTED.
01  IN-RECORD             PIC X(72).
FD  PRINT-OUT
    LABEL RECORDS ARE OMITTED.
01  PRINT-LINE            PIC X(72).
WORKING-STORAGE SECTION.
77  STUDENT-COUNT         PIC 9(3)     VALUE ZEROES.
01  FLAG.
    05 END-OF-FILE-FLAG   PIC X        VALUE "N".
    05 NO-MORE-DATA       PIC X        VALUE "Y".
01  STUDENT-RECORD.
    05 NAME-RD            PIC X(20).
    05 GRADE-PT           PIC 9V99.
    05 FILLER             PIC X(49).
01  HDG.
    05 FILLER             PIC X(5)     VALUE SPACES.
    05 FILLER             PIC X(9)     VALUE "OAKRIVER ".
    05 FILLER             PIC X(11)    VALUE "UNIVERSITY ".
    05 FILLER             PIC X(17)    VALUE "HONOR ROLL REPORT".
    05 FILLER             PIC X(30)    VALUE SPACES.
01  HDG-1.
    05 FILLER             PIC X(10)    VALUE SPACES.
    05 FILLER             PIC X(15)    VALUE "THE HONOR ROLL ".
    05 FILLER             PIC X(8)     VALUE "STUDENTS".
    05 FILLER             PIC X(39)    VALUE SPACES.
01  HDG-2.
    05 FILLER             PIC X(5)     VALUE SPACES.
    05 FILLER             PIC X(12)    VALUE "STUDENT NAME".
    05 FILLER             PIC X(18)    VALUE SPACES.
    05 FILLER             PIC X(3)     VALUE "GPA".
    05 FILLER             PIC X(34)    VALUE SPACES.
01  HDG-3.
    05 FILLER             PIC X(72)    VALUE SPACES.
01  STUDENT-LINE.
    05 FILLER             PIC X(5)     VALUE SPACES.
    05 NAME-IN            PIC X(20).
    05 FILLER             PIC X(10)    VALUE SPACES.
    05 GRADE              PIC 9.99.
    05 FILLER             PIC X(33)    VALUE SPACES.
```

```
01   TOTAL-LINE.
     05 FILLER              PIC X(5)      VALUE SPACES.
     05 FILLER              PIC X(14)     VALUE "THE NUMBER OF ".
     05 FILLER              PIC X(11)     VALUE "HONOR ROLL ".
     05 FILLER              PIC X(12)     VALUE "STUDENTS IS:".
     05 STUDENT-NUMBER      PIC ZZ9.
     05 FILLER              PIC X(27)     VALUE SPACES.

PROCEDURE DIVISION.

MAIN-PROGRAM.
     PERFORM START-PROCESS.
     PEFORM DECISION-FOR-HONOR-ROLL
       UNTIL END-OF-FILE-FLAG = "Y".
     PERFORM WRAPITUP.
     STOP RUN.
START-PROCESS.
     OPEN INPUT RECORDS-IN OUTPUT PRINT-OUT.
     MOVE SPACES TO STUDENT-LINE.
     WRITE PRINT-LINE FROM HDG AFTER ADVANCING 2 LINES.
     WRITE PRINT-LINE FROM HDG-1 AFTER ADVANCING 2 LINES.
     WRITE PRINT-LINE FROM HDG-2 AFTER ADVANCING 2 LINES.
     WRITE PRINT-LINE FROM HDG-3 AFTER ADVANCING 1 LINE.
DECISION-FOR-HONOR-ROLL.
     READ RECORDS-IN INTO STUDENT-RECORD
       AT END MOVE NO-MORE-DATA TO END-OF-FILE-FLAG.
     MOVE NAME-RD TO NAME-LN.
     MOVE GRADE-PT TO GRADE.
     IF (GRADE-PT > 3.49)                                 IF THEN ELSE
       WRITE PRINT-LINE FROM STUDENT-LINE
       AFTER ADVANCING 1 LINE ADD 1 TO STUDENT-COUNT.
     MOVE STUDENT-COUNT TO STUDENT-NUMBER.
WRAPITUP.
     WRITE PRINT-LINE FROM TOTAL-LINE AFTER ADVANCING 3 LINES.
     CLOSE RECORDS-IN, PRINT-OUT.

RUN

      OAKRIVER UNIVERSITY HONOR ROLL REPORT

           THE HONOR ROLL STUDENTS

      STUDENT NAME               GPA

      MARY SMITH                 3.75
      TOM TOSHIBA                3.95
      SUSAN O'MALLEY             3.50
      MICHAEL RAMIREZ            3.65


THE NUMBER OF HONOR ROLL STUDENTS IS:  4
```

Source: Figure 15–7, "The honor roll problem in COBOL," from *Computer Information Systems* by Jerome S. Burstein and Edward G. Martin, p. 514–515, copyright © 1989 by The Dryden Press, a division of Holt, Rinehart and Winston, Inc. Reprinted by permission of the publisher.

COBOL does not handle complex mathematical calculations well, however, and its programs tend to be very wordy and lengthy. Figure 5.8 shows the honor-roll program in COBOL.

PL/1 · IBM created **PL/1** (which stands for Programming Language 1) in 1964 as a general-purpose programming language to support both business and scientific problem solving. PL/1 is very powerful but not widely used. Companies that had already invested heavily in COBOL and FORTRAN

PL/1

A programming language developed in 1964 by IBM for business and scientific applications; not as widely used as COBOL or FORTRAN.

software and programmers did not want to convert to another language. They were reluctant to spend millions of dollars rewriting software when software written in COBOL and FORTRAN was already solving problems well. It has also been difficult to teach PL/1 to programmers versed in COBOL.

BASIC
A programming language frequently used for teaching programming and for microcomputers; although it is easy to learn, it does not easily support sound programming practices.

BASIC · **BASIC** (which stands for Beginner's All-purpose Symbolic Instruction Code) was developed in 1964 to teach Dartmouth College students how to use computers. It has become an extremely popular programming language for microcomputers and for teaching programming in colleges and high schools. BASIC is easy to learn and has minimal memory requirements for conversion into machine code. Beginners with only a few hours of instruction can use the software to solve small problems. Figure 5.9 illustrates the honor-roll program in BASIC.

BASIC can handle many kinds of problems, although experts point out that it performs few tasks very well. BASIC also lacks strong structures for enforcing clear flow of logic and well-organized programs, so it is not conducive to teaching good programming practices.

Pascal
A programming language that consists of smaller subprograms, each of which is a structured program in itself; it is used on microcomputers and for teaching programming but has relatively few business applications.

Pascal · Named after Blaise Pascal, the seventeenth-century mathematician and philosopher, **Pascal** was developed by the Swiss computer science professor Niklaus Wirth of Zurich in the late 1960s. Wirth wanted to create a language that would teach students structured programming techniques. Pascal programs consist of smaller subprograms, each of which is a structured program in itself. Figure 5.10 illustrates the honor-roll program in Pascal.

Pascal programs can be used on microcomputers, but Pascal itself is used primarily in computer science courses to teach sound programming practices. Pascal has limited features for input and output, so it is not well suited for most business problems.

Ada
A programming language developed for the Department of Defense to be portable across diverse brands of hardware; it also has nonmilitary applications and can be used for business problems.

Ada · **Ada** was developed in 1980 to provide the U.S. Defense Department with a structured programming language to serve as the standard for all of its applications. In addition to military command and control systems, Ada is used in some nonmilitary government applications. The language is also useful for business problems: it can operate on microcomputers, is portable across different brands of computer hardware, and promotes structured program design. Ada also supports concurrent tasks and real-time programming.

Ada may be the only computer language named for a woman: Ada, Countess of Lovelace, daughter of the English poet Lord Byron. The Countess was an able nineteenth-century mathematician who developed the mathematical tables for an early calculating machine. For this reason she is sometimes called the first programmer.

An example of a nonmilitary application of Ada is the Stanfins-R (Standard Finance System Redesign) project. It involves a complete renovation of the Army's financial systems and is the largest information management system ever undertaken using Ada. Stanfins-R will automate functions, such as management of accounts payable, calculation of travel vouchers, and dispersal, that are currently done manually.

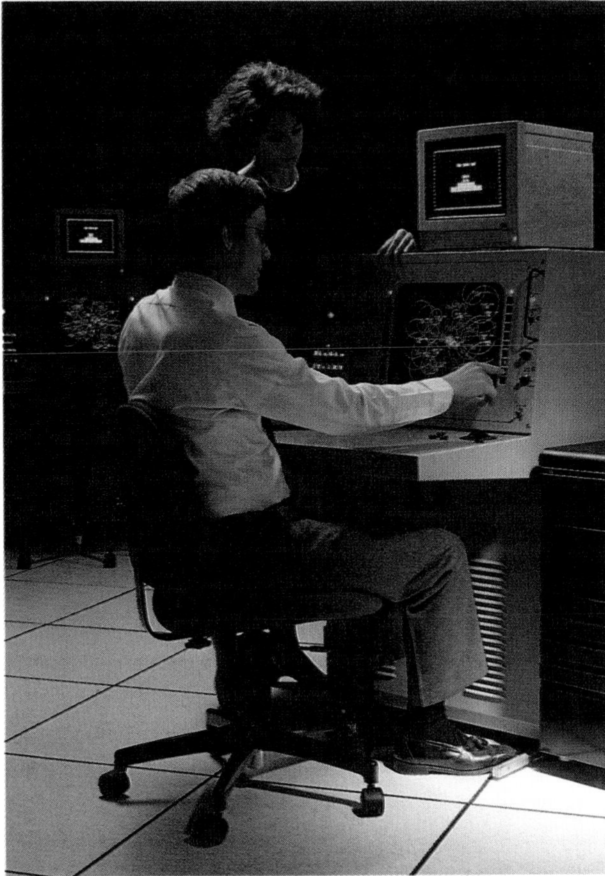

This real-time artificial intelligence trainer by IntelliSys, Inc. uses Harris Corporation's Night Hawk computer system. The simulation software is programmed in Ada using the Harris Ada Programming Support Environment (HAPSE).

Source: Courtesy of Harris Corporation.

Management information systems specialists have had some reservations about developing large-scale systems with Ada because it does not yet have a good compiler for IBM's mainframe MVS operating system. However, Ada has many attractive features. The language was initially conceived for weapons systems for which software is developed on a processor and then embedded in the weapon. It was explicitly designed so that it could be uniformly executed in diverse hardware environments. The language also promotes structured software design. According to Glenn Hughes, a former major with the Army's Ada Programming Office, Ada systems should be more cost-effective over the long term because they facilitate more clearly structured code than COBOL.[2]

Nevertheless, the question remains as to whether Ada will ever be widely applied to business problem solving. Many firms are not convinced that it is worth the investment and risk to abandon COBOL as the business standard. A large firm would have to retrain hundreds, even thousands, of COBOL programmers and scrap millions of dollars worth of COBOL software.

Figure 5.9

The Honor-Roll Program in BASIC

Here we see the BASIC instructions for performing the same task. BASIC is a popular language for microcomputers; it is similar to English and thus is easy to learn. However, it is not very good at performing sophisticated calculations or complex manipulations of data.

```
100 REM  HONOR PROGRAM
110 REM  This program prints NAMES and GPA for students
120 REM  whose GPA is 3.5 or higher. It also prints the
130 REM  total number of honor roll students printed on report.
140 REM  VARIABLES: N$ = Student Name  G = Grade Point Average
150 REM             S  = Total         I = Array counter
160 REM  * * * * * MAIN PROGRAM * * * * *
170 LET  S=0
180 OPEN  "i",1,"SCORES"
190 PRINT  "         Oakriver University Honor Roll Report"
200 PRINT
210 PRINT  "              The Honor Roll Students"
220 PRINT
230 PRINT  "         Student Name              GPA"
240 PRINT
250 FOR  I = 1 TO 10
260 IF  EOF(1)  THEN 320
270 INPUT  #1,N$,G
280 IF G>3.49 THEN 290 ELSE 310
290 PRINT USING "    \                    \          #.##";N$,G
300 LET S=S+1
310 NEXT  I
320 CLOSE #1
330 PRINT
340 PRINT
350 PRINT  "   The number of honor roll students is: ";S
360 END

RUN

    Oakriver University Honor Roll Report

         The Honor Roll Students

    Student Name                GPA

    Mary Smith                  3.75
    Tom Toshiba                 3.95
    Susan O'Malley              3.50
    Michael Ramirez             3.65


    The number of honor roll students is:  4
```

Source: Figure 15–5, "The honor roll problem in BASIC," from *Computer Information Systems* by Jerome S. Burstein and Edward G. Martin, p. 511, copyright © 1989 by The Dryden Press, a division of Holt, Rinehart and Winston, Inc. Reprinted by permission of the publisher.

C
A programming language with tight control and efficiency of execution like assembly language; it is portable across different microprocessors and easier to learn than assembly language.

C · Developed under the auspices of AT&T's Bell Laboratories in the early 1970s, **C** is the language in which most of the UNIX operating system is written. C has much of the tight control and efficiency of execution of assembly language, yet it is easier to learn and portable across different microprocessors. Figure 5.11 illustrates a sample C program that determines the smallest of two numbers supplied by the user.

Figure 5.10

Pascal: Programs within Programs

The Pascal language was developed to teach students the techniques of designing logical, easy-to-read programs. Each Pascal program contains subprograms written to follow consistent patterns of instructions. Today Pascal is rarely used in business because its input and output features are limited.

```
PROGRAM HONOR(INPUT/,OUTPUT,SCOREP);

(*  This program extracts the names of those students who *)
(*  have a grade-point average (GPA) greater than or equal *)
(*  to 3.50.  The name and GPA of each qualifying student, and *)
(*  the total number of the qualifying students is printed out. *)

TYPE
     STRING = ARRAY[1..20] OF CHAR;

VAR
     COUNT, I, J: INTEGER;
     GRADEPT: REAL;
     NAME: STRING;
     SCOREP: TEXT;
BEGIN (* START OF PROGRAM *)
     RESET(SCOREP);
     COUNT := 0;
     WRITELN('      Oakriver University Honor Roll Report');
     WRITELN;
     WRITELN('             The Honor Roll Students');
     WRITELN;
     WRITELN('      Student Name             GPA');
     WRITELN;
     WHILE NOT EOF (SCOREP) DO
        BEGIN
           FOR J := 1 TO 20 DO
              READ(SCOREP, NAME[J]);
           READLN(SCOREP, GRADEPT);
          +---------------------------------------+
          |IF GRADEPT > 3.49 THEN                 |
          |   BEGIN                               |
          |      COUNT := COUNT + 1;              |
          |      WRITE(' ':5);                    |
          |      FOR I := 1 TO 20 DO              |   IF THEN ELSE
          |         WRITE(NAME[I]);               |
          |      WRITELN(' ':10, GRADEPT :3:2);   |
          |   END;                                |
          +---------------------------------------+
           END;
     WRITELN;
     WRITELN;
     WRITELN('      The number of honor roll students is:', COUNT :3);
END.

RUN

           Oakriver University Honor Roll Report

                 The Honor Roll Students

           Student Name                   GPA

           Mary Smith                     3.75
           Tom Toshiba                    3.95
           Susan O'Malley                 3.50
           Michael Ramirez                3.65


           The number of honor roll students is:  4
```

Source: Figure 15–6, "The honor roll problem in Pascal," from *Computer Information Systems* by Jerome S. Burstein and Edward G. Martin, p. 512, copyright © 1989 by The Dryden Press, a division of Holt, Rinehart and Winston, Inc. Reprinted by permission of the publisher.

Figure 5.11

C: A Newer Version of Assembly Language

C is the programming language of the UNIX operating system. Like earlier assembly languages, it executes very efficiently, but it is easier to learn. It also has the advantage of operating with different microprocessors, which makes it more flexible than assembly languages.

```
/ *
  * M I N I M U M
  *
  * This program determines the lesser of two
  * numbers supplied by the user.
  */

main()
{
        int lesser;                 /* the result */
        int number1, number2;       /* the input values */

        /*
         * Prompt the user for two numbers and read them.
         */
        printf("Type the first number and press Enter: ");
        scanf("%d" &number1);
        printf("Type the second number and press Enter: ");
        scanf("%d", &number2);

        /*
         * Find the lesser value and report it.
         */
        if (number1 < number2)
               lesser = number1;
        else
               lesser = number2;
        printf("The lesser of %d and %d is %d.\n".
                  number1, number2, lesser);

        return (0);
}
```

Source: From *Learn C Now*, p. 96, reprinted by permission of Microsoft Press. Copyright © 1988 by Augie Hansen. All rights reserved.

Much commercial microcomputer software has been written in C, but experts believe this language will not dislodge COBOL for mainframe business applications. C will more likely be used for commercial microcomputer software and for solving scientific and technical problems.

Fourth-generation language
Programming languages that are less procedural than conventional languages (i.e., they need only specify what is to be done rather than provide the details of how to do it) and contain more English language–like commands; they are easier for nonspecialists to learn and use than conventional languages.

Fourth-Generation Languages

Fourth-generation languages offer two major advantages: they allow business specialists to develop software on their own with little or no technical assistance, and they offer dramatic productivity gains in software development.

Fourth-generation languages tend to be less procedural than conventional languages, making them more suitable for business specialists. Thus, these languages have created the technical platform for business specialists to play a larger role in problem solving with information systems. In addition, fourth-generation languages can be employed by less skilled programmers, a quality that helps improve productivity. Indeed, studies have shown that fourth-generation languages can produce productivity gains of 300 to 500 percent over conventional languages.[3]

There are several major types of fourth-generation software tools:

1. Query languages
2. Graphics languages
3. Report generators
4. Application generators
5. Very-high-level programming languages

Query languages are high-level, easy-to-use languages for accessing data stored in information systems. They are valuable for supporting ad-hoc requests for information that are not predefined (as opposed to routine, predefined requests). These are one-time requests for information that cannot be produced by existing applications or reporting software.

Query language
A high-level, easy-to-use, fourth-generation language for accessing stored data.

Query languages tend to be very end-user oriented, although some may have sophisticated capabilities for updating data as well. Some query languages have strong natural-language features, such as statements that use English-like words and syntax. An example of an ad-hoc query might be, "List all products with a unit price over $12.00." (Compare this with a similar request in COBOL.)

Figure 5.12 compares queries in two different kinds of query languages, Nomad2 and Intellect. Nomad2 is an application generator with a query language. An application generator is a software package that uses a high-level or fourth-generation language and/or graphical screen painting tools to quickly generate a software application. Intellect is a natural-language system that accepts English-like queries. Most query languages are highly interactive, allowing users to satisfy requests for information immediately on-line.

Graphics languages are specialized software for displaying computerized data in graphical form, for cases in which information can be assimilated more rapidly and trends spotted more easily than when data are presented numerically. Graphics software can retrieve stored data and display them in the graphic format requested by users. Some graphics languages can manipulate data and perform calculations as well. VP Graphix, Harvard Graphics, BPS Graphics, and GraphPlan are leading graphics packages for microcomputers.

Graphics language
A fourth-generation language for displaying computerized data in graphical form.

A popular mainframe graphics language, Statistical Analysis Software (SAS), is primarily a statistical analysis tool, but it also has easy-to-use graphics capabilities. It features English-like commands and menus that enable end-users to perform statistical operations, such as regression analysis and variance analysis, and to create reports. SAS has easy-to-use yet powerful color graphics features for charts, plots, maps, and three-dimensional displays. The graphs can be customized, and multiple displays can be presented on a single page.

Report generators are software tools that extract stored data to create customized reports that are not routinely produced by existing applications.

Report generator
A software tool that extracts stored data to create customized reports that are not routinely produced by existing applications.

Figure 5.12

Nomad2 and Intellect, Two Different Query Languages

Query languages are fourth-generation languages that make it easier than ever before to access stored data. They allow nonprogrammers to "ask" computers questions pertaining to stored information. The query in panel a uses Intellect and prints total sales in 1989 for four cities. The Nomad2 query in panel b lists total salary for each department in a firm.

(a) Natural-Language Query Using Intellect

RANK TOTAL COPIER SALES BY MARKET
PRINT THE RANKED TOTAL 1989 ACT YTD $
IN EACH MARKET OF ALL SALES DATA WITH PRODUCT
LINE = COPIER & PRODUCT = TOTAL & MARKET NOT
TOTAL & CHANNEL = TOTAL

MARKET	1989 ACTUAL YTD SALES
CHICAGO	$33,340,528
LOS ANGELES	$30,211,200
WASHINGTON	$20,295,200
NEW YORK	$18,848,800

(b) Query Using Nomad2

>LIST BY DEPT SUM (SALARY)
PAGE 1

DEPARTMENT	SUM CURRENT SALARY
MARKETING	66,700
PERSONNEL	54,900
SALES	77,300

Source: David H. Freedman, "Programming without Tears," *High Technology,* April 1986.

Application generator
Software that can generate entire information system applications without customized programming; the end-user specifies what needs to be done, and the generator creates the appropriate program code.

Very-high-level programming language
A programming language that produces program code with far fewer instructions than conventional languages; used primarily by professional programmers.

In contrast to query languages, report generators give users more control over the way data are formatted, organized, and displayed. For example, report generators such as RPG III have facilities for specifying report headings, subheadings, page headings, column positioning, page numbering, and totaling of numbers. Report generators may have on-line capabilities, but they typically run in a batch processing environment.

Application generators are related pieces of software that can generate entire information system applications without customized programming. The end-user need only specify *what* needs to be done, and the application generator will create the appropriate program code. The most versatile and powerful application generators integrate tools such as a query language, screen painter, graphics and report generators, modeling software, and a special programming language. Application generators typically are too complex for end-users to work with alone, but they require less technical assistance than conventional programming and can create entire applications more rapidly. Some features of application generators, such as the query language or graphics languages, can be employed directly by end-users.

Very-high-level programming languages are primarily tools for professional programmers, but they have some capabilities that can be employed by business specialists. These languages are distinguished by their productivity-promoting features, which produce program code with far fewer instructions than conventional languages such as COBOL or PL/1. APL, Nomad2, and ADS-Online by Computer Associates are examples of such very-high-level programming languages.

Selecting a Programming Language

To select the right software tool for problem solving, you must know the capabilities and limitations of the major programming languages (see Table 5.2 for a comparison of the various languages). The following are the most important considerations for selecting a programming language:

1. **The nature of the problem to be solved:** Is it a scientific problem, a business problem that requires mathematical modeling, or a problem that entails extensive file manipulation and input/output work?
2. **Computer hardware requirements:** Is the language compatible with your computer hardware resources? Is it essential that it be able to run on more than one kind of machine? Will it work on the operating system for your computer hardware (see Section 5.2)? Are there any limitations on memory size or computer resources? Do you need to use a microcomputer?
3. **Ease of use:** Is the language one that you can use, one that your technical staff is already familiar with, or one that can easily be learned?
4. **Maintainability:** Is it important that the language be highly structured? Can the language-support programs be modified and maintained by others over a long period of time?

5.4 Applications Software

A computer application is the use of a computer to solve a specific problem or to perform a specific task for a business specialist. Applications software is a major category of software that handles the processing for a particular computer application. There are myriad computer applications for which applications software has been written: business functions, such as accounts receivable or sales forecasting; scientific and engineering functions, such as molecular modeling or microprocessor design; law enforcement functions, such as computerized criminal-history record keeping; educational functions, such as computer-based mathematics instruction; artistic functions, such as the production of computer-generated music and art; and the transmission of data via telecommunications.

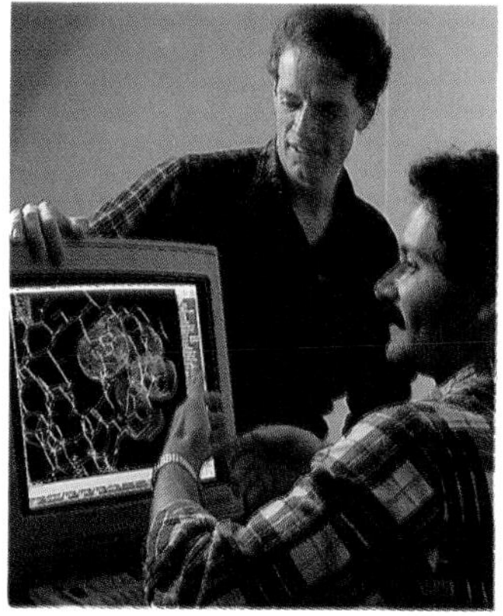

To facilitate drug design, Genentech scientists develop molecular models. The processing of commands and data that create these models is handled by applications software.

Source: Courtesy of Genentech, Inc.

Software Packages

Software packages are prewritten, precoded, commercially available programs that eliminate the need for writing software programs. Software packages are available for systems software, but the vast majority of software packages are **applications software packages.** The spreadsheet, database,

Applications software package
A prewritten, precoded, commercially available program that handles the processing for a particular computer application (e.g., spreadsheet or data management software for a personal computer).

Table 5.2

Comparison of the Major Programming Languages

Programming Language	Key Features	Appropriate Tasks
Assembly language	Machine dependent; highly efficient; symbolic; difficult to learn.	Systems software.
FORTRAN	Strong facilities for mathematical computations and formulas; poor input/output facilities.	Scientific and mathematical problems and business problems requiring complex formulas; modeling.
COBOL	Strong input/output and file manipulation facilities; weak facilities for mathematical computations.	Business problems requiring extensive reading and printing of records and file manipulation.
PL/1	Powerful, multipurpose language developed by IBM; complex and somewhat difficult to learn.	Both scientific and business problems.
BASIC	General-purpose language; easy to learn; runs on microcomputers; does not promote good program structure.	Problems that can be solved primarily with microcomputers; teaching programming.
Pascal	Used to teach structured programming; limited input/output capabilities.	Education; scientific problems that can be solved with microcomputers.
Ada	Developed by Defense Department for weapons systems and business applications; powerful; portable across different machine environments.	Weapons systems; business problems.
C	Highly efficient and portable across different computer machine environments; somewhat difficult to learn.	General-purpose problems, especially those that can be solved with microcomputers; development of systems software.
Fourth-generation languages	Query languages, report generators, application generators, graphics languages, very-high-level programming languages; largely nonprocedural with many "user-friendly" features.	Simple problems that can be solved primarily by nontechnical specialists.

and word processing software for your personal computer are all software packages. A mainframe-based payroll system that issues checks each week for 30,000 employees and the checking and savings account processing system of a bank also typically use software packages.

The following is a list of areas for which commercial applications software packages are available. Some of these applications are solely mainframe or microcomputer based, but many have packages available in mainframe, minicomputer, and microcomputer versions.

- Accounts payable
- Accounts receivable
- Arithmetic drill
- Automobile rentals
- Cash-flow analysis
- Check processing
- Client management
- Client write-up
- Desktop publishing
- Econometric modeling
- Equal Employment Opportunity reporting and compliance
- General ledger
- Hotel reservations
- Human resources
- Life insurance
- Mailing labels
- Management of personal finances
- Manufacturing resources planning
- Modeling
- Mortgage account calculation
- Payroll
- Pension calculations
- Presentation graphics
- Process control
- Property management
- Purchasing
- Statistical analysis
- Tax planning
- Tax preparation
- Videotape rental tracking
- Word processing

Popular Microcomputer Applications Packages

Some of the most popular pieces of applications software are the general-purpose applications packages that have been developed for microcomputers. Word processing, spreadsheet, data management, graphics, and desktop-publishing software have been widely adopted for business and other kinds of problem solving.

Word Processing Software · **Word processing software** has dramatically enhanced the productivity of clerical workers, managers, and knowledge workers by automating the creation, editing, and printing of documents. Text data are stored electronically rather than typed on paper. The word processing software allows changes to be made in the document electronically in memory so that it does not have to be typed again. Changes in line spacing, margins, character size, and column widths can be made with formatting options in the software. WordPerfect, Microsoft Word, WordStar, and MultiMate are examples of popular word processing packages.

Word processing software
Software that handles such applications as electronic editing, formatting, and printing of documents.

Most word processing software has advanced features that automate other aspects of the writing process. Spelling checkers utilize built-in dictionaries to locate and correct spelling errors. Style checkers analyze grammar and punctuation errors and may even suggest ways to improve writing style. The thesaurus program provides on-line lists of synonyms and antonyms. Mail merge programs link letters or other text documents with names and addresses in a mailing list.

Spreadsheet software
Software that provides the user with financial modeling tools; data are displayed on a grid and numerical data can easily be recalculated to permit the evaluation of several alternatives.

Spreadsheets · Electronic **spreadsheet software** provides computerized versions of traditional financial modeling tools—the accountant's columnar pad, pencil, and calculator. A spreadsheet is organized into a grid of columns and rows. The intersection of a column and row, which is called a cell, can store a number, formula, word, or phrase.

Spreadsheets are valuable for solving business problems in which numerous calculations with pieces of data must be related to each other. After a set of mathematical relationships has been constructed, the spreadsheet can be recalculated immediately using a different set of assumptions.

Spreadsheet software readily lends itself to modeling and "what if" analysis. A number of alternatives can easily be evaluated by changing one or two pieces of data without having to rekey in the rest of the worksheet. Figure 5.13 illustrates how spreadsheet software could be used to answer the question "what if sales revenue increased 10 percent each year over a five-year period?" Many spreadsheet packages include graphics functions that can present data in the form of line graphs, bar graphs, or pie charts. The most popular spreadsheet package is Lotus® 1-2-3®. Other leading spreadsheet packages are VP-Planner Plus, Quattro, Multiplan, and SuperCalc.

Data management software
Software that is used for such applications as creating and manipulating lists, creating files and databases to store data, and combining information for reports.

Data Management Software · Although spreadsheet programs are good at manipulating quantitative data, they are poor at storing and manipulating lists or at extracting parts of files from larger sets of data. **Data management software,** on the other hand, is weak at manipulating quantitative data but is very good at creating and manipulating lists and at combining information from different files for problem solving. It has programming features and easy-to-learn menus that enable nonspecialists to build small information systems.

Figure 5.13

Spreadsheet Software—An Important Business Tool

Spreadsheets have become very popular in business because they can perform "what if?" analysis. The top work sheet displays the results of asking the software to determine sales revenues over a five-year period if sales increased 10 percent each year. The bottom work sheet shows the formulas and data relationships that were entered to ask this question.

Breakdown of Sales by Region

SALES REGION	1990	1991	1992	1993	1994
Northeast	$2,304,000	$2,534,400	$2,787,840	$3,066,624	$3,373,286
South	$1,509,300	$1,660,230	$1,826,253	$2,008,878	$2,209,766
Midwest	$3,309,800	$3,640,780	$4,004,858	$4,405,344	$4,845,878
West	$2,667,000	$2,933,700	$3,227,070	$3,549,777	$3,904,755

% Annual Growth 10%

Breakdown of Sales by Region

SALES REGION	1990	1991	1992	1993	1994
Northeast	$2,304,000	+C23*(1+$C$11)	+D23*(1+$C$11)	+E23*(1+$C$11)	+F23*(1+$C$11)
South	$1,509,300	+C24*(1+$C$11)	+D24*(1+$C$11)	+E24*(1+$C$11)	+F24*(1+$C$11)
Midwest	$3,309,800	+C25*(1+$C$11)	+D25*(1+$C$11)	+E25*(1+$C$11)	+F25*(1+$C$11)
West	$2,667,000	+C26*(1+$C$11)	+D26*(1+$C$11)	+E26*(1+$C$11)	+F26*(1+$C$11)

% Annual Growth 10%

Data management software typically has facilities for creating files and databases (discussed in Chapter 6), storing data, modifying data, and manipulating data for reports and queries. Data management software and database management systems are treated in detail in Chapter 6. Popular database management software for the personal computer includes dBASE IV, Paradox, RBase, and Foxbase.

Integrated Packages · Problem solving often requires a combination of software skills—some writing, some quantitative analysis, and some record management. To produce a polished sales forecast report using unintegrated word processing and spreadsheet programs, one would have to develop a sales forecasting spreadsheet and then reformat that spreadsheet as a report by separately keying the data into both programs. **Integrated software packages** eliminate the redundant work by performing such tasks without having to switch from one program to the other. The spreadsheet data could be reworked in word processing mode by merely pressing a few keys on the keyboard.

Integrated software package
A software package that provides two or more applications, such as spreadsheets and word processing, allowing for easy transfer of data between them.

Integrated packages typically combine the most common kinds of personal computer applications software—spreadsheet, database, and word processing. Some have recently added data communications, graphics, and project management functions. Popular integrated packages include Symphony, Framework, Enable, Microsoft WORKS, and the Smart System.

Businesses are not the only organizations that require software that perform a variety of tasks. The Focus on Problem Solving describes some of the problems the Maine Department of Education faced when it was asked to produce a "report card" on Maine schools.

5.5 Leading-Edge Application: Maps that Can Read People's Minds

Instead of hanging on walls or cluttering automobile glove compartments, the maps of the 1990s are produced by computers using **geographic information systems.** Geographic information software uses vast amounts of data, such as the number and location of houses on a block, power lines, waterways, mineral deposits, crops, and even the occupation and income of an area's residents. Any combination of data, such as the relationship between waterways and iron mines, can be displayed graphically with the touch of a few keys.

Geographic information systems
Software used in producing maps or performing geographic modeling; such systems may be two dimensional or three dimensional.

The most advanced geographic information systems are three dimensional. A two-dimensional geographic information system can overlay layers of information for analysis and thematic maps. But a three-dimensional geographic information system allows scientists and geologists to chart underwater data, monitor the flight of birds, or generate perspective views of the surrounding environment before a tree is felled in a national forest or a tall building is added to a downtown skyline.

Three-dimensional capabilities are essential for solving such problems as predicting cross-country movement of military vehicles or predicting the

FOCUS ON Problem Solving

A Promise Fulfilled

Desktop publishing may not help balance the budget or lower taxes, but it did help Governor John R. McKernan, Jr., of Maine keep his campaign promise to give the voters more and better information on the status of their public schools. In his inaugural address, McKernan called for a "report card" on Maine schools. When he made the promise, however, the governor did not realize that he would have to overcome serious technical barriers to achieve it.

The task of developing a report card for each of the nearly 300 school administrative units fell to Maine's Commissioner of Education, Eve M. Blithes. She created a task force of about 20 people, which met monthly for most of a school year.

The group faced several problems. Not only would the report have to be completed two weeks after the data had been accumulated, but the report would also have to convert dry, sometimes unpalatable data into fare for mass consumption. "We had a diverse readership for the report card, technical educators and administrators, as well as the public with interest in the school budget," said the director of management information. "It had to be self-explanatory, avoiding overly technical statistics, while still addressing the audiences without compromising the quality of the information. We knew that to communicate to the man on the street, we had to do it graphically."

Using Aldus Pagemaker desktop-publishing software and Full Impact presentation graphics software, the group was able to complete the *Report Card for Maine Schools* on schedule. The report had an immediate impact and was widely discussed. Furthermore, the Department of Education was able to increase public awareness of the schools by producing new versions of the report, changing the format and presentation of data. Without desktop publishing, the report would not have been possible.

Source: Clay Andres, "A Promise Fulfilled: Maine's Department of Education Uses Automated Report Generation to Keep a Campaign Promise," *ITC Desktop,* 5, November–December 1989, pp. 38–42.

effects of rainfall runoff, when the results are affected by the slope of the surface and quality of the terrain. Such systems can handle problems that require a solid model for their solution.

Two-dimensional geographic information software represents spatial data as x, y coordinates. To view geographic data three dimensionally, a z coordinate must be implemented within a vector data structure. Developers of geographic information software have been experimenting with several data models for doing this. Three-dimensional models, in turn, must be integrated with three-dimensional graphics. To date, only a handful of geographic information systems actually have true three-dimensional characteristics.

A true three-dimensional geographic information system should be able to store data about the three-dimensional structure of, for example, a vast network of pipes, tunnels, and sewers under a city's streets. It should be able to respond analytically to questions such as "How can I run a pipe from this corner over to that building without intersecting all the other pipes, tunnels, and sewers?" To address such problems, commercial vendors

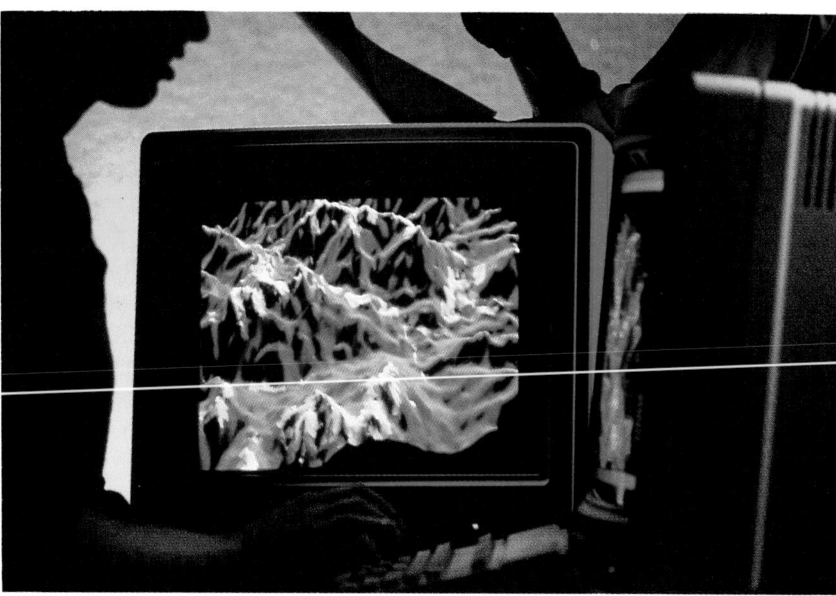

Displaying information is a key element in understanding it. Using Hewlett Packard's three dimensional modeling software, Northwest Digital Research developed a computer program that uses satellite data to make accurate topographical models of remote locations. These models are useful in exploration and development of natural resources.

Source: Courtesy of Hewlett-Packard Company.

are busy refining their software to handle three-dimensional computations and producing computer hardware with more levels of color display capability.

True three-dimensional geographic information systems hold great promise for both the military and business worlds. For the military, the location of mobile targets may change in minutes, hours, or days. Moreover, the Army, Navy and Air Force have different requirements for the same piece of information. The Navy will look at a land target from a slant angle, the Army will view it from the top of a ridge, and the Air Force will look down on it from several miles up in the air.

Even now, companies using geographic information systems claim they have gained a strategic edge.[4] Like all maps, geographic information systems present data in a form that can be absorbed more easily and intuitively than by reviewing and analyzing many reports. For example, the Federal Express Corporation plans to use up-to-the-minute digitized maps to dispatch its vans. General Motors Corporation uses color computerized maps to determine if dealers are maintaining their market share. With such data General Motors can plot the best location for its dealerships.

Unfortunately, geographic information software, like other types of software, may sometimes fall prey to what one commentator has called the "vaporware epidemic" of the computer industry—the tendency to announce new software long before it is ready to market (and sometimes before the company knows for sure that it can deliver the software). As the Focus on Technology explains, months and even years may pass before announced software appears.

FOCUS ON *Technology*

Stewart Alsop's All-Time Vaporware List

The vapors were a Victorian malady, but times change. Today, the computer industry has succumbed to a vaporware epidemic, leaving innocent consumers out in the cold.

Some companies in the personal computer industry had a habit of announcing products before they were sure they could finish building them. Companies engaged in this activity for one of two reasons. Either they wanted to judge potential consumer interest in the product before spending too much money on development, or they needed money to develop the product. If they were looking for funding, they wanted potential customers to pay in advance, or they wanted to show how much demand existed for the product so that venture capitalists would invest.

One of the reasons this vaporware list is published is that there is no good reason to announce products in advance of delivery, particularly when a company does not know if it can finish the job. Customers should not be burdened with the task of figuring out when—or whether—a product will be finished. The customer's only job should be to decide whether a product fits his or her needs, not to evaluate the reality of a company's delivery schedule. It not only hurts customers when products are preannounced, but it also usually hurts the companies that do the preannouncing.

The All-Time Vaporware List

Product	Company	Announced	Promised	Shipped	Vaportime*
Ovation	Ovation	October 1983	June 1984	Never	48
Magneto-Optical Disk	Verbatim/Kodak	July 1985	December 1987	—	27
Crosstalk Mk.4	Microstuf	April 1985	June 1985	May 1987	25
Windows	Microsoft	November 1983	September 1984	November 1985	24
Visi O	VisiCorp	November 1982	June 1983	November 1983	12
Atari PC	Atari	January 1987	April 1987	—	9
OS/2 version 1.1	IBM	April 1987	October 1988	—	6
OS/2 Extended Edition	IBM	April 1987	July 1988	—	6

*In months, as of October, 1987.

Source: Stewart Alsop, "Stewart Alsop's All-Time Vaporware List," *PC World,* January 1988, pp. 181–182. Reprinted with permission.

Summary

- There are two major types of software: systems software and applications software. Systems software consists of generalized programs to manage computer resources and mediate between applications software and computer hardware. Applications software consists of programs designed for applying the computer to solve a specific problem such as a business problem.

- There have been four generations of software development: (1) machine language; (2) symbolic languages such as assembly language; (3) high-level languages such as FORTRAN and COBOL; and (4) fourth-generation languages, which are less procedural and closer to natural language than earlier generations of software.

- The operating system acts as the chief manager of the computer system, allocating, scheduling, and assigning system resources and monitoring the use of the computer.

- Multiprogramming, multitasking, multiprocessing, virtual storage, and time-sharing enable operating system resources to be used more efficiently so that the computer can attack many problems at the same time.

- Multiprogramming (multitasking in microcomputer environments) allows multiple programs to use the computer's resources concurrently.

- Multiprocessing is the use of two or more CPUs linked together, working in tandem to perform a task.

- Time-sharing enables many users to share computer resources simultaneously by allocating each user a tiny slice of computing time.

- Virtual storage splits up programs into pages or segments so that primary storage can be utilized more efficiently.

- To be executed by the computer, a software program must be translated into machine language via special language translation software—a compiler, an assembler, or an interpreter.

- The leading microcomputer operating systems are DOS, OS/2, UNIX, and Multifinder. These operating systems can be classified according to whether they support multitasking and multiple users and whether they are command driven or use a graphical user interface.

- The most popular programming languages are assembly language, FORTRAN, COBOL, BASIC, PL/1, Pascal, C, and Ada. Each has been designed to solve a special class of problems.

- Fourth-generation languages are more nonprocedural than earlier programming languages and include query software, report generators, graphics software, application generators, and other tools that dramatically reduce programming time and make some software tasks easy enough to be performed by nontechnical specialists.

- Software packages are prewritten, precoded, commercially available programs that eliminate the need for writing software programs. The most popular software packages for microcomputers are productivity aids such as word processing software, spreadsheet software, data management software, and integrated software packages.

Key Terms

Program
Stored-program concept
Systems software
Applications software
Machine language
High-level language
Assembly language
Assembler
Operating system
Multiprogramming
Multitasking
Multiprocessing
Time-sharing
Virtual storage
Source code
Object code
Compiler
Interpreter
DOS
OS/2
UNIX
Graphical user interface
FORTRAN
COBOL
PL/1
BASIC
Pascal
Ada
C
Fourth-generation language
Query language
Graphics language
Report generator
Application generator
Very-high-level programming language
Applications software package
Word processing software
Spreadsheet software
Data management software
Integrated software package
Geographic information systems

Review Questions

1. Why do we need software to use computers?
2. What are the major types of software? How can they be distinguished?
3. What are the major software generations? When were they developed? Describe the characteristics of each generation.
4. Define an operating system. What functions does it perform?
5. How do a compiler, an assembler, and an interpreter differ?
6. Define multiprogramming, multitasking, time-sharing, multiprocessing, and virtual storage.
7. Name the leading microcomputer operating systems. How can they be distinguished?
8. What is a graphical user interface?
9. Name and describe four popular high-level programming languages.
10. What is a fourth-generation language? Give examples of fourth-generation software tools.

11. What is an applications software package? Name and describe the four major kinds of software packages used with microcomputers.

Discussion Questions

1. Why is the operating system considered the chief manager of a computer system?

2. Software will continue to become more user friendly. Discuss.

Problem-Solving Exercises

1. David Ashton is the superintendent of schools for the Herron Lake School District. His staff consists of a business manager, who performs all of the accounting for the district and manages the budget; a manager of pupil and personnel services, who maintains enrollment and test score data; and two secretaries. The secretaries are in charge of the superintendent's appointments and correspondence with district staff and parents. The District Office has one terminal connected to a countywide computer system that maintains student enrollment data and prints mailing labels. Otherwise, all work is performed with calculators, electric typewriters, or pen and pencil. Write a memo describing how the leading microcomputer software packages could help the superintendent and his staff. Identify applications that should be computerized and the type of software most suitable for each. What software selection criteria should be considered?

2. Using computing magazine articles, write an analysis comparing DOS and OS/2 operating systems for IBM microcomputers.

Notes

1. Daniel Lalonde and A. Duane Donnelly, "Voice Technology Speaks for Itself," *Computerworld,* May 16, 1988.
2. Michael Puttre with Jeffry Oppenheim, "Army Rearms with ADA," *Information Week,* February 27, 1989.
3. Jesse Green, "Productivity in the Fourth Generation," *Journal of Management Information Systems* 1 (Winter 1984–85).
4. Laura Lang, "GIS Goes 3D," *Computer Graphics World,* March 1989; Mimi Bluestone and Evert Clark, "These Maps Can Almost Read People's Minds," *Business Week,* May 11, 1987.

Problem-Solving Case

UNIX Solves Publishing Problems at Kaiser Electronics

Kaiser Electronics of San Jose, California, holds government and military contracts to manufacture display systems for aircraft and spacecraft, including the NASA space shuttle. Its publications must conform to military specifications, and demand for presentation graphics and literature for sales, overhead graphics, and ads is very high. Kaiser produces between 50,000 and 100,000 pages of documentation a year.

Kaiser has a technical support group to support its word processing, graphics, and publishing software and to maintain its stored data. The group works without programmers or technical specialists from Kaiser's management information systems department. Faced with an outmoded word processing system, the group had to devise a plan for meeting Kaiser's needs for marketing graphics, data management, and product support.

The solution required a system that would improve the quality of presentations, accommodate a huge volume of word processing, and provide room for future growth. The technical support group evaluated stand-alone publishing systems and personal computers and eventually selected a UNIX-based system. The system runs on two AT&T 3B1 and one 3B2/400 computers, supporting between 30 and 40 clerical and administrative people.

One 3B1 system is used for typesetting, overhead slides, and other presentation material; the second keeps maintenance records; and the 3B2/400 machine provides product support. Once a process has been analyzed, reports can be easily created using a boilerplate menu. Popular business productivity software—spreadsheets, word processors, and data management software—is also utilized. Kaiser uses 20/20, Multiplan, Crystal Writer, File-it, Informix, and UNIX tools. UNIX facilitates conversions from one application to another.

As a long-term goal, Al Montoya, the principal writer for the technical support group, envisions a distributed electronic publishing system. A person will be able to retrieve a manual stored electronically on a workstation and print any number of copies. The only barrier at this time is cost.

Source: Irene Fuerst, "Solving a Publishing Problem," *UNIX Today!*, December 12, 1988.

Case Study Questions

1. What were the business problems that had to be addressed by the Kaiser Electronics technical support group?
2. What kinds of solutions were available for this problem?
3. Were there any constraints on the software options for this firm?
4. Was the UNIX operating system an appropriate choice for the solution?

CHAPTER · SIX

Organizing Information: Files and Databases

Chapter Outline

6.1 Introduction
- Why Are File Organization and Management Important?
- Data Organization Terms and Concepts

6.2 The Traditional File Environment
- Sequential File Access Methods
- Random File Access Methods
- Problems with the Traditional File Environment

6.3 The Database Vision
- Logical versus Physical Views of Data
- Components of a Database Management System
- Advantages of Database Management Systems
- The Three Database Models

6.4 Applying Database Concepts to Problem Solving
- Designing Database Solutions
- Choosing a Traditional File Access Method or a Database Approach

6.5 Distributing Information: Distributed and On-Line Databases
- Distributed Databases
- On-Line Databases and Information Services

6.6 Leading-Edge Application: HyperCard

Learning Objectives

After reading and studying this chapter, you will:

1. Understand how the usefulness of information is affected by file organization.
2. Be familiar with traditional file organization methods.
3. Know how to overcome the limitations of a traditional file environment by using a database approach.
4. Be able to describe the components of a database management system.
5. Be familiar with the three database models.
6. Know how to design a simple database.
7. Know how distributed databases and on-line information services are used.

Cracking the Welfare Data Shell

Researchers have long been studying how people move on and off welfare and looking for ways to make the welfare program more efficient. But, since 1983, data that could show connections between marriage rates, welfare, and other government-funded programs sat largely untouched in a U.S. Census Bureau computer. Most researchers were aware the data existed but had no way to access or analyze them.

This situation has changed, thanks to Alice Robbin and Martin David, two scientists at the University of Wisconsin's Institute for Research on Poverty. As part of a U.S. Census Bureau study called the Survey of Income and Program Participation (SIPP), they developed a prototype system to improve the storage, access, and retrieval of data in the government's antiquated data processing systems.

The prototype system, called SIPP Access, was explicitly designed to tackle massive pools of data. A 1984 study alone contained nearly 7 million units of analysis and 20,000 data elements on details such as a respondent's employment, education, fertility, health, household composition, and government program participation. The information was stored on more than 30 tapes, totaling about 2.2 gigabytes, in nine separate hierarchical files. An additional 300 megabytes are entered into the statistical database every four months.

Robbin and David made the data more manageable by restructuring them into a relational database management system using a VAX computer from Digital Equipment Corporation and microcomputer versions of Oracle and Ingres database software. This new method of organization reduced storage requirements for the data by 75 percent without losing any information. The original 20,000 data elements were restructured into 8,000. SIPP Access also utilizes three telecommunications networks to make the data available to researchers across the country and an optical archive storage disk for the massive amounts of data.

Retrieval of the data has become extremely rapid since the researchers found a way to organize the data. The relational database organization format has drastically reduced research time. Harlene Gogan, a research demographer at the Research Triangle Institute, who formerly spent two to three years organizing her research data, can now do the same work in six months. Statistics that formerly took six months to two years to find can now be located in a couple of hours to a few days.

Source: Sharon Baker, "University Scientists Crack High-Tech Welfare Data Shell," *Computerworld,* May 22, 1989.

The usefulness of information depends a great deal on how it is stored, organized, and accessed. One cannot solve problems unless the requisite information is easily available in the right form. Consequently, an understanding of files and databases is crucial for deploying information systems effectively in business.

6.1 Introduction

Information systems cannot provide solutions unless their data are accurate, timely, and easily accessible. Various file organization and management techniques have been developed to achieve these objectives. Each of these techniques works best with a different class of problems.

Why Are File Organization and Management Important to Problem Solving?

In all information systems, data must be organized and structured so that they can be utilized effectively. But unless information can be easily processed and accessed, the system cannot achieve its purpose. Due to disorganized methods of storing and retrieving information, many firms with excellent hardware and software cannot deliver timely and precise information. Poor file organization prevents some firms from accessing much of the information they maintain.

Imagine how difficult it would be to write a term paper with your notes on 3-by-5-inch index cards if the cards were in random order. No matter how neatly they were stacked and stored, you would have no way of organizing the term paper. Of course, with enough time, you might be able to arrange the cards in some order. But often imposing an organization scheme after the fact, or modifying it to accommodate a change of viewpoint in your paper, will cause you to miss your deadline. Thus the role of file organization and management cannot be underestimated.

Data Organization Terms and Concepts

Data are structured in information systems in a manner that keeps track of discrete data elements and related groupings of information. The data are organized in a hierarchy that starts with bits and bytes and progresses to fields, records, files, and databases (see Figure 6.1).

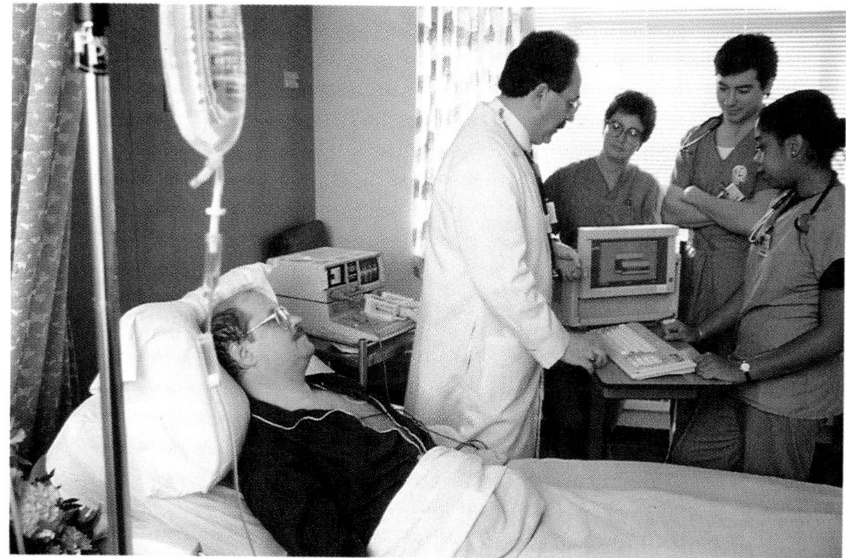

A Compaq Portable III computer helps cardiologist Jeffrey M. Zaks, M.D., diagnose patients, design treatments, prescribe drugs, and teach medicine. Records of Dr. Zaks' more than 3,000 patients include patient name and address, medical problems, allergies, and prescribed medications.

Source: Courtesy of Compaq Computer Corporation.

Figure 6.1

The Data Hierarchy

In an information system, pieces of data are organized into a hierarchy. The smallest piece of data that computers can handle is the bit (the 1s and 0s of binary representation). Next is the byte, a group of bits that forms a character such as a letter, number, or punctuation mark. A field is a group of characters that forms a word, a group of words, or a number. A record is a collection of related fields; a file is a collection of related records. The largest element in the hierarchy, a database, consists of related files.

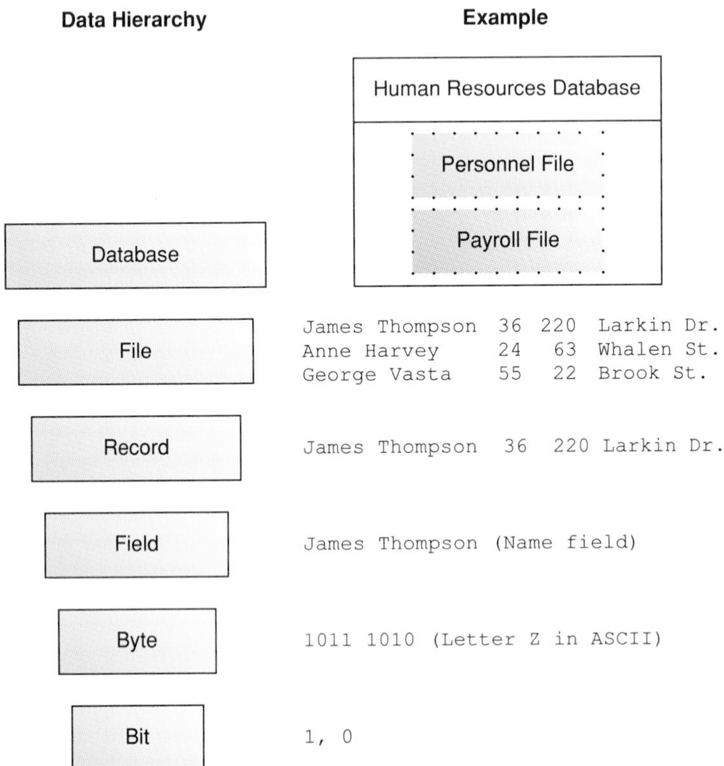

Field
A grouping of characters into a word, a group of words, or a complete number.

Record
A grouping of related data fields, such as a person's name, age, and address.

File
A group of related records.

Database
A group of related files; more specifically, a collection of data organized so they can be accessed and utilized by many different applications.

Entity
A person, place, or thing on which information is maintained.

A bit, as we have seen, represents the smallest piece of data the computer can handle. A byte is a group of bits that represents a single character, which can be a letter, number, or other symbol. A grouping of characters into a word, group of words, or complete number, such as a person's name or age, is called a **field.** A collection of related data fields, such as a person's name, age, and address, is called a **record.** A group of related records is called a **file.** For example, we could collect all of the records described in Figure 6.1 into a personnel file. Related files, in turn, can be grouped into a **database.** For example, our personnel file could be grouped with a payroll information file into a human resources database.

Entities and Attributes · An **entity** is a person, place, or thing on which information is maintained. For example, employee is a typical entity in a personnel file, which maintains information on people employed by the firm. Each characteristic or quality describing a particular entity is called an

Figure 6.2

A Sample Record Containing Data about the Entity "Employee"

A personnel record with information about employees contains separate fields for attributes such as last name, first name, and so on. Social Security number is the key field because each employee has a unique Social Security number that can be used to identify that employee.

Entity = "Employee"

SSN Field	Last Name Field	First Name Field	Birth Date Field	Address Field
444367890	Johnson	Maureen	01/02/60	12 Valley Road, Croton, NY 10520
113467098	Kanter	Steven	11/04/44	33 Hillsdale Dr., Peekskill, NY 10566
224569801	Minton	Helen	08/04/57	46 Wood Road, Bedford, NY 10593
576018935	Thomas	George	04/04/59	11 Avery Drive, Croton, NY 10520

Key Field

Attributes

attribute. For example, name, address, or number of dependents would each be an attribute of the entity employee. Attributes correspond to data fields on a record about a particular category of information. Thus, a record can be considered a collection of attributes about a particular entity.

Key Fields · Every record in a file or database must contain at least one field that uniquely identifies that record so that it can be retrieved (accessed), updated, or sorted. This identifier field is called a **key field.** An example of a key field would be an employee number or Social Security number for a personnel file or a product number for an inventory file. In the sample personnel record in Figure 6.2, which contains information about the entity employee, the Social Security number is the key field for the record, since each employee has a unique Social Security number.

Attribute
A characteristic or quality of a particular entity.

Key field
A field in a record that uniquely identifies that record so that it can be retrieved, updated, or sorted.

Traditional file environment
The storage of data so that each application has its own separate data file or files and software programs.

Sequential file organization
A way of storing data records so that they must be retrieved in the physical order in which they are stored; the only file organization method that can be used with magnetic tape.

Random file organization
A way of storing data records so that they can be accessed in any sequence, regardless of their physical order; used with magnetic disk technology.

6.2 The Traditional File Environment

The way data are organized on storage media determines how easily they can be accessed and utilized. In Chapter 4 we discussed the difference between sequential-access storage devices, such as magnetic tape, and direct-access storage devices (DASDs), such as magnetic disk. In a **traditional file environment,** data records are physically organized on storage devices using either sequential file organization or random (or direct) file organization.

Sequential File Access Methods

In **sequential file organization,** data records must be retrieved in the same physical sequence in which they are stored. In **random** (or direct) **file or-**

Indexed sequential-access method (ISAM)
A way of storing records sequentially on a direct-access storage device that also allows individual records to be accessed in any desired order using an index of key fields.

ganization, data records can be accessed in any sequence, independent of their physical order. Sequential file organization is the only file organization method that can be used with magnetic tape. Random file organization is utilized with magnetic disk technology.

Sequential files are becoming outmoded, but they are still used for older batch processing applications, which access and process each record in sequential order. The classic example is a payroll system; the system must process all of the employees in a firm one by one and issue each a check. Most applications today, however, including those based on microcomputers, rely on some form of random file organization method.

Figure 6.3 compares sequential file access with the **indexed sequential-access method (ISAM),** which stores records sequentially on a DASD but

Figure 6.3

Two Methods of Organizing Data

The sequential file access method (panel a) retrieves records in the same sequence in which they are physically stored. It is useful for batch processing, in which records on a file are processed one after the other in sequential order, and is the only access method for magnetic tape storage. In the indexed sequential-access method (ISAM) (panel b), records are also stored sequentially but can be accessed directly by using an index. The index lists every record by its unique key field and gives its storage location. With ISAM, records are stored on a direct access storage device (DASD) such as a disk.

(a) Sequential File Access Method

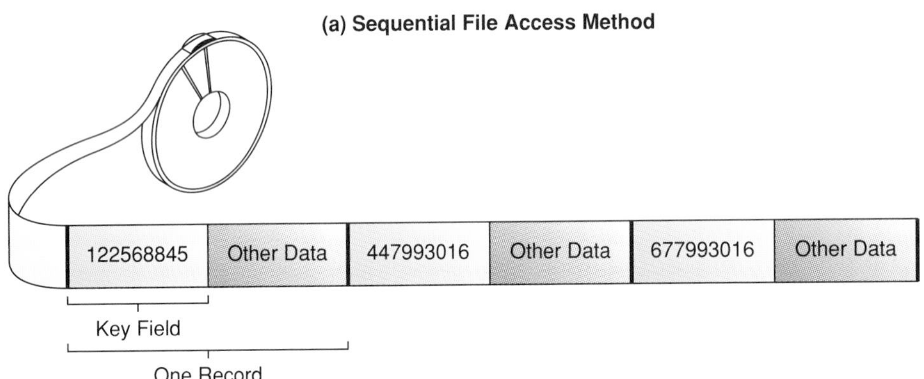

(b) Indexed Sequential Access Method (ISAM)

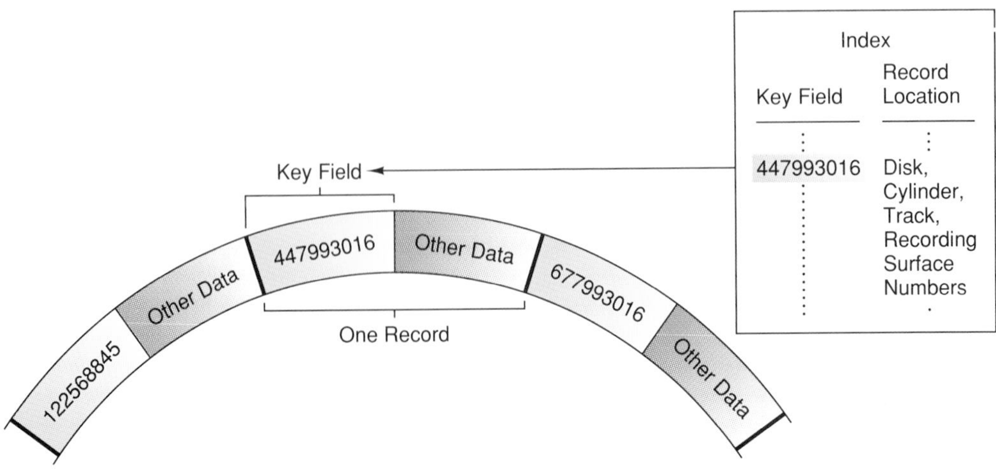

also allows individual records to be accessed in any desired order using an **index** of key fields. Like the index for a book, the index for a file consists of a listing of record keys and their associated storage location. The index shows the actual physical location on disk of each record that can be referenced with its key field. Any specific record can be located directly by checking the index for its storage address. ISAM is most useful for applications requiring sequential processing of large numbers of records in batch mode but with occasional direct access of individual records.

Index
A list, for a file or database, of the key field of each record and its associated storage location.

Random File Access Methods

Random, or direct, file organization also uses a key field to locate the physical address of a record but accomplishes this without an index. This access method uses a mathematical formula called a randomizing algorithm (also called a transform or hashing algorithm) to translate the key field directly into the record's physical storage location on disk. The algorithm performs some mathematical computation on the record key, and the result of that calculation is the record's physical address. For example, in Figure 6.4 the randomizing algorithm divides the record's key field number (4467) by the prime number closest to the total number of records in the file (997). The remainder designates the address on disk for that particular record.

This access method is most appropriate for applications requiring individual records to be located directly and rapidly for immediate on-line processing. Only a few records in the file need to be retrieved, and the records are selected randomly, in no particular sequence. An example might be an on-line order processing application.

Problems with the Traditional File Environment

All of these methods of file organization are associated with individual files and individual software programs. But what if the information required to solve a particular problem is located in more than one file? Often extra

Figure 6.4

Direct File Access Methods Direct file access methods let users access individual records more quickly than either the sequential or indexed sequential methods. Direct file access involves a mathematical operation called a randomizing algorithm. In this example the algorithm involves dividing the record's key field (4467) by the prime number closest to the total number of records in the file (997). The remainder (479) is the storage address on disk of the record. Thus we can go directly to this record rather than sifting through all the records that may be stored ahead of it.

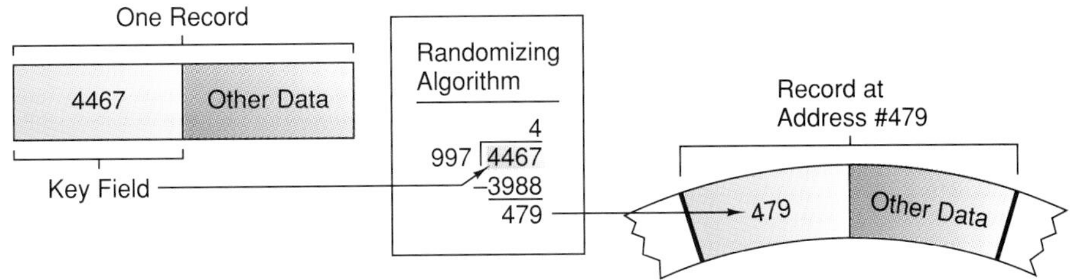

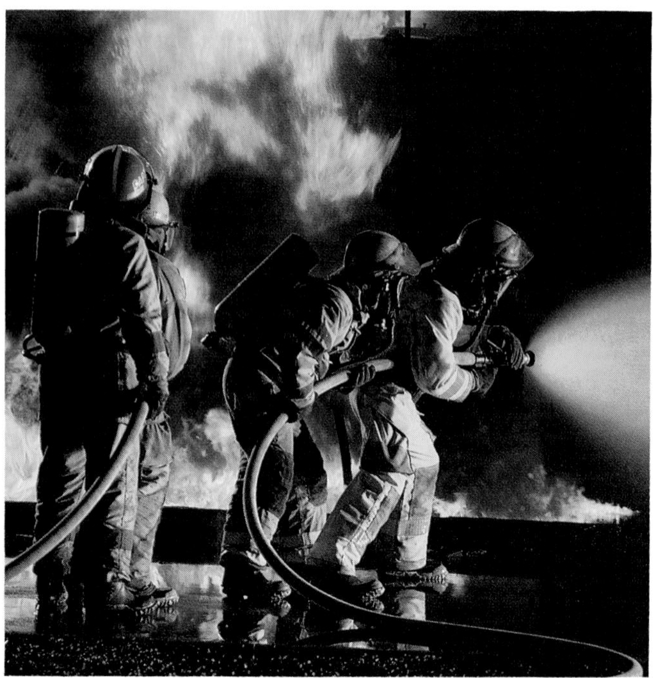

By linking telephones with computers and databases, Ohio Bell and other local telephone companies throughout the nation provide, install, and maintain 9-1-1 emergency service. In situations like emergency service, for which individual records must be retrieved immediately, direct or random file organization is necessary.

Source: © Mike Steinberg.

programming and data manipulation will be required to obtain that information.

For example, suppose you want to know all of the orders outstanding for a particular customer. Some of the information is maintained in an order file for an order entry application. The rest of the information is contained in a customer master file. Thus the required information is stored in several disparate files, each of which is organized in a different way. To extract the required information, you will need to sort both files repeatedly until the records are arranged in the same order. Records from the two files will have to be matched, and the data items from the merging of both files will have to be extracted and output. Obtaining this information entails additional programming and the creation of more files. Sometimes the effort to extract this information is so enormous that the problem remains unsolved.

Even with the most up-to-date computer hardware and software, the traditional file environment has spawned a host of obstacles to efficient and effective problem solving—high costs, poor performance, inflexible response to information requests, and information processing chaos. Most organizations have developed information systems one at a time, as the need arose, each with its own set of software programs, files, and users (the people in the organization who use that system). Over time, these independent applications and files proliferated to the point where the firm's infor-

Figure 6.5

The Traditional Approach to Organizing Data

Most organizations have developed information systems one at a time, as they needed them, each with its own set of software programs and files. All too often this involves storing duplicate information in each system. The same piece of data might be updated in one system but not in others. Another problem is that the format in which the same piece of data was stored in different files could be inconsistent. Such a situation also drives up costs because there are so many files and applications to maintain, each serving a separate group of users in an organization. Can you identify any other potential problems?

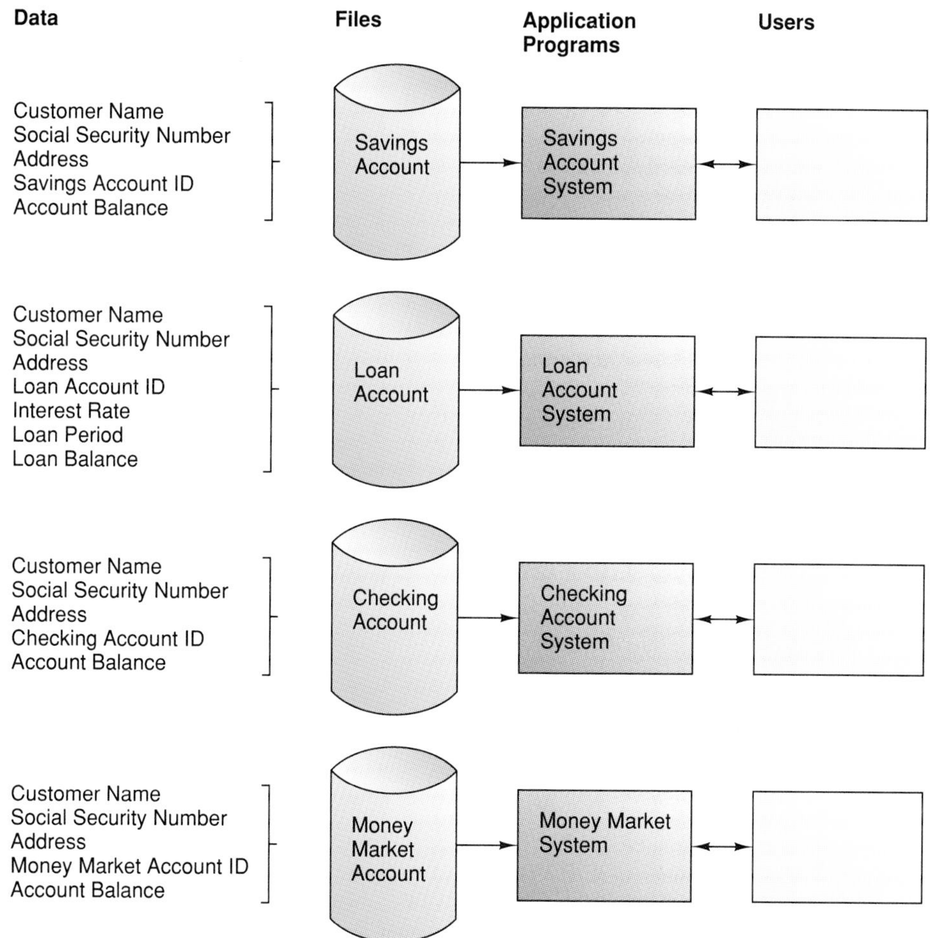

mation resources may be out of control. Some symptoms of this crisis are data redundancy, program/data dependence, data confusion, and excessive software costs. This predicament is illustrated in Figure 6.5 for a bank in which customers maintain several accounts.

Data redundancy refers to the presence of duplicate data in multiple data files. The same piece of data, such as employee name and address, will be maintained and stored in several different files by several different systems. Separate software programs must be developed to update this information and keep it current in each file in which it appears.

Data redundancy
The presence of duplicate data in multiple data files.

Program/data dependency
The close relationship between data stored in files and the specific software programs required to update and maintain those files, whereby any change in data format or structure requires a change in all the programs that access the data.

Program/data dependence refers to the close relationship between data stored in files and the specific software programs required to update and maintain those files. Every computer program must describe the location of the data it uses. In a traditional file environment, any change to the format or structure of data in a file necessitates a change in all of the software programs that use these data. The program maintenance effort required, for example, to change from a five-digit to a nine-digit zip code may be exorbitant.

Data confusion refers to inconsistencies among various representations of the same piece of data in different information systems and files. Over time, as different groups in a firm update their applications according to their own business rules, data in one system become inconsistent with the same data in another system. For example, the student names and addresses maintained in a school student enrollment system and in a separate system to generate mailing labels may not correspond exactly if each system is updated with different software programs, procedures, and time frames.

Excessive software costs result from creating, documenting, and keeping track of so many files and different applications, many of which contain redundant data. Organizations must devote a large part of their information systems resources merely to maintaining data in hundreds and thousands of files. New requests for information can only be satisfied if professional programmers write new software to strip data from existing files and recombine them into new files.

6.3 The Database Vision

Many of the problems of the traditional file environment can be solved by taking a database approach to data management and storage. A stricter definition of a database than we presented earlier is a collection of data organized so that they can be accessed and utilized by many different applications. Instead of storing data in separate files for each application, data are stored physically in one location. A single common database services multiple applications. For example, instead of a bank storing customer data in separate information systems and separate files for savings accounts, money market funds, loans, and checking accounts, the bank could create a single common client database, as in Figure 6.6.

Logical view
The presentation of data as they would be perceived by end-users or business specialists.

Physical view
The presentation of data as they are actually organized and structured on physical storage media.

Schema
The logical description of an entire database; it lists all the data items and the relationships among them.

Logical versus Physical Views of Data

The database concept distinguishes between logical and physical views of data. In the **logical view,** data are presented as they would be perceived by end-users or business specialists. The **physical view** shows how data are actually organized and structured on physical storage media. One physical view can support many logical views. A database management system uses special database management software to make the physical database available for different logical views presented by various application programs.

The **schema** is the logical description of the entire database; it lists all of the data items and the relationships among them. The specific set of data

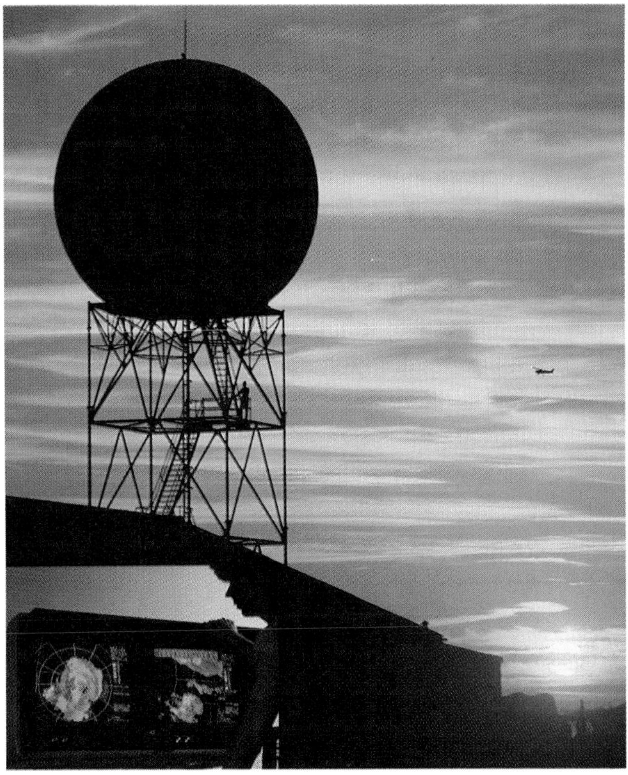

To improve the detection of severe weather, data on storms, such as wind speed and direction, are collected and analyzed by the NEXRAD system created by Unisys Corporation. The information is stored in a database and sent to U.S. government weather bureaus and air traffic controllers.

Source: Courtesy of Unisys Corporation.

from the database that is required by each application program is called the **subschema.** The subschema could be considered the portion of the database that is used to solve a particular problem presented by a business specialist. For example, for the Bank Customer Database in Figure 6.6, the savings account application would have a subschema consisting of client name, address, Social Security number, and specific savings account data such as savings account number and account balance.

Subschema
The specific set of data from a database that each application program requires.

Components of a Database Management System

Special software called a **database management system (DBMS)** permits these data to be stored in one place while making them available to different applications. Database management software serves as an interface between the common database and various application programs. When an application program calls for a data element like hourly pay rate, the database management software locates it in the database and presents it to the application program. There is no need for the application programmer to specify in detail how and where the data are found. Database management software

Database management system (DBMS)
Software that serves as an interface between a common database and various application programs; it permits data to be stored in one place yet be made available to different applications.

Figure 6.6

How a Database Management System Helps a Business Organize Data

Here we see how a database management system could help the bank solve its data problems as shown in Figure 6.5. The bank can combine all its data into a single customer database, and the database management system can make the data available to multiple applications and users. Combining all data into one database avoids duplicating data. It also means that a particular data element needs to be updated only once; all systems will be using the same updated piece of information.

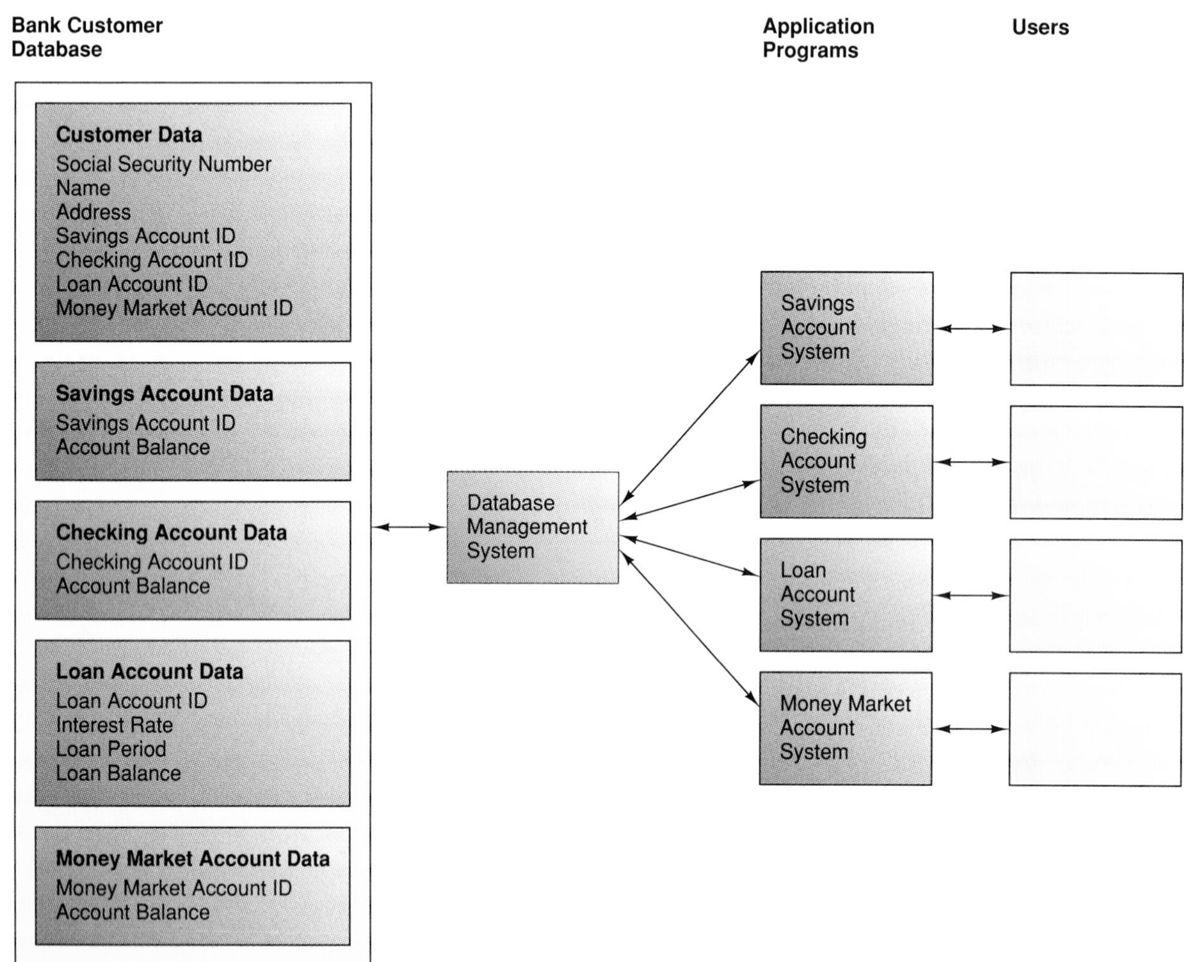

Data definition language
The part of a database management system that defines each data element as it appears in the database before it is translated into the form required by various application programs.

Data manipulation language
A special tool in a database management system that manipulates the data in the database.

has three components: a data definition language, a data manipulation language, and a data dictionary.

The **data definition language** defines each data element as it appears in the database before it is translated into the form required by various application programs. Database programming specialists use this language when they are developing the database.

The **data manipulation language** is a special tool for manipulating data in the database. It has features that can be utilized by both business and technical specialists for satisfying information requests and for application development. The most prominent data manipulation language today is

SQL, or **Structured Query Language,** which is the data manipulation language for mainframe database management systems such as IBM's DB2, with versions for microcomputer database management software.

A **data dictionary** is an automated file that stores definitions of data elements and other characteristics such as usage patterns, ownership (who in the organization is responsible for maintaining the data), relationships among data elements, and security. If properly documented, the data dictionary is an important problem-solving tool. It identifies for business specialists what data reside in the database, their structure and format, and their business usage.

Figure 6.7 shows a sample data dictionary entry for a Human Resources database. This report from the dictionary describes the size, format, meaning, alternate name (alias), and usage of the data element AMT-YTD-EARNINGS, which is an employee's accumulated year-to-date earnings. The dictionary also shows which individuals, programs, reports, and business functions use this data element and what business function "owns" or

Structured Query Language (SQL)
A data manipulation language for relational database management systems that is an emerging business standard.

Data dictionary
The component in a database management system that stores definitions and other characteristics of data elements; it identifies what data reside in the database, their structure and format, and their business usage.

Figure 6.7

An Example of a Data Dictionary Entry

Here is a sample report from a data dictionary for a Human Resources database. The data element is AMT-YTD-EARNINGS; its "alias" or alternative name is YTD-EARNINGS. The entry gives such helpful information as the size of the data element, what programs and reports use it, and which department "owns" it (i.e., is responsible for updating it).

```
NAME:  AMT-YTD-EARNINGS
ALIAS:  YTD-EARNINGS

DESCRIPTION:  EMPLOYEE'S YEAR-TO-DATE EARNINGS

SIZE:  9 BYTES

TYPE:  NUMERIC

OWNERSHIP:          PAYROLL

UPDATE SECURITY:    PAYROLL DATA ENTRY CLERK

ACCESS SECURITY:    PAYROLL DATA ENTRY CLERK
                    PAYROLL MANAGER,
                    ACCOUNTS PAYABLE MANAGER
                    PERSONNEL COMPENSATION ANALYST
                    BENEFITS ADMINISTRATOR

BUSINESS FUNCTIONS USED IN:   PAYROLL
                              PERSONNEL
                              BENEFITS

PROGRAMS USED IN:   PLP1000
                    PLP2020
                    PLP4000
                    PLP6000

REPORTS USED IN:   PAYROLL REGISTER
                    PAYROLL CHECK STUB
                    W-2 FORMS
                    941A REPORT
                    PENSION BENEFITS REPORT
```

has the responsibility for maintaining this piece of data. The "security" entries identify the people who have the right to access this information.

Advantages of Database Management Systems

Database management systems and a database approach to organizing information overcome many of the limitations of the traditional file environment:

- Data are independent of application programs. The DBMS distinguishes between logical and physical views of data so that many different application programs can use data from a common, shared database.
- Data redundancy and inconsistency are reduced. Because data are independent of application programs, there is no need to build isolated files in which the same data elements are repeated each time a new application is called for. Data are maintained in one and only one place.
- Complexity is reduced by consolidated management of data, access, and utilization via the database management system.
- Data confusion can be eliminated because there is one and only one source and definition for data.
- Information is easier to access and utilize. The database establishes relationships among different pieces of information. Data from different records and applications can be more easily accessed and combined.

The Focus on People shows how one publication uses its subscriber database to tailor its articles and advertisements to the needs of individual farmers.

The Three Database Models

The way data are organized in a database depends on the nature of the problems they are required to solve. There are three principal logical database models: the hierarchical model, the network model, and the relational model. Each model is best suited to solving a particular class of problems.

Hierarchical database model
The organization of data in a database in a top-down, treelike manner; each record is broken down into multilevel segments, with one root segment linked to several subordinate segments in a one-to-many, parent-child relationship.

The Hierarchical Model · The **hierarchical database model** organizes data in a top-down, treelike manner. Each record is broken down into pieces of records called segments. The database looks like an organization chart with one root segment and any number of subordinate segments. The segments, in turn, are arranged into multilevel structures, with an upper segment linked to a subordinate segment in a parent-child relationship. A "parent" segment can have more than one "child," but a subordinate "child" segment can have only one "parent."

The hierarchical model thus works best for one-to-many relationships among pieces of data. Figure 6.8 shows a hierarchical database for personnel in a work department. The root segment, Department, is the point of entry into the hierarchy. Data are accessed by starting at the root and moving progressively downward in the hierarchy. Thus, to find information about employees, jobs, and performance ratings, one must start at Department,

People

A Farm Journal for Every Farmer

What do a hog raiser in Texas, a corn farmer in Iowa, and a cotton farmer in Georgia have in common? Aside from being farmers, not very much. But the Philadelphia-based *Farm Journal* is able to reach out to each of their individual interests by maintaining a detailed database of subscribers.

Approximately 900,000 farmers read *Farm Journal* nationwide. *Farm Journal* has increased its revenue and market share during hard times for the farming industry by "custom-building" hundreds of editions, which are tailored to a particular group or individual. For each edition, a core of editorial pages is combined with special-interest articles and advertisements to create many different issues. Wheat farmers, for instance, would receive an issue related to wheat farming but not dealing with corn or livestock.

Farm Journal maintains a detailed database on its readers, including type of farm, location, and operational interest. This information is collected when a reader subscribes or renews and through annual telephone surveys of thousands of readers. With information on three million farmers, this represents the nation's largest agricultural database. Advertisers can use this database to target their ads to just dairy farmers of a certain size or Midwestern wheat farmers, for example. Neighboring farmers could conceivably receive issues of *Farm Journal* that differ by as much as 50 pages.

Source: Amy Cortese, "Greener Acres Ahead in Publishing," *Computerworld*, September 4, 1989.

then access related data about the employees and jobs in a particular department. IBM's IMS (Information Management System) is the most widely used hierarchical DBMS.

Hierarchical DBMSs thus have well-defined, prespecified access paths. Any piece of data in the database must be accessed from the top downward, starting with the root segment and proceeding through successive layers of subordinate segments. Hierarchical DBMSs are best suited for problems that require a limited number of structured answers that can be specified in advance. Once data relationships have been specified, they cannot easily be changed without a major programming effort. Thus the hierarchical model cannot respond flexibly to changing requests for information.

Hierarchical DBMSs are also noted for their processing efficiency, making them ideal for systems in which massive numbers of records and changes to the database must be processed. Hierarchical DBMSs would be

Figure 6.8

A Hierarchical Database: A Child Has Only One Parent

The design of a hierarchical database resembles a tree: it has a single "root" segment (in this case, "department") connected to several lower-level "segments" ("employee"). Each employee segment, in turn, connects to other subordinate segments ("performance ratings" and "job assignments"), each subordinate segment being the "child" of the "parent" segment immediately above it in the design. In a hierarchical database, each child segment can have only one parent; in order to access that child, we must "go through" the parent.

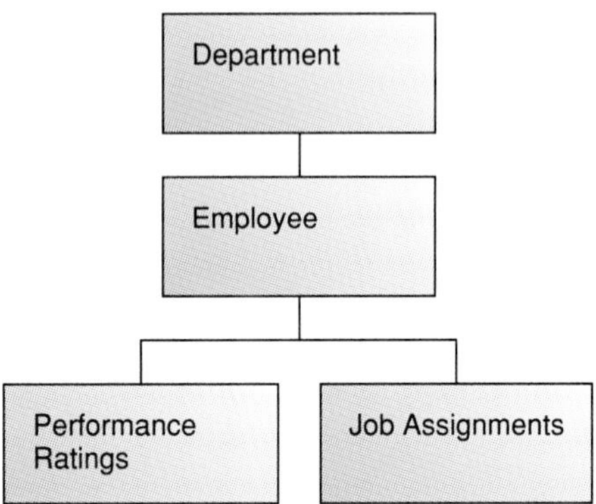

ideal for solving problems such as the processing of millions of airline reservations or automated teller banking transactions daily.

For example Security Pacific National Bank continues to use IBM's IMS, a hierarchical DBMS, for its automated tellers and other applications with heavy inputs, outputs, and updates to databases. The bank's Host Authorization System supports a large network of automated teller machines (ATMs) and bank card readers that check payment authorizations. The system utilizes IBM's IMS Fastpath (a version of IMS tuned for exceptionally high database access rates), registering a response time of 0.1 seconds and a "hit rate" of 15 transactions per second. Security Pacific's ATMs have an up-time of over 99 percent, including the time the machines must be shut down for daily service. The bank also uses IMS Fastpath for its Total On-us Processing and Services (TOPAS) system, which keeps every customer checking and savings account transaction on-line for 65 days. TOPAS can process 4 million transactions in less than one hour each night.[1]

Network database model
The organization of data in a database so that each data element or record can be related to several other data elements or records in a many-to-many relationship.

The Network Model · The **network database model** is best at representing many-to-many relationships between data. It allows a data element or record to be related to more than one other data element or record. In other words, a "child" can have more than one "parent." For example, in the network structure for personnel in work departments in Figure 6.9, an employee can be associated with more than one department. Computer Associates' IDMS is a popular network DBMS for computer mainframes.

Network DBMSs are more flexible than hierarchical DBMSs, but access paths must still be specified in advance. There are practical limitations

Figure 6.9

A Network Database: A Child Can Have More than One Parent

A network database permits many-to-many relationships. If we wanted to retrieve information on Employee 3, for example, we could access that information by going through either Department A or Department B. This means that network databases are somewhat more flexible than their hierarchical counterparts, although there are practical limits to the number of links that can be designed into them.

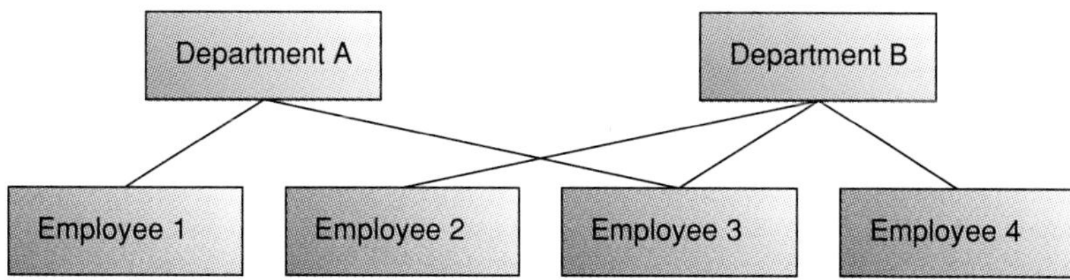

to the number of links, or relationships, that can be established among records. If they are too numerous, the software will not work efficiently. Neither network nor hierarchical database management models can easily create new relationships among data elements or new patterns of access without major programming efforts.

The Relational Model · The most recent database structure, the **relational database model,** was developed to overcome the limitations of the other two models in representing data relationships. The relational model represents all data in the database in simple two-dimensional tables called relations. The tables appear similar to flat files, but the information in more than one file can be easily extracted and combined.

Relational database model
The organization of data in a database in two-dimensional tables called relations; a data element in any one table can be related to any piece of data in another table as long as both tables share a common data element.

The strength of the relational model is that a data element in any one file or table can be related to any piece of data in another file or table as long as both tables share a common data element. IBM's DB2 and Oracle from the Oracle Corporation are examples of mainframe relational database management systems. dBASE IV from Ashton-Tate, Foxbase+ from Fox Software, Inc., and Paradox from Borland International, Inc., are examples of microcomputer relational database management systems. (Oracle also has a personal computer version.)

Figure 6.10 illustrates how personnel in work departments would be treated by a relational database. The relational database consists of four tables or files: a department file (Department), an employee file (Employee), a performance rating file (Performance), and a job assignment file (Job). Each file or table consists of columns and rows. Each column represents a different field, and each row represents a different record in the file. The database was arranged this way because most of the time these files or tables are updated and accessed independently. When information is needed from more than one table, however, it can be combined by using commands from the database management software. Therefore, a request to show which department is associated with a particular job assignment and the department's name and location could easily be satisfied by a relational database model.

Figure 6.10

A Relational Database: The Most Flexible Approach to Data Retrieval

A relational database arranges data into tables or relations. What makes this approach so flexible is that a data element in one table can be related to any data element in any other table, as long as the two tables share a common data element. Thus, in the example here, the employee table can be combined with the job assignment table, because each of these tables has a field containing a job code. Similarly, the employee table can be combined with the performance rating table, because each one holds an employee number field.

Table (Relation)

Columns

Department

Dept Code	Dept Name	Dept Location	Cost Center
398	Shipping	Warehouse 2	B1209
447	Accounting	Office Building 1	C4428
112	Purchasing	Office Building 2	C1133

Rows

Employee

Employee ID	Employee Name	Address	Age	Hire Date	Term Date	Salary	Job Code
113223394	David Sniffen	11 Scenic Dr, Rye, NY 11233	33	02/04/90		22,000	S88
432669764	Paula Hayes	22 Brook St, Croton, NY 10520	67	05/03/49	04/30/90	27,000	C42
135770964	Mark Hastings	6 Nordica, Elmsford, NY 11677	44	11/01/85		66,000	M55
445890264	Robert Flynn	3 Oak Pl, Harrison, NY 10767	55	11/01/77		46,000	M77

Job

Job Code	Job Description	Date Created	Salary Range	Dept Code
C42	Clerk	01/01/45	13,000-29,000	447
S88	Shipping Clerk	05/01/49	15,000-25,000	398
M55	Manager	01/01/45	40,000-150,000	112

Performance

Employee ID	Performance Rating	Evaluation Date
113223394	2	12/14/89
432669764	3	11/23/89
135770964	1	12/07/89
445890264	2	12/14/89

The standard data manipulation language for relational database management systems is Structured Query Language, or SQL. SQL was developed by IBM in the mid-1970s for mainframe and minicomputer environments and commercially introduced in 1979. It has recently been incorporated into some microcomputer environments. Using SQL, we can combine information from several tables or files, using the operations SELECT, FROM, and WHERE.

The basic structure of a SQL query for retrieving data is as follows:

```
SELECT <columns>
FROM <tables>
[WHERE <condition>]
```

The SELECT command identifies the columns or data fields to retrieve. The FROM clause specifies the tables or files this information is retrieved from. The WHERE clause restricts the information output to only those records or rows matching a specified condition.

Figure 6.11 illustrates a typical SQL query to extract data from the Department and Job tables illustrated in Figure 6.10. The two tables share a common field, Dept_Code, which identifies each department. In the SQL query, the department code field in the Job table, called Job.Dept_Code, is given a prefix of Job to distinguish it from the department code field (Department.Dept_Code) in the Department table. The query described in Figure 6.11 joins the Department and Job tables to form a new table with the required information.

6.4 Applying Database Concepts to Problem Solving

In applying database concepts to problem solving, several points must be kept in mind: (1) how the database should be designed; (2) whether a traditional file access method or a database approach should be chosen; and (3) if a database approach is appropriate, which model should be selected.

Figure 6.11

A Sample Query Using SQL

SQL (Structured Query Language) is a popular data manipulation language for retrieving information from relational databases. Here we see an SQL query to obtain information by joining two different tables.

```
SELECT  Job.Job_Code,Job_Description,Job.Dept_Code,Dept_Name,
Dept_Location
FROM  Job, Department
WHERE  Job.Dept_Code = Department.Dept_Code
```

Wetterau Incorporated's Maintenance Control Management System tracks nearly 15,000 warehouse and transportation equipment parts, identifying minimun and maximum inventory levels, determining lead times for automatic reordering, tracking repairs, and analyzing operating costs. In order to work efficiently and effectively, databases such as those used in the Wetterau system must be carefully designed.

Source: Courtesy of Wetterau Corporation.

Designing Database Solutions

Since file or database organization has a profound effect on how information can be delivered, the design of a database must be very carefully thought out. An information system solution must include the logical design and physical design of the database.

The logical design of the database shows how data are arranged and organized from a business perspective, as opposed to a technical perspective. There are three steps in logical database design:

- Identifying the functions the solution must perform.
- Identifying the pieces of data required by each function.
- Grouping the data elements in a manner that most easily and efficiently delivers the solution.

We will illustrate the data modeling for a simple purchasing system. (Real-world systems of this sort are more complex, but we have simplified here for instructional purposes.) The problem consists of finding a way to keep track of orders for all of the parts a ventilator manufacturer purchases from outside vendors. There may be more than one order for each part. The solution consists of a purchasing system with three basic functions:

1. Issuing and tracking purchase orders.
2. Keeping track of parts on order.
3. Tracking parts suppliers.

The system will need to maintain the following data for each function:

1. Issue purchase orders:
   - Order number
   - Part number
   - Part description
   - Unit cost
   - Number of units
   - Total cost of order
   - Vendor identification code
   - Vendor name
   - Vendor address
   - Order date
   - Delivery date
2. Track parts:
   - Part number
   - Part description
   - Unit cost
   - Vendor identification code
   - Vendor name
   - Vendor address

3. Track suppliers:
   - Vendor identification code
   - Vendor name
   - Vendor address
   - Vendor payment terms

This laundry list of data must then be analyzed to identify redundant data items and to ascertain the most natural way to group data elements. From our list and description of functions, we can identify three basic data groupings or entities: orders, parts, and suppliers. Each of these groupings represents a single subject, or entity, and defines an individual file or record. The data elements are the details that are appropriate for describing each entity. We also need to add key fields so that we can identify unique records. Thus part number is the key field for the parts file, vendor identification code is the key field for the supplier file, and order number is the key field for the order file.

The final logical design describes all of the data elements to be stored in the database, the records and files into which they will be grouped, the relationships among these data elements, and the structure of the database (hierarchical, network, or relational). Figure 6.12 shows that the logical design for solving this problem uses a relational model with three separate tables, or files: a suppliers file, a parts file, and an order file. The key field in each table is marked with an asterisk.

Note that vendor name, vendor address, part description, and unit cost appear in only one file, although they are required for more than one function. Ideally, redundant data elements should be represented only once—in the group in which they are most appropriate. The data elements in each file pertain to the subject of that file, but they can be combined with each other if required. This is accomplished by using certain fields to establish links or relationships between files, a task facilitated by the relational

Figure 6.12

The Logical Design for Building a Relational Database for a Purchasing System

The logical design for a database organizes the data according to a business perspective rather than a technical perspective. The final design groups the data elements into records and files that will best serve the information needs of the organization. It must also identify the key field of each file. In this illustration, we have marked the key field with an asterisk. It is essential to develop a useful and workable logical design before creating the physical database.

Order File	*Parts File*	*Suppliers File*
Order number*	Part number*	Vendor identification code*
Part number	Part description	Vendor name
Number of units	Unit cost	Vendor address
Total cost of order	Vendor identification code	Vendor payment terms
Order date		
Delivery date		

database model. The vendor identification code in the parts file, for example, allows us to access further details about the vendor of a particular part from the suppliers file.

Once the logical database design has been finalized, it is translated into a physical database, the form in which the data are actually arranged and stored on computer storage media. The goal of physical database design is to arrange data in a manner that makes updating and retrieval as rapid and efficient as possible. Business specialists' data access patterns and frequency of data usage are important considerations for the physical design. The physical database design for our purchasing system using dBASE III+ or dBASE IV software appears in Figure 6.13.

Choosing a Traditional File Access Method or a Database Approach

Problem solving must consider alternative file organization and access methods. The nature of the problem at hand largely determines whether one of

Figure 6.13

Building a Physical Database from a Logical Design

Here we see the physical database design developed from the logical plan in Figure 6.12. In this case we have used dBASE III+ software to create the physical version. A well-designed database must take into account users' access patterns and how often they need to retrieve specific data elements.

```
Structure for database:   C:insuppl.dbf
Number of data records:       0
Date of last update     :  12/03/89
 Field    Field Name        Type            Width        Dec
     1    VEND_ID           Character           4
     2    VEND_NAME         Character          40
     3    VEND_ADDR         Character          50
     4    PAY_TERMS         Numeric             2
**  Total **                                   97

Structure for database:   c:inparts.dbf
Number of data records:       0
Date of last update     :  12/03/89
 Field    Field Name        Type            Width        Dec
     1    PART_NO           Character           4
     2    PART_DESC         Character          30
     3    UNIT_COST         Numeric             4          2
     4    VENDOR_ID         Character           4
**  Total **                                   43

Structure for database:   c:inorder.dbf
Number of data records:       0
Date of last update     :  12/03/89
 Field    Field Name        Type            Width        Dec
     1    ORD_NUM           Character           5
     2    PART_NUM          Character           4
     3    NUM_UNITS         Numeric             5
     4    ORDER_COST        Numeric             6          2
     5    ORDER_DATE        Date                8
     6    DELIV_DATE        Date                8
**  Total **                                   37
```

the traditional approaches to file management or a database approach should be built into the solution design.

Very few application solutions of the 1990s will be based on magnetic tape sequential files. But files using indexed sequential or random-access methods may be appropriate if the solution best stands alone as an independent application, or if the firm does not have the economic or organizational resources to commit to a database approach.

Stand-alone microcomputer databases for personal or small business applications are relatively easy to implement compared to large company-wide databases residing on mainframes or minicomputers. The data requirements of personal or small business databases tend to be quite simple; microcomputer database management software is much less complex and easier to master than mainframe DBMSs. However, a true database approach for a large corporation is a large-scale, long-term effort requiring deep-rooted organizational and conceptual change. In order to fashion an application-independent database, organizational discipline must be applied to enforce common standards for defining and using data among diverse groups and functional areas. Defining and building files and programs that take into account the entire organization's interest in data is a long-term effort.

If a database approach is selected, the nature of the problem likewise dictates the most appropriate database model. For example, the Astronautics Group of Martin Marietta Corporation chose a relational DBMS for two reasons: (1) the group uses a matrix system of management in which an employee reports to two managers (this cannot be handled well in a hierarchical system because a many-to-many relationship would be needed); and (2) the database is changed frequently as employees move to new job assignments. The relational system solution is based on Version 5 of the Oracle database management system and runs on a DEC Vaxcluster.[2] The system is composed of eight databases, each with 15 to 150 tables. The largest table holds 750,000 records. Table 6.1 shows the kind of problems each database model is best able to solve.

Confronted by the problem of drivers who fail to tell the whole truth on automobile insurance applications, the insurance industry created a database that enables it to obtain more accurate information on applicants' insurance claims. The Focus on Organizations describes this system.

Table 6.1

A Problem-Solving Matrix for Database Models

Problem Dimension	Hierarchial DBMS	Network DBMS	Relational DBMS
Data relationships	One to many	Many to many	Flexible
Transaction volume	High	Medium	Medium to low
Flexibility of information retrieval	Low	Low	High
Ease of use for business specialists	Low	Low	High

FOCUS ON *Organizations*

A New Weapon for Car Insurers

You lie about that fender-bender two years ago, or maybe innocently forget a speeding ticket when applying for auto insurance. Lies and memory lapses are haunting consumers more these days because the insurance industry has a new weapon to get the truth.

A growing number of insurance companies are using a computer database—the Comprehensive Loss Underwriting Exchange—to share information on customers' auto claims. The database reports insurance claims from the past three to five years, their status, and their cost to insurers, updating the information monthly. The companies use the system to screen some or all applicants for auto insurance. The information the database turns up that is not on a customer's application could cause a company to cancel a policy or raise premiums, depending on the company and the nature of the information. Companies say the database will save them money and thus help restrain rising insurance premiums.

The system was created and is operated by Equifax, Inc., of Atlanta. Equifax and insurance companies created the database because "motor vehicle records in many states don't really provide a full story," said John J. Javaruski, an assistant vice president in personal lines at ITT Hartford Insurance Group.

A company may invest more than $1 million in staff time and money to become part of the system, and then spend an average $2.25 for each application check. Aetna Life & Casualty Company estimates its startup costs at $1.2 million. It expects, however, a return in 1990 of $2 million to $3 million in extra premiums it will charge and in claims it will avoid by rejecting high-risk drivers.

The database now has 280 insurance company members owned by 72 insurance groups and representing 60 percent of the U.S. market for personal auto insurance, said Joseph L. Cash, vice president of Equifax property and casualty-industry group.

More than 1.8 million database searches have been done, and they turn up claims 20 percent of the time. Of those, 90 percent were not listed on the customer's application, Cash said.

When a company decides to cancel a policy or raise premiums because of a database report, a customer must be notified about the system, Cash said. The customer can obtain a free copy of his or her file and challenge it, forcing Equifax to verify information with the company that supplied it. If the company stands by its information, the customer can still enter his or her own statement into the file, Cash said.

Source: Diane Levick, "A New Weapon for Car Insurers: Database Allows Companies to Check Drivers' Records," *New York Newsday,* February 22, 1990, Business Section, p. 49.

6.5 Distributing Information: Distributed and On-Line Databases

Two recent trends in information distribution are distributed databases and on-line databases.

Distributed Databases

Databases can be centralized in one location or distributed among multiple locations. The movement away from centralization toward distribution of computing resources and the growth of computer networks has also spawned a trend toward **distributed databases.** With a distributed database, a complete database or portions of a database are maintained in more than one location. As Figure 6.14 shows, there are essentially two kinds of distributed databases: replicated and partitioned.

With a **replicated database,** a central database is duplicated at all other locations. This is most appropriate for problems in which every location needs to access the same data. A **partitioned database** is subdivided so that each location has only the portion of the database that serves its local needs.

Distributed databases provide faster response time and service at each business location. Firms can fill orders or service customer requests faster if

Distributed database
A complete database or portions of a database that are maintained in more than one location.

Replicated database
A central database that is duplicated at all other locations.

Partitioned database
A database that is subdivided so that each location has only the portion of the database that serves its local needs.

Figure 6.14

The Two Types of Distributed Databases: Replicated and Partitioned

As its name implies, a distributed database distributes data among several locations. There are two ways of doing this. A replicated data base (panel a) places copies of the central database in each location. Every database is a duplicate of the central one. A partitioned database (panel b) "partitions" its data according to the needs of each location. Thus each local database contains a different portion of the organization's data, and none of the local databases contains all the data.

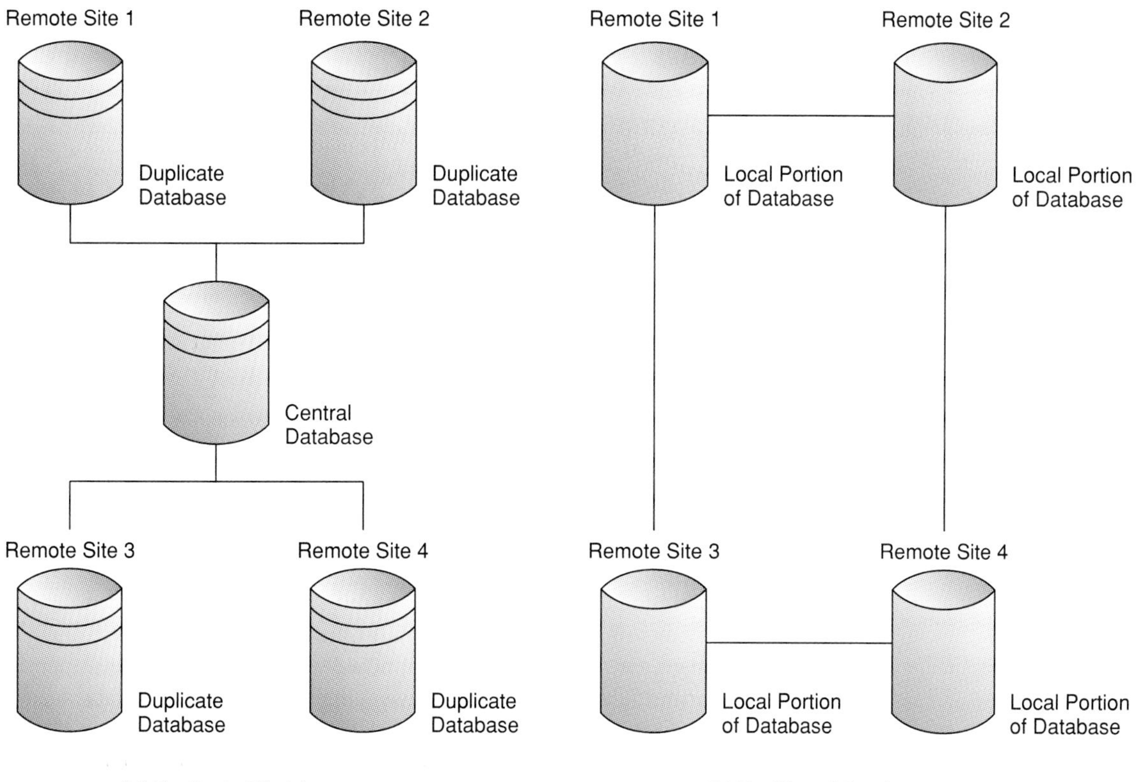

FOCUS ON Problem Solving

Why the Fuss over SQL?

Why all the fuss over SQL? SQL (Structured Query Language) was designed by IBM in the mid-1970s. A data manipulation language, it is used to create, maintain, and query databases. It represents all data as a collection of relational tables, made up of rows and columns. SQL offers sophisticated database control through its concise, flexible commands. With them, databases can be created and updated with great attention to security issues. And, of course, data can be selected and reported.

Shortly after IBM brought SQL to the mainframe marketplace, the American National Standards Institute (ANSI) approved a SQL standard. IBM's mainframe database product, DB2, uses a superset of ANSI SQL. This has been informally accepted as the real standard.

But why is SQL important? First of all, all major producers of database software for personal computers are incorporating SQL—one way or another—into their products. Such firms as Ashton-Tate, Borland, IBM, Lotus, and Microsoft are adopting SQL because it has become the lingua franca of the distributed database concept.

With SQL, users can efficiently speed data between personal computers, local area networks (LANs), mainframes, and minis and micros, and between databases from different vendors. Each workstation runs the database product most suited to it. Volumes of program code do not have to flow over network lines—just queries. Gigantic data dumps do not choke the net either. The database traffic comprises nothing but succinct SQL queries and the data actually needed at their destination. Queries need only specify the data needed—not their location.

Because the queries specify only data and because the dozen or so core command verbs and 30-odd total commands are so powerful, SQL queries tend to be much shorter than their equivalents in other database languages. So they conserve network overhead and, for those who master SQL syntax, such queries take less time to program.

Moreover, training is simplified when all systems use this common language—especially for mainframe database programmers now working with personal computers. Most of them already know SQL. And once coded on any kind of hardware, an SQL application can be easily moved to other hardware environments.

Less work for the users does come at the price of running distributed databases that have great underlying complexity. Fortunately, SQL comes with excellent tools both for access security and for recovering from system crashes. Properly implemented with SQL, distributed databases will be marvels of information in motion.

Source: Ed Jones, "Why the Fuss over SQL?" *Business Software*, July 1988, p. 60.

their data are locally available. Distributed databases also reduce the vulnerability of consolidating all the firm's essential data at only one site. They can also increase security problems, however, because of their dependence on telecommunications links and widened access to sensitive data.

Distributing databases increases data redundancy, especially if a replicated database is chosen. Inconsistencies can easily arise among the data in central and local systems, especially if changes to the data in one system are not immediately captured by the other. These problems can be compounded if data from a central database are informally "distributed" by downloading portions of them to microcomputers.

As the Focus on Problem Solving explains, SQL (Structured Query Language) is becoming the most popular language for distributed databases.

On-Line Databases and Information Services

In addition to information maintained internally, many firms are taking advantage of **on-line databases** and information services. Such services supply information external to the firm, such as stock market quotations, general news and information, or specific legal and business information. A valuable feature of these services is the ability to search the databases for specific information, such as key words and phrases, and to extract reports. If you were researching CAD workstations, for example, you could request references on the key words *workstation*, *CAD*, and *computer-aided design* and receive a list of articles containing those key words in the title. In addition to supplying information, these services may provide a network that lets two different users communicate with each other.

On-line database
A service that supplies information external to the firm, such as stock market quotations, general news and information, or specific legal and business information.

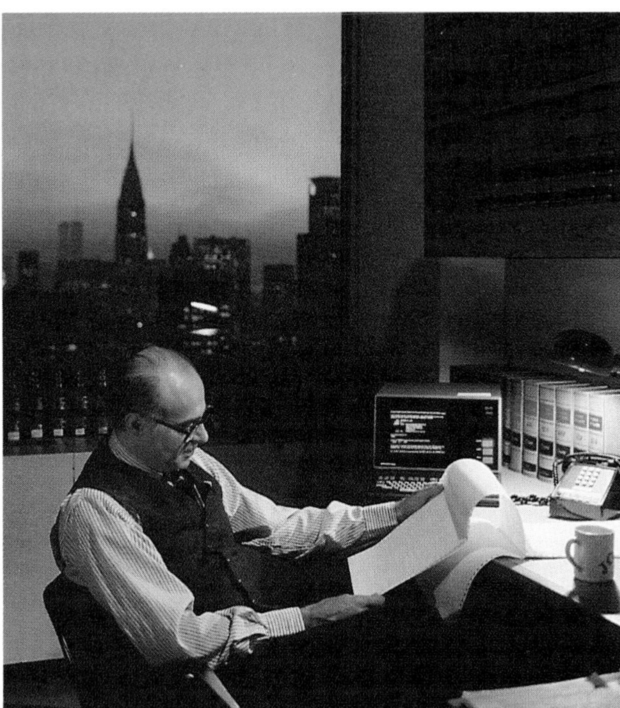

LEXIS®, Mead Data Central's computerized legal research service, gives users immediate access to the laws and court decisions of all 50 states and the federal government plus all the U.S. patents filed since 1968. Like many on-line databases, LEXIS searches the database for key words and phrases and generates reports based on the specified information. The feature that makes the LEXIS service unique, however, is that even a combination of *unconnected* words can be used to retrieve pertinent information.

Source: Dennis Brack/Black Star.

Firms such as Edward D. Jones & Company, a St. Louis–based brokerage firm with 1,300 offices in 37 states, have found that on-line databases can provide them with valuable information much more easily and cheaply than maintaining their own internal research staff. Unlike Wall Street firms at which five or seven terminals on each desktop might be dedicated to different services tracking stock and bond prices, E. D. Jones wanted to display as much information as possible on one terminal. E. D. Jones receives current stock price data from Quotron, historical information on the prices and yields of stocks and bonds from Interactive Data Corporation, and information from major investment funds, such as the Putnam Fund in Boston. All of this information pours into the company mainframe, where it is combined into one feed. E. D. Jones brokers across the country can access any of this information from a single terminal. In-house software presents information from disparate sources in a consistent format.[3]

Table 6.2 lists the leading on-line database services. For example, a "general interest" supplier, Compuserve, provides not only on-line information but also electronic bulletin boards and airline reservation and shopping services.

6.6 Leading-Edge Application: HyperCard

Hypertext
A way of delivering information that transcends the limitations of traditional methods by branching instantly to related facts rather than following a predetermined organization scheme.

HyperCard, a program Apple Computer Corporation includes with every Macintosh computer sold, is one of the few personal computer products to be called revolutionary. It is based on the concept of "hypertext." **Hypertext** is a way of delivering information that transcends some of the limitations of traditional database and list methods. Searching for information does not have to follow a predetermined organization scheme. Instead, one can branch instantly to related facts. The information is "eternally cross-referenced," with fact linked to fact linked to fact.

Table 6.2

Leading On-Line Database Services

Company	Service Provided
ADP/Bunker Ramo	Financial information
Citicorp Quotron	Financial information
Compuserve	Business and general-interest information
Dialcom	Information retrieval
Dow Jones News Retrieval	Business and financial information
Easylink	Information retrieval
Genie	Information retrieval
Lexis	Legal services
Nexis	News and business information
The Reuter Monitor	Business and financial information

Source: "MIS Taps into On-line Databases," *Information Week*, May 23, 1988.

Programs are constructed as if they were stacks of individual cards, each of which can be linked to one or more other cards in any way the user chooses. The links do not have to follow the structured formulas of conventional databases or lists, and they can contain digitized sounds, photographs, drawings, and video images as well as text. The pattern behind the links can be anything you want it to be. High-tech prophets claim that our lives will be transformed by this radical new way to access information.

Facts can be linked across traditional subject boundaries. For example, if you were studying chemistry, you could link a chemical compound to the biographical information about the compound's creator that is located in an entirely different reference work. Or you could connect the compound to grocery products containing it or to long-term health studies of the compound. You could call up a card containing the picture of a cardinal in a cedar tree from a stack of "trees." By pointing a button linked to the cardinal, you could access a stack of other birds, a stack of bird call sounds, or a stack of baseball team names. Or, by pointing at the tree itself, you could call up a card listing symptoms of cedar fever, with a button that produces the sound "ah-CHOO!"

HyperCard is a toolkit encouraging freedom to associate. It can be used to access applications by other HyperCard authors, adding personal information to what is already there. Individuals can create their own applications as well.

The basic unit of information in HyperCard is the card. In contrast to traditional DBMSs, cards can contain text, music, or graphics—whatever one wishes to put in them. Each card fills an entire Macintosh screen. Cards are grouped together with other cards called stacks. Cards in a common stack typically have the same look and contain similar information. For example, a stack might consist of name and address cards; an appointment calendar with cards for days, weeks, or months; a photo collection; or a library card catalog. One HyperCard stack even teaches ear-training skills for music. Clicking a note on the keyboard plays the note and causes the corresponding note to appear on the staff.

The card contrasts with the list metaphor for organizing information in a traditional DBMS. The relationship between records is less structured than in a traditional DBMS. In HyperCard one can follow a rigid structure, but it is not required. A tree in one card can be linked to other tree cards or to a card for a country such as Norway, where pine trees are found. The linkages can change from card to card and are established by the application developer. A single click directs the browser to what he or she is interested in—whether it is in the same stack or a different one. Clicking a "button" causes the program to move from one card to another. In addition to moving from one card or stack to another, buttons can also dial a phone, keep track of money, teach a new subject, or control a video disk player.

HyperTalk is HyperCard's built-in programming language. The commands are very English-like, and the syntax rules are more flexible than other programming tools. Commands can be placed in special scripts that HyperCard performs whenever certain events happen, such as using a certain button. Scripts can look up information or post information into another card without bringing the other card into view. A script can also run another application, such as a communications or word processing program.

FOCUS ON *Technology*

Mapping out Database Information

Database management software teams up with graphics software to form the Geographical Information Systems (GIS). GIS began as software for displaying and analyzing geographical data on mainframes and minicomputers. It has since been adapted for the more expensive lines of microcomputers, making it available for a wider variety of applications.

What distinguishes GIS from simpler products is its links between maps and databases. When a user creates and stores a map on the system, the program treats the information in the map as data for the database.

For example, users at Indianapolis Water Company have stored a high-resolution map on the system. The map shows details as fine as fire hydrants and manholes, as well as buildings, property lines, and streets. According to Larry Stout, a civil engineer with Indianapolis Water, "We'll be able to say, 'Show me a picture of all the 12-inch water mains that we installed in 1982,' and just those lines will show up [on the map produced by the system]." The system would search the database to find which water mains fit the designated criteria, then would use the data to create a map.

As in Stout's example, the software enables users to create graphic displays of data from the database. Besides data retrieved from maps stored on the system, the data might also consist of demographic information.

Indianapolis Water's GIS system is installed on a network of personal computers. Such hardware arrangements are particularly attractive because they cost less than mainframes and minicomputers. Furthermore, cartographic data in digitized form—available from the Census Bureau and the U.S. Geological Survey—are more economical than ever. The low cost is especially attractive to organizations that wish to create a GIS by combining geographic information with internal data such as customer lists.

Source: Barbara Darrow, "Geographical Software Moves Down to PC Level," *Info World*, January 22, 1990, pp. 13, 16.

HyperCard provides more freedom to relate information than a traditional DBMS, but there appears to be no way to display what the linkages are, unless cards are well written and well designed. Another HyperCard limitation is that one can view only one card at a time. Lists and reports typical of conventional DBMSs cannot be generated if they are derived from different cards. In addition, many kinds of applications, such as word processing, desktop publishing, or number crunching, do not fit well into the card metaphor.

Database tools that can store and link graphical data are becoming increasingly important. The Focus on Technology describes an important application of graphical databases: geographic information systems.

Summary

- Data are organized in computerized information systems in a hierarchy that starts with bits and bytes and proceeds to fields, records, files, and databases.

- In the traditional file environment, data records are organized using either a sequential file organization or a random file organization.

- Problems associated with the traditional file environment include data redundancy, program/data dependence, data confusion, and excessive software costs.

- A true database approach to organizing information stores data physically in only one location and uses special database management software so that this common pool of data can be shared by many different applications.

- The three components of a database management system are a data definition language, a data manipulation language, and a data dictionary.

- Advantages of using a database approach to organizing information include independence of data from application programs, reduction of data redundancy and inconsistency, elimination of data confusion, consolidation of data management, and ease of information access and use.

- The three principal database models are the hierarchical model, the network model, and the relational model. The suitability of each model depends on the nature of the problem to be solved—specifically, the nature of the data relationships (one to many or many to many), the need for flexibility, and the volume of requests or changes to the database to be processed.

- The standard data manipulation language for relational database management systems is Structured Query Language (SQL).

- With a distributed database, a complete database or portions of a database are maintained in more than one location. There are two major types of distributed databases: replicated databases and partitioned databases.

- Commercial on-line databases such as Compuserve, Quotron, and Dow Jones News Retrieval can provide essential external information to firms easily and inexpensively.

- The hypertext approach to a database, utilized in Apple Computer's HyperCard, organizes textual, numeric, and graphic information or digitized sounds in stacks of cards. The links between cards are more flexible and freeform than traditional database structures.

Key Terms

Field
Record
File
Database
Entity
Attribute
Key field
Traditional file environment
Sequential file organization
Random file organization
Indexed sequential-access method (ISAM)
Index
Data redundancy
Program/data dependence
Logical view
Physical view
Schema
Subschema
Database management system (DBMS)
Data definition language
Data manipulation language
Structured Query Language (SQL)
Data dictionary
Hierarchical database model
Network database model
Relational database model
Distributed database
Replicated database
Partitioned database
On-line database
Hypertext

Review Questions

1. Why should businesses be concerned about file organization and management?
2. List and define each of the components of the data hierarchy.
3. Why are indexes and key fields important tools for file management?
4. What is the difference between the indexed sequential-access method and the sequential-access method? Distinguish between the indexed sequential-access method and the random-access method.
5. Define a database and a database management system.
6. What problems associated with a traditional file environment can be overcome by a DBMS?
7. What is the difference between a logical view and a physical view of data?
8. List and describe the components of a DBMS.
9. Why are data dictionaries important tools for businesses?
10. Describe the three principal database models and indicate the strengths and limitations of each.
11. What are the three steps in logical database design?
12. What is a distributed database? List and define the two major types of distributed databases.

13. List two major commercial on-line databases and the services they provide.
14. How does HyperCard differ from a traditional database? What kinds of problems is it most useful for solving?

Discussion Questions

1. Compare the database approach to the traditional approach to file management. What are the advantages and disadvantages of each?

2. It has been said that you do not need database management software to have a database environment. Discuss.

3. Which of the components of a DBMS (data definition language, data manipulation language, data dictionary) would you use for each of the following?
   a. The field for annual salary must be expanded from six to seven digits.
   b. A report listing all employees who work in the purchasing department must be produced.
   c. A new data element, taxable life insurance, must be added to the database. Personnel and payroll programs must be modified to keep track of the amount of company-funded life insurance that is taxable.

Problem-Solving Exercises

1. Develop a data dictionary for the purchasing system described in this chapter. List all of the data elements in the system and show their format, size, definition, and business usage.

2. A university typically maintains information about students and courses. Some of the pieces of data that must be maintained are student names and addresses, student identification numbers, course names, course descriptions, course numbers, grades, majors, course enrollments, number of credits per course, faculty member teaching each course, term offered, and department giving the course. Using the guidelines presented in Section 6.4 of this chapter, design a database for this application.

Notes

1. Richard Skrinde, "The Imperative of Coexistence," *Computerworld*, August 10, 1987.
2. Alan Radding, "Relational DBMS," *Computerworld*, February 27, 1989.
3. "MIS Taps into On-Line Databases," *Information Week*, May 23, 1988.

Problem-Solving Case

Cutting Electricity Bills at Ontario Hydro

Ontario Hydro, Canada's second largest publicly owned power company, must spend $3 million a day to keep lights on and motors running in Ontario Province. One of this company's main concerns is dealing with 5,000 power

outages per year. Left unchecked, this problem could add millions to the company's operating costs.

When Ontario Hydro experiences an outage, it usually must shift power generation to more costly generating systems. The company must pay thousands of dollars per hour while power is generated from another source. Proper scheduling and coordination are essential to ensure that the power system is secure and reliable when transmission equipment is out of service.

A Transmission Utilization Department Outage System (TUDOS) was built to schedule and coordinate power outages. The original COBOL-based TUDOS system ran on a Unisys mainframe in the company's Computer Services Division. Its chief problem was its inflexibility. Adding a one-character field, for example, entailed modifying the entire database at a cost of $70,000. It was also a single-user system that was unbearably slow at times.

Ontario Hydro's Power System Operations Division came up with a list of 16 undesirable features of the old system and 21 requirements for a new one. The new system had to be highly functional, flexible, fast, and secure. It also had to be easy to use and prototype, with a strong fourth-generation language and user support.

In early 1987 Ontario replaced the old TUDOS system with one using relational database management software. Since users were unable to specify all of their functional and data requirements before the system was built, Ontario Hydro needed a database that would allow changes to be made when needed without reprogramming. It adopted the Ingres relational database management system (RDBMS) because of its performance, reliability, and ability to meet these requirements.

The new TUDOS system runs on a VAX 8650 machine and eventually will be accessed by 200 business specialists at Ontario Hydro. Information in the database includes code numbers, dates, times, outage locations, affected equipment, previous outage history, special instructions and operating strategies, personnel contacts, and job status.

Ontario Hydro reported that the tools provided with the new database management system, which are based on the concept of visual forms, have reduced development time by a factor of five. These tools allow business specialists to enter, retrieve, and updata data easily and to produce specialized reports without any programming knowledge. Business specialists can select various data manipulation functions themselves and control the flow of the whole scheduling application. The company claims that it has saved 250 hours per user per year.

Ontario Hydro Power System Operations Division is also using its RDBMS for other applications, including a tactical operations planning system to determine cost-effective outage strategies.

Source: Brian Worth, "Ontario Hydro Saves $$$ with RDBMS," *Canadian Data Systems*, April 1989.

Case Study Questions

1. Why was the old TUDOS system a problem for Ontario Hydro?
2. Why was a relational database management system important to the new system solution?
3. What factors do you think Ontario Hydro had to take into account when choosing a database management system?

CHAPTER · SEVEN

Telecommunications

Chapter Outline

7.1 Introduction
- Types of Signals
- Digital Transmission Modes

7.2 Telecommunications Technology
- Telecommunications System Components
- Types of Transmission Media
- Measuring Transmission Rates

7.3 Telecommunications Networks
- Network Topologies
- Private Branch Exchanges and Local Area Networks
- Wide Area Networks
- Problem Solving with Networks: Cautions and Concerns

7.4 Applying Telecommunications to Business Problems
- Electronic Mail
- Teleconferencing
- Electronic Data Interchange
- Integrated Services Digital Network

7.5 Leading-Edge Application: New Networks Speed Air Travel

Learning Objectives

After reading and studying this chapter, you will:

1. Understand the basic components of a telecommunications network.
2. Know how to measure telecommunications transmission rates.
3. Be familiar with the three basic network topologies.
4. Know the major types of telecommunications networks.
5. Be able to address telecommunications issues when designing a solution.
6. Be aware of important business applications using telecommunications.

Telecommunications Keeps Domino's Delivering on Time

Domino's Pizza is a nationwide chain whose popularity is based on its ability to deliver pizza to customers' homes within 30 minutes. One reason it can make this guarantee is its automated ordering service. Domino's developed special software to keep track of the number of pizzas sold in one day, the most popular pizzas, customer names and addresses, and the time orders are placed.

Approximately 400 of Domino's 1,200 corporate-owned outlets use the telecommunications-based ordering system. The firm's 3,300 franchised outlets also have the option of using this system. The ordering system uses a wide-area network of leased telephone lines linking eight cities in an area extending from Columbus, Ohio, to Miami, Florida. There is an NCR 9300, 9400, or 9500 mid-range computer at each of eight nationwide order centers and an NCR 386 microcomputer at each pizza outlet.

Customers never have to search phone books for the number of the nearest Domino's, because Domino's lists only one phone number for a region and has situated calling centers so that every order is a local call. At the calling centers Domino's employees enter the telephone orders and transmit them to the closest store. The microcomputer at each pizza outlet processes the orders and sends them to a printer. The printout serves as both an order record and

customer receipt. Without this automated ordering service, employees at each store would have to answer the phones and scribble orders on tickets.

The ordering system has trimmed delivery time by 5 percent. Domino's can now deliver pizzas in 23 minutes or less, with much less chance of delivering cold pizza to the wrong address.

Source: Kathy Chin Leong, "Network Delivers for Domino's," *Computerworld,* June 13, 1988.

Domino's, like many firms, depends on telecommunications-based information systems as solutions for improving service and streamlining its basic operations. Today, telecommunications networks are a critical ingredient for linking people, factories, stores, and offices in different locations and for providing immediate on-line access to information.

7.1 Introduction

Telecommunications can be defined as communication by electronic means, usually over some distance. A telecommunications system transmits information, establishes an interface or path between sender and receiver, directs messages along the most efficient paths and makes sure they reach the right receiver, edits data by performing error checking and reformatting, converts messages so they flow from one device to another, and controls the overall flow of information. Telecommunications systems can transmit text, graphic images, voice, or video information.

It is impossible to talk about contemporary information systems without addressing telecommunications issues. Today, most information systems for nonpersonal use feature on-line processing and remote access to information. Without communications technology, it would be impossible to solve problems requiring immediate, on-line access to information, sharing of information among different geographic locations, or transmission of information from one location or one information system to another. Table 7.1 lists some of the typical business applications based on telecommunications and the business problems they solve.

Recent changes in communications technology and in the ownership and control of telecommunications services have blurred the distinction between telecommunications and computing. Before 1984, telecommunications in the United States was virtually a monopoly of American Telephone and Telegraph Company (AT&T). But, in that year, legal action by the Department of Justice forced AT&T to give up its monopoly and allowed competing firms to sell telecommunications equipment and services. Other

Table 7.1

Common Uses of Telecommunications in Business

Application	Purpose
Finance Automated teller machines Electronic funds transfer Electronic clearinghouses Securities trading On-line account inquiry On-line access to accounts receivable data	Reducing the time and cost of funds transfer
Sales and Marketing Point-of-sale terminals Telemarketing Airline and hotel reservation systems On-line order processing Credit cards and credit authorization	Making it easy for customers to purchase
Manufacturing and Production Process control On-line inventory control Computer-integrated manufacturing	Reducing production costs
Human Resources On-line personnel inquiry On-line applicant tracking	Managing human resources
Communication and Knowledge Work Electronic mail Groupware On-line information services Shared design databases and specifications	Reducing the cost of knowledge and information transfer

Banks rely heavily on their telecommunications systems for the fast, efficient, accurate flow of information. To improve this flow of information, Ameritrust in Cleveland upgraded its Ameritech Centrex system from analog to digital.

Source: © Mike Steinberg.

companies promptly began to offer telecommunications services, presenting firms with a bewildering array of alternative vendors and technologies from which to choose. AT&T, for example, now markets its own line of computers and computing services, while IBM has ventured into the telephone equipment market.

Consequently, since many more communications choices are available than in the past, you will need some background knowledge on business telecommunications systems in order to choose wisely among them. To understand how telecommunications systems work, you must become familiar with certain characteristics of data transmission, the capabilities of various transmission media, the manner in which the components of a telecommunications network work, and alternative ways of arranging these components into networks.

Types of Signals

Analog signal
A continuous sine wave form over a certain frequency range, with a positive voltage representing a 1 and a negative charge representing a 0; used for voice transmissions.

Digital signal
A discrete flow in which data are coded as 0-bits and 1-bits and transmitted as a series of on-and-off electrical pulses; used for communication between computers and by some telephone systems.

Modulation
The process of converting digital signals into analog form.

Demodulation
The process of converting analog signals into digital form.

Modem
A device used to translate digital signals into analog signals and vice versa, a necessity when computers communicate through analog lines; stands for MOdulation and DEModulation.

Two types of signals are used in telecommunications systems: analog and digital (see Figure 7.1). An **analog signal** takes the form of a continuous sine wave over a certain frequency range. A positive voltage charge represents a +1 and a negative charge represents a 0. Analog signals are used to handle voice traffic and to reflect variations in pitch.

A **digital signal** is a discrete burst rather than a continuous wave; it represents data coded into two discrete states: 0-bits and 1-bits, which are transmitted as a series of on-and-off electrical pulses. Most computers communicate with digital signals, as do many local telephone companies and some larger networks. (Although telephone lines used to be analog only, digital lines, which can transmit data faster and more accurately than analog lines, are beginning to be used.) If computers communicate through analog lines, all digital signals must be converted into analog form and then reconverted into digital form for the receiving computer.

The process of converting digital signals into analog form is called **modulation,** and the process of converting analog signals back into digital form is called **demodulation.** A device called a **modem** (MOdulation and DEModulation) is used for this translation process. As Figure 7.2 shows, when computers communicate through analog telephone lines, two modems will be needed—one to convert the first computer's digital signals to analog, the other to convert the analog signals back to digital for the second computer.

Figure 7.1

Analog and Digital Signals

An analog signal is a continuous wave over a particular range of frequencies. A positive voltage charge represents a "1," and a negative voltage charge represents a "0." A digital signal contains discrete bursts representing "on" and "off" electrical pulses. Digital lines tend to be faster and more accurate than analog. Telecommunications systems are moving toward using digital signals exclusively, but some telephone lines are still carrying information in analog form.

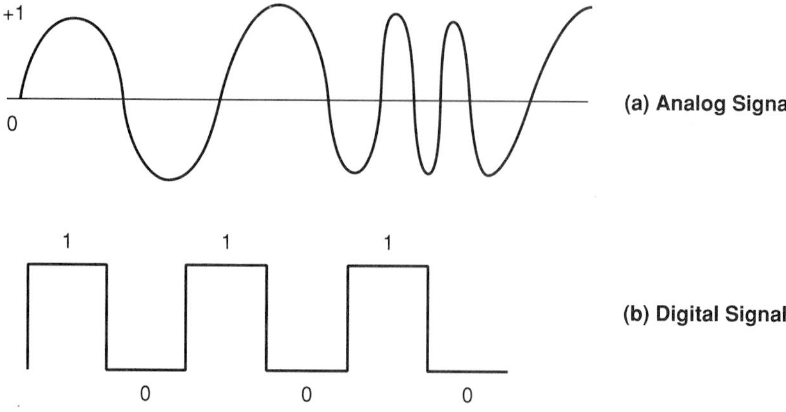

Figure 7.2

The Function of Modems in Telecommunications

A modem (short for MOdulation/DEModulation) is a device that translates digital signals into analog, and vice versa. It is a vital piece of equipment in telecommunications systems that employ both types of signals.

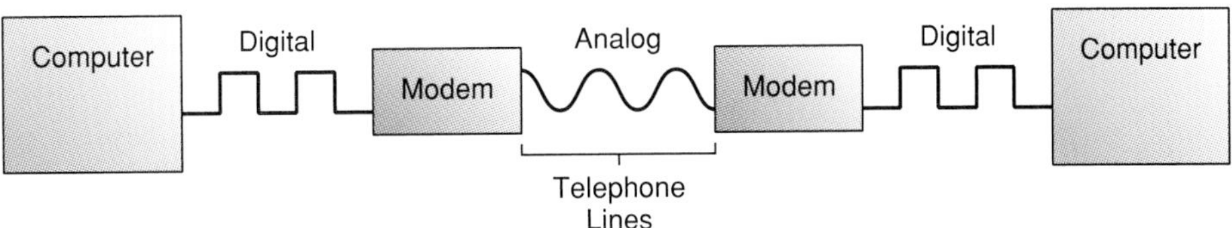

Digital Transmission Modes

Once the signal type has been determined, the user must be aware of the alternative ways of arranging bits of data for transmission and must also consider the direction of data flow supported by the telecommunications medium.

Asynchronous and Synchronous Transmission · Data are transmitted from one computer to another as a stream of bits. How then does a receiving computer know where one character ends and another begins? Several conventions have been devised for communicating when a character begins or ends. In **asynchronous transmission,** characters or bytes are transmitted one at a time over a line. Each string of bits composing a character is "framed" by control bits—a start bit, a parity bit, and one or two stop bits. The parity bit is set on or off, depending on whether the parity scheme is odd or even (see Chapter 3).

In **synchronous transmission,** several characters at a time are transmitted in blocks, framed by header and trailer bytes called flags. Synchronous transmission is faster than asynchronous transmission because the characters are transmitted as blocks with no start and stop bits between them. Consequently, it is used for transmitting large volumes of data at high speeds. Figure 7.3 compares synchronous and asynchronous transmission.

Simplex, Half-Duplex, and Full-Duplex Transmission · Transmission must also consider the direction of data flow over a communications line. In **simplex transmission,** data can travel only in one direction at all times; thus data can flow from a computer processing unit to a printer but cannot flow from the printer to the computer. **Half-duplex transmission** supports two-way flow of data, but the data can travel in only one direction at a time. In **full-duplex transmission,** data can move in both directions simultaneously. Figure 7.4 compares the simplex, half-duplex, and full-duplex transmission modes.

Asynchronous transmission
A method of transmitting one character or byte at a time when data are communicated between computers, with each string of bits comprising a character framed by control bits.

Synchronous transmission
The transmission of characters in blocks framed by header and trailer bytes called flags; allows large volumes of data to be transmitted at high speeds between computers, because groups of characters can be transmitted as blocks, with no start and stop bits between characters as in asynchronous transmission.

Simplex transmission
A form of transmission over communications lines in which data can travel in only one direction at all times.

Half-duplex transmission
A form of transmission over communications lines in which data can move in both directions, but not simultaneously.

Full-duplex transmission
A form of transmission over communications lines in which data can be sent in both directions simultaneously.

Figure 7.3

Asynchronous and Synchronous Transmission

Asynchronous and synchronous transmission represent two ways of sending bits of data along telecommunications lines. Asynchronous transmission sends one byte (one character) at a time; each byte is preceded by a start bit and followed by a parity bit (for error checking) and a stop bit (to signal the end of that particular byte). Synchronous transmission sends several bytes at one time, preceded and followed by bytes called flags. Not surprisingly, synchronous transmission is much faster than asynchronous because there are fewer intervening bits slowing down transmission of data. Both of these examples use an ASCII representation of data.

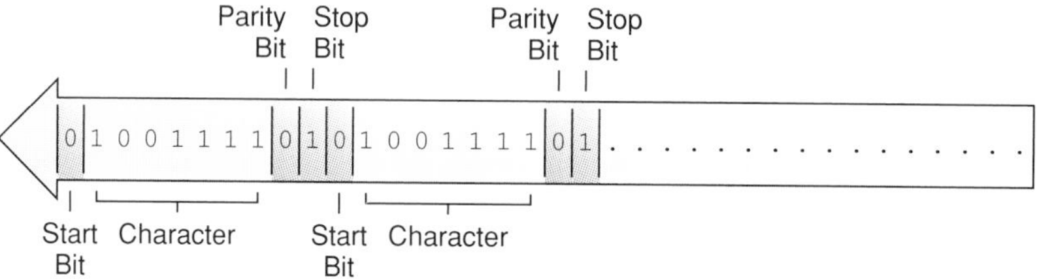

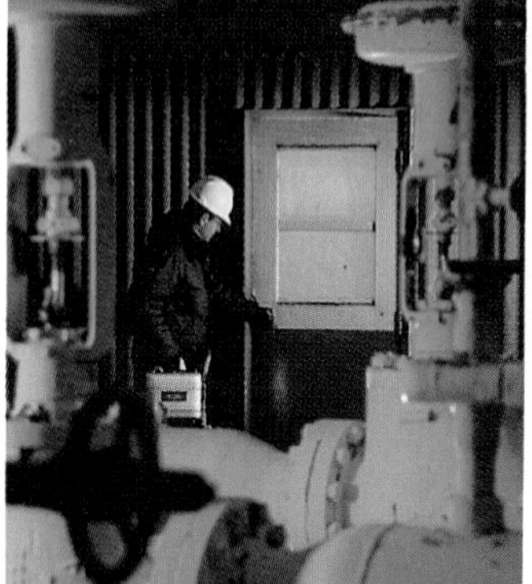

A Panhandle Eastern Corporation technician makes a routine check of a gas pipeline measurement station near Indianapolis. A telecommunications system at this station electronically sends volume data to the Houston operating headquarters.

Source: Courtesy Panhandle Eastern Corporation.

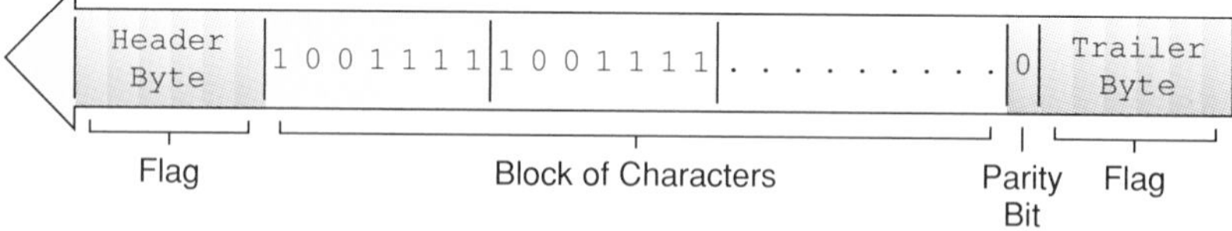

7.2 Telecommunications Technology

A telecommunications system is a collection of both hardware devices and the software needed to control these devices. We will examine the major components of telecommunications systems in this section and then describe how these components are used to build networks in the following section.

Telecommunications System Components

A telecommunications system is a network of interconnected hardware and software components that perform the telecommunications functions described above. Its essential components are as follows:

1. Computers to process information.
2. Terminals or any input/output devices that send or receive data.
3. Communications **channels,** the links by which data or voice communications are transmitted between sending and receiving devices in a network. Communications channels use various communications media,

Channel
A link by which voices or data are transmitted in a communications network.

Figure 7.4

How Data Flow: Simplex, Half-Duplex, and Full-Duplex Transmission

There are differences in how telecommunications lines transmit data. Simplex transmission (panel a) allows data to flow in only one direction—in this case, from a computer to a receiving device. Half-duplex transmission (panel b) allows two-way flow, but data can travel in only one direction at a time. Full-duplex transmission (panel c) can transmit data in both directions at the same time.

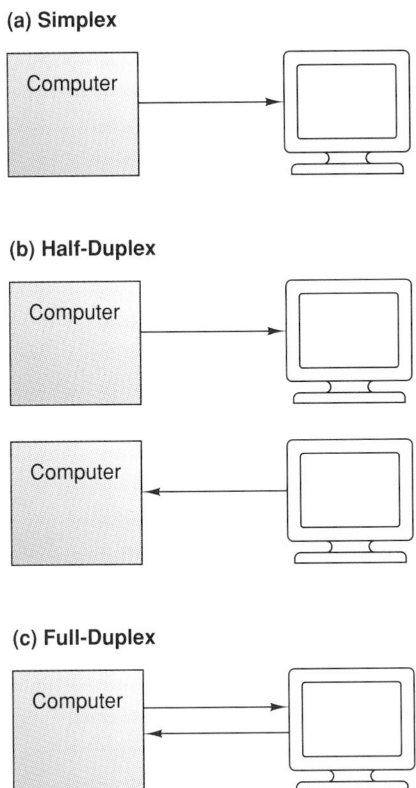

such as telephone lines, fiber optic cables, coaxial cables, and satellite systems.

4. Communications processors, such as modems, front-end processors, multiplexers, and concentrators, which provide support functions for data transmission.
5. Telecommunications software, which controls input and output activities and other functions of the communications network.

Communications Processors · A telecommunications system contains a number of computer-like "intelligent" devices, each of which plays a special role in a network.

The **front-end processor** is a computer (often a programmable minicomputer) that is dedicated to communications management and attached to the **host computer** (main computer). It takes some of the load off the host

Front-end processor
A computer that manages communications for a host computer to which it is attached; the front-end processor is largely responsible for collecting and processing input and output data to and from terminals and performing such tasks as formatting, editing, and routing for the host computer.

Host computer
The main computer in a network.

computer by performing error control, formatting, editing, controlling, routing, and speed and signal conversion. The front-end processor is largely responsible for collecting and processing input and output data to and from terminals, and it also groups characters into complete messages for submission to the central processing unit (CPU).

Multiplexer
A device that enables a single communications channel to carry data transmission from multiple sources simultaneously.

A **multiplexer** is a device that enables a single communications channel to carry data transmissions from multiple sources simultaneously. The multiplexer divides the communications channel so that it can be shared by several transmission devices. The multiplexer may divide a high-speed channel into multiple channels of slower speed or may assign each transmission terminal a very small slice of time in which it can use the high-speed channel. Figure 7.5 illustrates components of a telecommunications system that includes two multiplexers.

Concentrator
A device that collects and temporarily stores messages from terminals in a buffer or temporary storage area and sends bursts of signals to the host computer.

A **concentrator** is a type of "store and forward" device (often a specialized minicomputer) that collects and temporarily stores messages from terminals in a buffer, or temporary storage area. When the messages are ready to be sent economically, the concentrator "bursts" signals to the host computer.

Controller
A device that supervises communications traffic between the CPU and peripheral devices such as terminals and printers.

A **controller,** often a specialized minicomputer, supervises communications traffic between the CPU and peripheral devices such as terminals and printers. The controller manages the flow of messages from these devices and communicates them to the CPU, and it also routes output from the CPU to the appropriate peripheral device.

Telecommunications Software · Special software is required to control and support the activities of a network. This software resides in the host computer, front-end processor, and other processors in the network. The

Figure 7.5

The Components of a Telecommunications System

The five major components of a telecommunications system are a computer, communications processors, communications channels, terminals (or other input/output devices), and telecommunications software. Here we see a telecommunications system that uses two multiplexers as communications processors. The multiplexers divide the communications channel to allow several devices to share it. The separate streams of data entering from terminals are routed through the channel into the computer. Multiplexers operate by splitting a high-speed channel into several channels of a slower speed, or by giving each terminal only a very small piece of time for using the high-speed channel.

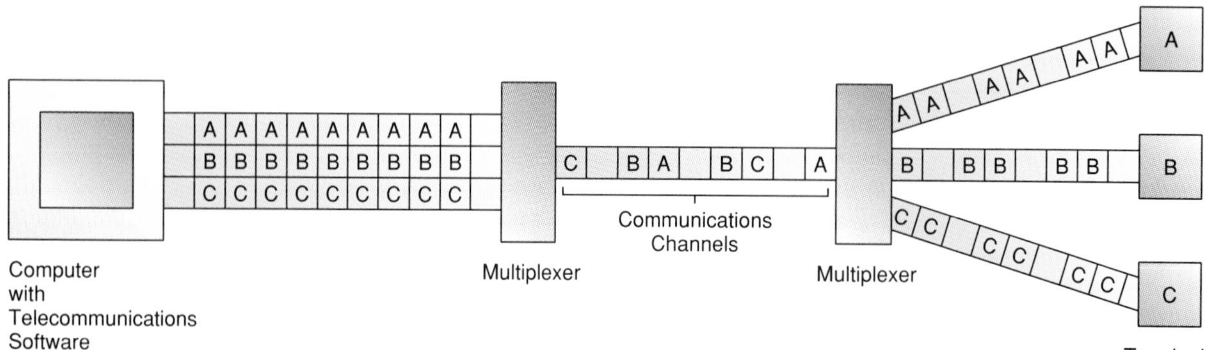

main functions of telecommunications software are network control, access control, transmission control, error detection/correction, and security.

Network control software routes messages, polls network terminals, determines transmission priorities, maintains a log of network activity, and checks for errors. Access control software establishes connections between terminals and computers in the network and controls transmission speed, mode, and direction. Transmission control software enables computers and terminals to send and receive data, programs, commands, and messages. Error control software detects and corrects errors, then retransmits the corrected data. Security control software utilizes log-ons, passwords, and various authorization procedures (see Chapter 16) to prevent unauthorized access to a network.

Protocols · Telecommunications networks typically consist of a wide variety of hardware and software technologies. In order for different components in a network to communicate, they must adhere to a common set of rules, called a **protocol,** that enables them to "talk to" each other. Each device in a network must be able to interpret the other devices' protocols. Protocols perform the following functions in a telecommunications network:

Protocol
The set of rules governing transmission between two components in a telecommunications network.

1. Identify each device in the communication path.
2. Secure the attention of the other device.
3. Verify the correct receipt of a transmitted message.
4. Verify that a message requires retransmission because it cannot be correctly interpreted.
5. Perform recovery when errors occur.

Although the need for standard protocols is widely recognized, different vendors have developed their own systems. For example, IBM developed a system of protocols called Systems Network Architecture as a standard for transmitting data through a network controlled by a host computer. Other computer manufacturers have also devised their own systems. In 1978, the International Standards Organization issued a model of network protocols called Open Systems Interconnection (OSI), which will enable any computer connected to a network to communicate with any other computer on the same network or a different network, regardless of the manufacturer. Computer hardware and software vendors are developing products to conform to the OSI model, but no universal standard is in effect as yet. One emerging standard for extending common carrier digital service to homes and offices from central telephone company centers is the Integrated Services Digital Network (ISDN) discussed at the end of this chapter.

Types of Transmission Media

There are five different kinds of telecommunications transmission media: twisted wire, coaxial cable, fiber optics, microwave (and other forms of radio transmission), and satellite. Each has certain advantages and limitations.

Twisted wire
The oldest transmission medium, consisting of strands of wire twisted in pairs; it forms the basis for the analog phone system.

The oldest transmission medium is **twisted wire,** which consists of strands of wire twisted in pairs. Most of the telephone system in a building relies on twisted wires installed to operate the analog phone system. Most buildings have extra cables installed for future expansion, so every office usually has a number of unused twisted wire cables that can be used for digital communications. Although it is low in cost and is already in place, twisted wire is relatively slow for transmitting data, and high-speed transmission causes interference called crosstalk. On the other hand, new software and hardware have raised the capacity of existing twisted wire cables up to 10 megabits per second, which is often adequate for connecting personal computers and other office devices.

Coaxial cable
A transmission medium consisting of thickly insulated copper wire; it can transmit a larger volume of data than twisted wire and is faster and more interference-free; cannot be used for analog phone conversations.

Coaxial cable, like that used for cable television, consists of thickly insulated copper wire that can transmit a larger volume of data than twisted wire. It is often used in place of twisted wire for important links in a telecommunications network because it is a faster, more interference-free transmission medium. Speeds of up to 200 megabits per second are possible. However, coaxial cable is thick and hard to install in many buildings; it also has to be moved when the computer and other devices are moved, and it does not support analog phone conversations.

Fiber optics
A transmission medium consisting of strands of clear glass fiber bound into cables through which data are transformed into beams of light and transmitted by a laser device; it is faster, lighter, and more durable than wire media but also more expensive and harder to install.

Fiber optics technology consists of thousands of strands of clear glass fiber, the thickness of a human hair, that are bound into cables. Data are transformed into beams of light that are sent through the fiber-optic cable by a laser device at a rate of 500 kilobits to 1,000 megabits per second. Fiber-optic cable is considerably faster, lighter, and more durable than wire media and is well suited to solutions requiring transfers of large volumes of data. On the other hand, fiber-optic cable is more difficult to work with,

In Marietta, Ohio, an Ohio Bell cable crew installs a fiber optic cable. Fiber optic cable delivers information much faster than copper wire cable, thus improving service to both business and residential customers.

Source: © Mike Steinberg.

more expensive, and harder to install. It is best used as the "backbone" of a network rather than for connecting isolated devices to a backbone. In most networks, fiber-optic cable is used as the high-speed trunk line, while twisted wire and coaxial cable are used to connect the trunk line to individual devices.

For example, Track Data Corporation, a New York financial information services firm, changed to a reconfigurable fiber-optic–based network because its clients' intensive information needs could not be met with traditional wire networks. Track Data provides stock quotations, financial news, and information to approximately 700 subscribers in the New York area. The company sends 10 megabytes of data daily to each customer from its data center. Retail and institutional traders use Intel 80386–based microcomputers to access resulting charts, graphs, spreadsheets, arbitrage news, and stock quotations. Data used to be transmitted on 9.6-kilobit-per-second analog leased lines, but the analog system became inefficient when the stock market opened each morning—price data on a fast trading day tended to back up.[1]

Therefore, Track Data decided to build its own private fiber-optic–based network called Tracknet. The fiber-optic network delivers information to the building level. Then multiplexers enable customers to link up with the fiber network using an ordinary telephone line hookup to New York Telephone Company switches. The fiber-optic network supports multiple digital 56-kilobit-per-second lines and will be able to reroute communications automatically in the event of network failure.

Microwave systems transmit high-frequency radio signals through the atmosphere and are widely used for high-volume, long-distance, point-to-point communication. No cabling is required. Because microwave signals follow a straight line and do not bend with the curvature of the earth, terrestrial transmission stations must be positioned 25 to 30 miles apart, which adds to the expense of microwave. This problem can be solved by using microwave systems with other communications methods, such as satellites.

Microwave
A transmission medium in which high-frequency radio signals are sent through the atmosphere; used for high-volume, long-distance, point-to-point communication.

Communications satellites are preferred for transmitting large quantities of data over long distances because they do not have the distance limitations of terrestrial microwave transmission stations. Communications satellites orbiting more than 22,000 miles above the earth can receive, amplify, and retransmit microwave signals; thus the satellites act as relay stations for earth stations (microwave stations on the ground).

Satellite is not optimal for problems requiring extremely rapid exchanges of data, because delays occur when data are sent thousands of miles up into space and back down again. However, satellite is very appropriate for transmission of large quantities of information in one direction at a time. Figure 7.6 shows a typical VSAT (very small aperture terminal) private satellite communications system. Satellite networks are typically used for communications in large, far-flung organizations with many locations that would be difficult to tie together through cabling media. For example, as the Focus on Organizations describes, Holiday Inns replaced its terrestrial network with a private VSAT network to connect its corporate headquarters in Memphis, Tennessee, with all of its 1,500 lodging sites throughout the United States.

Figure 7.6

A VSAT Satellite Communications System

Satellite-based telecommunications are useful for systems that transmit large amounts of information over great distances. A VSAT (very small aperture terminal) satellite system uses a satellite that orbits over the equator. At the central site, a hub earth station and a host computer with a front-end processor manage the system. At the remote sites—there can be hundreds of these—an outdoor VSAT or antenna links the remote site with the central location by picking up transmissions from the satellite. A control center at the remote site handles data from telephones, facsimile machines, and closed-circuit television broadcasts.

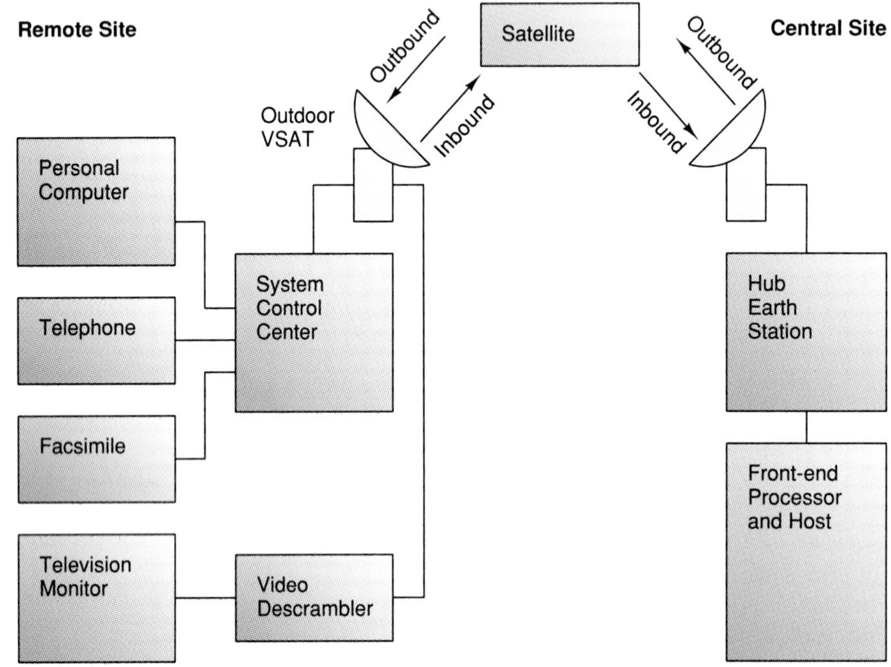

Source: The New York Times, October 26, 1988. Copyright © 1988 by The New York Times Company.

Measuring Transmission Rates

The total amount of information that can be transmitted via any telecommunications channel is measured in bits per second (BPS). Sometimes this is referred to as the **baud** rate; a baud represents a voltage switch (signal change) from positive to negative or vice versa. The baud rate is not always identical to the bit rate, however. At higher speeds, more than one bit at a time can be transmitted in a single signal change, so the bit rate will generally surpass the baud rate. Since one signal change, or cycle, is required to transmit one or several bits per second, the transmission capacity of each type of telecommunications medium is a function of its frequency—that is, the number of cycles per second that can be sent through that medium measured in hertz (see Chapter 3). The range of frequencies that can be accommodated on a particular telecommunications medium is called its

Baud
A change in voltage from positive to negative and vice versa. The baud rate at lower speeds corresponds to a telecommunications transmission rate of bits per second. At higher speeds the baud rate is less than the bit rate because more than one bit at a time can be transmitted by a single signal change.

FOCUS ON Organizations

Holiday Inns Uses Satellite Network to Maintain Lead in Customer Service

Holiday Corporation, the world's largest hotel chain, replaced its terrestrial network with an all-digital, fully integrated satellite network to maintain its position as an industry leader in customer service. The VSAT network links the firm's corporate headquarters in Memphis, Tennessee, with all of its 1,500 lodging sites throughout the United States. Staff at any Holiday Inn can access the central reservations database and obtain timely information about room availability at any other site.

Holiday decided to replace its terrestrial communications facilities with satellite to reduce costs and to increase network reliability. A typical terrestrial network has many switching centers—each a potential problem spot—and is vulnerable to a cable being dug up or a microwave tower going out of order because of the weather. Holiday critically depends on the network to book reservations for all of its Holiday Inn, Crown Plaza, Embassy Suite, and Hampton Inn hotels. Holiday's reservation data are also used to improve marketing and customer service: a reservation agent can obtain a complete information file on frequent customers in a matter of seconds and tailor services to the customer's preferences without having to ask the customer a list of questions each time. Holiday can also track "soft times" in the year when it should offer discount rates.

Source: "Holiday Inns Books a 1,500 Site Communications Network," *Uplink* (Hughes Communications Publication, Spring 1988).

bandwidth. The bandwidth is the difference between the highest and lowest frequencies that can be accommodated on a single channel. The larger the range of frequencies, the greater the bandwidth and the greater the medium's telecommunications transmission capacity.

Bandwidth
The range of frequencies that can be accommodated on a particular telecommunications medium.

Deciding which telecommunications medium to employ depends not only on cost but also on how often the channel is used. For example, the monthly charges for satellite links are much higher than for twisted wire, but if a firm uses the link 100 percent of the time, the cost per bit of data could be much lower than leasing a line from the telephone company. Table 7.2 compares the speed and cost of the various transmission media.

7.3 Telecommunications Networks

There are several ways of organizing telecommunications components to form a network and hence several ways of classifying networks. They can be classified by their shape or **network topology;** they can also be classified by their geographic scope and the type of services they provide. Wide area networks, for example, encompass a relatively wide geographic area, from several miles to thousands of miles, whereas local area networks link local

Network topology
The shape or configuration of a network; the most common topologies are the star, bus, and ring.

Table 7.2

Transmission Capacity of Telecommunications Media

In general, the high-speed transmission media are more expensive, but they can handle higher volumes (which reduces the cost per bit). A wide range of speeds is possible for any given medium, depending on the software and hardware configuration. Most microwave and satellite commercial systems support a standard of 6.2 MBPS for high-speed communication but theoretically have much higher transmission rates.

Medium	Speed
Twisted wire	300 BPS to 10 MBPS
Microwave	256 KBPS to 100 MBPS
Satellite	256 KBPS to 100 MBPS
Coaxial cable	56 KBPS to 200 MBPS
Fiber-optic cable	500 KPBS to 1,000 MBPS

Note: BPS = bits per second; KBPS = kilobits per second; and MBPS = megabits per second.

resources such as computers and terminals in the same department or office of a firm. This section will examine both the topological and the geographical classification of networks.

Network Topologies

The three most common network topologies are the star, the bus, and the ring, which are compared in Figure 7.7. Each configuration is appropriate for a particular class of problems.

Star network
A network in which a central host computer is connected to several smaller computers and/or terminals; all communications between the smaller computers or terminals must pass through the host computer.

In the **star network** (panel a), a central host computer is connected to a number of smaller computers, terminals, and other devices such as printers. This topology is popular for organizations in which some aspects of business information processing must be centralized and others can be performed locally. For instance, company-wide files like the master customer list are best stored on a central file. A star network allows data from the master list to be downloaded, or transferred to local computers for processing, and then uploaded back to the central file when the work is complete.

One problem with the star network is its vulnerability. All communication between points in the network must pass through the host computer. Because the host computer is the traffic controller for the other computers and terminals in the system, communication in the network will come to a standstill if the host computer stops functioning.

Bus network
A network in which a number of computers are linked by a single loop circuit made of twisted wire, coaxial cable, or optical fiber; all messages are transmitted to the entire network and can flow in either direction, with special software identifying which component receives each message.

The **bus network** (panel b in Figure 7.7) links a number of computers and other equipment by a single loop circuit made of twisted wire, coaxial cable, or optical fiber. All of the messages are transmitted to the entire network, with special software to identify which components receive each message; messages can flow in both directions along the cable. The most common network for microcomputers is a bus network called Ethernet. Ethernet is a protocol that allows many digital devices to share a common cable for communicating with one another and with central computers. No central host computer controls the network, although a host computer can

Figure 7.7

Three Common Types of Networks: Star, Bus, and Ring

The star network (panel a) is managed by a central or host computer, which is connected to all the other devices in the network. All communications must pass through the host computer; another computer cannot send output to a printer, for example, without first channeling it through the host. The bus network (panel b) connects equipment via a single circuit. There is no host computer to control the network, and all data are transmitted to the entire network. Bus networks are more reliable than ring networks, since they do not depend on one computer to run the network. A third topology or shape is the ring network (panel c), in which the connecting channel (whether wire, cable, or optical fiber) forms a closed loop. This allows each member of the network to communicate directly with any of the others, with data always flowing in one direction.

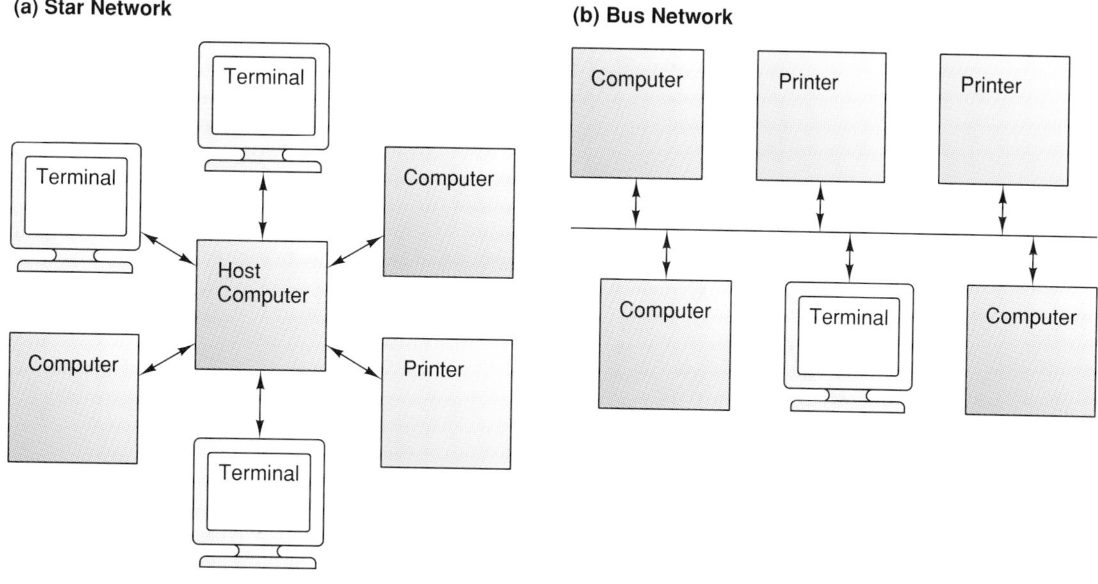

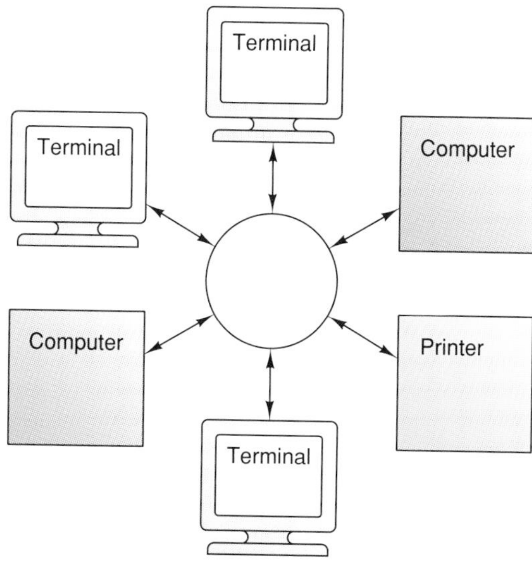

be one of the devices on the network. If one of the computers in the network fails, none of the other components in the network is affected; hence the network is far less vulnerable than a star network to a machine failure. The bus and ring topologies are commonly used for local area networks (LANs), discussed in the following section.

One difficulty of bus networks is that with many users, the system slows down because messages start colliding with one another and have to be re-sent. This network topology is also not appropriate for storing large business data files that must be shared, such as a list of customers in a mail-order firm. The reason is that too many inquiries to the central file will collide and have to be retransmitted. For these reasons, bus networks perform best for applications such as electronic mail, sharing of resources like printers, and file transfers from one machine to another.

Ring network
A network in which a number of computers are linked by a closed loop of wire, coaxial cable, or optical fiber in a manner that allows data to be passed along the loop in a single direction from computer to computer.

Like the bus network, the **ring network** (panel c in Figure 7.7) does not rely on a central host computer and will not break down if one of the component computers malfunctions. The connecting wire, coaxial cable, or optical fiber forms a closed loop that allows each computer in the network to communicate directly with any other computer. Data are passed along the ring from one computer to another, always flowing in one direction, but each computer processes its own applications independently. The most common ring network for personal computers is IBM's Token Ring Network. Ring networks offer similar advantages and disadvantages as bus networks.

Private Branch Exchanges and Local Area Networks

The most common kinds of local networks are local area networks and private branch exchanges.

Private branch exchange (PBX)
A central private switchboard that handles a firm's voice and digital communications needs.

Private Branch Exchanges · A **private branch exchange (PBX)** is a private telephone exchange that handles a firm's internal voice and digital communications needs. A branch exchange is simply the equipment—found in many buildings—that switches incoming and outgoing telephone calls from the telephone company trunk line to individual offices. In the past, most premise exchanges were owned by the telephone company and manually operated by human operators. Today, many are fully automated and owned by the building or business firm.

Like the switching equipment in central offices, today's PBX is a special computer originally designed for handling and switching voice telephone calls. PBXs not only store, forward, transfer, hold, and redial telephone calls, but they also can carry both voice and data to create local networks, switching digital information among computers and office devices. For example, a person can write a letter on a microcomputer, connect to the PBX using his or her own modem and telephone, and distribute a copy of the document to other people in the office or have it printed on the office copying machine. The PBX serves as the connection among all of these devices. The Focus on Technology shows how powerful and versatile PBXs can be.

PBXs offer several advantages. First, PBXs handle both data and voice communications and, in the future, may even handle video signals. For voice

FOCUS ON *Technology*

PBXs Get Smarter

AT&T, Mitel, Hitachi America Telecommunications, and other PBX vendors are all integrating more intelligence into a device that has traditionally been regarded as little more than a voice-traffic cop. According to Dave Leone, PBX marketing manager for Siemens/Rolm in Santa Clara, California, today's PBX is a very powerful computer, with more power than traditional minicomputers in some cases.

Earlier PBXs served mainly as "traffic cops" for voice messaging, but today's PBXs can manage both voice and data via 64 kilobit-per-second lines and act as high-speed bridges between local area networks. The Digital Equipment Corporation paved the way for such breakthroughs with its Computer Integrated Telephony (CIT) project, which proposed a standard for improved PBX-to-host computer interworking so that other computers could help the PBX manage the activity of the telephone network. AT&T and other computer vendors have begun work to enable host processors to interwork with their PBXs.

While recognizing that PBXs have limitations, PBX vendors claim that today's souped-up PBXs can be a good deal. They offer a single platform from which to administer a network, support recognized communications standards, offer powerful resource-sharing features, and allow much of a business firm's installed base of computers and networking equipment to remain in place.

Source: J. B. Miles, "PBXs Get Smarter," *Information Week,* March 12, 1990.

communications, they allow a firm to exercise more control over its internal telephone system than systems provided by the telephone company. For data communications, they create networks without the expense of installing new cable or wire because they rely on the existing phone wires. Devices can be linked wherever there is a phone jack. Therefore, personal computers can be networked together or linked to mainframes or minicomputers using existing telephone lines. Because PBXs rely on a local branch exchange, communications outside the local area must rely on the AT&T long-distance network or common carriers such as MCI or Sprint, which are quite slow (usually 2,400 BPS).

The primary disadvantage of PBXs is that they are limited to telephone lines and therefore cannot easily handle large volumes of data. Although they are good at connecting low-volume digital devices, they are less well developed than local area networks for accessing massive central databases like customer files.

Local area network (LAN)

A transmission network encompassing a limited area, such as a single building or several buildings in close proximity; widely used to link personal computers so that they can share information and peripheral devices.

Local Area Networks · A **local area network (LAN)** encompasses a limited area, usually one building or several buildings in close proximity. Most LANs connect devices located within a 2,000-foot radius and are widely used to link personal computers. In contrast to PBXs, which utilize existing telephone lines, LANs require their own wiring. A cable connects all of the network components.

LANs have higher transmission capacities than PBXs. LANs generally have bus or ring topologies and a high bandwidth. A very fast PBX may have a transmission capacity of over 2 megabits per second, whereas LANs typically transmit at a rate ranging from 256 kilobits per second to over 100 megabits per second, depending on the model and cabling. They are recommended for solutions requiring high volumes of data and high transmission speeds. For example, a problem requiring a solution expressed with graphics would need a LAN because graphic output is so data-intensive.

LANs have become popular for network-based solutions for several reasons: Networks can be built independently of central computer systems. Instead of relying on a central main computer for processing (which can fail), LANs can be installed wherever the business need is the greatest. A LAN solution can be economical, since hardware and software can be shared by many locations. For instance, several offices or departments in a firm may share an expensive laser or color printer. Finally, LANs may be the only viable alternative for electronic mail, video conferencing, graphics, and on-line applications requiring a high-capacity network solution.

LANs are most commonly used to link microcomputers within a building or office so that they can share information and expensive peripheral devices such as laser printers. For instance, United Illuminating, an electric utility corporation in New Haven, Connecticut, uses two LANs ranging from 6 to 12 microcomputers each for preparing documents and providing shared access to printers and shared storage of "boilerplate" document forms (commonly used paragraphs or sections of documents). Another popular application of LANs is in factories, where they link computers and computer-controlled machines. Figure 7.8 shows a typical LAN for an office environment. It consists of several microcomputer workstations, a file server, a network gateway, and a laser printer. We have shown a LAN that uses the ring topology.

File server

A computer with a large hard disk whose function is to allow other devices to share files and programs.

Network gateway

The software that links a local area network to another network, such as the public telephone system or another corporate network.

A **file server** is a computer—often a high-capacity microcomputer—with a large hard disk, and its function is to allow other devices to share files and programs. The file server typically contains the LAN's network management software, which manages the file server and routes and manages communications on the network. The **network gateway** connects the LAN to public networks, such as the telephone network, or to other corporate networks so that the LAN can exchange information with networks external to it. The network operating system works with application software, such as word processing or electronic mail, to keep data traffic flowing smoothly.

LAN technology components consist of metallic or fiber-optic cable that links individual computer devices, special adapters that serve as interfaces to the cable, and software that controls LAN activities. There are four

Figure 7.8

A Local Area Network (LAN)

LANs are becoming very common in business. They are networks that link a limited area, such as one office building or several buildings located close to each other. They are often used for electronic mail, graphics, and shared on-line applications. Here we show a LAN with the ring topology. LANs with the bus topology are also common.

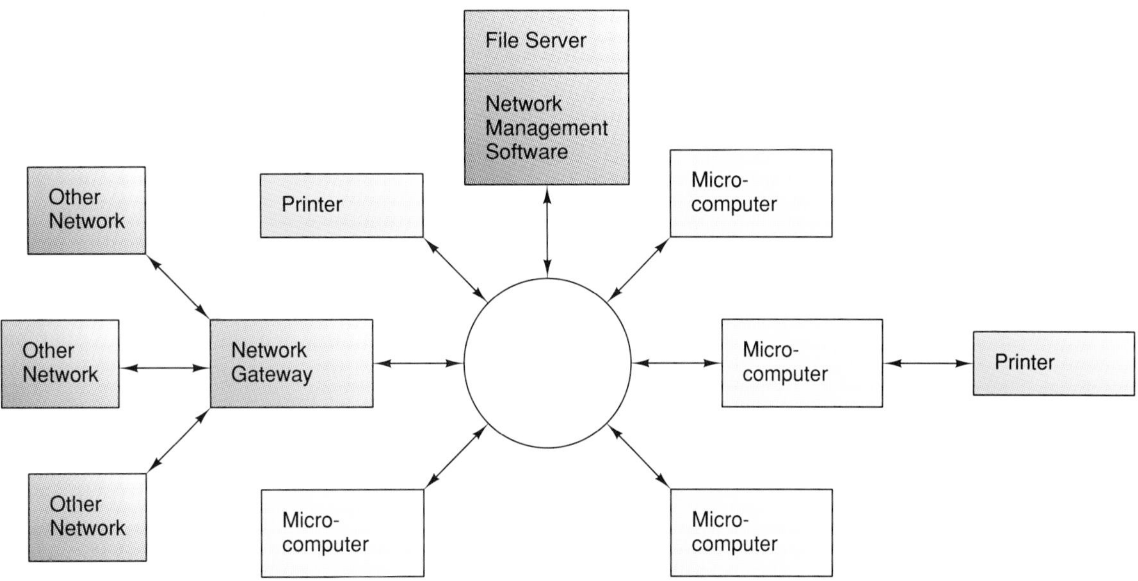

principal LAN technologies for physically connecting devices: Ethernet, developed by Xerox, Digital Equipment Corporation, and Intel; Appletalk from Apple Computer Corporation; Token Ring, developed by IBM and Texas Instruments; and Arcnet, developed by Datapoint. LANs employ either a baseband or a broadband technology. Baseband products, such as thin Ethernet, provide a single path or channel for transmitting text, graphics, voice, or video data. Broadband networks provide several paths or channels so that different types of data, or different messages, can be transmitted simultaneously.

LAN capabilities are also defined by the network operating system employed. The network operating system can reside on every microcomputer in the network (as is the case with the Appletalk network for the Macintosh), or it can reside on a single designated microcomputer, which acts as the server for all the applications on the network.

The primary disadvantages of LANs are that they are more expensive to install than PBXs and are more inflexible, requiring new wiring each time the LAN is moved. LANs also require specially trained staff to manage them and run them.

Wide Area Networks

Wide area network (WAN) A telecommunications network covering a large geographical distance; provided by common carriers that are licensed by the government.

Wide area networks (WANs) span a broad geographical distance, ranging from several miles to entire continents. WANs are provided by common carriers, which are companies (such as AT&T or MCI) that are licensed by the government to provide communications services to the public. The common carrier typically determines transmission rates or interconnections between lines, but the customer is responsible for the content and management of telecommunications. In other words, individual firms are responsible for establishing the most efficient routing of messages, error checking, editing, protocols, and telecommunications management.

WANs may consist of a combination of switched and dedicated lines and microwave and satellite communications. Switched lines are telephone lines that a person can access from his or her terminal to transmit data to another computer; the call is routed or switched through paths to the designated destination. Dedicated lines, or nonswitched lines, can be leased or purchased from common carriers or private communications media vendors and are continuously available for transmission. The lessee typically pays a flat rate for total access to the line. Dedicated lines are often conditioned to transmit data at higher speeds than switched lines and are more appropriate for transmitting high volumes of data. Switched lines, on the other hand, are less expensive and more appropriate for low-volume applications requiring only occasional transmission.

The retailer J. C. Penney uses an extensive WAN to link its 180,000 employees in 1,800 stores. Penney was an early adopter of IBM's Systems Network Architecture (SNA) to connect its 2,000 facilities with seven regional data centers. The WAN is the pipeline that carries credit authorization requests from Penney's 1,800 stores, data from Penney's point-of-sale systems, catalog orders, IBM's Professional Office System, stock quotations data, and other information and services.[2]

Penney's stores exchange information with data centers throughout the United States that are linked with 56-kilobit-per-second land lines. The company also leases satellite circuits for backup. Each data center is equipped with IBM front-end communications processors. Each Penney's store uses an IBM Series/1 minicomputer to attach to the network.

Figure 7.9 shows Penney's wide area network. It handles 350 million credit authorization requests per year (186 per second during peak times), since 52 percent of purchases at Penney's involve charge cards. The network handles an additional 300 million business transactions per year through J. C. Penney Systems Services, a Penney's subsidiary that sells credit card authorization, bill processing, electronic messaging, and other processing services to outside companies.

The Penney's point-of-sale system has utilized optical scanners since 1981. Each store item carries a tag containing machine-readable information, such as price, color, size, and store location. When an item is purchased, a sales clerk scans the tag with a wand scanner attached to an NCR cash register that forwards the information to an IBM Series/1 minicomputer. At the end of each day, the information is transmitted over the network to the closest of the three principal data centers. Overnight processing creates records of each store's sales, which are returned to the store within 24 hours. The sales data can be analyzed for local and regional sales trends or for redistribution of merchandise at the warehouse level. For example, shipments of air conditioners bound for a chilly Boston can be quickly reassigned to a steamy Atlanta.

Figure 7.9

A Wide Area Network (WAN)

A WAN spans a wide geographical area, often covering whole countries or continents. Its lines are provided by common carriers such as MCI or AT&T. This map shows a WAN that serves the retailer J. C. Penney, with data centers distributed over the entire United States. The data centers in Reno, Lenexa, and Columbus handle credit authorization, catalog sales, and store processing, with 13 Tandem TXP-class computers serving as network gateways to credit card company and bank data centers. The Milwaukee and Atlanta data centers support catalog distribution centers, and the Dallas site supports corporate accounting, personnel, and systems development.

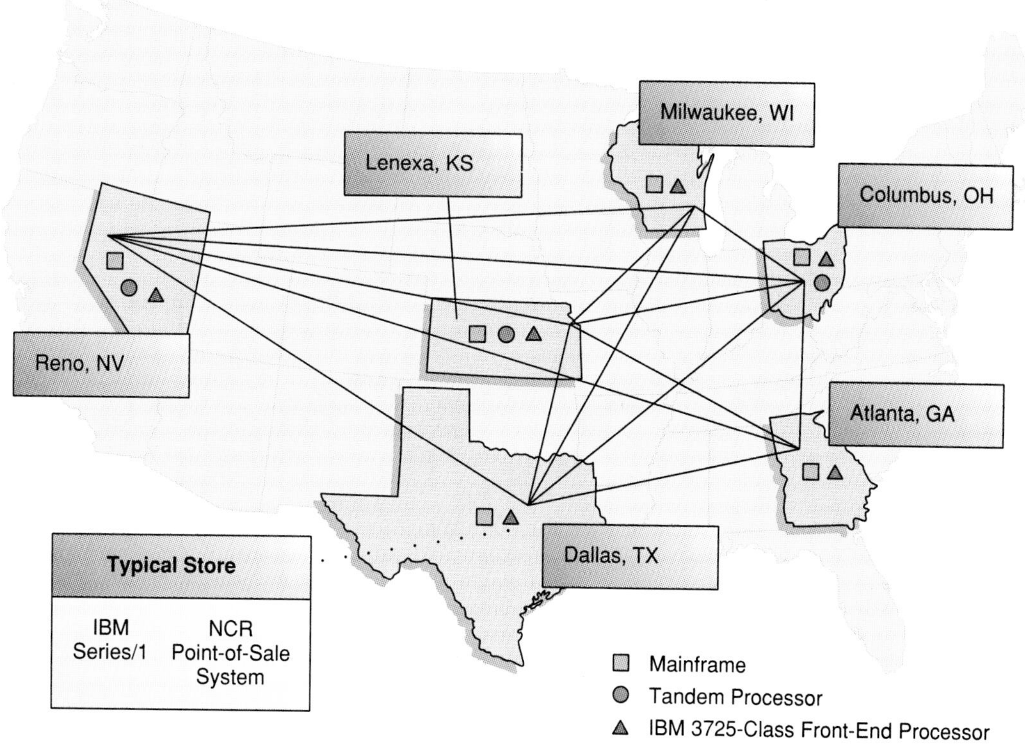

Source: Alan Alper and James Daly, "Penney Cashes in on Leading Edge," *Computerworld*, June 20, 1988. Copyright 1988 by CW Publishing Inc., Framingham, MA 01701—Reprinted from *Computerworld*.

Value-Added Networks · **Value-added networks (VANs)** are an alternative to firms designing and managing their own networks. VANs are private, multimedia, multipath networks managed by third parties that can provide economies of service and management to participating businesses. A private firm establishes and manages the VAN and sells subscriptions to other firms wishing to use it. The network may utilize ordinary telephone or voice-grade lines, satellite links, and other communications channels leased by the value-added carrier. Subscribers pay only for the amount of data they transmit plus a subscription fee. Note that VANs are not common carriers in the sense that they are not regulated monopolies; instead, they are private firms offering a service for a fee. They cannot provide long-distance voice service, however, which is reserved for common carriers.

Value-added network (VAN)
A multimedia, multipath network managed by a private firm that sets up the network and charges other firms a fee to use it.

The term *value added* refers to the extra "value" added to communications by the telecommunications and computing services these networks provide to clients. Customers do not have to invest in network equipment and software or perform their own error checking, editing, routing, and protocol conversion. They may also save on line charges and transmission costs because the costs of using the network are shared among many users. Thus the resulting rates may be lower than if the clients had leased their own lines or satellite services.

Packet switching
The breaking up of a block of text into packets of data approximately 128 bytes long; a value-added network gathers data from its subscribers, divides the data into packets, and sends the packets on any available communications channel.

Another way VANs achieve economies is through **packet switching.** This entails breaking up a lengthy block of text into packets, or small bundles of data approximately 128 bytes long. The VAN gathers information from many users, divides it into small packets, and continuously searches for available communications channels that it leases from common carriers and others on which to send the packets. In contrast, an individual firm might use a single leased line for one hour and then not use it for two or three hours. Packets of data originating at one source can be routed through different paths in the network, then reassembled into the original message when they reach their destination. Packet switching enables communications facilities to be utilized more fully and shared by more users.

VANs are also attractive because they provide special services, such as electronic mail and access to public databases and bulletin boards. Compuserve, Tymnet, and Telenet are popular VAN suppliers.

For example, Manpower, Inc., the world's largest temporary employment service, uses a Tymnet VAN for file transfer, electronic mail, and on-line access. An IBM 4381 host computer at Manpower's Milwaukee corporate headquarters runs applications such as payroll and employee training. The firm's 1,400 offices around the world, all equipped with IBM Personal Computers (PCs), collect client records and transmit them to corporate headquarters, where they are centrally stored. The Tymnet VAN is used to transfer this information from the PCs to the host and vice versa. Manpower uses Tymnet's electronic mail facility to send memos automati-

CompuServe, the on-line information service, provides its customers with information over an Ameritech Direct High Capacity Service and Packet Switched Network. Packets—data in small bundles—from several calls can share the same channels between switching offices, computers, and data banks.

Source: © Mike Steinberg.

cally to all 1,400 offices at once. It also uses the VAN to train its temporary workers on mainframe-based software, such as PROFS and Display-write. Training packages for these products reside on Manpower's Milwaukee host, where they can be accessed from any of Manpower's remote PCs.[3]

Problem Solving with Networks: Cautions and Concerns

Several factors must be considered when a solution involves the use of a network:

1. **Response time:** This refers to the amount of time an on-line system takes to send a transaction or query over a network and receive a response. An example might be an inquiry about the balance in a client's checking account in an on-line banking system. Many factors affect response time, including the processing speed of application software and the ease of extracting information or records from databases. Many of these factors are network related, however, such as the transmission capacity of a telecommunications channel and related equipment, the distance data must be communicated, and the amount of traffic on the network. High error rates, which are primarily caused by line noise or power surges, also degrade response time because messages must be retransmitted.

2. **Reliability:** A network may be unable to deliver the required solution if it is crippled by excessive "downtime" (the period of time a network is nonoperational). Businesses such as Mastercard would come to a standstill if their network operations were interrupted for more than a few minutes. Network reliability is a function of the quality of telecommunications channels and equipment, error rates, and the quality of the personnel managing the network.

3. **Cost:** There are extra costs for using a network solution, such as the cost of installing or renting the channels, purchasing telecommunications equipment, and employing and training personnel to manage the network. Alternative network solutions may have different cost structures that should be considered—for example, a PBX is less costly to install than a LAN but has a lower transmission capacity. Savings may also be realized by increasing response time or by reducing transmission errors. The cost and performance trade-offs of alternative network structures must be figured into the solution design.

4. **Security:** Networks are vulnerable to disruption and penetration by outsiders at many points. A network solution must consider the critical nature of the data flowing through the network and the extent to which they need to be safeguarded by special security measures. This issue is discussed in detail in Chapter 16.

7.4 Applying Telecommunications to Business Problems

Firms are making more intensive use of telecommunications to "compete against the clock," accelerating the time it takes to bring their products to market. This is especially true of firms with operations in multiple geographic locations that must be closely coordinated throughout the production cycle. Many of the applications discussed throughout this text employ telecommunications technology to make decisions faster and to accelerate the production cycle. Here we discuss some of the leading telecommunications applications for communicating, coordinating, and speeding the flow of information throughout business firms.

Electronic Mail

Electronic mail
The computer-to-computer exchange of messages.

Electronic mail, or E-mail, is the computer-to-computer exchange of messages that has become a way of eliminating telephone tag and costly long-distance telephone charges. By 1992, 16 billion messages will be transmitted annually by this technology. It is possible for a person with a personal computer attached to a modem or a terminal to send notes and even lengthier documents just by typing in the name of the message's recipient. Leading commercial (public) E-mail services, such as EasyLink, Telemail, Dialcom, MCI Mail, and AT&T Mail, offer mailboxes to individual subscribers. Western Union's EasyLink will also transmit a message to a fax machine or send it by messenger if it cannot be received electronically.

By providing faster and more efficient communication between different functional areas of the firm, E-mail can speed up the production process. For example, Liz Claiborne, a leading U.S. clothing manufacturer, uses electronic mail to coordinate activities between its corporate headquarters in New York and New Jersey and its offices in Hong Kong, Korea, Taiwan, Singapore, the Philippines, and Shanghai. Marketing and administrative decisions are made in the United States, but Claiborne's production is handled in hundreds of factories in the Far East. Manufacturing activities and design and production decisions must be carefully coordinated. In a given fashion season, separate items must be color-coordinated, with matching dyes and consistent sizing. Since matching pieces may be produced in different factories, this is a complex process. Claiborne tried telex communication overseas but found it too cumbersome: telex messages could not be sorted by recipient, and critical messages that needed immediate attention could not be singled out. Clairborne now uses E-mail, which can automatically sort messages by department and route them to the appropriate recipient. Using Infonet's value-added network, Claiborne sends 4,500 E-mail messages a day.[4]

Voice mail
A telecommunications system in which the spoken message of the sender is digitized, transmitted over a telecommunications network, and stored on disk until the recipient is ready to listen; at this time the message is reconverted to audio form.

Voice Mail · In a **voice mail** system, the spoken message of the sender is digitized, transmitted over a telecommunications network, and stored on disk for later retrieval. When the recipient is ready to listen, the messages are reconverted to audio form. Various "store and forward" capabilities notify recipients that messages are waiting. Recipients have the option of saving these messages for future use, deleting them, or routing them to other parties. Sophisticated mainframe- or minicomputer-based voice mail systems can store hundreds of hours of messages and handle over 100 incoming phone lines, while personal computer–based systems are much smaller in scope.

The voice mail system in Figure 7.10 has an "auto-attendant" feature for automatically routing incoming calls. Calls can be transferred automati-

Figure 7.10

A Voice Mail System

A voice mail system routes incoming telephone calls. If there is no answer at the requested telephone extension, the caller can leave a voice message that the system digitizes, transmits over a telecommunications channel, and stores on disk for later retrieval. When the recipient retrieves the message, it is converted back into audio form. This voice mail system uses an "auto attendant," which automatically routes calls and either rings the extension, screens calls, or holds calls.

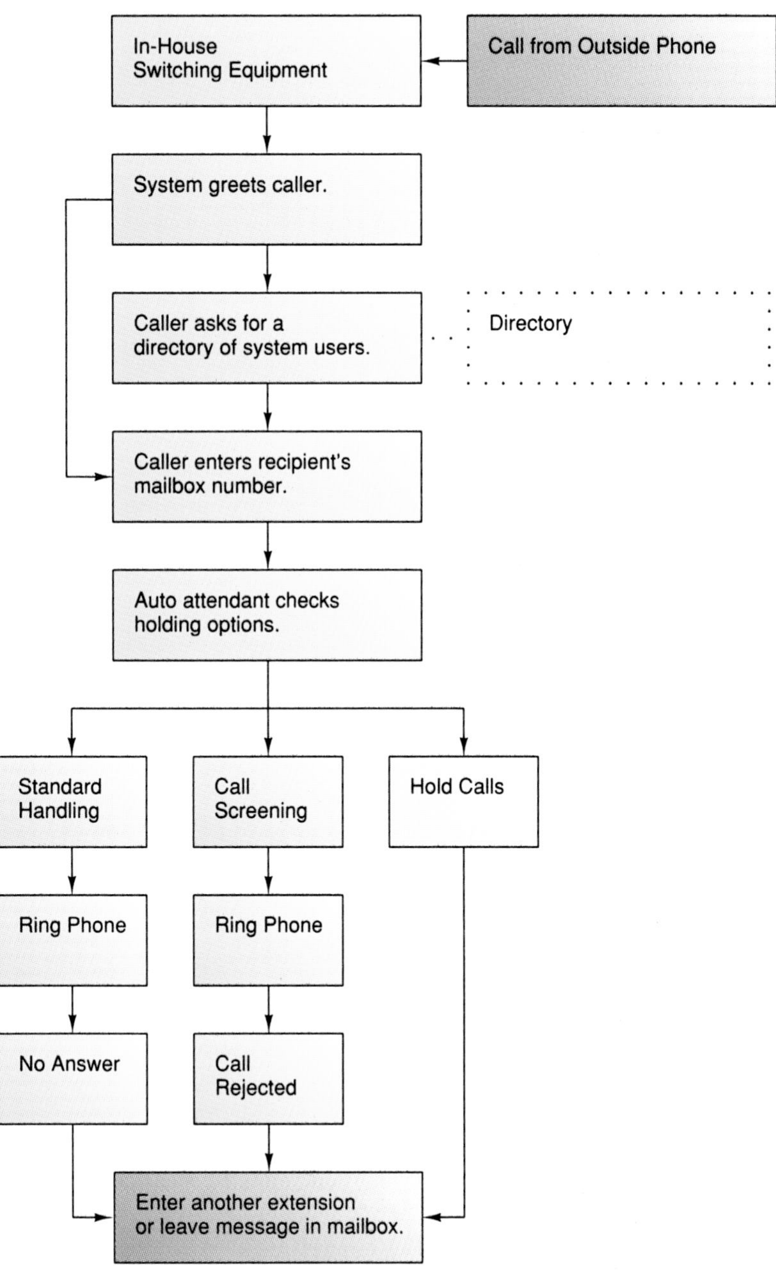

The Union Pacific Railroad uses a network of 450 Pitney Bowes facsimile machines to link rail yards across the U.S. to a customer service center in St. Louis. This network allows Union Pacific to tell customers about how, when, and where their shipments are moving as they are moving.
Source: Courtesy of Pitney Bowes Facsimile Systems.

cally to any phone extension; the system can also screen or hold calls. If the specified extension does not answer, the system will leave the message in the mailbox set up for that extension. The message can then be retrieved at a later time.

Facsimile (fax)
A machine that can transmit documents containing both text and graphics over telephone lines; the sending machine digitizes and transmits the image, which is reproduced as a facsimile (fax) by the receiving machine.

Facsimile · **Facsimile (fax)** machines can transmit documents containing both text and graphics over ordinary telephone lines. The image is scanned, digitized, and transmitted by a sending fax machine and reproduced in hard-copy form by a receiving fax machine. The process results in a duplicate, or facsimile, of the original.

Teleconferencing

Teleconferencing
The use of telecommunications technology to enable people to meet electronically; can be accomplished via telephone or electronic mail.

Telecommunications technology has provided **teleconferencing** capabilities that allow people to meet electronically. In electronic meetings, several people "confer" via telephone or E-mail group communications software (see Chapter 13). With video teleconferencing or videoconferencing, participants can see each other over video screens.

Video teleconferencing requires complex video conference facilities, technology to integrate images with data and voice transmission, and appropriate technology and transmission media for relaying the massive volume of data required to transmit images. In the past, most firms could not afford this technology, but advances in transmission technology have now made video teleconferencing more affordable and easier to implement.

FOCUS ON *Problem Solving*

GE Bases Global Net Strategy on Video Teleconferencing

The General Electric Corporation (GE) has launched a two-phase, three-year plan to use video teleconferencing to promote information sharing between its U.S. operations and its international joint-venture businesses. Implemented by AT&T, France Telecom, and British Telecom, the network will link 20 U.S. offices with offices in 25 countries, providing seven-digit dialing for GE offices worldwide. The network, which will be managed by GE's network-control center in Princeton, New Jersey, will comprise many T-1 links and three intelligent nodes in Princeton, London, and Paris with the Rembrandt series of Codecs by Compression Labs, Inc., as the computer system driving the video teleconferencing. (A T-1 link is a telephone line, leased from a common carrier, that can carry both voice and digital messages at 1.544 megabits per second.)

Teleconferencing will help GE customize its products for specific markets in different countries and implement new production and engineering techniques. The firm will be able to use a few dozen internal video conference rooms to hold meetings with 30 to 40 customers and suppliers around the world. It hopes this technology will help the firm solve day-to-day problems as if the factory were in the same building rather than thousands of miles away.

Source: "GE Enters the Video Age," *Information Week*, June 5, 1989.

Teleconferencing helps bring ideas and people together from remote locations, reducing the need for costly business travel and saving travel time. For example, as the Focus on Problem Solving describes, the General Electric Corporation has adopted video teleconferencing as a means of reducing executive travel and facilitating global sharing of technical information.

Electronic Data Interchange

Electronic data interchange, or **EDI,** is the direct computer-to-computer exchange of standard business transaction documents, such as invoices, bills of lading, and purchase orders, between two separate organizations. EDI saves money and time because transactions can be electronically transmitted, eliminating the printing and handling of paper at one end and the inputting of data at the other. Figure 7.11 illustrates how EDI streamlines information processing.

Electronic data interchange (EDI)
The direct computer-to-computer exchange of standard business documents, such as invoices, bills of lading, and purchase orders, between two separate organizations.

EDI differs from electronic mail in that it transmits an actual transaction, as opposed to a primarily text message, and features standardized transaction formats, content-related error checking, and actual processing of the information.

Various transaction documents, such as purchase orders and invoices, can be generated electronically and passed from one organization's information systems to another using a telecommunications network. Routine

Figure 7.11

Electronic Data Interchange (EDI)

EDI is the computer-to-computer exchange of standard business documents, such as purchase orders, invoices, and bills of lading, between two separate organizations. Transmitting these documents electronically, or on-line, saves time and money by cutting down on paperwork and data entry. This diagram illustrates an EDI system that transmits a purchase order (P.O.) from the buyer to the seller.

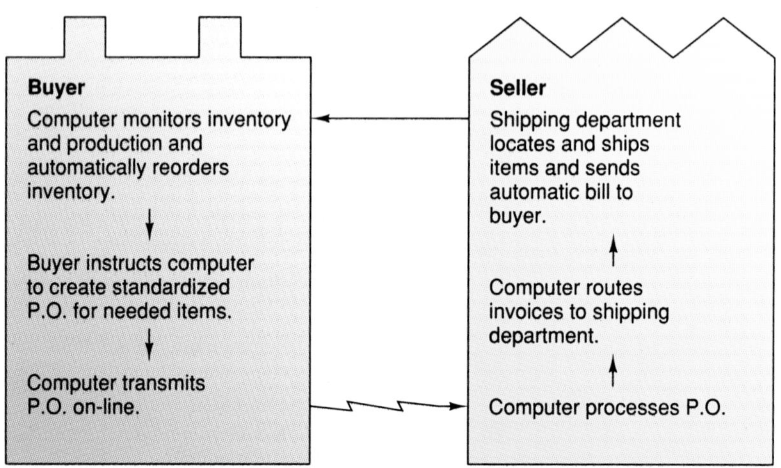

processing costs are lower, because there is less need to transfer data from hard-copy forms into computer-ready transactions. EDI also reduces transcription errors and associated costs that occur when data are entered and printed out many times.

For example, United Refrigerated Services, Inc., in Atlanta, Georgia, has found that EDI helps it reduce both costs and errors. Receiving invoices and purchase orders on a real-time basis through EDI eliminates the peaks and valleys that occur when companies mail documents daily or weekly. There are no more "panic afternoons" and overtime when a bundle of release orders arrives by mail at 4 P.M.. Instead, orders flow in all day and staff can pace themselves. By reducing transcription errors, EDI has also produced savings at many points in the order-processing cycle. As a public warehouse for the grocery industry, United Refrigerated receives more than 1,000 release orders a day. Each time an error occurs, the firm pays freight both ways. It has to restock the product, and it loses customer goodwill. EDI has almost eliminated errors.[5]

EDI can produce strategic benefits as well; it helps firms increase market share by "locking in" customers—making it easier for customers or distributors to order from them rather than from competitors. EDI also reduces transaction processing costs and can cut inventory costs by reducing the amount of time components are in inventory. For example, by handling 80 percent of its general merchandise orders through EDI, the K Mart Corporation in Troy, Michigan, has reduced lead time for ordering most stock by three or four days, resulting in substantial interest savings.

For EDI to work properly, three key components are required:

1. **Transaction standardization:** Participating companies must agree on the form of the message to be exchanged. Transaction formats and data must be standardized.
2. **Translation software:** Special software must be developed to convert incoming and outgoing messages into a form comprehensible to other companies.
3. **Appropriate mailbox facilities:** Companies must select a third-party value-added network with mailbox facilities that allow messages to be sent, sorted, and held until needed by the receiving computer.

Integrated Services Digital Network

Integrated Services Digital Network (ISDN) is an emerging international standard for extending common-carrier digital service to homes and offices from central telephone company facilities. Imagine sitting in your office or dormitory room looking at your computer screen; in one window is a spreadsheet, and in the other is the moving picture of a friend or colleague located across the country with whom you are working. You can both share voice messages, digital information, and video pictures. All of this information comes over a single twisted wire telephone line that is totally managed by the local phone company. That means you have integrated voice, digital, and video service and great flexibility with no expensive rewiring with coaxial cable; you just plug your computer/telephone into the wall socket. This is the promise of ISDN.

Integrated Services Digital Network (ISDN)
An emerging international standard for extending common carrier digital service to homes and offices from central telephone company centers.

ISDN is a product of local and long-distance telephone companies that delivers two 64-kilobit-per-second channels and one 16-kilobit-per-second channel to the desk top or room through ordinary phone wire. Currently, there are about 70,000 ISDN installations in the United States, all of which are limited to regional areas served by a single Bell operating company (local phone companies). National ISDN service will emerge in the 1990s as local Bell companies upgrade their equipment. Currently, implementation of ISDN is restricted by its cost, regional limitations, and the difficulties business firms have experienced in learning how to use the technology. Once the technology is fully developed, however, and prices fall, ISDN will become a leading network alternative in the 1990s.

For an example of the difficulties ISDN can present for firms, consider the experience of Harrah's Reno, one of the largest gambling resorts in Reno, Nevada. Harrah's recently installed an information kiosk at Reno International Airport connected to Harrah's Hotel complex via an ISDN network installed by the local Bell phone company. The idea was that customers would exit their plane and walk to the kiosk, where they would enter their room request using a screen menu. A desk clerk from the resort would appear on a monitor and help the guest register. A magnetic card reader attached to the terminal would take credit card information, while a camera captured an image of the guest and transmitted it to a fax machine at the resort. When customers reached the hotel, they would not need to register or sign in. A doorman would recognize the guests from the fax picture, greet them personally, and walk them to their rooms (or to the casino tables).

Unfortunately, while the technology worked perfectly, it tended to scare guests, who were frightened when the clerk appeared on the screen. Only 10 of 70 or 80 people who walked up to the terminal would use it. The rest were intimidated. Harrah's has withdrawn the experiment for now, but it expects to use ISDN services throughout its operation in the future once the needs of customers and the technical abilities of ISDN are more fully understood.[6]

In addition to implementing E-mail, EDI, and ISDN, firms are also discovering the potential of another form of electronic information exchange—the bulletin board system. The Focus on People describes how CBS Records is using such a system to save time and reduce costs and errors.

7.5 Leading-Edge Application: New Networks Speed Airline Travel

Covia, the systems company that runs United Airline's Apollo computerized reservation system, is linked to 60,000 reservations terminals. It is in the midst of a ten-year, $1 billion plan to replace its centralized mainframe-based network with a distributed network that will integrate personal computer LANs at every travel office with 13 regional minicomputers or mainframes.[7]

The system comprises 23 subnetworks and can handle up to 2,000 nodes (computerized devices). The personal computers are linked in LANs using IBM's Token Ring Network, which works by passing an electric "baton" around until it is picked up by a computer that needs to use the network. When the computer completes its work, it releases the baton for others to use. Covia has developed Open Systems Manager software, which enables equipment from different venders to share data and applications.

Each LAN has a database for airlines and other travel information required at that site. Orders placed at these sites are communicated to the regional computers, which distribute updates to the other sites and coordinate services such as maintenance schedules for aircraft and gates. The LAN is also attached to application computers that handle such tasks as determining meals and assigning crew members to specific flights. The LAN accepts radio information from incoming planes to monitor arrival times.

Covia has already installed this system at United's terminal at Chicago's O'Hare International Airport. Desktop workstations now handle tasks that were formerly handled by central mainframes, such as scheduling the departure of an airplane or assigning a crew change. The mainframe computers have become electronic "librarians," handling information requests from smaller computers in the network. This network arrangement is particularly appealing to airlines, for whom information processing must reflect demand for services and employees are spread over a wide area.

To the observer, Covia functions like a seamless network of personal computers and other microprocessor-controlled devices that manage vir-

FOCUS ON *People*

Electronic Bulletin Board Speeds Catalog Preparation

Thomas Del Otero's job is easier thanks to the help of a computer bulletin board system (BBS). A BBS is a system for exchanging information. On such a system, a user can post public messages that others can read. The user can also send an electronic mail message or data to a specific individual.

Del Otero uses a BBS to carry out his job of producing catalogs at CBS Records. The catalogs provide retailers with listings of CBS's classical, rock, jazz, and other recordings. To produce a catalog, Del Otero retrieves information about each record—title, musician, selection number, and so forth—from the company's mainframe computer. The software that retrieves this information automatically eliminates duplicate entries and converts the information into a format that Del Otero's typesetter can transform into type for the catalog.

The BBS saves Del Otero from performing the tedious task of making sure that the entries precisely reflect CBS's inventory. He also avoids the need to coordinate the transmission of data with the typesetter: He merely sends the complete file, which the typesetter retrieves at its convenience.

This automated process has reduced the several weeks required to produce the catalog to several days. Because Del Otero can retrieve up-to-date inventory data on such a short schedule, he need not incur the trouble and expense of having the typesetter make last-minute changes to the catalog.

According to Del Otero's estimate, besides making his job easier, the bulletin board system saves CBS $100,000 a year.

Source: Russ Lockwood, "The Corporate BBS," *Personal Computing*, March 20, 1990, pp. 63–68.

tually all of United's operations at O'Hare Airport. Using their desktop workstations, reservation agents can communicate with Denver mainframes that handle reservations and send data to the Unisys mainframes in Chicago that manage scheduling of crews. They also print tickets, plan airline schedules, and provide timely scheduling data to ground crews. A broadband cable TV network connects the LAN and desktop workstations with the TV monitors that display arrivals and departures. Tiny network-connected computers synchronize the dozens of clocks in United's O'Hare terminal. Figure 7.12 illustrates how this network operates.

The Covia system is still in its early stages and is only operational at O'Hare. At other United hub airports, United's terminals still perform all

Figure 7.12

The Covia Network

An ambitious, extensive network connects United Airlines' reservation and information systems. (Covia is the systems company that runs the system.) Information from regional mainframes and even incoming airplanes is transmitted to a local area network. The LAN manages multiple computers, desktop workstations, and TV monitors so that all sites have access to continually updated information.

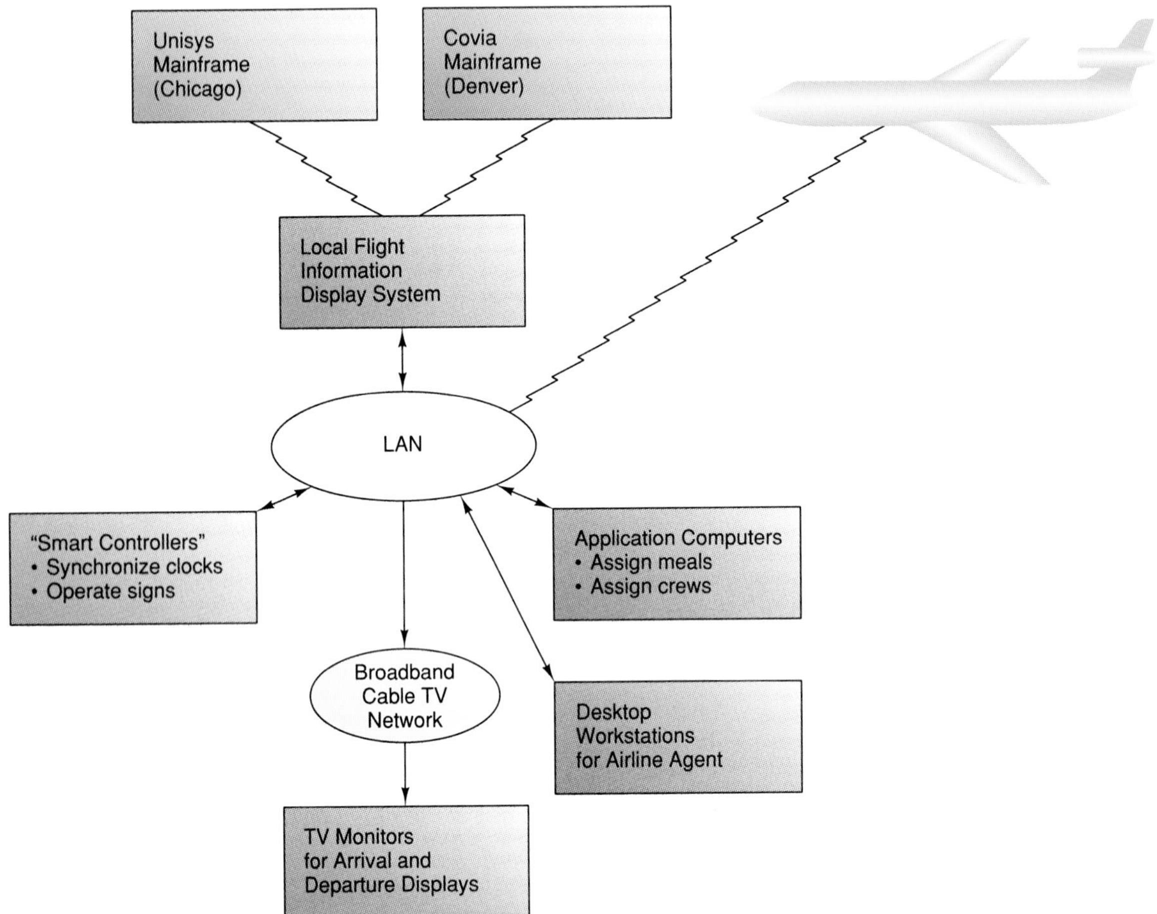

Source: John Markoff, "A System to Speed Airline Travel," *The New York Times*, September 6, 1989, p. D6. Copyright © 1989 by The New York Times Company. Reprinted by permission.

their processing on a central mainframe with dumb terminals. Remote locations like boarding areas still do not have their own local processing power. If the main computer goes down, boarding and ticketing grind to a halt.

Covia recently added a service for travel agents called Focalpoint, which allows agents to capture and sort lists of discount seats in any categories they choose. This enables agents to locate discounts tailored to specific corporate clients more easily. About 10,000 Focalpoint workstations have been installed.

Summary

- Telecommunications can be defined as communication by electronic means.

- Asynchronous transmission and synchronous transmission are two conventions for determining where a character begins or ends when data are transmitted from one computer to another.

- There are three different transmission modes governing direction of data flow over a telecommunications medium: simplex transmission, half-duplex transmission, and full-duplex transmission.

- Two types of signals are used in telecommunications systems: analog and digital. Analog signals are used primarily for voice transmission, whereas digital signals are used for data transmission and some voice transmission. A modem can be used to convert digital signals to analog form and vice versa.

- The essential components of a telecommunications network are computers, terminals or other input/output devices, communications channels, communications processors (such as modems, multiplexers, and front-end processors), and telecommunications software.

- Different components of a telecommunications network, which typically use a wide array of hardware and software technology, can communicate with each other with a common set of rules called protocols.

- The principal telecommunications media are twisted wire, coaxial cable, fiber-optic cable, microwave, and satellite.

- Telecommunications transmission rate is measured in bits per second. The transmission capacity of a particular telecommunications medium is a function of its bandwidth, the range of frequencies that the medium can accommodate.

- The three common network topologies are the star network, the bus network, and the ring network.

- Local area networks (LANs) and private branch exchanges (PBXs) are used for local, short-range office and building systems. A PBX is a central, private switchboard that can be used for digital transmission among computers and office devices as well as for voice transmission. A LAN typically consists of a group of microcomputers linked together with a cable. LANs are useful for large-volume, high-speed communications among computers, whereas PBXs are most useful for mixed voice and data traffic involving low volumes and lower speeds.

- Wide area networks (WANs) cover large geographical areas and are provided by common carriers.

- Value-added networks (VANs) are privately owned and managed networks that carry digital information over long distances. In addition to providing baseline communications, VANs also provide editing, storage, and redistribution of information for a firm.

- Four factors should be considered when designing a business communications network: response time, reliability, cost, and security.

• Electronic mail, voice mail, teleconferencing, EDI, and ISDN are some of the leading and fastest growing telecommunications solutions available in the 1990s.

Key Terms

Analog signal
Digital signal
Modulation
Demodulation
Modem
Asynchronous transmission
Synchronous transmission
Simplex transmission
Half-duplex transmission
Full-duplex transmission
Channel
Front-end processor
Host computer
Multiplexer
Concentrator
Controller
Protocol
Twisted wire
Coaxial cable
Fiber optics
Microwave
Baud
Bandwidth
Network topology
Star network
Bus network
Ring network
Private branch exchange (PBX)
Local area network (LAN)
File server
Network gateway
Wide area network (WAN)
Value-added network (VAN)
Packet switching
Electronic mail
Voice mail
Facsimile (fax)
Teleconferencing
Electronic data interchange (EDI)
Integrated Services Digital Network (ISDN)

Review Questions

1. Name and briefly describe the principal functions of telecommunications systems.
2. What is the difference between an analog signal and a digital signal?
3. What is the difference between synchronous and asynchronous transmission? How do half-duplex, full-duplex, and simplex transmission differ?
4. Name and briefly describe the components of a telecommunications network.
5. How do a modem, a concentrator, and a controller differ?
6. What are the five principal telecommunications media? Compare them in terms of speed and cost.
7. What are the measures of telecommunications transmission speed? What is the relationship between the bandwidth and the transmission capacity of a channel?

8. Name and briefly describe the three principal network topologies.
9. What is the difference between a local area network and a private branch exchange? Between a wide area network and a value-added network?
10. What is the difference between electronic mail and electronic data interchange (EDI)?
11. Distinguish between teleconferencing and video teleconferencing.

Discussion Questions

1. Which type of transmission medium is most suitable for the following situations? Why?
   a. *USA Today* uses a network to relay each day's newspaper layout to 31 print locations across the world.
   b. The law firm of Sidley & Austin wants to link 1,000 personal computers used for legal document preparation and to send electronic mail between the firm's primary offices in Chicago and its branches in New York, Los Angeles, and Washington, D.C.
   c. Lloyd's of London wants to link all of its 1,000 underwriters, located in the same building in corporate headquarters.

2. Nathan Kaplan is a prominent obstetrician-gynecologist in Fairfield County, Connecticut, who is starting to use personal computers in his busy office. His office staff includes one receptionist, one secretary, and one nurse. The office uses an IBM Personal Computer (PC) for writing letters, simple office accounting (payroll, accounts payable, billing), and maintaining patient files. Business has grown to the point where one PC is not enough. Kaplan wants to purchase another so that one PC can be utilized by the receptionist in the front office and one by the secretary in the back room. Both need access to the same data and files. What networking options should he consider? What factors should be taken into account in the final selection?

Problem-Solving Exercises

1. Using Table 7.2 for reference, calculate approximately how long it would take to transmit this chapter over the following media: twisted wire, coaxial cable, fiber-optic cable, and satellite.

2. Newton's is a discount appliance and electronics retail chain with outlets in over 50 locations throughout the Northeast. Its inventory and other major application systems are processed by a minicomputer in corporate headquarters in Hartford, Connecticut. If an outlet runs out of a popular item, such as large air conditioners, it can obtain that item from another outlet or from the firm's central warehouse. Newton's currently has no way to maintain up-to-date data on inventory. Outlets collect purchase transactions at the checkout counter and mail them to corporate headquarters. Customer complaints have mounted, because customers are frequently told that an item is in inventory when it has been sold out for the season.

Newton's is afraid it will lose market share unless it develops an on-line point-of-sale system with up-to-date inventory data for each outlet and for the central warehouse. Write a proposal for an on-line, real-time, point-of-sale system using telecommunications technology. Draw a diagram of the proposed network and write an analysis of appropriate hardware, transmission media, and network topology. Provide reasons for your recommendations.

Notes

1. Robert Moran, "Financial Network Hits New York Streets," *Computerworld,* March 27, 1989.
2. Alan Alper and James Daly, "Penney Cashes in on Leading Edge," *Computerworld,* June 20, 1988.
3. International Data Corporation, "Networking Technology and Applications," special advertising supplement, *The New York Times,* March 27, 1989.
4. Ibid.
5. Lawrence Stevens, "Users Say EDI Cuts Inventory Costs, Speeds Product Delivery," *Computerworld,* May 2, 1988.
6. Alan Radding, "Small Wagers Can Pay Off but Don't Bet the Farm," *Computerworld,* November 20, 1989.
7. John Markoff, "A System to Speed Airline Travel," *The New York Times,* September 6, 1989; "Cooperative Processing: Solving the Network Problem," *Information Week,* November 14, 1988; International Data Corporation, "Networking Technology and Applications," special advertising supplement, *The New York Times,* March 27, 1989.

Problem-Solving Case

Tying in Acquisitions at First Union Bank

Since 1985, First Union Bank of Charlotte, North Carolina, has grown from a statewide bank with $8 billion in assets to a superregional bank with $28 billion in assets. With 723 branches in five southeastern states, First Union has become the third largest bank in North Carolina and the nineteenth largest in the United States.

First Union's major acquisitions include the Florida-based Atlantic Bancorporation, First Bankers Corporation of Florida, Florida Commercial Banks, Inc., Northwestern Financial Corporation in North Carolina, Southern Bancorporation, Inc. in South Carolina, and First Railroad & Banking Company of Georgia. In the past three years alone, First Union bought 20 banks with branches in both rural and urban areas.

First Union's acquisitions motto is "Common name, common systems, and common products with a pricing differential." It will price the same financial product differently in different states. When a new bank is acquired, it is immediately consolidated with First Union, and its applications migrate to common, company-wide systems. The consolidation process takes approximately 18 months. First Union has merged over 40 institutions in the past five years.

First Union's common-system/common-product approach is designed to bring new services to new markets. Many of the acquisitions did not offer

the same financial services and products as First Union. By integrating their systems with First Union's, they can sell the same products as First Union and make more money.

First Union's branches and acquisitions are linked via a network that must process an average of 500,000 transactions per day and support 500 ATMs (automatic teller machines). In 1985 the bank had 1,500 CRTs; now it has 7,800, with 1,500 in Georgia alone. Previously, First Union used terrestrial circuitry, but it switched to satellite links in 1988. Under a $22 million multi-year contract with GTE Spacenet of McLean, Virginia, each bank branch is equipped with a 1.8-meter VSAT satellite antenna dish and other peripheral equipment.

In North Carolina, First Union had to deal with more than 50 providers of land-based communications. In rural areas these often amounted to mom-and-pop telecommunications companies with no data communications experience. In North Carolina, the bank paid about 60 cents per circuit mile of analog data communications channel, but in other southeastern states the equivalent might cost $1.50.

When the bank bought two other banks in the same area, the existing terrestrial network had to be modified. First Union either had to add on to the existing network or replace it with a larger one, entailing high rearrangement charges. Installing terrestrial circuitry can take 150 to 180 days.

VSAT can ordinarily be installed within 30 days, but it can be done overnight if an emergency requires. First Union's management information systems department only needs to make sure the satellite can be seen from each new location, install the VSAT on the roof, run a cable, and plug in the indoor unit and terminals.

First Union has realized cost savings from switching to satellite. It used to pay $100,000 a month to more than 50 providers of land-based lines. The satellite network saves approximately $90,000 per month. Reliability has increased to 99.6 percent, compared to 98–98.5 percent using land-based lines. Every 0.1 percent increase in channel availability translates into 7.44 more hours per month of availability at the company's 500 ATM machines. First Union estimates that the new network's higher speed saves one second per transaction, or 120 work hours per day throughout its five-state network.

Case Study Questions

1. What problems did First Union encounter with land-based telecommunications networks?
2. Why was a satellite-based network an appropriate solution for this firm?
3. Many other banks do not use a satellite network. Why not?
4. What benefits did a satellite network bring to First Union?

C H A P T E R · E I G H T

Artificial Intelligence *in* Business

Chapter Outline

8.1 Introduction
- The Nature of Artificial Intelligence
- The Family of Artificial Intelligence Techniques
- The Development of Artificial Intelligence

8.2 Expert Systems
- The Nature of Expert Systems
- The Components of an Expert System
- Building Expert Systems
- The Role of Expert Systems in Business Firms
- Leading-Edge Application: Taking Intelligent Orders at Westinghouse
- Limitations of Expert Systems

8.3 Other Intelligent Techniques
- Neural Networks
- Leading-Edge Application: A Neural Network Mortgage Insurance Underwriter
- Parallel Sensor Systems
- An Intelligent Database Search Machine
- Assessing Machine Intelligence

Learning Objectives

After reading and studying this chapter, you will:

1. Know what artificial intelligence is and how it has evolved.
2. Be familiar with the many varieties of artificial intelligence.
3. Be able to define and describe expert systems.
4. Know what neural networks are and how they operate.
5. Understand what is meant by "intelligent" techniques and how they are used in the computer-based decision process.
6. Know how and why business organizations use artificial intelligence techniques.

Looking for Hot Prospects at R.R. Donnelley

R.R. Donnelley & Sons is the largest mailing list house in the United States, supplying mail-order catalog companies, retailers, magazine publishers, and political candidates with lists of people who might buy, contribute, or respond to advertising campaigns. Donnelley maintains names of millions of citizens arranged into countless groups, subgroups, census tracks, and regions.

How does Donnelley identify the persons who are most likely to respond to an advertisement or an appeal for contributions? In the past, Donnelley, like other mail-order firms, developed elaborate statistical models based on region, income, status group, education, job, and census track (zip code) location to predict the most likely customers for a product. But these early models were expensive to produce and run, difficult to maintain, and therefore infrequently updated. Consequently, Donnelley has now turned to a new computer technique called artificial intelligence to cull the millions of names in its files and produce a much smaller list of people most likely to respond.

Recently, Selectronic Services of Chicago, a division of Donnelley, purchased an artificial intelligence software package called More/2. More/2 is an expert system with built-in rules that judges the effectiveness of mailing lists. The system looks at two sources of data: the results of previous mailings and limited test mailings sent to prospects. Judgments about whether to include a

given person on a list are made on the basis of age, sex, income, zip code, region, marital status, and 15 other background factors.

What makes More/2 especially interesting is that the rules or model can be changed if necessary. For example, an initial analysis may determine that a food catalog selling specialty seafood should be sent to single, working women living in apartments in major metropolitan areas with average incomes above $24,000. More/2 would create a mailing model and a list based on these key variables, and a promotion would be conducted. The response rates would then be analyzed and used to change the model automatically as needed. It might turn out that both married and single women should receive the mailing. If the catalog publisher later decided to add meat products to its line, the profile of responders would change again.

Initial results of More/2-directed mailings have been encouraging. Selectronic Services has learned that it can mail to just 50 percent of an existing list and, by targeting just the right people, can achieve 70–80 percent of the responses obtained when the entire list is used. As a result, Selectronic can send more frequent mailings to groups most likely to respond.

More/2 serves as an expert adviser, not a final decision maker. Selectronic's human experts note that the system sometimes overweights a factor. In that case, the human experts correct the factor by weighting it downward.

Source: Based on Dwight B. Davis, "Artificial Intelligence Goes to Work," *High Technology,* April 1987.

The R.R. Donnelley example indicates how powerful computers can be if they display some intelligence. In many areas of business life, from banks and credit card companies to machine manufacturers, new kinds of information systems based on artificial intelligence technology are being used to guide human experts, help managers make decisions, diagnose problems, and in limited instances make decisions.

8.1 Introduction

Imagine that someday you could go to a desktop computer in your room and in simple English speak into a microphone attached to the computer: "Summarize the major points of all articles dealing with artificial intelligence in computer magazines published since 1988! Then print the summaries on my printer and give me an oral report of no longer than five minutes!" What would your desktop computer need in terms of hardware and software to be able to handle your request? Here are some requirements:

- Your desktop machine would have to understand and speak English.
- Your desktop machine would have to be linked to a main library collection of magazines or have access to a very large optical disk on your desktop.
- Your machine would have to know something about how to conduct research in order to summarize articles; that is, your software would need some real expertise.
- Your software would have to read and "understand" natural English language statements found in articles and newspapers.

No machine or software yet in existence has these capabilities, but information scientists are working on building such machines and some with other capabilities as well. The promise of artificial intelligence is in part the promise of providing humans with some intelligent assistance so that people can do their work more efficiently and effectively and stay out of danger as well.

The Nature of Artificial Intelligence

Put simply, **artificial intelligence (AI)** is the study and creation of machines that exhibit humanlike qualities, including the ability to reason. Even the seventeenth-century scientists and engineers who built the first calculators and mechanical robots that could play musical instruments may have dreamed of this goal, but none of these early machines had quite so ambitious a program as contemporary efforts in artificial intelligence. Experts in artificial intelligence believe that one day, computers will be able to learn natural languages like English, perceive objects just as humans do, and exhibit all the qualities that we think of as human reason—the ability to think, make judgments, arrive at conclusions, and make comparisons. These systems will not look like robots, or R2-D2 in the film *Star Wars.* Instead

Artificial intelligence (AI)
The study and creation of machines that exhibit humanlike qualities, including the ability to reason.

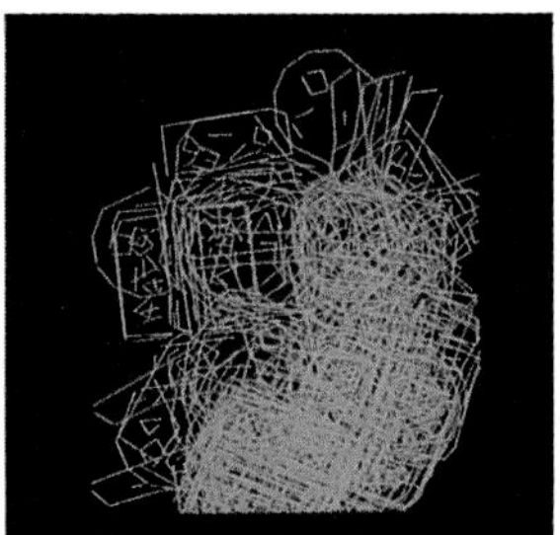
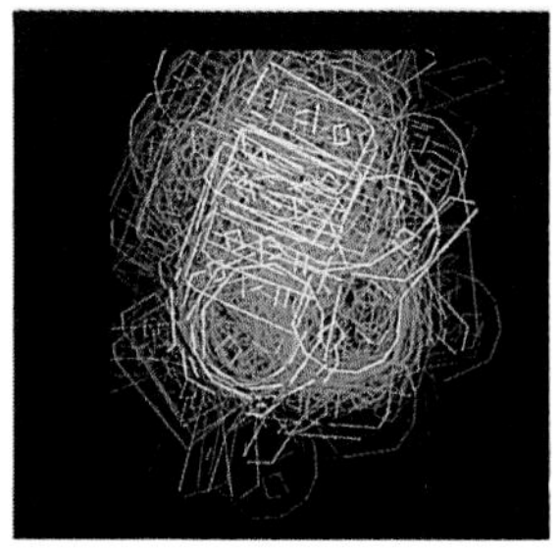
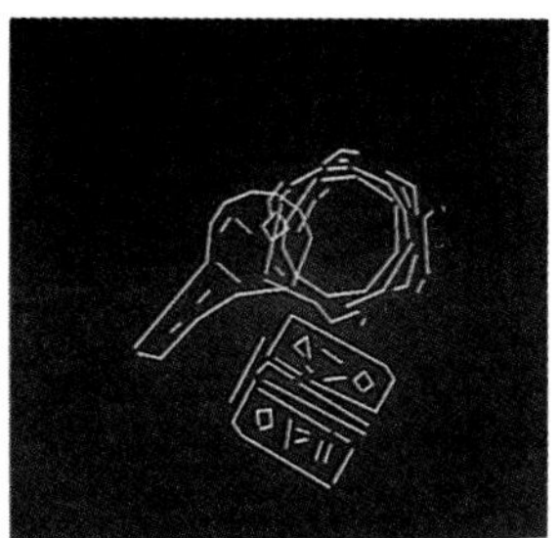

Scientists and engineers working in the field of artificial intelligence are creating machines that can "see." These machines break the task of "seeing" into several steps, matching the shape of the objects on view to objects they know, then eliminating the options before "recognizing" the objects.

Source: Courtesy of Thinking Machines Corporation.

these systems will reside inside desktop computers, similar to the ones we now call personal computers. Artificial intelligence is also the stuff of military dreams in which AI machines fight future wars largely independent of human intervention.

How would we know if a machine possessed these qualities of intelligence? How could we tell that we had built a war machine capable of conducting an autonomous war? One test was proposed by the British computer scientist Alan Turing in 1948. In the so-called **Turing test,** a human and a computer are placed in separate rooms connected by a communications link; if the person cannot tell whether he or she is talking to a machine or another human, then the machine is intelligent. So far no machines have passed Turing's test. What has been accomplished is quite remarkable, however, as we describe below.

Turing test
A test devised by Alan Turing to determine if a machine is intelligent. A computer and a human are placed in separate rooms connected by a communications link; if the human is not aware that he or she is communicating with a machine, the machine is intelligent.

The Family of Artificial Intelligence Techniques

Artificial intelligence is not a single phenomenon but a family of sometimes related activities, each of which seeks to capture some aspect of human intelligence and being (see Figure 8.1). Computer scientists, electronic engineers, psychologists, linguists, physiologists, and biologists are all involved in that search, which leads them into research on natural language, robotics, perceptive systems, expert systems, neural networks, and intelligent machines.

Natural Language · **Natural language** focuses on computer speech recognition and speech generation. The basic goal is to build computer hardware and software that can recognize human speech and "read" text, and that can speak and write as well. A related goal is to build software that can do research requested by humans. The major impetus for this research began in the 1950s when the military attempted to develop computers that could automatically translate Soviet texts and speech for national security pur-

Natural language
Languages, including idioms, that are used by humans (e.g., English, Swahili, French).

Figure 8.1

Artificial Intelligence (AI) Involves Many Fields of Study

Artificial intelligence is not one discipline; it is many. Shown here are the major initiatives that AI currently includes: natural language, robotics, perceptive systems, expert systems, neural networks, and intelligent software. What do all these activities have in common? In brief, they are attempting to emulate human abilities.

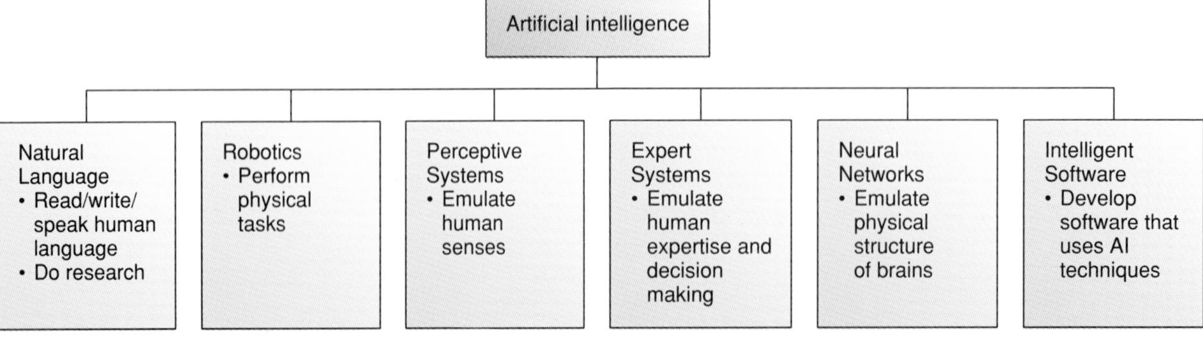

FOCUS ON *Technology*

Coping with Information Overload: Let Machines Do It

In the information age, terrabytes of text, data, and information are bombarding us from all sides (a terrabyte is a trillion bytes of information). The problem is how to shrink this information overload into something useful and small, like a few hundred megabytes (the size of an encyclopedia or one optical disk). In the past, computers used a simple keyword search strategy to search large databases. LEXIS and NEXIS, for instance, are large databases operated by Mead Data Corporation. Both of these databases require the user to specify a keyword to search the database (e.g., print all articles that use the word "computer security.")

But what happens if articles use the word "encryption" (a computer-security method that disguises data or programs so they cannot be accessed by unauthorized users) rather than "computer security"? New software developed by Verity Corporation of Mountain View, California, permits the user to specify a main keyword and a number of related terms, weighted according to importance—in this example, "access control" and "cryptography." In turn, each of these terms can have subterms and appropriate weights. As the figure illustrates, a user interested in computer-security articles can specify a number of interrelated criteria for the search and suggest how important each factor should be. The system then scans the database and assigns an overall score to each item that reflects its relevance for the main keyword. A list of items rank ordered by relevance is then presented to the user.

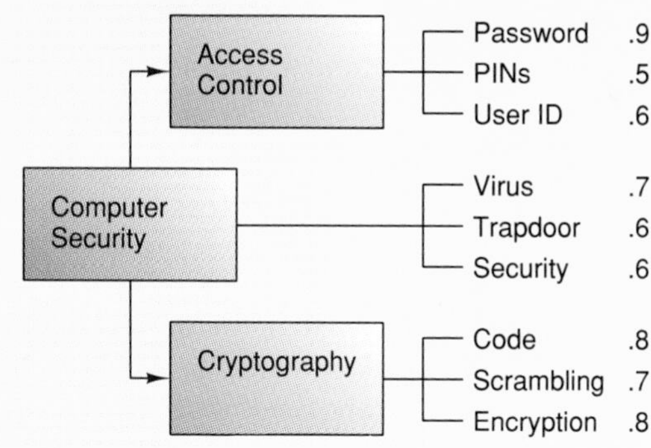

Source: Andrew Pollack, "Computers that Read and Analyze," *The New York Times,* June 7, 1989.

poses. These early efforts largely failed: machines have a very difficult time understanding idiomatic expressions or translating sentences such as "Jane took a swing at the ball." A computer would not know whether "swing" refers to a movement or an object and might produce a translation in which Jane used something like a porch swing. Nor would the computer know that "bat" is implicit in the sentence even though just about every child knows that you swing at balls with a bat. Nevertheless, as the Focus on Technology explains, some progress has been made in large database text searching when the domain of knowledge (i.e., the subject matter) is narrow.

Robotics · The goal of robotics research is to develop physical systems that can perform work normally done by humans, especially in hazardous

The OPTI-III™ automated optical inspection system, a product of GM Hughes Electronics, uses pattern recognition to analyze the inner layers of printed circuit boards. This system combines laser scanning with sophisticated algorithms and high-speed parallel processing of images to perceive defects in the boards.

Source: Courtesy of GM Hughes Electronics Corporation.

or lethal environments. The origins of robotics lie in seventeenth-century clockworks in which human forms mimicked human actions. Modern **robotics** is more concerned with the development of numerically controlled machine tools and industrial fabrication machines that are driven by CAM (computer-aided manufacturing) systems.

Robotics
The study of physical systems that can perform work normally done by humans, especially in hazardous or lethal environments.

Perceptive Systems · Like humans, robots need eyes and ears in order to orient their behavior. And humans who look for patterns in huge data streams need extensions of their own senses (see the visualization techniques described in Chapter 4). Since World War II, computer scientists and engineers have worked to develop **perceptive systems,** or sensing devices that can see and hear in the sense of recognizing patterns. This field, which is sometimes called "pattern recognition," has focused largely on military applications like photo reconnaissance, submarine echo sounding, radar scanning, and missile control and navigation. Progress has been uneven, however, as the following example illustrates.

Perceptive systems
Sensing devices used in robots that can recognize patterns in streams of data.

During a NATO exercise involving an attack on a hill defended by 11 enemy tanks, the U.S. Third Infantry relied on the Army's M-1 tanks, which are armed with heat-seeking missiles, and on airborne missiles that can seek out tanks and other shapes. Both missile systems are based on pattern recognition technology. Although the infantry succeeded in taking the hill, the Army commanders were embarrassed to learn that their perceptive systems had been fooled by decoys. In fact, the Red Army mock opposition had hired TVI Corporation of Beltsville, Maryland, to build plastic laminated tank replicas with heat-generating pads built into their faces. Small generators kept the tanks warm, while the main Red Army force sneaked off the hill during the night. In a real war, the Red Army group would have been poised for a morning flank counterattack.

Since this experience, the Army, Navy, and Air Force have begun to realize the limitations of their weapons and have initiated decoy research. The goal now is to develop "brilliant" precursor missiles that can fly into enemy territory, distinguish between the real targets and the decoys, and identify the targets for the following "smart" missiles.[1]

Expert Systems · **Expert systems** are relatively recent software applications that seek to capture expertise in limited domains of knowledge and experience and apply this expertise to solving problems. Perhaps more media attention has focused on expert systems than on any other member of the AI family. In part, this is because such systems can assist the decision making of managers and professionals in areas where expertise is expensive or in short supply. These systems are described at greater length in Section 8.2.

Expert systems
Software applications that seek to capture expertise in limited domains of knowledge and experience and apply this expertise to solving problems.

Neural Networks · People have always dreamed of building a computer that thinks, a "brain" modeled in some sense on the human brain. **Neural networks** are usually physical devices (although they can be simulated with software) that electronically emulate the physiology of animal or human brains. We describe in detail how these systems work in Section 8.3.

Neural network
Hardware or software that emulates the physiology of animal or human brains.

Intelligent Software · Many products now on the market claim to use AI techniques or to be "intelligent." Some of this is pure advertising hype, but software design is advancing beyond the contemporary Von Neuman computer model described in Chapter 3 in which a single processor executes one instruction at a time. Later sections of this chapter will describe some of these developments, including parallel coordinated computing, in which many small computers work on a problem at once; "information refineries," in which thousands of parallel sensors summarize huge data streams; and intelligent databases, in which parallel processors search very large files for patterns.

The Development of Artificial Intelligence

Research into artificial intelligence has actually been conducted in two directions, each of which has its own story.[2] One involves the history of efforts to develop **intelligent machines** that mimic what people at the time think is the way an animal or human brain works. This is called the **bottom-up approach;** it is essentially the effort to build a physical analog to the human brain. The second story involves the **top-down approach,** the effort to develop a logical analog to how the brain works.

Intelligent machines
Physical devices or computers that mimic the way people think.

Bottom-up approach
An approach to intelligent machines that concentrates on trying to build a physical analog to the human brain.

Top-down approach
An approach to intelligent machines that concentrates on trying to develop a logical analog to the human brain.

The effort to develop intelligent machines is hardly new. In fact, Charles Babbage, who invented a mechanical calculator in 1834, called his

Figure 8.2

A Brief History of the Top-Down and Bottom-Up Approaches to AI

Since World War II there have been two main thrusts in AI research. The top-down approach seeks to develop a logical model of human intelligence and the workings of the human brain. The bottom-up school tries to build a physical analog to the human brain and thus reproduce human thought patterns. Both techniques have played an important role in current AI research.

(a) Top-Down Approach (Logic Analog)

Simon and Newell's Logic Theorist

General Problem Solver

Pattern Recognition Software

Chess Playing Systems
Natural Language Software

Expert Systems

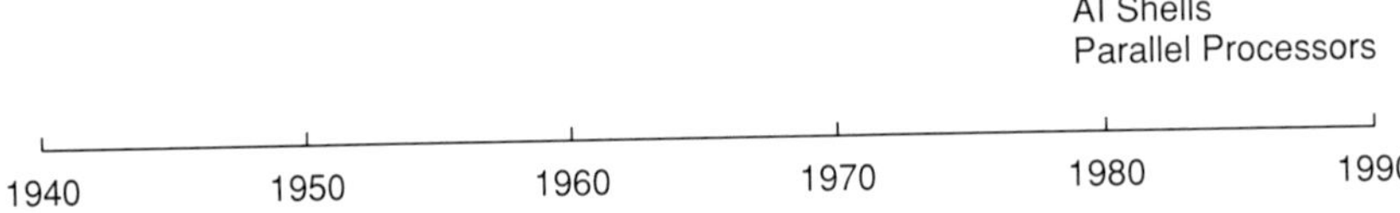

(b) Bottom-Up Approach (Physical Analog)

Image Recognition
Neural Network Simulation

Neural Chips

Word Recognition
Process Monitor

Neural Concepts Discredited

Rosenblatt's Perceptron

McCulloch and Pitt's Neural Brain Theories

Wiener's "Feedback" Machines

proposed calculating machine an "analytical engine," or thinking machine, and believed it could play chess at some point. This was perhaps the first top-down intelligent device. Figure 8.2 illustrates major developments in the top-down and bottom-up methods over the last 50 years.

Feedback
The return to a machine of part of the machine's output; the machine then uses the input information to improve its performance.

Contemporary AI research can be traced to World War II and the concept of **feedback.** In feedback, part of a machine's output is returned to it as input, and the machine then uses the input information to improve its performance. Norbert Wiener, a scientist and mathematician at the Massachusetts Institute of Technology (MIT) in the 1940s, developed a method of radar control of antiaircraft guns for the U.S. Army in which the expected location of an aircraft was calculated based on new information—feedback—from radar. Wiener went on to propose in several books that feedback could explain how humans think and suggested that the principle could be applied to make machines think like humans.

Thus started the physiological or bottom-up approach to artificial intelligence. Warren McCulloch, a biologist interested in brain function, and Walter Pitts, a mathematician, used Wiener's idea of feedback to develop a theory of how the brain works. In this theory, a brain was composed of millions of neuron cells that both processed binary numbers (they were either "on" or "off") and were connected into a network that took in feedback or information from the environment. Learning was simply a matter of teaching the neurons in a brain how to respond to the environment.

These ideas were taken further by Frank Rosenblatt, a Cornell psychologist and scientist, who in 1960 demonstrated a machine he called a **Perceptron.** This machine was composed of 400 photoelectric cells that could perceive letters or shapes and 512 neuronlike relays that conveyed information from the photoelectric cells to response units. The machine could recognize letters (as long as they were all of the same size and type) and could be taught: operators would increase or decrease voltages in certain areas of the machine when mistakes were made.

Perceptron
A machine devised by Frank Rosenblatt that could perceive letters or shapes and could be taught, or corrected, when it made mistakes; an example of the bottom-up approach to artificial intelligence.

In 1969 the top-down logical school led by Marvin Minsky and Seymour Papert, both at MIT, published a book called *Perceptrons,* which "proved" mathematically that such devices could never approach the intelligence of even lowly animals. This book ended serious research in the bottom-up, or cybernetics, school for many years. Since then, Minsky has withdrawn his critique and now supports neural network machine research. The resurgence of interest in neural networks is discussed in Section 8.3.

Although machines like the Perceptron received more media attention, the theorists of the logical, top-down school of AI were also hard at work. This school has developed through three stages. In its earliest stage, the goal was to develop a general model of human intelligence. This was followed by a period in which the extraordinary power of third-generation computers—the machines of the 1960s—was applied to more limited problems, like playing chess, or specialized areas, such as machine tool control. Finally, beginning in the 1970s, expert systems emerged in which the goals were scaled down to understanding knowledge in specific and highly limited areas.

In 1956 at the Dartmouth Summer Research Project on Artificial Intelligence, Herbert Simon (a Carnegie Mellon psychologist and scientist) and Alan Newell (a Rand Corporation scientist) announced they had developed a thinking machine, which they called a **Logic Theorist.** This software could prove certain mathematical theorems found in the famous mathematical treatise *Principia Mathematica* by Alfred North Whitehead and Bertrand Russell. The software mimicked deductive logic: that is, it selected the correct rules and postulates to create a coherent logical chain from premises to conclusion.

Logic Theorist
Software developed by Herbert Simon and Alan Newell that mimicked deductive logic; that is, it selected correct rules and postulates to create a coherent logical chain from premises to conclusion.

Unfortunately, the Logic Theorist could not easily be adapted to other areas of life where deductive reasoning was used. The problem with following chains of "if a, then b" statements is that hundreds of thousands, or millions, of such rules are required for even simple real-world problems. In response to the difficulties of applying the Logic Theorist to real-world problems, Simon and Newell attempted in the late 1950s to discover the

FOCUS ON *People*

The Chess Grandmaster Is a Machine

After 25 years of development, a chess-playing computer finally beat a chess grandmaster. The Carnegie-Mellon machine, Hitech, triumphed over grandmaster Arnold Denker in a four-game match. Denker complained that he was not in good form, and experts agreed that Denker, who is known for his innovative combination plays and sacrificial attacks that confuse the opposition, was not at his best. At 74, Denker does not play much chess anymore, and some critics called the game a "setup" to make the computer look good.

Still, Hitech's games were impressive. In previous competition, Hitech had been victorious over international masters (a lesser caliber of player than grandmaster). Grandmaster Edmar Mednis, who witnessed the game, said that Hitech was impressive, but he felt he could beat it. Mednis noted that the difficulty in playing a machine is that, unlike humans, it does not experience psychological pressure. Nothing bothers it.

Hitech, which runs on a mainframe computer at Carnegie-Mellon, can scan 165,000 different chess positions each second. The creator of Hitech is Dr. Hans Berliner, a chess player himself. Berliner says Hitech scans "in sort of a dumb way." Berliner is working on another machine that will only scan 100,000 positions per second but will do it in a smart way, with more attention to strategy and more focus on the current situation.

Source: Harold C. Schonberg, "For the First Time, a Chess Computer Outwits Grandmaster in a Tournament," *The New York Times*, September 26, 1988.

Combinatorial explosion
The difficulty that arises when a problem requires a computer to test a very large number of rules to reach a solution; even a very fast computer cannot search through all the possibilities in a reasonable amount of time.

general principles of human problem solving. If a few principles could be found, then perhaps a few simple rules of thumb could be used to avoid a **combinatorial explosion.** This is the problem that arises when a computer must test more rules to solve a problem than it has the capacity to examine. Regrettably, no general or simple principles of human problem solving were discovered. The search for a General Problem Solver ended.

In the 1960s advances in hardware offered some hope of coping with the combinatorial explosion. The newly developed third-generation computers—the first computers to use integrated circuits—made it possible to consider thousands of computations per second. Attention turned to pure "power" approaches: using the new machines to test out millions of rules, one at a time. But even a simple game like chess contains 10^{120} possible moves, so ways had to be found to pare down the search tree in order to avoid a combinatorial explosion. An exhaustive search through all possibilities on a chess board would have quickly swamped all the computers known to exist in the 1960s. On the other hand, in restricted domains—like chess—and with sufficient processing power, a number of problem-solving rules or strategies that are specific to the game of chess can be pursued and processed with some success, as the Focus on People describes.

One result of these developments was the first expert system—a system of rules limited to a very specific domain of human expertise (like chess). Unfortunately, the rules and strategies developed to play chess are not really applicable to any other area of life. Expert systems, which use heuristic, or rule-guided, searches, have helped to solve some of these difficulties.

Random or exhaustive searches through all the possible rules can be extremely time-consuming and can lead to a combinatorial explosion; in contrast, a heuristic search, based on certain rules of thumb that guide the search by indicating the most promising branch at a given point, can pare down the decision tree and make searching more efficient. In limited areas of expertise, such as diagnosing a car's ignition system or classifying biological specimens, expert systems have succeeded in codifying the rules of thumb used by real-world experts and placing them in a machine.

8.2 Expert Systems

Expert systems represent the latest evolution of top-down artificial intelligence thinking in which the computer is used to assist or even replace human decision makers. Unlike robotics or perceptive systems, expert systems have a very wide potential application to many areas of human endeavor in which expertise is important.

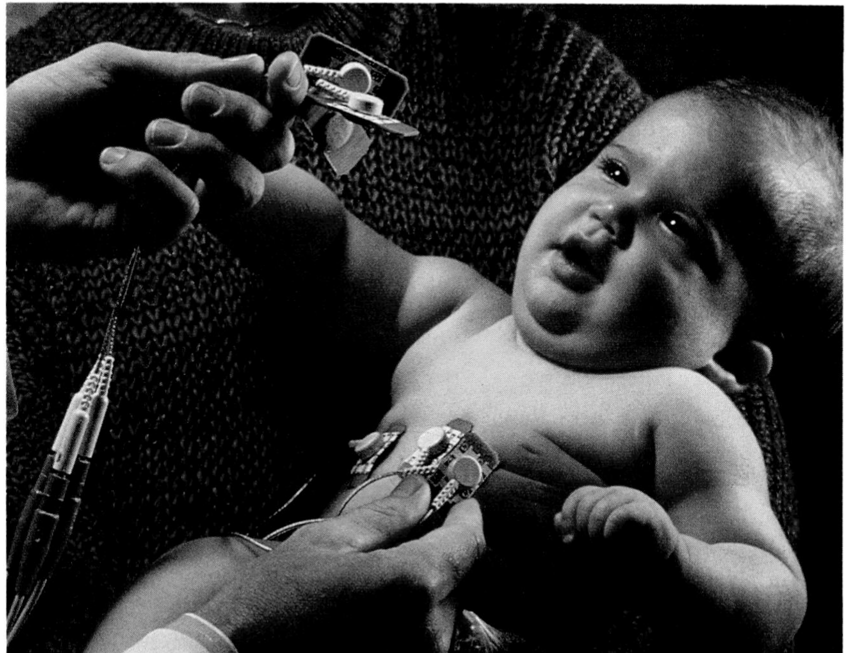

In 1978 Hewlett-Packard introduced one of the first commercial products to use a rule-based expert system, the HP 5600C ECG Management System. The system compares data from an electrocardiograph to a set of rules or criteria it has previously "learned" to detect heart abnormalities in infants or adults.

Source: Courtesy of Hewlett-Packard Company.

The Nature of Expert Systems

As we noted earlier, expert systems can be defined as systems that model human knowledge in limited areas or domains. Such systems are intended to solve problems as well or better than human decision makers, to apply human knowledge to well-understood problems, and to be able to account for how they arrive at decisions. At the same time, it is important to recognize the limitations of expert systems: they do not draw analogies, they cannot reason from first principles (i.e., they have no understanding of the larger world beyond their expertise), and they are hard to teach. Briefly, expert systems lack common sense and for this reason may not be applicable to some areas of business, such as general management, that require an open-ended search for solutions.[3]

The Components of an Expert System

An expert system contains four major components: the knowledge domain, or base, in which one is building the system; the development team, which tries to capture relevant portions of the knowledge base; the shell, or programming environment in which the system is programmed; and the user, who must interact with the system to guide it. Figure 8.3 illustrates these components.

Knowledge base
A model of human knowledge used by artificial intelligence systems; consists of rules, semantic nets, or frames.

The Knowledge Base · What is human knowledge? Artificial intelligence developers sidestep this thorny issue by asking a slightly different question: how can human knowledge be modeled or represented so that a computer can deal with it? Three ways have been devised so far to represent human knowledge and expertise: rules, semantic nets, and frames. These constitute the **knowledge base** in an expert system.

A standard programming construct (see Chapter 10) is the IF-THEN construct in which a condition is evaluated and, if it is true, an action is taken. For instance:

IF
    INCOME > $50,000 **(condition)**
    PRINT NAME AND ADDRESS **(action)**

A series of these rules can be used to represent a knowledge base. Indeed, as you can easily see, virtually all traditional computer programs contain IF-THEN statements, and one can argue that these programs are intelligent. What, then, is the difference between an expert system and a traditional program?

The difference between a traditional program and a rule-based expert system program is one of degree and magnitude. AI programs can easily have 200 to 3,000 rules, far more than traditional programs, which may have 50 to 100 IF-THEN statements. Moreover, as Figure 8.4 indicates, in an AI program, the rules tend to be interconnected and nested to a far larger degree than in traditional programs.

The order in which rules are searched depends in part on the information the system is given. There are multiple paths to the same result. If the system is given "F" in Figure 8.4, then "H" will be performed, and if

Figure 8.3

The Four Basic Elements in an Expert System

An expert system represents an effort to reproduce human expertise in a computer. There are four major components that combine to create an expert system. First, there is the knowledge base, the area of expertise for which the system is being built. Second, a development team composed of experts and knowledge engineers works to discover and develop the rules of thumb used by experts into a programmable and coherent whole. The third element consists of the development environment, which can either be a special purpose AI language such as LISP or PROLOG or a more user friendly expert system shell (described more fully later). The final element is the user, who must guide the system with instructions, data input, and questions.

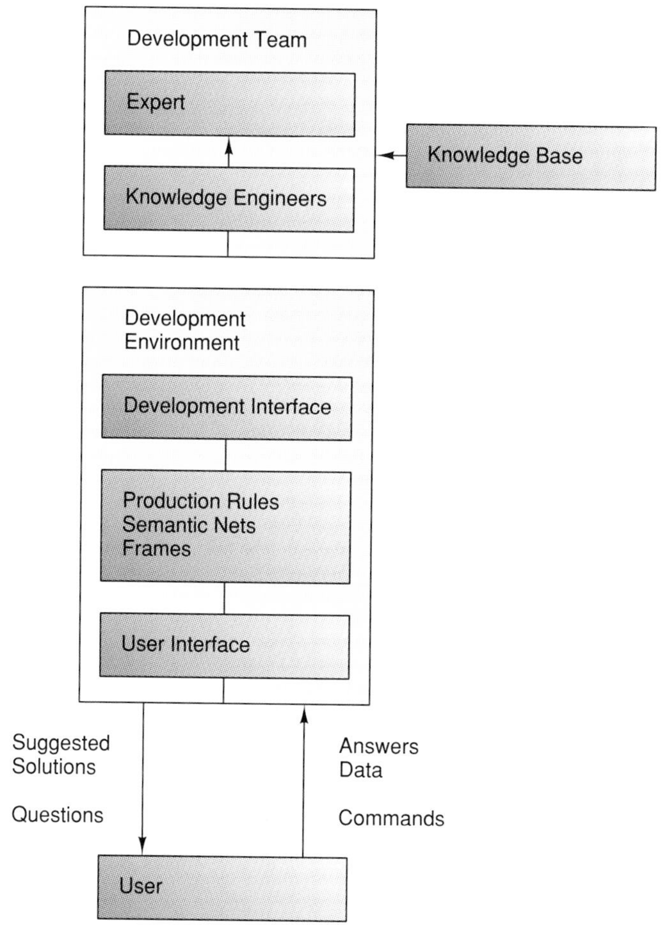

the system is given "A", "H" will also be performed. The system is also nonsequential: if "H" occurs when rule #5 fires, then rule #3 will be fired on a second pass through the rule base.

Could you represent the knowledge in the *Encyclopedia Britannica* this way? Probably not, because the rule base would be too large, and not all the knowledge in the encyclopedia can be represented in the form of IF-THEN rules. In general, expert systems can be efficiently used only in

Figure 8.4

Production Rules in an Expert System

A simple credit-granting expert system contains a number of rules to be followed when interviewing applicants on the telephone. The rules themselves are interconnected, the number of outcomes is known in advance and is limited, there are multiple paths to the same outcome, and the system can consider multiple rules at the same time.

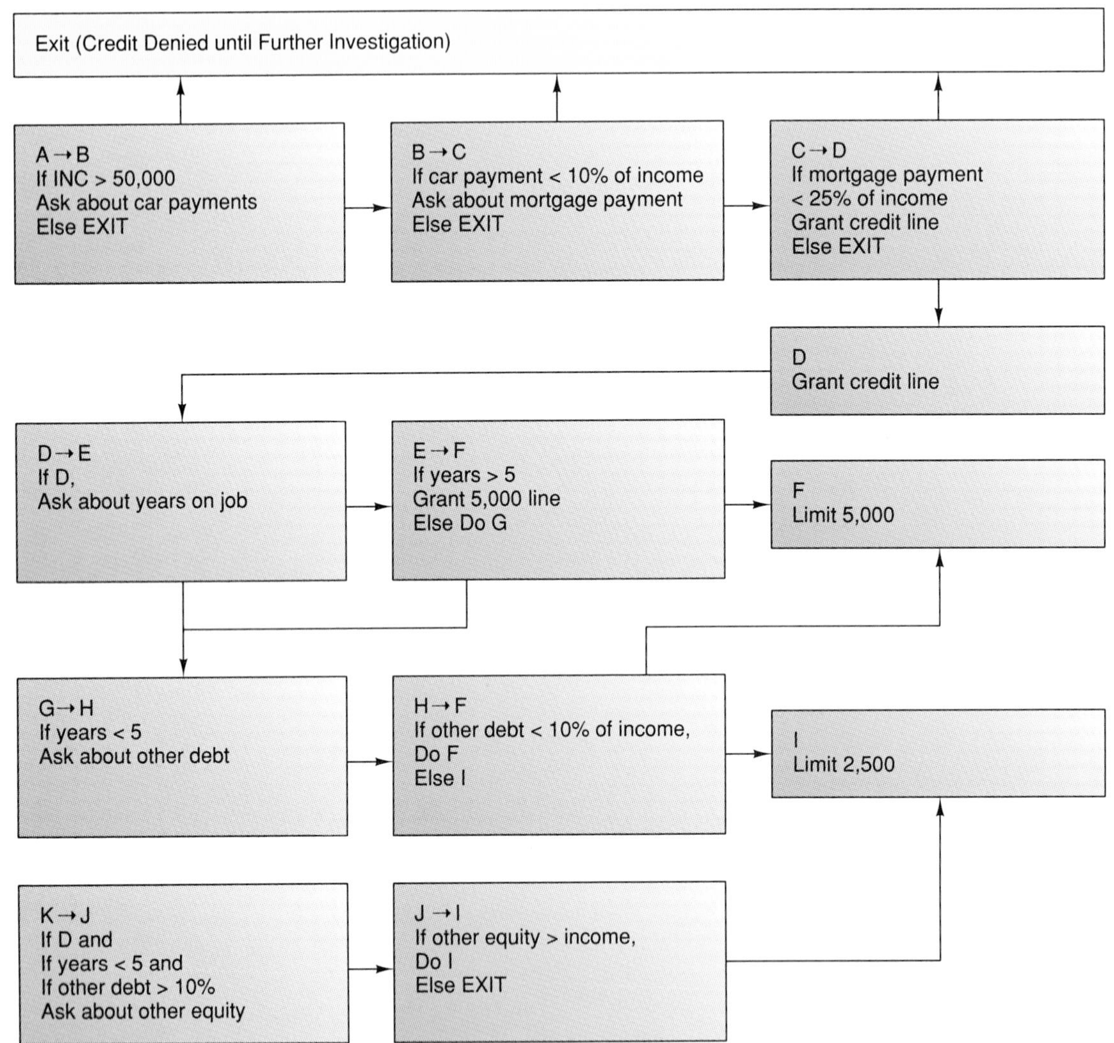

Exit (Credit Denied until Further Investigation)
A → B
If INC > 50,000
Ask about car payments
Else EXIT
B → C
If car payment < 10% of income
Ask about mortgage payment
Else EXIT
C → D
If mortgage payment
< 25% of income
Grant credit line
Else EXIT
D
Grant credit line
D → E
If D,
Ask about years on job
E → F
If years > 5
Grant 5,000 line
Else Do G
F
Limit 5,000
G → H
If years < 5
Ask about other debt
H → F
If other debt < 10% of income,
Do F
Else I
I
Limit 2,500
K → J
If D and
If years < 5 and
If other debt > 10%
Ask about other equity
J → I
If other equity > income,
Do I
Else EXIT

Source: Copyright 1990 Azimuth Corporation. Used with permission.

Semantic nets
A way of representing knowledge when the knowledge is composed of easily identified objects with interrelated characteristics; objects are classified according to the principle of inheritance so that the objects in lower levels of the net "inherit" all the general characteristics of the objects above them.

situations in which the domain of knowledge is highly restricted (such as granting credit) and involves only a few thousand rules.

Semantic nets can be used to represent knowledge when the knowledge base is composed of easily identified chunks or objects of interrelated characteristics. Figure 8.5 shows a semantic net used to classify kinds of automobiles, based on size, high or low drag coefficient, and other traits. Semantic nets use the property of inheritance to organize and classify objects and also use a condition like "IS A" to tie objects together. "IS A" is a

Figure 8.5

Expert System Using Semantic Nets

Semantic nets employ the characteristic of inheritance to form associations between objects and traits. For instance, in this semantic network, which is used to classify cars, each item "inherits" characteristics from the item above it. Thus, all Dodge Caravans and Ford Escorts are family cars, and all family cars are automobiles.

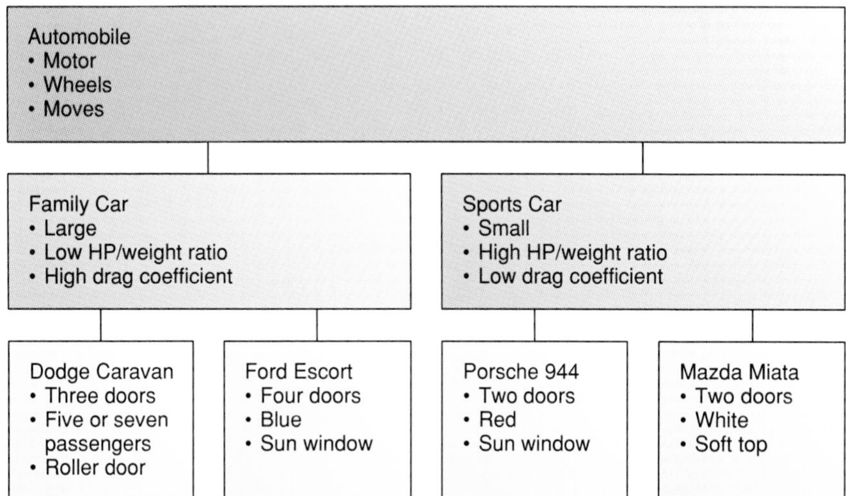

pointer to all objects of a specific class. For instance, all specific automobiles in the lower part of the diagram inherit characteristics of the general categories of automobiles above. Insurance companies, for instance, can use a semantic net to classify cars into rating classes. A clerical worker merely types the name and model of a car into a terminal, and the system can properly classify the car and decide on a rate.

Frames
A way of organizing knowledge based on shared characteristics; an object is defined by its characteristics and can be related to any other object in the database that shares those characteristics.

Knowledge **frames** are similar to semantic nets in that knowledge is organized into chunks, but the relationships between chunks is less hierarchical and is based on shared characteristics rather than inherited characteristics. Figure 8.6 shows a part of a knowledge base organized by frames. A "CAR" is defined by characteristics or slots in the frame as a vehicle, with four wheels, a gas or diesel motor, and an action like rolling or moving. This frame could be related to just about any other object in the database that shares any of these characteristics. The manner in which the frames are connected can be determined by the user. Frame-based AI systems are somewhat similar to a HyperCard database, which is organized into cards (see Chapter 6) with each object described on a card.

The Development Team · An expert system development team is composed of one or several "experts," who have a thorough command of the knowledge base, and one or more **knowledge engineers,** who can translate the knowledge (as described by the expert) into a set of production rules, frames, or semantic nets. A knowledge engineer is a specialist trained in eliciting information and expertise from other professionals.[4] The knowledge engineer interviews the expert or experts and determines the decision rules and knowledge that must be embedded into the system. Thus the

Knowledge engineer
Specialist trained in eliciting information and expertise from other professionals in order to translate the knowledge into a set of production rules, frames, or semantic nets.

Figure 8.6

Expert System Using Knowledge Frames

In a manner similar to semantic nets, knowledge and information can be organized by "frames" that capture the relevant and important characteristics of objects of interest. This approach is based on the belief that humans use "frames," or concepts to narrow the range of possibilities when scanning incoming information, to make rapid sense out of perceptions. For instance, when a person is told to "look for a tank and shoot when you see one," experts believe humans invoke a concept or frame of what a tank should look like. Anything that does not fit this concept of a tank is ignored. In a similar fashion, AI researchers can organize a vast array of information into frames. The computer is then instructed to search the database of frames and list connections to other frames of interest. The user can then follow the various pathways pointed to by the system. To some extent, HyperCard, the Apple Computer software described in Chapter 6, can be organized as a series of frames with embedded pointers controlled by the user.

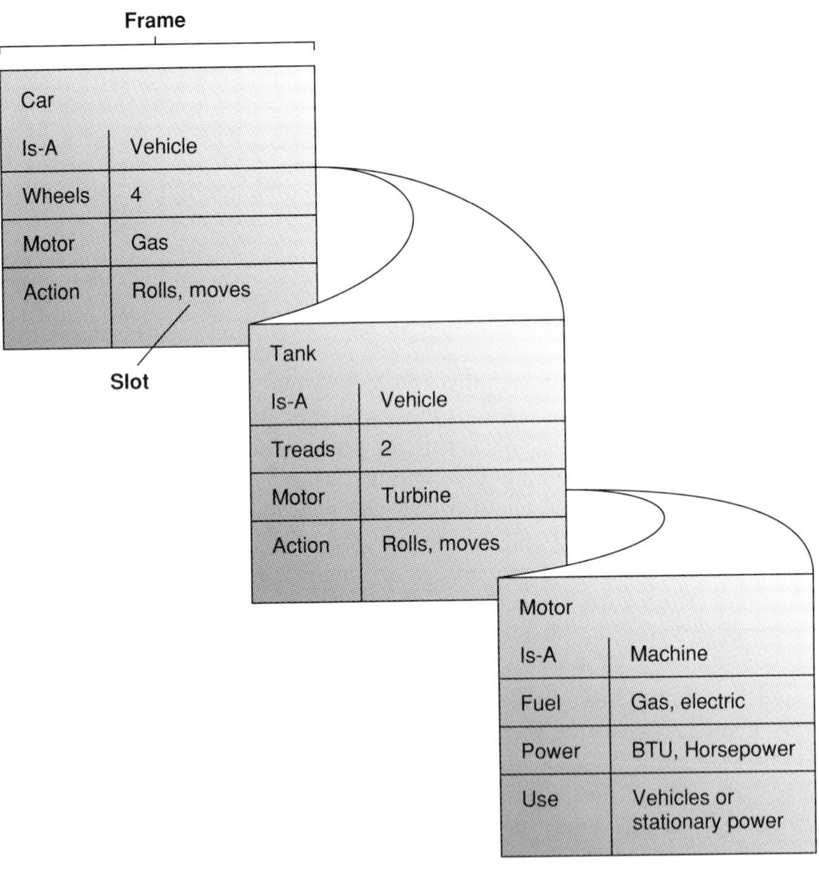

knowledge engineer works with the expert to refine and improve the system until a useful system has been created. While AI software continues to improve, the process of eliciting knowledge from an expert remains a major challenge. Because knowledge engineering requires some background in diverse fields (such as software design, clinical psychology, and anthropology) plus finely tuned communications skills, knowledge engineers are rare.

Indeed, according to many experts, the hard part of writing an expert system is knowledge engineering. Knowledge engineer Helen Ojha, employed by Coopers and Lybrand, a prominent accounting and consulting firm, describes knowledge engineers as "visitors to another culture they have not grown up in." At work, they're much like anthropologists, who are trained to observe things they do not fully understand.

The steps taken by knowledge engineer Sajnicole Joni of Gold Hill Computers in Cambridge, Massachusetts, when she developed a system that qualifies sales leads, illustrate the role knowledge engineers play. Joni first asked all the salespeople to write down what they did and selected roughly 20 representative scenarios of how the salespeople performed in the field. Then she analyzed the salesperson's thinking process, looking for critical variables that allowed the salesperson to make decisions very quickly. From there, Joni assembled the pieces of information comprising the knowledge base and determined how to string the pieces together. Her task was difficult because, on the one hand, the system had to be confined to a single problem, such as targeting potential customers above a certain income level, yet on the other hand it had to incorporate some details, such as the customer's hobby or favorite drink, that were not necessarily part of any decision-making process.[5]

The Artificial Intelligence Shell · The **artificial intelligence shell** is the programming environment of an expert system. Currently, expert systems can be developed in just about any programming language, including BASIC, C, or Pascal. In the early years of expert systems, computer scientists developed specialized programming languages, such as Lisp and PROLOG, that could process lists of rules efficiently. Although these languages were efficient, they have proved difficult to standardize and even more difficult to integrate into a traditional business environment. Hence a growing number of expert systems today are developed using either C or, more commonly, AI shells, which are user-friendly development environments capable of quickly generating user interface screens, capturing the knowledge base quickly, and managing the strategies for searching the rule base.

Artificial intelligence shell
The programming environment of an artificial intelligence system.

For example, Neuron Data Corporation of Palo Alto, CA, produces an AI shell for Macintosh and personal computers systems called Nexpert Object. This shell, like many others on the market, reduces the time and cost of expert system development and opens up AI systems to nonexperts.

One of the most interesting aspects of the AI shell is the **inference engine;** this is simply the strategy used to search through the rule base. Two strategies are commonly used: forward reasoning and backward reasoning.

Inference engine
The process of searching through the rule base in an expert system; either a forward reasoning strategy or a backward reasoning strategy is used.

In **forward reasoning,** the inference engine begins with information entered by the user and searches the rules in a knowledge base to arrive at a conclusion. The strategy is to "fire," or carry out the action of the rule, when a condition is true. Figure 8.7 shows two sets of rules that allow a user to search a rule base in order to decide whether a client is a good prospect for a visit from an insurance sales representative. If the user enters the information that the client has an income greater than $100,000, the inference engine will fire all rules in sequence from left to right. If the user then enters the information that the same client owns real estate (panel b), another rule base will be searched again, and more rules will fire. The rule base can be searched each time the user enters new information. Processing continues until no more rules can be fired.

Forward reasoning
A strategy for searching the rules in a knowledge base in which the inference engine begins with information entered by the user and searches the rule base to arrive at a conclusion.

Figure 8.7

How the Inference Engine Works

The inference engine is the strategy that has been programmed into an expert system to guide its search through the rule base. In forward reasoning, the inference engine takes its cue from the information entered by the user. In this example, if the user tells the machine that a certain client has an income greater than $100,000, the inference engine "fires," or carries out, a series of further rules based on additional information. If the user tells the machine that the same client owns real estate, this spurs a separate set of rules, some of which branch into the income rules. In backward reasoning, the engine would begin with the information at the right side of the diagram and reason "backward" through the same decision points.

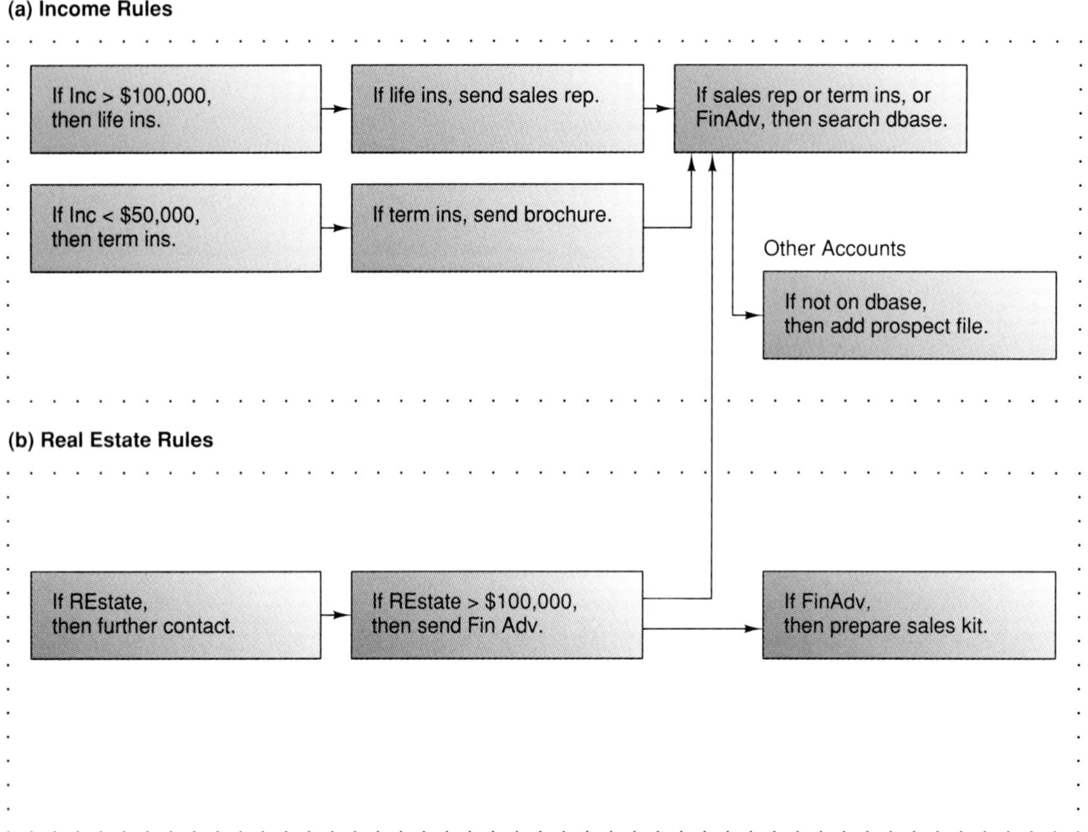
(a) Income Rules
If Inc > $100,000, then life ins.
If life ins, send sales rep.
If sales rep or term ins, or FinAdv, then search dbase.
If Inc < $50,000, then term ins.
If term ins, send brochure.
Other Accounts
If not on dbase, then add prospect file.
(b) Real Estate Rules
If REstate, then further contact.
If REstate > $100,000, then send Fin Adv.
If FinAdv, then prepare sales kit.

Backward reasoning
A strategy for searching the rules in a knowledge base in which the inference engine begins with a hypothesis and proceeds by asking the user questions about selected facts until the hypothesis is either confirmed or disproved.

In **backward reasoning,** an expert system acts more like a problem solver who begins with a hypothesis and seeks out information to evaluate the hypothesis by asking questions. Thus, in Figure 8.7, the user might ask the question "Should we add this person to the prospect data base?" The inference engine begins on the right of the diagram and works toward the left. Thus the person should be added to the database if a sales representative, term insurance brochure, or financial adviser will be sent to the client. But will these events take place? The answer is yes, if life insurance is recommended.

The User · The role of the user in an expert system is both to pose questions for the system and to enter relevant data to guide the system along. In most cases, the expert system will simply be an adviser to human experts and users, but on rare occasions, decision making may be turned over to the expert system entirely.

Building Expert Systems

Building an expert system is basically similar to building any information system. A systems analyst (here a knowledge engineer) sits down with a user of the system (called an expert), and together they work out what the system should be able to do. They develop a preliminary version, which is tested and refined to produce the final expert system. Figure 8.8 depicts the process of expert system development.

Developing expert systems differs from building conventional systems in that expert systems rely much more heavily on experimental versions of the system and frequent, intense interactions with the user. Thus, as in Figure 8.8, much time is spent on the preliminary version(s), testing, and improvement. One reason for this is that experts often discover that they cannot clearly articulate the rules they actually use when making decisions.

The Role of Expert Systems in Business Firms

Expert systems were at first developed as stand-alone applications, largely unrelated to the business systems that surrounded them. This has changed, however, as developers realized that expert systems often required data directly from mainstream corporate systems and often had to work cooperatively with knowledge workers' and managers' desktop computers. This has led to a significant reform in expert systems' development and a rethinking of their role. The extent to which an expert system can be integrated into mainstream business systems is illustrated by the leading-edge application in the next section.

Leading-Edge Application: Taking Intelligent Orders at Westinghouse

Although many expert systems are used to extend and maintain expertise in an organization, a growing number of expert systems are being integrated into the mainstream of business procedures and day-to-day activities. One such system is CORA (Customer Order Relaying Assistant), which was developed by the Relay and Telecommunications Division at Westinghouse Electric Corporation.[6]

Westinghouse's Relay and Telecommunications Division makes relay protection systems for power companies. Relays are used to protect circuits when power lines are destroyed in a storm, transformers fail, or other interruptions occur. The relays "trip off" generators in much the same way as a fuse acts in a house.

There are thousands of different kinds of relays and related equipment, ranging in cost from a few hundred dollars to hundreds of thousands of dollars. The types of relays used depend on the voltage ratings, length of lines, and environmental conditions. In the past, a customer order engineer would work closely with the customer, using several huge catalogs to put

Figure 8.8

The Process of Developing an Expert System

The first step in developing an expert system is to capture the relevant information from the knowledge base. A knowledge engineer works with an expert in the knowledge base to determine what the system needs to know. Then they develop a preliminary version of the system, which is tested for accuracy and completeness. The final step involves implementing the finished system.

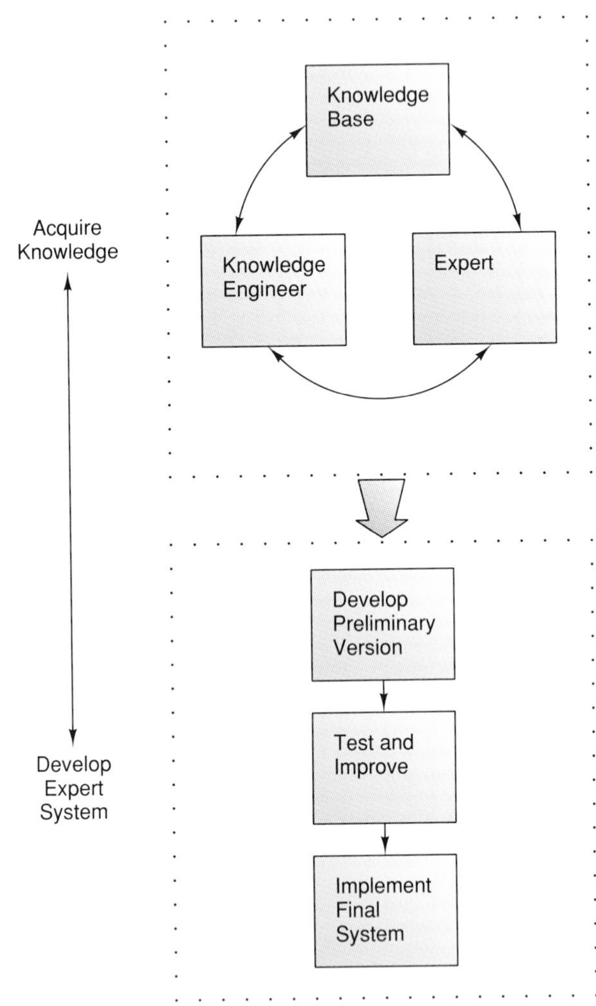

together orders for entire systems. Since a single order may involve hundreds of parts, and no on-line system was available to track styles of relays, engineers used to spend days paging through the catalogs to find out what styles existed.

CORA was developed to alleviate this problem and to assure order consistency and completeness. CORA is a frame-based expert system. A frame is dedicated to each object or component that the system needs to know about. Within each frame are slots with each object's attributes. The frames can be arranged in a hierarchy so that lower-level frames inherit the characteristics of their "parent" frames, and relationships can be defined. Altogether, CORA has 3,000 frames to keep track of 600 components. CORA was written in a special language called Lisp (List Processing language) and has 10,000 lines of code. The program was developed on a VAX 11/780 super minicomputer, but it can run just as well on an IBM desktop AT personal computer.

Installed as a production system in 1988, by 1989 CORA was being used every day by customer order engineers. The engineers take the customer's order specifications for relays one at a time, directing the system at each stage. As the components are specified, CORA searches the product database and prompts the user to specify which style of relay is required.

After the components are specified, CORA verifies the entire list to make sure the parts will work together. If so, an engineering bill of materials is produced. CORA is interfaced directly to a Burroughs mainframe system that contains a bill of materials file and produces an invoice. In turn, the two systems produce a manufacturing bill that contains all the parts needed for the system down to the last nut and bolt.

Since Westinghouse implemented the system in 1988, new uses have been found. In 1990 the system was extended to the marketing division. Marketing engineers can use CORA to ensure that they have not overlooked necessary components when bidding on customer orders.

Limitations of Expert Systems

In many respects, expert systems are not much different from traditional programming techniques, and the entire exercise might even be called "advanced programming" rather than artificial intelligence. After a decade's experience, some limitations in the technique are also becoming clear.

First, it takes a very long time and a large commitment of resources to build interesting expert systems. Many institutions have found it cheaper to hire an expert than to hire a team of knowledge engineers to build an expert system. Although simple expert systems of up to one hundred rules can be built quickly using one of several AI shells sold for personal computers, these applications tend not to be particularly important or powerful. Second, expert systems are brittle and cannot learn. They must be reprogrammed whenever knowledge changes in a field. Because knowledge does change often in an information society, expert systems maintenance costs are considerable. Third, expert systems require that knowledge be organized in an IF-THEN format. This is appropriate for some knowledge and expertise, but much expertise cannot be organized in this fashion without producing erroneous results. Fourth, for all of these reasons, expert systems are limited in application to taxonomy problems (i.e., problems in which the goal is to diagnose or assign objects to classes). Expert systems are not very good at typical management problems, which tend to be open ended, involve synthesis rather than deduction, require many different kinds of expertise, and rely on expertise that is widely distributed in an organization.

As the Focus on Organizations points out, companies specializing in producing hardware and software for expert systems have found that the market for their products is not as large as they anticipated.

FOCUS ON *Organizations*

Where Lisp Slipped

Of the half-dozen companies that spun out of the Massachusetts Institute of Technology's Artificial Intelligence Laboratory in the early 1980s, Symbolics, Inc., seemed to hold the most promise. Led by Russell Noftsker, former director of MIT's lab, Symbolics boasted some of the best software talent in the artificial intelligence world. And it was well funded: $72 million from the public and venture capitalists who believed that artificial intelligence—the design of "expert systems"—was the next growth area of technology.

Alas, Symbolics made the mistake of believing all the hype that surrounded artificial intelligence in the early days. "They were spending the money before it got here," says John S. Wurts, who was brought in as chairman and chief executive to rescue the company in May 1988.

Under Wurts, the company is surviving, barely. After a $46 million loss in the year ended June 1988, it eked out a $1.8 million profit in fiscal 1989, on revenue of $67 million. If the company attracts investors now, it will be on the strength of very reduced expectations and a humbler attitude toward its market.

From the beginning, Noftsker insisted that the only way to really do AI applications was on a proprietary piece of hardware optimized to run software written in Lisp (for List Processing), the somewhat obscure programming language used extensively in artificial intelligence. He made a mistake.

Symbolics made a $75,000 special-purpose AI computer. Specialized, proprietary systems are hard to sell even in the market for general-purpose business computers; in a market as narrow as that for artificial intelligence, they can be a disaster.

Over time, it became hard to justify $75,000 for a machine that doesn't share information with anyone else. Most commercial users didn't need the level of intensity that the Symbolics machine gives you.

Despite the hurdles, Symbolics can point to a lot of satisfied customers. Manufacturers Hanover uses Symbolics machines to help traders trade foreign currency. American Express uses them to help credit authorization clerks clear customer purchases. Houston Lighting & Power uses them for scheduling maintenance at its 56 power plants. Symbolics is reportedly talking to a number of airlines about developing expert systems to help reservation clerks.

Source: Adapted from Julie Pitta, "Where Lisp Slipped," *Forbes,* October 16, 1989, pp. 262–263. Adapted by permission of Forbes Magazine.

8.3 Other Intelligent Techniques

It is clear that the pursuit of artificial intelligence will be a persistent theme of the 1990s. Although progress will continue to be made in expert systems, the development of parallel processing at the hardware level—the idea of breaking up a problem into many small components and then processing each component simultaneously using hundreds or even thousands of computers operating in parallel—is likely to unleash a host of new possibilities.[7] Here we review briefly four of the intelligent computing techniques that stand the best chance of developing into major fields for business applications in the 1990s.

Neural Networks

There has been an exciting resurgence of interest in bottom-up approaches to artificial intelligence in which machines are designed to imitate the physical thought process of the biological brain. Figure 8.9 illustrates the natural version—in this case, two neurons from the brain of a leech—and its man-made counterpart. In the leech's brain, the soma or nerve cell at the center acts like a switch, stimulating other neurons and being stimulated in turn. Emanating from the neuron is an axon, which is an electrically active link to the dendrites of other neurons. Axons and dendrites are the "wires" that electrically connect neurons to one another. The junction of the two is called a synapse. This simple biological model is the metaphor for the development of neural networks.

The human brain has about 100 billion (10^{11}) neurons, each of which has about 1,000 dendrites, which form 100 trillion (10^{14}) synapses. The brain operates at about 100 HZ (each neuron can fire off a pulse 100 times per second)—very slow by computer standards. For example, an Intel 80386 chip operates at up to 33 megahertz, or millions of cycles, per second, executing one instruction at a time. But the brain's neurons operate in parallel, enabling the human brain to accomplish about 10 quadrillion (10^{16}) interconnections per second. This far exceeds the capacity of any known machine—or any machine now planned or ever likely to be built with current technology. The human brain weighs 3 pounds and occupies about 0.15 square meters.

No technology now known can come close to these capabilities, but elementary neuron circuits can be built and studied, and far more complex networks of neurons—neural networks—have been simulated on computers. Panel b in Figure 8.9 shows an artificial neural network with two neurons. The resistors in the circuits are variable and can be used to "teach" the network. When the network makes a mistake—that is, chooses the wrong pathway through the network and arrives at a false conclusion—resistance can be raised on some circuits, forcing other neurons to fire. If this learning process continues for thousands of cycles, the machine "learns" the correct response.

One feature that distinguishes neural networks from digital computers is the inherent parallelism: the simple neurons or switches are highly interconnected and operate in parallel. Instead of a single personal computer executing a single instruction at a time, imagine 64,000 personal computers all connected to one another and working simultaneously on parts of the same problem.

A digital neural network computer can be defined, then, as an interconnected set of parallel switches or processors that can be controlled by intervention. Neural networks are very different from expert systems, in which human expertise has to be modeled with rules and frames. In neural networks, the physical machine emulates a human brain and can be taught from experience.

The first commercial hardware and neural network systems are being prototyped now. An interesting hardware development is the production of computer chips that can emulate a neural network. For example, the research arm of the local Bell operating companies, Bellcore, has packaged a

Figure 8.9

Two Neural Networks: A Computer and a Leech

Neural networks are an area of research in artificial intelligence in which programmers attempt to emulate the processing patterns of the biological brain. Panel a illustrates part of an animal brain, that of a leech. Each neuron contains a soma, or nerve cell. Axons and dendrites are the branches by which it connects to other neurons; each connection point is called a synapse. Panel b is the man-made version, in which each neuron becomes a switch or processing element. Axons and dendrites are wires, and the synapses are variable resistors that carry currents representing data.

(a) Natural Neuron

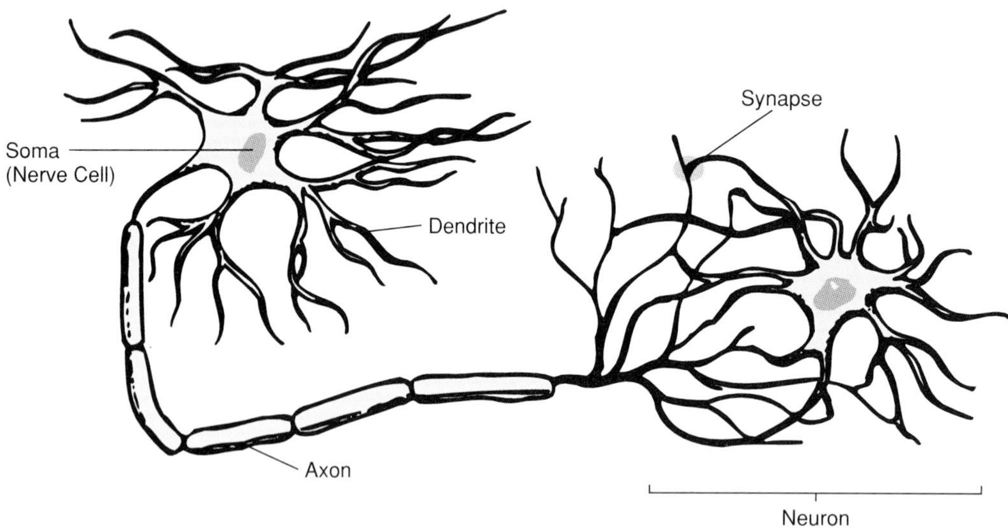

(b) Man-Made Neurons

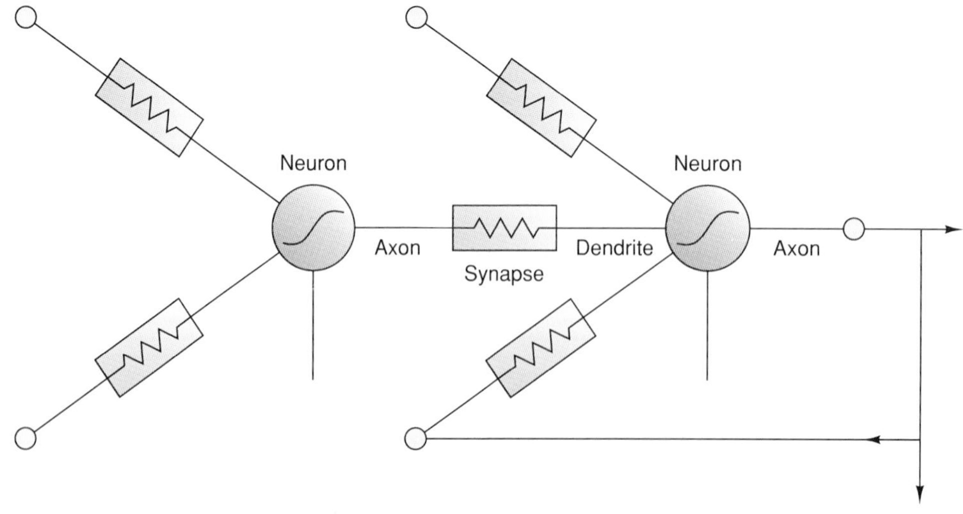

Source: Defense Advanced Research Projects Agency (DARPA), "DARPA Neural Network Study, October 1987–February 1988," DARPA 1988.

neural network on a chip. The chip performs about 100,000 times faster than neural networks simulated in traditional machines.

By packaging a neural network on a chip, Bellcore will make it easier for developers to integrate artificial intelligence applications into existing business applications. For instance, a traditional order entry system may need some intelligent input for some of its operations. With a neural network chip closely integrated to an order entry system, the system could learn about new products or new customers and automatically update the order entry system. Other corporations, including Motorola, Intel, and Texas Instruments, Inc., are also working on neural network chips.[8]

An interesting example of a complete neural network system is Nestor's mortgage underwriting neural network, which is described in the next section.

Leading-Edge Application: A Neural Network Mortgage Insurance Underwriter

Nestor, Inc., of Providence, Rhode Island, is a leading builder of neural network simulation machines. Under contract to one of the nation's largest mortgage insurance underwriters, Nestor developed a neural network on an experimental basis to demonstrate the technology.

Before a bank approves a mortgage on a house, the bank may require the applicant to take out mortgage insurance to ensure that the mortgage will be repaid should the borrower be unable to pay. Human underwriters take many features into account when deciding whether to insure borrowers: credit rating, number of dependents, years employed, income, other debt, loan-to-value ratio (the value of the loan relative to the value of the

Neural net technology mimics the brain's network of neurons to solve a problem. GTE installed a net to track variations in heat, pressure, and the chemicals used to make fluorescent light bulbs. This neural net will help reveal the best manufacturing conditions.

Source: Hank Morgan—Rainbow.

property), type of mortgage, and the ratio of income to mortgage payments. Also important is the nature of the property, the number of units, age, cash flow if any, appraised value, and even location. Although only 3 percent of insured borrowers become delinquent in a year, over six years this amounts to almost a 20 percent default rate. During this time period, criteria for granting insurance change, as do underwriting practices, making an expert system solution somewhat unlikely. The knowledge base is too unstable.

The process of insurance underwriting is complex, lengthy, and costly. Nestor's system was designed to reduce cost, increase consistency, and enhance understandability of the process by providing a clear account of why insurance is turned down. Human underwriters exercise a considerable amount of discretion and often cannot explain why they denied someone, or why two people with seemingly similar characteristics will receive different treatment.

Nestor has developed a system it calls a Multiple Neural Network Decision System to handle problems like these. Nine different networks arranged in a grid are used to divide a problem into manageable parts. Each network is "trained" to become an expert at assessing a particular part of the problem; then it passes the results to a controller, which can poll other networks for other parts of the solution.

In a test using 5,048 applicants from all parts of the United States, about half of whom had been denied insurance and the other half accepted, the Mortgage Underwriter was taught to discriminate between acceptable and unacceptable applicants. Mortgage Underwriter succeeded in correctly classifying applicants about 90 percent of the time. Thus, in a short while, this system learned the geographic knowledge and skills of all underwriters in the agency across the United States.[9]

The Mortgage Underwriter system is still in the experimental stages. At present, it provides an estimate of how certain the system is about a case and lets the human underwriter make the final judgment. In addition, the system can quickly give a list of reasons for acceptance or denial.

Parallel Sensor Systems

One of the problems of the Star Wars defense program (officially called the Strategic Defense Initiative) was that it proposed that the heavens be seeded with thousands upon thousands of sensors, all of which would be aimed at countries that might launch missiles against the United States. How could a computer, or collection of computers, keep track of all this information? Similar problems arise in hospitals: how can all patients be watched and monitored at once, or how can all the indicators on a single patient be closely monitored simultaneously to alert nurses in case something is wrong or to analyze the health status of the patient continually?

Parallel sensor systems
A system in which each node continually receives information from lower-level sensors, evaluates the information, requests more if needed, and reports to higher-level machines.

One possibility is a **parallel sensor system** called a Trellis machine by one of its inventors, David Gelernter, a computer scientist at Yale (see Figure 8.10). One might think of each node in the machine as a processor or computer that continually receives information from lower-level sensors, evaluates the information, requests more if needed, and reports to higher-level machines. Notice how each piece of information leads upward to possible diagnoses of the cause. The machine depicted in Figure 8.10 is only

Figure 8.10

A Medical Application for Artificial Intelligence: A Trellis Machine

A Trellis machine is one attempt to apply AI principles to the problem of monitoring a large amount of data on an ongoing basis and drawing conclusions based on continual changes in the data. The Trellis machine monitors a hospital patient's condition through sensors that track such measures as blood pressure and heart rate and send this information (blue) upward through the "trellis" to computers that evaluate the data. As data rise, they travel through a hierarchy of processors that evaluate them and direct them to other processors as indicated by preliminary diagnoses. Higher-level units may send queries and comments (orange) downward to elicit additional information or change the behavior of a lower-level unit based on a high-level hypothesis.

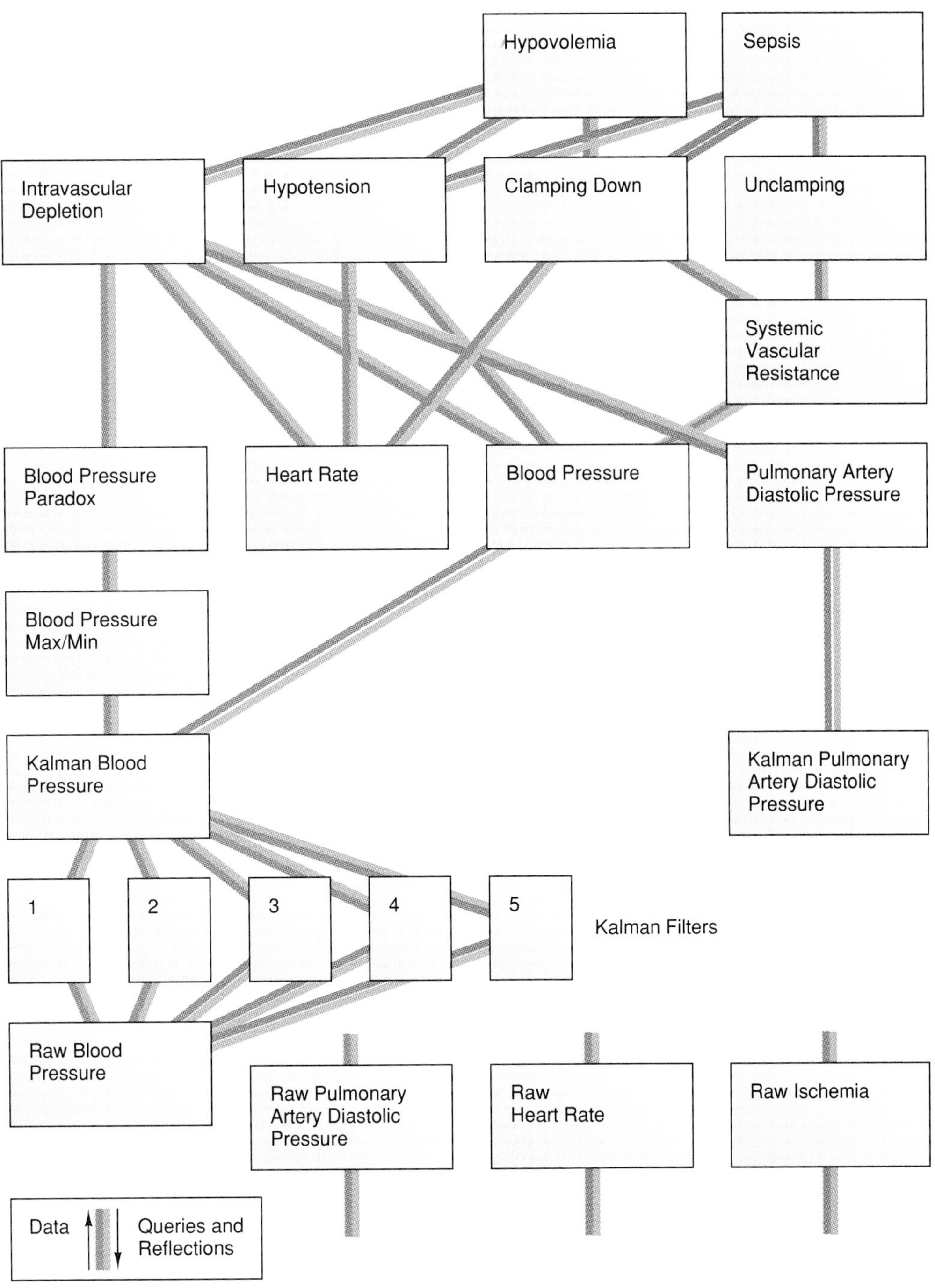

one portion of a Trellis machine showing how blood pressure is tracked. Other parts of the machine monitor other indicators of health.

An Intelligent Database Search Machine

Imagine you have to search the Library of Congress (90 million items including journals and technical reports) for all articles or book chapters having to do with computer security. One possibility, of course, is to have a massively large computer go through each volume, one by one, looking for articles that match the descriptions you have given. Another possibility is to use an **intelligent database search machine.** Instead of working alone, an intelligent database search machine, called the master, would give your descriptions to many machines, called workers, which would search the database simultaneously. When a lower-level machine finds a possible match, it passes it back to the master for a final assessment. Figure 8.11 shows an

Intelligent database search machine

A "master" machine that can direct a search of a very large database by giving the target pattern to many machines that search simultaneously; when a machine finds a possible match, it sends it to the controller machine, which makes the final assessment.

Figure 8.11

The Intelligent Database Search Machine

The intelligent database search machine applies principles of artificial intelligence to the problem of searching a large database. In this example the machine has been asked to match a certain DNA sequence against an enormous database of all known sequences. It accomplishes the task by delegating. A controlling computer, the master, copies the sequence and transmits it to many smaller computers called workers. The workers search the database simultaneously. When they locate a possible matching sequence, they send the information back up to the master for evaluation. The master selects the correct answer.

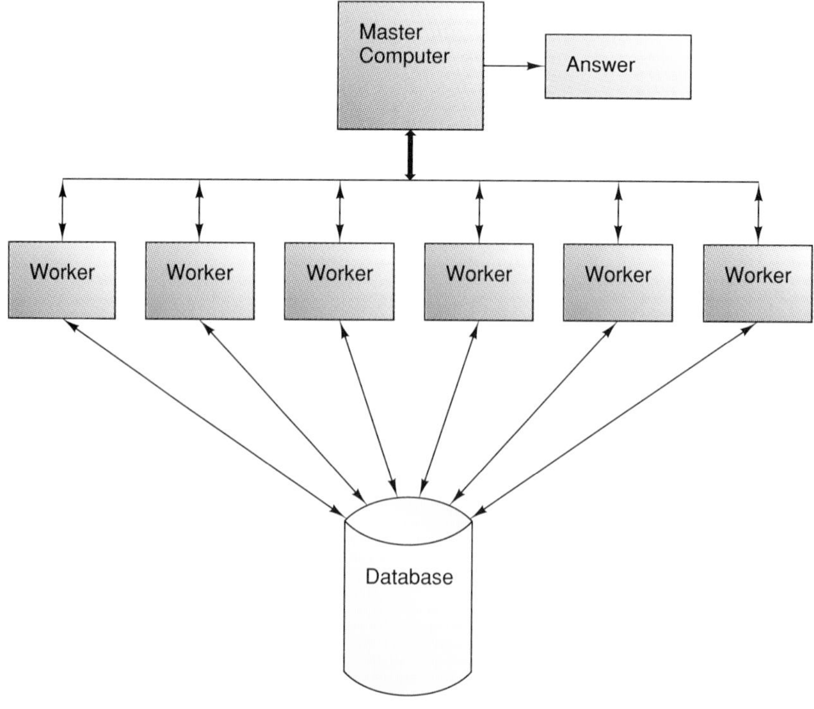

FOCUS ON *Problem Solving*

Smart Sam?

Sam is one computer that just might pass the Turing test—at least if its intelligence were evaluated by someone with a small vocabulary.

Sam is a robot built by researchers at AT&T Bell Laboratories to demonstrate artificial intelligence capabilities in a machine that uses high-speed parallel computing to integrate several sensors with artificial intelligence. Thus, using its AI programming, Sam can interpret and respond to spoken words, objects it "sees" through video cameras, and objects it "feels" through other sensors. Separate computers process the inputs Sam receives from each type of sensor. According to the scientists at Bell Labs, Sam is the first system to combine so many human capabilities in a single robotic system.

Sam's programmers gave the robot a vocabulary of 127 words. Although this vocabulary is small by human standards, it is possible to construct about 300 quintillion meaningful sentences from those words. The robot can interpret communications using those words and can use them in its replies.

For example, the user can place a few objects in front of Sam and ask the robot to put the small cube next to the tall cylinder. Sam interprets the user's words, then identifies and moves the object. Try to fool the robot—say, by describing the tall cylinder as short—and you may be surprised by what has been called Sam's "sense of humor." According to one observer, the robot may reply, "I don't think the cylinder is short. But I'll take your word for it."

Source: William D. Marbach, "A Robot with Human Senses—Including a Sense of Humor," *Business Week*, October 2, 1989, p. 105.

intelligent database search machine used to match a particular DNA sequence against a massively large database of all known sequences. In a test of the concept, 64 Intel 80386 processors wired in parallel completed the job in four minutes.

Assessing Machine Intelligence

Assessing the intelligence of machines is no different from assessing the intelligence of people. This is an obvious corollary of the Turing test described at the beginning of the chapter. Intelligence is in the eye of the beholder and reflects the culture and zeitgeist (or spirit) of every age. Machines like the Trellis and intelligent database search machines, as well as Sam, the robot described in the Focus on Problem Solving, exhibit such power in the sense of mastery over an environment that, in the eyes of many, they assume the quality of "intelligence," a quality normally reserved for humans.

But we must always remember that we are using the word "intelligence" metaphorically. These machines are not human. Instead they are programmed reflections of human intelligence, artifacts of humans that we hope are under our control. And it is well to remember their limitations.

Summary

• Artificial intelligence refers to a number of different techniques and practices that have as their common goal the emulation of human intelligence and perception.

• The artificial intelligence family has six members: natural language, robotics, perceptive systems, expert systems, neural networks, and intelligent machines.

• There are two approaches to artificial intelligence: top-down approaches seek to emulate the logic of human problem solving, and bottom-up approaches seek to emulate the biological brain.

• Expert systems exemplify the top-down approach by modeling human reasoning in restricted domains.

• Expert systems are composed of four major components: the knowledge base, the development team, the AI shell, and the user.

• Artificial intelligence systems have come to play a more integral role in traditional business systems, such as order entry, accounting, and manufacturing.

• Neural networks exemplify the bottom-up approach to artificial intelligence because they are based on a biological metaphor of the brain.

• Neural networks can learn and, in that sense, are more flexible than expert systems.

• The hardware available for building neural networks is primitive, but the capabilities of these systems are nevertheless impressive.

• Intelligent machines provide another approach to artificial intelligence. Because of their massive parallelism, these machines offer the prospect of greatly expanding computing power by performing "intelligent" functions we might expect of humans. The Trellis machine and the intelligent database search machine are two examples.

Key Terms

Artificial intelligence (AI)
Turing test
Natural language
Robotics
Perceptive systems
Expert systems
Neural network
Intelligent machines
Bottom-up approach
Top-down approach
Feedback
Perceptron
Logic Theorist
Combinatorial explosion
Knowledge base
Semantic nets
Frames
Knowledge engineer
Artificial intelligence shell
Inference engine
Forward reasoning
Backward reasoning
Parallel sensor systems
Intelligent database search machine

Review Questions

1. How would you define artificial intelligence?
2. What are the members of the AI family?
3. What is meant by a domain of knowledge?
4. How would you characterize the history of AI? What were the major stages in its development, and when did they happen?
5. What is meant by a "combinatorial explosion"? How can intelligent systems solve this problem?
6. How would you define an expert system?
7. What are the major components of an expert system?
8. Name and describe the three different ways in which a knowledge base can be modeled.
9. Define and describe forward and backward reasoning.
10. How does building an expert system differ from developing a traditional system?
11. How has the relationship between expert systems and other business systems changed?
12. What is a neural network?
13. Describe a biological neuron, and then describe a physical or artificial neuron.
14. How can a neural network learn?
15. Define a parallel sensor system and explain how it differs from an ordinary information system in a business.

Discussion Questions

1. Many people say that someday intelligent expert systems will replace high-level business managers. Do you think this will be possible?

2. Examine an office in your college or in a local business, and describe how a small expert system might be used to make work more efficient and pleasant.

3. What is the proper role of expert systems or neural networks in a business or a government agency? Should key decisions be left to AI devices? Describe a range of possible roles.

Problem-Solving Exercises

1. Locate a small business in your neighborhood, and within that business locate a single occupation—for example, supervisor, clerk, shelf stocker, and the like. Interview the person who occupies this position, and try to discover at least ten "rules of thumb" that that person follows in order to accomplish his or her job. Write a short paper about what you discovered.

2. Look through several microcomputer magazines, such as *PC World*, *PC Magazine*, *Macworld*, and *Computer World*, for a case study of an expert

system. Review this article and write a three-page critical report. Was the system as successful as originally planned? How did the system fall short?

3. Some people argue that artificial intelligence will have its greatest impact on low-level, relatively simple jobs in a business. Others argue that professionals and managers will be most affected by expert systems. In a short paper, analyze these two positions.

Notes

1. " 'Smart' Arms' Failure to Distinguish Decoys Has Pentagon Alarmed," *The Wall Street Journal,* February 17, 1989.
2. Actually, the story of AI is much more complex and controversial than can be presented here in such a brief introduction. Involved in this larger debate are questions about the nature of human beings and knowledge, the proper relationship between responsible human beings and machines, and the difference between promise and reality. The interested student is directed to two diametrically opposed books. For a positive view of AI, see Edward A. Feigenbaum and Pamela McCorduck, *The Fifth Generation: Artificial Intelligence and Japan's Computer Challenge to the World* (Reading, Mass.: Addison-Wesley, 1985). For a counterview of AI, see Hubert L. and Stuart E. Dreyfus, *Mind over Machine: The Power of Human Intuition and Expertise in the Era of the Computer* (New York: The Free Press, 1986).
3. For an interesting discussion of the difficulties of applying expert systems methods to general management, see Vasant Dhar, "On the Plausibility and Scope of Expert Systems in Management," *Journal of Management Information Systems* (Summer 1987).
4. For a compact review of the differences between a systems analyst and a knowledge engineer, see Jon A. Turner, "A Comparison of the Process of Knowledge Elicitation with that of Information Requirements Determination," Center for Research on Information Systems, Working Paper, New York University, Stern Graduate School of Business, March 1989.
5. Eric Bender, "The Knowledge Engineers," *PC World,* September 1987.
6. Dwight B. Davis, "Artificial Intelligence Goes to Work," *High Technology,* April 1987.
7. This section benefits from an article by David Gelernter, "The Metamorphosis of Information Management," *Scientific American,* August 1989. This article outlines a number of possibilities for extending computing through parallel processing.
8. Amy Cortese, "Bellcore Puts Neural Nets on a Chip," *Computerworld,* September 19, 1988.
9. Edward Collins, Sushmito Ghosh, and Christopher Scofield, Nestor, Inc., Providence, Rhode Island, in DARPA, 1988.

Problem-Solving Case

Taking Care of Sick Robots at Ford Motor Company

When people get sick, they complain. Often a human can "feel a cold coming on" and take precautions. Robots, however, give no warning that they are developing sore arms, aches, and pains. Moreover, when robots get sick, they fail, and an entire production line can come to a halt. Recognizing this, the Big Three automakers often have to keep several spare robots of every type on hand just to back up the production robots. This can be expensive. And when a $2 million, handmade robot fails, chances are the local repair crew will not have the expertise to repair it.

Ford Motor Company realized it had a problem: its maintenance crews were being overwhelmed by the company's 3,000 robots. Soon Ford expects to have 5,000 robots on line. Rather than hire thousands of new maintenance engineers, Ford turned to the Robotics and Automation Consulting Center in Dearborn, Michigan, for help. The company hoped a simple system could be developed quickly and then promoted to Ford robot suppliers as a generic diagnostic and repair system. In this way, Ford could get others—the suppliers—involved in designing and paying for maintenance of the expert system. In return, suppliers would get Ford's business and develop a competitive edge by offering robots with a built-in diagnostic system.

The Robotics Center was determined to keep the project simple and ended up spending only $5,000 for a preliminary model of the system, which was built by two people in six weeks. They were rather special people, however; one had 30 years' programming experience, and the other was one of Ford's leading hands-on experts on robots used at Ford and made by ASEA Corporation. The development team was critical.

The developers used an AI shell developed by Texas Instruments called Personal Consultant. The system ran on a Texas Instruments personal computer. The expert system had about 100 rules designed to take maintenance personnel step by step through the complicated process of diagnosing sick robots.

The preliminary version was a rough cut. It contained approximately 20 percent of the rules that ultimately will be needed for a complete system. But, according to Morgan M. Whitney, the center director, 20 percent of the rules are sufficient to cover 60 to 80 percent of the problems experienced by robots. A graduate student wrote a powerful graphics extension to the program, which gave color graphic representations of the robots' parts. Users of the system could use these color "X-rays" to distinguish layers of parts.

The system is now running on IBM Personal Computers at three Ford factories. A maintenance engineer at one installation complained, "You guys are really hoping to replace us, aren't you?" But Whitney and Ford officials explained time and again to field engineers that the system is designed to be a tool used by field personnel, not a replacement for them. Once this was understood, maintenance personnel started demanding the product. Basically, the system makes a maintenance engineer's job easier and helps train new maintenance personnel.

After the system was built, Ford began distributing the product on a floppy disk, with source code, to robot manufacturers. The company hopes to use this preliminary version as a seed for commercial diagnostic programs sold by robot manufacturers as a part of their package of goods and services. Demand for the source code is strong, with several calls coming in a year.

Source: Based on Dwight B. Davis, "Artificial Intelligence Goes to Work," *High Technology,* April 1987.

Case Study Questions

1. What kind of problem does Ford's expert system solve? To what other kinds of problems can this system be applied?
2. Who was on the development team and why? What other kinds of people should have been included in the development team?
3. How could a system with only 100 rules be helpful to field engineers?

Slaying the Paper Dragon

In 1965, when IBM began mass-producing its third-generation commercial mainframe computers (large computers using computer chips rather than vacuum tubes or transistors that made possible the widespread use of computers in business), many experts predicted that the "paper dragon" would be slain. No more would offices round the industrial world be deluged with mountains of paperwork. Since then, still more experts have predicted the paperless office and even the paperless society, but all to no avail: paper production in the United States has increased over 300 percent since 1965.

Today American business and American government each produces 1.4 trillion pages a year. With a U.S. population of 240 million, that's about 10,000 pieces of paper per person in the United States each year! Similarly, the promised "checkless society" did not come about: 60 billion checks are cleared each year in the United States.

The Information Age has not been a "paperless" age: business and government generate billions of documents and files each year. Systems like Kodak's PC-based KIMS eliminate the need for paper files by storing document images on optical disks and distributing them to users on a PC network.

Source: SUPERSTOCK, Inc.

But information technology may yet slay the paper dragon, thanks to a convergence of several technologies. These technologies are multimedia software and hardware, the workstation, the network, and the user interface.

Multimedia software working with multimedia hardware is beginning to provide the ability to integrate voice, data, text, and image. For instance, a CD-ROM optical disk working with special compression software can now be used to store page-size, full-image documents in about 50 kilobytes of space, and hence the entire 500 megabyte optical disk can hold about 10,000 image documents. Imaging technology is a rapidly expanding technology because it gives business quick access to the images of the original documents, including hand-written notes and signatures. The price of the digital scanners that translate a document into a digitized image has decreased significantly. If the user desires, character recognition software working with a scanner can translate the digitized image into text characters for inclusion into a word processing program that permits the document to be stored in a much smaller space. Whether documents are stored as images or text files, they offer businesses an increasingly inexpensive alternative to the filing cabinet.

To work with images and large text files, clerical and sales personnel need direct access to a large amount of high-speed processing power. For example, sales and service personnel should have access to a complete customer information database no matter where it is stored in the company—even if it is stored in several different files on different machines. This is where the workstation and network technology are important.

One example of network technology is Hewlett-Packard's New Wave environment. New Wave enables users to combine information such as text, numbers, and graphics from multiple applications that may be operating on different machines in a local area network (LAN). With New Wave, for instance, a user could access the corporate database stored on a LAN, download information to his or her workstation, and analyze the data in a spreadsheet. The user could produce a graph of the data and send it to a customer or to a co-worker at another workstation. New Wave is a graphical user interface. Using a mouse, the user points to an icon or symbol representing what he or she wants to do or the information he or she needs and clicks to navigate toward the desired information.

One company that has made good use of such technology is la Compagnie de Location d'Equipement Cle Ltée., an equipment-leasing company in Trois-Rivières, Quebec, which was drowning in paperwork. The head office had developed 15,000 client files, and with its branch offices in Montreal, Quebec City, Sherbrooke, and Chicoutimi, was generating 6,000 pieces of paper per month—200 pieces per employee.

The president of Cle could see the flood of paper would get worse as the company expanded. He hired a consulting firm, Sogi Informatique Ltée., to eliminate paper at all five of Cle's offices.

After evaluating the company's needs and shopping for the equipment and tools, Sogi designed an image management system that enables users to open and review on screen all the documents within a client file, make written notations in the file (with a light pen using ordinary handwriting), and order printed copies of necessary documents. The hardware for this system is a Wang minicomputer running Wang imaging software and supporting Wang's Freestyle system. Freestyle is a combination of hardware and software that permits computers

Applying New Wave

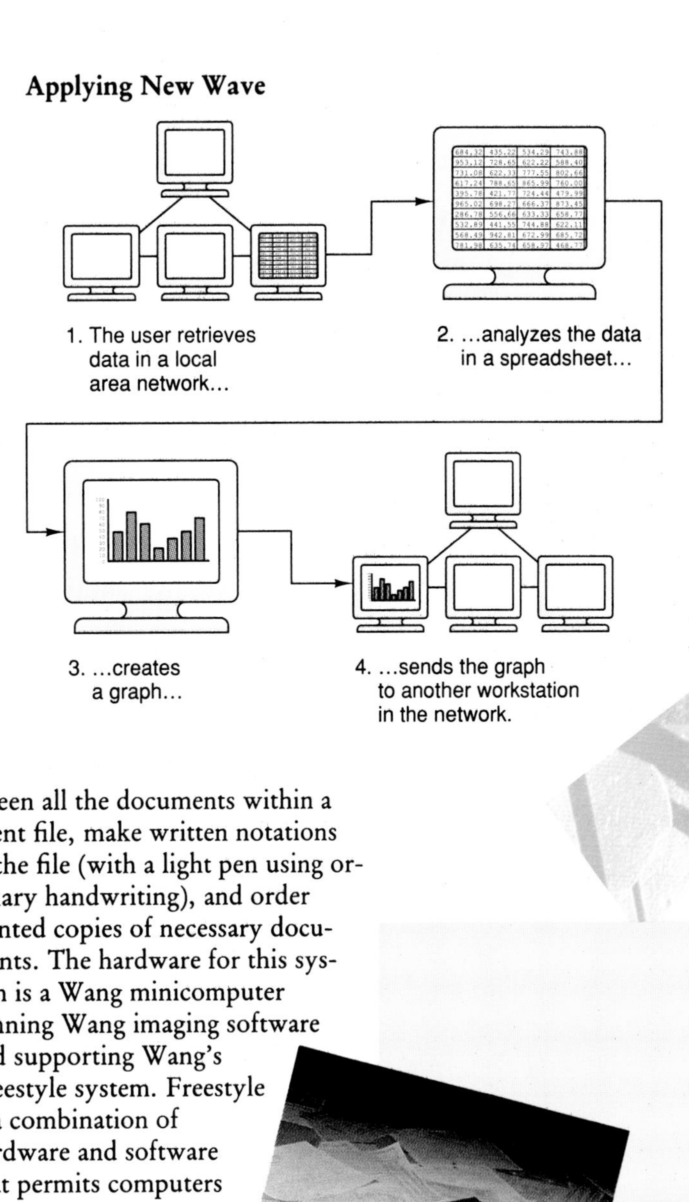
1. The user retrieves data in a local area network...
2. ...analyzes the data in a spreadsheet...
3. ...creates a graph...
4. ...sends the graph to another workstation in the network.

One way to cut down on paper is to decrease the amount of data put on paper forms before it is input into computer systems. GRiDPAD is a clipboard-sized, lightweight computer that allows data to be collected from handprinted fill-in fields, check-off boxes, and multiple-choice lists.

Source: Courtesy of GRiD Systems Corporation.

using the DOS operating system to work with Wang equipment, automating office communication to a degree that heretofore was impossible. With Freestyle, the user can attach handwritten notes, images, and spoken conversations to Wang image documents and store them with any text or image file. Freestyle also allows documents to be sent via fax or electronic mail.

What this means for Cle is that an employee in any of its offices can open a client file (no matter where it is stored, even in remote offices), do a credit check, evaluate the business risk, listen to a salesperson's recorded impressions of the client, approve equipment rental, order equipment, and insure and expedite the order. Even handwritten letters from the client can be included! All of this client service takes place without a single piece of paper being generated.

Imagine what this might mean in terms of savings. Experts tell us that it costs a firm an average of about $3.00 to handle each piece of paper it generates. For a firm like Cle, which generates about 72,000 pieces of paper per year (not to mention storing and handling the paper from previous years), eliminating paper would therefore save around $216,000 each year.

Companies such as Hewlett-Packard continue to refine existing technologies and develop new ones for the paperless office. H-P's New Wave environment lets users integrate information from many sources onto different computers in a local area network.

Source: Courtesy of Hewlett-Packard Company.

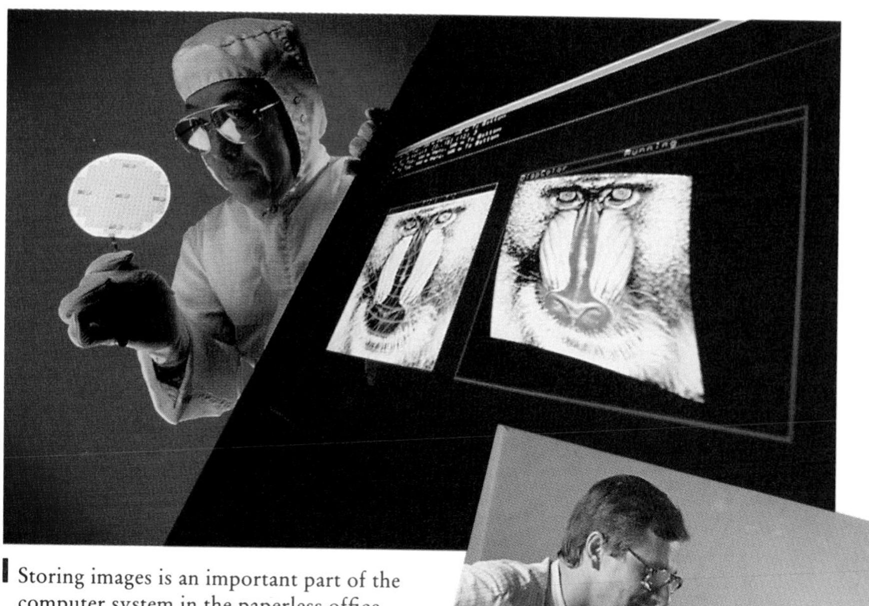

Storing images is an important part of the computer system in the paperless office because information is found not only in words and numbers but in drawings, video, and photographs. A TRW technician holds a chip that can store and manipulate images such as the baboon shown.

Source: Courtesy of TRW Inc.

For a small business, slaying the paper dragon once and for all could boost profits tremendously by lowering costs. For society as a whole, movement toward a paperless office would unleash the enormous financial resources now devoted to managing, tracking, and sending paper.

Source: Based on Pat Atkinson, "State of the Art Office," *Canadian Datasystems,* March 1990.

Systems for paper-intense industries such as publishing not only cut the amount of paper used, but also cut the amount of time needed for various functions. The Harris 8900 Integrated Newspaper System offers page makeup functions for classified advertising, news editing and layout, and display-ad composition.

Source: Courtesy of Harris Corporation.

P A R T · T H R E E

Problem Solving with Information Systems

CHAPTER · NINE

Business Problem Analysis: Critical Thinking Skills

Chapter Outline

9.1 Introduction: Concepts
- Defining the Problem
- The Problem-Solving Funnel of Real-World Decision Making
- Critical Thinking

9.2 A Five-Step Model of Problem Solving
- Step 1: Problem Analysis
- Step 2: Problem Understanding
- Step 3: Decision Making
- Step 4: Solutions Design
- Step 5: Implementation

9.3 Typical Business Problems: Analysis and Understanding
- Technology Perspectives
- Organizational Perspectives
- People: Strategic Human Resource Issues

9.4 Problem Solving: Making Decisions
- Establish Objectives
- Establish Feasibility
- Choose Cost-Effective Solutions

9.5 Problem Solving: Designing Solutions
- Making a Logical Design
- Making a Physical Design

9.6 Problem Solving: Implementing Solutions
- Steps in the Implementation of a System Solution
- Conversion Strategies

Learning Objectives

After reading and studying this chapter, you will:

1. Know how to solve problems using a simple five-step model.
2. Know how to develop your critical thinking skills.
3. Understand the three major factors to consider when approaching a business problem.
4. Be able to design logical and physical system solutions for a business.
5. Be familiar with the three major factors to consider when implementing a system solution.

What's Wrong at Ryder?

Until the end of the 1980s, Ryder Systems, Inc., was prospering, with revenues and profits growing rapidly. Then the Miami-based transportation conglomerate seemed to stall out. Profits lagged, revenue growth slowed to a crawl, and the price of the company's stock began to fall. Consequently, stockholders began pressuring Ryder's chairman, M. Anthony Burns, either to break up the company, selling its various businesses, or to sell some of the nontransportation businesses Burns had acquired during the latter half of the 1980s.

What is Ryder's problem? At least some of the difficulties stem from changes in the economy. As growth in the overall economy has slowed, businesses that rent trucks from Ryder have reduced their orders. Furthermore, sales of automobiles to consumers have declined, meaning that Ryder trucks began transporting fewer new cars to showrooms. These trends have hurt Ryder's core business of renting trucks.

Other sources of trouble lie within Ryder itself. As the company has grown from a relatively simple truck rental company into a conglomerate comprising more than 100 companies with assets of $6 billion, Ryder has added layers of bureaucracy. The company has been criticized for having too many managers and too little resolve in trimming inefficiency. Furthermore, the company's businesses are in mature industries, meaning that they have passed

their time of rapid growth. Therefore, the company's prosperity is more directly tied to that of the economy. Finally, to finance the many acquisitions it made during the 1980s, Ryder assumed a giant debt load of $2.4 billion. Thus, much of the company's revenues go to repaying debt.

Despite Ryder's complex problems, Burns has so far resisted selling off all or part of the company. Instead, Burns hopes to increase profits through internal growth rather than through acquisitions. This solution is by no means an easy one.

Source: Pete Engardio and Eric Schine, "Suddenly, Ryder's Engine Is Sputtering," *Business Week*, June 19, 1989, p. 56.

The difficulties facing Ryder are typical of many American service firms that grew through acquisitions during the 1980s. The problems these firms face are multifaceted and the potential solutions complex. Although technology offers a partial answer in many cases, experience shows that changes in organization and people are also required to save business firms like Ryder. Where would you start looking for solutions? Learning how to solve these and simpler problems is the subject of the next four chapters.

In this chapter you will learn some very important concepts about problem solving that can be applied in virtually all business settings. This will be demonstrated in Chapter 10, in which these conceptual skills will be applied to real-world cases. This conceptual framework is not tied to technology, although, as you will see, information technology can be useful in solving some business problems.

9.1 Introduction: Concepts

At first glance problem solving in business seems to be perfectly straightforward: a machine breaks down, parts and oil are spilling all over the floor, and obviously somebody has to do something about it. So, of course, you find a tool around the shop and start repairing the machine. After a cleanup and proper inspection of other parts, you start the machine and production resumes.

No doubt some problems in business are this straightforward. But few problems are this simple, and, in general, when they are, they are not very interesting. Most business problems are considerably more complex. In a real-world business organization, a number of major factors are simultaneously involved in problems. These major factors can be grouped into three categories: technology, organization, and people. When a business problem occurs, it is usually not a simple technology or machine problem, but some mixture of organization, people, and technology problems. In other words, a whole set of problems is usually involved. Even establishing the existence of a problem, or declaring that a problem exists, can be controversial in a business or other organization. Why is this so?

Defining the Problem

Contrary to popular conception, problems are not like basketballs on a court just waiting to be picked up by some "objective" problem solver. There are an infinite number of solutions in the world, each with its own advocates. Choosing the right solutions in an organization depends on the ability of key actors in the organization to define the problem correctly.

Before problems can be solved, there must be agreement in an organization about what the problem is, what its causes are, and what can be done about the problem given the limited resources of the organization. Problems have to be properly defined by people in an organization before they can be solved. Once you understand this critical fact, you can start to solve problems creatively.

Consider the following example. As you read the next paragraph, try to answer these questions: Is technology the solution to Dow Jones's problems? How have different people defined the problem in different ways?

The on-line database business has so far failed to meet expectations. Back in the 1980s, people were predicting that on-line data services provided by huge information firms like Dow Jones & Company, Mead Corporation, Knight-Ridder, Inc., and H&R Block would put librarians and even newspapers out of business. With 73 million knowledge and information workers in the U.S. labor force and 17 million personal computers in use, many people predicted there would be a huge industry and consumer market for on-line databases, amounting to at least $10 billion in revenue.[1]

This huge market has failed to materialize. As of 1989, the major firms shared a mere 500,000 active subscribers and combined revenues of about $600 million.

William L. Dunn, executive vice-president of Dow Jones & Company, wanted to know what the company was doing wrong. He decided the problem was technology. Users, Dunn figured, were scared off by the difficulties of using Dow Jones News/Retrieval. Dunn thinks he has found the solution.

Rather than have users dial and ask for information, Dow Jones will ship it out to them automatically. Thus, when subscribers use their computers, they can access the information automatically using everyday language, not arcane computer codes. Currently, customers cannot type in "Russia" and receive news on Russia because the Dow Jones software only understands "Soviet Union." In the new system, a user will automatically receive information in the form he or she wants, say, a spreadsheet. The system will also be able to handle English-like queries such as, "Compare the views of Bush and Gorbachev on free speech." Dunn calls the new concept "information broadcasting."

To implement the new concept, Dunn ordered a pair of $2.5 million Connection Machines, supercomputers that will permit users to converse in English-like commands with the system. For corporate subscribers, Dow Jones has built a $3 million network that will automatically feed corporate local area networks.

But industry skeptics and investors are not so sure Dunn has found the answer. Critics feel the changes are too narrow to attract new customers and will not increase usage by existing subscribers. Part of the problem, in the critics' view, is that many new technologies and competitors are challenging the on-line services. Lotus Development Corporation's product, called One Source, offers financial and corporate text and statistics updated weekly on compact disks (CD-ROM disks). The traditional newspapers are stronger than ever and clearly are not being challenged by the on-line databases. People still like to hold hard copy, and no form of information delivery yet available is as convenient as a newspaper (you can carry it with you and read it in the rain, and it requires no batteries).

Furthermore, lurking in the background are AT&T and the local Bell phone companies with massive marketing clout and an installed base of customers. AT&T, which was recently granted the right to originate information, could be a powerful competitor. The local Bell operating companies are now developing fiber-optic links to households; at some future date, these will permit the delivery of video pictures as well as data to home owners. When this occurs, the traditional on-line database companies will lose any competitive advantage they had in delivery of information. They will be consigned to mere wholesalers of information. Consequently, given all these factors, critics wonder if Dow Jones has properly understood the problems facing the company.

Obviously, people inside Dow Jones define the problems facing the company differently than outside critics and competitors do. Depending on how one defines Dow Jones's problem, different courses of further research and action can be recommended. For instance, if Dow Jones's problem is defined as one of competing with totally different technologies—like CD-ROM—then the company should begin exploring these technologies with the ultimate goal of developing new products based on the new technology. Alternatively, Dow Jones's problem could be defined as a management failure to perceive the changing environment. Investors with this view would encourage a buy-out and breakup of the company; then the cash realized from selling parts of the company could be used to invest in faster growth areas of information management.

As it turns out, Dow Jones management has defined its problem rather narrowly: it is pursuing a change in software and hardware without fundamentally questioning the product line, alternate technologies, or product expansion. Dow Jones management may be right in its definition of the problem given its resources, historical assets, and trained personnel.

Our point here is that "the problems" facing all companies are usually subject to interpretation, complex, and often controversial. These problems are not objective objects but, rather, subjective interpretations involving competing views of the world by powerful actors both inside and outside the company.

The Problem-Solving Funnel of Real-World Decision Making

The Dow Jones example illustrates the typical stages that problem solving goes through. Real-life problem solving can usefully be seen as a kind of funnel (see Figure 9.1) involving five stages.[2] The model begins by recogniz-

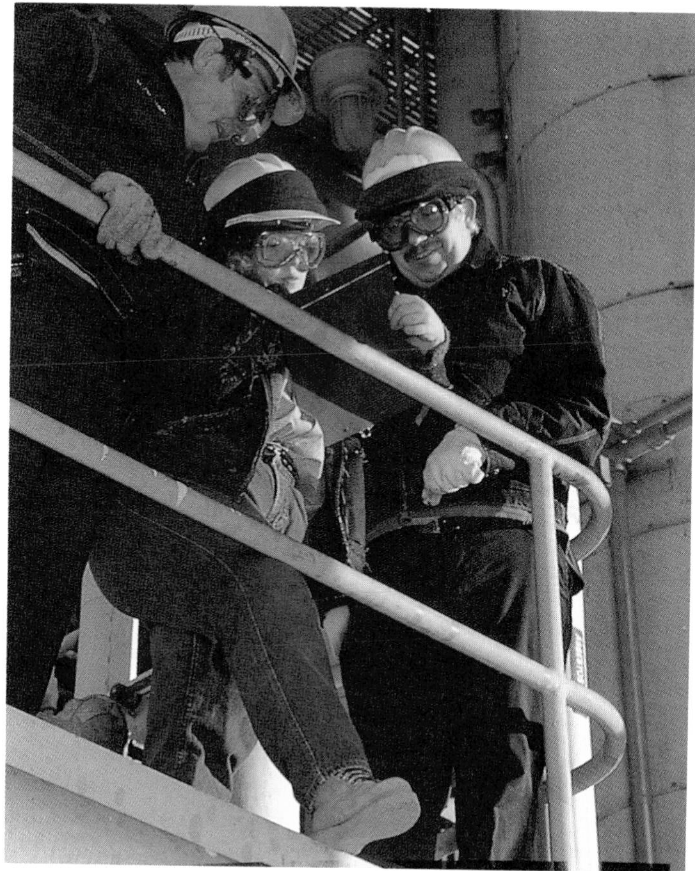

By investigating, analyzing, and defining problems, businesspeople can design and implement effective solutions. To solve a problem with the production of chemicals, Dow Corning manufacturing engineer Sue Jacob and her team studied procedures and analyzed production data. Their solution was an operating guideline that, when implemented, exposed a new problem: lack of communication between machine operators and their supervisors. Their solution to the second problem included clarifying the manufacturing process to both operators and supervisors to improve communications and training for operators.

Source: Courtesy of Dow Corning Corporation.

ing that there are a large number of solutions in the environment; our goal is to capture the correct solution from the many possibilities. A first step in problem solving typically involves the search for a consensus on what—in very general terms—the problem is and what general kinds of solutions might be appropriate. This is a critical period of **problem analysis** and definition in which the definition of the problem is narrowed considerably. The second stage is **problem understanding;** this is a period of investigation—fact gathering and more analysis—hopefully leading to better understanding. Next comes a period of **decision making** when objectives and feasible solutions are debated, and the best option is chosen. Fourth, once options are identified, the process of **solutions design** can begin. Note that each of the stages in the model has narrowed the possible solutions down to a smaller number. Finally, a period of **implementation** is entered, during

Problem analysis
The consideration of the dimensions of a problem to determine what kind of problem it is and what general kinds of solutions may be appropriate; the first step in problem solving.

Problem understanding
The investigation—fact gathering and analysis—of a problem to gain better understanding; the second step of problem solving.

Decision making
The process of debating objectives and feasible solutions and choosing the best option; the third step of problem solving.

Solutions design
The development of a solution to a problem, including both logical and physical design; the fourth step of problem solving.

Implementation
The process of putting the solution of a problem into effect and evaluating the results and performance in order to make improvements; the fifth, and last, step of problem solving.

Figure 9.1

The Five Stages in the Problem-Solving Process

We can think of problem solving as a five-step process. There are many possible solutions to a problem; the goal is to select the right solution through following these five steps. The first task is to define the problem. This may be more difficult than it sounds, since various people in an organization may have various ideas on what the exact problem is. The second step is to gather and analyze information, helping us to understand the problem better. Third is the decision-making stage, in which we look at possible solutions and select the best one. Next comes the process of designing the solution, and last is solution implementation, during which the solution is tested and refined. It is important to evaluate the results of each phase, including implementation, to make sure that the solution is indeed solving the problem.

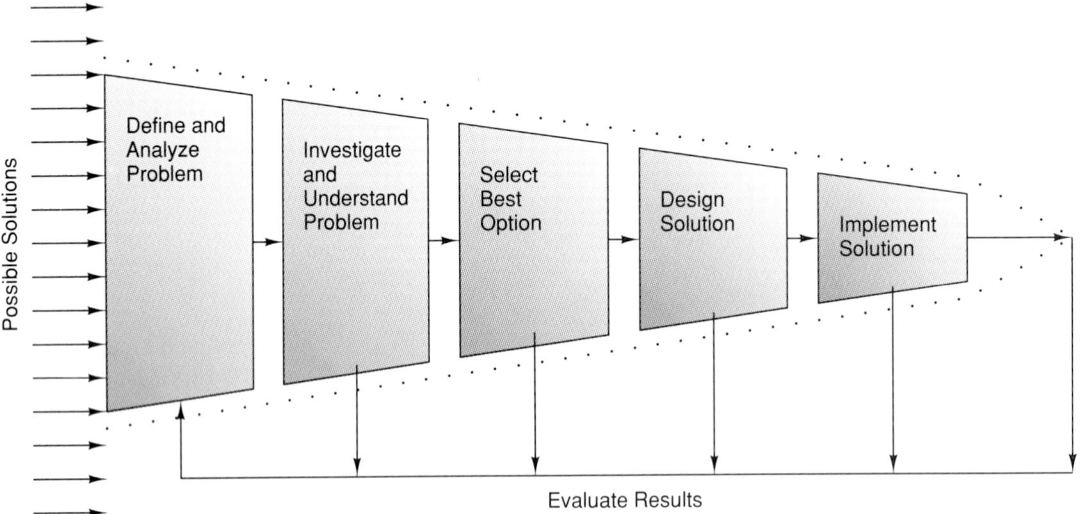

which theoretical designs and concepts are tested in the real world and final changes are made in the design based on field experience. Evaluating the results and performance of this solution helps the firm to improve and refine it. As the business environment changes, feedback may signal that it is time to go through the decision-making process again.

We will use this real-world view of decision making later as the basis for a five-step model of how you can solve problems. First, however, we need to examine the early process of problem solving a little more closely.

Critical Thinking

It is amazingly easy to accept someone else's definition of a problem or to adopt the opinions of some authoritative group that has "objectively" analyzed the problem and offers quick solutions. You should try to resist this tendency to accept existing definitions of the problem. Throughout the natural flow of decision making, it is essential that you try to maintain some distance from any specific given solution until you are sure you have properly identified the problem, developed understanding, and analyzed alternatives. Otherwise you may leap off in the wrong direction, solve the wrong problem, and waste resources. Wise decision makers wait until decisions are necessary and until they are as certain as they will ever be that the correct solution is at hand. Even then, wise decision makers carefully observe the early implementation period to see if they were right. To do this, you will have to engage in some critical thinking exercises.

Critical thinking can be defined briefly as the sustained suspension of judgment with an awareness of multiple perspectives and alternatives. It involves at least four elements:

Critical thinking
The sustained suspension of judgment with an awareness of multiple perspectives and alternatives.

- Maintaining doubt and suspending judgment.
- Being aware of different perspectives.
- Testing alternatives and letting experience guide.
- Being aware of organizational and personal limitations.

Simply following a rote pattern of decision making, or a model, will not guarantee a correct solution. The best protection against incorrect results is to engage in critical thinking throughout the problem-solving process.

First, maintain doubt and suspend judgment. Perhaps the most frequent error in problem solving is to arrive prematurely at a judgment about the nature of a problem. By doubting all solutions at first and refusing to rush to a judgment, you create the necessary mental conditions to take a fresh, creative look at problems, and you keep open the chance to make a creative contribution. Second, recognize that all interesting business problems have many dimensions and that the same problem can be viewed from different perspectives.

In this text we have emphasized the usefulness of three perspectives on business problems: technology, organizations, and people. Within each of these very broad perspectives there are many sub-perspectives or views. The **technology perspective,** for instance, includes a consideration of a firm's hardware, software, telecommunications, and database. The **organization perspective** includes a consideration of a firm's formal rules and procedures, culture, management, production process, and politics. The **people perspective** includes consideration of the firm's employees as individuals and their interrelationships in work groups.

Technology perspective
A way of viewing a problem in which emphasis is placed on information technology hardware, software, telecommunications, and database as sources of business problems and the way in which they can contribute to a solution.

Organization perspective
A way of viewing a problem in which emphasis is placed on the firm's formal rules and procedures, production process, management, politics, bureaucracy, and culture as sources of its problems and the way in which they can contribute to a solution.

People perspective
A way of viewing a problem in which emphasis is placed on the firm's employees as individuals and their interrelationships as sources of its problems and the way in which they can contribute to a solution.

You will have to decide for yourself which major perspectives are useful for viewing a given problem. The ultimate criterion here is utility: does adopting a certain perspective tell you something more about the problem that is useful for solving the problem? If not, reject that perspective as being not meaningful in this situation, and look for other perspectives.

The third element of critical thinking involves testing alternatives, or model solutions to problems, letting experience be the guide. Not all contingencies can be known in advance, and much can be learned by empirical experience. The experience of A. O. Smith's Automotive Products Company is a good example of how a firm may have to test several alternatives before it arrives at a solution.

Smith is one of the worlds' largest producers of auto frames and parts for the Detroit Big Three automakers. By 1981, despite concerted efforts to automate with new technology, Smith had reached a low point in productivity growth and quality. Up to 20 percent of the auto frames had to be reworked before shipment. Bored workers toiled on assembly lines performing robotlike, repetitive actions; strong union work rules prevented any sharing of work; and union shop stewards spent much of the day arguing with shop foremen over speed and work rule enfringements.[3]

But in 1981, Smith started out on an eight-year odyssey of change. Its goal was not only higher productivity, but its very survival. Smith started with an employee involvement program (EI) that centered on creating quality circles. The union was not asked to participate. From 1981 to 1984, productivity improved somewhat, but without union involvement, there was little real change on the shop floor.

By 1984, as the Big Three automakers forced Smith to lower its prices, the union agreed to work with Smith to set up Problem-Solving Committees on the shop floor, Advisory Committees at the plant level, and a Top Planning Committee involving senior union and company management. With this move, the union gained a large say in both day-to-day decision making and long-term strategic planning.

Even with this change, however, workers still lifted, welded, and riveted in 20-second cycles, and absenteeism remained at around 20 percent on some days. The piecework pay system resulted in an enormous amount of poor-quality product.

By 1987, the Big Three had forced another round of price reductions on Smith. A decline in orders followed, and then 1,300 workers were laid off. In their 1987 negotiations, the union and Smith's management agreed to eliminate the old piecework pay system, set up production teams of workers, and freeze wages for four years so that no one lost money. In the production-team concept, small groups of workers perform integrated tasks in teams, switching off as needed to keep production rolling or just to change jobs. The teams elect a team leader and engage in most management activities, including setting work standards, ordering replacement parts, and stopping the line if problems arise. As one worker noted, "They just turned control of the shops over to us." The 1987 agreement eliminated the need for foremen, and many were let go. The ratio of foremen to workers went from 1 to 10 in 1987 to 1 to 37 in 1989.

With these changes, productivity has finally improved. Workers were recently issued a $123 payment under a new profit-sharing plan. Although small difficulties still exist, Smith's management believes it has finally solved its basic production problems on the shop floor.

Careful examination of the A. O. Smith story makes it clear that the company ended up with quite a different solution than it originally anticipated. This is commonplace: solutions generally evolve over time rather than being "frozen" in time.

The fourth and final element of critical thinking involves an awareness of the limits on the human and organizational resources at your command. Remember, there is a difference between what an organization "should do" and what it "can do." And there is a difference between an "optimal" solution and a "satisfactory" solution. Generally, so-called optimal solutions may not be feasible, whereas satisfactory solutions are feasible, indeed even economical. Some solutions may be so expensive that the organization would go bankrupt if it adopted them (creating a whole new set of problems). An awareness of the feasibility of a solution—whether it is actually doable—will not only help you choose the right solution to problems, but will also help you save time and money by avoiding solutions that are beyond your organization's resources.

9.2 A Five-Step Model of Problem Solving

As we noted in Figure 9.1, real-world decision making can be summarized in a simple five-stage model of problem solving, which is applicable to personal problems as well as to business decisions. In the world of information systems, the first three stages are usually called systems analysis, and the last two stages are called systems design. Thus, "systems analysis and design" is another word for problem solving.

Step 1: Problem Analysis

Problem analysis is somewhat analogous to "ball parking"—that is, estimating the dimensions of a problem. The most important question answered in this step is, "What kind of a problem is it?" The State Department of Motor Vehicles Office at White Plains, New York, discovered this when it set out to improve the quality of service.[4] As you read through the saga of the Motor Vehicles Office in the next paragraphs, pay particular attention to the way the office defined its problems.

In 1984, the office seemed to have nothing but problems. The average waiting time to register a car was two and a half hours. The building itself was a crumbling relic. Office hours were set for the convenience of employees (8:00 A.M. to 4:00 P.M.), making it difficult for working people to register.

Registrants had to wait in three separate lines: document examination, eye examination, and billing. New York State had instituted a four-year license renewal program in which driver's licenses expired at the end of the month in which they were originally issued. Thousands of people would descend on the office at the end of each month, causing long lines. If any document was missing, or if applicants forgot to bring some documents, they had to leave the line and reenter at a later time.

There was no way for people to call in to ask questions and no information service on the premises. Therefore, people had to stand in line just to get information. Although cars could be registered by mail, few people were aware of this and came in to register their cars in person because that is how it had always been done. Computer capacity was stretched to the limit, with four- and five-minute delays in computer terminal response at peak hours.

What kind of a problem does the Motor Vehicles Office have? Is this a people or labor problem related to poor attitudes of public workers or poor training? Is this a business problem related to outdated procedures and unnecessary bureaucratic red tape? Is the Motor Vehicles Department being starved for funds by the state legislature? Or is this a technology problem that more powerful computers could easily solve?

Let's look at how these problems actually were solved in the period 1984–1988.[5] First, the State Department of Motor Vehicles renovated and modernized the entire building and physical plant. Second, a new commissioner who was publicly committed to radical improvements in service was appointed in 1986. Third, in 1986, evening hours were added to serve working people. Fourth, computer capacity was expanded 20 percent to permit sales tax collection and registration in one operation, and a new cash accounting system was written to speed up service. Fifth, the end-of-the-month rush in license renewals was eliminated by making expirations effective at dates throughout the month. Sixth, a new employee training program was instituted involving three weeks of in-class training on subjects ranging from computer operations, dress codes, and courtesy to how to keep cool under pressure. Seventh, a centralized telephone information service was initiated in 1987; it now handles up to 6,000 inquiries a day. Eighth, mail-in registration was initiated for those who wanted to use it, reducing the load on local offices.

As a result of these improvements, a person now has to wait in only one line at the Motor Vehicles Office and can check his or her documents at a central information booth before entering the line. The average time to register a car or obtain a license has been reduced to less than 30 minutes at peak times. In estimating the dimensions of the solution, planners at the New York State Department of Motor Vehicles identified a number of interrelated problems involving people, technology, and organization. The solution was multifaceted, took many years to implement, and was largely incremental—that is, it was implemented one step at a time.

Step 2: Problem Understanding

What causes the problem? Why is it still around? Why wasn't it solved long ago? Those are some of the questions that must be asked in the second step of problem solving. Finding the answers involves some detailed detective work, some fact gathering, and some history writing. Facts may be gathered through personal interviews with people involved in the problem, analysis of quantitative and written documents, or attitude questionnaires. Generally, the more different kinds of data you have, the better understanding you will achieve.

Interviews and surveys can be used to gather facts about a problem or to verify satisfaction. Here, employees of TDS Telecom, Inc., a subsidiary of Telephone and Data Systems, Inc., conduct surveys to determine subscribers' needs and perception of service quality.

Source: Courtesy of Telephone and Data Systems, Inc.

In the case of the Motor Vehicles Office described above, managers used personal observation and interviews to understand the problems, along with agency documents, administrative data, and employee questionnaires.

At the end of this second step, you should be able to give a rather precise, brief account of what the problem is, how it was caused, and what major factors are sustaining it.

Step 3: Decision Making

Once a problem is analyzed and a sense of understanding is developed, it is possible to make some decisions about what should and can be done. We emphasize these two aspects of decision making because they are quite different.

What should be done has to do with objectives; these are the goals that the business hopes to attain. Is the firm's objective short-term profit maximization, intermediate-term growth, or long-term survival? Sometimes, to your surprise, you may find out that no one has ever asked that question. It is your job to understand precisely what the firm's objectives are.

Second, whatever the firm's objectives may be, it has resources to pursue only selected options. Your job is to understand what can be feasibly done within the resources of the business. Generally, a business cannot hire a whole new labor force, develop new products overnight, or enter entire new markets in the short term. All these may be things the firm should do but cannot do in the short term because of resource limits.

Step 4: Solutions Design

Most people think that once a decision is made to pursue a given option, the process is over. Actually, only the beginning is over. Solutions have to be designed and planned. In the process, the solutions will continue to be modified and changed. As we describe in Section 9.5, a design may be logical or physical. In a **logical design,** the general level of resources, the general operational process, and the nature of outputs that the solution should require are described. A **physical design** involves a more detailed description of equipment, buildings, personnel, and inventories than the logical design provides.

Logical design
The part of a solutions design that provides a description of the general level of resources, the operational process, and the nature of outputs that the solution should require; it describes what the solution will do, not how it will work physically.

Physical design
The part of a solutions design that translates the abstract logical system model into specifications for equipment, hardware, software, and other physical resources.

Step 5: Implementation

Once a solution is designed, the last step in problem solving is implementation. The world's best solutions do not implement themselves. Virtually all real-world business solutions require a planned implementation strategy in order to work properly. You will have to consider when and how to introduce the solution, how to explain the solution to your employees, how to modify the planned solution to account for field experience, how to change existing business procedures so the solution can work, and how to evaluate the solution so you know it is working.

Figure 9.2 summarizes the five-step model of business problem solving described here. It is a very general model that can be used in a variety of business or personal settings. But we also need to be more specific in describing the problems businesses typically face. In the next section, we look at the first two steps and three major sources of business problems and their related solutions. In later sections, we describe logical and physical designs of solutions and illustrate some charting tools used to depict solutions graphically.

9.3 Typical Business Problems: Analysis and Understanding

We have suggested throughout this book that all business problems (and solutions) can be seen as some combination of technology, organization, and people issues. These three perspectives can be applied throughout the problem-solving process. They are especially helpful in the first two steps of problem solving—problem analysis (what kind of problem are we facing?) and problem understanding (where did the problem come from and why does it persist?)—but can also be valuable in the decision-making and implementation steps.

Figure 9.2

Systems Analysis and Design

In order to design effective solutions for business problems, we must first analyze and understand the problem. Systems analysis includes the first three stages in our five-step model, during which we identify the problem, gather information about it, and make a decision about the best solution. The best solution is not always the ideal solution, since the ideal may be too expensive or too difficult considering present resources. The final two steps encompass systems design: designing the logical and physical specifications of the solution and implementing this solution. Feedback from each step, and from the post-implementation evaluation, helps us judge the effectiveness of the solution: has it solved the problem it was intended to solve?

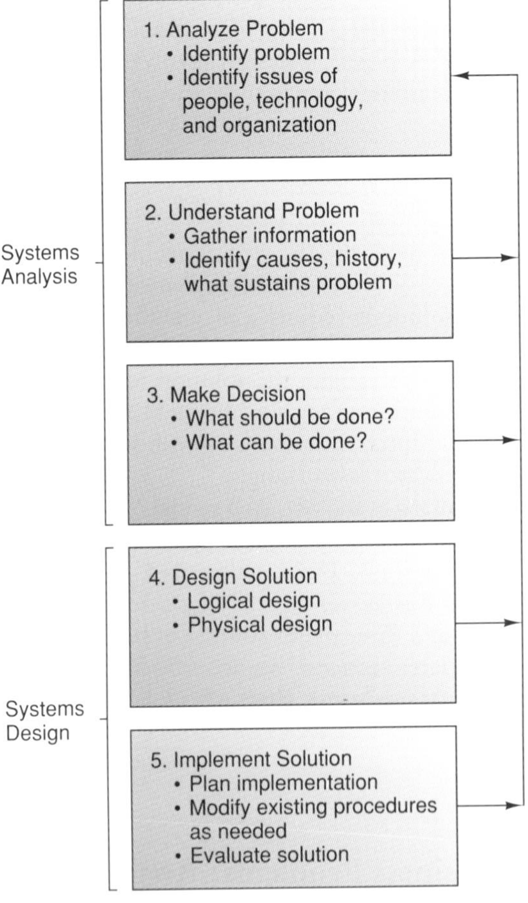

Table 9.1 has been compiled to help you relate these perspectives to the real-world examples in the text. Table 9.1 shows the matrix of perspectives we use throughout the book to guide the problem-solving process and lists the real-world examples in this chapter along with the particular perspective each illustrates.

Table 9.1

Problem-Solving Perspectives and the Examples in This Chapter that Illustrate Them

Perspective	Example
Technology	
Hardware	Dow Jones News/Retrieval
Software	Sun Microsystems, Inc.
Telecommunications	
Database	
Organization	
Culture	Ryder Systems, Inc.
Management	New York State Department of Motor Vehicles
Politics	
Bureaucracy	Department of Defense
Resources	Sun Microsystems, Inc.
Turbulence	
Complexity	
People	
Ergonomics	A.O. Smith
Evaluation and Monitoring	
Training	TRW, Inc.
Employee Attitudes and Involvement	Sun Microsystems, Inc.
Legal and Regulatory Compliance	

Technology Perspectives

Business problems—and solutions—are rarely technology problems per se. However, information technology is often one of the major sources of organizational problems. There are several kinds of technology problems, as shown in Figure 9.3. In general, when problem solving, you should ask yourself, "What changes in information technology hardware, software, telecommunications, and database are required to solve this problem?"

For all types of technology, the most common hardware problems are capacity, compatibility, and change. The growth in desktop computers has quickly overwhelmed the central mainframe computers installed in the 1980s. You can usually tell when capacity is exceeded by looking at response time: when response times approach 30 seconds to a minute, you know a capacity problem exists. The experience of Atlantic Casualty and Insurance Company is typical. Its four-year-old Data General Corporation MV/10000 minicomputer could no longer keep up with the company's rapidly expanding computational needs. Response times of 45 seconds were common, and some reports were taking up to 10 hours to run, impairing the firm's ability to process the flood of policies coming in every day.[6]

In Thailand, barges shuttle cases of Pepsi from a bottling plant on the Chao Phaya river to warehouses in Bangkok. Pepsi International replaced its 15-year-old mainframe computer system with COMPAQ DESKPRO personal computers.

Source: Courtesy of Compaq Computer Corporation and Pepsi-Cola International.

The firm's 75 programmers were waiting up to a minute just for a command to register.

The slowdown began to have an impact on business. The six-year-old company specializes in nonstandard automobile insurance policies. Most insurance companies will not insure race-car drivers, but when Mario Andretti needs a policy for the Indy 500, he comes to Atlantic Casualty. Atlantic receives hundreds of requests daily for strange and unusual policies. It must be able to respond rapidly, but with its capacity problems, that seemed impossible.

Fortunately, Data General had just released its new, more powerful MV 40000, which could process at 14 MIPS (millions of instructions per second), as compared to the old 2.5 MIP machine. The cost was $500,000 for the new machine. After three weeks of testing, prodding, and poking, the new machine went on-line. Response time for programmers and most customer requests went from 45 seconds down to an average of 4 seconds. The new machine's total MIP capacity can be quadrupled by adding up to four processors, and it can be extended further by adding intelligent workstations, each of which can handle 17 MIPS. Other benefits of the new system include its smaller size and its compatibility with existing software.

Expanding capacity is not as simple as it sounds. Often, a firm will want to change from one generation of computer to another to take advantage of new technology. But this may necessitate a change in software. What starts out as a simple hardware upgrade may end up as an expensive rewriting of all the organization's software. Compatibility issues must be considered as well: will the new computer be compatible with all the older computers and related equipment, such as printers and communication networks?

Software often presents a problem when an organization wants to do something new or to accomplish traditional tasks in a new way. Existing

Figure 9.3

Looking at Business Problems from a Technology Perspective

Information technology can often contribute to organizational problems. The most common technology issues are capacity (is the system overloaded?), compatibility (can the system's various components "talk" to each other?), and change (is the system still meeting organizational needs?). These issues affect hardware, software, databases, and telecommunications. It is wise to look at all of these aspects before ruling out technical problems.

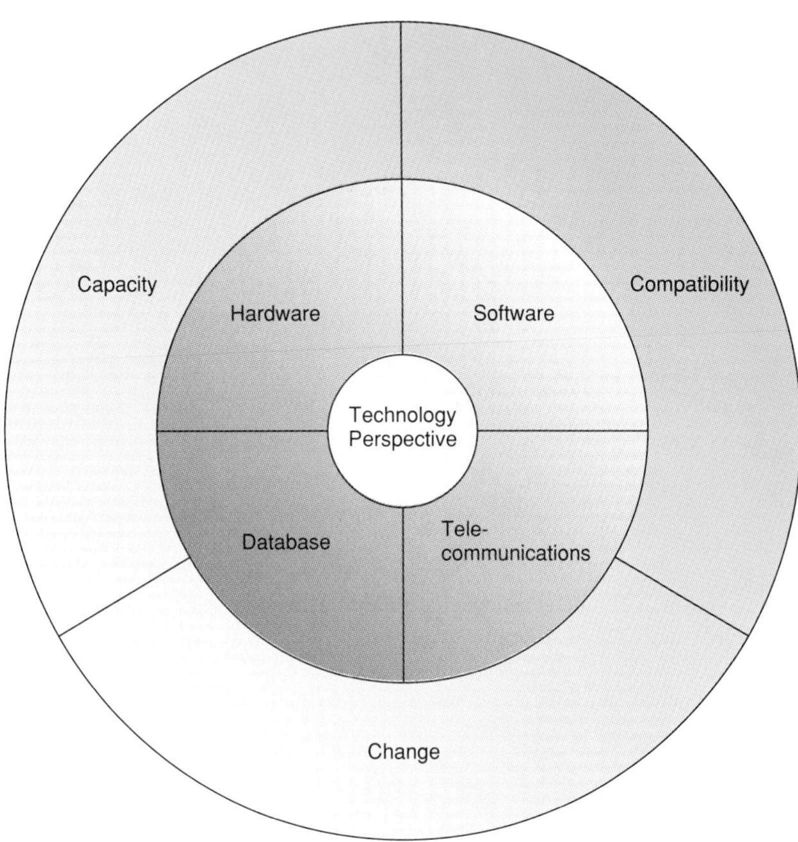

software will have to be replaced with new software when the organization changes, develops new products, institutes new organizational structures, or initiates new procedures.

The most common software issues involve the creation of interfaces with existing software, management of cost and projects, and personnel. Organizations build large libraries of software applications over many years. New software typically will require inputs from the old software and may be required to output information to the old systems. Generally, software interfaces have to be built. This is a time-consuming, expensive, and difficult process. It is no secret that the typical software project is 50 to 100 percent over budget and behind schedule.[7] What looks like a six-month project costing $100,000 can quickly turn into a year-long extravaganza costing $200,000 or more.

Part of the problem with the management of software projects involves personnel. Typically, organizations do not have in-house personnel trained in the techniques of building new software. Most of the existing staff is involved in maintaining the old software, not writing new software. Hence organizations must often hire outside consultants to write new software, and the outsiders may take many months to master the complexities of the organization.

Telecommunications has recently become a major source of problems for organizations because of the need to network large numbers of desktop computers and the desire to develop integrated systems that can link mainframes, minicomputers, and microcomputers into single networks. Typically, telecommunications issues involve standards (compatibility) and capacity planning.

Computers existed long before computer networks. This is quite different from the telephone system. Telephones were developed at the same time networks evolved, and there were well-established standards to assure that one phone could talk with all others on the network (this came about because the telephone companies in all cultures have been regulated monopolies that both manufactured the equipment and owned, operated, and defined the networks).

This is not the case with computers. Apple computers talk a different language than IBM PCs, and both talk a different language than mainframe computers, which in turn talk a different language than minicomputers. Overcoming these differences and developing standards are major difficulties for organizations.

Fortunately, vendors are providing a growing number of communications solutions to the standards problem. Mainframes and personal computers could effectively communicate in limited ways by 1990. Capacity planning, however, remains a guessing game. To put it simply, the problem is that it is extremely difficult to predict the demand on a communications network. Like improved highways that attract new traffic, when communications networks are made user friendly, the message traffic often skyrockets. The system can be overloaded the day it is installed.

A final technology area that causes problems for organizations is database. A firm often learns that it has a database problem when it discovers that needed information is located somewhere in the organization's computers, but it cannot be easily found or used. A second indicator of a database problem is an inability to write new software because the organization has no central repository or library showing what information is stored and where it is located.

Frequently, organizations inherit outmoded file structures that cannot adequately meet contemporary demands. Sometimes, organizations have thousands of application files but no real integrated database. Other organizations may have an integrated database, but it is an older hierarchical system that cannot easily be changed.

There are solutions to these database problems but they are expensive. Typically, the database has to be completely redesigned. This requires a major and fundamental software effort.

Although technology problems are usually not the sole cause of an organization's difficulties, and they certainly are not the only solution, information technology is increasingly playing a larger role in problem solu-

FOCUS ON People

The "Electric Army" Battles Support Problems

An organization that is faced with a microcomputer support problem that is baffling its staff has a new option: it can call on the "electronic army"—an all-volunteer force that's available around the clock. The electronic army is that band of brothers (and sisters) who frequent the wires. They drop everything from macros to pearls of wisdom into CompuServe Forums or subscription-based bulletin board systems. There are hundreds of these systems nationwide. For the price of a modem, an inexpensive subscription, and an occasional long-distance phone call, you can contact some of the best people in the business.

The CompuServe-based WordPerfect Support Group, NetWire, and the Graphics Forum are all places where they can be found. Nested within the messages, you can find out about every trick, trap, or technique imaginable. It is a great place to find useful utilities, inventive macros, drivers, or bug fixes.

The price of admission is pretty cheap. It might cost a few hundred dollars a year to get the subscriptions set up, but chances are that is cheaper than devoting months of staff time to debugging a technical glitch.

A corporate microcomputer support department will never have enough experts on hand to deal with every technical issue. Be glad that you can get to high-quality reinforcements. It's comforting to know there's a well-trained army out there to help.

Source: Cheryl Currid, "Turn to the 'Electric Army' to Battle Support Problems," adapted from *PC Week*, December 18, 1989, p. 75. Copyright © 1989, Ziff Communications Company.

tion. In large part, this is because, in the 1990s, what organizations want to do in terms of new products, new methods of manufacture, new organizational designs, and new methods of product delivery often directly involve information technology. But it should be remembered that information technology is only the servant of larger organizational purposes and issues.

The Focus on People describes a new option for firms facing technology problems—the "electronic army."

Organizational Perspectives

As Figure 9.4 shows, the organizational perspective on problem solving can be divided into internal institutional areas and external environmental areas (see Chapter 2). Let's look at some internal sources of problems first.

Figure 9.4

Issues to Consider in an Organizational Perspective

The organizational perspective requires a multifaceted approach. Factors in the internal environment that can play a role include the organization's culture, management, company politics, and bureaucratic structure. Forces in the external environment must also be considered: resources that are available to the firm, the turbulence or rate of change in such important areas as technology and prices, and the complexity in inputs and products with which the firm must cope.

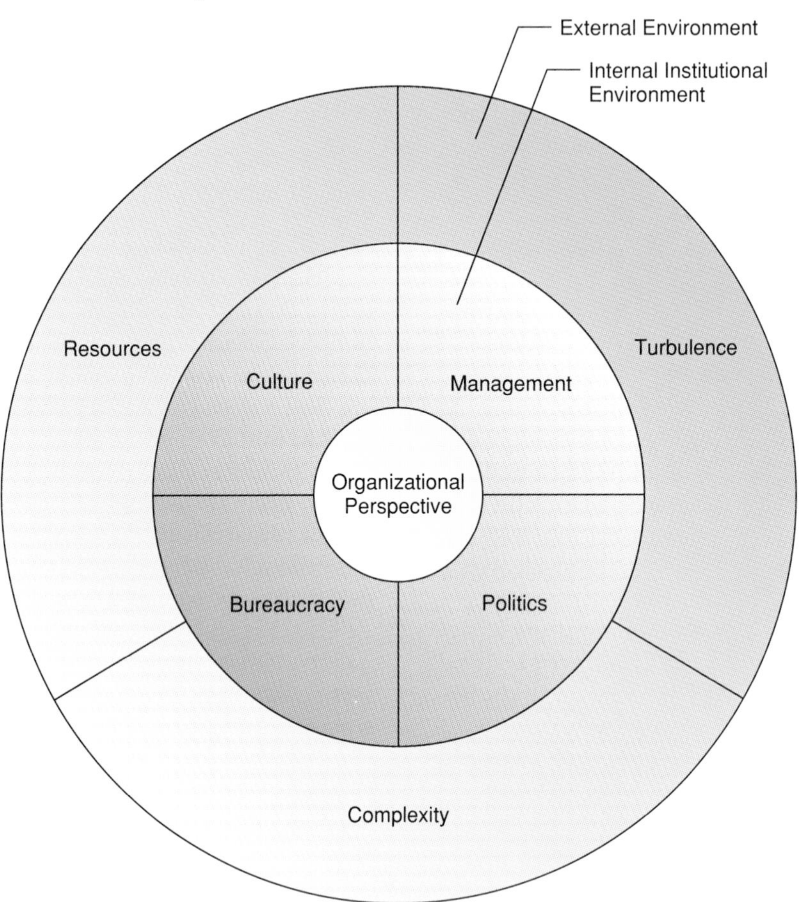

Internal Institutional Perspectives · At the most general level, organizational problems should be related to an organization's culture, management, politics, and bureaucracy. Organizational culture refers to the rarely questioned bedrock assumptions and publicly espoused values that most members of the organization freely accept. In the case studies presented earlier in the chapter, for example, employees of Dow Jones tend to accept the notion that Dow Jones' principal product is distributing access to its existing databases; at A. O. Smith it was simply assumed (until recently) that employees should be paid on a piecework basis. But times change, and old cultural assumptions often become outdated and even dangerous. When looking at an organization, you should ask, "Are the cultural assumptions of the organization still valid; that is, can the firm still survive doing what it always did in the past?" Can the business survive with its traditional values, or are new public statements of its purpose needed?

How can an organization change its culture? Think again of A. O. Smith's experiences over eight years. The answer is that cultures change over long periods of time, with great difficulty, and largely through experimentation. Strong leadership from both management and employees is required. Many businesses cannot survive extensive cultural changes.

Management is expected to both control the existing organization and guide it into the future. Management problems become obvious when unexpected events happen and the business seems out of control. For instance, when profits fall due to cost overruns on major projects, you will know there is a management problem. And although all managements have a strategic plan that purports to guide the future activities of the organization (this is a skill taught in business school and widely disseminated), not all plans work or are appropriate. Therefore, you should question strategic plans in terms of their ability to meet the challenges of a changing environment. When problem solving, ask yourself, "Can this management team control the business and, in addition, adequately plan for the future?"

Whatever organizations in fact do is often the result of a political struggle among major organizational players. One of the questions to ask when problem solving in an organization is, "Will the political struggles in this organization impede the adoption of suitable solutions?" If the answer is yes, you will have to devise ways to change the political landscape or tilt the balance in the political competition. You will have to chose sides and work for the side you believe in.

A last, very broad feature to consider when problem solving is business bureaucracy. Bureaucracy simply refers to the fact that all successful, large organizations develop specialized subunits (structure) over time that do most of the work; these specialized units, in turn, develop finely tuned procedures to get the work done in an acceptable manner. These standard operating procedures are difficult to change. In general, whatever a large organization does is an output of its bureaucratic subunits and their standard operating procedures.

When problem solving, you should ask yourself, "Are changes in bureaucratic structure or procedure required to solve the problem?" If the answer is yes, you will have to develop new, highly trained specialized groups to accomplish the solution and new bureaucratic procedures. The example above of the New York Motor Vehicles Office illustrates how simple changes in bureaucratic procedure can do wonders for customer service.

External Environment · Once you have examined these internal organizational issues, you should look further at the external constraints facing an organization. The most powerful environmental dimensions are resources, turbulence, and complexity.

All businesses need financial, political, cultural, and other resources from the environment. Some environments are rich with support for certain business firms but poor for other firms. For instance, for the last 20 years, computer manufacturers of all kinds have existed in an environment of growing market demand, growing legitimacy and acceptance by the broader culture (computers do not pollute like oil refineries), and large financial investments. Although these features do not guarantee survival, they are vital ingredients to longevity and prosperity and have been crucial to the success of many computer firms that may have been poorly managed but were fortunate enough to exist in a rich, forgiving environment. The same applies to home insulation manufacturers: during the last 20 years, the price of heating a home with oil or gas has tripled, leading to increased demand for insulation and keeping prices up as well.

When you examine an organization in trouble and are looking for solutions, you should ask, "Is this firm in a rich or poor environment? Is its market growing or declining?" Often firms fall into financial difficulty not simply because they are poorly managed, but because they are in declining markets and have failed to identify areas of growth to invest in. Obviously, if a firm is starved for funds, the solutions it ultimately chooses will have to be inexpensive and will have to show a return on investment in the very short term (one year). In a cash-rich environment, a firm has many more options and can afford to take a longer-term view (three to five years).

Turbulence refers to rates of environmental change in such areas as production technologies, sales, and prices. While computer manufacturers in general have benefited from expanding demand for their products (resource richness), they have been subject to incredible change in production technologies—that is, a turbulent environment. One result is a high level of failure among computer manufacturers. Having become competent in one set of production technologies, most firms find it difficult to adopt new techniques. Young, new firms built around the new technologies quickly rise to dominate older firms.

When you examine a problem at an organization, ask yourself, "Is this problem related in any way to broad environmental changes in production technology, sales, or prices?" If the answer is yes, you will have to consider ways in which the organization might respond.

Complexity refers to the number of inputs and products that a firm has as well as the geographical diversity of its production. Firms operating in a complex environment have many suppliers, a vast array of products, and widely distributed production facilities. The automobile industry and the petrochemical industry are typically identified as complex: they have a small number of suppliers but widely distributed production facilities and a vast array of products and niche markets. A chain of hamburger stands is marvelously uniform and not complex: a limited menu is served worldwide, and each store is a carbon copy of the others.

In complex industries, administrative overhead is high, and decision making is difficult. Complex firms tend to have very large bureaucracies, with layer upon layer of middle management, whose job it is to control the complex organization. Profits and return on investment tend to be lower in complex industries than in "simpler" industries.

When you begin the analysis of an organization or seek better understanding, you should ask yourself, "To what extent are the problems visible here the result of a complex environment?" If environmental complexity is a problem, what solution might reduce that complexity?

People Perspectives: Strategic Human Resource Issues

One of the major findings of research on information systems in the last five years is that systems frequently do not achieve the hoped-for productivity gains because insufficient attention has been paid to the "people" perspective, or human resource issues. Because business organizations are made up of people, just about any problem in a business is a "people" problem. Research has identified five strategic human resource issues (see Figure 9.5). By "strategic" we mean simply those issues that must be accounted for or dealt with to assure success in problem solving.[8]

Ergonomics is the science of designing machines, operations, systems, and work environments in general so that they best meet the needs of the human beings involved and optimize economic returns. This is a very broad field, which encompasses the study of the physical design of hardware and furniture, the design of jobs, health issues, and the user/software interface design (e.g., the software logic and its presentation on the screen). Some

Figure 9.5

The People Perspective: Strategic Human Resources Issues

Research has identified five key areas that are especially important for identifying problems related to people in an organization. They are ergonomics, or the design of effective work environments to meet the needs of the human beings involved; evaluating and monitoring employees' work, which can backfire because it creates pressure and resentment; training employees, which is vital but all too often ignored; employee involvement, a controversial issue in many firms that can affect productivity; and legal and regulatory compliance, or making sure the organization protects its employees' legal rights. It is important to consider all of these areas when analyzing a problem.

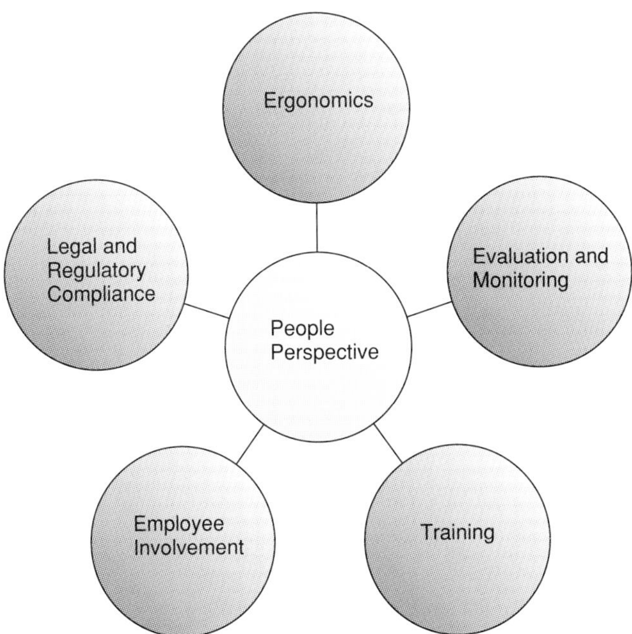

typical ergonomic issues raised by information systems are VDT screen radiation (VDT means visual display terminal or computer screen) and its potential to harm; the height of terminals above the floor, which can contribute to back strain and fatigue; the collection of too many (or too few) tasks into jobs, which can lead to fatigue and high absenteeism; and the way in which screens display information (software interface), which can also produce fatigue, monotony, and boredom. In addition, ergonomics has expanded its concerns to include the social psychology and physical results of screen design and software design. The "user interface" that the software creates has turned out to have an important impact on the productivity of information technology. Figure 9.6 illustrates many of the physical relationships that have to be taken into account when designing human-machine interfaces.

All jobs involve evaluation and monitoring by superiors to gauge the quality and quantity of work performed by employees. This evaluation can be fair and unobtrusive, or it can be perceived by workers as unfair and

Figure 9.6

Some Physical Ergonomic Considerations in Designing a Computer System

There are many more issues to consider in designing a system than you might think. Such features as screen angle, viewing angle, and viewing distance can make the difference between comfortable viewing and eye strain. The correct knee angle, seat back angle, and back support can greatly reduce the possibility of back strain. The next time you sit down at a personal computer or terminal, notice how all these different factors feel to you. Making computer systems more comfortable to use pays off in higher employee morale and productivity and lower absenteeism.

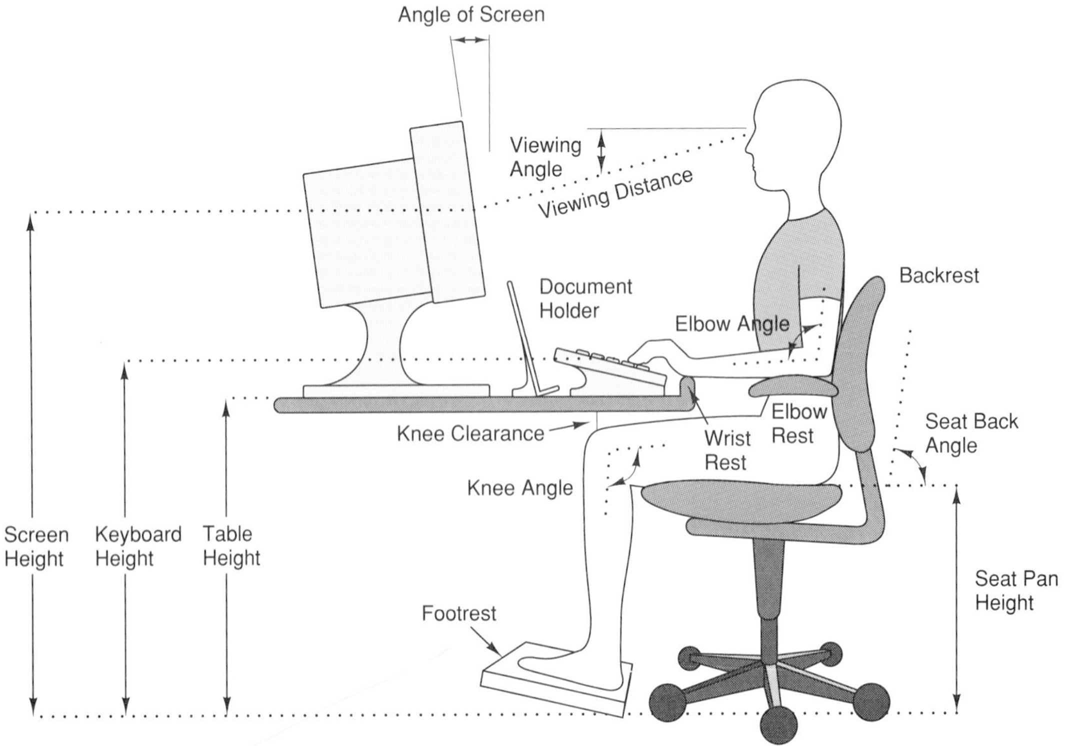

Aircraft mechanics for USAir participate in training programs that exceed Federal Aviation Administration requirements. Although training usually does not carry the life-and-death consequence of aircraft maintenance, it is a key factor in smoothly operating computer systems.

Source: © Jeff Zaruba.

intrusive. Computers permit much closer monitoring of the output of workers than the traditional means of monitoring and evaluating work, but they may be resented by workers. Computer monitoring of workers may at first appear to be a "solution" to a productivity problem, but it can backfire into a human relations disaster.

It is obvious that training employees is a vital part of a successful human relations program. Training involves an investment of resources, however, and although many employers are willing to spend a great deal to ensure that employees are properly trained, many businesses and government agencies view formal training as an unnecessary expense. It is often the first budget to be cut when fortunes turn down. Inadequate training is a major source of information system failure, or at least disappointment.

Traditionally, American management has adopted a hostile attitude toward employee involvement, participation, and feedback. Since the turn of the century, a dominant attitude on the part of management has been that employees should follow orders, and if they disagree, they should resign. With very few exceptions, employment law allows employers great discretion in determining whom to hire, how the job will be done, and whom to terminate.

But these old attitudes are changing for many reasons. In a knowledge- and information-driven economy, skilled employees are in short supply and their views must be heeded. The overall productivity growth of the American economy is low relative to that of Japan, where a somewhat more participative style of management is encouraged. Hence many American managers have sought to imitate their Japanese counterparts by encouraging employee feedback, reducing the social distance between senior management and middle management, and promoting a family-like atmosphere.

Still other managers have adopted Swedish and European-style employee participation schemes in which employees operate in teams with less direct supervision (see the example of A. O. Smith above). Finally, a number of federal and state laws have been enacted that have established a body of employee rights (described below).

When examining an organizational problem, you should ask yourself, "To what extent is this problem a result of poor employee attitudes related to lack of involvement, participation, and communication?" If this seems a problem, try to find solutions in this area.

A last human resource issue to consider is legal and regulatory compliance. Because the American public is concerned about the welfare of all working people, since the 1930s both the federal government and most states have enacted legislation establishing a number of employee rights. The following are the most important:

- The right to join a union.
- The right to "no fault" worker compensation for injury on the job.
- The right to equal employment opportunity regardless of race, gender, or ethnicity.
- The right to a safe and healthy workplace.
- The right to have a pension and to have it protected.
- The right to freedom from reprisal for reporting violations of federal public-protection laws.
- The right of access to selected management information concerning toxic chemicals in the workplace.

Some states have also enacted laws that protect workers from arbitrary termination; under these laws, fired workers are entitled to a due process hearing.

These rights are often a source of organizational problems as well as part of the solution. The growth of information technology, the development of new systems, and their utilization by organizations have raised legal issues in health areas (as we explained above in the discussion of ergonomics), in matters related to employees' access to corporate information, and in the equal opportunity area. Briefly, the growth in management information made possible by computers has led employee groups and courts to subpoena information from the firm to support litigation against the firm. Women and minorities, for instance, who believe they have been discriminated against may demand that corporations release management and statistical information on employment practices. Likewise, workers who believe they have been illegally exposed to toxic chemicals can demand corporate management information on product composition, exposure levels, and internal reports. Employers cannot use the defense of claiming they did not or could not collect and analyze the information: statutes and court decisions make clear that, in this information age, it is the responsibility of employers to maintain complete employee data for periods of up to 60 years.

Usually, it will be obvious if legal and regulatory issues are a cause of the problems facing an organization. Generally, unions or groups of employees bring suits against the corporation for alleged violations of rights.

Rather than waiting for suits to arise, however, wise managers periodically review their organization's compliance with existing regulations.

If employees were fearful of using VDTs, how could you resolve some of their fears? If employees believed they had been unfairly compensated for their work with information systems, how could you address this concern? If minorities and women claimed that they were unfairly relegated to low-level data entry jobs, or were not receiving promotions as rapidly as others, how could you address their complaints?

9.4 Problem Solving: Making Decisions

If you have done a good job of analysis and understanding, the next step of the problem-solving process will be to choose among several alternative solutions. This should be a relatively simple process if you are properly prepared. What at first seemed like a hopelessly complex problem should at this point appear much clearer. The number of potential "solutions" or options should now be reduced to a manageable number—a few that stand some chance of working. In choosing among them, what criteria should be foremost? Figure 9.7 illustrates the steps involved in making a good decision.

Establish Objectives

The process of establishing objectives may be the most complicated part of decision making if only because many people in a firm have different perspectives. Nevertheless, in a firm, objectives must be carefully chosen and agreed on in a group process; otherwise, people will not be committed to a common course of action. One way to begin is to consider the overall corporate objectives as well as the major divisional or subunit objectives. The following might be a firm's overall corporate goals:

- Long-term survival.
- Meeting a competitive challenge at any cost.
- Improving productivity.
- Increasing employee morale and loyalty.

Subunit goals might include the following:

- The introduction of new products.
- More effective marketing.
- Lower administrative costs.
- Lower manufacturing costs.
- Better financing terms.

Because a firm can pursue several objectives, you may want to list the goals in order of importance or establish the critical success factors that are absolutely essential for the firm to attain.

Figure 9.7

What's Involved in Step Three: Making Decisions

In order to make an effective decision, first make sure that everyone agrees on the organization's objectives, both the broad corporate goals and the more focused subunit goals. Then determine the feasibility of each proposed solution, considering both internal and external constraints. Perform a cost-benefit analysis to determine the most appropriate solution for your firm. Remember to consider intangible benefits as well as tangible gains.

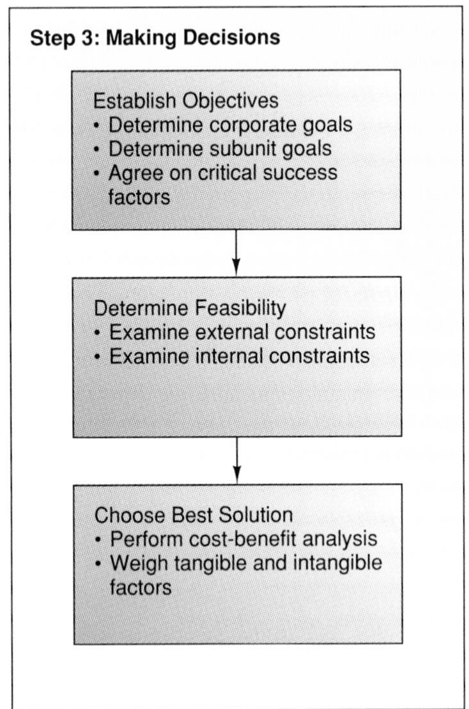

It is very important that problem solvers agree on a time frame over which a solution can and should be put in place. This entails deciding whether a short-term solution (starting this week) or a long-term solution (a program that lasts for several years) is appropriate. Some solutions can be staged: a short-term emergency action can head off imminent disaster while a long-term program is undertaken.

Establish Feasibility

By now the number of possible solutions should have been pared down to a handful of options. At this point, you must decide which of the remaining solutions are doable given your firm's resources. Here you should consider both the external and internal constraints on your organization.

As we noted earlier, external constraints include the following:

- Financial resources.
- Legal/regulatory demands.
- The action of competitors.

- Suppliers.
- Customers.

You must consider how each of the proposed solutions is affected by these factors. For instance, it may be financially feasible to install a network of personal computers in your customers' order rooms (thus assuring customers they have easy access to your products), but you may fear the reprisals of competitors, which may lead to an unending technology war for customers.

Internal constraints are just as important. Can the subunits in the organization carry out the solution? Is the solution compatible with your company's culture? Are there major opposition groups that will try to scuttle your solution?

In addition to considering external and internal constraints, you should also ensure that your solution is really as feasible as it seems. The Focus on Organizations describes a solution that turned out to be considerably less than feasible.

Choose Cost-Effective Solutions

In the end, you will be left with a very small number of realistic solutions. Realistic solutions are those that meet your firm's objectives and are feasible. The last question is, "What solution is best in a financial sense?" In other words, you must try to determine the **cost-effectiveness** of a solution, or

Cost-effectiveness
Being economical in terms of providing benefits that exceed costs; measured by cost-benefit analysis.

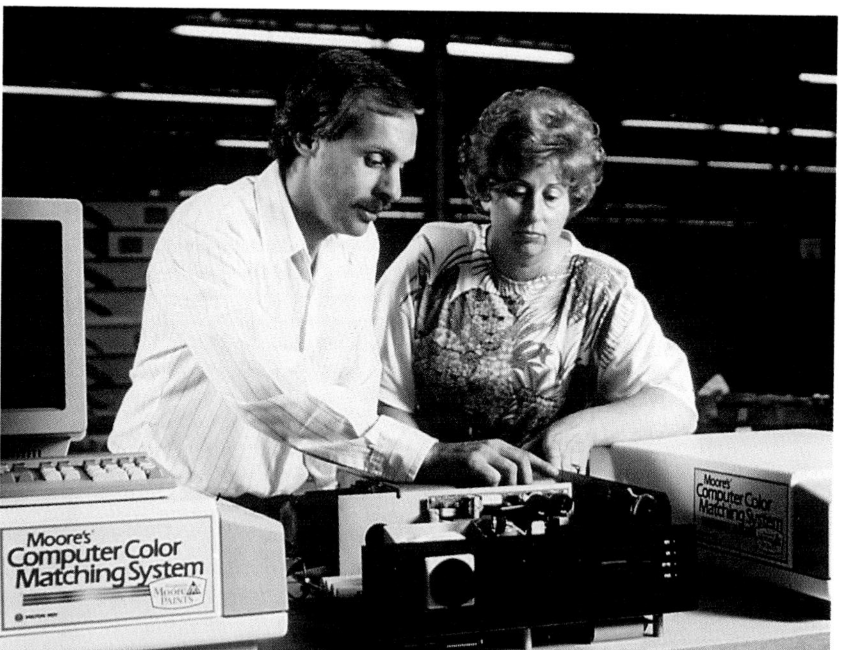

Solutions to business problems must be practical and based on the company's resources and constraints. Milton Roy's Analytical Products division solved a production problem by creating ministockrooms throughout the manufacturing area to ensure that parts are located where they are needed.

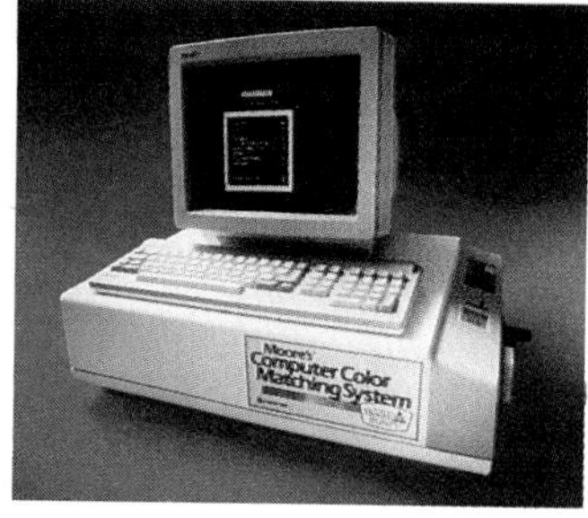

Source: Courtesy of Milton Roy Company.

FOCUS ON *Organizations*

A Not-So-Feasible Solution

Geophysical Systems Corporation found that its choice of a computer system supplier was not as feasible as it had originally thought. Geophysical had developed a device that uses sonar to analyze the worth of oil and gas discoveries. The company hired Seismograph Service Corporation to create a $20 million computer system that would process its sonar-generated data.

Unfortunately, Geophysical found that the Seismograph system could not handle the complex computations it was required to perform. Geophysical's clients began canceling their contracts, and the company went from earning profits of $6 million in one year to filing for bankruptcy two years later.

Geophysical sued Seismograph, claiming that not only did the supplier's system fail to perform as promised but that Seismograph had known this before it started putting the system together. The jury agreed, awarding Geophysical over $48 million in compensation for lost profits and the cost of the computer system. (Seismograph has appealed on the basis that its system did work and that Geophysical's sales decline resulted from a slump in oil prices.)

As carefully as decision makers try to evaluate the feasibility of their purchases, suppliers can intentionally or inadvertently deliver less than they promise. Consequently, buyers of computer systems can benefit from requiring a variety of protections:

- ***Acceptance test:* The customer can require the supplier to run the customer's actual data through the system and demonstrate that it works.**
- ***Guarantee:* The customer may agree to pay only after the system has been operating correctly for two months.**
- ***Binding arbitration:* The sales agreement may provide that the customer may elect to have an outside arbitrator resolve any disputes concerning the system.**
- ***Ownership of software:* The supplier may agree to give the customer the rights to the system's source code, leaving it in the customer's possession so that the customer can have problems corrected without depending on the supplier.**
- ***Support:* The customer may demand that the supplier guarantee that it will provide support and service for the system for at least a year, even if the supplier goes out of business.**

Source: Jeffrey Rothfeder, "Using the Law to Rein in Computer Runaways," *Business Week,* April 3, 1989, pp. 70, 71.

whether it is economical in terms of providing sufficient benefits for the cost.

The answer to this question can be estimated by conducting a cost-benefit analysis. Cost-benefit analysis involves adding up all the costs of a project and dividing by all its benefits. You will arrive at a ratio of costs to benefits. Ideally, you should chose the option or solution that is the least costly for a given amount of benefit.

For instance, if you had two options, one that delivered $2.00 in benefit for each $1.00 in cost and the other that delivered only $1.50 in benefit for each $1.00 in cost, you would choose the first option.

As it turns out, adding up all the costs and benefits of feasible solutions is not easy, especially with large projects. Many factors, such as "speed of decision making," cannot be assigned a monetary value. These factors are called intangible, as opposed to tangible, factors. If a bank can process a loan in one hour, instead of in three days, how much is that "worth" to the bank in terms of increased loan activity from enthusiastic customers and decreased clerical cost? Here, only "guesstimates" can be obtained. But good guesses are usually better than no estimate at all.

9.5 Problem Solving: Designing Solutions

Just because you have arrived at a solution that has broad support in your organization does not mean you have "solved" the problem. Once you have arrived at a feasible option, you will have to design the solution. At first, in the problem-solving process, solutions and options are only vaguely understood, even though many organizational actors pretend they understand precisely what is involved. When you get down to the nuts and bolts of specific solutions, however, you almost always discover new aspects of the solution—and the problem.

A design is a detailed description of a proposed solution in the form of a document. The document includes both textual description and graphs, charts, lists, and figures. As we mentioned earlier, there are two aspects to the design document: logical and physical design (see Figure 9.8).

Figure 9.8

The Two Stages in Step Four: Designing Solutions

There are two parts to the process of designing a solution: creating a logical design and translating it into a physical design. The logical design phase comes first; it involves developing a document that describes a conceptual model for the system. The emphasis is on what the system will do rather than on how it will work. The physical design translates the logical model into design specifications for hardware, software, manual procedures, and other physical considerations.

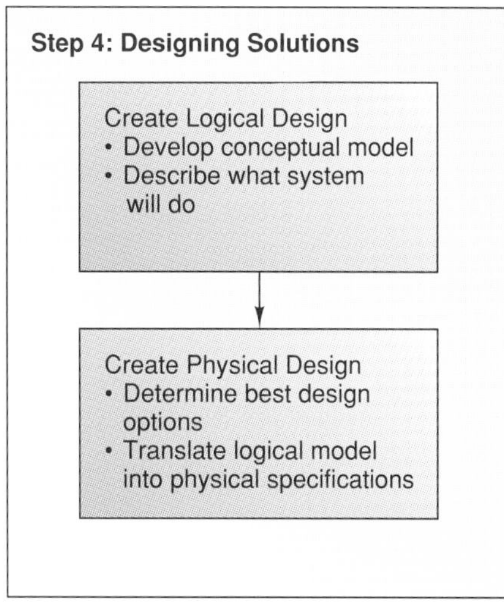

FOCUS ON *Problem Solving*

U.S. Defense Department Software Standards Put Requirements First

The U.S. Department of Defense has issued standards for software development that recognize the importance of establishing requirements prior to the program code. The process calls for a high-level "System Specification Document," which is carefully worded to specify requirements, not the realized solution. The most recent revision of the Defense Department's guidelines deleted any references in this document to processor memory and word size until later in the development process. Only after the System Specification Document is completed are detailed Software Requirements Specification Documents produced.

Source: Peter C. Coffee, "Outfitting the End User: Desirements and Dreams," *PC Tech Journal*, November 1988.

Making a Logical Design

The most critical steps in problem solving take place before the hardware or software for an application is considered. Unless the requirements for solving a problem are clearly understood beforehand, they can become obscured or even overshadowed by concerns with programming languages or hardware, and the result is an incorrect solution. This principle is recognized in the Department of Defense's guidelines for software development described in the Focus on Problem Solving.

Therefore, in order to develop an information system application, a logical design, or model, of the proposed system is needed. This model must be built and understood in logical or conceptual terms before it can be translated into a specific, detailed system solution. The logical design presents the functional, or business, requirements of the proposed application solution as opposed to the technical requirements. It describes what the solution will do, not how it will work physically. The following are the basic components of a logical design:

- **Outputs:** The information to be produced by the system. This includes reports, files, and on-line displays. The model must consider what pieces of output information are required and how they are to be organized and displayed.
- **Inputs:** The data required to be input into the system in order to create the desired output. The model must consider what pieces of data must be input and how they can best be arranged.

The solution to 8,000 square feet of storage space full of files was a Wang Integrated Image System, which captures documents and stores them on optical disk. Creating a model or logical design of a solution before hardware or software are chosen ensures that the end-user's business requirements are met.

Source: Courtesy of Wang Laboratories, Inc.

- **Processing:** The activities, both manual and automated, required to transform input data to output. The model must consider what kinds of decision rules, calculations, and modeling are required to perform the required manipulations on data.
- **Database:** The method of organizing and storing information in the system, through either computerized or manual means. The model must consider what pieces of data to store, when and how to update them, the relationships among them, and how they should be arranged.
- **Procedures:** The activities that must be performed by end-users and operations staff to run and use the system. The model must consider manual activities required to produce the desired information, business policies, and rules governing these activities, as well as the sequence of these activities.
- **Controls:** The manual and automated processes and procedures that ensure that the system is accurate, secure, and performing as required. The model must consider tests and measures for ensuring that the information produced is accurate and secure.

These components may be arranged in a number of ways. In problems where one alternative is an information system application, the application itself can have alternative design solutions.

Although it may seem rather easy to find out what outputs a system should have (e.g., what reports should be produced, what screens of information are needed, and the like), in many cases the users themselves do not know or are not very good at describing what they want from their software. On the other hand, people are quite definite in their desires and tastes once they see a product. Many companies have developed software development systems that permit software engineers to build a mockup or model of the software product before actual programs are written. Users can critique the prototype before large investments are made, and the end result is a more useful piece of software.

Most such prototyping systems do not take the human side of computing into account. But TRW, Inc., has developed a $5 million program that does just that. A central part of TRW's program involves using a psychologist and a sociologist on the staff. The manager of TRW's office of system engineering technology says that "the sociologist is there to help us understand the interdynamics of the workplace—how users are organized and the protocol of the office. We need the psychologist to help us understand the individual because each user responds to a system differently based on his or her psyche."[9]

Some users think intuitively while others think systematically. The intuitive thinker wants the computer system to produce charts, graphs, and line drawings, while the systematic thinker wants quantitative information. It's possible to build a system that produces both kinds of reports, but first these needs must be identified.

TRW's prototyping systems works in four steps. First, the TRW staff and the user try to define what the system is supposed to do and for whom. Second, the staff observes prospective users in the workplace, asks them questions, and measures how they perform certain tasks. Next, an analysis of these data is used to produce the first prototype. In the last step, the prototype is tested, and corrections are made before a final version of the system is built.

In one project TRW was asked to automate the work of a cartographer who worked with satellite intelligence photographs of foreign countries. The cartographer found many faults with TRW's prototype. The position of the menu overlaid important intelligence details, so it was moved and highlighted in black; the resolution was poor and had to be enhanced; and, finally, the system did not project the photographs in a true north position, which was corrected by permitting the cartographer to rotate the map on the screen in any direction.

Making a Physical Design

During the physical design process, the abstract, logical system model is translated into specifications for hardware, software, processing logic, input/output methods and media, manual procedures, and controls. The following are some of the detailed specifications that must be addressed by physical design:

- **Databases:**
  What is the file and record layout?
  What are the relationships among data items?
  How much storage capacity is required?
  Through what path will data be accessed?
  How often will data be accessed or updated?
- **Software:**
  Is much complex logic required to transform input data to output?
  Do large files and lists need to be combined and manipulated?

Does the application require modeling and mathematical formulas among interrelated pieces of data?

- **Hardware:**
  What hardware is already available?
  What processing power is required?
  Does the application require a special environment, such as a telecommunications network?
- **Input:**
  What medium should input data be collected on?
  How should data be collected for input?
  How often should data be input?
- **Output:**
  What medium should output information be displayed on?
  How should output be arranged and organized?
  How often should output be produced?
- **Controls:**
  What technology and procedures will make the system secure?
  How can the accuracy and integrity of data be ensured?
  How will the system be supervised?
- **Procedures:**
  What personnel are required to run the system?
  What activities must be performed for input, processing, and output?
  Where will these activities be performed?

As with logical design, there may be physical design alternatives. Some applications could be implemented on a personal computer or a mainframe; with software packages or custom programs; on a sequential file or a database; using on-line data entry or keypunched cards. The physical design options are myriad. But clearly the nature of the application plus the solution constraints will determine which design options are the most desirable.

Problem solvers must also remember that new technologies will make new solutions available. In the Focus on Technology, two leaders in the computer field comment on the advances they believe will occur in the 1990s.

9.6 Problem Solving: Implementing Solutions

In the last step of problem solving, the solution must be implemented. Often firms arrive at correct decisions, but their implementation is a failure. Effectively implementing solutions and decisions is a complex topic involving questions of psychology, organizational design, sociology, and finance. Here we will present only a summary of the steps needed for effective implementation.[10] (See Figure 9.9.)

Steps in the Implementation of a System Solution

If the problem called for an application solution, the following activities would be performed:

FOCUS ON *Technology*

Today's Leaders Look to Tomorrow

Alan Kay, 49, resident guru at Apple Computer, dreamed up the as-yet unrealized concept of a notebook-size computer that could tap every digitized information source in the world. In an interview, he commented on the developments he foresees in the 1990s:

> *The next phase in the 1990s and for some time beyond is what I've been calling* intimate computing. *The intimate computer will always be on. The magnitude of resources you'll be connected to will be enormous. Your computer will become an agent roaming through many networks 24 hours a day, looking for whatever you need.*
>
> *Say a college student has research to do on a disease. He immediately retrieves some of the things you'd expect. But when he comes in the next morning, he finds more—for example, unexpected items from the military. During the night, the system has dug deeper. It has much more sense of the world people live in than today's computers. In effect, it watches you and tries to figure out what you want.*
>
> *Will human-level intelligence come along in computers? There's no philosophical reason why it won't.*

Bill Gates, the 34-year-old billionaire CEO of Microsoft, is probably the single most influential person in the personal computer business. Gates also commented on his predictions for the 1990s:

> *As businesses focus more on service and on quality tracking, and get by with fewer layers of management, there's a lot of recognition that data can be a competitive tool. The goal for the 1990s is information at your fingertips, so you can come into your office and with a few clicks of the mouse not only read your messages and see your schedule but also check sales results by product or region and all your interaction between your company and a customer.*
>
> *You don't just think about what a company does and try to do it faster. You want to empower somebody like a product manager to be able to digest more things. Why do you have meetings? Well, the top executive has more data than other people, so he has to have meetings to share his data. What if everybody had the same data and had a better way to look at it? Would you need as many meetings, as many levels of management? Maybe not.*
>
> *Beyond that, new technologies are coming. We're doing some work on a technology for accepting handwriting into a computer. Say I had a handwriting machine: I could take notes, find out when I saw you last and what I said. It's a great thing because everybody's trained to use handwriting. One thing I've learned in the past five years is that new technologies take time, but they are worth the wait.*

Source: Joel Dreyfuss, Brenton Schlender, "Today's Leaders Look to Tomorrow," *FORTUNE,* March 26, 1990, pp. 30–31, 68–72, 149–150.

- **Software development:** Software would be developed to perform any processing that had to be automated. Custom programs might be written, or the software might be based on an application package or on a personal computer spreadsheet or database management system.

Figure 9.9

A Close-up of Step Five: Implementing Solutions

Four procedures make up the final step in the systems analysis and design process. First, we must develop software for the new system, whether it means writing totally new software or modifying existing programs. Second, we must select the right hardware to run the software we've written. In the testing phase, we run the programs and try out the hardware and manual procedures to ensure that everything is working properly. Finally, users must be trained to use the new system, and documentation must be written for it.

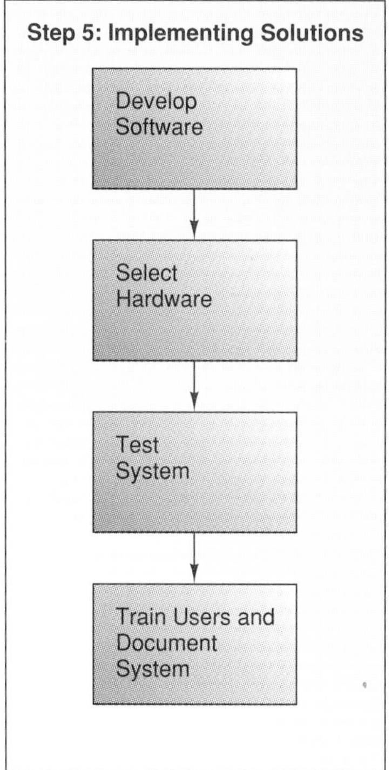

- **Hardware selection and acquisition:** Appropriate hardware would be selected for the application and purchased if it was not immediately available.
- **Testing:** Each component of the system would be thoroughly tested to make sure that the system produced the right results. The testing process requires detailed testing of individual computer programs and of the entire system as a whole, including manual procedures. The process of testing each program in a system individually is called unit testing. System testing tests whether all the components of a system (program modules, hardware, and manual procedures) function together properly.
- **Training and documentation:** End-users and technical specialists would be trained in using the new application. Detailed documentation generated during the development process for end-users and technical systems specialists would be finalized for use in training and everyday operations. Without proper documentation, it would be

TRW Inc. assigned a design integration manager to work with the U.S. Air Force to integrate and test new equipment for the underground command center of the Strategic Air Command. Testing components, training users, and providing documentation are integral parts of all systems' solutions.

Source: Courtesy of TRW Inc.

impossible to run or use an information system. The importance of technical and user documentation cannot be overemphasized.

Conversion Strategies

A final matter to consider is the strategy used to convert from the old system to the new system. In complicated systems, this will involve changes in personnel, procedures, databases, processing, inputs, and outputs. Such changes cannot be accomplished overnight and must be planned carefully beforehand.

Conversion strategies
Plans and methods for changing from an old system to a new system; include parallel conversion, direct cutover, pilot study, and phased approach.

Parallel conversion
A conversion strategy in which the old system and the new system run in tandem until it is clear that the new system is working correctly.

Direct cutover
A conversion strategy in which the old system is replaced entirely with the new system on an appointed day; no system is available if the new system fails.

Pilot study
A conversion strategy in which a new system is introduced to only a limited part of an organization; if the system is effective there, it is installed throughout the rest of the organization.

Phased approach
A conversion strategy in which a new system is introduced in steps.

The following are the most important **conversion strategies:**

- **Parallel conversion:** The old system and the new system are run in tandem until it is clear that the new system works correctly. The old system can serve as a backup if errors are found, but additional work is required to run the extra system.
- **Direct cutover:** The old system is replaced entirely with the new system on an appointed day. This carries the risk that no system is available to fall back on if errors are discovered.
- **Pilot study:** The new system is introduced to a limited part of the organization, such as a single department. Once the pilot is considered safe, the system is installed in the rest of the organization.
- **Phased approach:** The new system is introduced in steps. For example, a new payroll system could be phased in by introducing the modules for paying clerical employees first and managerial employees later.

In complicated projects, in which you expect that the solution will change as you gather field experience, the safest strategies are a pilot study or a phased approach. They will enable the solution to be deployed slowly over time. Direct cutover strategies are suitable for simple substitutions (when one kind of machine replaces another) and when human and social organizational changes are minimal. Perhaps the safest strategy is to run both the old system and the new system in parallel for a short period of time. In case the new system collapses, you will always have the old system to fall back upon. The disadvantage of this strategy is that it is expensive.

Summary

- Problem solving in business involves a number of conceptual steps and is usually not a simple process. There are an infinite number of solutions looking to be exercised. The right solution depends on defining the problem correctly.
- Problems are not simply objective situations but depend greatly on how organizations and people define matters. Solutions depend on how problems are defined.

• Critical thinking is an important attribute of wise decision making. You should suspend judgment and sustain a skeptical attitude until you become convinced of the true nature of a problem.

• Problem solving involves five steps: analysis, understanding, decision making, solutions design, and implementation.

• Most organizational problems involve a mix of technology, organizational, and people problems.

• Designing solutions requires both a logical and a physical design. A logical design describes the functional performance of a solution—what it is supposed to do—and a physical design describes how the solution actually works.

• Logical design presents the functional or business requirements of an application solution independent of technical considerations. It presents a model for solving a problem from an end-user or business standpoint. An information system will not be successful unless this business model is clearly visualized before technical factors (such as hardware and software) are considered.

• Physical design consists of detailed specifications for hardware, software, processing logic, input/output methods and media, manual procedures, and controls. Physical design will be shaped by the requirements of the logical business design and existing technical, economic, or operational constraints.

• Solution implementation involves four steps: software development, hardware selection, testing, and training. Four conversion strategies for implementing a solution are parallel conversion, direct cutover, pilot study, and phased approach.

Key Terms

Problem analysis
Problem understanding
Decision making
Solutions design
Implementation
Critical thinking
Technology perspective
Organization perspective
People perspective
Feasibility
Objectives
Logical design
Physical design
Cost-effectiveness
Conversion strategies
Parallel conversion
Direct cutover
Pilot study
Phased approach

Review Questions

1. In what sense are problems "not like basketballs on a court"? Does this mean problems are not real?
2. What is the problem-solving funnel? Do all problems go through these stages?

3. What is meant by critical thinking?
4. What are the five steps involved in problem solving?
5. What is a technology perspective on problems? What makes technology problems easy (or difficult) to solve? Give some examples.
6. What is an organizational perspective on problems? What makes organizational problems difficult to solve? Give some examples.
7. What is a people perspective on problems? Give some examples.
8. What are the three facets of decision making that are required to arrive at a specific solution?
9. What is the difference between a logical design and a physical design?
10. What are the key features of the logical design of an information system?
11. What are the key features of the physical design of an information system?
12. Describe the steps involved in implementing a system solution. What factors should be taken into account when implementing a solution?
13. Name and describe the most important conversion strategies.

Discussion Questions

1. Review the Dow Jones example. With a group of students, make a list of the company's possible problems. Then make a list of solutions for each problem you identify. If you were a Dow Jones senior executive, which solutions (and problems) would you prefer?

2. With a group of students, identify a problem at your college or university that you all agree is indeed a problem. Next, identify the technology, organizational, and people features of this problem. Last, identify some feasible solutions.

3. Calculate the costs and benefits of each of the solutions you identified in Question 2. What does this tell you about establishing the cost-effectiveness of solutions?

Problem-Solving Exercises

1. Locate a small business firm in your neighborhood and interview the owner. Make a list of the five most important problems identified by the owner and a list of the solutions (if any) the owner currently uses to "solve" or cope with the problems. Write a short paper analyzing how well the owner's solutions fit the problems. Can you suggest better solutions?

2. In *Business Week, Fortune, The Wall Street Journal,* or some other business publication, find and read a story about a business failure or mistake. Write a short paper describing the situation and the errors made in the problem-solving process. How might you have improved on the problem-solving process?

3. By interviewing a local small business manager or reading a business publication, find an example of poor implementation—for example, a situation in which the solution appeared to be correct but implementation was not. Write a short paper analyzing the causes of the problem and how you might have improved implementation.

Notes

1. "Dow Jones Makes a Young Dog Do New Tricks," *Business Week,* January 16, 1989.
2. We do not argue that all real-world decision making follows this sequence in lockstep fashion, but rather that it is useful to conceive of problem solving with this sequence. Some real-world problem solving follows this sequence; other sequences are possible, even likely. See Michael D. Cohen, James G. March, and Johan P. Olsen, "A Garbage Can Model of Decisionmaking," *Administrative Science Quarterly,* 17 (1972). See also Karl E. Weick, "Educational Organizations as Loosely Coupled Systems," *Administrative Science Quarterly,* 21 (March 1976); and James G. March and Zur Shapira, "Managerial Perspectives on Risk and Risk Taking," *Management Science,* 33 (November 1987).
3. John Hoerr, "The Cultural Revolution at A. O. Smith," *Business Week,* May 29, 1989, pp. 66–68.
4. Penny Singer, "Long Lines Gone at Motor Vehicle Office," *The New York Times,* November 6, 1988.
5. *Ibid.*
6. James Daly, "Playing with the Speed of MIPS," *Computerworld,* April 3, 1989.
7. See Glenn L. Helms and Ira Weiss, "The Cost of Internally Developed Applications: Analysis of Problems and Cost Control Methods," *Journal of Management Information Systems* (Fall 1986); and Donald H. Bender, "Financial Impact of Information Processing," *Journal of Management Information Systems* (Fall 1986). For large-scale systems, see General Accounting Office, "Automated Information Systems: Schedule Delays and Cost Overruns Plague DOD Systems," GAO/IMTEC 89-36 (Washington, D.C.: U.S. Government Printing Office, May 1989).
8. An excellent description of "strategic human resource issues" can be found in Alan F. Westin, et al., *The Changing Workplace: A Guide to Managing the People, Organizational, and Regulatory Aspects of Office Technology* (White Plains, N.Y.: Knowledge Industry Publications, 1985).
9. Calvin Sims, "Personalizing Software," *The New York Times,* July 17, 1986.
10. The interested student can consult more advanced texts for a full treatment of the subject. See Kenneth C. Laudon and Jane P. Laudon, *Management Information Systems: A Contemporary Perspective* (New York: Macmillan, 1991).

Problem-Solving Case

Clouds at Sun Microsystems, Inc.

In 1983, at his kitchen table, Scott McNealy started Sun Microsystems, Inc., with a pen and a notepad. By 1988 the company was producing over $1 billion in revenue based on a 40 percent share of the RISC (Reduced Instruction Set Computing, described in Chapter 3) workstation market and a similar large share of the regular workstation market. Sun was known for flouting tradition and taking on the big players such as IBM, Digital Equipment Corporation (DEC), and Hewlett Packard by selling powerful desktop workstations at roughly half the cost per MIP as competitors. It had a loyal following among

engineers and technical specialists in the UNIX workstations market with machines that were designed to work easily in networks. The strategy was so successful that it literally forced IBM, DEC, and Hewlett Packard to alter their corporate strategies and to begin paying more attention to the desktop workstation market.

But in 1989, Sun's stupendous growth started to catch up with it, as the company began to suffer a series of problems:

- To compete in new markets, McNealy, the president and founder, created dozens of autonomous units within the company. Spending in these units was beyond the control of the chief financial officer. One result was the creation of overlapping and competing fiefdoms of power largely unchecked by central controls. Divisions began competing with one another for the same customers.
- In the first six months of 1989, Sun introduced five major new computers. Some of these new computers offered more power at a lower price than older machines still manufactured by Sun. The most popular new machine was the Sparcstation 1, a powerful desktop workstation called the "pizza box" because of its low profile and low cost. As a result, sales of the older machines plummeted, while demand for the new machines skyrocketed. Unfortunately, the lack of powerful order entry and manufacturing systems did not permit senior management to realize what was happening in time (see below for an explanation). In fact, demand for the new machines was ten times the initial forecasts. Hence the older machines were produced in record numbers, while the new machines were in short supply. Sales revenue plummeted in these divisions.
- In June 1989, Sun announced that its outdated and troublesome order entry system based on a Hewlett Packard minicomputer had been replaced by a new, centralized IBM mainframe order entry, inventory, and accounting system. Although Sun was pleased with the IBM system, unfortunately the implementation of the project was badly fumbled. As a result, Sun lost track of orders, was unable to find out what was in inventory, overproduced certain machines and underproduced others, and could not complete the books at the end of the quarter without a great deal of hand calculating.
- The chief financial officer quit with this announcement of system failure, alleging the company was out of control.
- Earlier in the year, Hewlett Packard and Apollo Computer merged to form the largest single workstation conglomerate. The newly formed company immediately announced forthcoming products based on Hewlett Packard's RISC chips and sent Sun owners a "Sun Survival Kit" that promised to help owners "get out of the sun." Simultaneously, IBM let it be known that it planned a very powerful workstation product to be announced in the fall.
- In July, a hiring freeze went into effect, but managers continued to hire more than 1,000 new workers in one month. Sun's labor force now totals 10,000 and is growing rapidly despite the announced "freeze."

- **In August, Sun announced a $27 million loss for the third quarter—the first in its history. No profits are expected in the fourth quarter.**
- **The financial press began questioning McNealy's managerial ability and started to call for a transition at Sun similar to that which occurred at Apple when John Sculley, a marketing executive at Pepsi Cola, was brought in to take over Apple Computer from its founder, Steven Jobs.**

Case Study Questions

1. Use the three perspectives outlined in the chapter—technology, organization, and people—to analyze and categorize the problems at Sun Microsystems. Describe some of the possible interrelationships. Rank the problems in order from the most significant to the least significant.
2. What steps would you take to obtain a better understanding of the problems you identified in Question 1?
3. Design a solution for one problem faced by Sun Microsystems in a short paper (three to five pages).

C H A P T E R · T E N

Designing Information System Solutions

Chapter Outline

10.1 Introduction
- Problem Solving and Systems Analysis and Design
- Systems Analysis and Design: The Five Steps

10.2 Problem Solving in Action: New Technology
- Maimonides Medical Center
- Applying the Methodology

10.3 Problem Solving in Action: Management and Procedures
- Consolidated Chemical Corporation
- Applying the Methodology

10.4 Problem Solving in Action: Database Application
- The Patient Billing System
- Applying the Methodology

10.5 Problem Solving in Action: Spreadsheet Application
- Partnership Allocation at Haskell, Simpson, and Porter
- Applying the Methodology

10.6 Problem Solving in Action: Mainframe Application
- Variable Rate Mortgages at North Lake Bank
- Applying the Methodology

10.7 Systems-Building Tools and Methodologies
- Data Flow Diagrams
- The Data Dictionary
- System Flowcharts
- Structured Design and Programming
- Computer-Aided Software Engineering

Learning Objectives

After reading and studying this chapter, you will:

1. Be able to apply the five problem-solving steps to systems analysis and design.
2. Be able to devise and evaluate alternative systems solutions.
3. Be able to determine when a solution requires an information system application.
4. Understand the functional requirements of an information system application solution.
5. Be able to translate a logical or conceptual system design into a physical system design.
6. Know how to choose among alternative hardware and software configurations for the physical design of an application solution.
7. Understand how to use data flow diagrams, system flowcharts, and data dictionaries as tools for solution design.

Maimonides Experiences a Paper Glut

Maimonides Medical Center, a 700-bed nonprofit hospital serving the Borough Park section of Brooklyn, New York, must comply with very stringent record retention requirements mandated by New York State law. Maimonides must retain patient financial records a minimum of six years and health records indefinitely.

These records come from a variety of sources. When a patient is admitted to Maimonides, his or her medical history and insurance data are entered into a terminal connected to a Burroughs Corporation Model 3955 mainframe. Each night all such information entered that day is transferred onto tape. During the patient's hospital stay, other information from various departments, such as cardiology or radiology, generated manually on paper, is added to the patient's files. This information consists mainly of freeform textual comments, observations, and reports of test results.

So many documents have piled up in this manner that Maimonides has found itself in the midst of a "paper glut." A request for information from an outside organization, such as Medicaid or Medicare, takes a week or ten days to fulfill. The hospital has considered renting warehouse space, which would cost a minimum of $18 per square foot, because it no longer has room to store this paperwork.

Maimonides tried to relieve this situation by transferring many of the documents to microfilm. However, the staff complained that locating patient records still took a long time and that not enough microfilm readers were available.

Source: "Hospital Cures Paper Plague," *Computerworld,* May 16, 1988.

Maimonides had a records management problem and eventually solved it by implementing optical disk storage technology. This case and other examples in this chapter illustrate how our problem-solving methodology can be applied more specifically to the analysis of information system–related problems and the development of information system solutions.

10.1 Introduction

The critical thinking skills you have learned in earlier chapters can be applied to a variety of situations. They can be used to analyze everyday business problems for which the answer lies in better procedures or better management. These skills can also be applied to the building of new information systems or the improvement of existing ones. In many instances, the solution to a problem will be a "system solution."

Indeed, this problem-solving framework lies at the heart of the analysis and design of information systems. No matter what hardware, software, and software development methodology you use, you must first be able to understand a problem, describe it, and design a solution. Thus this process lays the groundwork for all subsequent systems development activities. Unless it is carried out properly, it can result in major errors in a new system or even total failure.

Alternative systems-building approaches will be discussed in subsequent chapters. The purpose of this chapter is to illustrate the core problem-solving methodology that is the foundation for all of them.

Systems analysis
The study and analysis of problems of existing information systems; it includes the identification of both the organization's objectives and its requirements for the solution of the problems.

Systems design
A model or blueprint for an information system solution to a problem; it shows in detail how the technical, organizational, and people components of the system will fit together.

Problem Solving and Systems Analysis and Design

When the problem-solving methodology introduced in Chapter 9 is applied specifically to information system–related problems, it is called systems analysis and design. **Systems analysis** is the study and analysis of problems of existing information systems; it involves both identifying the organization's objectives and determining what must be done to solve its problems. While systems analysis shows what the problems are and what has to be done about them, **systems design** shows how this should be realized. The systems design is the model or blueprint for an information system solution that shows in detail how technical (hardware and software), organizational (procedures, data), and people (training, end-user interfaces) components will fit together. Sometimes a problem will not require an information system solution but an adjustment in management or existing procedures. Even so, systems analysis may be required to arrive at the proper solution.

Systems Analysis and Design: The Five Steps

The most important steps in systems analysis and design are the five steps in problem solving introduced in the preceding chapter. (You may want to review Figure 9.2.) Let's review them as they apply to systems analysis and design:

1. **Problem analysis:** Investigate the problem to determine what kind of problem it is. Gather preliminary information about the problem.
2. **Problem understanding:** Accumulate detailed information about the problem by conducting interviews and studying documents, policies, and procedures, including those pertaining to existing information systems. Analyze the problem, considering its technical, organizational, and people dimensions. State exactly what the problem is and what its causes are.
3. **Decision making:** Specify solution objectives. State what the solution should be in precise terms. Typical solution objectives might be more efficient operations, reduced costs, tighter control, higher revenues, or improved decision making. Consider constraints. Evaluate each solution for feasibility. Evaluate alternative solutions. Decide which alternative best meets the solution objectives within the specified constraints.
4. **Solution design:** Develop a logical design capturing functional business requirements if the solution requires an information systems application. Develop general specifications for how input, output, processing, database, procedure, and control components can meet the requirements of the proposed solution (see Figure 10.1, which illustrates some of the issues and requirements that the logical design must address). Translate the logical design into a physical design if the solution requires an information systems application. Decide which among several configurations of hardware and software best meets solution objectives given the functional requirements and specified constraints. Develop detailed specifications for input/output methods and media, database or file structure, processing logic, manual procedures, and control methods. Figure 10.2 shows options for hardware, software, input/output, storage media, and procedures that can be used in the physical design.
5. **Implementation:** Implement the solution. Code, test, and install the system if an **application solution** (the use of an information system to solve a problem) is required. Make the necessary modifications in procedures and management.

Application solution
The use of an information system to solve a problem.

Figure 10.1

Scope of the Logical Design

The logical design is a document that specifies a system's functional business requirements. Here we show some of the issues and requirements that are crucial to building an effective information system. For instance, input procedures must take into account the content, format, and source of the input data, as well as the volume, frequency, and timing with which it enters the system. The design must also include controls to ensure the system's security, accuracy, and validity and must allow adequate supervision to maintain it on an ongoing basis. Note that these logical considerations are independent of specific types of hardware and software.

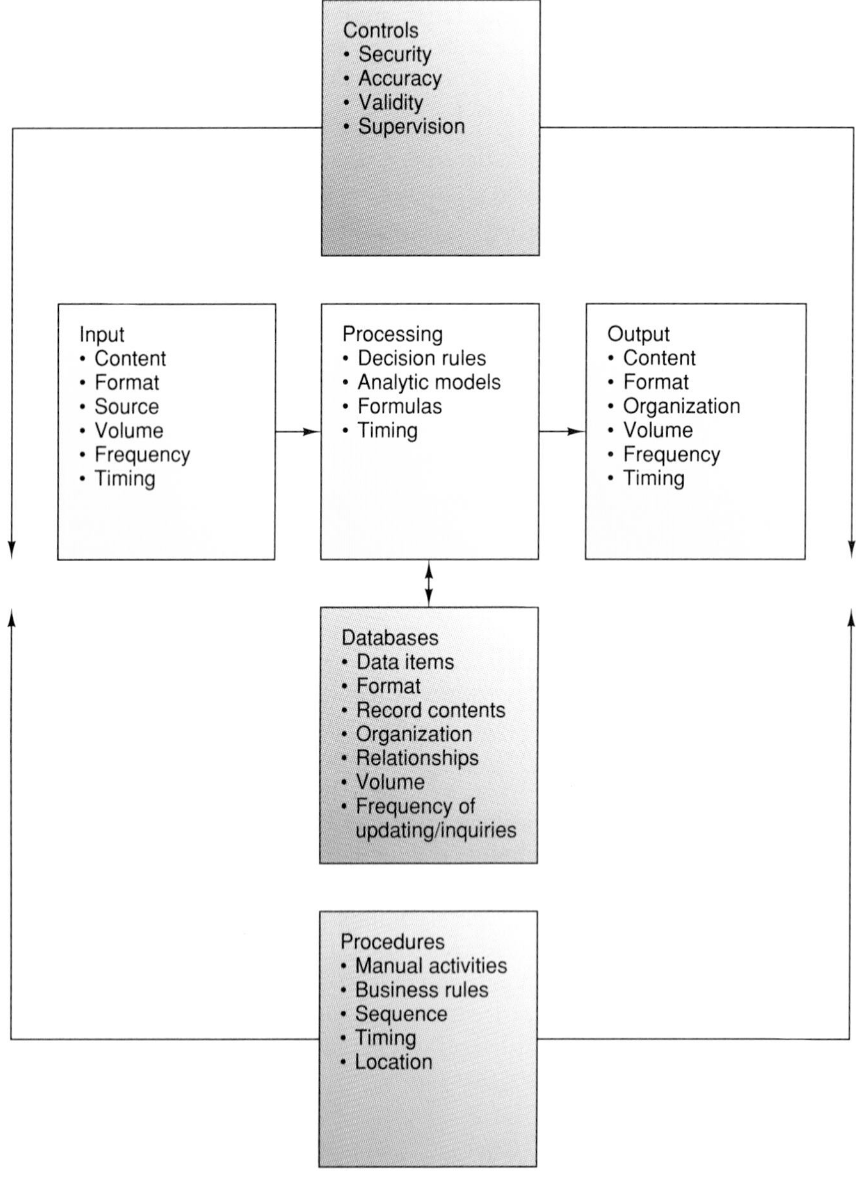

Figure 10.2

Physical Design Specifications

As you can see, there are many options for translating a logical design into a physical system. The physical design chooses among these possibilities to create the most effective design to meet business needs. Note that the physical design, like its logical counterpart, also includes specifications for procedures and controls.

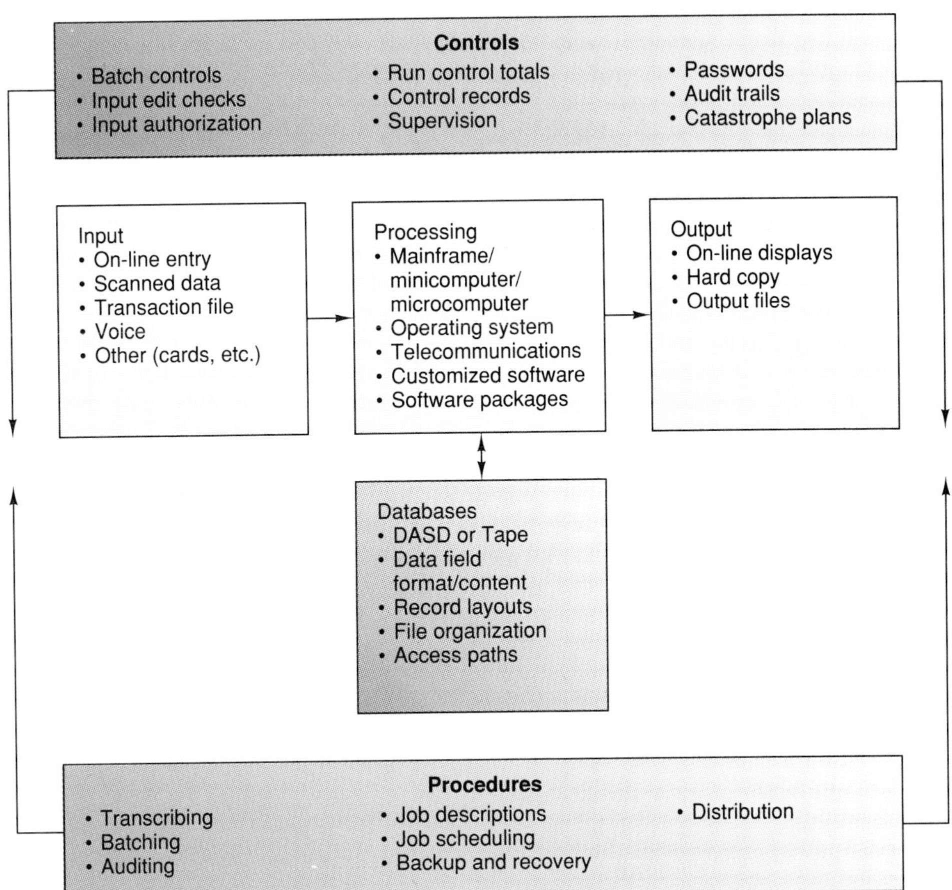

10.2 Problem Solving in Action: New Technology

Throughout this chapter, we will use real-world cases to illustrate how problem solving and systems analysis and design actually work step by step. Our purpose is to focus on the process of analyzing a problem and visualizing the right business solution. Accordingly, we have simplified these cases for instructional purposes; their actual analysis and solution required many more details than can be presented here.

Maimonides Medical Center

Let's start by looking at Maimonides Medical Center again. For this case, as well as for all the other cases in this chapter, we need to answer the following questions:

1. What exactly was the problem?
2. What were its causes, and what was its scope?
3. What was the solution objective?
4. What alternative solutions were available?
5. What were the constraints on these solutions?
6. Why was a particular solution chosen?

In other words, how and why did Maimonides select optical disk storage for its solution? Let's put our problem-solving methodology to work.

Applying the Methodology

Step 1: Problem Analysis · The chapter-opening description of Maimonides provides sufficient facts for our investigation.

Step 2: Problem Understanding · To determine the cause and dimensions of Maimonides' problem, we must examine the array of technical, organizational, and people factors that we discussed in Chapter 9. As the matrix shows, Maimonides' problem involves mainly organizational factors.

Technology	Organization		People
Internal:			
Hardware	Culture		Ergonomics Evaluation and Monitoring
Software	Management		Training
Telecommunications	Politics		Employee Attitudes and Involvement
Database	Bureaucracy	X	Legal and Regulatory Compliance
External:			
	Resources	X	
	Turbulence		
	Complexity	X	

The Problem · Maimonides lacked sufficient space to store patient records, given the extensiveness of documentation and record retention requirements. Moreover, the documents were so numerous that records could not be located quickly and timely information could not be provided to patients or external agencies.

Problem Dimensions · The problem had both external and internal dimensions:

- **External:** Maimonides must comply with state record retention requirements, which mandate that hospitals retain patient information for many years. Alternatives are limited because storage space in the New York metropolitan area is so costly.

- **Internal:** Maimonides lacks sufficient space to store the records it has accumulated on patients. It has too many records to locate manually or via microfilm. Documents originate from many sources and time frames, and consolidating one patient's records is difficult. Rules and procedures for hospital treatment require that detailed records be kept on each patient upon admission and when he or she receives treatment. Maimonides' use of technology for records management is very primitive. Only admissions data are computerized. All other hospital records are maintained manually and dispersed throughout the organization.

Step 3: Decision Making · Our solution objective would be to make the numerous records on each patient easily retrievable. But we would have to consider the following constraints:

- **Economic:** Like all hospitals, Maimonides is under pressure to keep health care costs down. Warehouse space in New York City costs a minimum of $18 per square foot.
- **Operational:** Maimonides staff would like to access documents quickly to service requests for information. Neither microfilm readers nor hard-copy storage in warehouses can deliver information rapidly.

Given these constraints, Maimonides has three alternatives: (1) rent additional warehouse space; (2) provide more microfilm readers; or (3) implement optical disk storage technology. Maimonides eventually selected the third alternative. It installed an optical disk–based document storage and retrieval system that provides instantaneous access to patient admission, billing and medical records from networked workstations. Scanners transfer the information from paper to optical disk for storage and retrieval.

Step 4: Solution Design · We could consider this solution primarily a technology solution, since it was solved with a new information technology. Of course, it represented a new information system application as well, because additional analysis and design work were required to devise the format for storing and accessing the documents and the hardware and network options. Organizational and people changes (not described here) were also required to make this new application work. For this case, we will simplify the logical design requirements.

Inputs

Admissions data (medical history, billing address, insurance data).
Test results.
Physician evaluations and comments (textual data).

Processing

Translate hard-copy document into digital form and store on optical disk.
Update the patient database with admissions data entered on-line.

Outputs

Same as inputs.

Database

Store each document in patient files using Social Security number as the identifying key field.

Procedures

Batch all documents and enter into the system using an optical scanner.

Enter patient data on-line during hospital admissions.

Retrieve documents on request.

Controls

Back up the computerized files periodically.

Audit admissions and insurance data against signed patient forms.

The physical design, shown in Figure 10.3, consists of an Ungerman-Bass token ring network over twisted-pair wiring that enables admissions records to be accessed throughout the hospital by workstations using an IBM Personal Computer AT or Personal System/2.® The network links five locations: administration, cashiers, financial services, patient accounting, and the computer room. Eventually, the radiology and cardiology departments will be linked to the network as well, using modems and twisted-pair telephone wiring.

When a patient is admitted, his or her medical history and insurance information are entered on-line into a Burroughs Corporation Model 3955 mainframe. Each night, this information is downloaded from the mainframe onto tape and then put into the network's file server via a tape-to-tape transfer. Scanners attached to workstations enable hard-copy patient information to be entered from various locations. Related data and documents on each patient are grouped into patient files using dBASE III Plus and Nantucket Corporation's Clipper. Instead of taking a week, information requests can now be fulfilled within a day.

Optical storage technology was chosen because it is an appropriate medium for permanently storing large quantities of data, yet it can make those data easily available if required. Some hospital data already resided on the hospital's mainframe, but personal computers were selected as workstations because they could provide some local processing while accessing patient information through the network.

Eventually, the hospital hopes to create an interface that will transfer data automatically from the mainframe to the optical system and convey test results via voice messaging from the radiology laboratory to attending physicians.

Step 5: Implementation · Maimonides had to install optical scanners, IBM Personal Computers, a token ring network, and optical disk storage devices. It wrote programs with dBASE III Plus and Clipper to create a new patient file structure that combined both basic admissions data and accounting data. Individual pieces of software and the entire system, including the new procedures, had to be tested thoroughly before the system was put into place. Optical scanners converted the old hard-copy records to optical disk files. Maimonides changed procedures so that records from various sources are scanned and transferred to optical disk rather than being stored in a warehouse.

We will discuss more detailed aspects of application solutions in subsequent cases.

Figure 10.3

Physical Design for the New Maimonides Medical Center Network

The new system allows staff to access patients' admission records from a variety of workstations and departments throughout the hospital. The network currently links five locations (administration, cashiers, financial services, patient accounting, and the computer room); future plans are to add the radiology and cardiology departments to the network. Optical storage lets the hospital store large amounts of data, yet allows speedy random access to the data when needed.

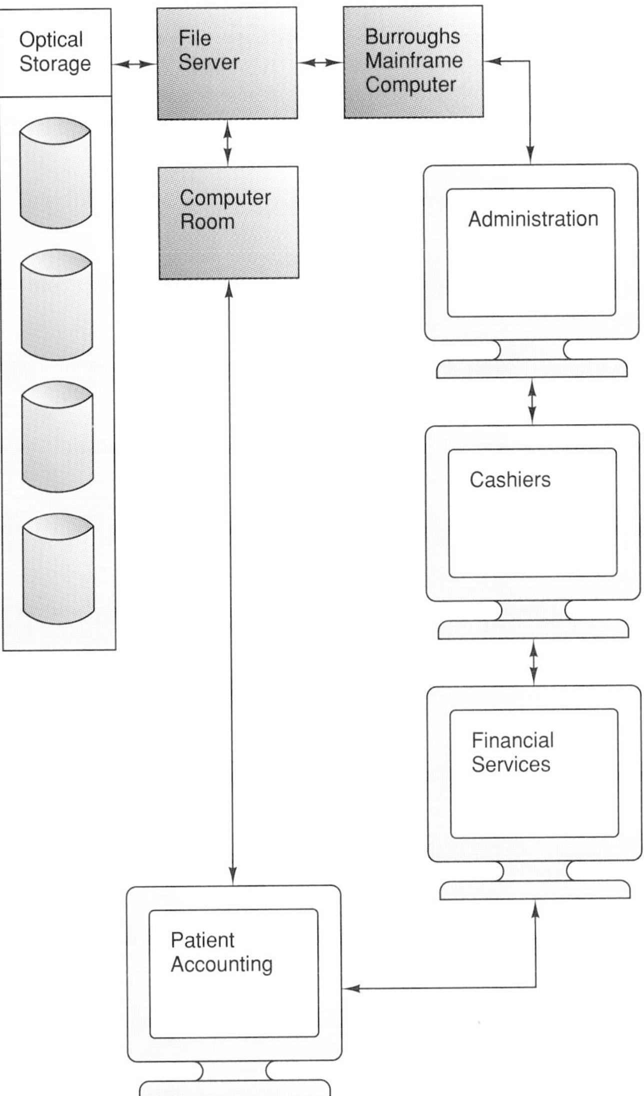

10.3 Problem Solving in Action: Management and Procedures

The next case illustrates a problem that primarily involved the organizational and people dimensions of the firm.

Consolidated Chemical Corporation

The Consolidated Chemical Corporation consists of four separate divisions that manufacture plastics, pharmaceuticals, agricultural chemicals, and dyes and additives. Its 20 different operating units, located in North Carolina, Pennsylvania, New Jersey, Illinois, and Alabama, have their own local systems for order entry and production, but there are company-wide systems for personnel and payroll processing.

Each operating unit fills out its own time cards and forwards them to the corporate Payroll Department at corporate headquarters in Tarrytown, New York. Clerical and production employees, whose wages are based on an hourly rate (such as $8.50 per hour), are paid weekly. Managers and professionals, whose compensation is based on an annual salary, are paid monthly and do not require time cards. The time card data are entered online by Payroll Department clerks and held in a batch transaction file until it is time to update the payroll.

Other changes in payroll data, such as year-end salary increases or promotions, are initiated by the Personnel Department of each operating unit. After receiving management authorization, the local Personnel Department makes these changes on an employee profile form. The profile is sent to the corporate Personnel Department, where data entry clerks enter these data into the personnel system. An additional transaction is created for any payroll-related change, such as a salary increase, and this transaction is passed to the transaction file for the Payroll Department.

Recently, Consolidated has experienced a high incidence of errors in the payroll transactions that originated in the Personnel Department. Sometimes a salary increase for an hourly employee will be expressed as a change in annual salary rather than in hourly rate or will have the monthly payroll code rather than the weekly payroll code. Sometimes the transaction will have the payroll code of the wrong operating unit.

Since the Payroll Department cannot afford to be wrong, it has hired a clerk who does nothing but scrutinize the transactions originating in the Personnel Department. When she finds an error, she either corrects the transaction or telephones the Personnel Department where it originated for the correct information. Then she informs the Personnel Department of the errors she has detected so that they can be changed on the personnel information system, too.

The errors must be resolved immediately. The company cannot afford the ill will of employees who have not been paid on time. The Payroll Department runs four or five different payrolls each night, so there is only a very short time in which to fix changes. But the volume of errors has grown so large that one person cannot handle them all. Consolidated suffered a 10 percent decrease in earnings last year and has instituted a freeze on hiring and information systems budgets.

The data entry clerks of the personnel information system have also been trained to filter out erroneous transactions. Their manager originally hailed from the Payroll Department, and one of his prime responsibilities was ensuring the accuracy of the personnel data that fed the payroll system. He recently retired and with him went two of his oldest, most experienced data entry clerks.

What exactly is the problem at Consolidated? How can it be solved?

Applying the Methodology

Step 1: Problem Analysis · Again, the preceding discussion can be used for fact finding.

Step 2: Problem Understanding · Applying our three-part matrix, the dimensions of Consolidated's problem appear to involve mainly organizational and people factors.

Technology	Organization		People	
Internal:				
Hardware	Culture		Ergonomics	
			Evaluation and Monitoring	
Software	Management	X	Training	X
Telecommunications	Politics		Employee Attitudes and Involvement	
Database	Bureaucracy	X	Legal and Regulatory Compliance	
External:				
	Resources	X		
	Turbulence			
	Complexity			

The Problem · The incidence of errors in data passed from the Personnel Department to the Payroll Department is too high. The accuracy of both the personnel and payroll systems is seriously jeopardized.

Problem Dimensions · Consolidated has a very complex structure and procedures. The corporation maintains centralized, comprehensive payroll and personnel systems that must serve and distinguish between 20 different operating units. There are many different payroll codes to maintain and payrolls to run. Personnel Department staff preparing the employee profiles have not been trained well enough to put in the correct codes or amounts or to check their work. The most experienced data entry clerks in the Personnel Department just retired, as did their manager. Management is poor with little, if any, management accountability. There is no management directive specifying exactly what the responsibilities of the Personnel Department versus the Payroll Department are. Payroll is correcting data that essentially "belong" to or are the responsibility of the Personnel Department. Personnel management is not being held accountable for errors that originate in its department. Management is also relying on the data entry clerks in the personnel information system and the payroll system to act as "filters" for the bad data passed by Personnel. The white portion of Figure 10.4 illustrates the old arrangement. It is clear from this diagram that the Payroll Department was shouldering most of the responsibility for accuracy.

Step 3: Decision Making · The solution objective is to increase the accuracy of payroll-related data originating in the Personnel Department. The constraints here are primarily economic: Consolidated's earnings were poor last year. The chemical business in general is highly competitive and depen-

Figure 10.4

Information Flow in the Personnel and Payroll Departments of Consolidated Chemical Corporation: Old and New

The white portions of this chart show the old arrangement at Consolidated, in which the Payroll Department had the thankless task of auditing all of the Personnel Department's transactions to catch the errors. The white brackets on the right compare the relative responsibilities of the two departments. The blue portions illustrate differences in the new system. Note that, unlike the Maimonides system, adopting a new solution did not mean adopting new technologies. The new Consolidated solution involves changes to management, staff responsibilities, and training. It also transfers the responsibility for auditing Personnel transactions back to the Personnel Department. The blue brackets at the right show how the departments' relative responsibilities have shifted.

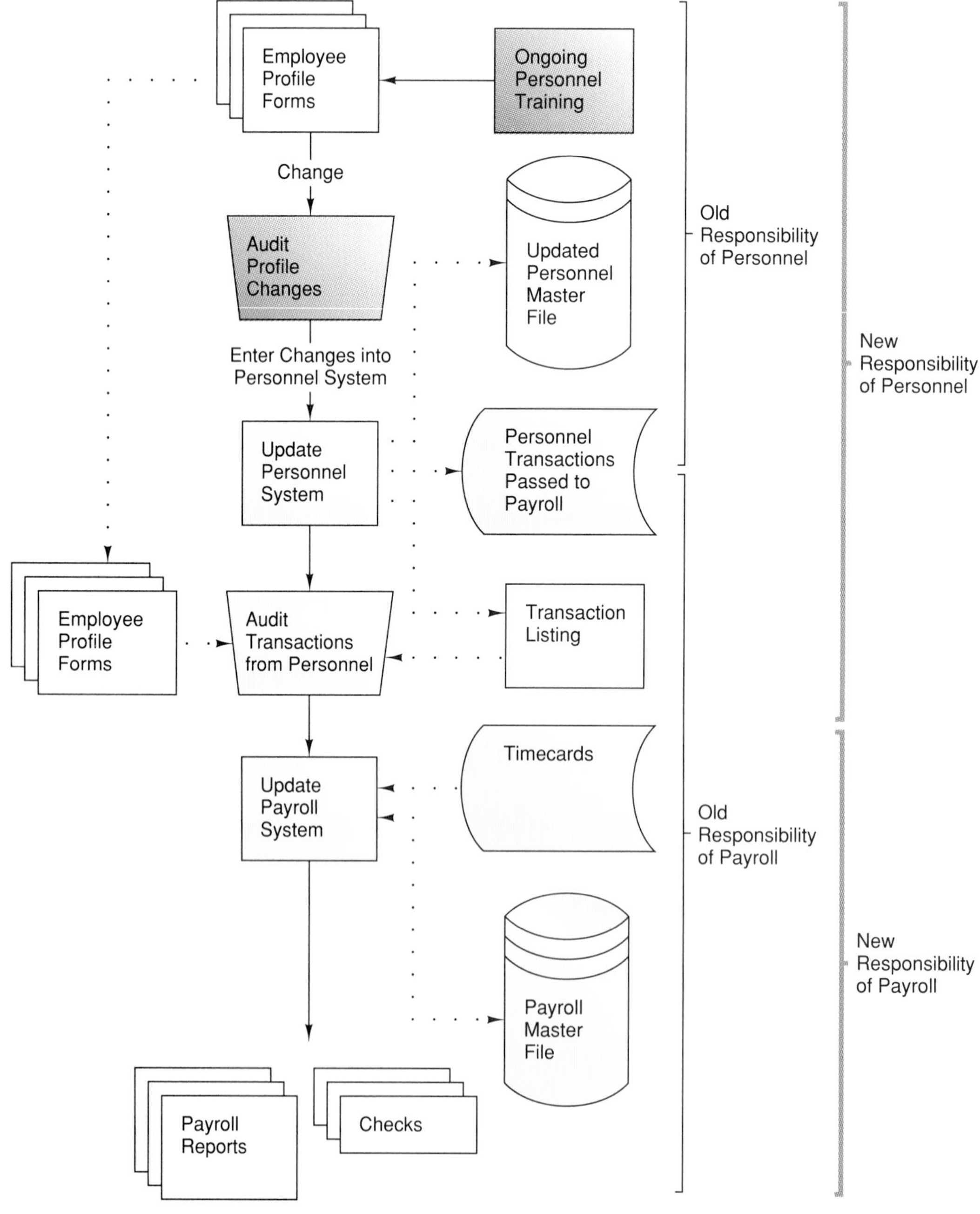

Pitney Bowes Credit Corporation conducts programs and workshops for employees that emphasize customer service. Employee training—whether in customer service or systems procedures—will often solve business problems and prevent new ones.

Source: Courtesy of Pitney Bowes Credit Corporation.

dent on worldwide economic trends and interest rates. To keep costs in line, Consolidated has instituted a freeze on hiring.

Under the circumstances, Consolidated has three solution alternatives:

- **Alternative 1:** Hire an additional person to audit the transactions passed from the Personnel Department to the Payroll Department.
- **Alternative 2:** Tighten procedures and training. Institute an intensive training program for personnel staff so they know precisely how to fill out the payroll data on the profile. Establish a procedure requiring them to audit the data they pass into the system. Institute greater management accountability so that Personnel is held responsible for the erroneous data it passes to Payroll. The Payroll manager should inform higher authorities if Personnel is remiss, not try to do its work or cover up for that department.
- **Alternative 3:** Enhance the payroll and personnel systems with tighter controls on input data so that some of these inconsistencies would be eliminated. For example, software programs could be written to cross-check payroll codes against an employee's operating unit location code so that incorrect codes would be rejected.

We selected alternative 2 because it was operationally feasible and could cut errors without the expense associated with hiring additional employees or making major modifications to the personnel information

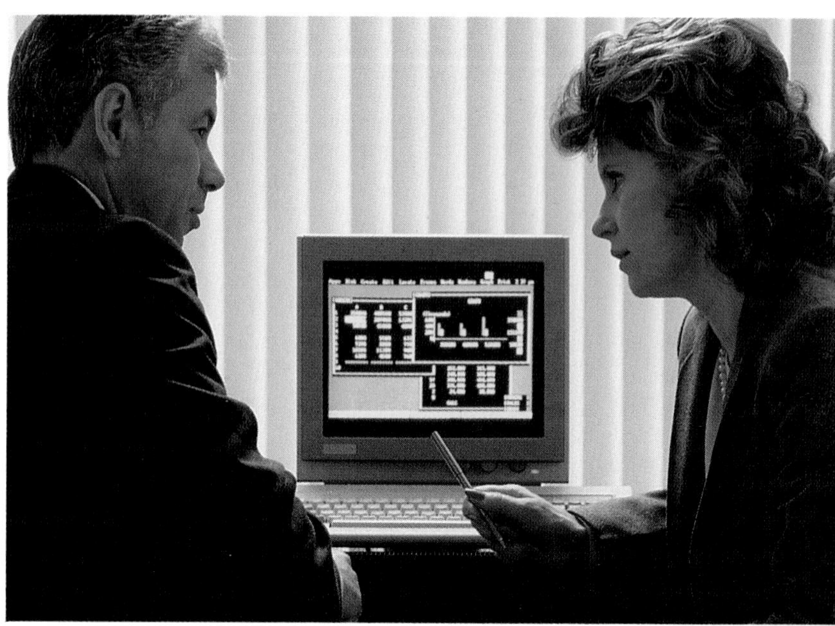

Personal computers and database software allow small businesses to automate functions such as client billing. Not only does database software do the basic bookkeeping, it prints invoices and mailing labels.

Source: Copyright 1990, Comstock.

system. Alternative 3 was not immediately feasible because of budgetary constraints. It also might not solve the problem because it originates where the data are created—at the Personnel Department. Personnel staff might continue to be sloppy in filling out other profile data that could not be easily scrutinized by computerized checking, such as the actual amount of salary increases. Alternative 1 is ruled out by the company's hiring freeze.

Step 4: Solution Design · This problem was largely nontechnical in nature and could be solved without changing existing technology or information flows. Given the constraints, the most viable alternative did not involve a new application solution but focused instead on improving management, procedures, and end-user training for the existing system.

Step 5: Implementation · Consolidated must develop a training program and additional documentation that teach Personnel Department staff how to enter the right codes for payroll data on the employee profiles and how to check their work. Senior management must inform Personnel managers that they, rather than Payroll, will be held accountable for all wrong payroll-related data that originate in the Personnel area. The blue portions of Figure 10.4 show the management, procedural, and training changes required by the solution design. As you can see, much of the responsibility has been shifted to the Personnel Department, where it belongs.

10.4 Problem Solving in Action: Database Application

Problems such as Consolidated's are typical of large corporations with many different operating units and thousands of employees. The next case is representative of a small business in a start-up situation.

The Patient Billing System

Myron and Adrienne Springer are two up-and-coming child psychologists. After working in clinics for a decade, they decided to form their own private practice in Norwalk, Connecticut, an area with no therapists who could handle child disorders. Because of their excellent credentials and expertise with children, their practice is flourishing, and they have had to open a second office in nearby Bridgeport. But this leaves them with virtually no time for office record keeping.

Both psychologists must maintain detailed records of therapy sessions and periodic patient evaluations. They must also prepare a biweekly bill for each patient and keep records of payments. The Springers charge $75 per session, and most patients have sessions once or twice a week. Each patient's session is scheduled for the same day and time every week. The Springers find that they barely have time to maintain their patient evaluations, let alone send bills. Since they are still in a start-up situation, they do not have the resources to hire secretarial help.

In addition to patient charts, the Springers maintain patient records with the patient's name, address, date therapy started, time and day of the week for each session, and number of sessions per week. Do the Springers have a problem? If so, how can it be solved?

Applying the Methodology

Step 1: Problem Analysis · The preceding case discussion serves as our fact-finding results.

Step 2: Problem Understanding · Once again, we apply our matrix and find that the Springers' problem involves mainly organizational factors.

Technology	Organization		People
Internal:			
Hardware	Culture		Ergonomics Evaluation and Monitoring
Software	Management		Training
Telecommunications	Politics		Employee Attitudes and Involvement
Database	Bureaucracy	X	Legal and Regulatory Compliance
External:			
	Resources		
	Turbulence	X	
	Complexity		

The Problem · The Springers do not have time to maintain adequate billings records or perform all the other record keeping required for a therapy practice.

Problem Dimensions · The Springers' problem has both external and internal dimensions:

- **External:** There is enormous demand for child therapist services in the Springers' area, so they are very busy.
- **Internal:** The Springers are in a start-up situation with very little capital or need for a permanent clerical employee. They have heavy record-keeping requirements. In addition to patient billings, very detailed patient charts and evaluations must be maintained. Higher priority is placed on patient charts and evaluations because they are critical to the treatment process. There is no systematic way to ensure that patient billing records are kept up to date.

Step 3: Decision Making · The solution objective would be to reduce the time and effort required to maintain patient records and send out bills. But we must also consider certain economic and operational constraints: The Springers cannot afford a full-time secretary or bookkeeper. In addition, they must maintain the patient evaluation records themselves and do not have any time left over for other kinds of record keeping.

Given these constraints, the Springers have three solution alternatives: (1) hire an office temporary to do the billing every two weeks; (2) develop an automated patient record-keeping and billing system; or (3) automate patient evaluations.

The most time-saving alternative would be an automated patient billing and record-keeping system. This would consist of a simple file with patient name, address, number of sessions per week, amount due, amount paid, and outstanding balance. Automating patient evaluations using word processing would not save as much time as automating the billing process. Hiring a temporary to prepare bills would have little impact, because the Springers themselves would still have to keep track of payments on an ongoing basis.

Step 4: Solution Design · The logical design for a patient billing and record-keeping system might look like this:

Inputs

Basic patient data: Patient name, address, number of sessions per week.
Payment transaction data: date paid and amount paid.

Processing

Create and maintain patient records.
Calculate amount owed by each patient every two weeks.
Accumulate and total payment transactions for each patient every two weeks or on request.
Adjust balance due every two weeks.

Outputs

Semimonthly bill for each patient.

Payment transaction listing that shows payment amounts and dates over each two-week period.

Amount of bill and payment for each month.

Listing of patients with overdue balances.

Mailing labels.

Database

A simple patient file with all of the fields for basic patient data.

A payment transaction file showing patient name, payment amount, and payment date would also be required.

Procedures

Input basic patient data when patient starts therapy.

Update patient data for address changes or therapy session changes.

Input payment data whenever a payment is received.

Generate bills and mailing labels once every two weeks.

Generate payment transaction listing on request.

Controls

Reconcile checks with daily transaction listing report.

Several physical design options are possible. The Springers could use a time-sharing service. (A time-sharing service is a commercial firm that allows other firms to use its hardware and software for a fee for their information processing on a time-sharing basis.) A printer and terminal networked to the time-sharing company's mainframe or minicomputer could be installed in their office, but this would be too costly for such a small business with simple processing needs. The Springers require a very elementary application with small files that could be easily and inexpensively developed on a personal computer using database software. Patient bills could be calculated with spreadsheet software, but the advantage of database software is that it could generate individual patient invoices and many different kinds of reports. This application requires flexibility and file management capabilities that are more readily available with database software. The personal computer could also be used for word processing and other office tasks.

Figure 10.5 compares the physical design and sample contents of two files in the new system: the patient file and the payment transaction file. The designs were done on a personal computer using dBASE IV or dBASE III Plus database software.

Step 5: Implementation · The Springers would have to transfer required patient data from their manual records to the database. They would also have to develop and test the database software programs for printing the patient bills, mailing labels, lists of overdue payments, and payment transaction logs and for calculating payments due (see Figure 10.9). Finally, they would have to change procedures for updating their patient files when they received payments or address changes and for generating patient bills.

Figure 10.5

Physical Design and Sample Contents of Two Files from a Patient Billing System

This system, to be used on a personal computer with dBASE III Plus or dBASE IV, is the result of applying our problem-solving approach to the needs of a small start-up business. The Springers must do a great deal of record keeping but cannot afford clerical help. The solution was to design a patient billing system that they could use themselves on a personal computer. This figure compares the physical designs of the client and payment transaction files with the sample contents after information has been entered into the computer.

(a) Design of the Client File

```
Structure for database :   A:CLIENT.dbf
Number of data records :    5
Date of last update    :   01/01/80
Field Field Name     Type        Width    Dec
    1 LAST_NAME      Character      15
    2 FIRST_NAME     Character      15
    3 STREET         Character      25
    4 CITY_ZIP       Character      20
    5 TIMES_WEEK     Numeric         1
    6 AMT_DUE        Numeric         5
    7 AMT_PAID       Numeric         5
    8 BALANCE        Numeric         5
** Total **                         92
```

(b) Sample Contents of the Client File

Record #	LAST_NAME	FIRST_NAME	STREET	CITY_ZIP	TIMES_WEEK	AMT_DUE	AMT_PAID	BALANCE
1	Smith	Janet	33 Harmon Drive	Ossining, NY 10563	2	150	0	150
2	Harrison	Thomas	111 Cleveland Road	Danbury, CT 06601	1	75	0	75
3	Grover	Cynthia	88 Pleasant Ave.	Norwalk, CT 06888	1	75	0	75
4	Robertson	Hilary	99 Saw Mill Road	Danbury, CT 06502	2	150	0	150
5								

(c) Design of the Payment Transaction File

```
Structure for database :   A:PAYMENT.dbf
Number of data records :    3
Date of last update    :   01/01/80
Field Field Name     Type        Width    Dec
    1 PLAST_NAME     Character      15
    2 PFIRST_NAME    Character      15
    3 PAY_AMT        Numeric         5
    4 PAY_DATE       Date            8
** Total **                         44
```

(d) Sample Contents of the Payment Transaction File

PLAST_NAME-----	PFIRST_NAM-----	PAY_AMT	PAY_DATE
Smith	Janet	150	09/15/88
Harrison	Thomas	150	09/15/88
Smith	Janet	150	10/01/88

In the Springers' case, a simple database was sufficient to solve their problem. As the Focus on Organizations explains, the Department of Justice is preparing to implement a much more complex database to solve a nationwide problem.

FOCUS ON *Organizations*

Justice Aims Database at Gun Sales

The U.S. Department of Justice has decided to build a complete computerized database that lists convicted felons so that local firearms dealers throughout the country will be able to check the criminal histories of gun buyers at the point of sale. Before the database can be implemented, however, the Federal Bureau of Investigation and state authorities will have to fully automate and standardize their criminal-history records and make the data much more accurate and complete.

When the system is fully operational, local firearms dealers will be able to call a state police official, who will then use a computer terminal to find out if the intended purchaser has a criminal record in the national database. If a felony record exists, the sale could not go through.

The point-of-sale system selected by the Justice Department is estimated to cost up to $44 million to develop and up to $70 million a year to operate. The department chose the least costly of the technical options offered by the Task Force on Felon Identification in Firearm Sales, which also considered preapproval systems using smart cards, fingerprint scanning, and biometric scanning.

Source: Mitch Betts, "Justice Aims Database at Gun Sales," *Computerworld*, December 4, 1989, pp. 1, 141. Copyright 1989 by CW Publishing Inc., Framingham, MA 01701—Adapted from Computerworld.

10.5 Problem Solving in Action: Spreadsheet Application

This case shows how a simple spreadsheet application can cut through a complex web of procedures and red tape in a firm with several hundred employees.

Partnership Allocation at Haskell, Simpson, and Porter

Haskell, Simpson, and Porter is a medium-sized New York City law firm specializing in trusts and corporate law. Its 35 partners and 150 associates generate annual revenues of over $25 million, with $5 million in total assets.

Haskell, Simpson, and Porter's accounting department consists of a controller, assistant controller, and ten staff members. At the end of each fiscal year, one of the major public accounting firms audits Haskell, Simpson, and Porter's books, determines the accuracy of its financial statements, and approves the figure for net income.

In addition to a fixed salary, the 35 partners receive shares in the net income of the partnership. The percentage of each partner's share is determined by seniority and the amount of partnership revenue generated by the partner. Once the auditor approves the net income of the firm, the accounting department allocates partnership income. At year end, the law firm's accounting department also summarizes tax information for each partner, a task that requires numerous calculations of each partner's income and deductions.

The public accounting firm issues a first draft of financial statements during the first week in January, and then Haskell, Simpson, and Porter's accounting department finalizes the partnership income allocations. The auditing firm typically revises the bottom line of the drafted financial statements several times before the final version is approved.

Each time a change is made, the accounting department must prepare a new allocation of each partner's income. Each calculation is performed manually, including calculations for allocated partnership income, total income, unincorporated business tax, nondeductible insurance (which must be treated as additional income for tax purposes), retirement plan contributions, charitable contributions, and financial statement income.

Total income consists of each partner's fixed salary plus his or her allocated partnership income. (Total income is reported as ordinary income from the partnership on the federal income tax form 1040 Schedule E.) Each partner takes 6 percent of total salary for nontaxable retirement plan deductions, 0.3 percent of total salary for charitable contributions, 4.16 percent of total income for New York City unincorporated business tax (the law firm is a partnership), and 0.5 percent of total income for nondeductible insurance. Financial statement income consists of total income minus unincorporated business tax. It is reported as net earnings from self-employment on federal income tax form 1040 Schedule SE.

Mathematical errors are common, and the process of correcting them is tedious and even more time-consuming. For example, if the sum of the individual partners' allocations for an insurance deduction does not equal the partnership's total for that deduction, the assistant controller is forced to recalculate each number until the error is located.

In addition, the accounting department must prepare a tax letter for each partner listing his or her share of the firm's taxable income and deductions. This letter is required for individual record keeping and for preparation of the partners' federal, New York State, and New York City income tax returns.

Partners continually pressure the accounting department to complete their income allocation calculations and tax letters. During the past few years, several changes were made to the bottom line of the firm's income statement after the allocation calculations were completed. Since all the calculations are based on this figure, all of the partnership allocation calculations had to be performed again, taking an extra three days. Let's analyze this problem.

Applying the Methodology

Step 1: Problem Analysis · Again, we can use the facts from the preceding discussion.

Step 2: Problem Understanding · Using our matrix, we find that this law firm's problem has both organizational and people dimensions.

Technology	Organization		People
Internal:			
Hardware	Culture		Ergonomics Evaluation and Monitoring
Software	Management		Training
Telecommunications	Politics	X	Employee Attitudes and Involvement
Database	Bureaucracy	X	Legal and Regulatory Compliance
External:			
	Resources		
	Turbulence	X	
	Complexity		

The Problem · Partnership allocations and tax calculations cannot be performed in a timely manner.

Problem Dimensions · The problem has both external and internal dimensions:

- **External:** The law firm is dependent on an external auditing firm for finalizing its bottom-line financial statement figures. It must base all of its partnership allocation calculations on input from an external source and work within a very narrow time frame to complete tax letters and income distributions for partners.
- **Internal:** Calculations for partnership allocations are complex and variable and require special approvals and bureaucratic procedures. The controller's office operates with primarily manual tools and technology and resists efforts to automate.

Step 3: Decision Making · The objectives here are to expedite and increase the accuracy of partnership allocations and tax calculations. At the same time, several constraints must be considered: The time frame for finalizing partnership allocations and tax calculations will remain very narrow because business rules require that the firm use an external auditor. The firm's internal accounting department is very resistant to extensive automation.

Given these constraints, the law firm appears to have two solution alternatives: (1) hire extra staff for the controller's office to perform the calculations manually once figures have been finalized. (2) Develop an automated model for partner income allocation that can be easily revised when bottom-line figures are changed.

Determining income and tax liability from a partnership such as a law firm requires many interrelated calculations. Spreadsheet software is specifically designed to simplify these accounting tasks.

Source: Copyright 1988, Comstock.

The first alternative is not very desirable, since this process leads to mathematical errors and repetition of effort. The second alternative is feasible, provided that it can be done with minimum disruption to the accounting department.

Step 4: Solution Design · A system model for partnership income allocation would incorporate these requirements in a logical design.

Inputs

Final bottom-line figure for net income.
Each partner's percentage.
Each partner's fixed salary.
Unincorporated business tax percentage.
Nondeductible insurance percentage.
Retirement plan contribution percentage.
Charitable contributions percentage.

Processing

Compute each partner's gross partnership income allocation.
Compute each partner's total income.
Compute unincorporated business tax.
Compute nondeductible insurance.
Compute retirement plan contribution (deduction).
Compute charitable contributions deduction.
Compute financial statement income.
Compute firm totals for each of the above.

Outputs

Schedule of partner allocations.

Individual tax letters.

Database

A record must be kept for each partner with the following fields:

Partner's name
Partner's fixed salary amount
Percentage of net income
Amount of net income allocation
Total income
Nonincorporated business tax amount
Nondeductible insurance amount
Retirement plan contribution amount
Charitable contribution amount
Financial statement reporting income amount

Procedures

Input the net income figures after approval by the auditor and management.

Mail tax letters and partnership income allocation statements to each partner.

Controls

Require management's as well as the auditor's authorization of the final net income figure before it is input for partner income calculations.

Total all partners' shares of income and reconcile this total with the firm's net income figure used as input.

The physical design requires a very small file, with records on only 35 partners. Since the law firm does not need to have its own mainframe or minicomputer, the application could be farmed out to a time-sharing service. But the application is so small that it is most appropriate and cost-effective on a microcomputer, which could also be used for word processing and other office tasks. This application requires many calculations that are interrelated in a very small file. Spreadsheet software would be preferable to database software in this instance because it handles such problems more easily.

Figure 10.6 shows the physical design of the partnership allocation worksheet and a sample of the output. Panel a displays the organization of the worksheet, cell relationships, and calculation formulas. Panel b is a printout of the partnership allocation report. Data are extracted from the partnership allocation report for the tax letter sent to each partner, so the letters can be created much faster than before.

Step 5: Implementation · The firm would have to purchase a personal computer and printer and compatible spreadsheet software. With the spreadsheet software, a template could be developed to produce the required partnership allocation calculations. Data formerly maintained manually (such as all of the partners' names and fixed income) would have to be entered into the template. The accuracy of the template would be tested by comparison with the same calculations performed manually. Procedures would have to be modified so that the calculations were performed on the template rather than by hand. The accounting department would have to be trained to use the personal computer and spreadsheet software.

Figure 10.6

Using Spreadsheets at Haskell, Simpson, and Porter: The Physical Design and Sample Output

This New York City law firm benefited greatly from a simple microcomputer-based spreadsheet (in this case, Lotus 1-2-3). Panel a is the worksheet that was developed for the partnership allocation system. The calculation factors are grouped at the lower left and are referenced by the formulas. The factor entitled "firm's net income" is the bottom-line figure, supplied by the auditor, that drives the rest of the calculations. Panel b shows a sample of the output, which displays the figures for each partner.

(a) Physical Design for Spreadsheet

PARTNER	PARTNERSHIP PERCENT	FIXED SALARY	ALLOCATED INCOME	TOTAL INCOME	UNINCORPORATED BUSINESS TAX
Donaldson, Paul	2.52%	48000	+$B5*$C$20	+$C5+$D5	+$E5*$C$21
Grover, Pauline	1.81%	48000	+$B6*$C$20	+$C6+$D6	+$E6*$C$21
Naskell, Thomas	3.83%	46000	+$B7*$C$20	+$C7+$D7	+$E7*$C$21
Porter, Arnold	4.42%	48000	+$B8*$C$20	+$C8+$D8	+$E8*$C$21
Simpson, Jeffry	2.76%	41000	+$B9*$C$20	+$C9+$D9	+$E9*$C$21
Thomas, Linda	3.12%	48000	+$B10*$C$20	+$C10+$D10	+$E10*$C$21
Westheimer, Charles	6.61%	55000	+$B11*$C$20	+$C11+$D11	+$E11*$C$21
TOTALS		@SUM($C5..$	@SUM($D5..$D1	@SUM($E5..$E1	@SUM($F5..$F11)

CALCULATION FACTORS

FIRM'S NET INCOME	$5,125,000
UNINCORPORATED BUSINESS TAX	4.16%
RETIREMENT PLAN CONTRIBUTION	6.00%
NON-DEDUCTIBLE INSURANCE	0.50%
CHARITABLE CONTRIBUTION	0.30%

(b) Sample Output

PARTNER	PARTNERSHIP PERCENT	FIXED SALARY	ALLOCATED INCOME	TOTAL INCOME	UNINCORPORATED BUSINESS TAX
Donaldson, Paul	2.52%	$48,000	$129,150	$177,150.00	$7,369.44
Grover, Pauline	1.81%	$48,000	$92,763	$140,762.50	$5,855.72
Naskell, Thomas	3.83%	$46,000	$196,288	$242,287.50	$10,079.16
Porter, Arnold	4.42%	$48,000	$226,525	$274,525.00	$11,420.24
Simpson, Jeffry	2.76%	$41,000	$141,450	$182,450.00	$7,589.92
Thomas, Linda	3.12%	$48,000	$159,900	$207,900.00	$8,648.64
Westheimer, Charles	6.61%	$55,000	$338,763	$393,762.50	$16,380.52
TOTALS		$334,000.00	$1,284,837.50	$1,618,837.50	$67,343.64

As Haskell, Simpson, and Porter grows in the future, it might wish to consider other software, such as the groupware described in the Focus on Problem Solving.

10.6 Problem Solving in Action: Mainframe Application

Most information system solutions based on mainframe computers have large files and fairly complex inputs and outputs. This problem has been simplified to focus only on redesigning the output part of an existing information system.

(a) Physical Design for Spreadsheet

RETIREMENT PLAN CONTRIB.	NON-DEDUCT. INSURANCE	CHARITABLE CONTRIBUTION	FINANCIAL STAT INCOME
+$E5*$C$22	+$E5*$C$23	+$E5*$C$24	+$E5-$F5
+$E6*$C$22	+$E6*$C$23	+$E6*$C$24	+$E6-$F6
+$E7*$C$22	+$E7*$C$23	+$E7*$C$24	+$E7-$F7
+$E8*$C$22	+$E8*$C$23	+$E8*$C$24	+$E8-$F8
+$E9*$C$22	+$E9*$C$23	+$E9*$C$24	+$E9-$F9
+$E10*$C$22	+$E10*$C$23	+$E10*$C$24	+$E10-$F10
+$E11*$C$22	+$E11*$C$23	+$E11*$C$24	+$E11-$F11
@SUM($G5..$G1	@SUM($H5..$H1	@SUM($I5..$I1	@SUM($J5..$J1

(b) Sample Output

RETIREMENT PLAN CONTRIB.	NONDEDUCT. INSURANCE	CHARITABLE CONTRIBUTION	FINANCIAL STAT INCOME
$10,629.00	$885.75	$531.45	$169,780.56
$8,445.75	$703.81	$422.29	$134,906.78
$14,537.25	$1,211.44	$726.86	$232,208.34
$16,471.50	$1,372.63	$823.58	$263,104.76
$10,947.00	$912.25	$547.35	$174,860.08
$12,474.00	$1,039.50	$623.70	$199,251.36
$23,625.75	$1,968.81	$1,181.29	$377,381.98
$97,130.25	$8,094.19	$4,856.51	$1,551,493.86

Variable Rate Mortgages at North Lake Bank

North Lake Bank is an old, well-established savings and loan institution headquartered in Montpelier, Vermont. One of North Lake's fastest-growing services has been supplying mortgages to purchasers of vacation homes and condominiums. The majority of these mortgages have been adjustable rate mortgages. North Lake will not issue fixed rate mortgages on condominiums, and many home owners have opted for the variable rate mortgages in the hope of later converting them to fixed rate mortgages when interest rates drop.

Under variable rate mortgages, the interest rate is adjusted annually. Effective September 1, the bank computes a new interest rate for the year, based on the Federal Savings and Loan Insurance Corporation (FSLIC)

FOCUS ON Problem Solving

Not Just Another Spreadsheet

Recently, Sheldon Laube, Price Waterhouse's national director of information and technology, bought 10,000 copies of Lotus Notes, a new software tool that offers several advantages over traditional spreadsheets.

Lotus Notes is a groupware tool—software that helps build applications for groups of people working together. How does groupware differ from ordinary software? With a spreadsheet or a word processor, one person works with a computer to produce information. With groupware, several people work together through their computers to produce and share information.

Notes' data structures are a cross between a table-oriented database and an outline. Using Notes, you can display data in tables or forms and select whatever levels of detail you wish to see from a list of what look like headings and subheads (but are actually titles of individual records or documents). Data can be sorted in any number of ways, such as by customer, person responsible (for a set of tasks or customers), date, problem type, and the like. Data can also be classified automatically based on selected words found within a text, such as a news item or a memo. What makes Notes more useful than a standard relational database is its implicit awareness of individual users, so it can be used as a medium for exchange of messages, assignment of responsibilities, and routing of work through a sequence of tasks or approval performed by different people.

Lotus has included a number of templates with the first release. These cover simple applications, such as group discussions in which users' comments are maintained and organized by topics. They also cover client tracking (name, address, phone, contact dates and subject), electronic mail, project status reporting, and "newswire" (news item filtering and categorization).

Laube and his staff looked at a variety of electronic-mail packages to run over the local networks installed in 50 offices. The mail systems he considered at first did not scale up and had insufficient security. What he needed was neither point-to-point nor central broadcasting, but a medium in which everyone could be both broadcaster and recipient—without creating total confusion and a surplus of unusable information as the system grew.

Source: Adapted from Esther Dyson, "Not Just Another Spreadsheet," *Forbes*, February 5, 1990, p. 161. Adapted by permission of Forbes Magazine. © Forbes Inc. 1990.

monthly median cost of funds index. This new interest rate is entered, via a control card transaction, into the bank's automated mortgage account system. North Lake then sends out statements notifying each customer of the new interest rate and the change this will make in the customer's monthly mortgage payment. Customers are told to switch to the new monthly payment amount starting with the mortgage payment due October 1.

Most North Lake customers, especially the out-of-staters, pay their mortgages by mail. Until recently, each was issued a mortgage account passbook, which keeps track of his or her account (see Figure 10.7, panel a).

Amounts on the TOTAL line are entered by hand. They display changes in the amount of monthly mortgage payment, with the most recent payment amount listed on the right. The amounts in the other columns are entered via a passbook machine when customers send in their monthly

Figure 10.7

North Lake Bank's Mortgage Payment Reports: Old and New

Panel a is the old report. Amounts on the TOTAL line had to be filled in individually by hand, which sometimes caused trouble. If bank employees forgot to enter changes in monthly mortgage payments, customers would be unaware that the payments had changed—leading to some very angry telephone calls. Customers also complained that the old statements were difficult to interpret. Panel b shows the new report, on which the new software automatically updates mortgage payments and reports mortgage account information more precisely.

(a)

Acct. No 9999-99

DATE	ESCROW PAYMENT	ESCROW BALANCE	INTEREST & CHARGES	LOAN PAYMENTS	LOAN BALANCE
020188	12.00	24.00	492.29	530.86	58,268.08
TOTAL	$623.41	$542.86	$		

(b)

ANNUAL RATE: 09.125 ACCOUNT NUMBER 9999-99
DATE: 2/1/88

BALANCES:

PRINCIPAL	ESCROW
$58,268.08	$24.00

DATE DUE	PRINCIPAL	INTEREST	ESCROW	LATE CHARGE	TOTAL PAYMENT
2/16/88	$38.57	$492.29	$12.00		$542.86

TOTAL PAYMENT DUE: $542.86

payments. The ESCROW PAYMENT and ESCROW BALANCE columns shows how much of that monthly payment is held in an escrow account and the accumulated balance in that account. The LOAN PAYMENTS column lists the amount of the monthly payment actually applied to the loan after escrow payments have been deducted, and the INTEREST & CHARGES column lists the portion of the loan payment consisting of interest. The LOAN BALANCE column shows the outstanding balance of the loan.

North Lake has received many calls from customers complaining about their statements. They claim they are difficult to interpret and that the portion of the loan payment that consists of repayment of principal is not clearly spelled out. Sometimes the bank forgets to enter changes in monthly mortgage payments in the TOTAL fields. Some of the customers will forget to change their monthly mortgage payment on October 1. Those whose monthly mortgage payment has gone up will be billed a penalty for underpayment. Those whose mortgage payment has gone down will pay more than they owe. The difference will be applied to reducing the principal.

Applying the Methodology

Let's apply our methodology to this problem.

Step 1: Problem Analysis · We can use the facts from the preceding discussion.

Step 2: Problem Understanding · As the matrix shows, this problem has both organizational and people dimensions.

Technology	Organization		People
Internal:			
Hardware	Culture		Ergonomics X Evaluation and Monitoring
Software	Management	X	Training X
Telecommunications	Politics		Employee Attitudes and Involvement
Database	Bureaucracy	X	Legal and Regulatory Compliance
External:			
	Resources		
	Turbulence	X	
	Complexity		

The Problem · Customers are making erroneous monthly payments toward mortgage accounts. The Mortgage Department's time is not being used efficiently to resolve such complaints.

Problem Dimensions · North Lake's problem has both external and internal dimensions:

- **External:** North Lake's customer base is increasing, due to the Vermont vacation real estate boom. The bank's existing procedures are not sufficient to handle the influx of new customers.
- **Internal:** North Lake's procedures are very poor to begin with. There is no way to ensure that the new monthly mortgage payment amount will be entered manually on every passbook. Inconsistent information concerning changing monthly payments and interest rates is passed to clients. There is no management supervision to ensure that passbooks are consistently updated. Data in the mortgage payment passbook are broken out and displayed in a confusing manner.

Step 3: Decision Making · The objective here is to ensure that each customer's correct monthly payment amount appears on the monthly passbook when the payment amount changes. This must be done within the constraint that North Lake's mortgage payment system contains sensitive financial data that must always be accurate and timely. The bank cannot afford any errors or major disruptions.

Given these constraints, North Lake has two alternatives:

- **Alternative 1:** Tighten procedures to ensure that changes in the monthly payment amount will always be entered on the bottom of the passbook.
- **Alternative 2:** Develop an application that produces an improved mortgage payment form, one that both notifies the customer of the correct monthly payment and tracks the same pieces of information in the customer's account. The application should also display the mortgage payment components in a clearer way.

Step 4: Solution Design · Alternative 2 was selected. North Lake maintained all of the required data on its customer database internally and did not need any new inputs or changes to its databases. What had to be improved were the content and organization of its output document to customers.

The logical design for this solution would mainly involve changes in outputs.

A BellSouth Corporation representative shows a customer the new design of a telephone bill. By improving the content and organization of the output document, companies can make transactions simpler and less prone to error.

Source: © 1989 Chipp Jamieson for BellSouth Corporation. Reprinted with permission.

Inputs
Unchanged

Processing
Unchanged

Outputs
Design a new output document that can serve as both a mortgage payment coupon and a record of past payments and outstanding balances.
Field contents:
- Account number
- Annual mortgage rate
- Date
- Balance of mortgage principal
- Balance in escrow
- Date payment is due
- Amount of payment allocated to principal
- Amount of payment allocated to escrow
- Amount of payment allocated to interest
- Amount of late charge (from delay in previous month's payment)
- Total monthly payment amount

Database
Same as before

Procedures
Eliminate need to enter changes in monthly payment manually on mortgage payment passbooks.

Controls
Same as before

North Lake did not need to make any physical design changes in existing hardware or files for its mortgage payment system. It did have to revise software programs to produce a different output report for customers. The new report, shown in panel b of Figure 10.7, serves as a turnaround document and payment form.

The bank also modified procedures so that mortgage interest changes were no longer entered manually on mortgage passbooks but were automatically updated on the payment report form.

Step 5: Implementation · In order to produce the new mortgage payment statement, the bank had to modify and test the output-reporting programs from its mortgage account system. No new hardware was required. The bank replaced its old mortgage payment passbooks with mortgage payment statement forms. No special training or documentation was required for this modification, since the mortgage payment statement is self-explanatory.

Most problems you will encounter in the real world will be more complex than the preceding examples. Their solution will require considerable research, analysis, and consideration of other factors, such as organizational culture or conflicting interest groups, that were not addressed here. In these cases, information system solutions were deliberately kept very simple so we could focus on the problem-solving process itself.

What stands out in all these cases is the importance of analyzing all the dimensions of a problem in order to derive the right solution. If an information systems application is called for, these cases demonstrate that the solution must be visualized first in business terms, as a business solution or logical systems model, before any details concerning computer hardware or software are addressed.

10.7 Systems-Building Tools and Methodologies

A number of tools and methodologies have been developed to document various aspects of the systems-building process. The most widely used are data flow diagrams, data dictionaries, and system flowcharts. These can be used during analysis of a problem to document an existing system or during solution design to help visualize a new solution. They are most useful for describing large, complex information systems. Simple, microcomputer-based applications are often developed without these tools, especially if they involve only a limited number of data elements and one or two basic processes.

Data flow diagram
A graphic diagram that shows both how data flow to, from, and within an information system and the various processes that transform the data; used for documenting the logical design of an information system.

Data Flow Diagrams

Data flow diagrams are useful for documenting the logical design of an information system. They show how data flow to, from, and within an information system and the various processes that transform those data. Data flow diagrams break a system down into manageable levels of detail so

Figure 10.8

Data Flow Diagram Symbols

Data flow diagrams are a useful tool for depicting the flow of data and processes of a system. They can be constructed using only four basic symbols, shown here. Arrows represent the flow of data in a system. A box with rounded edges represents a process, whether manual or computerized, that changes input data into output. The open rectangle symbolizes a data store, a collection of data such as a file or database. Finally, a rectangle or square is an external entity, which lies outside the system and serves as a source or destination of data.

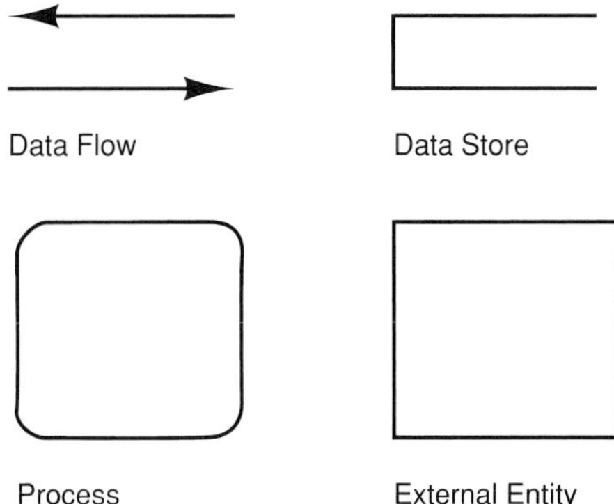

that it can be visualized first at a very general or abstract level and then gradually in greater and greater detail.

Basic data flow diagram symbols are shown in Figure 10.8. The arrow is used to depict the flow of data. The rounded box (sometimes a "bubble" or circle is used) is the process symbol; it signifies any process, computerized or manual, that transforms data. The open rectangle is the data store symbol; it indicates a file or repository where data are stored. A rectangle or square is the external entity symbol; it is used to indicate an originator or receiver of data that is outside the boundaries of a system.

Data flows can consist of a single data element or of multiple data elements grouped together. The name or contents of each data flow are listed beside the arrow. Data flows can be manual or automated and can consist of documents, reports, or data from a computer file.

Data flow
The movement of data within an information system; a data flow can consist of a single data element or multiple data elements grouped together and can be manual or automated.

Data flow diagrams can break a complex process into successive layers of detail by depicting the system in various levels. For example, Figure 10.9 shows a general picture of the patient billing and record-keeping system described earlier in this chapter. It is called a context diagram. The context diagram depicts an information system at the most general level as a single process with its major inputs and outputs. Subsequent diagrams then break the system down into greater levels of detail. Panel a of Figure 10.10, which is called a zero-level data flow diagram, shows the same system at the next level of detail. It explodes the context diagram into multiple processes that are the major processes of the system: capturing patient details; tracking payments; and producing bills, mailing labels, patient listings, and other reports. Panel b is a first-level data flow diagram; it shows more specific detail about process 3.0, Prepare Bills and Reports. If necessary, lower-level

Figure 10.9

A Context Diagram of a Patient Billing System

A context diagram is a data flow diagram that gives a broad picture of a system: a single process with its principal inputs and outputs. The process in this case is the patient billing and record-keeping system, which we discussed earlier in the chapter. The patient and the therapist are the principal external entities, and the arrows depict the data flowing between the external entities and the system.

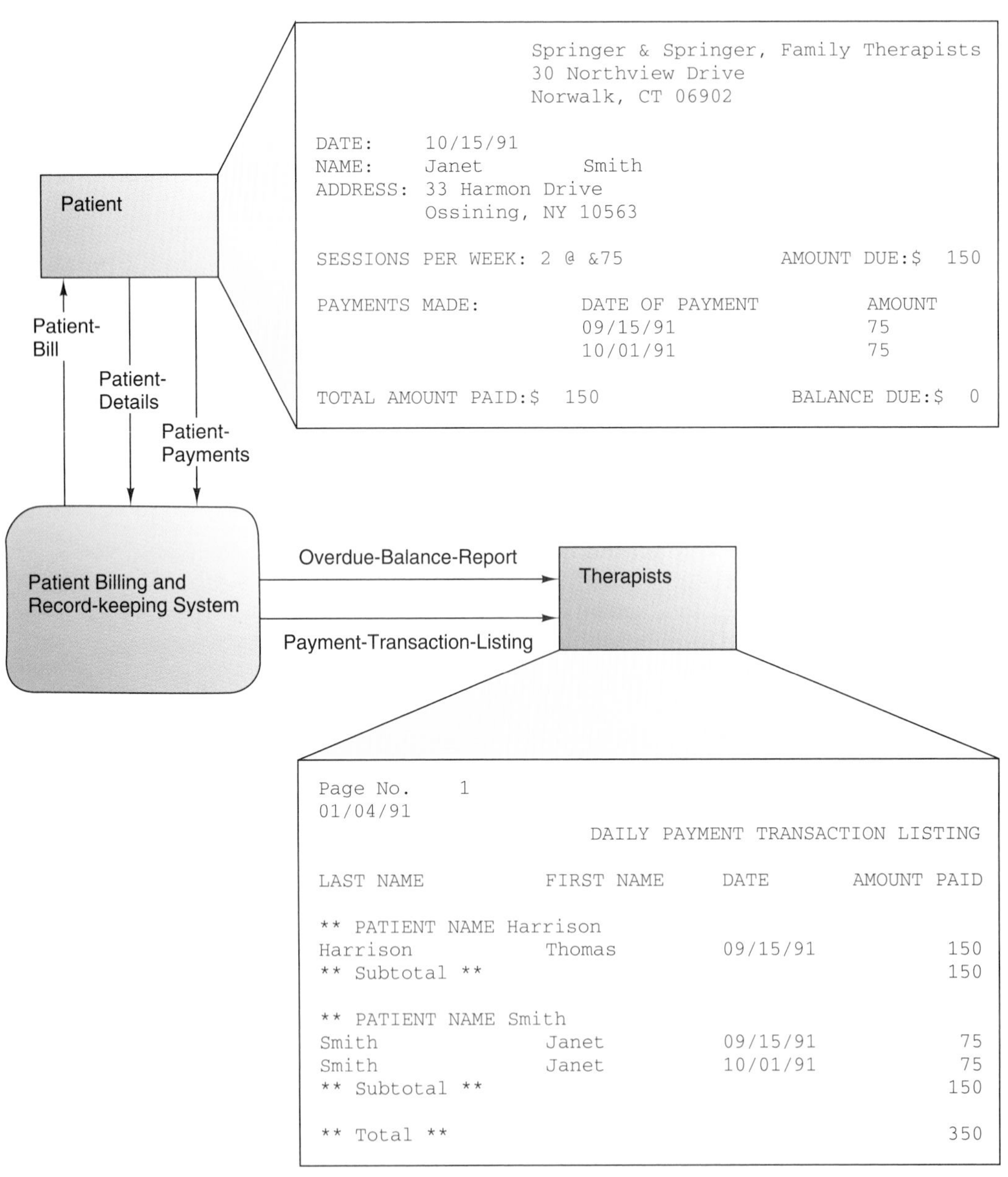

Figure 10.10

Zero-Level and First-Level Data Flow Diagrams and Process Specifications

Data flow diagrams can be "exploded" into greater and greater levels of detail. Panel a shows a zero-level data flow diagram, the next step in terms of detail after the context diagram shown in Figure 10.9. Here we see that the patient billing system includes three major processes: Capture Patient Details, Track Payments, and Prepare Bills and Reports. Panel b is a first-level data flow diagram that explodes process 3.0, Prepare Bills and Reports, into the next level of detail. We see that this process itself consists of three processes: Calculate Balance Due, Generate Bills and Reports, and Generate Mailing Labels. Panel c illustrates process specifications for process 3.3, Generate Mailing Labels. Process specifications are a type of documentation that gives further information.

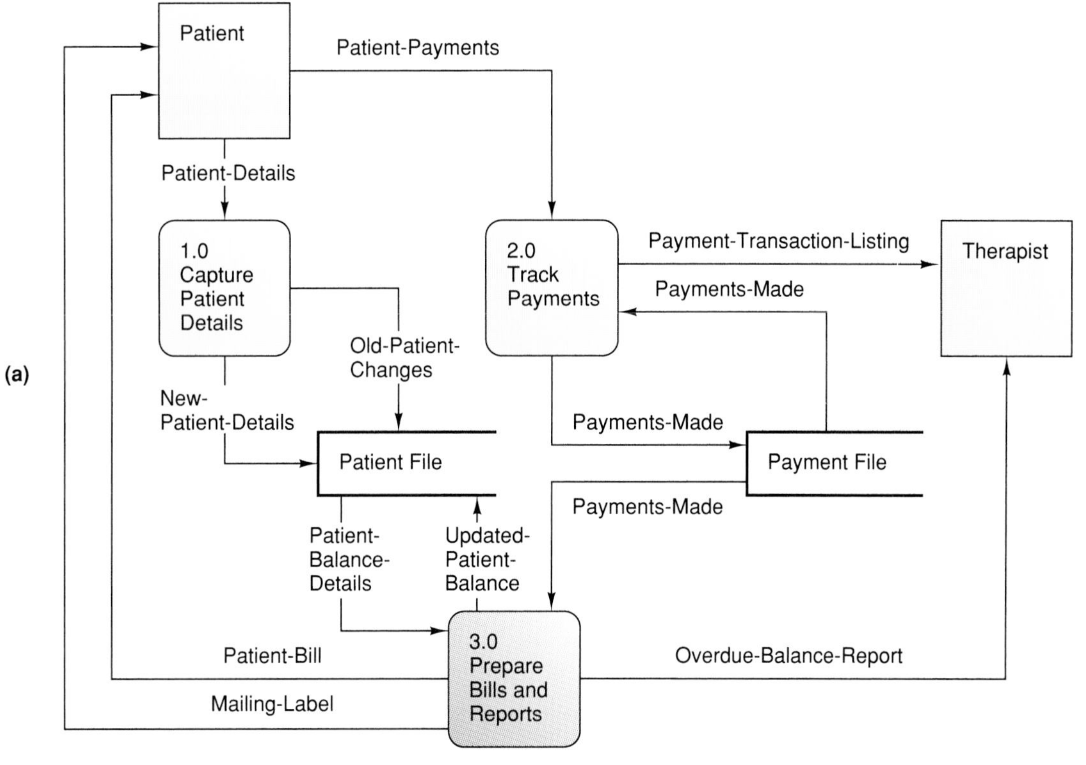

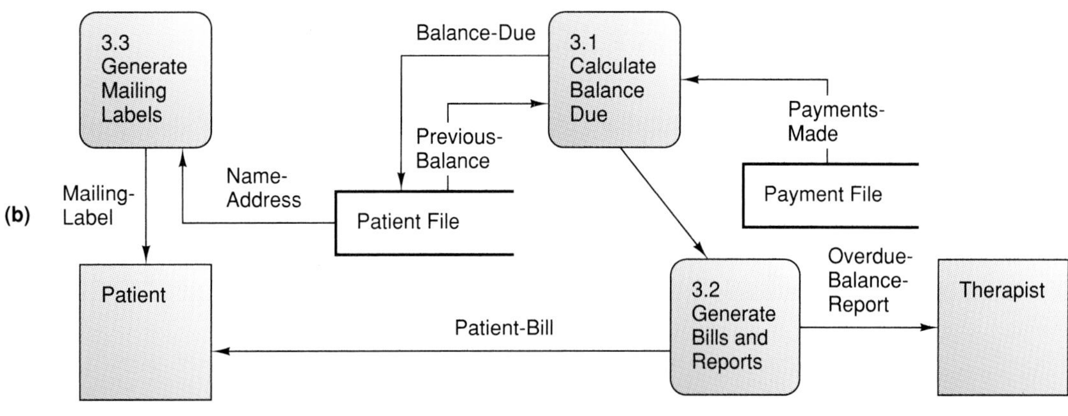

(c)

```
Generate Mailing Labels

For each patient in the patient file do the following:
    IF the amount due is greater than 0,
          Print client's first name, last name, street,
          city, state, and zip code on mailing label report.
```

data flow diagrams can be used to break this process and others into even greater detail.

Process specifications
The logical steps for performing a process; they appear in documents accompanying lower-level data flow diagrams to show the various steps by which data are transformed.

Accompanying the data flow diagrams is additional documentation with more detail about the data in the data flows and the logical steps in each process. For example, panel c illustrates the **process specifications** (the logical sequence of steps for performing a process) for process 3.3, Generate Mailing Labels, in our first-level data flow diagram.

The Data Dictionary

Detail about each piece of data and the data groupings used in the data flows is maintained in a data dictionary. The data dictionary contains information about each data element, such as its name, meaning, size, format, and the processes in which it is used. Figure 10.11 shows some sample data dictionary entries for our patient billing and record-keeping system. Panel a is a sample description of an individual data element from the patient file, the patient's last name. Panel b is a dictionary entry for a group of data elements traveling together as the data flow called Payments-made.

The data dictionary can be in paper and pencil form, but it is often automated, since a large or medium-size information system application must keep track of many pieces of data, processes, and interrelationships. Data dictionaries are not used only when a new system is being developed.

Figure 10.11

Two Data Dictionary Entries for the Patient Billing System

A data dictionary is a valuable tool for documentation. It "defines" each data element in a system by giving information such as its meaning, size, format, and the processes in which it is used. Panel a defines a data element called "Last_Name," which represents the patient's last name in the patient file. Panel b is an entry that defines a data flow, a group of elements that "travel" together through the system. This particular group is called Payments-made. What information would you expect to find in that data flow?

(a)

Data Elements

NAME:	Last-Name
DEFINITION:	Designates the patient's last name
TYPE:	Character
LENGTH:	15 positions
ALIASES:	LAST_NAME PLAST_NAME
FILE WHERE FOUND:	CLIENT.DBF PAYMENT.DBF
PROCESSES WHERE USED:	1.0: Capture Patient Details 2.0: Track Payments 3.0: Prepare Bills and Reports 3.1: Calculate Balance Due 3.2: Generate Bills and Reports 3.3: Generate Mailing Labels

(b)

Data Flow

NAME:	Payments-Made
DESCRIPTION:	Patient's payment transaction
CONTENTS:	Last-Name First-Name Payment-Amount Payment-Date
PROCESSES WHERE USED:	2.0: Track Payments 3.0: Prepare Bills and Reports 3.1: Calculate Balance Due

They can also be used to help a business keep track of all of the data and groupings of data it maintains in existing systems. As discussed in Chapter 6, the data dictionary is a key component of a database management system. Data dictionaries thus provide a multipurpose data management tool for a business.

System Flowcharts

System flowcharts document the sequence of processing steps that take place in an entire system. They show the sequence of the flow of data and the files used by each processing step.

Figure 10.12 shows the basic symbols for system flowcharting. The most important are the plain rectangle, representing a computer processing

System flowchart
A diagram that documents the sequence of processing steps that take place in an entire system; most useful for physical design, in which such diagrams show the sequence of processing events and the files used by each processing step.

Figure 10.12

Basic System Flowchart Symbols

System flowcharts document the sequence information flow and processing steps within a system. Notice that there are more symbols involved in building a system flowchart than in drawing a data flow diagram.

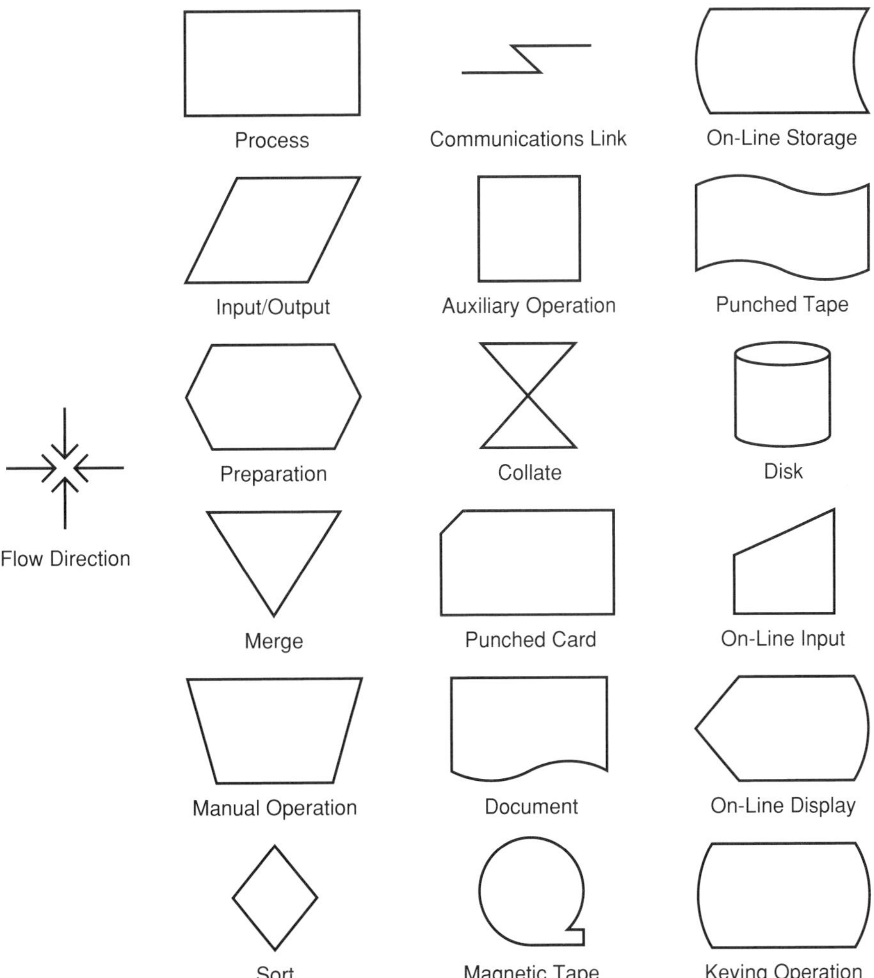

Figure 10.13

A System Flowchart Depicting the Patient Billing System

This system flowchart illustrates the major steps involved in the patient billing system discussed earlier in this chapter. Note that this flowchart is more specific than a data flow diagram about the sequence and physical characteristics of processes, inputs, and outputs in this system. From the symbols, we learn that Payments and Patient Data both enter the system as documents and that they are entered on-line. We can also see that the system contains two major files and produces three output documents and updated patient and payment files.

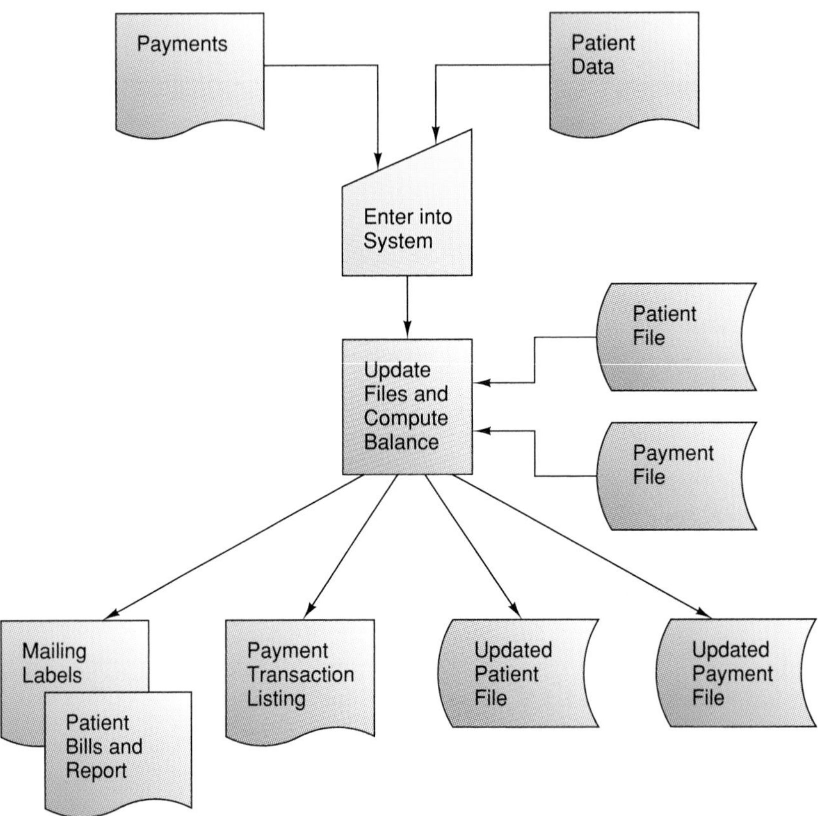

function; the flow lines, which show the sequence of processing steps; and the arrows, which show the direction of information flow. Figure 10.13 illustrates how our patient billing and record-keeping system would be represented as a system flowchart.

System flowcharts differ from data flow diagrams in that more attention is payed to the sequence of processing events and the physical media used in processing. Data flow diagrams, in contrast, are a more logical and abstract way of representing a system. Data flow diagrams do not show the physical characteristics of the system or the exact timing of steps taken during processing.

Structured Design and Programming

In order to develop good software, programs must be carefully thought out and designed. In the earliest days of computing, programmers wrote software according to their own whims, with the result that programs were often confusing and difficult to work with. Software today is expected to follow recognized design principles. The prevailing design standards today are called structured design and structured programming.

Structured Design · According to **structured design** principles, a program should be designed from the top down as a hierarchical series of modules. A **module** is a logical way of partitioning or subdividing a program so that each module performs one or a small number of related tasks. In **top-down design,** one should first consider the program's main functions, subdivide this function into component modules, and then subdivide each component module until the lowest level of detail has been reached.

The structured design is documented in a structure chart showing each level of the design and its relationship to other levels. Structure charts resemble corporate organization charts, but each box represents a program module. The chart shows how modules relate to each other but does not depict the details of the program instructions in each module.

Figure 10.14 shows a structure chart for a simple order processing program. There are three high-level program modules for the major functions of the program: inputting orders, updating inventory, and generating appropriate output documents. The structure chart shows that the modules for Input Orders and Output Order Reports can be further broken down

Structured design
A software design principle according to which a program is supposed to be designed from the top down as a hierarchical series of modules with each module performing a limited number of functions.

Module
A logical way of partitioning or subdividing a program so that each component (i.e., module) performs a limited number of related tasks.

Top-down design
A principle of software design according to which the design should first consider the program's main functions, subdivide these functions into component modules, and then subdivide each component module until the lowest level of detail has been reached.

Figure 10.14

A Structure Chart for an Order Processing Program

A structure chart is a tool for documenting levels and relationships within a computer program. Each box represents a module, a logical subdivision that performs one task or a few related tasks. We can see that the basic functions of this program are to input orders, update the inventory, and produce order reports as output.

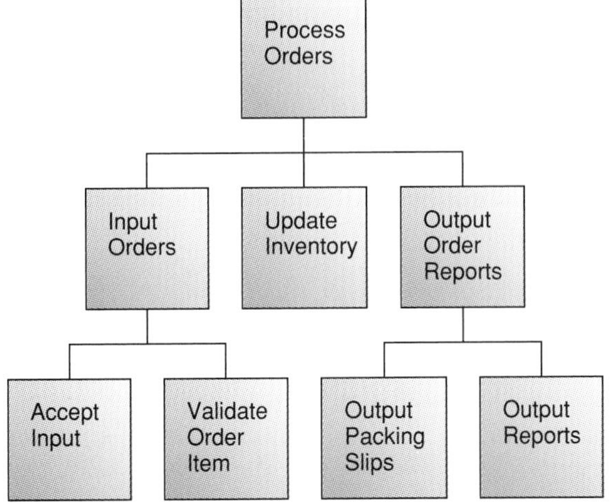

into another level of detail. The Input Orders module has subsidiary modules for accepting input and validating orders. The Output Order Reports module has subsidiary modules for generating packing slips and for generating various reports.

Structured programming
A way of writing program code that simplifies control paths so that programs can be easily understood and modified by others; it relies on three basic control constructs—the sequence construct, the selection construct, and the repetition construct.

Sequence construct
A series of statements that are executed in the order in which they appear, with control passing unconditionally from one statement to the next; one of three basic control constructs in structured programming.

Selection construct
A series of statements that tests a condition; depending on whether the results of the test are true or false, one of two alternative instructions will be executed. One of three basic control constructs in structured programming.

Repetition construct
A series of statements that repeats an instruction as long as the results of a conditional test are true; one of three basic control constructs in structured programming.

Structured Programming · **Structured programming** is a way of writing program code that simplifies control paths so that programs can be easily understood and modified by others. A structured program uses only three basic control constructs, or patterns, for executing instructions. These are the sequence construct, the selection construct, and the repetition or iteration construct (see Figure 10.15).

The **sequence construct** consists of a series of statements that are executed in the order in which they appear, with control passing unconditionally from one statement to the next. Panel a shows a sequence construct in which a program executes statement A, then statement B.

The **selection construct** tests a condition. Depending on whether the results of that test are true or false, one of two alternative instructions will be executed. In panel b of Figure 10.15, a selection construct tests condition D. If D is true, statement E is executed. If D is false, statement F is executed. Then control passes to the next program statement.

The **repetition construct** repeats an instruction as long as the results of a conditional test are true. In panel c of Figure 10.15, statement H will be executed as long as condition G is true. Once G is found false, H is skipped and control passes to the next program statement.

Proponents of structured programming claim that any program can be written using one or a combination of these control constructs. There is a single entry and exit point for each construct so that the path of the program logic remains clear.

Figure 10.15

The Three Constructs of Structured Programming: Sequence, Selection, and Repetition

These three constructs, or patterns for executing instructions, are the building blocks of structured computer programs. Panel a shows the sequence construct, a series of statements that are executed in the order in which they occur. Panel b is the selection construct, which tests a given condition and then branches to one of two possible alternatives ("true" or "false"), depending on the outcome of the test. The repetition construct, Panel c, repeats an instruction as long as the outcome of a test is "true."

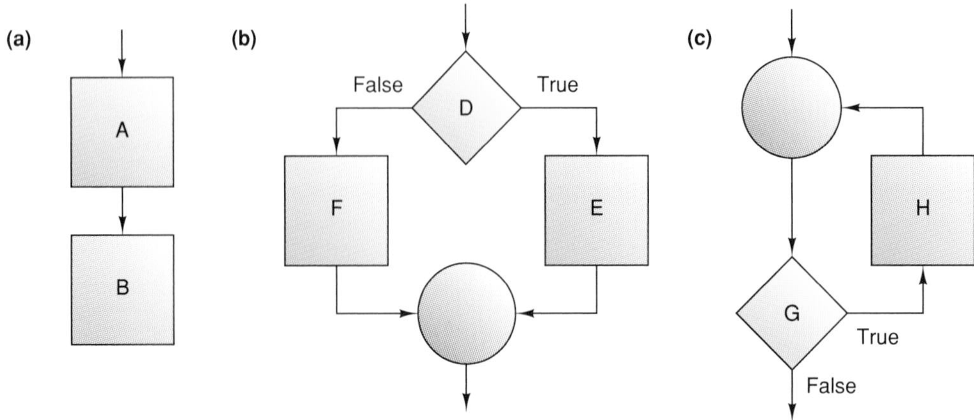

FOCUS ON *Technology*

OOPS: Object-Oriented Programming Software

American President Cos., Ltd., the Oakland, California, shipper, had an ambitious goal in 1984: doubling its trans-Pacific volume in five years. To do that required access to vast amounts of data: month-by-month figures for each commodity being shipped to different regions in the Pacific Rim. The company's computers were not up to the task. As for the software that would be needed to manipulate the data, that could have taken years to create.

The dilemma was resolved in early 1986 with a $250,000 purchase from Metaphor Computer Systems built around a new style of computation called object-oriented programming. Metaphor sells the software tools that make this kind of programming possible.

With Metaphor's workstations in hand, American President's data processing department was able to concoct custom software in a fraction of the time that it would have taken with traditional programming techniques. According to a department manager, the programming time for one market share report was cut from seven months to seven weeks.

Object-oriented programming software (OOPS) has been around for a number of years. The idea goes back to the computer language Smalltalk, developed by Xerox PARC (Palo Alto Research Center) scientists in the early 1980s. Now OOPS is finding a number of applications. The operating system on Steven Jobs' Next computer is, in part, object-oriented. IBM has begun to sell a version of its Personal System/2 personal computer with Metaphor software.

The advantage of OOPS is that it turns software writers from weavers into quiltmakers. Using OOPS, programmers produce programs by stitching together prefabricated modules—"objects"—instead of laboriously weaving threads every time someone orders up a new coverlet.

In the broadest sense, modular programming has always been the best kind of programming. You conceptually divide the problem into separate and self-contained tasks, or modules, and then write a program for each task. One module may handle the way a customer order is flashed on a screen, another how it is stored in a database, another how it gets printed on paper. The idea is to make it possible to make adjustments to one module without having to redesign them all. Also, later programmers can build on your work by borrowing some of your modules.

The drawback is that an application created using OOPS is slower than an identical application written in a conventional computer language. Because boxes are hierarchical, the object-oriented program ends up being larger—hence, it takes longer to run on a computer. Sacrificing the running speed of a computer program to get more speed out of a programming department makes perfect sense these days, however. Hardware is cheap. Programmers are expensive.

Source: Adapted from Julie Pitta, "OOPS," *Forbes,* March 19, 1990, pp. 162, 164. Adapted by permission of Forbes Magazine.

Structured analysis and design embody a more traditional approach to developing software, which treats data and procedures as independent components. A separate programming procedure must be written every time someone wants to take an action on a particular piece of data. Newer approaches to designing software, such as object-oriented programming, do not use such distinctions.

Object-oriented programming departs from traditional software design practices by combining data and the specific procedures that operate on those data into one "object." The object combines data and program code. Instead of passing data to procedures, programs send a message for an object to perform a procedure that is already embedded into it. For example, an object-oriented financial application might have Customer objects sending debit and credit messages to Account objects.

An object's data are hidden from other parts of the program and can be manipulated only from inside the object. Each object is thus an independent software building block that can be used in many different systems without changing the program code. Object-oriented programming is expected to reduce the time and cost of writing software by producing reusable program code or software "chips" that can be reused in other related systems. The Focus on Technology discusses the characteristics of object-oriented programming in more detail.

Figure 10.16

Program Flowchart Symbols

Program flowcharts graphically document the steps that are followed in a specific computer program (as opposed to system flowcharts, which depict an entire information system). Structured program flowcharts are drawn using the three control structures of structured programming—sequence, selection, and repetition.

Process

Represents a group of instructions performing a processing function.

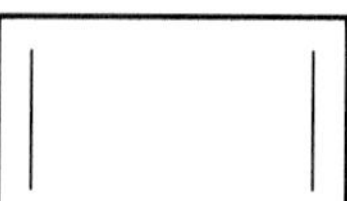

Predefined Process

Designates program instructions not detailed in the flowchart.

Input/Output

Designates movement of data into or out of a program's processing flow.

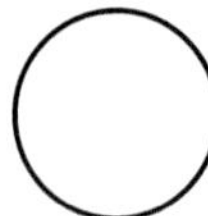

Connector

Links portions of a flowchart on the same page or separate pages.

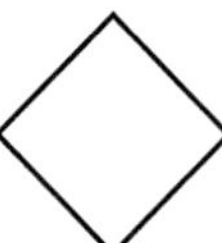

Decision

Designates a point in a program where the decision construct is used and the program flow can take one of two alternative paths.

Terminal

Indicates the beginning or end of a program.

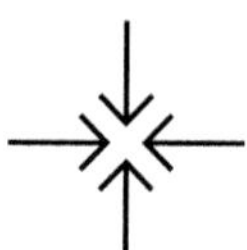

Flow Lines

Show the direction of the flow of program logic.

Documenting Program Logic · Two popular methods of documenting the logic followed by program instructions are structured program flowcharts and pseudocode. **Structured program flowcharts** use graphic symbols to depict the steps that processing must take in a specific program, using the three control structures of structured programming. Figure 10.16 explains the flowcharting symbols. Panel a of Figure 10.17 shows a structured program flowchart for a program that reads student records and prints out each record. Panel b is a second flowchart that details the steps involved in the predefined process "Process Records Routine."

Pseudocode uses plain English-like statements rather than graphic symbols or programming language to describe processing steps and logic. Once the outline for processing has been established, pseudocode can easily be translated into a programming language. Pseudocode uses the same control structures as structured programming. Panel b of Figure 10.17 shows the pseudocode for the first flowchart in panel a.

Structured program flowchart
A method of documenting the logic followed by program instructions; uses graphic symbols to depict the steps that processing must take in a specific program, using the three control structures of structured programming.

Pseudocode
A method of documenting the logic followed by program instructions in which English-like statements are used to describe processing steps and logic.

Figure 10.17

Program Flowcharts and Pseudocode for a Program that Reads and Prints Out Student Records

Somewhere in its information system, your school probably has a program that follows this logic. Panel a illustrates the program flowchart showing the sequence of instructions for a program that reads student records and then prints them out. Notice that there is a predefined process, Process Records Routine. To the right is another flowchart that represents the steps followed in Process Records Routine. Panel b shows the pseudocode statements that describe the logic in the first flowchart. Pseudocode is not a computer language itself, but it can easily be translated into a programming language.

(a) Flowcharts

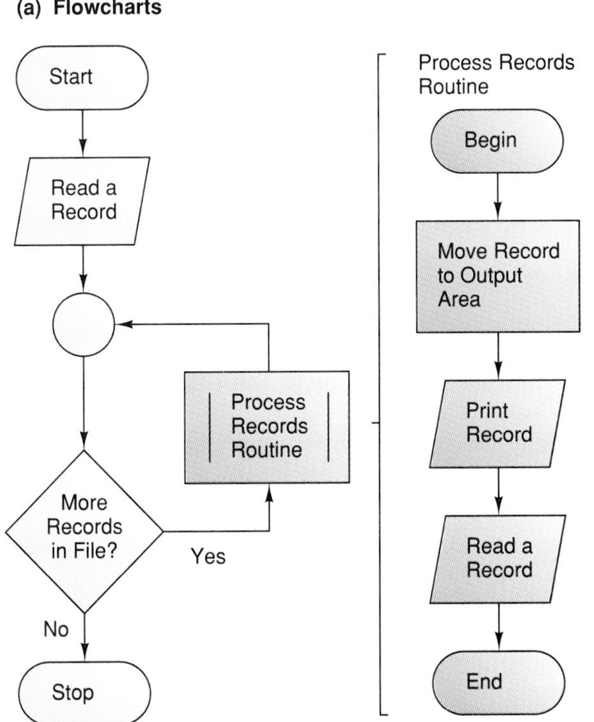

(b) Pseudocode

```
Start
Read a record
DOWHILE more records in file
   Perform Process Records Routine
ENDDO
Stop
```

FOCUS ON *People*

CASE Training Must Begin before Tools Are Installed

For organizations that want to obtain bottom-line results from the use of computer-aided software engineering (CASE), the formal training of systems analysts and programmers in the use of the tools is only the tip of the CASE training iceberg. Developing a standard environment of techniques and methodologies related to the CASE tools you plan to use, and training your staff within that environment, must precede the training of your staff on the actual tools if your investment is to be more than just shelfware.

Companies that look to CASE tools for a quick, low-cost fix to applications backlogs will end up with a negative return on their investment, which can be considerable. The price of a code-generator system can exceed $200,000, not including front-end software and installation and support costs.

To avoid a loss on the investment in CASE, companies must be committed to adequate planning and training. Creating a procedural environment for CASE tools can be a lengthy process—in some instances, it can take up to two years—and it is expensive. Experienced users estimate that for every dollar spent on the tools, you should be prepared to spend $2 on standardization and training.

A measure of how extensive and long-lasting the commitment to CASE training can be is provided by the program for more than 400 information systems professionals now under way at Kodak Park, the Rochester, New York, photographic film and paper production facility of Eastman Kodak Company.

Margaret A. Tomczak, director of the Kodak Park software engineering technology unit, said her unit began a comprehensive training and support program two years ago for each of two tools and methodologies it uses for application design and project management. In addition, she said she expects to select reengineering software to modify existing applications, which will require an additional training sequence. Training, carried out on-site in a classroom with ten workstations, consists of both lectures and hands-on instruction, Tomczak said.

Training in specific tools must initially come from the vendors. Consultants will be required first to train your staff in CASE techniques.

However, Jerrold M. Grochow, vice-president of American Management Systems, Inc., in Arlington, Virginia, says, "In the long run, training should be done by

Source: Mike Feuche, "CASE Training Must Begin before Tools Are Installed," *MIS Week*, February 19, 1990, p. 30.

Computer-Aided Software Engineering

Special software has been developed to automate the generation of data flow diagrams, system flowcharts, data dictionaries, program code, and other tasks in the systems development process so that systems can be fashioned much more rapidly and efficiently. The automation of methodologies for software and systems development is called computer-aided software engineering, or CASE. Many different kinds of CASE tools are commercially available. The most sophisticated integrate multiple tasks, such as linking a description of a data element in a data dictionary to all data flow diagrams or process specifications that use this piece of data. More detail on CASE can be found in the Focus on People.

knowledgeable internal personnel. This reduces training costs but, more importantly, these individuals can use examples from within the organization, which are going to make a lot more sense to the people they train."

Training suppliers generally recommend that user companies send only a limited number of people to their courses. Afterward, these individuals can serve as on-site resources.

Among potential trainees two questions inevitably come up whenever a training program is organized: "Will I lose my job?" followed by "When do I get started?"

Carol Thomas, systems analyst at Overland Park, Kansas-based United Data Services, the programming arm of United Telecom, said that when her organization standardized on an application generator in 1988, she had to figure out how to address disquieting rumors among her 400 programmers that their jobs would be made obsolete by the new tools. "The solution which we found effective," she said, "was to hold short presentations, about 30 minutes in length, to reassure small groups of programmers about their jobs, explain how CASE could help them, and get them involved from the beginning."

Once the staff became accustomed to the idea of using CASE tools, there was a great rush of volunteers eager to learn the coming thing. This was resolved by training people only on an as-needed basis. Otherwise, it was believed that individuals who had been trained in the new tools but did not use the tools right away would lose their new skills.

Companies that have implemented CASE suggest the following guidelines for CASE training:

- Plan a substantial budget for training—approximately two dollars for every dollar spent on the tools.
- Create a CASE environment based on standard procedures and methodologies, and acclimate your staff to that environment prior to introducing the tools.
- Keep programmers informed when you are installing a new CASE tool to prevent "FUD."
- Limit on-site classes to about 15 people at one time and install an adequate number of workstations for hands-on training in on-site classrooms or laboratories.
- Develop your own internal training resources by sending one or two staff members to external courses; these staffers can then work with the rest of your staff.
- Use vendor personnel to work alongside your staff and get them up to speed on initial CASE projects.
- Plan overview courses for corporate and end-user department management to inform them of what their expectations from CASE should be.

Summary

- One cannot successfully build an information system without first understanding a problem, describing it, and designing a solution using the five-step approach to problem solving introduced in the text.
- Systems analysis is the study and analysis of problems of existing information systems and the identification of the requirements for their solution.

- Systems design shows how to realize a solution to a problem requiring an information system application by providing a detailed blueprint of the technical, organizational, and people components for a system and indicating how they fit together.
- If a problem does not involve an information system application, the implementation of the solution would still require changes in procedures, management, and personnel.
- Data flow diagrams are most useful for documenting the logical design of an information system. They show how data flow to, from, and within an information system and the various processes that transform those data.
- A data dictionary is used in solution design to define and describe each piece of data and the data groupings used in information systems.
- System flowcharts document the sequence of processing steps that take place in an entire system. They are most useful for physical design, in which they show the sequence of the flow of data and the files used by each processing step.
- Structured design and structured programming are software design principles that promote software with a simple, clear structure that is easy to follow and maintain.
- Structured design organizes a program into a hierarchy of modules from the top down, with each module performing a limited number of functions.
- Structured programming is a method of writing programs using only three basic control constructs: sequence, selection, and repetition.

Key Terms

Systems analysis
Systems design
Application solution
Data flow diagram
Data flow
Process specification
System flowchart
Structured design
Module
Top-down design
Structured programming
Sequence construct
Selection construct
Repetition construct
Structured program flowchart
Pseudocode

Review Questions

1. What is the difference between systems analysis and systems design? How are they related to the general model of problem solving introduced in this text?
2. List three details that must be considered in the logical design specifications for each of the six information system components (input, processing, output, database, procedures, controls).
3. Name two physical design options for each of the six information system components.

4. Why should the solution to an application problem be worked out before hardware and software are considered?
5. How can you distinguish between a problem that requires an information system application solution and one that does not?
6. What is a data flow diagram? How is it used in systems analysis and design?
7. What is a data dictionary? How is it used in systems analysis and design?
8. What is a system flowchart? How is it used in systems analysis and design?
9. Define structured design and structured programming. How do they contribute to software design?
10. Name and describe the three basic control structures in structured programming.
11. Describe how each of the following is used in software development: structure charts, structured program flowcharts, and pseudocode.

Discussion Questions

1. How would you decide whether an information system application should be processed on a microcomputer? How would you decide whether an application should be processed with spreadsheet or database software?

2. Why is programming such a small part of the development of an information system?

3. Why must procedures be considered in solution design as well as in hardware and software?

Problem-Solving Exercises

1. Develop a context data flow diagram and a high-level system flowchart to document the solution design for North Lake Bank.

2. Use several levels of data flow diagrams, a data dictionary, and a system flowchart to document the solution design for partnership allocation at Haskell, Simpson, and Porter. Your data dictionary need not contain all of the data elements in the solution, but it should contain a description of at least one individual data element and one data flow.

3. Use a structured program flowchart to document a program that reads a student file and outputs a report of names of students qualifying for the dean's list. To qualify, students must have a grade point average of at least 3.5. Then document the same program using pseudocode.

Problem-Solving Case

Solution Design Projects

Grand Union Supermarket

The Grand Union Supermarket in Croton-on-Hudson, New York, is one of the smaller, older facilities of this nationwide chain. Profit margins in the supermarket business are only 1 to 2 percent of gross sales. This particular branch is fighting against stiff competition from new Shoprite and Food Emporium markets several miles away. It has been able to survive on much lower sales volumes than its competitors by keeping operating costs to a bare minimum and specializing in fresh fruits, vegetables, baked goods, and natural beef for an upscale local village clientele.

Most products, with the exception of fresh produce, are marked with a price tag. The price of fruits and vegetables is calculated by weighing them and multiplying the weight by the cost of each item per pound. The cost of fresh produce changes daily and is posted above each cash register on a chart. However, some produce items, such as Idaho potatoes, are marked with a product code number, such as 547. The cashier at the checkout counter must consult the produce chart for the price of code 547. Sometimes the cashier rings up $5.47 instead. Grand Union has had trouble finding enough cashiers lately, and lines have been growing longer.

What is Grand Union's problem? How can it be solved?

The Off-Campus Housing Office

Finger Lakes University in upstate New York does not have sufficient dormitory space to house all of its liberal arts, agricultural school, and graduate students. It uses a lottery system to determine which students can live in dorm rooms and which must find housing elsewhere. About half of Finger Lakes' students seek off-campus housing.

The ultimate responsibility for locating suitable housing rests with each student, but Finger Lakes offers assistance through its Off-Campus Housing Office (OCHO). OCHO maintains bulletin board listings of available housing and provides legal counseling services for students and landlords with questions about their leases.

Only 10 percent of OCHO's resources are devoted to legal services. Its most critical function is listing available housing in the surrounding area. Some landlords advertise in local newspapers, but virtually all openings flow through OCHO.

Landlords fill out an OCHO card describing the type of lodging they have available. This card is then placed on a bulletin board. Students review the bulletin board listings and copy down those of greatest interest. Then they call the landlords for appointments to view the rooms.

Cards are often put up haphazardly on the wrong bulletin board. Occasionally, a student will pull a card off to prevent other students from learning of the opening. Both students and landlords complain that listings remain posted several months after they have been filled. OCHO has no idea how many students actually use its services or the amount of student housing available. It does know, however, that around the time of the on-campus dormitory lottery, its office is jammed to capacity, to the point of being dangerously overcrowded, and students have difficulty seeing the bulletin board.

What is the problem at OCHO? How can it be solved? If an application solution is required, develop a logical model for the solution and determine whether it is a personal computer, database, or mainframe application. If the application can be developed on a personal computer, develop it using spreadsheet or database software, whichever is more appropriate. Justify your design and your decision. Document your solution design using data flow diagrams, the data dictionary, and a system flowchart.

Video-Save Mail-Order Cassettes

James and Susan Branson found that they could make money in their own home by selling videocassette tapes through the mail at discount prices. They can sell a cassette that would normally retail for $29.95 at the video store for $10.00 less because they have almost no overhead expenses. Their inventory is stored in their garage and family room, and Susan Branson uses a home office with a WATS line to answer telephone orders. Many orders are also placed by mail as well.

The Bransons started out by advertising in several popular television and movie magazines. Now that they have a customer base of over 3,000, they would like to change their marketing strategy. Video-Save has an inventory of over 500 titles. Its full-color catalog with a description of each tape initially cost $15,000 to print and mail. The Bransons would like to find a more inexpensive way to contact customers, such as an occasional announcement of new releases or a special mailing directed to special interest group—for example, purchasers of "self-help" tapes. They want to avoid expensive catalog mailings that do not bring in sales.

The Bransons recently purchased a personal computer and printer with word processing, spreadsheet, and database software, but they are not sure what to do next. They do not need an elaborate accounts receivable system because all orders must be prepaid. Video-Save receives approximately 18 orders a day. Mrs. Branson uses preprinted invoice forms and types out the customer's name, address, charge card number, product number, quantity, title (product description), unit cost, shipping cost, and total cost of each order. The product numbers consist of five characters, with the first character designating the type of video: A designates adult-only videos; C, children's videos; S, sports videos; H, self-help videos; F, foreign films; and G, dramas or comedies of general interest. The Bransons maintain their customer list on index cards and have used a direct mail service to generate mailing labels for their catalogs and announcements.

Analyze the problem(s) at Video-Save. If an application solution is required, develop a logical model for the solution and determine whether it is a personal computer spreadsheet, personal computer database, or mainframe application. If the application can be developed on a personal computer, develop the application using spreadsheet or database software, whichever is more appropriate. Justify your design and your decision. Document your solution design using data flow diagrams, the data dictionary, and a system flowchart.

H. V. Construction Company

Real estate development is a very high-risk method of investment, but one in which rewards can be substantial. In addition to a strong vision of a project, correct timing and accurate profit calculations are essential. Moreover, without adequate bank financing at supportable interest rates, a project will never be built.

The real estate boom of the early 1980s coupled with rising interest rates left the real estate market very volatile. Costs of building materials and land spiraled upward, while mounting mortgage rates, an uncertain economy, and high levels of consumer debt made the demand for housing much more uncertain.

Under such conditions, the H. V. Construction Company, a small general contracting firm, has been moving into development of residential townhouse complexes. H.V. hopes to combine its track record for quality construction with competitive pricing. To do this, the company tries to minimize overhead by subcontracting out most of the construction work and maintaining a small office with a skeleton staff. The permanent staff consists of only the owner, a secretary, a carpenter/superintendent, an additional carpenter, a general utility man, and a laborer.

H. V.'s owner, Harold Larson, feels this is the only way his company can compete with the development giants. But he finds himself overwhelmed, since he must find prospective properties, complete all financial calculations, prepare all proposal and correspondence documents, and shop around various banks for project financing. At present, he prepares all of his project estimates with a hand-held calculator. Any changes in relevant costs that alter the profitability of a project, such as interest rates, must be changed manually and retabulated.

Larson also knows that preparing a good bid is critical for survival. A sound estimate has double-edged objectives: it must be low and solid enough that the construction company will be awarded the job yet provide enough extra that the company can make a profit from the contract. If the bid fails on one or the other count, the company will soon be out of business. There is no margin for error. In bidding a job, there is no prize for second place. The company is either awarded the contract or it isn't.

The formula for a successful bid requires many ingredients: labor requirements, current labor rates, materials required and material costs, and total labor-hours anticipated. The cost of each component shifts constantly. When labor rates and prices from suppliers are volatile, the longer a company can wait before submitting its estimate, the better its chances are of being the low bidder.

The following cost components must be considered:

- Up-front costs: Architect, developed lot, and legal and accounting.
- Sales and marketing.

- Total number of units.
- Estimated labor-hours per unit.
- Labor costs per hour.
- Financing costs: Loan principal, interest rate, and financing period.
- Profit margin.

The company has an ATT 6300 (XT class) personal computer with a 20-megabyte hard disk drive and an Epson FX-286 wide column NLQ printer. H. V. uses it primarily for word processing, and it has been a very cost-effective tool for generating correspondence and proposals.

Analyze the problem(s) at H. V. Construction Company. If an application solution is required, develop a logical model for the solution and determine whether it is a personal computer spreadsheet, personal computer database, or mainframe application. If the application can be developed on a personal computer, develop the application using spreadsheet or database software, whichever is more appropriate. Justify your design and your decision. Document your solution design using data flow diagrams, a data dictionary, and a system flowchart.

C H A P T E R · E L E V E N

Alternative Approaches to Information System Solutions

Chapter Outline

11.1 Introduction

11.2 The Traditional Systems Life Cycle
- The Relationship of the Life Cycle to Problem Solving
- Problems with the Traditional Life Cycle
- Alternatives to the Life Cycle

11.3 The Prototyping Alternative
- Steps in Prototyping
- When to Use Prototyping
- Limitations of Prototyping

11.4 Developing Solutions with Software Packages
- Advantages of Packages
- Packages and the Solution Design Process
- Disadvantages of Packages

11.5 Fourth-Generation Development
- Fourth-Generation Solution Design
- Fourth-Generation Software Tools
- Disadvantages of Fourth-Generation Development
- Information Centers

11.6 Leading-Edge Application: On-Demand Mortgage Reports for Merrill Lynch Brokers

Learning Objectives

After reading and studying this chapter, you will:

1. Be able to apply the most important methodologies for designing information system solutions: the traditional systems life cycle, prototyping, the use of software packages, and fourth-generation development.
2. Understand the relationship of each design methodology to the core problem-solving process.
3. Know the steps and processes of each design methodology.
4. Be aware of the kinds of problems for which each design methodology is most appropriate.
5. Know the roles assigned to business specialists and technical specialists in each of the design methodologies.
6. Understand the strengths and limitations of each design methodology.

"Fast-Tracking" Solution Design

Ken Robertson, a director with the LGS Group, Inc. in Vancouver, British Columbia, recently participated in a "fast-track" project to design and build a management reporting and tracking system. This system was quite complex, involving 110 on-line screens, 55 physical data tables in a relational database, and 7 batch reports. Using fast-tracking techniques, Robertson's team completed the system's design in 8 man-months. The system was actually built in 20 man-months. Testing and implementation took another 5 man-months. For a system this size, progress was remarkably rapid.

Robertson believes that the fast-tracking approach expedites solution design because it focuses on a 90 percent solution and then "backfills" the remaining 10 percent. Traditional methodologies, on the other hand, insist on a 100 percent solution design right away. A person using the traditional systems-building approach would interview everyone who had anything to do with the new system and list 100 percent of the requirements for the system, a process that normally takes from two to eight weeks. In a few sessions with key users, Robertson's group was able to specify 90 percent of the solution requirements. The remaining 10 percent were determined during the logical design process itself.

The group used IBM's Cross System Product to create prototypes, or "mock-ups," of the screens and then built program code around these models. Robertson believes that targeting 90 percent of information requirements and filling in the missing pieces later can deliver the same quality solution as conventional methods with much greater speed.

Source: Ken Robertson, "Application Building on the Fast Track," *Computing Canada,* February 16, 1989.

Fast tracking is one of several alternative methodologies that can be used for designing information system solutions. Different problems call for different rules, procedures, and philosophies for building information systems.

11.1 Introduction

The actual development of an information system solution can take many paths. The solution may require a large central mainframe connecting 20,000 people or a laptop personal computer, elaborate programming and testing or a simple word processing and graphics package. The problem to be solved may be fully structured or only semistructured. A structured problem is one for which the solution is repetitive, is routine, and involves a definite procedure that can be used each time the same problem is encountered. For a semistructured problem, only parts of the problem have a clear-cut answer, provided by a definite procedure. Depending on the size, scope, complexity, and characteristics of the firm, different kinds of systems require different approaches to put them in place.

Some methodologies entail a more formal approach to solution design than others. Some call for clearly demarcated roles of business and technical specialists; others blur this distinction. What is common to all of them is the core problem-solving methodology described in the preceding chapter.

11.2 The Traditional Systems Life Cycle

Traditional systems life cycle The oldest methodology for building an information system; consists of six stages (project definition, systems study, design, programming, installation, and postimplementation) that must be completed sequentially.

The oldest methodology for building an information system is called the **traditional systems life cycle.** This method of developing systems originated with large operational systems in the 1950s and is still the predominant method for building large and medium mainframe-based systems today.

The "life cycle" metaphor partitions the development of a system into a formal set of stages, in much the same way as the life cycle of a human being or other organism can be divided into stages—a beginning, middle, and end. The systems life cycle has six stages, however:

1. Project definition
2. Systems study

3. Design
4. Programming
5. Installation
6. Postimplementation

Each stage is assigned activities that must be completed before the next stage can begin. Thus the system must be developed sequentially, stage by stage. Formal sign-offs, or agreements between technical staff and business specialists, are required to mark the completion of each stage.

Another characteristic of life cycle methodology is its clear-cut and formal division of labor between business specialists and technical specialists. Much of the solution design is relegated to technical staff such as professional systems analysts and programmers. Systems analysts are responsible for the analysis of problems in existing systems and for solution design specifications. Programmers are responsible for coding and testing the software components of a system. Both analysts and programmers use information and feedback provided by business specialists to guide their work, but the business specialists play a relatively passive role.

The Relationship of the Life Cycle Stages to Problem Solving

The stages of the life cycle correspond to some degree to the steps in our problem-solving methodology. Figure 11.1 illustrates the stages of the life cycle, the corresponding steps in problem solving, and the appropriate division of labor between business and technical specialists throughout the cycle. Notice that there is not always a one-to-one correlation between stages in problem solving and the systems life cycle, but they follow a similar process. The **project definition** stage of the life cycle investigates whether a problem actually exists and whether it requires further analysis and research. If so, a formal project to build a new information system or modify an existing system will be initiated. Thus this stage incorporates some aspects of our first step in problem solving.

The **systems study** stage incorporates some of the first step of problem analysis as well as the next two steps. Activities during this stage focus on describing and analyzing problems of existing systems, specifying solution objectives, describing potential solutions, and evaluating various solution alternatives. Constraints on solutions and the feasibility of each solution alternative are examined.

All of the information gathered from studying existing systems and interviewing business specialists will be used to specify information requirements. A systems solution must identify who needs what information, where, when, and how. The requirements must be specified in detail, down to the last piece of data, and must consider organizational procedures and constraints as well as hardware, software, and data.

It is important to emphasize that an information system solution will not work unless it is built around the correct set of requirements. If it is not, the system will have to be revised or discarded, often with a great waste of time and money. Perhaps the most difficult aspect of system building is capturing complex information needs when there are disagreements among users, poorly defined procedures, and data that are not clearly understood.

Project definition
The process of investigating a perceived problem to determine whether a problem actually exists and, if so, whether it requires further analysis and research; the first stage of the traditional systems life cycle.

Systems study
The process of describing and analyzing problems of existing systems, specifying solution objectives, describing potential solutions, and evaluating various solution alternatives; the second stage of the traditional systems life cycle.

Figure 11.1

The Systems Development Life Cycle

The traditional methodology for building an information system is the systems development life cycle, so called because it divides the process into a series of stages (similar to the life cycle of a human being, for instance). These stages correspond to the steps in the five-step problem-solving process that we discussed in earlier chapters. As this diagram shows, the systems life cycle can be a very formal process. Each step of the cycle requires certain tasks from both business and technical specialists, although with this approach, business specialists play a relatively passive role.

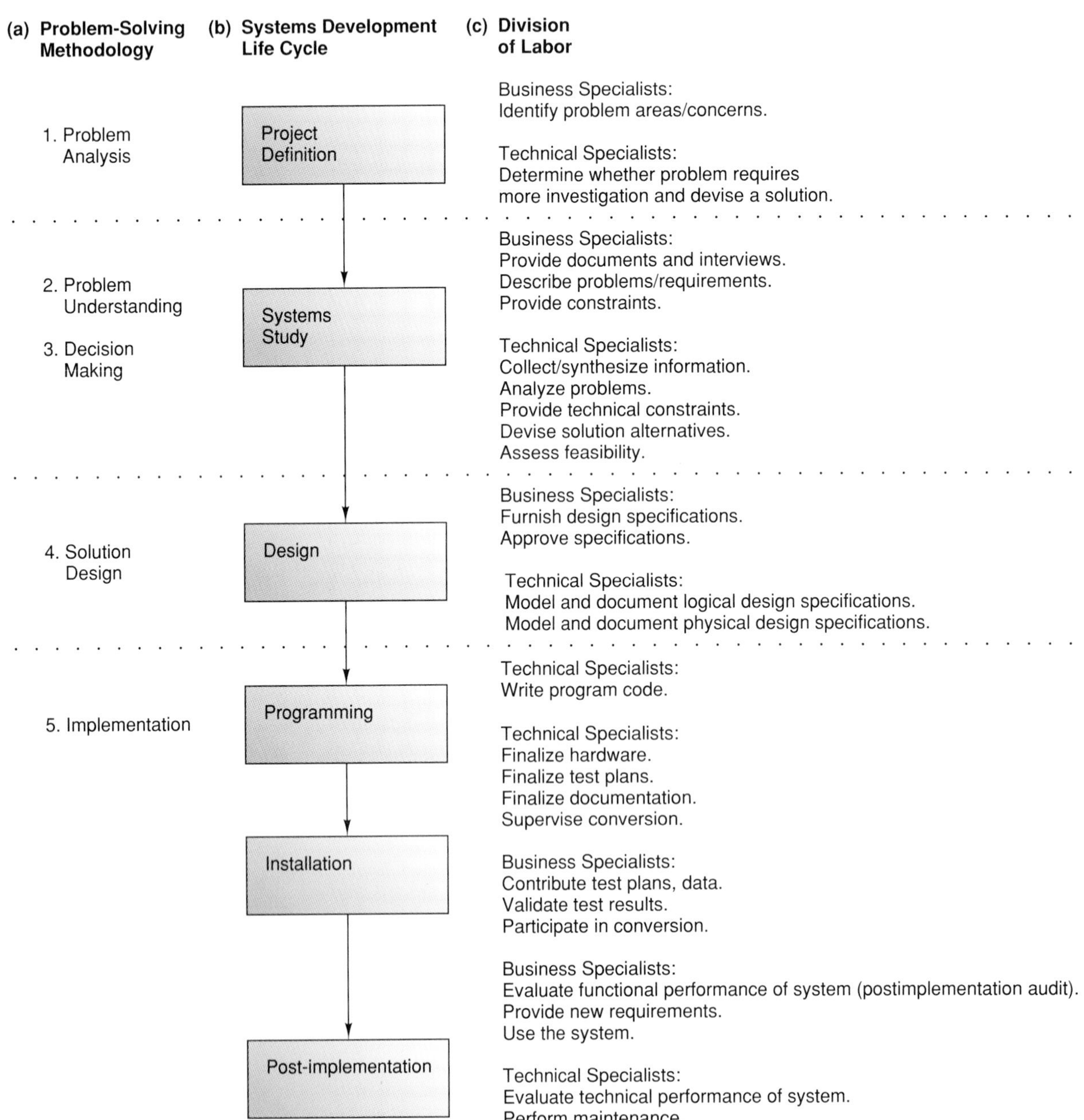
(a) Problem-Solving Methodology
(b) Systems Development Life Cycle
(c) Division of Labor
1. Problem Analysis
Project Definition
Business Specialists:
Identify problem areas/concerns.
Technical Specialists:
Determine whether problem requires more investigation and devise a solution.
2. Problem Understanding
3. Decision Making
Systems Study
Business Specialists:
Provide documents and interviews.
Describe problems/requirements.
Provide constraints.
Technical Specialists:
Collect/synthesize information.
Analyze problems.
Provide technical constraints.
Devise solution alternatives.
Assess feasibility.
4. Solution Design
Design
Business Specialists:
Furnish design specifications.
Approve specifications.
Technical Specialists:
Model and document logical design specifications.
Model and document physical design specifications.
5. Implementation
Programming
Technical Specialists:
Write program code.
Technical Specialists:
Finalize hardware.
Finalize test plans.
Finalize documentation.
Supervise conversion.
Installation
Business Specialists:
Contribute test plans, data.
Validate test results.
Participate in conversion.
Business Specialists:
Evaluate functional performance of system (postimplementation audit).
Provide new requirements.
Use the system.
Post-implementation
Technical Specialists:
Evaluate technical performance of system.
Perform maintenance.

Once requirements have been captured, the design stage can proceed. At this point, logical design specifications are generated, usually with voluminous formal documentation and paperwork. Design and documentation tools such as the data flow diagram, data dictionary, and system flowchart introduced in Chapter 10 are likely to be employed, because the life cycle puts so much emphasis on detailed specifications and paperwork. Business specialists and technical staff must review and approve these documents before physical design and programming can begin.

During the programming stage, detailed design specifications for files, processes, reports, and input transactions are translated into software for the proposed information system. Technical specialists will write customized program code using a conventional programming language, such as COBOL, FORTRAN, or a high-productivity fourth-generation language.

There is a widespread misconception that programming is the focal point of building an information system. In fact, the programming stage typically occupies only 10 percent of the system development effort. The bulk of time and resources are spent investigating and analyzing the problem, generating design specifications, and testing and installing the system.

During the installation stage, the software is tested to make sure it performs properly from both a technical and functional, or business, standpoint, and the old system is converted to the new one. Business and technical specialists are trained to use the new system. The activities surrounding programming, testing, conversion, and training correspond to the fifth and last step of our problem-solving methodology.

The systems life cycle also includes a stage for using and evaluating a system after it is installed. This is called the **postimplementation** stage. When a system is actually used on a day-to-day basis as the system of record, it is in production. At this point, it will be evaluated by both business and technical specialists to determine if the solution objectives specified earlier have been met. This formal evaluation is called the post-implementation audit.

The results of the audit may call for changes in hardware, software, procedures, or documentation to fine-tune the system. In addition, systems may have to be modified over the years to meet new information requirements or increase processing efficiency. Such changes to systems after they are in production are called maintenance. As time goes on, an information system may require increasing amounts of maintenance to continue meeting solution objectives. When maintenance becomes overwhelming, the system is usually considered to have come to the end of its useful lifespan. The problem-solving process initiates a call for a completely new system.

The bulk of time and resources needed to build an information system is not spent programming. When William M. Mercer, Inc. was hired by Bechtel Group, Inc., one of the world's largest multinational engineering firms, to evaluate its employee benefits program, the team analyzed and evaluated existing benefits and alternatives; obtained management's opinion on cost and administrative concerns and employees' reaction to the existing plan; and designed several alternative plans and used a computer system to project costs and administration. After Bechtel selected its final plan, Mercer used its enrollment and administration computer system to implement it.

Source: © Steve Chenn/Westlight.

Postimplementation
The use and evaluation of a new system after it is installed; the last stage of the traditional systems life cycle.

Problems with the Traditional Life Cycle

Large mainframe- or minicomputer-based systems and systems with highly complex, technical requirements will continue to use the traditional life cycle methodology. But 90 percent of the applications of the 1990s will be based on workstations and personal computers. Generating the paperwork and voluminous specifications and sign-off documents for life cycle methodology is very time-consuming and costly and may delay the installation of a system for several years.

Moreover, this approach may not be appropriate for simpler, less structured, and more individualized applications such as personal computer workstations or systems for which there are no well-defined models or procedures. The life cycle methodology is rather rigid and inflexible. Volumes of new documents must be generated and steps repeated if requirements and specifications have to be revised. Consequently, the methodology encourages freezing of specifications early in the development process. If a system solution cannot be visualized immediately—as is often the case with decision-oriented applications (see Chapter 15)—this methodology will not help.

Many firms have a two- to three-year backlog of application solutions requested by business specialists that cannot be implemented because of shortages of time, financial resources, and data processing personnel. Alternative system-building approaches focus on ways of reducing the time, cost, and inefficiencies of solution design.

Alternatives to the Life Cycle

There are other ways of building information systems that can overcome some of the limitations of the life cycle. They too are founded on the problem-solving methodology we have outlined. However, the means of establishing requirements, developing software, and finalizing the system solution differ from the traditional life cycle, and business specialists play a much larger role in the solution design process. The usefulness of alternative solution design approaches depends on the nature of the information system solution and the level of uncertainty in establishing information requirements. The three most important alternatives to the traditional life cycle are prototyping, the use of software packages, and fourth-generation development.

Prototyping
Building an experimental, or preliminary, system or part of a system for business specialists to try out and evaluate.

Prototyping entails building an experimental system or part of a system quickly and cheaply so that business specialists can evaluate it. As users interact with this prototype, they get a better idea of what their needs are, and the features of the final system can be adapted accordingly.

Application software packages are an alternative to writing software programs and developing a custom system internally. Instead, a firm can buy a software package in which all of the programs have already been written and tested and all of the input and output forms and screens have been designed. Software packages are most appropriate when the information system solution is one required by many organizations, and software packages to meet such needs are on the market. Software packages may present other problems, however, as the Focus on People explains.

Fourth-generation development
The construction of information systems with little or no formal assistance from technical specialists; useful for smaller, informal systems and personal computer applications.

Fourth-generation development promotes the development of information systems with little or no formal assistance from technical specialists. This approach is useful for smaller informal systems and for personal computer applications such as desktop file management or graphics applications. Much of the solution design process can be performed by business specialists themselves. When business specialists understand the requirements, they can design their own information system solutions with user-friendly fourth-generation software tools.

FOCUS ON *People*

Consumers, Legislators, and Publishers Consider Rules to Cover Programmers

The software world has been rocked by an unprecedented series of tremors in the last year. Bugs in software brought some of the biggest publishers to their knees. As a result, the software industry itself is looking for ways to make software more reliable and less vulnerable.

The problem is a very real one. A small amount of errant code can have a very large effect as software becomes more dependent on other software. The damage caused by a single bug or miscalculation grows exponentially when the data are used by hundreds of workers or by hundreds or thousands of other programs. A recently released House study said the government is risking lives and wasting billions of dollars because it is unable to ensure that its computer software operates reliably and is sufficiently debugged.

In one effort to cope with the problem, various state legislatures are considering bills that would impose criminal sanctions on individuals whose code threatens business operations and property. At the federal level, the first step has been to toughen computer crime statutes to catch malicious programmers.

Three bills are before the House of Representatives: H.R. 55, the Computer Virus Act of 1989, sponsored by Rep. Wally Herger of California; and two similar bills. Herger's bill—which has won partial support of software industry trade groups—mandates criminal penalties for anyone who "knowingly inserts into a program . . . information or commands, knowing or having reason to believe that such information or commands may cause loss, expense, or risk to health or welfare."

But the laws that have already been enacted apparently have had little effect. Part of the difficulty is proving that the programmer had a malicious motive in planting the destructive code.

Another approach has been to call for the software industry to police itself. This is not new. Since the middle of the 1980s, buyers have begun exerting pressure on the software industry to improve program quality and reliability. Today, most of the major publishers have responsible warranties, promising that applications will live up to a publisher's printed claims and be free of manufacturing defects.

But getting the software industry to set standards also presents difficulties. "If someone intentionally does something, then they should be penalized and held accountable, but not the accidental, not the erroneous," said Jerry Schneider, founder and secretary of the Association of PC User Groups. "It is possible we could evolve [a system of] certification of data processing professionals. But you always get the questions: Who does the certification, what are the standards, who affects the standards, and things like that." Schneider is urging groups such as the Software Publishers Association, Adapso, and the Windows/Presentation Manager Association to get involved in creating and promoting good programming practices.

Regardless of how well the software industry improves its programming standards, though, Schneider believes human expertise is likely to be more reliable. "When someone asks for my opinion on something, if I'm using software tools to come to that opinion, I always will check or double-check."

Source: Scott Mace, "I Swear: Consumers, Legislators, and Publishers Are Considering Establishing Rules to Cover Programmers," *Infoworld,* January 1, 1990, pp. 30, 31.

11.3 The Prototyping Alternative

A prototype is a preliminary model of a system solution for end-users to interact with and analyze. The prototype is constructed quickly and cheaply, within days or weeks, using personal computer software or fourth-generation software tools. Business specialists will then try out this experimental model to see how well it meets their requirements. In the process, they may discover new requirements they overlooked or suggest areas for improvement. The prototype is then modified, turned over to business specialists again, and enhanced over and over until it conforms exactly to what they want.

Using software to automate one of its warehouses, a large corporation establishes a prototype distribution center. Prototypes allow users to handle the experimental model, make improvements, and work out problems before the system is implemented.

Source: Margaret McCarthy, 1985/The Stock Market.

With prototyping, solution design is less formal than with the life cycle methodology. Instead of investigating and analyzing a problem in detail, prototyping quickly generates a solution design, assuming an application solution is called for. Requirements are determined dynamically as the prototype is constructed. Problem analysis, problem understanding, decision making, and solution design are rolled into one.

The prototyping approach is more explicitly iterative than traditional life cycle methodology. Unlike the traditional life cycle, which must capture the correct version of a system the first time around, prototyping encourages experimentation and repeated design changes. Prototyping is also highly interactive, with business specialists working directly with solution designs at a much earlier stage of the development process.

Compared to the traditional life cycle, prototyping calls for more intensive involvement of business specialists in the problem-solving process. Business specialists must be in close contact with the technical specialists who fashion the prototype. With fourth-generation or personal computer–based software tools, business specialists may actually design the prototype themselves. (This is discussed in more detail later in this chapter.) They will also have to make frequent decisions about further improvements each time the prototype is revised.

Steps in Prototyping

As Figure 11.2 illustrates, prototyping involves four steps, which incorporate the steps of our problem-solving methodology:

1. **Identify preliminary requirements:** A technical specialist or analyst will work briefly with the business specialist to capture a basic solution model and information needs. The process is more rapid and less formal than life cycle methodology. Several steps of solution design are consolidated into one.
2. **Develop a working prototype:** A functioning prototype will be created rapidly. It may consist of only on-line screens or reports for a proposed system or an entire system with very small files of data.
3. **Use the prototype:** The end-user works with the prototype to see how well it meets his or her needs. The user is encouraged to make recommendations for improving the prototype.

Figure 11.2

Prototyping: A Quicker Way to Develop a System

Prototyping can be faster and often cheaper than going through the more formal systems development life cycle. It involves constructing a prototype, or preliminary model, of a system aimed at solving business users' needs. The business specialists then try out this model and suggest ways to refine it. The technical specialists enhance the prototype, and the users try it again. This process continues—as shown by the repetitive construct in this diagram—until the prototype is acceptable. Only then is the final version produced.

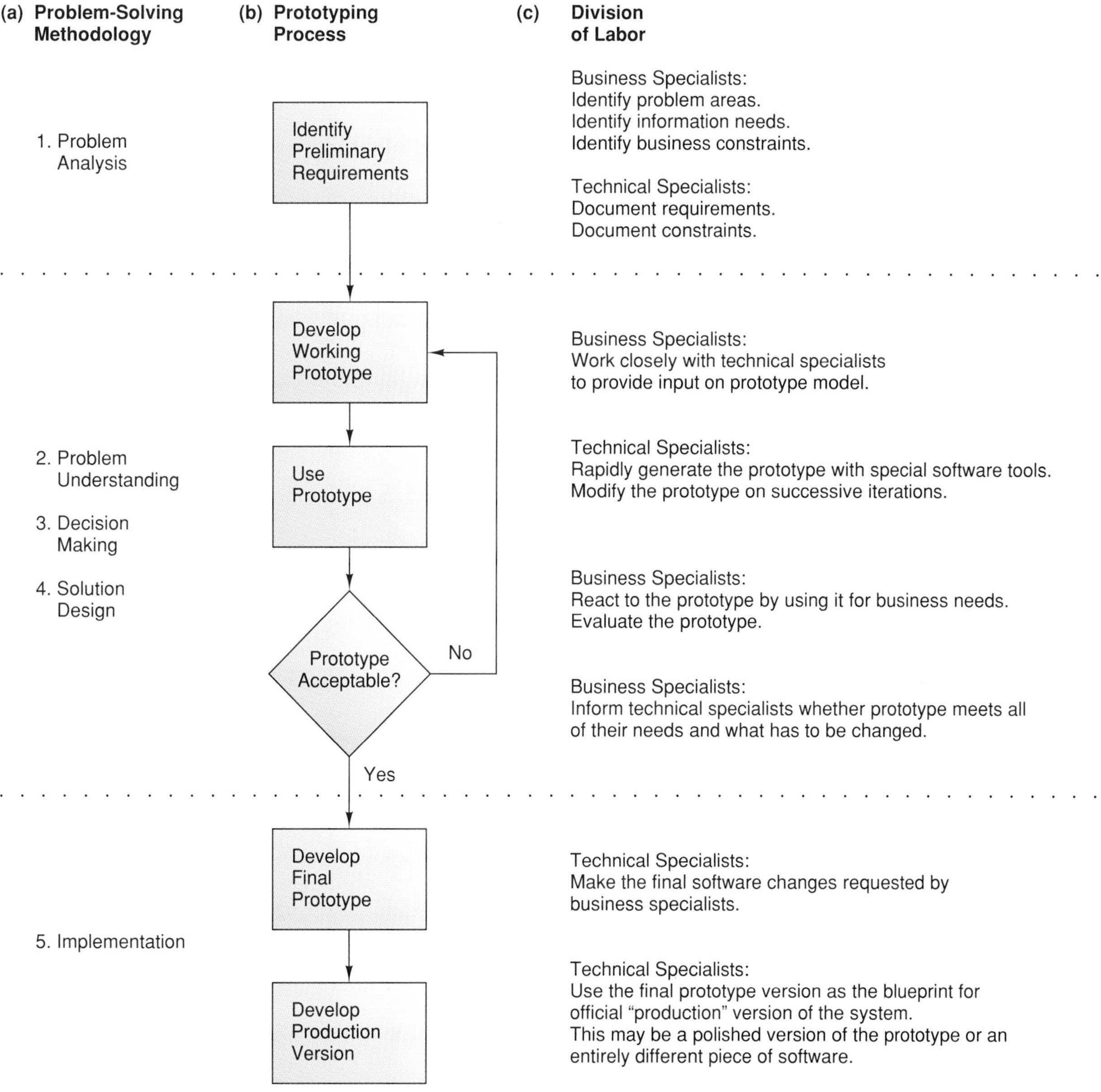

(a) Problem-Solving Methodology
(b) Prototyping Process
(c) Division of Labor
1. Problem Analysis
Identify Preliminary Requirements
Business Specialists:
Identify problem areas.
Identify information needs.
Identify business constraints.
Technical Specialists:
Document requirements.
Document constraints.
2. Problem Understanding
3. Decision Making
4. Solution Design
Develop Working Prototype
Use Prototype
Prototype Acceptable?
No
Yes
Business Specialists:
Work closely with technical specialists
to provide input on prototype model.
Technical Specialists:
Rapidly generate the prototype with special software tools.
Modify the prototype on successive iterations.
Business Specialists:
React to the prototype by using it for business needs.
Evaluate the prototype.
Business Specialists:
Inform technical specialists whether prototype meets all
of their needs and what has to be changed.
5. Implementation
Develop Final Prototype
Develop Production Version
Technical Specialists:
Make the final software changes requested by
business specialists.
Technical Specialists:
Use the final prototype version as the blueprint for
official "production" version of the system.
This may be a polished version of the prototype or an
entirely different piece of software.

4. **Revise and enhance the prototype:** On the basis of end-user recommendations, the technical specialist or analyst revises the prototype. The cycle then returns to step 3. Steps 2, 3, and 4 are repeated over and over again until the user is completely satisfied. The approved prototype furnishes the final specifications for the information system solution. Sometimes the prototype itself becomes the final version of the system.

When to Use Prototyping

Prototyping is most effective when user requirements are unclear. This is characteristic of many decision-oriented systems. Often the final system cannot be clearly visualized because the decision process itself has not been fully worked out. For example, TRW, Inc., discussed in Chapter 9, has used prototyping to accommodate both users who think "intuitively" and those who think "systematically." The intuitive thinkers typically prefer graphs, charts, and trend lines, whereas the systematic thinkers generally want information displayed quantitatively as dates, numbers, and places. The advantage of working with a prototype is that business specialists can use a working system as a mechanism for clarifying the problem-solving process, which helps them arrive at a solution rapidly.

Business interface
The parts of an information system that business specialists must interact with—for example, on-line data entry screens or reports.

Prototyping is also useful for testing the end-user or **business interface** of an information system—those parts of the system that business specialists must interact with, such as on-line transaction screens or reports. The prototype enables users to react immediately to the parts of the system they will be using. Figure 11.3 shows how a data entry screen for a human resources system was improved via prototyping. The old screen (panel a) was difficult to read and work with. Experienced human resources data entry clerks suggested ways of streamlining the arrangement of input data to create a clearer display (panel b).

One large manufacturing firm feared that a multifacility labor scheduling system could not be automated because of disparate data needs. Members from key areas of the firm then developed on-line screen layouts that would meet the needs of all of the firm's plants and operating units. With a screen generator/code generator tool, and assistance from technical staff, they found that all the company's needs could be met with just three screens.[1]

Limitations of Prototyping

Some studies have shown that prototypes that fully meet user requirements can be created in 10 to 20 percent of the time estimated for conventional development.[2] To balance the impressive advantages of this approach, however, we should note that prototyping is not suitable for certain types of information systems.

Prototyping is most effective for smaller applications. It cannot be applied easily to massive, mainframe-based systems with complex processing instructions and calculations; in those cases, the traditional life cycle methodology is more appropriate. Prototyping a large system would require partitioning so that prototypes could be developed for one part at a time.[3]

Figure 11.3

The Benefits of Prototyping: A Data Entry Screen, Before and After

One advantage of prototyping is that it encourages participation and feedback from the people who will actually be using the system to do their jobs. This can result in improvements that technical specialists, with no experience in doing those jobs, might not have considered. Here we see a data entry screen for a Human Resources system, both before (panel a) and after (panel b) prototyping. Human Resources clerks tested the screen and suggested improvements, leading to the much more readable version below.

(a) Old Screen

```
            1            2            3            4            5            6            7

                      CONSOLIDATED Corporation Personnel System
                                  Employee Profile

 Search Value: |||||||||||||||||||| |||||||||||||||||||| PEND DATE: xx/xx.

 Name:   xxxxxxxxxxxxxxxxxxxx  xxxxxxxxxxxxxxxxxxxx  x
 Employe #:    xxxxxx                     Position #:     xxxxxxx
 HR Center:    xxxxx   xxxxx              SSN #:          xxx-xx-xxxx
 Budget Cntr:  xxxxxxxx                   Admin Center:   xxxxx
 Ben Group:    xxx                        Ben Location:   xx
 Co/Pay Level: xx xxx                     Co of Origin:   xx
 Work St Loc Code:   xxx                  Site Loc:  xx  xxxxxxxxxxxxxxxxxxxx

 Addr Line 1:  xxxxxxxxxxxxxxxxxxxxxxxxx  Telephone:      xxx/xxx-xxxx
 Addr Line 2:  xxxxxxxxxxxxxxxxxxxxxxxxx  Birth Date:     xx/xx/xx
 Addr Line 3:  xxxxxxxxxxxxxxxxxxxx       High ed Lvl:    xx       xx/xx
 Zip:          xxxxx-xxxx                 Emp Status:     x
 Sex Race Code:      x  x                 AAP#:               xxxxx
 Date of Empl:       xx/xx/xx             Orig date of Hire:  xx/xx/xx
 Termination:    xx/xx/xx   Reason:  xxxxxxxxxxxxxxxxxxxxxxxxxxxxxxxxxxxxxxxxx

 |||||||||||||||||||| error message area ||||||||||||||||||||
 PF1/EMP#   PF2/EMP NAME   PF3/HRCNTR   PF4/BUDCNTR   PF5/COMP   PF6/position
 PF7/PREV   PF8/NEXT       PF9/PENDING  PF10/         PF11/      PF12/menu   CLE
```

New Screen

```
    CONSOLIDATED    Corporation Personnel System
                    Employee Profile

Search Value: |||||||||||||||||||| |||||||||||||||||||| PEND DATE: xx/xx/xx

                 Employee #:  xxxxxx                 Position #:  xx xx xxxxxxx
Name:  xxxxxxxxxxxxxxxxxxxx  xxxxxxxxxxxxxxxxxxxx  x SSNO:         xxx-xx-xxxx
    Addr Line 1:  xxxxxxxxxxxxxxxxxxxxxxxxx          Birth Date:  xx/xx/xx
    Addr Line 2:  xxxxxxxxxxxxxxxxxxxxxxxxx          Sex/Race:    x  x
    Addr Line 3:  xxxxxxxxxxxxxxxxxxxx
    Zip:          xxxxx-xxxx                         Telephone:   xxx/xxx-xxxx

Emp Status:     x         Date of Empl:  xx/xx/xx     Orig Date of Hire:  xx/xx/xx
Phys Work St:   xx        Site Loc:        xxx  xxxxxxxxxxxxxxxxxxxxxxxxx
Term Date:      xx/xx/xx  Reason:  xxxxxxxxxxxxxxxxxxxxxxxxxxxxxxxxxxxxxxxxxx

    HR Ctr:       xxxxx  xxxxx    AAP #:         xxxx       Ben Loc:      xx
    Admin Ctr:    xxxxx           Co/Pay Lvl:    xx  xxx    Ben Group:    xxx
    Budget Ctr:   xxxxxxxxxxxx    High Ed Lvl:   xx         Co of Orig:   xx

|||||||||||||||||||| error message area ||||||||||||||||||||
PF1 EMP#         PF3 HRCTR     PF7 NEXT     PF9  PENDING        PF11 POSITIONS
PF2 EMP NAME     PF4 BUDCTR    PF8 PREV     PF10 COMPENSATION   PF12 MENU
```

Another option would be to use prototyping for parts of the system such as data entry screens and reports.

In addition, prototyping is not a substitute for all of the detailed research and analysis required to build an information system. Large systems will still necessitate thorough problem investigation, analysis, and requirements specification before prototyping can begin.

Some of the advantages of prototyping are also disadvantages. Often, critical activities such as testing and documentation are glossed over because it is so easy to create a prototype. The system can be changed so effortlessly that documentation may not be kept up-to-date. Sometimes a prototype system will be immediately converted into a production system. Yet, under real business circumstances, it may not be able to accommodate large numbers of users, process numerous transactions, and maintain large quantities of records.

11.4 Developing Solutions with Software Packages

Chapter 5 introduced the topic of software packages—prewritten, precoded, commercially available programs that eliminate the need for writing software programs when an information system is developed. More and more systems today are being built with such packages for several reasons. For one thing, an increasing proportion of systems are based on desktop workstations and microcomputers, which lend themselves readily to packaged software. In addition, some problems encountered by organizations require the same or very similar information system solutions. For example, payroll, accounts payable, accounts receivable, and order processing are standard needs for almost all businesses.

Advantages of Packages

Packages offer a number of advantages, especially for firms that do not have a large staff of technical systems personnel or whose staff lack the requisite technical skills for a particular application. Not only does buying packaged software take the burden of developing systems off in-house staff, but it can also be a source of technical expertise in the future. Leading package vendors maintain their own technical support staff to furnish customers with expert advice after the system has been installed. Thus a firm that buys packaged software has less need to maintain its own internal specialists.

A related advantage is the cost savings that organizations may achieve by purchasing packaged software rather than developing their own. The Focus on Problem Solving suggests this may be one reason why government agencies have been seeking out package solutions. A typical package vendor will claim that a system can be fashioned with a package in one-third to one-fourth the time required for custom development at a fraction of the cost. Packages also eliminate some of the need to work and rework the specifications for a system because users must accept the package as it is. Many

FOCUS ON *Problem Solving*

Government Agencies Seek Package Solutions

Federal, state, and local government agencies have been exploring software packages in response to pressures to reduce costs. Although state treasury offices and accounting departments have shown particular interest in packages, other agencies, including the New York Transit Authority, are finding them useful as well. According to John Beasley, senior project coordinator for the New York City Transit Authority, the transit authority encourages the use of packaged software because "we know what we're getting without having to do a lot of feasibility studies." It uses standardized packages of dBASE III Plus and Lotus 1-2-3 for automating its reports.

Source: Mike Bucken, "Aging Software Base in Need of Updating," *Software Magazine,* January 1989.

features of the design solution have already been worked out, so the purchaser knows precisely what the capabilities of the system are.

The Information Systems Department at Harris Corporation realized all these benefits from packaged software. The package solutions did indeed reduce project development costs, lead times, and staff overhead. In fact, the advantages of packaged software extended far beyond their business benefits. As packages were implemented, the department's image in the company improved. Selecting packages turned out to be a way of demonstrating the ability of the Information Systems Department to find timely solutions to business problems.[4]

Packages and the Solution Design Process

How do packages fit into our solution design methodology? As Figure 11.4 shows, even when considering a package, system builders still have to investigate and analyze the problem, specify solution objectives, consider constraints, and evaluate solution alternatives. During these processes, they can determine whether a package solution alternative will meet information requirements. Then, when they evaluate solution alternatives, they can weigh the feasibility of a package solution against other solution options.

The formality of the solution design process with a software package depends on the dimensions and complexity of the problem. For example, a problem requiring a simple mailing label or client database package on a personal computer can be easily addressed, whereas a mainframe-based manufacturing resources planning package to link four different production

Figure 11.4

Pre-written Software Packages

Every organization is different, but most organizations perform many of the same functions, such as payroll, accounting, and order processing. This fact has led to the availability of pre-written software packages that reduce the number of new programs that must be written for a new system. Even if a firm is considering basing a system on a software package, however, this does not mean that it should bypass the step-by-step solution design process. This diagram shows that system builders should still analyze the problem and evaluate alternative solutions. If they choose a package, it will have to be installed, customized, and matched to the needs of that particular organization.

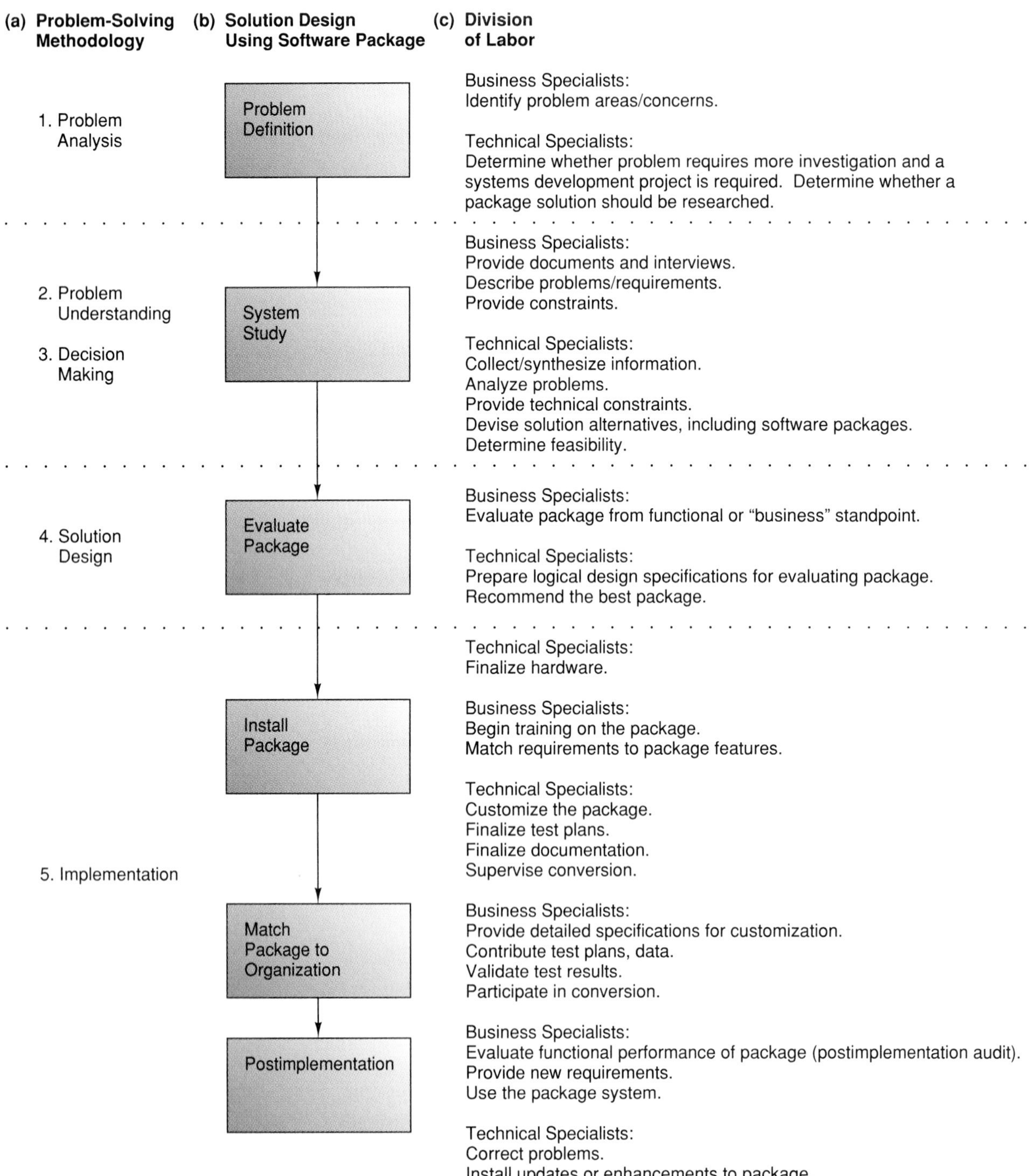

(a) Problem-Solving Methodology
(b) Solution Design Using Software Package
(c) Division of Labor
1. Problem Analysis
Problem Definition
Business Specialists:
Identify problem areas/concerns.
Technical Specialists:
Determine whether problem requires more investigation and a systems development project is required. Determine whether a package solution should be researched.
2. Problem Understanding
3. Decision Making
System Study
Business Specialists:
Provide documents and interviews.
Describe problems/requirements.
Provide constraints.
Technical Specialists:
Collect/synthesize information.
Analyze problems.
Provide technical constraints.
Devise solution alternatives, including software packages.
Determine feasibility.
4. Solution Design
Evaluate Package
Business Specialists:
Evaluate package from functional or "business" standpoint.
Technical Specialists:
Prepare logical design specifications for evaluating package.
Recommend the best package.
5. Implementation
Install Package
Technical Specialists:
Finalize hardware.
Business Specialists:
Begin training on the package.
Match requirements to package features.
Technical Specialists:
Customize the package.
Finalize test plans.
Finalize documentation.
Supervise conversion.
Match Package to Organization
Business Specialists:
Provide detailed specifications for customization.
Contribute test plans, data.
Validate test results.
Participate in conversion.
Postimplementation
Business Specialists:
Evaluate functional performance of package (postimplementation audit).
Provide new requirements.
Use the package system.
Technical Specialists:
Correct problems.
Install updates or enhancements to package.

units may require all of the stages, activities, and formal procedures of traditional life cycle methodology. But whether formal or informal, the process still involves the basic steps of problem solving.

The package evaluation process is often based on the results of a **Request for Proposal (RFP).** The RFP is a detailed list of questions that is submitted to vendors of packaged software. The questions are designed to measure the extent to which each package meets the requirements specified during the solution design process. An RFP is likely to include questions such as the following:

Request for Proposal (RFP) A detailed list of questions for software vendors to answer as part of the process of evaluating a software package; the questions are designed to determine the extent to which the software package meets the requirements specified during the solution design process.

1. **Business requirements:** What business functions are supported by the package? (For example, does a payroll package generate W-2 forms automatically?)
2. **Ease of use:** Is the package easy for end-users to learn and utilize? How much training is required?
3. **Technical requirements:** What model(s) of computer hardware can the package run on? What operating system does it use? How much primary and secondary storage is required? Does the vendor supply source code?
4. **Vendor quality:** Does the vendor have an established reputation? Will the vendor provide updates to the package or technical support? Does the vendor supply training?
5. **Cost:** What is the cost of the package? Are vendor support and training extra? What would it cost to use the package for the proposed system solution?
6. **Flexibility:** Can the package be easily modified to incorporate other requirements or data that are not standard with the package?

If a package solution is selected, the solution design step of problem solving will be carried out around the package. As a result, the work will proceed rather differently than in the other system-building methodologies we have examined. In particular, logical and physical design will not proceed from scratch, tailored to the requirements and specifications generated first. Instead, the design work will focus on adjusting user requirements and specifications to meet the characteristics of the package. In other words, instead of end-users designing their own payroll register, the payroll register report provided by a payroll package will be used. In this sense, the organization and end-users have less control over the shape and design of solution outcome.

Disadvantages of Packages

The main disadvantage of software packages is that they often are unable to meet all of an organization's requirements. As earlier chapters have pointed out, although organizations are alike in many ways, each has its own characteristics. Each organization treats even a standard function such as payroll a little differently. Consequently, there will be many instances in which a package will not be able to meet 100 percent of a firm's solution requirements. According to a study of corporations with payroll and personnel information systems, only 36.8 percent chose package software for person-

FOCUS ON *Technology*

"Customizable" Software from McCormack & Dodge

McCormack & Dodge, a leading application software vendor, announced major updates to its General Ledger: Millenium, Currency Management: Millenium, and Interactive PC Link software packages that provide wide latitude for customization. These changes will allow firms to tailor the software to their particular needs rather than having to alter their business practices and procedures to use the software. General Ledger: Millenium, for example, allows users to define key fields and record lengths, depending on reporting and storage requirements. A retailer can choose a weekly reporting system, and a utility can create specialized reports to meet regulatory requirements. The packages run on IBM 43XX and 30XX series machines with either OS or DOS operating systems. McCormack & Dodge plans to make the concept of "customer-controlled" software central to its products over the next few years.

Source: "M&D Announces 'Customizable' Software," *Information Week,* April 11, 1988.

nel and only 40.3 percent for payroll in spite of the fact that these are standard business functions with a vast array of commercial packages available.[5] The difficulty in finding a package that will meet a firm's special needs may be one reason for these relatively low percentages.

Customization
The modification of a software package to meet a firm's unique requirements.

Package vendors try to address this problem through **customization;** that is, the package includes features that allow it to be modified without destroying the integrity of the software. For example, the package may include areas on its files or databases where a firm can add and maintain its own pieces of data. As the Focus on Technology describes, McCormack & Dodge and other leading application package vendors are quick to tout these features in their promotional literature.

Some packages are modular in design; this allows clients to select only the modules that they need from an array of modules supporting different functions. Packages can also be customized through user exits, which enable clients to exit from the package programs to use programs they write themselves, then return to the package program. Figure 11.5 shows how a major payroll software package can be customized to accommodate different organizational reporting structures. This package allows firms to define different types of organizational structures, such as a corporation, a bank, or a university.

Even with customization features, there are limits to how much packages can be changed, however. Firms experienced in using package software

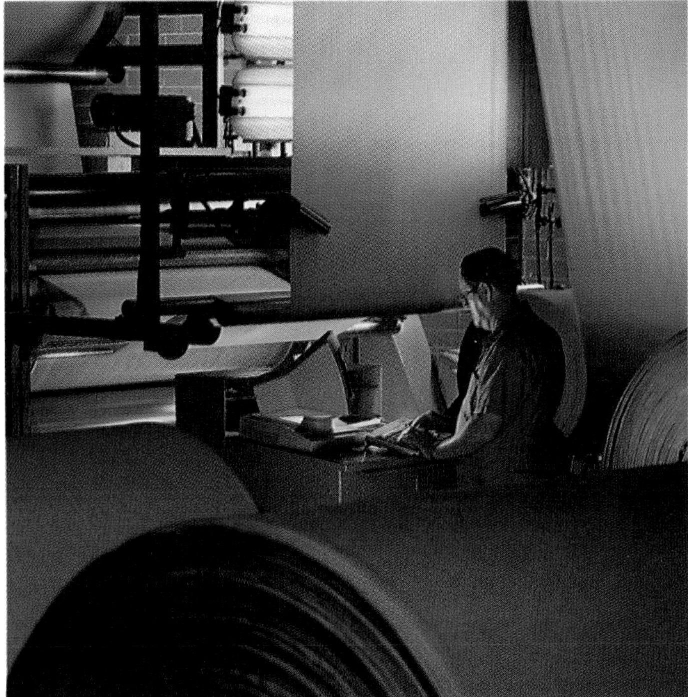

Customized manufacturing software, a mainframe, and workstations were included in the manufacturing control system that Unisys fashioned for Klopman Fabrics. Customized software packages accommodate firms' individual specifications, but don't require development from the ground up.

Source: Courtesy of Unisys Corporation.

for major business applications have noted that a good package may only satisfy 70 percent of their application requirements. If the package cannot be modified to meet a firm's unique needs, the firm will have to change its procedures and ways of doing business to conform to the package. This may help streamline the firm's operations, or it may create additional confusion and complexity.

11.5 Fourth-Generation Development

Many information systems can be developed by business specialists with little or no formal assistance from technical specialists. This approach is called fourth-generation development. It incorporates some of the software tools introduced in Chapter 5, such as fourth-generation languages, personal computer tools, and graphics languages, which make it possible for end-users to perform tasks that previously required trained data processing specialists. (As you may recall, fourth-generation languages are programming languages that are not only less procedural than conventional languages but also contain more English-language commands; consequently, they are easier for nontechnical specialists to use.)

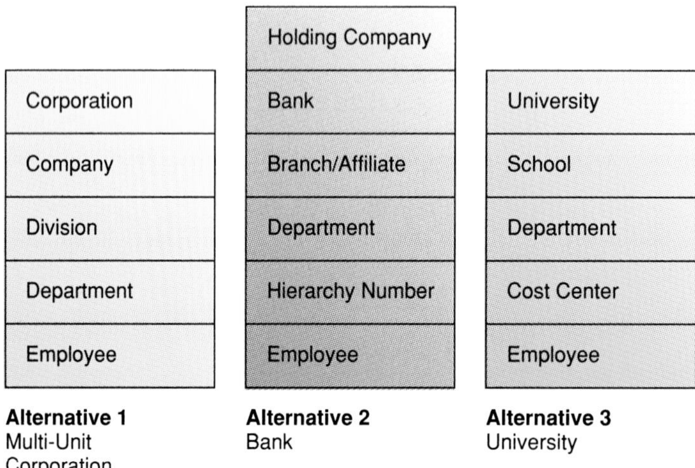

Figure 11.5

A Customized Software Package

These diagrams show three possible organizational structures that can be created by the payroll/personnel system package from Management Sciences of America, Inc. The package allows each customer to organize employees into groups for reporting and control purposes. Data can be gathered and calculated for each organizational level defined. Each of these examples lists the highest level of the firm first.

Fourth-generation development has been used to build systems for mainframes, minicomputers, and microcomputers, although the majority of such systems are microcomputer based. Many fourth-generation applications are decision oriented, although some have been built for operational tasks and management control. Some examples of fourth-generation systems are listed in Table 11.1.

Fourth-Generation Solution Design

Fourth-generation development puts business specialists more in control of the problem-solving process. They can investigate and analyze a problem, specify solution alternatives, perform logical and physical design, and implement the solution themselves or with much less intervention from technical specialists.

Figure 11.6 illustrates how fourth-generation development affects the solution design process. Note that solution design tends to be less formal than traditional systems development methodologies, with technical specialists playing a relatively smaller role. Depending on the application solution, fourth-generation development may include prototyping, personal computer packages, or more elaborate, custom-programmed software.

Generally, these fourth-generation systems tend to be quite simple and can be completed more rapidly than those using conventional life cycle methodology. This takes some of the pressure off the Information Systems or Data Processing Department, so its staff can be freed up for other, more technically demanding projects. The role of the Information Systems De-

Table 11.1

Examples of Fourth-Generation Systems

Application	Type
Market analysis: Provide comparative forecast versus sales history.	Tactical
Profitability report: Profitability analysis by product and customer.	Tactical
Billing ledger: Provide invoice amount, payment amount, and contract information.	Operational
Cost variance: Provide divisional cost data.	Tactical
Strategic planning: Furnish five-year strategic plan in income statement format.	Strategic
Quality reports: Provide quality measurements for various types of steel.	Operational
Freight cost savings: Summarize savings by shipping point and carrier.	Tactical

Source: Mary Sumner, "User-Developed Applications: What Are They Doing?" *Journal of Information Systems Management* (Fall 1986).

partment shifts from developing applications to ensuring that users have appropriate software and technology to create their own system solutions.

The solution design process may actually be facilitated because end-users are in charge of problem analysis and requirements specification. Since end-users are in the best position to understand their own problems, there is less chance of issues being misunderstood, as often occurs when the problem-solving process is dominated by technical specialists. End-users are also more likely to choose systems they have built themselves as their preferred problem-solving tools.

Fourth-Generation Software Tools

Fourth-generation development requires easy-to-use software tools that can be employed by end-users alone or by technical specialists as productivity aids. The following are the major types of software tools for end-users:

1. Personal computer tools
2. Query languages and report generators
3. Graphics languages
4. Application generators
5. Very-high-level programming languages
6. Application software packages

Figure 11.7 lists some representative, commercially available tools in each category and indicates the applications for which they are most appropriate.

Personal computer tools consist of the personal computer software described throughout this book: spreadsheet, database management, graphics, word processing, and communications software. Personal computer

Figure 11.6

Fourth-Generation Development

Fourth-generation development allows business specialists to do much of the development work themselves with easy-to-use software such as query languages and personal computer packages. This takes a great deal of pressure off the information systems staff, since the business specialists are responsible for identifying problems, designing and implementing solutions, and evaluating the results. Technical specialists take on a consulting role. Fourth-generation development works best with relatively simple applications and small files.

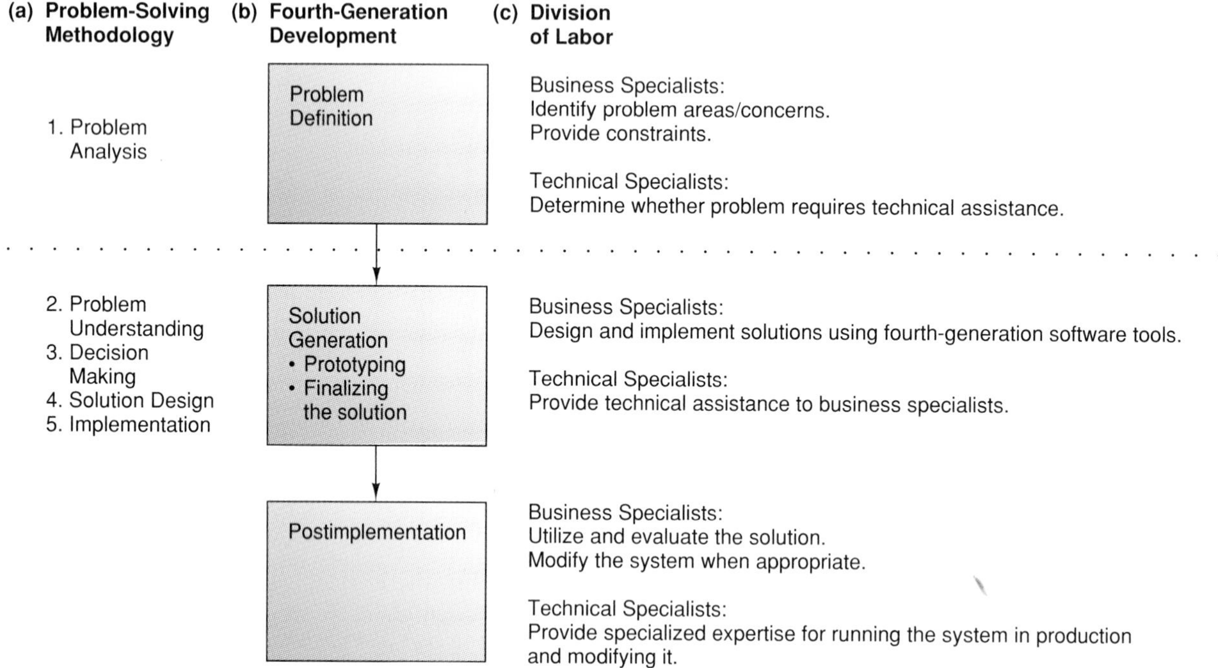
(a) Problem-Solving Methodology
(b) Fourth-Generation Development
(c) Division of Labor
1. Problem Analysis
Problem Definition
Business Specialists:
Identify problem areas/concerns.
Provide constraints.
Technical Specialists:
Determine whether problem requires technical assistance.
2. Problem Understanding
3. Decision Making
4. Solution Design
5. Implementation
Solution Generation
• Prototyping
• Finalizing the solution
Business Specialists:
Design and implement solutions using fourth-generation software tools.
Technical Specialists:
Provide technical assistance to business specialists.
Postimplementation
Business Specialists:
Utilize and evaluate the solution.
Modify the system when appropriate.
Technical Specialists:
Provide specialized expertise for running the system in production and modifying it.

software is especially well suited to end-user development both because it was designed for end-users rather than technical specialists and because personal computer operating systems are relatively simple.

Query languages, graphics languages, report generators, application generators, and very-high-level programming languages were introduced in Section 5.3 in Chapter 5. Query languages are easy-to-use fourth-generation languages that are used to access data stored in databases or files. Report generators extract data from files or databases to create customized reports. With an application generator, an entire information system application can be generated without customized programming; the end-user specifies what needs to be done, and the generator creates the appropriate program code. Very-high-level programming languages produce program code with far fewer instructions than are required by conventional languages.

Application software packages, described earlier in this chapter, can serve as fourth-generation computing tools if they are simple and can be installed by end-users. An example might be a mailing label or client database that can be installed by an end-user on a personal computer without any special programming or customization.

Figure 11.7

Fourth-Generation Solution Design Tools

The term "fourth-generation tools" actually describes a broad range of products, as is evident here. It includes software for personal computers such as Lotus 1-2-3 and query languages such as SQL, which are suitable for simpler problems. However, other tools, such as very high-level programming languages and application software packages, can address more technically sophisticated situations.

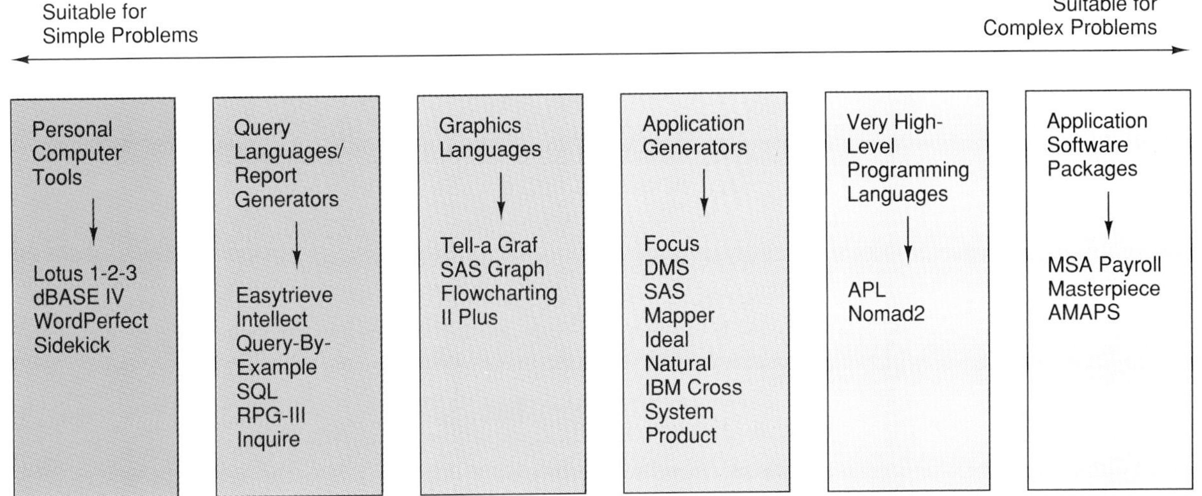

Disadvantages of Fourth-Generation Development

Although fourth-generation development offers many advantages, it can be used to solve problems only when the information system solution is relatively simple and easily understood by users. Fourth-generation languages and other end-user computing tools work best with small files and simple processing procedures. Such tools typically require more computer resources to process information than conventional languages, so they are unable to handle large transaction-based applications efficiently. For example, the New Jersey Division of Motor Vehicles faced a backlog of 1.4 million vehicle registration and ownership records when it built its system using Ideal, a fourth-generation tool. The high transaction volume necessitated reprogramming part of the system in COBOL.

Because these languages are heavily nonprocedural, they cannot easily handle applications that require complex procedural logic. Information systems such as production scheduling or designing nuclear reactors still require conventional languages.

Another disadvantage of fourth-generation development is the organization's potential loss of control over the solution design process and its information resources. Fourth-generation systems are developed much more informally and idiosyncratically than those using traditional data processing. Consequently, no professional programmers or systems analysts may be involved to assist with problem analysis, evaluation of solution alternatives, and solution design. User-developed systems thus lack the independent review mechanism provided by the technical specialist when both groups participate in solution design.

In addition, standards for ensuring data quality, security, or conformity with the information requirements of the firm as a whole may never be applied. For example, end-users may create many personal databases on desktop microcomputers containing data from corporate databases that, over time, have been updated, defined, and transformed so that they no longer match the same data in other systems. This leads to confusion about where to turn for reliable data.

Thus the firm that is considering a solution based on fourth-generation development should be aware that the following are common problems that may occur when fourth-generation and microcomputer tools are not used properly:

- **Report overload:** Miles of reports are generated to the point where everyone is swamped with paper.
- **Database deluge:** Redundant, trivial, inaccurate, and inappropriate data accumulate in computerized systems.
- **Excessive keypunching:** Source documents are transcribed to several forms before they are entered into the system, creating unnecessary work and transcription errors.
- **Unwieldy spreadsheets:** Spreadsheets are assigned tasks that would be more easily accomplished manually.
- **Vanishing documentation:** The system was developed too rapidly and informally without any explanatory documentation.

Information Centers

Information center
A facility that provides training, tools, standards, and expert support for solution design by end-users.

One way to manage fourth-generation development and maximize its benefits is through **information centers.** An information center is a facility that provides training and support for end-user computing. Its objective is to provide business specialists with tools to access computerized data and solve problems themselves. An information center furnishes computer hardware, software, and technical specialists, all of which are geared to fourth-generation systems development. The technical specialists serve as teachers and consultants; their primary goal is to train business specialists in the computing tools they will use, but they may also assist in the analysis, design, and programming of complex applications.

An information center may offer users access to mainframes and minicomputers as well as microcomputers, although some information centers contain only microcomputers. They support end-user software tools such as spreadsheets, word processing, graphics software, report generators, and query languages.

Some information centers, such as the Client Support Center at Exxon Corporate Headquarters in New York, support only applications that end-users can develop entirely on their own. Others will assist users with applications that may require technical specialists, provided they are based on end-user computing tools. IBM's Information Systems Productivity Center at its semiconductor manufacturing facility in Essex Junction, Vermont, has taken a proactive stance in teaching employees how to use computers to enhance productivity. Its approach is described in the Focus on Organizations.

FOCUS ON **Organizations**

Publicizing Productivity Tools

IBM's Information Systems Productivity Center at its semiconductor manufacturing facility in Essex Junction, Vermont, provides consulting services on three levels—to managers, business departments, and walk-in customers. Walk-in customers are individuals who seek out training or advice concerning an information center tool. The information center also schedules office visits in which managers can discuss their needs, such as how to automate a transparency presentation, and obtain suggestions for appropriate information center tools. Specific groups or business departments requesting information center support are treated to presentations describing the center's products and how they can increase productivity in that functional area. For example, the information center has demonstrated productivity tools for manufacturing technicians.

Some of the tools supported by the center include SAS, IBM's A Department Reporting System (ADRS/Business Graphics), SQL, and Professional Office System (PROFS). Clients can try out printers, plotters, software, and machines to make color overheads and slides in the information center before purchasing them. A Color Graphics Center features color graphics terminals for training sessions, meetings, and individual use. The information center also publishes a monthly newsletter to supply clients with information on new products, classes, and applications of interest.

Source: Roger L. Crouse, "An IC Approach to Productivity," *Infosystems,* February 1986.

Information centers support the solution design process at many stages. Their staffs are prepared to work intensively to help end-users understand their problems and solve them as much as possible on their own. The services provided by an information center can be summarized as follows (see Figure 11.8):

- Referring business specialists to existing information system applications that may help solve their problems.
- Providing technical assistance by suggesting appropriate hardware, software, and methodologies for solving a particular problem.
- Training business specialists in the tools supported by the information center.
- Providing documentation and reference materials for information center resources.
- Generating prototypes for business specialists to evaluate.
- Evaluating new pieces of hardware and software.
- Giving staff access to terminals, microcomputers, associated software, and databases.

Information centers offer a number of benefits:[6]

1. Better use of information.
2. Increased job productivity.

3. Greater computer literacy.
4. Better relations between business specialists and technical specialists.
5. Reduced application backlog.
6. Standards for hardware/software.

Another advantage of information centers is that they can establish standards for hardware and software so that end-users do not introduce too many incompatible pieces of equipment or data into a firm. Typically, an information center works with a firm's Information Systems Department to establish standards and guidelines for hardware and software acquisitions by the firm; then the information center will provide assistance with only those brands of equipment and software.

Figure 11.8

The Information Center Concept

An information center can help a firm provide fourth-generation development tools and benefits to all employees. It is a coordinating and consulting facility which, in addition to providing hardware and software, also provides services. This diagram illustrates the broad range of services that an information center typically performs, including training, documentation, and generating prototypes. A good information center can be a valuable resource for a company.

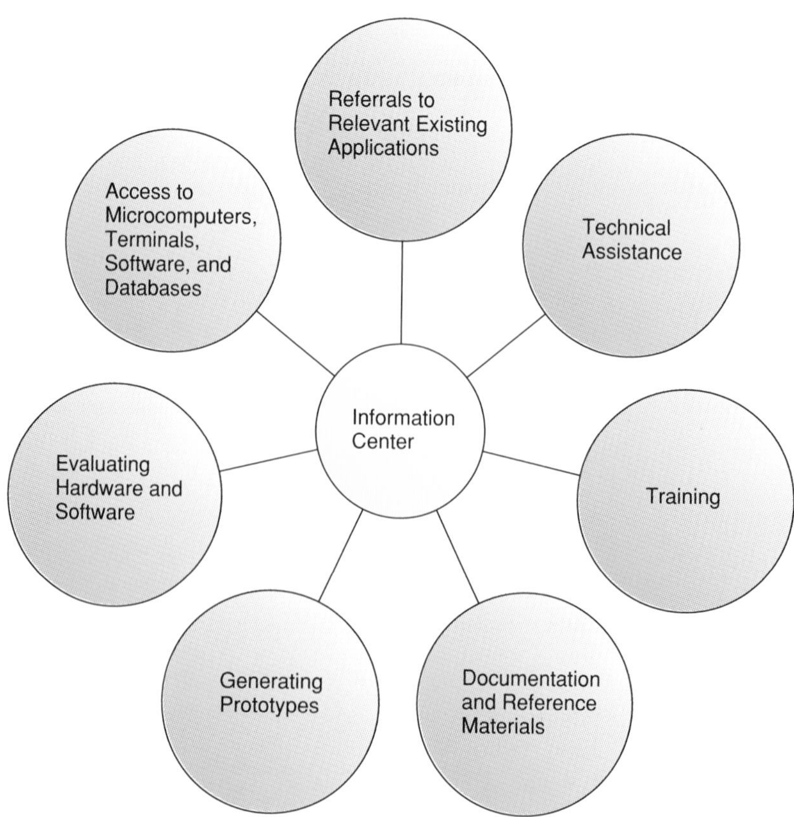

For example, an information center may provide training only on IBM's DisplayWrite II, as opposed to other word processing packages, because that is the company standard. Otherwise, its staff would have to learn several different types of word processing software, each of which would be used by only a small number of people. Such a policy also contributes to the efficient use of information in an organization. Files created by one kind of word processing software cannot easily be used by another; thus documents cannot be shared or transmitted to other departments if each uses a different word processing standard. This limits transportability of data across the organization.

11.6 Leading-Edge Application: On-Demand Mortgage Reports for Merrill Lynch Brokers

Due to changing market and competitive requirements, the traders and account executives of the mortgage-backed securities division of Merrill Lynch found themselves requesting a wide variety of new, ad hoc reports. These new information needs could not be satisfied by the firm's existing information systems, and Merrill Lynch's management feared its programming staff would be overwhelmed trying to satisfy them.

Instead, the firm implemented MASTIR (Mortgage-backed Accounting and Securities Trading Information Retrieval), which enables business specialists to generate their own ad hoc reports on demand without programmer intervention. The contents of the reports produced by the mortgage-backed securities division are so flexible that every user can be said to have a unique set of reports.

MASTIR was implemented in June 1988. Before that, traders and account executives had to use paper records or turn to professional programmers for historical inquiries about their customer base. The need for on-the-spot information mounted to the point where a full-time programmer was needed two and one-half days per week just to satisfy such ad hoc inquiries. The solution was to off load some of the reporting to the business specialists themselves.

MASTIR employs NonStop SQL, a relational database product from Tandem Computers, Inc., which can harness the query, information retrieval, and productivity-boosting features of SQL (Structured Query Language) in high-volume, on-line processing applications such as those in the brokerage industry. Each record in the MASTIR database consists of 35 fields, such as customer name, security type, branch office number, and account executive name and identification number. With NonStop SQL and a relational database model, these fields can be easily combined into complex reports within seconds.[7]

Using these fourth-generation tools, two programmers developed and implemented MASTIR in just two and one-half months. Development time would have doubled had traditional file management and programming tools been used. The real benefit of the system, however, is the day-to-day productivity gains from having business specialists fulfill their own reporting needs. Merrill Lynch plans to recoup the total development cost, including software purchase, development, and implementation, in one year.

The benefits that cannot be directly measured may actually be much greater. MASTIR enables brokers to obtain and use sales and marketing data immediately on-line to match available investments with customers' needs. For example, when interest in mortgage-backed securities drops off in summer, account executives can use the system to obtain reports on which customers were active purchasers the previous summer and which investments they favored. This information helps them target sales campaigns. Traders who want to repurchase a security to sell to someone else can obtain a list of current holders of that security and identify the account executive who handled the sale.

The MASTIR system is heavily menu driven. On an on-line screen, brokers can enter a report identification number and a report description of up to 30 characters. If the report is new, the broker selects the data fields for the report by typing an X next to each of the 35 possible fields listed on the screen. The system then moves to a screen that displays the fields just selected and prompts the broker to enter parameter restrictions, or limits on ranges of values, for each field. For example, if the broker selects the field for security type, he or she may want to retrieve only Ginnie Maes. The screen can also be used to specify fields to sort on, sort order, total, and subtotal. These report specifications can be stored for future use under the given report identification number.

If the broker selects an existing report identification number, he or she is directed to the screen controlling report formatting, parameter updating, and execution. If the broker is unsure of the report identification number, he or she can obtain a listing on-line by pressing the PF3 key. MASTIR is available on-line to Merrill Lynch branch offices as well. Through the data security features of NonStop SQL, each office is limited to its own data.

New trade data are fed into the MASTIR database daily, and this information is stored historically for two years. Eventually, the system will have seven years of historical data on trade activity. The application runs on a Tandem NonStop VLS computer with six processors and currently occupies only 3 percent of total storage capacity.

Summary

- The traditional systems life cycle is the oldest methodology for building information system solutions. It consists of a formal set of stages that must proceed sequentially, clearly demarcating the responsibilities of business and technical specialists.

- The six stages of the traditional systems life cycle are project definition, systems study, design, programming, installation, and post-implementation.

- The traditional life cycle is considered a very rigid and costly way to develop a systems solution. Moreover, it is not well suited for simpler, less structured applications for which requirements cannot easily be visualized.

- The most important alternatives to traditional life cycle methodology are prototyping, the use of software packages, and fourth-generation development.
- Prototyping entails building an experimental system or part of a system rapidly for business specialists to interact with and evaluate. The process is highly interactive and iterative.
- Prototyping involves four steps: identifying preliminary requirements; developing a working prototype; using the prototype; and refining and enhancing the prototype.
- Prototyping is most useful for simple, less structured applications for which solution requirements are vague. When the system solution is massive and complex, prototyping cannot substitute for comprehensive requirements analysis and careful programming, testing, and documentation.
- Software packages are commercially marketed, prewritten software that can considerably reduce system development costs if they meet solution requirements. Solution design using application software packages focuses on package evaluation and fitting the solution design to package characteristics.
- If a package does not meet an organization's unique requirements, it must be customized, or modified. However, extensive customization can elevate development costs to the point where a package solution is no longer feasible.
- Using fourth-generation development techniques, business specialists can construct information system solutions with minimal assistance from technical specialists. This is possible because of the productivity and ease of use provided by fourth-generation development tools: personal computer tools, query languages, graphics languages, report generators, application generators, very-high-level programming languages, and application software packages.
- Fourth-generation–developed solutions are most appropriate for applications with small files and relatively simple processing procedures. Potential problems from fourth-generation development include loss of organizational control and standards for solution design.
- Information centers can help control fourth-generation development by providing training, tools, standards, and expert support for solution design.

Key Terms

Traditional systems life cycle
Project definition
Systems study
Postimplementation
Prototyping
Fourth-generation development
Business interface
Request for Proposal (RFP)
Customization
Information center

Review Questions

1. Why is the oldest methodology for building an information system called the "systems life cycle"?

2. List and define each of the stages in the systems life cycle.
3. Why is it important to conduct a postimplementation audit of an information system?
4. What are the strengths and limitations of life cycle methodology?
5. What are the three most important alternatives to conventional systems-building methodology?
6. Define information system prototyping.
7. What kinds of situations benefit most from prototyping the solution?
8. What are the four steps in prototyping?
9. What are the limitations of prototyping?
10. What kinds of situations benefit from using software packages to develop a solution?
11. Describe two advantages and two disadvantages of software packages.
12. What is a Request for Proposal? How does it fit into the solution design process?
13. What is customization? Why is it an important feature to consider in a software package?
14. What is fourth-generation development? Name the major kinds of software tools employed with this approach.
15. What problems are associated with fourth-generation development?
16. Define an information center. How can information centers improve the management of fourth-generation development?

Discussion Questions

1. Discuss how the problem-solving methodology presented in this text is applied in the traditional systems life cycle, prototyping, software package–based development, and fourth-generation development.

2. Describe the roles of business specialists and technical specialists in each of the approaches to information systems solutions presented in this chapter.

3. Application software packages and fourth-generation computing tools eliminate the need for professional programmers. Discuss.

4. It is impossible to develop a good solution design the first time around. Discuss.

Problem-Solving Exercises

1. What kind of approach (methodology) would you choose for the following application solutions? Justify your decision.
   a. A system for tracking job applicants at six different branches of a nationwide retail chain.
   b. A money market account system for a major regional bank.
   c. A system to evaluate the financial and tax consequences of purchasing rental property.

d. A medical and dental claims administration and payment system for 14,000 employees of a major corporation.

2. Obtain product information about a microcomputer application software package, such as Peachtree Complete III or DacEasy Accounting. Write an analysis of the package. What are its strengths and limitations? Under what circumstances could it be used for a system solution?

Notes

1. Mark Teagan and Liz Young, "The Dynamics of Prototyping," *Computerworld*, August 8, 1988.
2. Richard Canning, "Developing Systems by Prototyping," *EDP Analyzer* 19 (September 1981).
3. Maryam Alavi, "An Assessment of the Prototyping Approach to Information System Development," *Communications of the ACM* 27 (June 1984).
4. Curt Hartog and Robert Klepper, "Business Software Pushes Software Sales Up 184%," *Computerworld*, August 22, 1988.
5. John E. Spirig, "New HRMS Challenge: Section 89 in 1989," *Software Magazine*, January 1989.
6. Wayne L. Rhodes, Jr., "The Information Center: Harvesting the Potential," *Infosystems*, November 1985.
7. "Merrill's Ad Hoc Approach Expands Mortgage Reports," *Wall Street Computer Review*, January 1989.

Problem-Solving Case

A Management System to Track Coast Guard Personnel

The Coast Guard, like the other branches of the U.S. armed forces, faces personnel constraints unknown to civilian agencies. The armed services must promote and fill a fairly rigid job structure. There is only one point of recruitment: at the bottom, when staff are initially recruited. No one is hired at middle or upper management levels. The available staff must be trained for these positions from the ground up.

To maintain a state of preparedness for defense and war, military jobs, or billets, must be filled at all times. Therefore, all branches of the service maintain a personnel supply that always exceeds the number of available jobs. Those not holding positions will be accounted for through extended training, hospitalization, or transfer from one unit to another. The increasingly sophisticated technical and educational requirements of military positions, along with the scarcity of personnel resources, make the need for effective management of resources much greater.

Until recently, the Coast Guard was unable to closely monitor its personnel cadre, called the General Detail. The Coast Guard maintains its primary personnel database on a mainframe-based personnel management information system (PMIS). However, PMIS data are considered too sensitive to permit easy access, and the system lacked user-friendly features as well. There was only a fixed set of standard reports written in COBOL. Any other requests for information had to be turned over to professional programmers.

Because of a backlog of requests, any new report required six to nine months to complete.

The PMIS could not measure personnel flow or deliver the kind of summary information Coast Guard planners required. Instead, the system primarily captured point-in-time transactions that were of little use. Data feeding the system were as much as three weeks out of date.

The enlisted programs branch within the Coast Guard Office of Personnel Management in Washington, D.C., decided to build a new general detail information system (GDIS) to capture, track, and monitor its use of critical personnel resources. Initial problem investigation ruled out the possibility of integration with the existing personnel management information system. Instead, the solution was developed using FOCUS, a popular fourth-generation language from Information Builders, Inc., in New York.

This software tool enabled end-users to design their own applications to meet changing requests for information. They could retrieve data from several sources and combine it into one database that could be stored on a Wang VS or IBM Personal Computer AT compatible. FOCUS Table Talk and File Talk utilities allow nonprogrammers to use menus to write their own applications.

Requirements were gathered informally from interviews and study of historical documents. There was no existing system to critique or analyze, so requirements were very fluid. Since different parties often could not agree on the purpose of the system, prototyping became a key feature of the development process.

Developers found that it was more difficult to capture the data required by the GDIS from five different system environments than they originally envisaged. They had to extract data from different pieces of hardware and software and transfer them to a common environment.

The GDIS creates a consumption file and a summary file on a personal computer. The consumption file provides a point-in-time snapshot of all of the individuals in the General Detail. The summary file is a database that captures and aggregates historical information as people pass through the General Detail. Updated monthly, the summary database will eventually feed a decision-oriented system within the Office of Personnel Management. The system features numerous standard reports. Some provide upper management with higher levels of summary data than were previously available for policy decisions.

In spite of the easy-to-learn features of FOCUS and modules to keep code free of syntax errors, the Coast Guard found that its expectations about mastering this software tool were too high. This could be attributed partly to the complexity of FOCUS and partly to the complexity of the application solution. The Coast Guard had an especially difficult time learning to extract data from the mainframe, since support staff were difficult to locate or lacking in experience and technical expertise. Delays also occurred because the project team was balancing many unrelated tasks.

Source: Michael J. Burgard, "Coast Guard's Management System Tracks Personnel," *Government Computer News*, July 31, 1987.

Case Study Questions

1. What problem did the Coast Guard have tracking and monitoring its personnel?
2. What external and internal constraints regarding personnel management did the Coast Guard face?

3. Was the GDIS an appropriate solution? Were any other solution alternatives feasible?
4. Did the Coast Guard have trouble defining a solution objective?
5. Why were prototyping and fourth-generation development appropriate for solving the problem? Could other methodologies and tools have been employed?
6. Why were difficulties in implementing the solution encountered during this project?

Automated Solutions with Computer-Aided Software Engineering

As Chapters 9–11 have shown, designing information systems to solve business problems can be a complex, multifaceted process. When a proposed solution entails a system with many inputs, outputs, and processing steps, developing it usually requires the joint efforts of information systems specialists and business specialists. The solution will need to be described using narrative and graphics. Much time is required to generate, revise, and refine these descriptions and then translate them into software code.

Now, through computer-aided software engineering (CASE), some of the repetitive aspects of developing system solutions have been automated, freeing time for the more creative aspects of problem solving. For example, CASE can automatically produce charts and diagrams, draw prototypes of screens and reports, generate program code, analyze and check design specifications, and generate documents in standard formats.

While some CASE vendors are trying to create software that addresses all aspects of the problem-solving process, most CASE tools either focus on the early stages of problem understanding, decision making, and solution design or else support implementation. Examples of the former are CASE tools that automatically produce data flow diagrams, structure charts, systems flowcharts, data dictionaries, and documentation. These are sometimes called front-end CASE tools.

In contrast, back-end CASE tools primarily support the implementation step of problem solving and some aspects of solution design. Thus, they address coding, testing, and maintenance activities. Examples of such tools include testing facilities, compilers, linkers, code generators (which generate modules of source code from higher-level specifications), and application generators. A number of CASE products allow system designers to model desired data entry screens and report layouts or menu paths through a system without complex formatting specifications or programming.

Many CASE tools contain a central information repository, which serves as an "encyclopedia" for storing all types of information related to a specific project: data descriptions, screen and report layouts, diagrams, project schedules, and other documentation. The people working on the project can easily look up the information, share it, and reuse it to solve other problems. Information is especially easy to share with CASE tools that are microcomputer-based and can be put on local area networks. Thus, not only do CASE tools help system designers create clear documentation, they also help coordinate group problem-solving activities.

As mentioned earlier, some CASE products, such as Andersen Consulting's FOUNDATION, attempt to support the entire problem-solving process. They contain design and analysis tools that can be integrated with tools for generating program code and for managing systems development. For instance, the DESIGN/1 component of FOUNDATION allows users to do word processing, design data entry screens and report layouts, diagram the flow of data through a system, generate structure charts, design databases, and prototype the flow of on-line screens. Figure 1 shows how this tool is used during database design to model relationships among the entities—customer order, invoice, product, and component.

As shown in Figure 2, the tools in DESIGN/1 are integrated through a shared repository. Problem solvers can define relationships among various design components, combine text and graphics within a single design component, and move or copy material from one component to another. For instance, one

Figure 2

Integration of DESIGN/1 Tools in Shared Repository

CASE tools such as FOUNDATION typically provide a shared design repository in which design data, images, and diagrams are automatically indexed and cross-referenced during the design process so that they can instantly relate to each other.

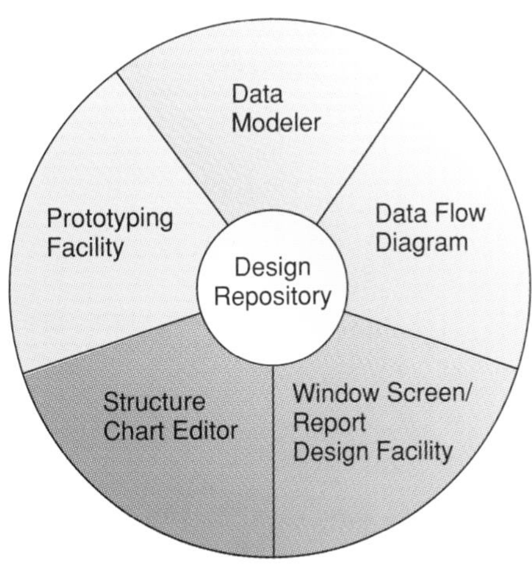

Source: © 1990 Andersen Consulting. All rights reserved. Reprinted with permission.

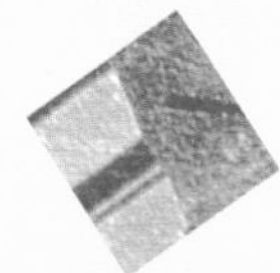

Figure 1

Use of FOUNDATION during Database Design

An entity-relationship diagram is a technique used to develop a model of a database that shows relationships among entities—one-to-one, one-to-many, many-to-one, or many-to-many. A user of FOUNDATION's Data Modeller can automatically define these relationships among entities by using a mouse, pull-down menus, symbols, and icons.

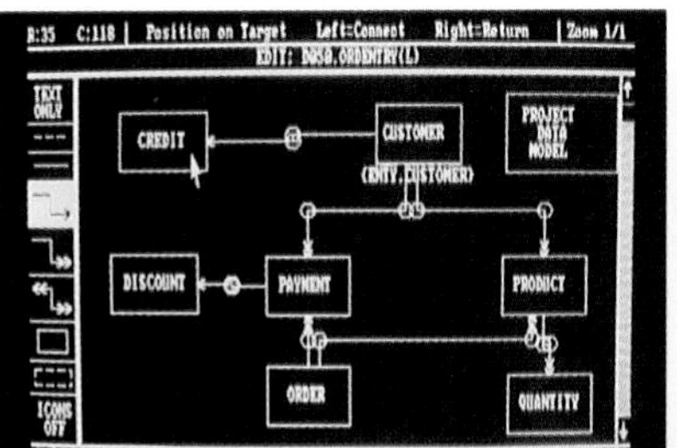

Source: © 1990 Andersen Consulting. All rights reserved. Reprinted with permission.

Figure 3

Capabilities of INSTALL/1

The INSTALL/1 capabilities of FOUNDATION provide automated tools for screen design, program code generation, test data management, database administration, production systems support, and technical support. The INSTALL/1 repository ties together all data elements, record layouts, programs, files, and documentation. The Test Data Management facility shown here streamlines testing by enabling each software developer to create isolated versions of test data for different test sessions.

Source: © 1990 Andersen Consulting.

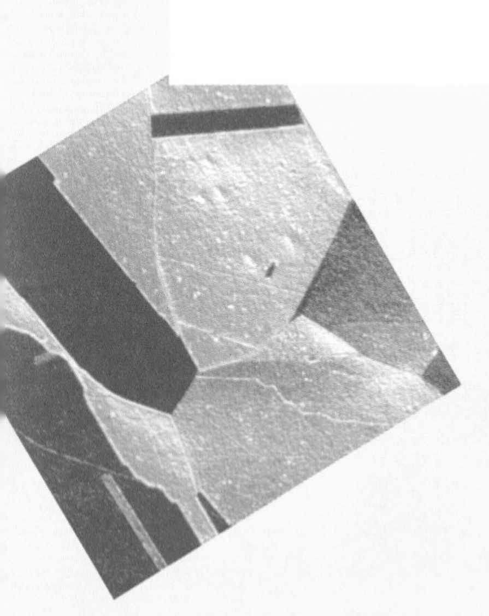

can establish relationships between a process in a data flow diagram and the data elements used in that process and use text to describe the process or to add personal notes. As information is changed in one diagram (for instance, a data flow might be deleted or added), the CASE software ensures that it will be automatically changed in related diagrams and other design components. DESIGN/1 also enables the user to review design data for completeness, accuracy, and consistency.

DESIGN/1 is integrated with INSTALL/1, the implementation and support component of FOUNDATION, which automates application generation. Design components stored in the DESIGN/1 repository are transferred to the INSTALL/1 repository where they serve as specifications for generating the program code for mainframe applications. Figure 3 illustrates the capabilities of INSTALL/1 and its facility for creating test data.

Another useful component of FOUNDATION is METHOD/1, which provides a comprehensive methodology and automated tools to support various approaches to systems development—a custom systems approach, a package system approach, and an iterative development (prototyping) approach. Figure 4 illustrates an inquiry screen

Figure 4

Inquiry Screen for the Custom Approach

METHOD/1 helps automate the management of systems development work by defining what to do and when to do it during each phase of the systems' development life cycle. The custom approach to systems development in METHOD/1 is used when a new system must be built from scratch. A methodology inquiry screen for systems design is illustrated here.

Source: © 1990 Andersen Consulting.

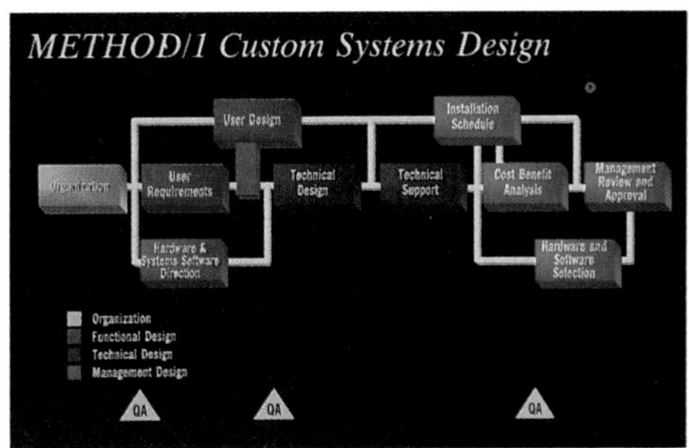

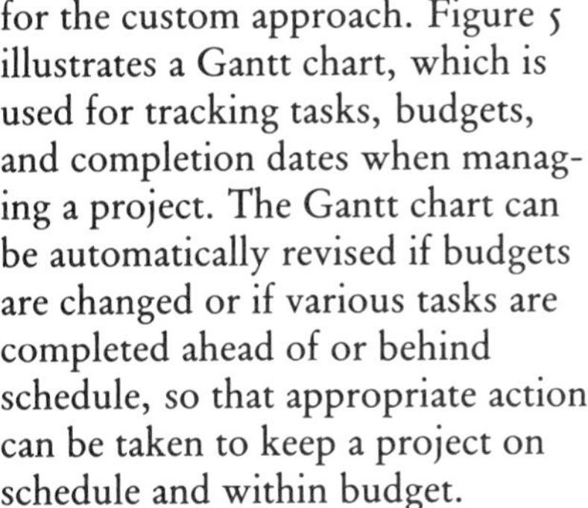

for the custom approach. Figure 5 illustrates a Gantt chart, which is used for tracking tasks, budgets, and completion dates when managing a project. The Gantt chart can be automatically revised if budgets are changed or if various tasks are completed ahead of or behind schedule, so that appropriate action can be taken to keep a project on schedule and within budget.

To use CASE tools effectively, members of a problem-solving team must adhere to common standards for diagramming, conventions for naming data flows, data elements, or program modules, and an agreed-upon solution design discipline. If each system builder were to cling to his or her own way of developing systems, the incompatibility between the old approaches and new tools could generate confusion.

Figure 5

Gantt Chart Used for Managing a Project

METHOD/1 contains automated project management tools with estimation, planning, and scheduling capabilities. The Gantt chart illustrated here details various tasks in a systems development project, their estimated duration, start and end dates, and which tasks overlap. The tasks depicted in red are identified as most critical to the project.

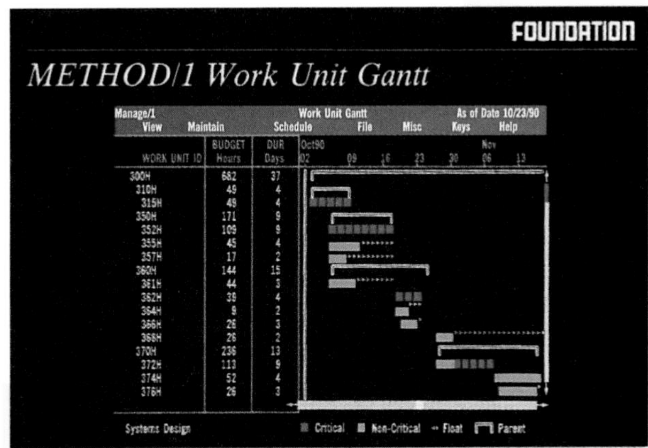

Source: © 1990 Andersen Consulting.

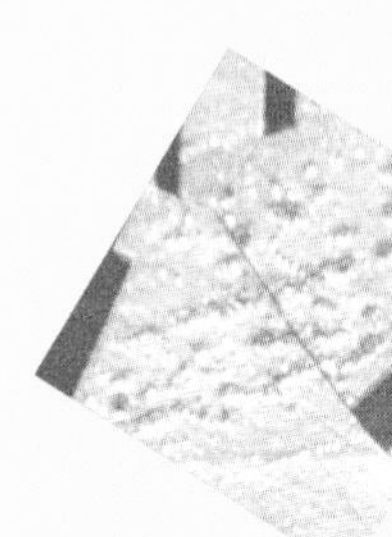

PART · FOUR

Overview of Business Information Systems

CHAPTER · TWELVE

*B*asic *B*usiness *S*ystems

Chapter Outline

12.1 Introduction: Basic Business Systems

12.2 Features of Basic Business Systems
- The Functions of Basic Business Systems
- Fault-Tolerant Systems

12.3 Examples of Basic Business Systems
- Basic Manufacturing and Production Systems
- Basic Sales and Marketing Systems
- Basic Accounting and Financial Systems
- Basic Human Resources Systems

12.4 The Challenges of Building Basic Business Systems
- Organizational Challenges
- People Challenges
- Technology Challenges

Learning Objectives

After reading and studying this chapter, you will:

1. Know how information systems are used at the most elemental level in each of the major functional areas of the firm: manufacturing and production, sales and marketing, accounting and finance, and human resources.
2. Be aware of the kinds of problems that basic business systems help to solve.
3. Understand the purpose of fault-tolerant computers.
4. Understand the organizational, technical, and people challenges of building basic business systems.

Pepperidge Farm Systems Promote Freshness and Quality

Pepperidge Farm runs a business based on freshness. Instead of churning out new food products, the Pepperidge Farm Corporation focuses on what it does best: baking. It has used information systems to halve the time between orders and deliveries, reducing the oven-to-shelf time to ten hours in the New York area.

The firm scrapped its old order system, which used cumbersome, oversized tickets to place orders through the mail. Workers at its headquarters in Norwalk, Connecticut, used to open, sort, keypunch, and process 50,000 order tickets each week. Now, 900 of Pepperidge's 2,500 independent distributors have switched to hand-held Fujitsu computers to place orders for bread and biscuits and to keep track of the inventory in their trucks. The distributors then send their orders to Norwalk headquarters via modem, where they are archived for billing and sent to the appropriate plant. The whole process takes less than five minutes, enabling Pepperidge Farm to deliver products to the distributor in less than 18 hours.

Pepperidge Farm has also installed quality control systems to monitor the company's baking formulas and make sure each day's baking progresses smoothly. Information on how each batch of bread is progressing is sent to a control room. The baking cycle can be modified on a computer terminal, if required.

Pepperidge Farm keeps 100 or so recipes and batching formulas for its breads and cookies on an IBM System 38 computer installed at each of its plants. Once the day's orders are received, a production schedule showing the quantity of bread and cookies to bake that day is sent to a VAX computer. This computer, in turn, keeps track of variations in the moisture content of flour and sugar. Operations staff use graphics terminals to review baking formulas and make sure the baking is progressing smoothly. By automating some of the basic sales and manufacturing activities at Pepperidge Farm, these systems have helped the firm do what it does best—run a business based on the freshness and quality of its baked goods.

Source: "Systems Give Pepperidge Farm Freshness," *Information Week,* March 20, 1989.

As this case study indicates, Pepperidge Farm has developed a powerful series of information systems that shorten the delivery process and give it greater control over the quality of its output. Like Pepperidge Farm, many businesses depend on information systems to monitor, record, and perform their most essential day-to-day activities.

12.1 Introduction: Basic Business Systems

Basic business system
A system that serves the most elementary day-to-day activities of an organization; it supports the operational level of the business and also supplies data for higher-level management decisions.

Transaction
A record of an event to which a business must respond.

Transaction processing system
A basic business system that keeps track of the transactions necessary to conduct a business and uses these transactions to update the firm's records. Another name for a basic business system.

At the most elementary level, information systems keep track of the day-to-day activities of a business, such as sales, receipts, cash deposits, credit decisions, and the flow of materials in a factory. These **basic business systems** perform and record the routine transactions necessary to conduct the business.

A **transaction** is a record of an event to which the business must respond. For example, data about an order that has just been recorded constitute a transaction. The company responds to this transaction by filling the order, adjusting its inventory to account for the items used to fill the order, generating a packing slip, packaging and shipping the order, and billing the customer. The transaction thus triggers a whole series of events that eventually update the firm's business records and produce appropriate documents. Another name for these basic business systems that use transactions to update company records is **transaction processing systems.**

Many organizations, especially those in banking or financial services, could not survive for more than a day if their basic business systems ceased to function. For example, MasterCard cannot even afford a few minutes' disruption to its system, which processes billions of credit cards transactions each day from all over the world. MasterCard employs multiple backup power supply systems for its World Data Center in St. Louis, which is the clearing center for all credit transactions. The First Interstate Bank of California in Los Angeles, which handles from $3 billion to $5 billion of securities trading transactions daily, continually reviews and tests its disaster recovery plan.

12.2 Features of Basic Business Systems

Basic business systems serve the most elementary level of an organization by processing data about the operations of that enterprise. Such systems keep records of routine business activities—bank deposits, long-distance calls and charges, tax returns, payrolls, and university grades and transcripts. They support the functions of recording, monitoring, and evaluating the basic activities of the business. These systems are important suppliers of data to the operational level of a business and to higher levels of the firm as well. Much of their output is critical to the day-to-day survival of the firm.

The Functions of Basic Business Systems

The principal purpose of basic business systems is to answer routine questions and to track the flow of transactions through the organization. How many parts are in inventory? What happened to Mrs. Talbert's payment? How many employees were paid this month? The kinds of problems solved by such systems involve very short-term issues. Information for their solution is structured and based on the firm's routine standard operating procedures.

Basic business systems support lower levels of the firm, where tasks and resources are predefined and highly structured. For example, the decision to pay an active employee is based on two predefined criteria: Is the employee on the company's payroll, and did the employee work that week? It does not require much management deliberation. All that must be determined is whether the employee meets those criteria. Consequently, these systems are utilized primarily by people with little or no management responsibility—payroll clerks, order entry clerks, or shop floor stewards. The systems require few, if any, decisions from the people who operate them.

Basic business systems enable organizations to perform their most essential activities more efficiently. Business firms need them to function on a day-to-day basis, but often the systems have far-reaching strategic consequences that make them valuable for more than just operational efficiency alone. For example, Pepperidge Farm's order entry and quality control systems described in the opening case study have boosted its reputation as a producer of fresh, quality baked goods, enabling the firm to double its share of the cookie market. The SABRE system for processing airline reservations, which is described in the Focus on Organizations, gave American

Agents and clients of The Travelers Corporation can call the customer hotline for instant access to insurance policy information such as cash value, coverage, and premium status. Basic business systems such as this one permit companies to efficiently perform their fundamental business activities.

Source: © R. J. Muna.

Airlines a lead in the computerized airline reservation market and helped it promote its flights over those of competitors.

Although much of the information in basic business systems comes from inside the firm, these systems must also deal with customers, suppliers, and factors external to the firm. For example, an order processing system will contain customer data; a purchasing system will contain supplier data; a personnel system must incorporate government regulations concerning occupational safety, unemployment, and benefits accounting practices; a payroll system must incorporate changes in federal, state, and local tax laws. Thus basic business systems help solve problems concerning the firm's relationship with its external environment.

Most basic business systems are in constant use because they are the underpinnings of the day-to-day activities that drive the business. Many (although not all) of these systems take a high volume of input and produce a high volume of output. A large firm may process thousands or millions of transactions daily. Input data can come from several sources: data entry, punched cards, scanning devices, or computerized files. The outputs may consist of finished pieces of goods or documents such as paychecks, packing slips, or purchase orders (see Figure 12.1).

Another form of output supplied by basic business systems is the data they provide for other systems used by managers. The basic business sys-

FOCUS ON *Organizations*

Computerized Reservation Processing Is a Formidable Competitive Weapon

During the 1950s, it took two hours to process an airline reservation and seats could not be sold more than 30 days in advance. Today, about two-thirds of all airline tickets issued in the United States are sold by travel agents using computerized reservation systems that can process close to 2,000 transactions per second. The lead was taken by American Airlines, which started working with IBM on an electronic reservation system in 1958. SABRE (standing for Semi-Automated Business Research Environment) was launched in 1964. Although other airlines have rival systems, American Airlines' SABRE and United Airlines' Apollo system control 75 percent of the computerized reservation system market. A smaller carrier that cannot afford to build its own computerized reservation system can have its flights listed on its bigger competitors' systems, but it must pay a fee to the airline owning the system every time it sells a ticket through the computerized reservation system. Medium-size air carriers have claimed unfair treatment by SABRE and Apollo because these reservation systems list American and United Airlines' flights first.

Source: Barbara Bochenski, "The OLTP Bandwagon Traces Back to SABRE," *Software Magazine*, February 1989.

tems are the primary suppliers of data for information systems that support middle-level managers, who use summaries of transaction data for monitoring and controlling the firm's performance. For example, a typical report for a middle manager in a firm's Sales Department would be a summary of sales transactions by each sales region for a month or a year. In many instances, the basic transaction data and summarization of that data for management control will be produced by the same system. Systems specifically serving managers are discussed in Chapter 15.

Fault-Tolerant Systems

Imagine the consequences to American Airlines if its reservation system was "down" for more than a few minutes or if a bank's customers were deprived of their automated teller machines. Such firms have heavy **on-line transaction processing (OLTP)** requirements, with multitudinous requests for information and changes to files occurring each instant. Their on-line

On-line transaction processing (OLTP)
A transaction processing mode in which transactions entered on-line are immediately processed by the CPU.

Figure 12.1

The Concept of Transaction Processing in Basic Business Systems

A transaction processing system is the mainstay of a company, because it performs the basic procedures that keep the firm in business. Exactly what kind of transaction is processed depends on the nature of the firm. However, the basic concept of transaction processing is the same, regardless of the company's line of business. The system accepts input related to a transaction event, processes it, and produces output that enables the firm to continue functioning. The primary users of transaction processing systems are staff at the operational or lowest level within a firm. However, these systems can supply data for other systems that serve different levels and functions.

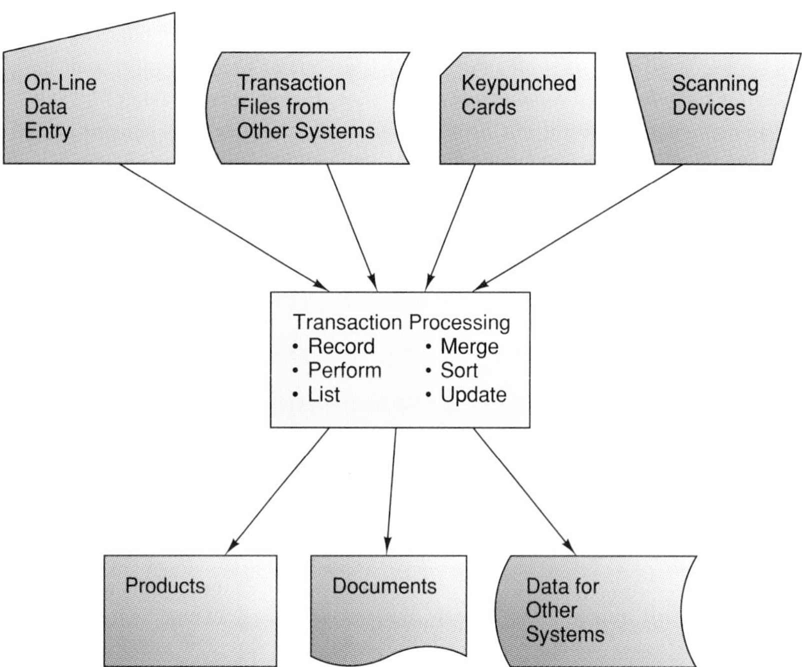

transaction processing systems, in which massive numbers of transactions are processed instantly by the CPU, can create major business disruptions if they break down.

Fault-tolerant computer systems
Systems with extra hardware, software, and power as backups against system failure.

To forestall such calamities, many firms with heavy OLTP requirements rely on **fault-tolerant computer systems** with extra hardware, software, and power supply as backups against system failure. Fault-tolerant computers contain extra processors, memory chips, and disk storage. They can use software routines or self-checking logic built into their circuitry to detect hardware failures and automatically switch to a backup device. Parts can be removed or repaired without disrupting the computer system.

About half of the systems of the Securities Industry Automation Corporation, the computing trading arm for both the New York and American Stock Exchanges, are fault tolerant. As the Focus on Technology describes, the First Florida Bank in Tampa needs fault-tolerant systems to keep its customers. Major airline and hotel reservation systems also depend on fault-tolerant technology.

FOCUS ON *Technology*

No Bad ATMs

According to Sam Triplett, vice-president and manager of telecommunications for First Florida Bank in Tampa, it takes just one bad experience with an automated teller machine (ATM) to lose a customer forever. First Florida relies on a Stratus XA600 fault-tolerant controller to manage line control and route data on its on-line transaction processing network, consisting of 175 ATMs across the state and 56 point-of-sale terminals in Cash n' Carry convenience stores. Since First Florida plans to put point-of-sale terminals in 50 more Cash n' Carry stores, it needs to ensure that its on-line transaction processing network remains up and operating.

Source: "Seamless Integration Sets OLTP Strategies," *Information Week,* March 6, 1989.

12.3 Examples of Basic Business Systems

A typical firm will have basic business systems for all of its major functional areas: manufacturing and production, sales and marketing, finance and accounting, and human resources. Depending on the nature of the firm's goods and services, these basic business systems will be more prominent in some functional areas than in others. For example, a bank or brokerage house may have only a small manufacturing system, since it primarily deals in financial services, but it will have extensive financial systems. Conversely, a firm that manufactures carburetors will put more weight on manufacturing systems; its financial systems will be less important.

Basic Manufacturing and Production Systems

Information systems support basic manufacturing and production functions by supplying the data to operate, monitor, and control the production process. They collect data and produce reports concerning the status of production tasks, inventories, purchases, and the flow of goods and services. Such manufacturing and production systems are not limited to manufacturing firms. Other businesses such as wholesalers, retail stores, financial institutions, and service companies use manufacturing and production systems to monitor and control inventories, goods, and services. Table 12.1 lists typical basic manufacturing and production systems.

Purchasing systems maintain data on materials purchased for the manufacturing process, such as files on vendors, prices of purchased items, and items on order. Receiving systems maintain data on purchased goods that

Table 12.1

Standard Manufacturing Systems

Application	Purpose
Purchasing	Enter, process, and track purchases.
Receiving	Track the receipt of purchased items.
Shipping	Track shipments to inventory and to customers.
Materials	Catalog usage of materials in production processes.
Labor costing	Track the cost of labor as a production cost.
Equipment	Track the cost of equipment and facilities as production costs.
Quality control	Monitor production processes to identify variance from quality control standards.
Process control	Monitor ongoing physical production processes.
Numerical control (machine)	Control actions of machines.
Robotics	Use programmed intelligence to control actions of machines.
Inventory systems	Record the number, cost, and location of items in stock.

have been received and their delivery dates and supply this information to the production, inventory, and accounts payable functions. Shipping systems track the placement of finished products into inventory and shipments to customers; this information is then passed on to inventory and accounts receivable. Inventory systems track inventory levels, stockout conditions, and the location and distribution of stock in the organization.

Materials systems track the usage of materials in the production process. The bill-of-materials system described in Chapter 2 inventories the raw materials and component parts needed to fashion a specific product. Labor-costing systems track the usage of personnel resources in the production process, and equipment systems track the costs of equipment and facilities for production.

Quality control systems
Manufacturing and production systems that monitor the production process to identify variances from established standards so that defects can be corrected.

Process control systems
Manufacturing and production systems that use computers to monitor the ongoing physical production processes.

Robotics
Devices with built-in intelligence and computer-controlled, humanlike capabilities that can control their own activities; used in manufacturing and production.

Quality control systems collect data using shop floor data collection devices, such as counters, assembly-line data entry terminals, or process control sensors. The latter might be used to monitor the gauge of metal as it is fabricated into sheets, bars, or wire. If the system detects any variance, signifying that an item fails to meet established standards, it notifies supervisory personnel. **Process control systems** use computers to monitor an ongoing physical process, such as the production of paper, food products, or chemicals.

Numerical control systems, also called machine control systems, use computers to control the actions of machines, such as machine tools in factories or typesetting machines. Numerical control programs for machine tools convert design specifications and machining instructions into commands that control the action of the machinery.

Robotics is a more intelligent version of machine control. Robotic devices are machines with built-in intelligence and computer-controlled, humanlike capabilities (such as movement or vision) that can control their own activities. For example, a robot might be used in automobile manufacturing to pick up heavy parts or to paint doors.

In addition to performing these tasks, manufacturing and production systems are important sources of data for other systems. They interact with the firm's inventory, order processing, and accounting systems and supply data for systems serving middle- and higher-level management, such as capacity planning, production scheduling, and facilities planning.

Significant economies, efficiencies, and competitive advantages have resulted from integrating basic manufacturing and production systems with management control systems and other functional areas. Many firms have implemented manufacturing resource planning (MRP-II) systems, which coordinate materials requirements planning, process control, inventory management, and capacity planning and exchange data automatically with the firm's financial accounting systems. Computer-integrated manufacturing (CIM) systems tie together all of the computer systems used in manufacturing—computer-aided design, computer-aided manufacturing, computer-aided engineering, and manufacturing resources planning, replacing uncoordinated islands of automation with seamless integration and control.

Elco's statistical process control system, which is described in the next section, illustrates key features of basic manufacturing systems. As you read this case study, ask yourself, Where does a basic manufacturing system obtain its data? What does it actually do with the data? What business problems does a manufacturing system solve? What difference does this manufacturing system make for the firm?

A Typical Manufacturing and Production System: Elco's Statistical Process Control System · A major producer of fasteners and precision metal components to the automotive and electronic industries, Elco Industries in Rockford, Illinois, must guarantee products with accurate dimensions. Elco uses the cold-heading method of production, in which rod or wire is fed into dies, cut to length, positioned, and struck by a punch. The force of the punch blow causes the metal to flow into the shape of the punch and die, thus forming the part. The firm must maintain tight tolerances, often in ten-thousandths of an inch, over long production runs. Variations in production will occur if any of the Ms—machine, materials, measurement, and man (the machine operator)—are slightly off. The company's inspection and quality control departments rely on constant production sampling and control charts.

Statistical process control measures groups of sample parts to plot averages and ranges in a production run. During production, a number of measurements of groups of sample parts will be taken. A particular group of sample measurements, such as dimensional measurements, are averaged, as are those for other groups. These averages are plotted on a chart along with the ranges of each sample group. Machine operators and quality control staff use this information to determine how a production run is progressing and whether some remedial action is required to bring the dimensions within acceptable range.

Elco found that manual methods of statistical process control took roughly two and one-half hours for a study of 20 groups of five samples

Figure 12.2

Sample Output from the Elco Statistical Process Control System

Elco's statistical process control system is a good example of a transaction processing system that improved a firm's manufacturing function. This system has automated Elco's quality control, which involves measuring sample products to gauge production performance. Output from the system includes charts, histograms, and bell curves. Also shown are measurements for the samples and acceptable limits.

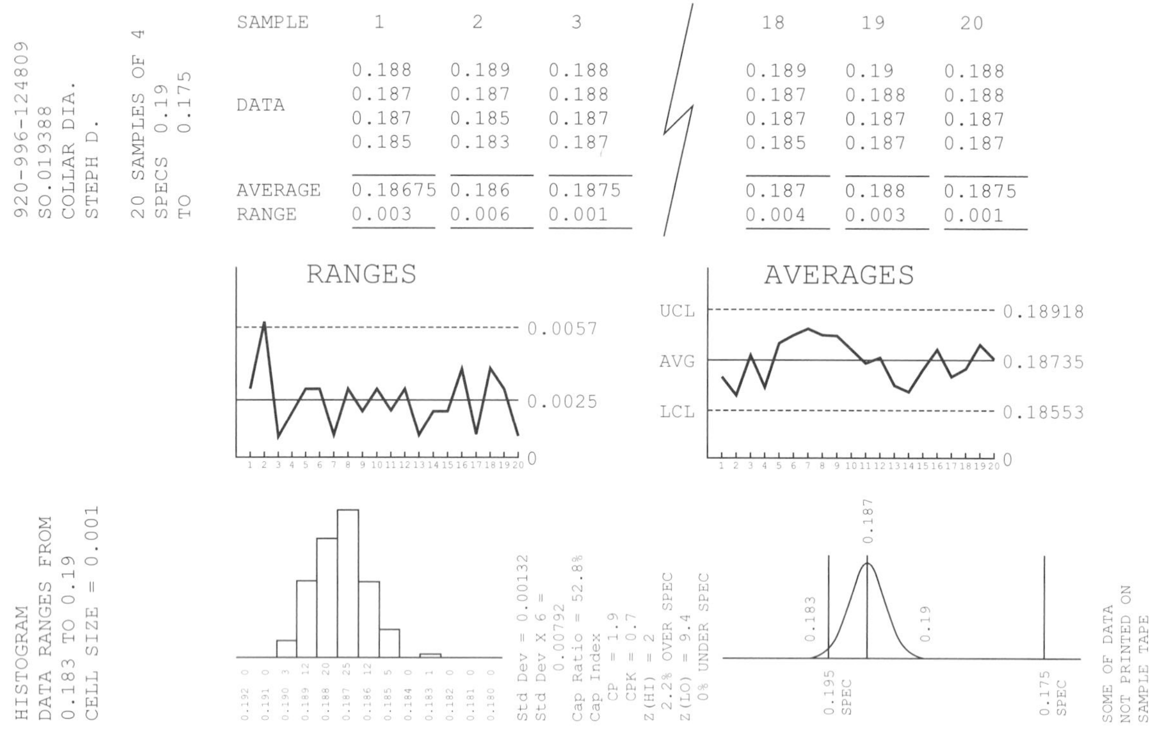

each—much too long to be practical. Ninety-five percent of this time was consumed by calculations and constructing charts. By the time production runs were measured and calculations performed, many defective units had been produced.

One of Elco's quality control engineers developed a computer program to produce the required calculations and charts. Utilizing a tiny handheld Sharp PC-1500A computer, the software calculates control limits, prints values that are entered, and draws charts, histograms, and bell curves. Figure 12.2 shows some sample output, which is generated on 2¼-inch tape. The system allows for corrections, deletions, recalculation of control limits, and redrawing of charts.

Elco's statistical process control system is so easy to use that anyone equipped with its brief *Operating Instructions* booklet can learn to run a statistical check in half an hour. Instructions carried on the display remain until answered. Data on a particular study are retained until new material is inserted. The program has been so successful that Elco now markets its system to other companies.[1]

Let's return now to the questions that we raised at the beginning of the case study:

- **Where does a basic manufacturing system obtain its data?** Elco's statistical process control system, shown in Figure 12.3, obtains its information from dimensional measurements of sample products—in this case, wires and fasteners—in a given production run.
- **What does a manufacturing system actually do with the data?** The statistical process control system performs calculations based on measurements of samples from the production line. It plots averages of sample measurements for each group studied in the production run. The averages and ranges for each sample group are plotted on a chart to provide a statistical and visual concept of how a production run is progressing. Machine operators and quality control staff monitor these charts to determine whether the output of a production run is within the acceptable range, or tolerances.
- **What business problems does a manufacturing system solve?** This system helps guide and monitor the flow of production by identifying output that does not conform to specifications so that machine operators can take corrective action before the dimensions of the products exceed the acceptable range.
- **What difference does this manufacturing system make for the firm?** The system reduced production costs by automating a calculation process that formerly took close to two and one-half hours. Man-hours consumed by calculations have been reduced by 95 percent. There is less wasted output from the production process because calculations are produced in time for machine operators to take corrective action against defects. The system promotes quality control by making it easier to measure whether production runs are falling within tight quality control limits. This enables the firm to back up its reputation for high-quality fasteners and wires, potentially increasing customer satisfaction and market share.

Figure 12.3

How the Elco Statistical Process Control System Works

Automating its statistical process control has allowed Elco Industries to reduce process control time by an impressive 95 percent, in addition to reducing defective output. Staff key the measurements of sample products into a handheld computer, which compares the samples to the control limits. Output includes reports and charts, such as those in Figure 12.2, on 2¼ inch tape.

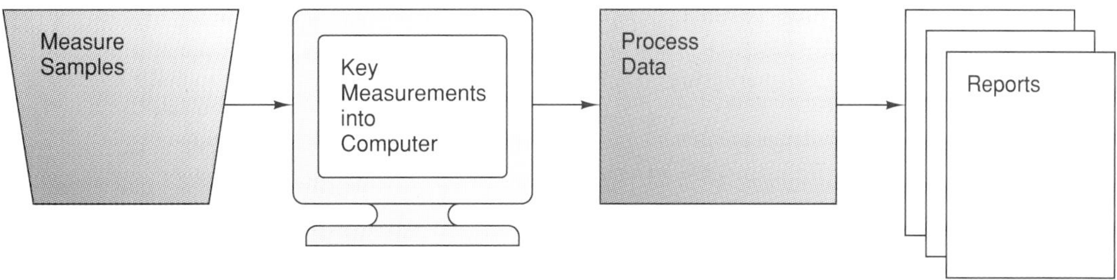

Selling Peterbilt and Kenworth trucks is quite complex because all trucks are custom built, and both lines have at least six models with some models offering more than 2,000 options. Using specialized sales and marketing software on COMPAQ portable computers, sales personnel can work up highly accurate estimates in 20 minutes.

Source: Courtesy of Compaq Computer Corporation.

Basic Sales and Marketing Systems

At the most elemental level, information systems support the sales and marketing function by facilitating the movement of goods and services from producers to consumers. These systems collect and process routine, repetitive data concerning locating customers, offering goods and services, processing sales and orders, and authorizing customer purchases. Table 12.2 lists typical sales and marketing information processing systems.

Sales support systems help sales staff identify potential customers, make customer contacts, and follow up on a sale. These systems record and keep track of prospective customers and customer contacts. They may include information such as the prospect or contact's name, address, and

Table 12.2

Standard Sales and Marketing Systems

Application	Purpose
Sales support	Track customer contacts and prospective customers.
Telemarketing	Track the use of the telephone to make contacts, offer products, and follow up on sales.
Order processing	Enter, process, and track orders.
Point-of-sale systems	Record sales data.
Customer credit authorization	Inform sales staff about a customer's maximum allowable credit.

product preferences. **Telemarketing systems** track the use of the telephone for contacting customers, offering products, and following up on sales.

Order processing systems record and process sales orders, tracking the status of orders, producing invoices, and often producing data for sales analysis and inventory control. **Point-of-sale systems,** which were described more fully in Chapter 2, capture sales data at the actual point of sale through the cash register or hand-held laser scanners.

Customer credit information systems provide sales representatives or credit managers with information concerning the maximum credit to be granted to a customer; they may contain credit history information. These systems are often integrated with the firm's order processing and accounting systems.

Like other basic business systems, sales and marketing transaction systems supply data to other systems. Data from order processing and point-of-sale systems, for example, are used not only to track sales but also in sales management information systems to help sales managers evaluate sales performance or to shape sales targets. Sales systems are also linked with information systems from other business functional areas, such as purchasing systems and accounts receivable systems.

The one-stop sales and payment system used by Circuit City Stores, Inc., and described in the next section, is an example of a leading-edge sales system. As you read this case study, ask yourself Where does a basic sales and marketing system obtain its data? What does it actually do with the data? What business problems does this system solve? What difference does this system make for the firm?

Telemarketing systems
Sales and marketing systems that track the use of the telephone for contacting customers, offering products, and following up sales.

Order processing systems
Sales and marketing systems that record and process sales orders, track the status of orders, produce invoices, and often produce data for sales analysis and inventory control.

Point-of-sale systems
Sales and marketing systems that capture sales data at the actual point of sale through the cash register or hand-held laser scanners.

A Typical Sales and Marketing System: No Lines at Circuit City Stores · Circuit City Stores, Inc., a national electronics and home appliance retailer based in Richmond, Virginia, makes shopping easier through a system that allows customers in its 125 branch stores to pay for different items from different departments at a single register. The system uses special internally developed software and an in-store minicomputer that can handle up to 64 devices, including point-of-sale terminals and printers.[2]

When a customer selects a microwave oven, for example, the salesperson enters the sale on his register and prints out the customer's number. The customer can then move on to another department and purchase a television by simply giving her customer number to the salesperson in that department. When the customer's shopping expedition is over, she goes to the checkout stand. The checker enters the customer's number and the total appears. In the meantime, the system has transmitted the order to the printer on the receiving dock. By the time the customer arrives with her car for the merchandise, the purchases are already waiting there. This system is shown in Figure 12.4.

Before Circuit City installed this system in 1981, it used a network of Hewlett Packard HP 3000 minicomputers based in company headquarters. The firm decentralized to in-store minicomputers to avert disruptions from telecommunications failures. A by-product of the new system is improved customer service, because each store maintains its own database of customer-buying records, which can be referenced by customer service representatives and equipment repair staff.

Figure 12.4

The Circuit City Sales System

Circuit City Stores, Inc., a large electronics and appliances retailer, has automated its sales/marketing system to allow customers to only pay once, regardless of how much they buy. With a customer's first purchase, a clerk enters the sale into the register and obtains a printout of the customer's number. This number is all that the customer needs to make further purchases. When the checker enters the number into the computer, the system tallies the total sale and forwards the data to the dock, where a printer outputs the customer's order and bill. The merchandise is ready for pickup when the customer drives up to the dock.

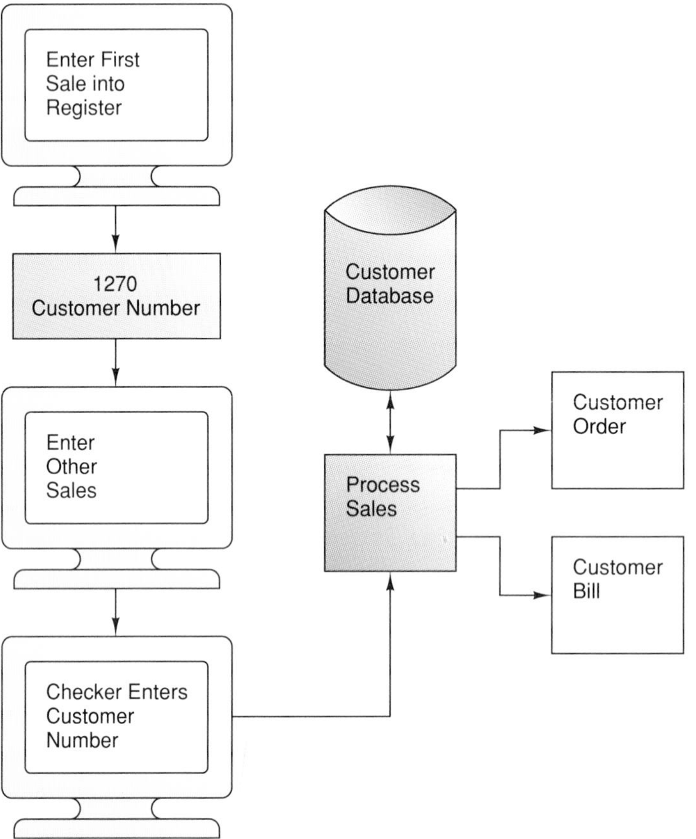

Let's return to our list of questions to examine more carefully what a sales and marketing system does:

- **Where does a basic sales and marketing system obtain its data?** The raw information comes from actual customer purchase transactions in each store. Each time a customer purchases an item, the purchase is recorded on the system. These sales transactions are tracked, recorded, and totaled by customer number, which is an identification number assigned to each customer when he or she comes to the cash register with the first item purchased.
- **What does a basic sales and marketing system actually do with the data?** Like other basic business systems, this system primarily re-

cords transaction events—that is, the purchase of each item. The system then transmits the order to the receiving dock printer. The order is printed out, and warehouse clerks retrieve the items for the customer. In other words, this sales system tracks purchases, totals sales by customer, and transmits order information to inventory.

- **What business problems does this system solve?** The system solves the problem of how to record individual purchase transactions and how to supply customers with their purchases. These are very routine, repetitive, structured problems that require no decision to be made: if a customer purchases an item (and has the means to pay for it), he or she must receive that item from the warehouse unless it is out of stock.

  In addition, customer purchase transactions from this system feed a database of customer-buying records. This provides information such as the brand and model of videocassette player a customer purchased and whether the customer purchased a service contract as well as the appliance. This information can be utilized by customer service representatives to assign appropriate repair staff and to stock the necessary repair parts.
- **What difference does this system make for the firm?** Circuit City's sales system primarily expedites the purchasing and delivery processes. Because purchase data are transmitted directly to the receiving dock, the customer can be supplied immediately from the warehouse. His or her order is immediate, direct, and not subject to discrepancies caused by time lags or transcription errors.

  The system creates some strategic advantage by providing superior service to customers. It reduces lines in individual departments, at the cash register, and at the receiving dock. Customers can make payments and receive delivery in a much smoother and more timely manner.

Basic Accounting and Financial Systems

Some of the earliest computer systems automated accounting and financial functions. Accounting systems maintain records concerning the flow of funds in the firm and produce financial statements, such as balance sheets and income statements. Financial systems keep records concerning the firm's use and management of funds. Table 12.3 lists the basic accounting and financial systems.

Accounts receivable systems keep records of amounts owed by customers and credit information, based on customer invoice and payment data. **Accounts payable systems,** in contrast, keep track of amounts owed to the firm's creditors. They generate checks for outstanding invoices and report payment transactions.

Accounts receivable systems
Accounting systems that keep track of amounts owed to the firm.

Accounts payable systems
Accounting systems that keep track of amounts owed by a firm to its creditors.

General ledger systems use data from the accounts receivable, payroll, accounts payable, and other accounting systems to record the firm's income and expenses. They produce the income statements, balance sheets, general ledger trial balance, and other reports. The Focus on Problem Solving describes some of the problems an accounting department may face and explains how the Brodart Company found a solution to its problems.

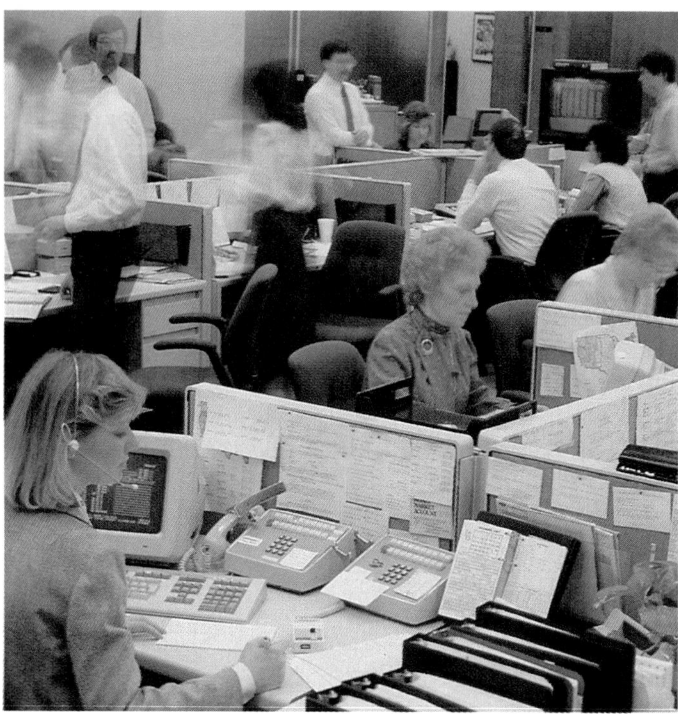

Ford Motor Credit Company's financial sales department sells securities directly to investors. Financial systems make the task more productive and efficient.

Source: Courtesy of Ford Motor Company.

Table 12.3

Standard Accounting and Financial Systems

Application	Purpose
Accounting	
Accounts receivable	Track money owed the firm; issue bills.
Accounts payable	Track money the firm owes.
General ledger	Summarize business accounts used to prepare balance sheets and income statements.
Payroll	Manage payroll records and produce paychecks.
Finance	
Cash management	Track the firm's receipts and disbursements.
Loan processing	Track transactions for consumer and commercial loans and credit card transactions; calculate interest and issue billing statements.
Check processing	Track checking account deposits and payments; issue statements of checking account activity and balances.
Securities trading	Track buying and selling of stocks, bonds, options, and other securities.

FOCUS ON *Problem Solving*

Brodart Decentralizes Corporate Accounting Applications

Brodart Company, a supplier of library equipment with revenues of $150 million a year, expects to save several hundred thousand dollars a year on computing expenses by pulling corporate accounting applications off its centralized IBM 4381 mainframe and putting them on a mid-range AS/400.

Brodart decided to switch to the AS/400 for several reasons. From the accounting department's point of view, centralized computing was expensive and not very effective. When accounting managers throughout the firm wanted reports or changes, they had to fill out a form for data processing, then wait. Control of reports and consolidation data were limited. In addition, hardware costs for storage and memory kept rising. Supporting mainframe financial software packages required four to six staff members dedicated to keeping the packages up and running and installing new releases.

Given these problems, the company's prime objective was to find an accounting solution requiring less programming and operations support. Since the accounting department handles 123,000 accounts payable, 30,000 invoices, and 37 companies on the general ledger, some skeptics questioned whether a mid-range system would be sufficient to handle all the department's needs. Nevertheless, the AS/400 has been successful. With the new system, data processing support for accounting now requires about 12 fewer programming and operations positions. In fact, one data processing manager and one operator run accounting's new processor. Accounting managers are responsible for their own data and even write most of the reports and run jobs themselves.

A welcome but somewhat unexpected benefit of decentralized accounting has been the degree of improved control accounting managers have over their own data.

Chris Daly, vice-president of finance and chief financial officer, noted that a decentralized approach does allow more users access to accounting data, which could raise data integrity questions. However, the software limits update authority and provides a "good audit trail." "More people enter data, but only into restricted areas," he noted.

In choosing software packages, the company settled on financial packages from Software 2000 Inc., in Hyannis, Massachusetts, because the packages "most closely replicated what we have on the mainframe," Daly said.

Source: John Mahnke, "Brodart Decentralizes Corporate Accounting Applications," *MIS Week*, January 22, 1990, p. 13.

Payroll systems are sometimes treated as human resources systems, but they also perform important accounting functions. They calculate and produce employee paychecks, earnings statements for the Internal Revenue Service and state and local taxing authorities, and payroll reports.

Cash management systems track receipts and disbursements of cash. Firms use this information to identify excess funds that can be deposited or invested to generate additional income. Cash management systems may also produce cash flow forecasts that managers can utilize for planning and development of alternative investment strategies.

Cash management systems
Financial systems that keep track of the receipt and disbursement of cash by a firm; they may also forecast the firm's cash flow.

The accounting and financial systems described above are found in virtually all firms, whereas loan processing, check processing, and securities trading systems are industry specific, serving primarily the banking and securities industries. Loan processing systems are used by banks to record transactions that initiate and pay for consumer and commercial loans and credit card transactions. Such systems keep track of principal and interest and issue customer billing statements. Banks use check processing systems to track deposits and payments in checking accounts and to produce customer statements of account activity.

Securities trading systems are used by the New York and American Stock Exchanges to track the purchase and sale of stocks, bonds, options, and other securities. The Globex trading system described in the next section is a leading-edge example of such a system. This case study can help us understand the workings of basic financial systems if we keep in mind the following questions: Where does a basic financial system obtain its data? What does it actually do with the data? What business problems does this system solve? What difference does this system make for the firm?

A Basic Financial System: Electronic Trading on the Chicago Mercantile Exchange · Globex, the electronic trading system developed jointly by the Chicago Mercantile Exchange and Reuters Holdings P.S.C., is in some ways the most advanced electronic trading system in the financial markets. It can handle orders of any size for financial futures contracts. Brokers can see what orders have been placed by other brokers and take the opposite side of, or "hit," any such order. However, in contrast to the traditional futures trading pits, where every trader can see who takes the opposite side of a trade, the Globex system is impersonal. There is no way of knowing who takes the other side of an order.

When an order is entered at terminals from Tokyo to Chicago to London, it will be recorded on the Globex system within one-hundredth of a second. The system provides automatic confirmation of all orders executed. If two brokers want to sell a financial futures contract at the same price, and there is only one buyer, the order entered first will prevail.[3]

As Figure 12.5 illustrates, in the Globex system, traders enter buy and sell orders on computer terminals, and the data are transmitted to a central computer. Customers' credit is screened, and buy and sell orders are matched based on time and price priority. Trades are executed instantaneously and files are updated accordingly. Confirmed trades are sent to the clearing system, where clearing member firms settle buyers' and sellers' accounts.

The Globex system claims to have an almost perfect audit trail, which makes trading violations much easier to detect. Under the traditional open-outcry system in the trading pits, it is sometimes difficult to know when a trade is executed because dozens of brokers are gesturing, yelling, and finalizing trades by eye contact. A difference of even a minute can make a big difference in price. Traders intent on cheating might find it easier to fabricate trades to benefit themselves at the customer's expense under the old system.

Globex trades financial futures contracts, notably currencies and Eurodollars, from the Chicago Mercantile Exchange from 6:00 P.M. to 6:00 A.M. Chicago time, but it is not used when the exchange itself is open. Although the hours when Globex is operational are not prime trading times in the United States, they do include the entire Japanese trading day and the

Figure 12.5

A Basic Financial System—Globex

Globex is an advanced electronic trading system developed by the Chicago Mercantile Exchange and Reuters Holdings P.S.C. Traders enter buy-and-sell orders into computer terminals. The central computer screens customers' credit, matches orders, and executes trades instantaneously. Confirmed trades are sent to the clearing system, where buyers' and sellers' accounts are settled. The Globex system makes it much easier to detect trading violations; unscrupulous traders cannot take advantage of price changes because orders are matched and executed so quickly.

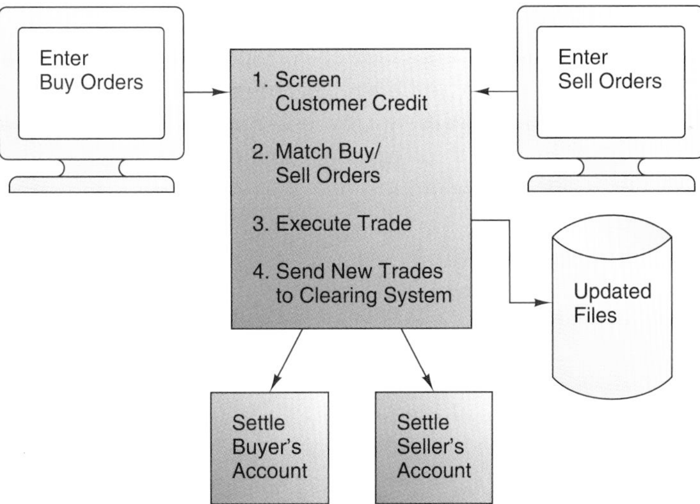

early London trading hours. The main users of Globex are not local Chicago traders, who spend most of the day in the pits, but commodities firms representing institutional clients.

The costs of the system discourage infrequent users. The Globex computer terminal rents for $800 per month with additional charges for telephone lines. A sophisticated system, complete with news reports that can affect prices, costs about $2,000 a month. A small fee must be paid to the Chicago Mercantile Exchange for each trade on the Globex system, whether the trade is in a Chicago Mercantile Exchange commodity or one from another futures exchange. The New York Mercantile Exchange and the Singapore Futures Exchange have some of their contracts traded on Globex.

Now let's return to the questions we posed at the beginning of this case study:

- **Where does a basic financial system obtain its information?** Information for the Globex system comes from buy and sell orders for financial futures contracts (currencies and Eurodollars) from the Chicago Mercantile Exchange. The orders are initiated by brokers and commodities firm traders who enter them on-line into terminals (as opposed to trading face to face in the futures pits). In addition to buy and sell transactions, the system maintains customer credit data.

- **What does a basic financial system actually do with the data?** This financial system primarily tracks buy and sell transactions for financial futures contracts. It records each customer's buy and sell order, authorizes each buy order using customer credit data, and matches different buy and sell orders based on their price and the time they are placed. The system then executes the trades and sends confirmed trade transactions to a clearing system. (The clearing system, in turn, settles buyers' and sellers' accounts.)
- **What business problems does this system solve?** In contrast to the traditional open-outcry system, this system instantaneously records and tracks buy and sell transactions for financial futures contracts. It provides a more precise and up-to-date record of trading activity than the traditional open-outcry system. It eliminates the ambiguity of face-to-face trading in the pits, preventing traders from cheating by fabricating trades and taking advantage of minute timing differences that can affect prices.
- **What difference does this system make for the firm?** The system opens trading activity to a wider number of players. It does not compete with the traditional Chicago exchange but operates during hours that are more convenient for foreign countries, such as Britain and Japan. The Globex system makes trading in financial futures contracts more accessible to commodities firms representing institutional clients.

Basic Human Resources Systems

At the most elementary level, human resources information systems deal with the recruitment, placement, performance evaluation, compensation, and career development of the firm's employees. Basic human resources systems collect data concerning employees and support repetitive, routine tasks such as tracking new hires, promotions, transfers, and terminations and maintaining records of employee benefits and beneficiaries.

Table 12.4 lists the most important basic human resources systems. In addition to the systems listed in the table, some firms treat payroll systems

Table 12.4

Standard Human Resources Systems

Application	Purpose
Personnel record keeping	Maintain employee records.
Applicant tracking	Maintain data about job applicants.
Positions	Track positions in the firm.
Training and skills	Maintain employee training and skills inventory records.
Benefits	Maintain records of employee benefits and perform benefits accounting.

as human resources systems because they maintain employee data that is used by the human resources function. Others consider payroll primarily an accounting function.

Personnel record-keeping systems maintain basic employee data, such as name, address, marital status, dependents, age, Equal Employment Opportunity (EEO) category, and job performance appraisals, and they also record hiring, termination, transfer, promotion, and performance evaluation transactions. **Applicant tracking systems** maintain data about applicants for jobs and provide reports to satisfy federal, state, and local employment regulations.

Applicant tracking systems
Human resources systems that maintain data about applicants for jobs at a firm and provide reports to satisfy federal, state, and local employment regulations.

Positions systems, by contrast, do not maintain information on employees but on the positions in the firm. A position can be defined as a slot in the firm's organization chart. Positions systems maintain data about filled and unfilled positions and track transactions concerning changes in positions and job assignments.

Positions systems
Human resources systems that maintain information about positions (slots in a firm's organization chart); they maintain data about filled and unfilled positions and track changes in positions and job assignments.

Training and skills systems maintain records of employees' training and work experiences, interests, and special skills and proficiencies. Such systems can identify employees with appropriate skills for special assignments or job requirements.

Training and skills systems
Human resources systems that maintain records of employees' training and work experience so that employees with appropriate skills for special assignments or job requirements can be identified.

Benefits systems maintain data about employees' life insurance, health insurance, pensions, and other benefits and track transactions such as changes in beneficiaries and benefits coverage.

Benefits systems
Human resources systems that maintain data about employees' life insurance, health insurance, pensions, and other benefits, including changes in beneficiaries and benefits coverage.

Basic human resources systems may also provide data for managers or supply data to other systems specifically serving management. For example, positions systems are used for management analysis of turnover problems and recruitment strategies as well as for succession planning.

Traditionally, the basic business systems in large firms have been based on mainframes and minicomputers, but given the processing power and capabilities of personal computers today, many high-volume transaction processing tasks can now be performed on a desktop computer. The Charitable Contribution Deduction System for the Hospital of the University of Pennsylvania in Philadelphia is an example of how transaction processing can be accomplished with personal computer technology. Again, as you read the following account, keep our list of questions in mind: Where does a basic human resources system obtain its data? What does it actually do with the data? What business problems does this system solve? What difference does this system make for the firm?

A Basic Human Resources System: University Hospital's Charitable Contribution Deduction System · Human resources departments traditionally sponsor events such as company-wide blood drives and fund-raising campaigns for charities. Such activities can elevate employee morale and directly affect employee benefits and compensation. Accurate tracking of employees' contributions is required.

The Human Resources Department of the Hospital of the University of Pennsylvania in Philadelphia solicits its 4,000 employees annually for contributions to several charities. The Technical Services Department of the division of information management worked with the hospital's Human Resources Department to develop a personal computer–based system that tracks United Way contributions. The system creates transactions to deduct contributions directly from employees' paychecks and to create participation records.[4]

Systems for managing earlier United Way campaigns required excessive data entry and could not verify known information. The United Way campaign director wanted a system that could provide current fund-raising information to his department canvassers and post the current total of pledged contributions by employees. The system also had to interface with the hospital's mainframe-based payroll system, since most employees wanted to have their charitable donations deducted directly from their paychecks.

The solution was an IBM Personal Computer (PC)–based system using dBASE III database management software. Most employee data are already maintained in the payroll system. Therefore, to eliminate redundant data entry, the system loads only select pieces of employee data from the payroll system onto the PC. The payroll system prints a set of labels with employee data snapshots, including the employee's name, department, employee number, and department and supervisor codes. The labels are fixed to pledge cards, with the employee number as the key, or identifying, field. If an employee's pledge card is lost, the employee's name can be looked up alphabetically.

Department canvassers distribute the pledge cards. Employees return their cards to the human resources offices. Employee numbers and pledges are then keyed in, which updates the PC contribution system. The system looks up and displays employees' records, which include name, department, supervisor, type of deduction (one-time or regular payroll deduction), and amount of donation.

Once data have been entered, the system can generate reports showing targets and results for both money raised and the number of participating employees. The reports are distributed to the lead canvassers and to contributors so that they can review their accounts. The system generates a transaction file on a floppy disk for the mainframe payroll system with the names and numbers of employees requesting payroll deductions. Updates and changes are processed using the standard human resources procedures. Figure 12.6 illustrates this system.

Once again, we return to the questions we raised at the beginning of the case study:

- **Where does a basic human resources system obtain its information?** This charitable contribution system obtains its data from two sources: (1) employee data (such as name, department, and employee number) extracted from another transaction processing system, the hospital's payroll system; and (2) employee pledges of charitable contributions, which are transmitted to the system on pledge cards.
- **What does a basic human resources system actually do with the data?** Employee pledge cards containing employee number and charitable contribution deduction amount are the transactions for the charitable contribution system. These transactions create or update the participation records on the personal computer. Outputs consist of reports listing employees who participated in the United Way campaigns and a floppy disk file of names, employee numbers, and

Figure 12.6

A Human Resources System Tracks Employees' Charitable Contributions

This microcomputer-based system provides current fund-raising information and eliminates excessive data entry. Programmed with dBASE III software, the system loads selected employee data extracted from the payroll system and prints a label for each employee. Staff place the labels on pledge cards, which are distributed to 4,000 employees. The information on returned pledge cards is entered into the system, which quickly updates the records of employee contributions. It also prints reports documenting the progress of the fund-raising campaign, as well as a transaction file passed to the payroll system allowing employees to have their contributions deducted from their paychecks.

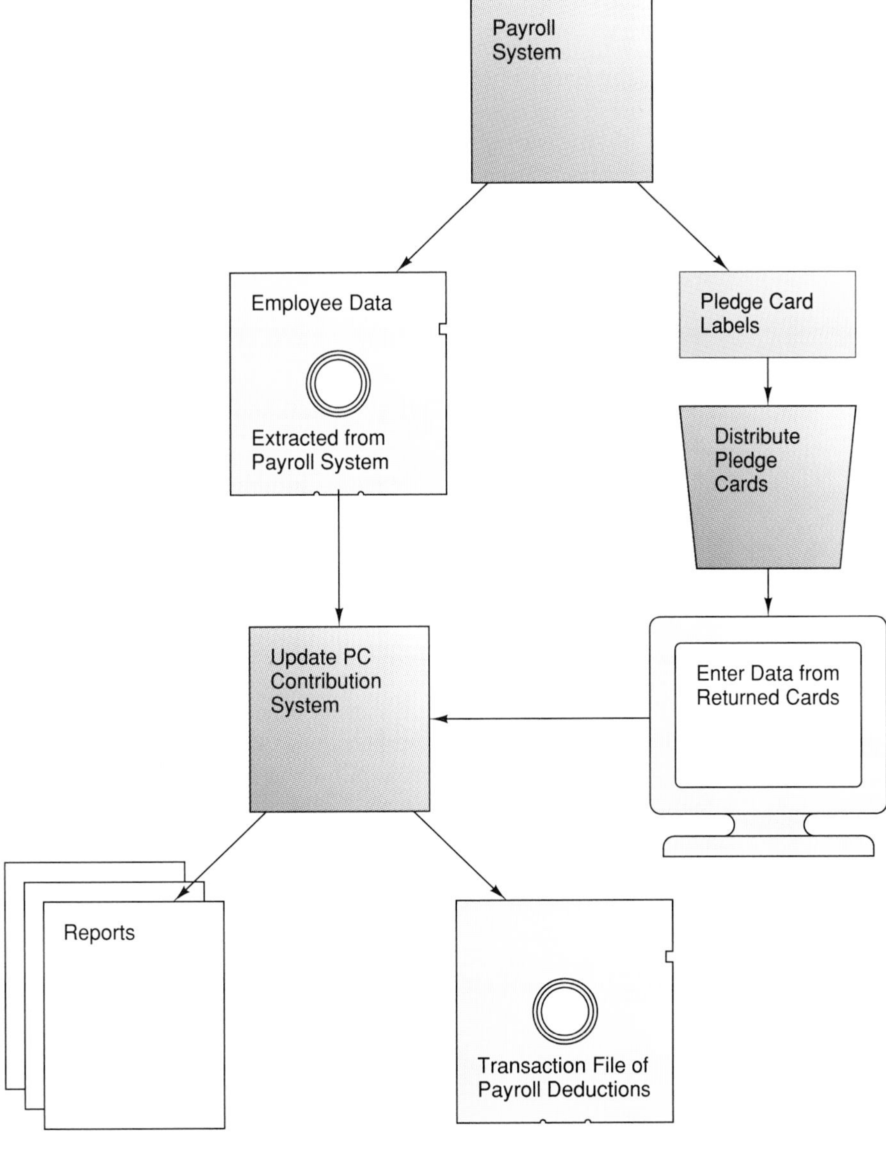

payroll deductions, which serve as transactions for the hospital's mainframe payroll system.

- **What business problems does this system solve?** To comply with both internal record-keeping and external legal requirements, all firms must accurately track employee payroll deductions, including charitable contributions. The system solves the operational problem of determining who made charitable contributions and who must have charitable contributions deducted from paychecks. The charitable contribution deduction system automates such record keeping and the transactions that feed related basic business systems (payroll).
- **What difference does this basic human resources system make for the firm?** Human resource experts believe that fund-raising for charities helps boost employee morale, although there is no way of tangibly measuring this. The charitable contribution deduction system supports such activities by saving time and administrative overhead.

12.4 The Challenges of Building Basic Business Systems

Because basic business systems are deeply engrained in the day-to-day operations of the business, organizational, people, and technical challenges are posed when such systems have to be built afresh or revised.

Organizational Challenges

Basic business systems are the lifeblood of organizations, embodying the organization's fundamental procedures. Although some of these procedures may be automated, many procedures may still have to be performed manually between the initiation of a transaction and the time it is finally recorded in a system.

A major organizational challenge is to fully understand, capture, and, if possible, rationalize or streamline these procedures so that a basic business system can function smoothly with as few steps as possible. Another challenge is to structure data so that they can flow smoothly into other systems and facilitate management decisions in higher levels of the firm.[5]

Perhaps the greatest challenge of this category of systems is the fear of rebuilding them. The basic business systems are so deeply embedded into a typical business's plans and day-to-day activities that they are exceedingly difficult to change and restructure. The sheer size and complexity of large basic business systems, such as the payroll system of the City of New York or the Internal Revenue Service Tax Administration system, make it impossible for them to be understood by one or a few individuals. Businesses typically resist changing their major business systems unless they are faced with a major crisis.

People Challenges

Information for basic business systems is relatively fixed, structured, and routine. People have less difficulty specifying the inputs, processes, and

FOCUS ON *People*

Wanted: Skilled Transaction Processing Specialists

For the past few years, American Airlines and other companies have searched as far away as Pakistan and Singapore for programmers skilled in their Airline Control Program/ Transaction Processing Facility (ACP/TPF). ACP/TPF is an operating system environment developed jointly by American and IBM in the 1950s, which is still widely used for high-volume transaction processing; it supports applications such as Walgreen Company's pharmaceutical network and American Express Company's credit authorization network.

Information systems professionals are responsible for maintaining TPF operations 24 hours a day, seven days a week. People who hire TPF specialists place a premium on their experience with this technology. In a transaction processing environment, an inexperienced programmer can do more harm than in other environments. Inexperienced programmers have been known to cause major outages to the most important system their company had.

According to Wolly Wilson, vice-president of American Express transaction services, working with TPF is challenging because high-volume transaction processing applications are very visible and represent the front end or lifeline of the company. For instance, American Express would lose its customers and cease to function if it could not immediately authorize credit card purchases.

Source: Sheryl Kay, "ACP/TPF Spreads Its Wings," *Computerworld,* April 24, 1989.

outputs for this class of systems than for higher-level systems. The primary people challenge is one of consistency and completeness—ensuring that all of the firm's operating procedures have been adequately defined, captured, and automated, when the procedures are multitudinous, complex, and poorly documented. Another people challenge is finding technical specialists with the requisite expertise to deal with critical transaction-oriented systems, in which mistakes and errors can trigger major business disruptions. The Focus on People examines this challenge in more detail.

Technology Challenges

Basic business systems have traditionally required hardware and software that can handle large numbers of discrete transaction events, collecting, updating, and listing up to millions of transactions each day. In the past, this required mainframe computing power and larger and larger machines as transaction volume soared. Fault-tolerant technology is essential for large-scale on-line transaction processing.

The primary technical question for basic business systems has become one of integration—how to link disparate islands of automation on the factory floor, in the warehouse, and in the accounting office so that their systems can exchange information with each other. Sometimes basic business systems do not efficiently supply the data required by management, and they need tighter integration with systems supporting higher levels of the firm.

Summary

• Basic business systems keep track of the most elementary, day-to-day activities of the firm, dealing with routine, repetitive problems for which the solution is based on the firm's standard operating procedures. These systems support the operational level of the business but also supply data for management decisions at higher levels of the firm.

• A transaction is a record of an event to which a firm's system must respond. Basic business systems, which keep track of the elementary transactions necessary to conduct a business, are also called transaction processing systems.

• In on-line transaction processing (OLTP) systems, transactions are immediately processed by the CPU. Firms that have to process massive numbers of transactions on-line are turning to fault-tolerant computer systems with backup hardware, software, and power supply to forestall major business disruptions if their on-line transaction processing breaks down.

• Basic business systems are utilized primarily by people at lower levels of the firm who have little or no management responsibility.

• Basic business systems help solve internal operating problems and problems concerning transactions with the firm's external environment—customers, suppliers, and government regulations.

• Output from basic business systems may consist of finished goods, paychecks, other documents, or data supplied to other systems. Basic business systems supply data to higher-level systems in the same functional area (for example, an order entry system supplies data for a sales management system) or to systems in different business areas.

• The basic business systems support the manufacturing and production functions by supplying data to operate, monitor, and control the production process. Materials, purchasing, receiving, shipping, process control, numerical control, equipment, quality control, labor-costing, and robotic systems are examples of basic manufacturing and production systems.

• The basic business systems support the sales and marketing function by collecting and processing routine, repetitive data concerning locating customers, offering goods and services, processing sales and orders, and authorizing purchases. Sales support, telemarketing, order processing, point-of-sale, and customer credit authorization systems are examples of basic sales and marketing systems.

• The basic business systems support the accounting and finance function by recording the flow of funds in the firm, by tracking the firm's use of funds, and by producing financial statements. There are also industry-specific financial systems for the banking and securities industries. Accounts receivable, accounts payable, general ledger, payroll, cash management, loan processing, check processing, and securities trading are examples of basic accounting and financial systems.

• The basic business systems support the human resources function by tracking the recruitment, placement, performance evaluation, compensation, and career development of the firm's employees. Personnel record-keeping, applicant tracking, positions, training and skills, and benefits systems are examples of basic human resources systems.

• The primary organizational challenge for basic business systems is to fully understand, capture, and, if possible, rationalize or streamline myriad operating procedures so that these systems can function smoothly with as few steps as possible. The primary technical question for basic business systems is how to integrate separate systems when there are disparate islands of automation throughout the firm. The primary people challenge of basic business systems is to ensure that all of the firm's multitudinous operating procedures have been adequately defined, captured, and automated in a system.

Key Terms

Basic business system
Transaction
Transaction processing system
On-line transaction processing (OLTP)
Fault-tolerant computer systems
Quality control systems
Process control systems
Robotics
Telemarketing systems
Order processing systems
Point-of-sale systems
Accounts receivable systems
Accounts payable systems
Cash management systems
Applicant tracking systems
Positions systems
Training and skills systems
Benefits systems

Review Questions

1. Define a basic business system. What functions do basic business systems serve?
2. What is a transaction? Give examples of three transactions used by businesses.
3. What kinds of problems do basic business systems solve? What kinds of positions in the firm use basic business systems?
4. What are the outputs of basic business systems?
5. What are fault-tolerant systems? Why are they necessary?
6. How do basic business systems support the manufacturing and production function? List and describe five kinds of manufacturing and production systems.
7. How do basic business systems support the sales and marketing function? List and describe four kinds of sales and marketing systems.
8. How do basic business systems support the accounting and financial functions? List and describe three accounting systems and four financial systems.
9. How do basic business systems support the human resources function? List and describe three human resources systems.

10. What are the principal organizational challenges of basic business systems? Technical challenges? People challenges?

Discussion Questions

1. An important function of basic business systems is to produce information for other systems. Discuss.

2. Why can failure of basic business systems for a few hours or days lead to a business firm's failure?

3. To be most effective, sales and marketing systems should be closely coordinated with basic business systems from other functional areas, such as manufacturing and production, and accounts receivable systems. Discuss.

Problem-Solving Exercises

1. As the director of Equal Economic Opportunity affairs for your firm, you are responsible for gathering the data concerning your firm's record in hiring and promoting women and minorities. How could you use human resources transaction processing systems for your work?

Develop two or three reports from the human resources systems described in this chapter that could assist you in this task. Then design a mock-up of each report, showing column headings, data fields required, and any kind of totals that would be useful.

2. Herman's Hardware is a mom-and-pop business in a neighborhood that is becoming increasingly gentrified on New York City's Upper West Side. Store space is limited, and rents have doubled over the past five years. Consequently, Herman and Ida Stein, the owners, are under great pressure to utilize every square foot of space as profitably as possible.

The Steins have never kept detailed records of stock in inventory or of their sales. Stock items are just automatically placed on shelves to be sold. Invoices from wholesalers are kept only for tax purposes. When an item is sold, the item number and price are rung up at the cash register. The Steins use their own judgment and observation in identifying stock items that are moving fast and might need reordering. Many times, however, they are caught short and lose the sale.

How could the Steins use the information they already maintain to help their business? What data would these systems capture? What reports would these systems produce?

Notes

1. "SPC Programmed Computer," *Manufacturing Systems,* March 1985.

2. Kathy Chin Leong, "Store Systems Help Retailers Give Shoppers What They Want," *Computerworld,* November 28, 1988.

3. Floyd Norris, "Computers for the Futures Pits," *The New York Times,* February 13, 1989.

4. Lawrence Sharrott, "The United Way," *Computers in Personnel* 1, no. 4 (Summer 1987).

5. Mary J. Culnan, "Transaction Processing Applications as Organizational Message Systems: Implications for the Intelligent Organization," Working Paper 88-10, 22nd Hawaii International Conference on Systems Sciences, January 1989.

Problem-Solving Case

Doing Away with Checks

The most popular way to pay bills is to mail a check. Currently, businesses in the United States write almost 10 billion checks a year to pay other companies. The attraction of this approach is that the time involved in writing and mailing a check is time that the company's money can be earning interest.

Despite this advantage, a number of large corporations have begun paying bills electronically. These companies include RJR Nabisco, General Motors, Du Pont, and Sears, Roebuck and Company. To pay, these companies simply have their bank transfer funds from their account to their suppliers' accounts. Sears currently makes about 40 percent of its payments—worth about $500 million a month—electronically. General Motors pays 1,200 suppliers electronically and plans to pay all 5,500 suppliers this way eventually.

The benefits of this approach, according to the companies that use it, include lower costs for processing transactions, fewer clerical errors, and cash flow that is more predictable. Compared to writing checks, Sears saves about 40 cents for each electronic payment it makes. At General Electric Company (GE), transactions paid by check are handled accurately 60 percent of the time; in contrast, the accuracy rate for transactions handled electronically is 95 percent. GE's manager for electronic payment systems, Charles Harp, credits this accuracy to less reentering of information into the system.

Even the government is in the electronic transfer act. According to Charles Schwan, director of the payment management division of the U.S. Treasury's financial management service, each check the federal government writes costs 30 cents, compared to only 4 cents for an electronic transfer.

The volume of payments handled electronically is expected to grow rapidly. As of 1988, Chase Manhattan Bank was expecting its volume of electronic payments to double within a year, to 4 million payments. The U.S. Treasury Department predicted that it would replace over 77 million checks a year with electronic payments by the early 1990s. As customers increasingly expect their banks to process electronic payments, institutions will have to be able to provide this service, or they will lose accounts.

To handle electronic payments, banks' computers must be linked with their customers' computers. With such a system in place, the transfer itself is a fairly simple process. What complicates the process of handling transactions is that companies not only send money to suppliers, they also send a form—a remittance—that tells the supplier how to apply the payment (for example, which account to credit).

A common feature in today's banking world is automated clearinghouses, which send data representing these transactions from the payer's bank to the supplier's bank. Thanks to automated clearinghouses, most banks have systems in place for transferring funds; however, many lack the ability to send remittance information electronically. These banks have difficulty telling companies they have been paid and for what, especially when a purchaser sends a single payment covering several invoices.

This poses a problem because most companies want their funds and documents to travel together; both are required to complete a transaction. For example, if funds arrive before the remittance, the payment may be credited to the wrong account. This may mean that the company cannot extend a customer credit even though the customer has already paid. Likewise, when remittances arrive before payments, they must be held until the funds arrive.

Banks that are technologically advanced can send remittance information to their corporate customers' computers. Unfortunately, most financial institutions today do not qualify as technologically advanced. Out of 18,000 financial institutions in the United States, only about 200 are well automated. And of those, only 30 have the capability to process the most advanced computer formats. Thus, many banks still document electronic payments by mailing paperwork to the supplier.

To fill this gap, nonfinancial institutions have responded by creating third-party networks. For example, General Electric Information Services and McDonnell Douglas Information Services provide networks for exchanging remittance documents. Sending an invoice on such networks can cost from 60 cents to over $75.

Some banks have hired information-handling companies to provide full electronic services for moving documents. For example, Marine Midland Bank in Buffalo, Citizens and Southern Bank in Atlanta, and First Bank System in Minneapolis use Atlanta-based Harbinger Computer Services.

Of course, electronic transfer of funds is not perfect. Outsiders interested in diverting funds or obtaining information may be able to penetrate the computer system. Also, the lack of paper documentation means that transactions might be difficult to trace if they are lost. Nevertheless, checks sent by mail also can be lost or stolen.

Source: Adapted from Teresa L. Petramala, "Why the Check Is No Longer in the Mail," *The New York Times,* March 26, 1989.

Case Study Questions

1. What problems does an electronic payments system solve for customers? For suppliers?
2. What are the basic transactions of an electronic payments system? What pieces of data are on each? Draw a diagram of what the Sears electronic payment system might look like.
3. What are the advantages of electronic payment systems for banks?
4. What problems are associated with electronic payment systems? Suggest possible solutions.
5. If a firm wants to switch to an electronic payment system, what factors must be considered?

C H A P T E R · T H I R T E E N

Knowledge and Information Work: Office Automation

Chapter Outline

13.1 Introduction: The Information and Knowledge Economy
- The Transformation of the American Economy
- The New Labor Force of the 1990s

13.2 The New Information and Knowledge Workers
- Information Workers: Data versus Knowledge Workers
- The Distribution of Information Workers
- The Productivity Connection: Information Workers and Offices

13.3 Office Automation: Automating Information Work
- The Three Roles of the Office in Business
- Roles, Activities, and Systems in the Office
- Groupware: A New Office Technology

13.4 Leading-Edge Application: Staying in the Fast Lane at BMW
- Office Automation at BMW

Learning Objectives

After reading and studying this chapter, you will:

1. Know what is meant by an "information and knowledge" economy.
2. Know who the new knowledge and information workers are.
3. Understand what office automation is and how it works.
4. Understand the role of office automation in contemporary business.
5. Be familiar with the principal types of office automation systems.

Environment Canada Networks Offices on a Grand Scale

Environment Canada is a public "super" agency that includes the National Parks Service, the Atmospheric Environment Service, and the Conservation and Protection Service. This super agency is roughly equivalent to the U.S. Department of the Interior. Environment Canada is a very decentralized organization with 11,000 employees, ranging from environmental engineers to secretaries, managers, and park rangers. A significant part of Environment Canada's work is technical, involving studies of natural resources, engineering plans for natural resource development, and measurements of air and water quality. All of this adds up to a tremendous paperwork burden.

Environment Canada's situation is complicated by the fact that 80 percent of its employees are dispersed across Canada, while the remainder work in headquarters at Hull, Quebec, and other locations in Canada's National Capital District. Communications are critical for coordinating all of its work groups and enhancing productivity.

Like many organizations both public and private, Environment Canada inherited a situation of technological chaos from the past. Employees were using a wide variety of word processors, personal computers, and minicomputers, none of which could talk with each other. Secretaries could not retype engineering reports easily because engineers and secretaries used different machines. Managers could not send documents electronically across country but instead had to rely on the mail.

"We recognized we needed an automated office system that was networked and coherent," said W. Evan Armstrong, assistant deputy minister of finance and administration. He continued, "We have to do things on a consistent basis across all locations to satisfy the needs of all levels of the department—from the individual data workstation right up to the top of the organization."

To improve productivity, interpersonal communication, and managers' access to information, Environment Canada decided to replace the crazy quilt pattern of systems with a single nationwide office technology system. Digital Equipment of Canada provided all of the necessary office automation products and networking technology to tie far-flung offices together.

To carry out the project, Environment Canada created a new department called the Department of Office Technology Systems (DOTS). The new DOTS system includes all of the standard office automation tools—word processing, electronic mail, filing/retrieval, time and resource management, spreadsheets, business graphics, and data management. A special feature is a bilingual version of office systems software that produces documentation in a unique side-by-side format, one column in French and the other in English.

The system has made it possible for people to share ideas and expertise more efficiently and make better use of ministry managers. Management and operational problems can be assigned to one of many locations or to several locations jointly, whereas previously they wound up in the larger locations. Plans can be drawn and approvals obtained in a fraction of the time it used to take. By expanding its electronic mail system to other agencies, Environment Canada has tied into the Department of Supply and Service's Automatic Procurement System to obtain purchasing approvals electronically rather than mailing requisitions between departments; the new system reduces delays and labor costs. When the system is fully implemented in the mid-1990s, the network is expected to have 4,500 terminals across Canada.

Source: George Collicott, "Heat's On: Environment Canada Doing More with Less," *Computing Canada,* June 1989.

This short case study of Environment Canada illustrates several themes. One is clearly the great extent to which modern organizations are dependent upon office clerical work to achieve their goals. Second, information technology has played, and will continue to play, a very large role in helping organizations cope with the flood of paperwork their offices produce. Electronic mail, digital calendars for entire work groups, word processing, and business graphics are just a few of the new information technology tools that we call "office automation." A third theme is less obvious: advanced industrial societies have shifted from industrial production to knowledge and information production as the basis of their wealth. The United States, Canada, and most European countries now employ more workers who create or work with information than workers who work with their hands. This shift toward information work and workers has had profound implications for the kinds of information technologies and systems found in businesses and the ways they are used. This shift is at the heart of the "information economy."

This and the next chapter will examine the information technology used to support knowledge and information work. This chapter focuses on office automation systems that support clerical, managerial, and some technical workers. Chapter 14 focuses on professional work systems that support knowledge workers—people with college educations and advanced degrees.

13.1 Introduction: The Information and Knowledge Economy

What is information work and what is an information worker? The Bureau of Labor Statistics defines **information work** as work that primarily involves the creation or processing of information. Information workers are, therefore, people who primarily create or process information to make a living.

Information work
Work that primarily involves the creation or processing of information.

At a conservative estimate, there are 63 million information workers in the U.S. economy alone (just over half the labor force). Information workers produce about 70 percent of the value—$3 trillion—in our $4 trillion economy. The 25 million personal computers now used in business are primarily used by information workers, and the productivity of the entire economy depends greatly on their productivity. Because information work and workers play such a large role in the American economy, scholars refer to our society, and other advanced societies, as **information and knowledge economies.** These can be defined as economies in which the majority of new wealth (gross national product) is produced by creating or processing information.

Information and knowledge economy
An economy in which the majority of new wealth (gross national product) is produced by creating or processing information.

The Transformation of the American Economy

Transformation of the American economy
The shift in the American economy from the production of manufactured goods toward the production of information and knowledge products and services.

The **transformation of the American economy** from an economy centered on the production of manufactured goods toward an economy based on the production of information and knowledge products and services is not new.

Figure 13.1

The Growth of White-Collar Occupations Since 1900

At the turn of the century, blue-collar workers formed the majority of the American work force. Since then the trend has been a steady decline in the number of blue-collar workers, while the number of white-collar workers has risen. White-collar workers produce economic value through the use of knowledge and information. Since 1976 white-collar workers have outnumbered their blue-collar counterparts in the U.S. economy.

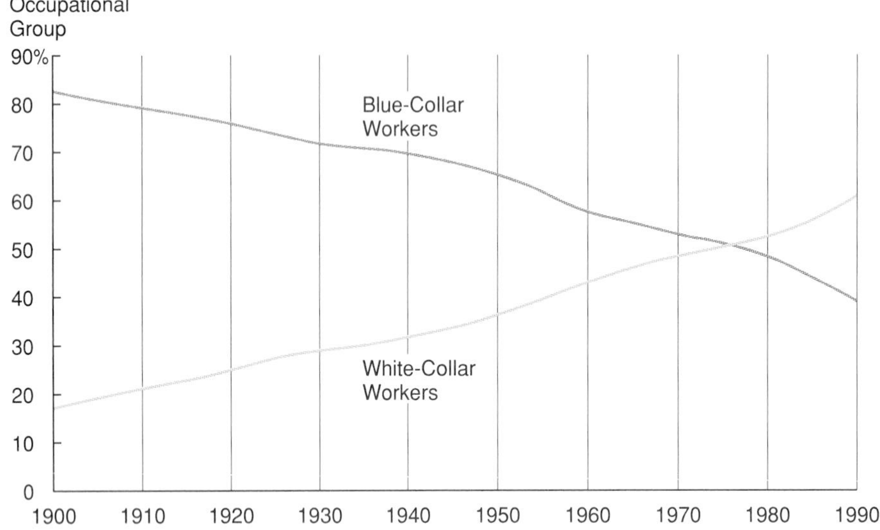

Source: Vincent E. Giuliano, "The Mechanization of Office Work," *Scientific American,* September 1982, pp. 148–152.

Since 1900, the percentage of people who work in offices using information and knowledge to produce economic value (white-collar workers) has been rising, and the percentage of workers who work with their hands in factories or on farms (blue-collar workers) has been declining (see Figure 13.1). Among these so-called white-collar workers, the fastest growing occupations have been clerical, professional, and technical workers and managers.[1] In the past, scholars called office workers "white-collar workers," but recently the terms "knowledge" and "information" workers have been used to describe these employees. They are distinguished not by the color of their shirt collars but, rather, by how they produce economic value through the use of knowledge and information.

These trends appear to have accelerated since 1960 in the United States and to have spurred worldwide changes in production and consumption. Since 1976, the value of goods produced in the information sector of the economy has been greater than the value of goods produced by manufacturing. Table 13.1 provides some examples of information, goods (manufacturing), and service industries.

Knowledge- and information-intense products
Products that require a great deal of learning and knowledge to create and often require information technologies to deliver in a timely fashion.

Information and service industries produce **knowledge- and information-intense products,** which are defined as products that require a great deal of learning and knowledge to create; often information technologies are required to deliver these products in a timely fashion. Nintendo and other video games and all computer software are knowledge- and information-

Table 13.1

Some Representative Information, Goods, and Service Industries

Information	Goods	Service
Telephone	Agriculture	Hotels
Retail and wholesale trade	Logging	Business service
Finance	Chemicals	Auto repair
Insurance	Steel	Medical service
Education	Farm machinery	Amusements

Source: Edward N. Wolff and William J. Baumol, "Sources of Postwar Growth of Information Activity in the U.S.," C.V. Starr Center for Applied Economics, New York University, June 1987; U.S. Census, 1980.

intense products because a great deal of knowledge and information is required to create them, and specialized information technology is needed to produce and use them. The airline industry, which provides a service—transportation—requires a vast computer network simply to book its seats and make a profit. Hence the airline reservation systems used in the United States are information-intense services. This is clearly less true of traditional industries such as mining and extraction, although even in these industries, information and knowledge are playing new roles, as we describe later.

The New Labor Force of the 1990s

The increased demand for information products and services has touched off a very rapid shift in the demand for labor: more and more information and knowledge workers are required to produce the new goods and services. The airlines have had to hire many more computer specialists than pilots in the last 20 years. Even within traditional manufacturing businesses, more knowledge and information workers are being used to produce manufactured goods. The automobile industry, for example, has cut back on blue-collar production workers but has dramatically increased its hiring of designers, engineers, and computer specialists.

Figure 13.2 provides an overview of the changing composition of the U.S. labor force since 1960. Clearly, goods workers—those who work in factories or manipulate physical objects—have declined relative to data workers (those who work with information), service workers (those who provide a service), and knowledge workers (those who create new information).

13.2 The New Information and Knowledge Workers

Before describing how information technology serves these new types of workers, we should develop a more precise understanding of what we mean by information and knowledge workers and what kinds of jobs they per-

Figure 13.2

Shifting Demands for Labor in the United States Since 1960

Since 1960 the increasing demand for information products and services has spurred the demand for—and the economic importance of—white-collar and service workers. This graph shows the sharp decline in manufacturing workers since 1960 and the corresponding increase in various types of white-collar and service occupations.

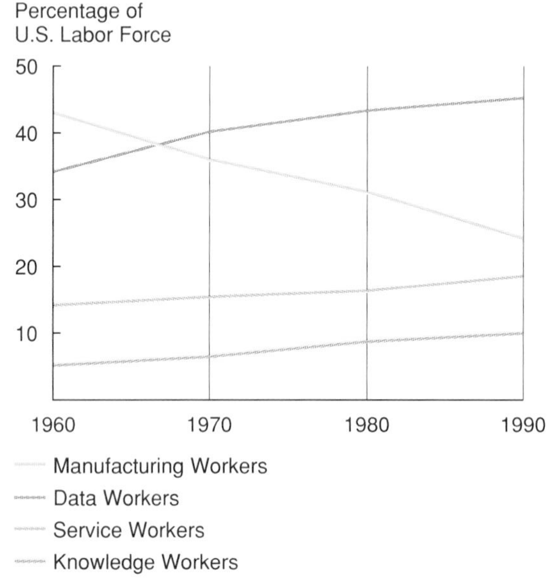

Source: Edward N. Wolff and William J. Baumol, "Sources of Postwar Growth of Information Activity in the U.S.," C.V. Starr Center for Applied Economics, New York University, June 1987. Reprinted with permission.

form. Only in this way can we understand the specific information requirements and technology solutions for information workers.

Information Workers: Data versus Knowledge Workers

The U.S. Department of Labor and the Bureau of the Census define information workers as all those people in the labor force who primarily create, work with, or disseminate information. The Department of Labor and the Bureau of the Census also distinguish two kinds of information workers: data workers and knowledge workers.

Knowledge work
Work whose primary emphasis is on the creation of new information or knowledge.

Data work
Work that primarily involves the processing, use, or dissemination of information.

Knowledge workers are defined as those who create new information or knowledge; thus, **knowledge work** refers to work that primarily involves the creation of new information or knowledge. Data workers are defined as those who use, manipulate, or disseminate information; **data work,** then, is work that involves the use, manipulation, or dissemination of information. This distinction between data work and knowledge work will become important in the next chapter, where we focus specifically on knowledge work. Service workers are those people who primarily deliver a service, while goods workers are those who work with physical

Table 13.2

Examples of Occupations of Various Types of Workers

Knowledge	Data	Service	Goods
Architect	Salesperson	Waiter	Teamster
Engineer	Accountant	Garbage collector	Welder
Judge	Lawyer	Cook	Machine operator
Scientist	Pharmacist	Nurse	Logger
Reporter	Railroad conductor	Hairdresser	Fisherman
Researcher	Foreman	Child care worker	Farmer
Writer	Draftsman	Gardener	Construction worker
Actuary	Real estate broker	Cleaner	Miner
Programmer	Secretary	Barber	Glazier
Manager*	Manager	Clergy*	Mechanic

*Many occupations—like managers and clergy—cannot be easily classified. Managers, for instance, sometimes create new knowledge and information when they write reports; hence they often act like knowledge workers. At other times, they read and disseminate reports like data workers. Scholars handle this situation by classifying half of the managers as knowledge workers and half as data workers. A similar situation exists with clergy: they provide a service and disseminate information. Obviously, in the future we will need better data on specific occupations.

Sources: Edward N. Wolff and William J. Baumol, "Sources of Postwar Growth of Information Activity in the U.S.," C. V. Starr Center for Applied Economics, New York University, 1987; Marc Uri Porat, *The Information Economy: Definition and Measurement,* U.S. Office of Technology Special Publication 77-12 (1) (U.S. Department of Commerce, Office of Telecommunications, May 1977).

objects or transform physical materials. Table 13.2 gives some examples of each kind of worker.

Notice in the table that knowledge workers are distinguished by the amount of formal schooling required to perform their jobs and by a large creative component in their work. Knowledge workers—for example, architects, engineers, judges, scientists, and writers—are required to exercise independent judgment and creativity based on mastery of large knowledge bases. In general, knowledge workers must obtain a Ph.D, master's degree, or certificate of competence before they are accepted into the labor force. In contrast, data workers typically have less formal training and no advanced educational degrees. They also tend to process information rather than create it and have less discretion in the exercise of judgment than knowledge workers do.

Given these differences, it is not surprising that these two types of workers have different requirements. Data workers are primarily served by office automation systems (described in Section 13.3). Knowledge workers, although they certainly rely on and use office automation, also require much more powerful professional workstations (described in Chapter 14).

The Distribution of Information Workers

Although all persons in an organization depend on the office for support, information workers all work in offices. Or, to put it another way, all office

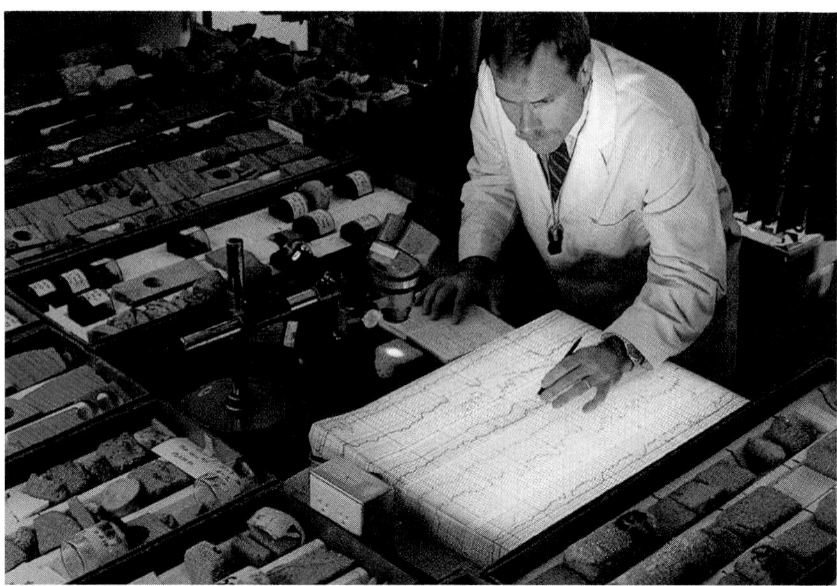

A Mobil Oil geologist studies core samples and well logs from an oil field. His analysis of the data and skill in interpreting it can lead to profits—or losses—for the company.

Source: © Dick Durrance II/Woodfin Camp.

workers are information workers of one kind or another. Sometimes the office is a "logical office"—anyplace like a car, plane, or train where you can get work done. These logical offices are possible because of information technology like cellular telephones, fax machines (electronic devices that read documents and transmit them through the telephone system to another machine that prints the documents), and a host of other office automation technologies described below.

But where are office workers concentrated? What industries do they work in, and what is the relationship between knowledge and data workers? Figure 13.3 shows the percentage of knowledge and data workers who work in the ten major industry groups.

This figure illustrates two important facts. First, some industries are almost entirely composed of information workers—especially data workers. The labor forces in finance, government, trade (retail and wholesale trade), and service are more than 50 percent information workers. In other words, some major American industries are largely composed of knowledge-intensive and information-intensive organizations.[2] In these organizations, most employees are either information or knowledge workers, and the product or service is very information or knowledge intense (composed mostly of information and knowledge).

Figure 13.3 also indicates that knowledge workers are much more evenly distributed across industries than data workers. Overall, knowledge workers are about 10 percent of the labor force and growing (though not as fast as data workers). With the exception of agriculture, where knowledge workers are only 3 percent of the labor force, most industries are composed of 7 to 10 percent knowledge workers. This indicates that the need for professional knowledge work systems is widespread.

Figure 13.3

Where Are the Knowledge and Data Workers?

This diagram displays the ten major industry groups in the United States and the percentage of knowledge and data workers within each group. As you can see, there are now information workers in every American industry, and in several industries, such as finance, government, trade, and services, they predominate. Thus, information systems that can increase the productivity of information occupations are vital to the American economy.

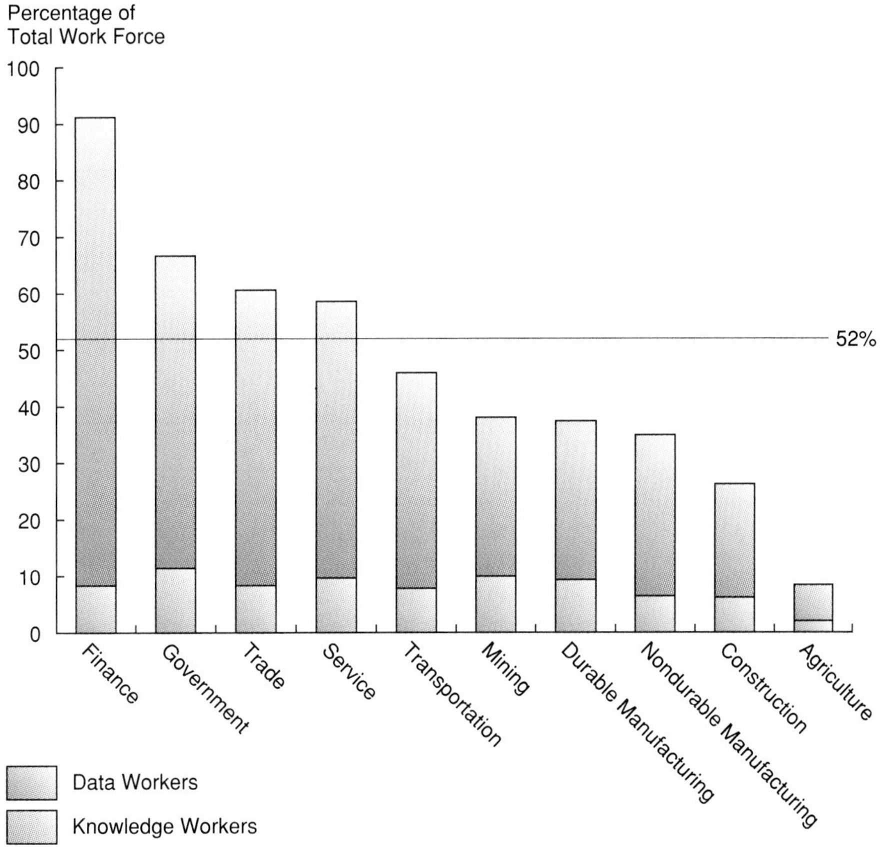

Source: Edward N. Wolff and William J. Baumol, "Sources of Postwar Growth of Information Activity in the U.S.," C. V. Starr Center for Applied Economics, New York University, June 1987. Reprinted with permission.

The Productivity Connection: Information Workers and Offices

With more than half of the labor force now composed of information workers who predominantly work in offices, and with most of our fastest growing industries being those that produce information- and knowledge-intense products utilizing very high proportions of information workers, it stands to reason that any overall advance in productivity for the U.S. economy will depend on increasing the productivity of information workers and knowledge workers. For this reason, there has been a massive increase in the capital investment in office workers. By the early 1980s, the amount of high-technology capital invested per information worker began to exceed the total capital invested per factory worker.

Although total capital spending in the United States has slowed since the 1950s, there has been a dramatic shift toward capital investment in information technology of all kinds, with most of this going to the information sector of the economy. To put it another way, over 70 percent of all capital investment in the United States in 1989 was investment in information technology! Although some of this went to factories, most ended up in offices.

For this reason, office automation systems and professional work systems were the fastest growing applications of information technology in the 1980s and will continue to grow in the 1990s. Thus, it is not an exaggeration to say that office and professional systems have come to symbolize computerization in American work life and the hope for future gains in productivity.

13.3 Office Automation: Automating Information Work

Office automation is simply any application of information technology that is intended to increase the productivity of information workers in the office. Office automation has been going on since the dawn of the Industrial Revolution or even earlier. In fact, one might trace the beginning of office automation to the year 1460, when Johannes Gutenberg and other German printers first used movable type to publish books and thereby semi-automated the printing process by permitting multiple strike-offs of single pages and rapid page composition.

The automation of specific office tasks accelerated in the nineteenth century with the first desktop mechanical calculators (1840) and desktop typewriters (1860) designed to semi-automate hand calculations and handwritten notes, respectively. With the advent of electricity in 1900, filing cabinets, typewriters, and adding machines were converted to electromechanical devices based on small motors. Added to these devices were entirely new technologies: teletype, telephone, dictation and recording machines, automatic telephone switching, duplicating machines, copiers, and small offset presses.[3] Large organizations like the Federal Bureau of Investigation (FBI) or the Internal Revenue Service had maintained huge manual files in large tubs. When these were motorized in the 1920s, the tubs of files could be spun to whatever three-letter combination a file clerk typed into a register box.

Notice, however, that, for much of the twentieth century, office automation involved simply motorizing existing equipment of the nineteenth century, miniaturizing equipment, and making it work faster. With the development of transistors and integrated circuits in the 1960s and the digital revolution, which saw the development of very-high-capacity digital storage devices like floppy disks and hard disks, much of this early electromechanical equipment was simply converted to digital machinery.

The contemporary office automation movement dates to the 1970s, when large mainframe manufacturers began to focus on ways in which large centralized computers could assist office workers. Until that time, large centralized computers were used almost entirely to process corporate data—payrolls, customer lists, inventories, and the like. In the late 1970s, however, IBM developed a number of tools, such as PROFS (Professional Office System) and DISOSS (Distributed Office Support System), which were designed to provide clerical workers with modern word processing capabilities, electronic calendars, communications capabilities, and some project management. These mainframe-based office automation tools were heavily oriented towards documents and required an IBM network called SNA (Systems Network Architecture) to connect desktop terminals.

Mainframe-based office systems are very expensive, however, and are suitable only for companies with large mainframe installations. With the development of personal computers in the 1980s, and the later emergence of powerful desktop machines such as the IBM XT, AT, and 386 machines and the Apple Macintosh, the focus of automation shifted from mainframes to desktop computing and networks of desktop computers. Suddenly, office automation became something that even small companies or individuals could develop.

The meaning of "office automation" has changed with each generation of technology. In 1980 office automation largely referred to document management and processing, but as hardware and software have improved, virtually all office activities—from sophisticated color graphics to personal databases to communications—can now be assisted by information technology. Before we describe office automation today, however, we must first take a look at the role of the office in the business firm.

The Three Roles of the Office in Business

At least three primary **office roles** in organizational life can be discerned:

Office roles
The functions played by an office in an organization, consisting of (1) coordinating and managing people and work, (2) linking diverse organizational units and projects, and (3) coupling the organization to the external environment.

1. Coordinating the work of a diverse collection of business professionals who work together to achieve some common goal.
2. Linking together diverse parts and units of the business both geographically and functionally.
3. Spanning the boundary between the business and its external environment, thereby coupling the firm to its clients, suppliers, and other organizations.

Many features of offices and their roles in business are not immediately apparent to the casual observer. Most people think that offices predominantly involve secretaries and clerical work, but this is just the most superficial aspect of office life. If you look closer, you will discover an incredibly diverse array of professional, managerial, sales, and clerical employees who work in the office or depend on the office to carry out their daily jobs (see Figure 13.4).

If you look even more closely at the typical business office, you will discover a rich, informal social life involving intense interpersonal interactions across professional and status lines. A kind of equality exists in offices

Figure 13.4

Primary Role of the Office

An office is more than a room with people sitting in it; it is an organizational group consisting of employees who work together to achieve a common goal. Within an office are staff members from many organizational levels, who perform a variety of information-intensive tasks. Office systems must therefore address various needs to help the office function more efficiently and coordinate the work of diverse groups of employees.

that is not found in the outside world. What unites diverse people in an office is a commonality of place, sometimes a sense of mission, and often their ultimate fate. When the organization no longer needs an office for a business purpose, everyone's life is changed—the boss, the secretary, the accountant are all either placed elsewhere or are let go. Offices are work groups composed of people who work together as individuals toward shared goals. Office work is complex and cooperative, yet highly individualistic. It is not so much a factory of collaborating workers as an orchestra of highly trained individuals.[4] The office, in other words, is the closest thing to a "family" or "team" that information workers experience when they go to work.

The office is a major tool for the coordination of diverse information work and the allocation of resources to projects; it also serves as a clearinghouse for information and knowledge flows. In much the same way that a market establishes a relationship between sellers and buyers, the office creates a relationship between creators of information and knowledge and those who use, disseminate, or work with that information. The centrality of offices to organizational life and work is a key feature of modern life.

In addition, the office plays a critical role in linking together diverse functional areas and physically distant units of the firm. The office is a significant node that gathers information and knowledge and distributes it to other work groups and offices in the organization. In this sense, the office is an information and knowledge conduit or channel. The office is the eyes and ears of the organization. The information and knowledge that

Figure 13.5

Two Other Major Roles of the Office

Offices connect the different functional areas of a firm. Each office gathers and distributes information according to its particular role in the organization. In addition, offices have a third major role; they connect an organization to its external environment. Offices in the production area deal with the firm's suppliers of raw materials, while those in finance deal with outside auditors. Sales and marketing offices are the organization's link to its customers. The human resources office is responsible for ensuring that the firm meets government standards for fair employment practices. Offices in several of these functional areas may also link up to databases, which provide businesses with pools of externally derived information.

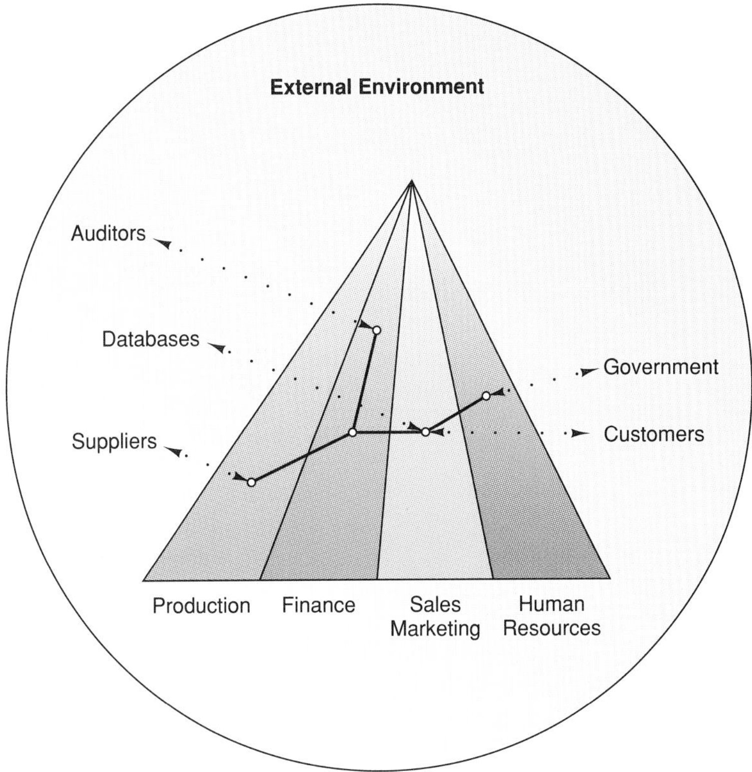

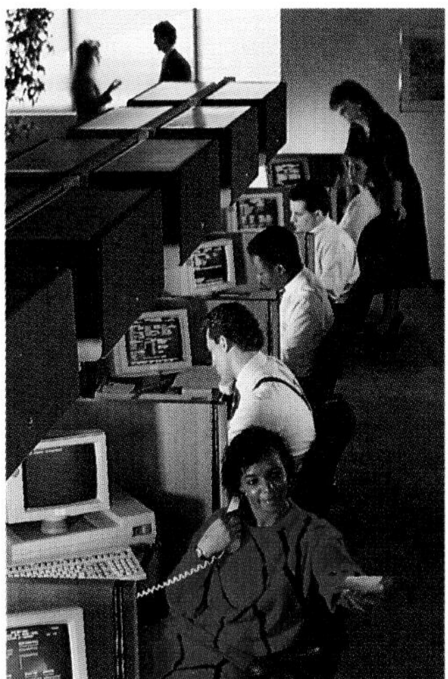

Public perception of a business often comes from one office: customer service. At MCI Communications Corporation, about 20 percent of the work force is dedicated to customer service.

Source: © John Madere for MCI Communications.

the office decides to send up or down or across the hierarchy critically affect the fate of organizations.

Figure 13.5 illustrates the role of the office in linking a firm's functional areas, as well as its third major role: the office also functions as the major link to the external environment. Just think for a moment. When you call an organization, you call an office. A specialized work group in that office handles your call in accordance with some well-established routine. The office is where the sales staff reports, where records are kept on customers, and where clients are tracked. Without the office, there would be no sales. Offices are also key purchasing units of the organization and are linked directly to vendors and suppliers of materials and to outside auditors.

The human resources office must ensure that the firm follows government standards for employment practices.

Viewing offices in terms of these three major roles can help you understand how and why businesses are using information technology in the form of the office automation systems described below. At the same time, you should remember that all offices do not face the same problems. Some offices are swamped by a crush of paperwork that engulfs the staff. Other offices have telephones ringing off the hook and going unanswered. Still other offices routinely lose engineering drawings.[5] Each of these problems has a different information systems solution.

Roles, Activities, and Systems in the Office

As Table 13.3 illustrates, the roles played by offices and the activities performed in them present different information challenges that can be met by various types of information technology.

Table 13.3

Offices and Office Automation: Functions, Activities, and Systems in the Modern Office

General Functions of Offices	Activities in an Office	Percentage of Effort*	Information Technology Assistance
Coordinating and managing people and work.	**Managing documents:** Creating, storing/retrieving, and communicating image (analog) and digital documents.	40%	**Document management** Word processing hardware and software. Desktop publishing. Optical and digital disk storage. Digital local area networks.
Linking organizational units and projects.	**Scheduling individuals and groups:** Creating, managing, and communicating documents, plans, and calendars.	10	**Digital calendars** Electronic calendars and schedules. Electronic mail.
Coupling the organization to outside groups and people.	**Communicating with individuals and groups:** Initiating, receiving, and managing voice and digital communications with diverse groups and individuals.	30	**Communications** Private branch exchanges and digital phone equipment. Voice mail. Group work support software.
	Managing data on individuals and groups: Entering and managing data to track external customers, clients, and vendors as well as internal individuals and groups.	10	**Data management** Desktop database for client/customer tracking, project tracking, and calendar information.
	Managing projects: Planning, initiating, evaluating, and monitoring projects; allocating resources; and making personnel decisions.	10	**Project management** Desktop project management tools. Critical Path Method (CPM) and Program Evaluation and Review Technique (PERT).

*Based on the authors' experience with office systems.

In the table, we have identified five major **office activities** that go on to some degree in every office: managing documents, scheduling, communicating, managing data, and managing projects. We have also provided an estimate—based on our own experience as office system implementors and software writers—of the average percentage of office effort involved in each activity. Effort can be defined either in terms of capital investment or time allocated to that type of activity. For instance, managing documents typically involves about 40 percent of the total hours worked in an average office. Communicating involves another 30 percent of office time.

Office activities
The activities performed by an office in an organization, consisting of (1) managing documents, (2) scheduling individuals and groups, (3) communicating with individuals and groups, (4) managing data on individuals and groups, and (5) managing projects.

At the far right of the table, we have identified five major groups of information technologies (both hardware and software) that are designed to support these five office activities. Some of these technologies support more than one activity.

In the next sections, we will examine each major group and explain what each of the technologies is and how it works. The hardware and software discussed here have already been described in previous chapters (see Chapters 2–7), so you may wish to review these chapters briefly to refresh your memory of some of these terms.

Document Management Technologies · **Document management technologies** are the information technologies used in the processing and management of documents; they include word processing, desktop publishing, and optical disk storage. The Focus on Organizations provides a good example of the quantity of documents that an organization may have to manage.

Document management technology
Information technology that is used for producing and managing the flow of documents in an organization; includes work processing, desktop publishing, and optical disk storage.

Word Processing · **Word processing** refers to the software and hardware used to create, edit, format, store, and print documents. Word processing systems are the single most common application of information technology to office work, in part because producing documents is what offices are all about. A word processing system has four basic components: input, processing, output, and storage. A typical word processing system includes many possible devices and software elements (see Figure 13.6). Most of the terms in Figure 13.6 were introduced in previous chapters. The following provides a brief review:

Word processing
Software and hardware that are used to create, edit, format, store, and print documents.

- **Scanner:** An electronic device that reads text or graphics and inputs the information into a computer automatically without human typing.
- **Disk-stored document:** A disk is a magnetic medium used to store digital information. Disks can be hard disks inside machines, which store a great deal of information, or floppy flexible disks, which can be removed from a machine but store less information.
- **Facsimile machine (fax):** An electronic device that reads a document and transmits it through the telephone system to another machine that prints a facsimile of the document.
- **Backup tape:** A device that makes a copy of files and disks on magnetic tape for safekeeping.
- **RAM:** Random-access memory is a computer's immediately available memory; it is used to store programs, data, and text.

FOCUS ON *Organizations*

Northrop Builds the First Paperless Airplane

In February 1989, Northrop Corporation completed its 842nd Hornet F-18 fighter/attack jet and delivered it to McDonnell Douglas for final avionics testing. This is the first time a major aerospace product of any kind has gone through assembly without mountains of paperwork. Northrop converted more than 16,000 pages of documents weighing 2,400 pounds associated with the F-18 contract to 36 microfiche cards weighing 6 ounces. The cards can be read from terminals located at assembly workstations.

Before the new system, at the beginning of every assembly line shift, clerks would use shopping carts to distribute thick blue binders containing the latest engineering and assembly guidelines and blueprints. Now a thousand assemblers and supervisors use 135 terminals on a quarter-mile assembly line linked to a Tandem Corporation computer. The computer updates the drawings automatically each day. Engineering changes that used to take days are now completed in 30 seconds. The $10 million system is expected to save $20 million for Northrop and the Navy.

Source: Charles Pelton, "Northrop Builds the First Paperless Airplane," *Information Week*, February 20, 1989.

- **CD-ROM:** Compact disk read-only memory is an optical disk similar to the 3-inch optical audio disks used for music. In the computer world, these disks are used to store very large amounts of data and text. The memory is "read only" in the sense that data can be placed on the disk only once and read many times. The data cannot be changed or updated, and the disk cannot be used to record new data.
- **Communications network:** A series of devices that work together to transmit information.

Many enhancements can be added to this bare-bones system. If we required access to large warehouses of information, we could add a CD-ROM storage unit with 500 megabytes of capacity as opposed to a mere 40-megabyte disk. Another option would be to add a magneto-optical disk, which would permit us to write on an optical disk as many times as we wanted. In addition, for a few hundred dollars, we could purchase desktop publishing software to produce higher-quality output. This software is used in conjunction with a laser printer ($1,000–$4,000).

Figure 13.6

A Typical Word Processing System

Word processing systems are the single most common application of information technology in today's offices. A word processing system consists of the hardware and software necessary for creating, editing, storing, and printing documents, and their importance reflects the importance of written documents in business transactions. As with other systems we have discussed, a word processing system includes devices for input, processing, storage, and output. This diagram shows possible devices that can perform or enhance the word processing function.

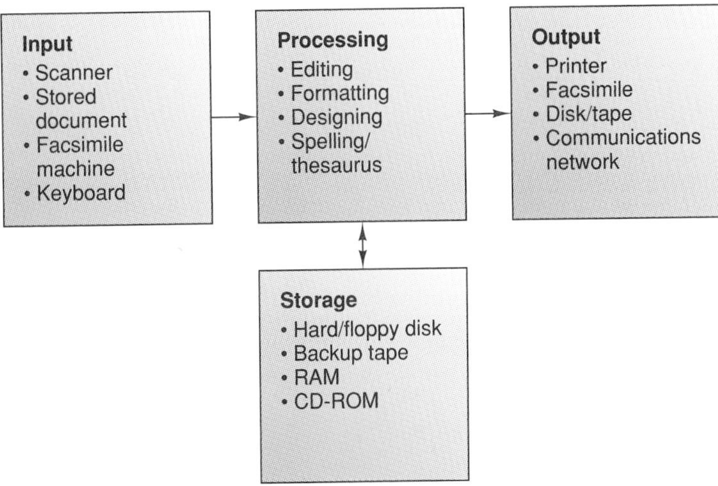

Desktop Publishing · The term **desktop publishing** covers a variety of systems and capabilities. In general, it refers to applications for producing documents that combine high-quality type, graphics, and a variety of layout options. Working on the computer screen, the user arranges words and graphics on pages. The user can type in words or charts, and if he or she has an electronic scanner, it can scan photographs and drawings, converting them into data that instruct the printer to generate a duplicate of the image by printing tiny dots. An advanced system can even reproduce color graphics. The system enables the user to enter commands for how the various elements are to be printed on the page. The user then sends the document to a laser printer, which produces the final output quickly and in excellent quality. "Postscript" (TM Adobe Systems), a computer language used to define a page, type fonts, and graphics, is one of several standard page description languages used to control high-quality laser printers and other output devices. Generally, advertising and graphic arts departments use Postscript printers because these business functions require very high-quality printed output. We should note that although laser printers are most commonly used in desktop publishing, other technologies are available, as the Focus on Technology explains.

Desktop publishing
Applications for producing documents that combine high-quality type and graphics with a variety of layout options, allowing users to produce professional-quality reports and documents.

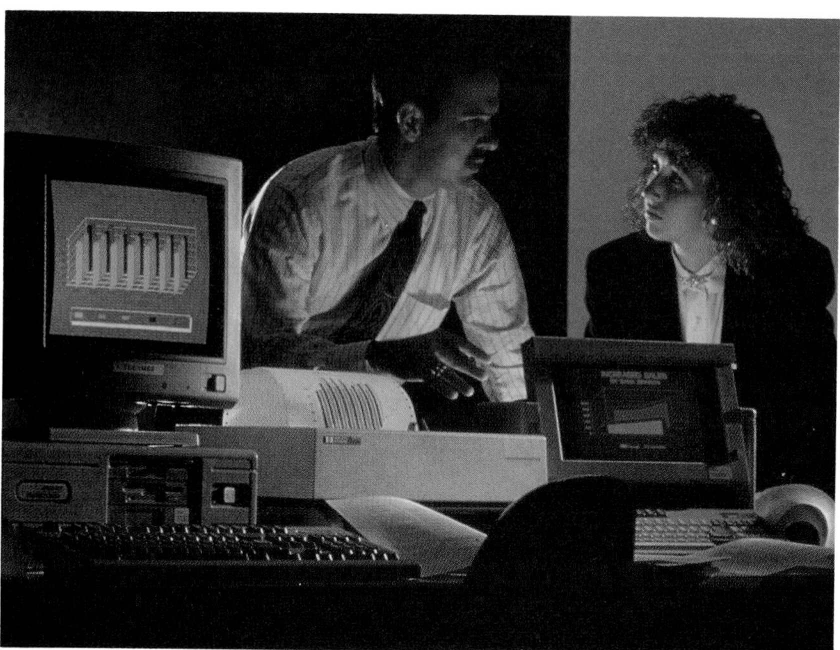

Many corporations use desktop publishing software on PCs to publish internal newsletters, sales brochures, and training documents. At the Texas Commerce Bank, staffers using COMPAQ personal computers produce sales proposals that look as if they were typeset and printed professionally.

Source: Courtesy of Compaq Computer Corporation.

If the user of such a system has good judgment in matters of design, he or she can use desktop publishing to single-handedly produce reports, advertisements, or other documents of a quality that closely approximates the work of professional typesetters and graphic designers. For example, the user can select various styles and sizes of type to fit a given design and layout for the document. Thus, desktop publishing enables users to do their own typesetting and page makeup at home or in the office. With a basic personal computer–based system, even the smallest businesses can afford ads, brochures, reports, or other documents that might be too expensive if they were prepared by professionals.[6]

But what good is all this equipment with its beautiful output if we cannot share the results with others? We need to add some communications to our typical office so we can connect workstations and communicate with our colleagues and the rest of the world.

Office Communications Technologies · For much of the early 1980s, the typical office relied on individual word processing workstations based on stand-alone personal computers. This did not present a problem for a person working alone in a tiny office or at home, but the purpose of documents is to communicate ideas, so stand-alone workstations in a large office made no sense. What if you wanted to send a document to another computer for processing, editing, formatting, or review?

The most common office communications systems are local area networks (LANs), which are digital communications systems that connect dig-

FOCUS ON *Technology*

Some Alternatives to Laser Printers

Although laser printers have garnered the lion's share of the page printer market, some competing technologies are starting to find their way into the mainstream. Two of the best-known alternatives are liquid crystal shutter (LCS) page printers and light-emitting diode (LED) array page printers. Both kinds of printers offer the same type of output as laser printers but create the images in different ways.

Apart from different methods of charging the drum with a pattern of dots, all page printers operate in a similar way. Toner (the black powder) is transferred to the drum and adheres only to the charged dots. When the paper passes under the rotating drum, the image is attracted to the paper. The paper then passes through a fusing station, where heated rollers press the image onto the paper, actually melting the toner. The charge on the drum is then neutralized, and the printing process starts again.

Proponents of the LCS and LED array technologies consider these more reliable since they have no moving parts and are not as susceptible to atmospheric contamination (such as smoke-filled air circulating through the machine) as laser printers are. Also, LCS and LED array page printers do not suffer from the linearity problems that some laser printers have. Proponents of laser technology argue that liquid crystals can be affected by heat and humidity—factors that impose limits on the operating environment—and LEDs can burn out. The marketing manager for LED array printheads at Rohm Corporation in Irvine, California, says that the life expectancy of LED arrays is 1,000 hours, or 10 million pages.

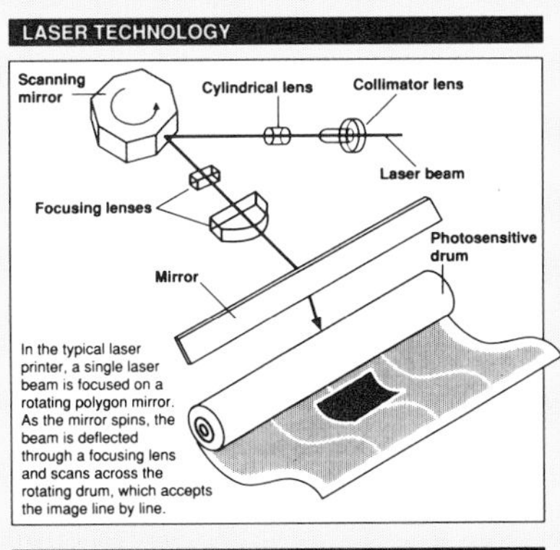

In the typical laser printer, a single laser beam is focused on a rotating polygon mirror. As the mirror spins, the beam is deflected through a focusing lens and scans across the rotating drum, which accepts the image line by line.

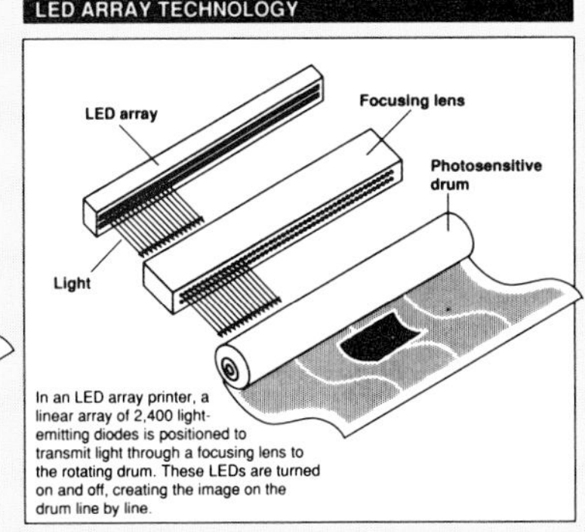

In an LED array printer, a linear array of 2,400 light-emitting diodes is positioned to transmit light through a focusing lens to the rotating drum. These LEDs are turned on and off, creating the image on the drum line by line.

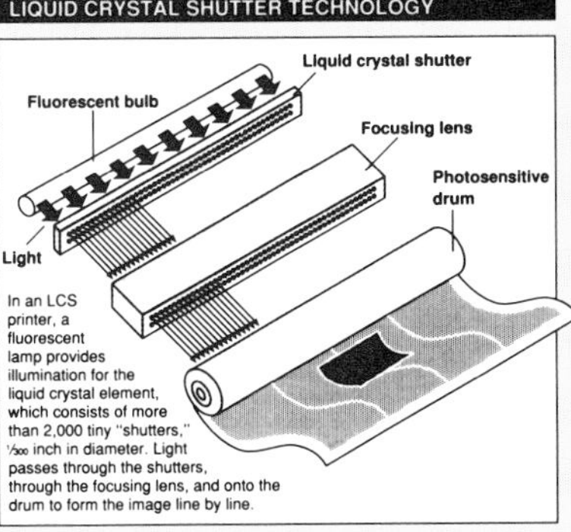

In an LCS printer, a fluorescent lamp provides illumination for the liquid crystal element, which consists of more than 2,000 tiny "shutters," 1/300 inch in diameter. Light passes through the shutters, through the focusing lens, and onto the drum to form the image line by line.

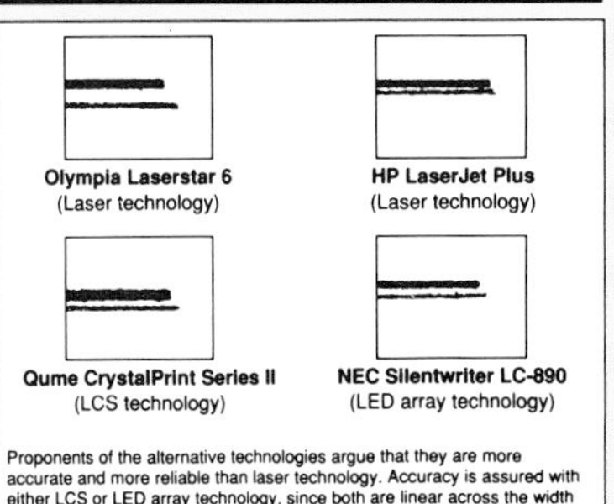

Proponents of the alternative technologies argue that they are more accurate and more reliable than laser technology. Accuracy is assured with either LCS or LED array technology, since both are linear across the width of the drum. In actuality, a laser printer's nonlinearity at the edges of a page is almost indiscernible.

Source: Joe Desposito, "The Science of Printing a Page," Reprinted from *PC Magazine*, October 31, 1988, p. 146. Copyright © 1988, Ziff Communications Company.

ital devices such as computers, printers, fax machines, and storage devices (see also Chapter 7). A LAN usually operates in a small area of up to half a mile; after that, a more powerful design is required. LANs are designed to integrate word processing and other personal computer–based or workstation projects (like spreadsheets or database applications) into a single, coherent system that permits documents, pictures, and related graphics to be shared and communicated. With a LAN, for instance, only one laser printer is needed in an office because many personal computer workstations have access to it through the network.

Office scheduling technology
Information technology used to coordinate individual and group calendars, such as electronic calendars.

Groupware
Software that attempts to expedite all the functions of a typical work group—for example, tracking the calendars of all or related individuals in an office, scheduling meetings, and sharing ideas and documents.

Office Scheduling Technology · Keeping track of appointments, activities, and meetings is an important job in the modern office. A variety of software tools, known collectively as **office scheduling technology,** is now available to coordinate individual and group calendars. A simple electronic calendar keeps track of personal appointments and activities.

More sophisticated software—sometimes referred to as **groupware**—tracks the calendars of related individuals, or all individuals, in an office and makes that calendar available to a central receptionist. In this way, for instance, if a customer calls and asks for an appointment with a specific salesperson who is out of the office, the receptionist can use an electronic group calendar to steer the customer to an available salesperson. Likewise, if a senior executive wants to meet with all his or her subordinates, a group calendar will show when all the subordinates are available. Other aspects of groupware will be discussed below.

Office data management technology
Information technology that centers around desktop databases for client or customer tracking, project tracking, calendar information, and other information required for office jobs.

Office Data Management Technology · Although business firms store basic transaction and client data in huge corporate databases on mainframes, the development of **office data management technology** has provided many office workers the opportunity to develop their own client tracking systems, customer lists, supplier and vendor lists, and the like using desktop machines. With contemporary database packages like dBASE IV, FoxBase, and Paradox, information workers can create their own databases on clients, customers, suppliers, and other data they need to do their jobs.

Most information workers do not create their own databases, however. In general, the personal computer database languages are still too difficult for most laypersons to use. Instead, they turn to personal information managers (PIMs), a new kind of software that is customized for specific positions such as salesperson, manager, real estate agent, stockbroker, and the like. Personal information managers are packaged database tools designed to support specific office tasks. They offer much greater flexibility than corporate databases and can easily be customized for individual preferences.

An example of a desktop database is The Financial Manager (Trademark Azimuth Corporation), which is designed to serve the desktop information needs of account executives and portfolio managers in the financial services industry. Financial managers typically have from five hundred to a thousand clients, each of whom has one or more portfolios of investments. In addition, financial managers usually have a full calendar of events, activities, and planned actions, as well as several routine projects such as contacting clients and prospecting for business. The Financial Manager keeps track of all these various activities and functions—clients, portfolios, calendars, and projects (see Figure 13.7).

Project Management Technology · Offices are a hotbed of individual projects. At the same time, offices are central control points that coordinate

Figure 13.7

Personal Information Management Software

Personal information management packages are a relatively new type of software tool that is proving to be very useful in offices. More flexible than traditional corporate databases, they can be customized for a variety of office functions. This figure shows two screens from "Financial Manager" (© 1990 Azimuth Corporation), a desktop information management package for account executives and portfolio managers in the financial services industry. The opening screen (top) presents a schedule of each day's events. The client screen (bottom) records background information and investment objectives for each client. This first screen is for prospects—people who are not yet clients. Additional screens with more detailed information, including the names of spouse and children, follow this screen.

File Edit Clients Portfolio Calendar Projects Utilities

Good morning Bill! Here is your calendar of events for today.

S	M	T	W	T	F	S
26	27	28	29	30	31	1
2	3	4	5	6	7	8
9	10	11	12	13	14	15
16	17	18	19	20	21	22
23	24	25	26	27	28	29

June

June 15, 1991

Done	Time	Activity	Tag	
	6:00 am			link
	7:00 am			link
	8:00 am	Breakfast with James Wyndham	Wyndham	link
	9:00 am			link
	10:00 am	Planning meeting for new building	Arenson	link
	11:00 am			link
	12:00 pm			link
	1:00 pm			link
	2:00 pm	Call George Plimpton	Plimpton	link
	3:00 pm			link
	4:00 pm			link
	5:00 pm			link
	6:00 pm			link
	7:00 pm			link

Month Next Day Previous Day To Do

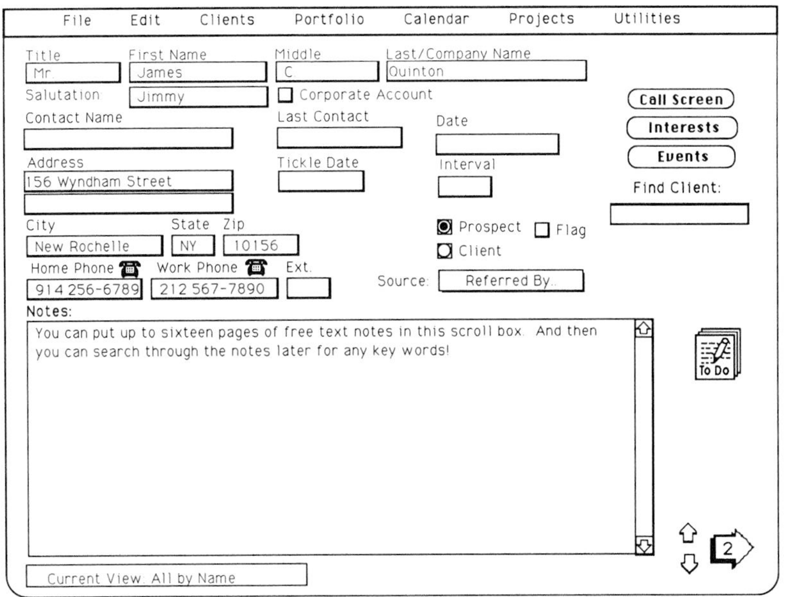

FOCUS ON *Problem Solving*

Project Management for the Olympics

After four years of planning and thinking, the official organizing committee (Olympiques Calgary Olympics—OCO 88) of the 1988 Winter Olympics had identified more than 5,000 separate projects that had to be completed by January 1988. With its 300 paid staff members and 7,000 volunteers, OCO 88 had, among other things, to build several mountain and ski resorts, 100 kilometers of cross-country ski trails, the first indoor speed skating rink, and a 17,000-seat hockey arena. In addition, the University of Calgary rooms that would house participants had to be improved, and provisions had to be made for transporting 1.3 million spectators to and from the airport. It was a massive undertaking.

John Rickards, supervisor of scheduling, realized he needed help. "We knew that we could have vast changes and growth in the project. We knew we couldn't handle this with a manual system. We felt we needed a mainframe application because of the size of the project. We needed a special project management tool that would handle a vast number of activities in multiple projects that could be combined or separated as needed."

To keep the project on track, OCO 88 used an Amdahl Corporation mainframe running software called Project/2. A standard project management technique called Work Breakdown Structure was used. Rickards explained: "The first thing we did was to list the facilities to be built. We looked at each one and broke it down into its component parts—including the buildings at each site and what is in each building room by room. Once that was done, you can start to schedule what you need to do." The project management system permitted the organizing team not only to analyze subprojects closely, but also to pull all the subprojects together for an overview of the Winter Olympics. Areas that were behind schedule could easily be identified, and more resources could be applied.

Source: Mickey Williamson, "Olympics Software Worth Its Weight in Gold," *Computerworld,* December 8, 1988.

Project management technology
Software that helps managers track and plan projects.

the flow of resources to projects and evaluate the results. **Project management technology** is software that helps managers track and plan this multitude of projects.

Project management software breaks a complex project down into simpler subtasks, each with its own completion date and resource requirements (see the Focus on Problem Solving box). Once a user knows what is needed, how much, and when, delivery schedules and resources can be provided precisely when needed. Some software provides suggestions about how resources should be allocated to tasks. Two traditional techniques of project management that most project managers use are CPM (Critical Path Method) and PERT (Program Evaluation and Review Technique).[7] These techniques can save thousands of dollars in inventory costs because a user does not have to stockpile resources.

Figure 13.8 shows how these information technologies might be used in a single office, such as a branch office of a large national stock brokerage firm. One would find clerical workers, office managers, account executives

Figure 13.8

Information Technologies Used by Employees in a Branch Office

In a branch office of a large stock brokerage firm, we would find several functional groups of employees, with each group being served by certain information technologies. The clerical staff, including receptionists, for instance, would be likely to use document management software and electronic calendars to do their jobs and a PBX system to route telephone calls. Account executives located in the same office would be more likely to utilize such tools as customer databases and personal information management software like that shown in Figure 13.7. All of the staff would use a network to communicate with each other and with customers.

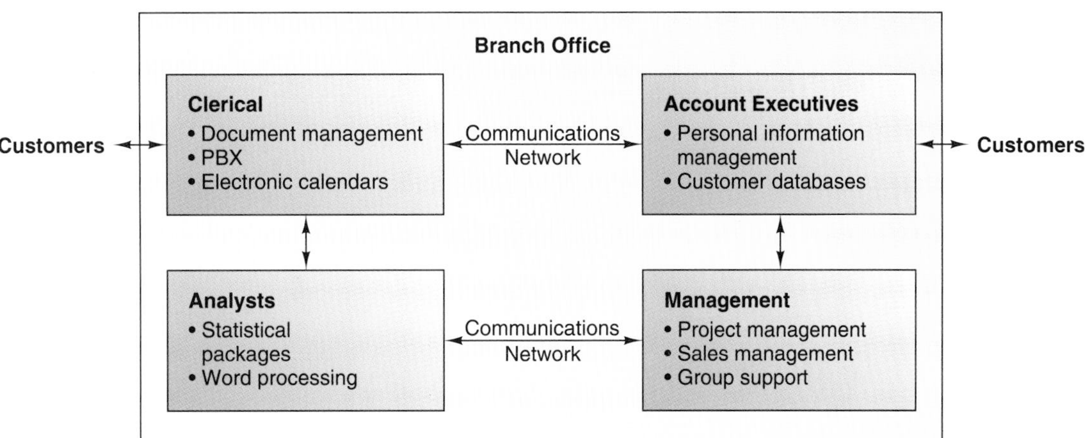

(the sales force), and a small professional support staff of analysts. The clerical group would primarily use document management software to keep track of sales and manage the flow of documents. The receptionist(s) would route calls through a private branch exchange (a central private switchboard that handles a firm's voice and digital communications needs) and use electronic calendars to schedule clients' appointments with account executives. Account executives would rely on personal information management software and customer databases to assist their sales. The management group would utilize project management, sales management, and group support software to set sales goals and track progress. The analysts would use statistical packages to measure office performance or track new trends in industry sales. In addition, each of these different office groups would utilize the communications network of the office to communicate with one another and with customers.

Groupware: A New Office Technology

A new kind of software aimed specifically at coordinating the work of work groups is now available. Called groupware as a generic category, this new software attempts to expedite all the functions of a typical work group (we introduced one form of groupware in the discussion of scheduling technology above). Whereas early office automation software and hardware focused on using a single personal computer to enhance the productivity of individual workers, there is a growing realization that much of what gets done in a business depends on the effective functioning of small work groups.

Table 13.4

Examples of Groupware and Logical Office Activities

Each of the five logical office activities can be assisted by software specifically designed to serve groups.

Managing Documents
- Group writing and commenting
- Electronic mail distribution
- Screen sharing

Scheduling
- Team and project calendars
- Office calendars and appointment books

Communicating
- Electronic mail
- Electronic meetings
- Conversation structuring
- Computer conferencing
- Screen sharing

Managing Data
- Group decision support systems
- Shared data files and databases

Managing Projects
- Shared time lines and plans
- Project management software on networks

But how can information technology help small work groups? To answer this question, think of what happens in work groups: ideas develop, documents are shared for comment, messages are sent, meetings are scheduled, and topics are discussed. Notice that these activities are similar to the five generic categories of office activities we identified earlier in Table 13.3. Groupware is developing in each of these areas (see Table 13.4). The following are some examples of groupware currently in use:

- **ForComment:** This is a group document-editing package that permits up to 16 users to comment on and edit a single document. ForComment permits all users to see others' comments and to retain the original and replacement language, with each of the 16 comments automatically initialed. This groupware is used primarily for the preparation of proposals.
- **Higgins:** One of the original group productivity tools, Higgins is a relational database package that permits access to group calendars, shared project information, and a personal filing system. It includes features like electronic mail, scheduling, project tracking, a calculator, a notepad, and a telephone dialer.
- **The Coordinator:** This groupware is a sophisticated tracker of "conversations" and interactions. The Coordinator keeps a record of all

the user's messages and the responses. This history of user interactions is then used to prompt further actions in the future.

- **Caucus:** Have you ever tried to hold a group meeting electronically? Actually, it was virtually impossible until systems like Caucus came along. Caucus can accommodate up to 16 users on personal computers in a single electronic meeting in which one person's comments are broadcast to other members of the group. Each electronic conference is linked to its own database, which can store prior decisions of the group, technical information, and data.

Other forms of groupware are being devised that will help make face-to-face meetings more productive. The Focus on People describes a conference room equipped with this new technology.

13.4 Leading-Edge Application: Staying in the Fast Lane at BMW

When people think about fast European sedans, they often think of BMW. When people think about office automation, they quite logically think of word processing by a secretary in a local office. But a corporation is a collection of offices—thousands of offices. And these offices coordinate the work of lawyers, managers, engineers, sales personnel, and marketing professionals. Therefore, any effort to automate offices in a corporation as a whole must take a systemwide view: not only must the firm automate word processing in many local offices, but it must develop a systematic approach to thousands of offices and consider many more capabilities than just word processing.

The case study presented in the next section illustrates how a multinational corporation solved these problems. It also exemplifies one approach to the problem: reliance on large central mainframes. The BMW case is a leading-edge example of this mainframe approach to office automation. Other approaches based on decentralized minicomputers or even supermicrocomputers are also feasible.

Office Automation at BMW

BMW of North America is the distribution and sales subsidiary of BMW AG of Munich, Germany. This distributor of cars and motorcycles, with headquarters in Montvale, New Jersey, operates across nine time zones—from Munich to Los Angeles. When Montvale opens for business in New Jersey, it is already afternoon in Munich and 2:00 A.M. in Los Angeles. When product engineers start their day in Los Angeles, their counterparts in Munich are going home for dinner. Like many multinational corporations, BMW needed to automate the communications and document management operations of the company as a whole. In addition, BMW needed to automate procedures in each local office.

BMW adopted a number of principles before automating. First, it decided to develop a worldwide office automation system within the context

FOCUS ON *People*

Computerized Meetings

The typical scenario most of us envision for computer use is a single operator engaged in some solitary task, pecking away at a keyboard. However, computers may also revamp the way people hold meetings.

The testing ground for computer-assisted meetings is at the University of Arizona's College of Business and Public Administration. There, a prototype electronic meeting room—the Arizona Room—is equipped with a variety of computer tools: 24 workstations, 2 rear-screen projectors, an electronic copyboard, and a video copy stand (in place of an overhead projector). On the podium are two workstations, video displays, and a bank of switches used to control the meeting room's video, sound, and lighting systems.

Complementing this hardware is a software system designed by a team of Arizona researchers. This software includes some programs with applications to almost any meeting: Brainstorming, Issue Analysis, and Prioritizing. Other, more specialized software called Policy Formation and Stakeholder Identification is suitable for top-level managers seeking to map out a formal strategy.

To use this software, a group needs a facilitator at the podium to control what appears on the screens of individual workstations. With this approach, the other participants need only minimal computer skills. Besides operating the software, the facilitator guides the group through the meeting process, and may work with another person familiar with the subject being discussed at the meeting.

Early applications of the Arizona Room suggest that computerized meetings are beneficial. IBM has installed the system in 18 U.S. locations. According to a study at one of those sites, the system reduced person-hours in meetings by more than 50 percent. Even more impressive, the time that the teams using the room needed to complete a project dropped by 92 percent.

How will such installations—called same-time, same-place groupware—affect the meetings of the future? Probably not dramatically at first. Most likely, companies will begin by gradually introducing computer technology into meeting rooms. People who use workstations at their desks will find it logical to apply this tool to other situations such as meetings. And as today's meeting rooms vary widely in their furnishings, so they will vary in use of technology.

The big surprise, of course, is that computers can be used to help people work face to face.

Source: Paul Saffo, "Same-Time, Same-Place Groupware," *Personal Computing,* March 20, 1990, pp. 57, 58.

of its existing IBM mainframe environment. BMW already operated several IBM System 370 systems and had some experience operating an IBM SNA network connecting mainframes in Germany and the United States (SNA stands for Systems Network Architecture, which is a proprietary IBM network based on large, centralized mainframe computers). This first decision, in turn, required BMW to adopt IBM's office system called DISOSS—a complex product line of programs, file structures, and capabilities for handling documents. Third, BMW did not want to be entirely dependent on mainframe computers and therefore vulnerable to centralized failures of the computers and/or the network. Therefore, BMW decided on a three-tier approach: all word processing would be done on local personal computers, with each user responsible for his or her work and data. Minicomputers would be used within departments to store some files and to act as a local communications network. The mainframe computer would be used to distribute information and supply functions—such as international electronic mail—that other systems could not supply. Finally, BMW wanted a system that could handle documents as images, not just computer files.

Phase 1 of the project began in 1984 and continued through 1986. In the first phase, BMW installed the international communications network, placed Scanmaster document scanners in all regional and national headquarters, and began installing minicomputers (System 36) in departmental offices.[8]

In 1986 Phase 1 was completed. The headquarters in Munich, the assembly plant in Regensberg, Germany, and a motor plant in Steyr, Austria, were all brought into an international network that permitted engineering drawings and product descriptions to be exchanged. The BMW sales force communicates with one another using either the DISOSS electronic mail system operated on a Munich host computer or a new DISOSS facility called Audio Distribution System, which digitizes voices. Salespersons can store and forward voice messages anywhere in the world by dialing into a local office minicomputer. Figure 13.9 illustrates BMW's three-tiered office automation system and lists the major functions of each tier.

The second phase of the project began in 1986 and was completed in 1989. It involved the development of local office personal computer systems and networks. Word processing was the first application developed using Display Write, an IBM word processor. Although documents are created on personal computers, they can be stored and communicated to other users anywhere in the world through the departmental computers connected to centralized mainframes in various parts of the world. Local electronic mail, group calendars, shared printers, and some limited graphics applications have also been developed.

BMW is now experiencing some significant payoffs from its long-term integrated approach. Telex and facsimile transmissions and their costs have nearly been eliminated because employees have an in-house capability of sending documents, data, and messages anywhere in the world. Management decision making has speeded up drastically. Product development periods have become shorter because engineers and other professionals can communicate complex documents and ideas in a rich environment.

Although many corporations have developed office automation independent of their mainframe environments by relying almost totally on local personal computers and personal computer–based local area networks, BMW feels it has achieved a system that can provide a more or less seamless integration of corporate, regional, and local information. On the other hand, BMW had a very stiff learning curve. Many of the capabilities of DISOSS are difficult to master and are not user-friendly. Significant training and learning costs were involved, and the difficulties of transferring information from local personal computers to corporate mainframes were greater than anticipated.

Figure 13.9

BMW's Three-Tier Network

BMW has developed an innovative office automation system that links offices around the world. The system combines IBM 370 mainframe computers, minicomputers, and microcomputers to give employees the ability to send documents and data anywhere else in the network. The first tier consists of mainframes using a SNA network that can exchange engineering drawings and descriptions, distribute information, and send electronic mail messages (E-mail) internationally. The second tier includes departmental minicomputers, which also provide a communications network and E-mail. Microcomputers form the lowest tier. Linked by local area networks, each microcomputer provides word processing, E-mail, and electronic calendars. BMW's office automation network has almost eliminated telex and facsimile transmissions and has speeded up decision making and product development. (For the sake of clarity, this diagram illustrates only a few machines at each level of the network.)

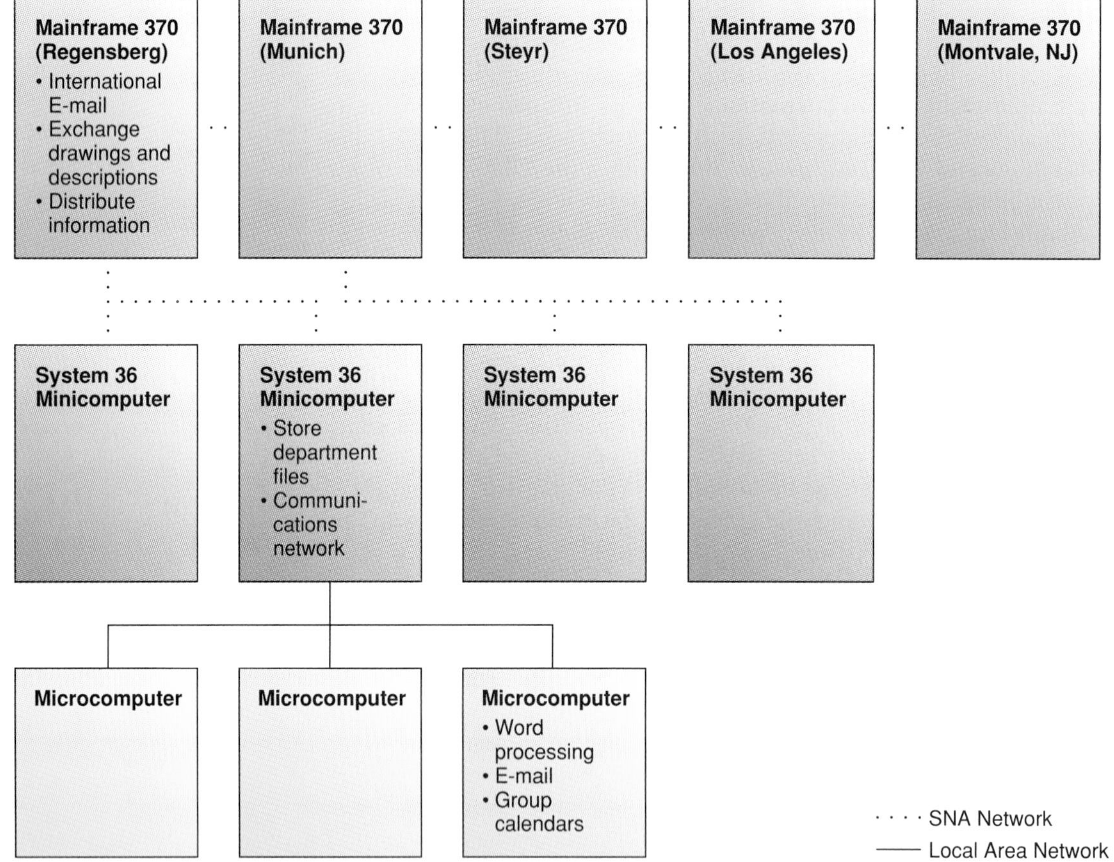

Now let's ask some questions about this leading-edge system.

- **Where does the BMW office automation system obtain its information?** Information in most office automation systems, including BMW's, originates with an individual—a local manager, clerical worker, or professional. From there the information is stored on a local personal computer or transmitted to and stored in a local minicomputer that acts as a file server (literally a machine that stores files and software).

- **What does the BMW office automation system do with this information?** The BMW office system, like most communications-based systems, stores and communicates information to a large number of users. As in most communications systems, a great deal of translating (from one kind of system to another) and error checking must go on.

  The largest transformations take place at the interface between the personal computers and the minicomputers (System 36). The minicomputers use a data code standard called EBCDIC inherited from the world of mainframes in the 1960s. Microcomputers are the new kid on the block, and they use a data code standard called ASCII (data codes were discussed in Chapter 3). Thus, microcomputers, minicomputers, and mainframes were not designed to talk with one another! They literally speak different languages. This means that all personal computer files (ASCII) must be transformed into EBCDIC files before they can be stored on the minicomputers.
- **What problems does the BMW office automation system solve?** If you return to Figures 13.4 and 13.5, which describe the functions of a modern office, you can see that the BMW system acts primarily to coordinate work within individual offices and to link separate organizational units and projects geographically. The third function of the office—linking the organization to the external world—is not yet served by BMW's system. The inclusion of external databases, or even providing dealers and customers with access to the BMW network, would extend the functionality of the BMW system.

  A number of contemporary office automation tasks probably cannot be performed on BMW's system. It would be difficult to do desktop publishing on this system, and desktop databases—personal information managers—are not possible. Many applications, in fact, would have to be designed by IBM and be compatible with the DISOSS standards. This limits the organization's options. But the payoff is a single, integrated system, operating with a more or less coherent set of standards.

Summary

- The American economy has been transformed from an industrial economy, in which most wealth came from the production of goods and most employees worked in factories and assembled goods, to an information economy, in which most wealth derives from information and knowledge production and the majority of workers process or create information. This new economy is known as an "information and knowledge economy."

- As our economy becomes more dependent on information and knowledge to produce economic value, our productivity and wealth as a nation depend on the effective use of knowledge work systems.

- Information workers are those whose primary job is to create or process information.

- There are two kinds of information workers: knowledge workers are employees whose primary job is to create new information; data workers are employees whose primary job is to process, use, or disseminate information.
- Data workers are concentrated in certain information-intense industries. Knowledge workers are more evenly spread across all industries.
- Office automation is any application of information technology that is intended to increase the productivity of information workers in the office.
- Offices coordinate work, link together diverse groups in the business, and couple the firm to its external environment. Offices and office work are therefore central to the success of any modern business.
- The major office activities are document management, communications, scheduling, data management, and project management. Information technology can support all of these activities.
- Word processing and desktop publishing systems support the document management activities of the office.
- Systems based on local area networks support the communications activities of the office.
- Electronic calendar and groupware systems support the scheduling activities of the office.
- Desktop data management systems and customized personal information managers support the data management activities of the office.
- Project management systems break down complex projects into simpler subtasks, producing delivery schedules, allocating resources, and supporting the project management activities of the office.

Key Terms

Information work
Information and knowledge economy
Transformation of the American economy
Knowledge- and information-intense products
Knowledge work
Data work
Office roles
Office activities
Document management technology
Word processing
Desktop publishing
Office scheduling technology
Groupware
Office data management technology
Project management technology

Review Questions

1. What does the phrase "transformation of the American economy toward an information economy" mean? When did this transformation begin?
2. What has happened to the value of information products and services relative to the value of manufactured goods?

3. Give some examples of information, goods, and service industries. Give some examples of knowledge, data, service, and goods occupations.
4. What are knowledge- and information-intense products? Give an example.
5. What is the difference between data work and knowledge work? Give some examples.
6. How is information work related to the productivity of a business?
7. What kinds of businesses have the highest concentration of data and knowledge workers?
8. Define office automation. How has office automation technology changed over time?
9. What are the three roles of offices in modern organizations?
10. What are the five major activities that go on in all offices? Give an example of how information technology supports each activity.
11. What is the difference between word processing and desktop publishing? Why are these such important office automation applications?
12. What is a personal information manager?
13. What is groupware and how does it differ from traditional office technology?
14. Why did BMW develop a mainframe office automation system as opposed to letting each office in the company decide what hardware and software to use locally?

Discussion Questions

1. Reread the BMW leading-edge example. What do you think are the advantages of the system that BMW put together, and what are some of the disadvantages? Diagram a different kind of office automation system for BMW and describe its advantages.

2. Some people argue that groupware produces a mindset of "group think," diminishes the role of the individual, and potentially harms business by reducing the role of individual brilliance and creativity. Divide into two groups to debate this issue after reviewing the actual groupware products described in the chapter. Alternatively, write a two-page paper that takes a position on this issue.

3. Some people argue that our country cannot survive as an information economy, that we need to produce manufactured goods as well, and that we should invest more money in factories and less money in offices. Divide into two groups to debate this issue.

Problem-Solving Exercises

1. Locate a small business firm in your neighborhood and write a short report that analyzes how the firm currently deals with office correspondence and publications—letters to customers, suppliers, sales force (if any), and

the general public. Identify where documents originate, how they are processed, and what communications technologies are used. Be sure to identify the people, hardware, and software separately. Trace the flow of example documents (letters to suppliers). The last page of your report should be a list of recommended improvements.

2. Find an office in a local business or your university, and write a report on the various occupational/social groups that are directly involved in office life. Identify these groups of workers in terms of knowledge work versus data work using the definitions supplied in this chapter. Consider how the information requirements of these groups differ, and comment on the usefulness of the distinction between data work and knowledge work.

Notes

1. Vincent E. Giuliano, "The Mechanization of Office Work," *Scientific American,* September 1982, pp. 148–152. See also Martin L. Ernst, "The Mechanization of Commerce," *Scientific American,* September 1982, pp. 132–145.
2. The phrases "knowledge-intensive organization" and "information-intensive organization" originated with Professor William Starbuck, Department of Management, Stern School of Business, New York University. The author is endebted to him for several stimulating conversations about the issue. Doubtless, over the next years, a great deal of attention will be paid to the various kinds of knowledge and information organizations, their peculiar work forces, and unique management problems.
3. Giuliano, "The Mechanization of Office Work."
4. Tora K. Bikson, J. D. Eveland, and Barbara A. Gutek, "Flexible Interactive Technologies for Multi-Person Tasks: Current Problems and Future Prospects" (Rand Corporation, December 1988).
5. Bikson, Eveland, and Gutek, "Flexible Interactive Technologies."
6. Keith H. Hammonds, "These Desktops Are Rewriting the Book on Publishing," *Business Week,* November 28, 1988, pp. 154, 156.
7. For a more complete description of project management techniques, see Roger G. Shroeder, *Operations Management: Decision Making in the Operations Function,* 2d ed. (New York: McGraw-Hill, 1985).
8. Kevin Tolly, "BMW Puts Network in Gear," *Computerworld,* April 1, 1987.

Problem-Solving Case

Unions Seek a Say in Office Automation Decisions

Many critical observers of office automation and knowledge systems argue that to achieve the full productivity benefits of information technology, employees must be allowed to participate in the design of their jobs. There is also a widespread belief that organizations must be redesigned prior to the introduction of new information technology. Otherwise, it is argued, technology will be used to automate archaic structures, and few benefits will result.

But in the real world, managers often resist having employees participate in the design of their jobs, and they fear permitting unions to participate in job design or technology plans. The following case study describes some of the issues.

The growing number of union contracts that address the implementation of office automation technology suggests the issue is of compelling inter-

est to office workers. Most of these contracts address concerns about the safety of video display terminals (VDTs), including the installation of antiglare screens, company-provided eye exams and radiation tests, and the temporary reassignment of pregnant employees who work on VDTs. An increasing number of contracts call for the creation of advisory or policymaking boards comprising management and union members. In a few cases, unions are fighting to eliminate electronic monitoring as a means of measuring employee performance.

The net effect of union gains is difficult to gauge, but it appears to be minimal. In several cases, managers in affected shops were unaware of clauses addressing office automation issues. Others noted that the concessions mainly concerned what they called peripheral office equipment—such as chairs, lighting, and antiglare screens—rather than computer hardware and software. Many managers praised the trend, calling it a way for workers to become more involved in the implementation of office systems.

Gary Haug, data processing director in New Mexico's Department of Human Services, applauds the joint implementation committee set up for management and employees. "It gives managers greater awareness of working conditions," he contends. Haug has solicited union representatives' help in developing screen layouts for a new welfare certification system. He says it is "just common sense" to give workers a voice in the design of applications they use. Glen Blahnik, employment relations specialist for the state of Wisconsin, believes the existence of a joint committee that has been reviewing VDT health and safety issues for the last two years "defuses potential problems" by increasing communication between management and the 10,000 to 13,000 state employees who use VDTs.

More executives are now dealing directly with workers' technology concerns, union officials say. For example, about 75 percent of the 120,000 workers belonging to the Office & Professional Employees International Union (OPEI, New York) are covered by contract language that addresses VDT safety issues. Sixty of the 200 contracts recently negotiated by the Newspaper Guild (Washington), the union that represents white-collar employees on newspapers, contain similar language. About 75 percent of the 100,000 members of District 925, a Boston-based affiliate of the Service Employees International Union (Washington), also work under contracts that contain VDT safety language.

Some unions are seeking to rein in management's use of computers for electronic monitoring of employee performance, although such demands seem to be the exception rather than the rule. Two years ago, District 925 won some concessions from the Syracuse, New York, claims-processing center of Equitable Life Assurance Society on the issue. Equitable continues to monitor employee performance electronically and uses the data to help determine promotions and pay increases. But the union's 110 members have access to the data and can appeal if they disagree with actions taken on the basis of the data. The Communications Workers of America (CWA, Washington) plans to seek a ban on electronic monitoring in its forthcoming negotiations on behalf of about 500,000 employees of AT&T and the Bell operating companies, about 60 percent of whom work with VDTs.

The CWA is also pushing for the inclusion of labor representation on technology change committees. These committees may review research liter-

ature on VDTs, initiate their own workstation research, disseminate findings to employees, make recommendations on workplace design, and sometimes set standards. The committees serve as the workers' pipeline to management on technology implementation. Prior to implementation, important changes in technology are supposed to be released to the committee and thus to the workers.

The American Federation of State, County, and Municipal Employees (AFSCME), which boasts more than a million members nationwide, reports that state employees in New Mexico, Illinois, Wisconsin, and New York, as well as employees of the city of Los Angeles, have won representation on joint labor-management committees. In Los Angeles, a five-member joint committee on VDT use has been meeting since 1983. But nothing specific has come out of the group to affect the city's 39,000 AFSCME employees.

Still, management is paying some heed to safety concerns. On its own initiative, management is training 50 to 100 supervisors on such worker concerns as lighting and screen glare. The managers insist, however, that these changes are not the result of the committee and that management was responsive to worker health and safety concerns prior to the committee's founding.

As the Los Angeles case shows, management-labor committees overseeing VDT safety and other office automation issues can be slow to act. In New York State, a joint safety and health committee set up four years ago will probably not see its recommendations implemented in the majority of state offices for several years.

Source: Anita Micossi, "Unions Seek Say in OA Decisions," *Computer Decisions,* April 22, 1986, pp. 18–20.

Case Study Questions

1. Describe what you think are legitimate areas of union participation in office automation projects. You might consider areas of overall design, organizational goals, implementation, evaluation, and so forth. Within each of these areas, you might separate out selected topics (e.g., health issues, productivity issues, job assignments, scheduling, and so on).
2. Should office automation systems monitor employees' work such as phone conversations, keypunch and typing, and/or absences from their desk?

CHAPTER · FOURTEEN

Knowledge and Information Work: Professional Work Systems

Chapter Outline

14.1 Introduction
- The Characteristics of Knowledge Work and Knowledge Workers
- The Role of Knowledge Work in the Business Firm
- The Setting of Knowledge Work

14.2 Knowledge Work Systems
- Generic Requirements of Knowledge Work Systems
- Workstations
- Some Examples of Knowledge Workstations

14.3 Leading-Edge Applications: Knowledge Work Systems
- Using Artificial Realities to Design Drugs with Computers at Novo-Nordisk
- CLARA: Expert Advice for the Legal Experts

14.4 Challenges of Building Knowledge and Information Work Systems
- Technology Challenges
- People Challenges
- Organizational Challenges

Learning Objectives

After reading and studying this chapter, you will:

1. Be familiar with the characteristics of knowledge work and knowledge workers.
2. Understand the role knowledge work and knowledge workers play in the modern business firm.
3. Understand the generic information requirements of knowledge work.
4. Know how information technology supports knowledge work.
5. Be familiar with the unique role of professional workstations.
6. Understand how professional workstations use information and knowledge to support professionals.
7. Understand the people, organizational, and technological challenges to supporting professional knowledge workers.

Toro's at the Cutting Edge of Lawn Mowers

Minneapolis-based Toro Company is one of America's leading manufacturers of high-quality lawn, garden, and snow removal equipment for homeowners. In years past, tried and true designs were slowly reworked and improved based on field reports and customer preferences. But the entire design and testing process had to be speeded up: competitors (some from Japan) were introducing new models and features very rapidly.

In the mid-1980s, Toro radically altered its design and manufacturing by introducing engineering workstations made by Computervision of Bedford, Massachusetts. The hardware is based on Sun Microsystems workstations using software designed by Computervision. Engineers now draft and design new lawn mowers and parts on the computer screen. Most parts are now carefully tested for strength, stress, and durability using finite element analysis (FEA)—a sophisticated engineering technique for understanding how assemblies and parts react to stress. In the past, only a few parts could be tested because of outdated computer software.

Dana Lonn, Toro's manager of advanced engineering, discovered with the new engineering workstations that some parts "which appear different from their drawings and were rejected in the past were all right. The structure differences didn't affect the parts performance or quality." In the past, these

parts would have been scrapped, raising costs. Overall, the new workstations have speeded up design, lowered new product development cost, and improved product quality.

According to Lonn, the new workstations have made possible new kinds of lawn mowers: "I'm not sure how we would have designed many of our larger mowers, which have complex lift arms that are subjected to very high loads of pressure. We spent hours analyzing these lift arms with our software, and we got solutions to our design problems relatively quickly—solutions that would have been difficult to obtain using traditional finite element analysis methods."

Source: Audrey Vaislopoulos, "FEA at Toro," *Computer Graphics World,* March 1989.

14.1 Introduction

Professional or knowledge workers—like most information workers—are critically dependent on office technology and office automation. But the needs of professional workers are different from those of data workers like secretaries or file clerks. In order to understand the different information problems and requirements of knowledge workers, we need to understand a little more about knowledge work and the role of professionals in the modern business.

The Characteristics of Knowledge Work and Knowledge Workers

What is the difference between technique, know-how, experience, and knowledge work? Doesn't all work involve the application of knowledge? Doesn't a lathe operator use knowledge and experience to cut a piece of metal in much the same way that a surgeon uses a knife to cut out an appendix?

These are all difficult questions. To some extent, the distinctions between knowledge workers, information workers, and just plain "workers" are arbitrary. But some important differences can be noted. Technique and know-how refer to rules of thumb gained from long experience in a line of work. Knowledge is quite different from know-how.

Knowledge work
Work that is (1) based on a codified body of findings and results; (2) can be taught in a school as principles, procedures, and methods; (3) is certified by the state or a university; and (4) is regulated by a professional body that sets standards.

Sociologists and economists who study occupations believe that four characteristics define **knowledge work** and knowledge workers (see Figure 14.1). This definition is accepted by the Bureau of the Census, the Bureau of Labor Statistics, and professional demographers. First, knowledge work is work that is supported by a body of knowledge, a collection of books, articles, and findings that are widely accepted as valid, can be tested, and

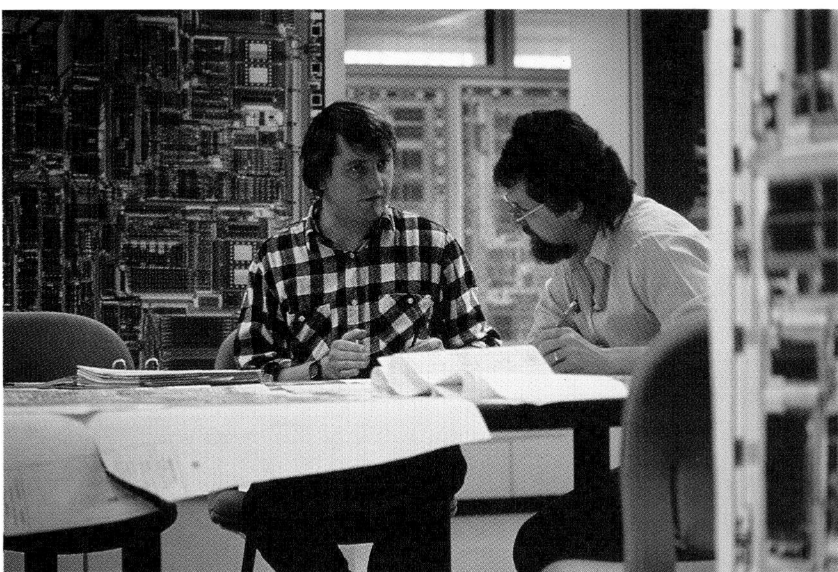

ITT engineers design digital signal processors for video and audio equipment. Like all knowledge workers, engineers rely on both a body of truths, facts, and principles learned in college and their own creativity when solving problems.

Source: Courtesy of ITT Corporation.

are stored somewhere (usually a library). In other words, knowledge is codified.

Second, this body of knowledge must be capable of being taught at major universities rather than merely being passed on as experience. Thus, principles, procedures, and methods must exist independent of pure experience for work to be labeled knowledge work.

Third, the people who learn the body of knowledge generally must be certified by the state (or university) to prove their mastery. Fourth, the field or profession must be regulated by independent professional bodies that maintain standards of admission and make independent judgments, based on their knowledge, of members' credentials as well as the social uses of their knowledge. At a minimum, these professional bodies maintain a published statement of ethics and educational or professional standards.

What kinds of work meet these qualifications? As we noted in Chapter 13, a list of knowledge workers would certainly include engineers, lawyers, doctors (to at least some extent), architects, biologists, scientists of all kinds, managers (to some extent), and even professors.

The Role of Knowledge Work in the Business Firm

As we described in Chapter 13, there has been a fundamental shift in developed economies toward the production of information- and knowledge-intensive products and services. More and more services, such as financial advising, ecological analysis and reporting, materials testing, and medical testing, require professional degrees. Some business firms are composed predominantly of knowledge workers. As time passes, it is becoming appar-

Figure 14.1

Four Characteristics of Knowledge Work

What exactly is knowledge work? Definitions can vary, but the one presented here is accepted by the Bureau of the Census and the Bureau of Labor Statistics. Knowledge work has four characteristics: it is based on a codified body of information; it can be taught in a school as a collection of principles and procedures; proficiency in knowledge occupations is certified by the state or the school; and knowledge workers are regulated by independent professional associations that set standards for their work.

Knowledge Work

- Based on codified body of findings and results
- Can be taught in school as principles and procedures
- Certified by the state or school
- Regulated by professional association

Two scientists in the fermentation research group at the Bristol-Myers Squibb Research Institute in Tokyo collect soil samples that will be screened for substances that might eventually become new therapeutic agents. New products and businesses are frequently the result of knowledge work.

Source: Courtesy of Bristol-Myers Squibb Company.

Figure 14.2

Three Unique Roles of Knowledge Workers in a Business

The roles of knowledge workers are unlike those of any other employees. Part of their mission is to interpret the always-growing external knowledge base for the organization so that the firm can remain competitive. A second role is to serve as internal consultants and advisers for management. Third, knowledge workers often serve as change agents who develop and facilitate projects that bring new knowledge into the firm. It can be difficult to manage knowledge workers, since their roles do not fit neatly into the traditional corporate hierarchy.

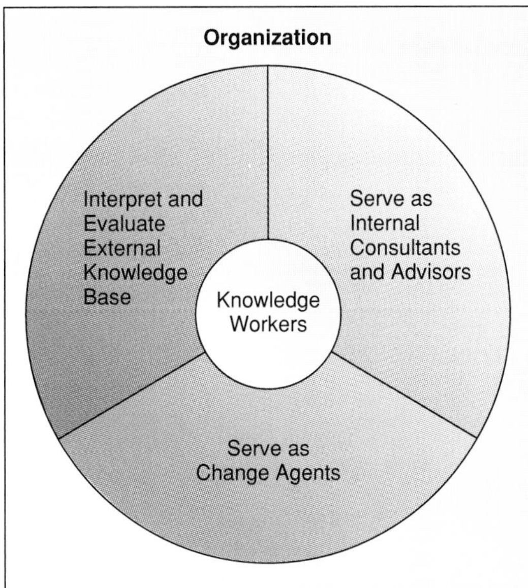

ent that **knowledge workers' roles in business** firms are both unique and becoming more important (see Figure 14.2).

Perhaps the most distinctive role of knowledge workers is to interpret the **external knowledge base** (which is always growing) for the organization. From the firm's point of view, a central purpose of hiring knowledge workers is to keep the business abreast of developments in science, technology, the arts, and social thought. Developments in these areas of knowledge often contain business opportunities. Consequently, knowledge workers are expected to refresh their skills and keep up-to-date so that the corporation may benefit from the latest developments in a field. This means knowledge workers must continually scan the environment and keep up with developments by participating in professional seminars, meetings, and the like.

Second, knowledge workers are uniquely qualified to play the role of advisers and internal business consultants. Rather than merely writing reports, business professionals are expected to use their expertise to play an active corporate role in advising managers. Although most business firms hire external consultants at one point or another, internal knowledge workers constitute a major source of advice and professional expertise on a continuing basis.

Third, knowledge workers are change agents. They are expected to initiate, promote, and evaluate change projects that incorporate develop-

Knowledge workers' roles in business
Business positions that involve interpreting the firm's external knowledge base; playing an active role as advisers and internal business consultants; and initiating, promoting, and evaluating projects that incorporate new developments and changes into the firm.

External knowledge base
A knowledge base that is outside the organization, such as libraries of articles, collections of scientific or legal findings, and links to other professionals in universities or other businesses.

ments in science, the arts, and other areas into the corporation. Knowledge workers are a little like evangelists: they are expected to believe strongly in their professional values and to share their views with other workers with the aim of improving the firm's behavior.

The Setting of Knowledge Work

As this analysis of their roles suggests, knowledge workers are really quite different from other information workers like file clerks or secretaries and quite different from lathe operators. Because their position depends on understanding a formal knowledge base, knowledge workers really cannot be told what to do and cannot be subject to the same kind of authority relationships that exist elsewhere in the firm. Knowledge workers often know more than the boss. Consequently, they tend to be independent and autonomous.

Generally, knowledge workers are physically segregated from other line workers and staff in special research areas, or research centers. In part, this is because knowledge workers tend not to conform readily to a corporate image or mold. Major American firms like IBM and AT&T have developed specialized research centers far removed from daily corporate life where knowledge-intensive work is conducted.

14.2 Knowledge Work Systems

Due to their unique roles and setting in the firm, knowledge workers as a group have very different information requirements from information workers and office workers. As a result, a new class of systems has emerged—called knowledge work systems—that uses different hardware and software to serve business knowledge workers. These systems must satisfy four requirements, as shown in Figure 14.3.

Generic Requirements of Knowledge Work Systems

The first requirement is easy access to electronically stored knowledge bases external to the organization. These knowledge bases could be libraries of articles, collections of chemical or legal findings, or electronic mail links to other professionals working in universities or other businesses. Thus, one characteristic of knowledge work systems is that they are more directed toward external data and information than typical corporate systems.

Second, knowledge work systems typically require different software than other corporate systems. They need much more powerful analytic, graphics, document management, and communications abilities than a typical personal computer can provide. Third, knowledge work often requires much more computing power than typical information work (see Focus on Problem Solving). Some intensive simulations (called artificial reality) require very large and very fast supercomputers (see Section 14.3 for more on artificial reality). Engineers may wish to run thousands of calculations before they are satisfied that a specific part is safe. Designers and draftsmen

Figure 14.3

Four General Requirements of a Knowledge Work System

Given that knowledge workers are unique, it follows that the information technologies they use must also be unique. Four characteristics distinguish knowledge work systems from the more usual corporate workstations. First, knowledge work systems must provide easy access to an external knowledge base. Second, they must provide software that differs from the usual business software by offering greater capabilities for analysis, graphics, document management, and communications. Third, they need to support "computing-intense" applications that may require unusual numbers of calculations and data manipulations. Finally, they should have a friendly, easy-to-use interface.

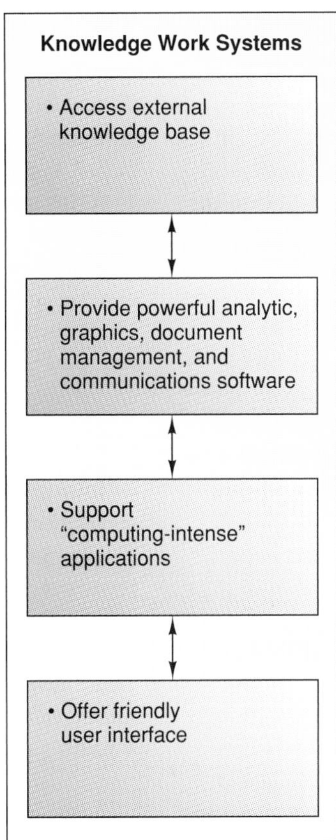

will frequently want to use three-dimensional graphics software to fully visualize a model of a product. Lawyers may want to scan thousands of legal findings before recommending a strategy.

And finally, knowledge work systems will also have a user-friendly interface so that professionals can gain access to knowledge and information without spending a great deal of time learning how to use the computer. A user-friendly interface is somewhat more critical for knowledge workers than for ordinary information workers because knowledge workers are expensive. Wasting a knowledge worker's time is more costly than wasting a clerical worker's time. Unfortunately, many knowledge work systems need a great deal of work before they can be said to be user-friendly.

FOCUS ON Problem Solving

3D Data Shed Light on Surgery

A good example of a knowledge worker is the physician. For years, physicians have diagnosed ailments by referring to images created with computed tomography (CT) and medical resonance imaging (MRI) techniques. But studying the two-dimensional, X-raylike images generated by these techniques is like trying to visualize what a puzzle will look like by examining its individual pieces.

Aesculys Research Corporation, a service bureau comprising physicians with extensive backgrounds in computer programming, is attempting to solve that problem by applying computer technology. This Lebanon, New Hampshire–based firm converts CT and MRI data supplied by radiologists and surgeons into high-resolution, computer-generated three-dimensional color renderings, complete with measurements and reports.

A surgeon forwards CT and/or MRI data slices of a patient's ailment, such as a compressed spinal nerve or herniated disk, to Aesculys on a magnetic tape. The Aesculys physician loads the data into the system and analyzes the data for abnormalities, "painting" or highlighting the abnormal areas with colors. (Sixteen million colors can be displayed simultaneously.) The Aesculys physician also generates low-resolution images of the areas taken from a variety of views; these allow him or her to see spatial relationships between bone and tissue.

The Aesculys system then uses the physician's data to automatically generate high-quality renderings of the images. The resulting 3D images are then printed in near photographic quality and sent back to the referring surgeon with a report explaining what each image shows. The surgeon uses the final images in the operating room or to determine whether surgery is appropriate at all.

Aesculys physicians use a sophisticated system that handles floating-point calculations to perform true 3D perspective calculations, generates three-dimensional images rapidly, and contains large amounts of memory. A typical CT or MRI study contains an average of 10 to 40 megabytes of data, whereas most computer graphics studies contain only 1 to 2 megabytes. High-speed processors also are required to render the images and write their RGB color values.

Dr. Dan Schlusselberg, a co-founder of Aesculys, observes that rendered three-dimensional images, such as those produced by this system, provide much more information than two-dimensional data. Thus, surgeons can recognize spatial relationships that wouldn't be evident otherwise.

Source: Audrey Vasilopoulos, "Operating in a New Light," *Computer Graphics World,* August 1989.

Workstations

The term "workstation" is typically used to describe the hardware platform on which knowledge work systems operate. As we saw in Chapter 3, workstations differ from simple personal computers in both power and applications. Personal computers are designed to meet the very general requirements of diverse groups ranging from secretaries to financial analysts. In contrast, a professional workstation—whether built for a sales manager

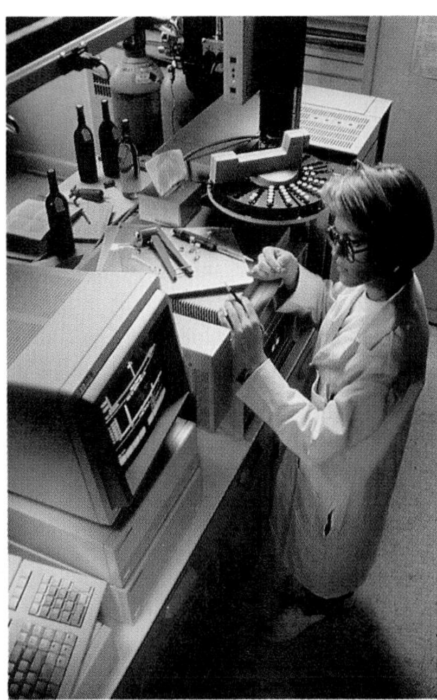

The Hewlett-Packard ChemStation, an analytical workstation combining analytical instruments and computers, is widely used in the food industry. It precisely identifies substances by matching their chemical fingerprints to information stored in its computer. Many California wineries have samples tested at this lab at the University of California at Davis.

Source: Courtesy of Hewlett-Packard Company.

(managerial workstation) or a chemist—must generally be fine-tuned and optimized for a particular occupation.

Some Examples of Knowledge Workstations

In 1990, the professional knowledge workstation market involved about $5 billion of annual purchases (see the Focus on Technology for a discussion of the market and one of the new entries). Whereas about 25 million personal computers and other microcomputers are used by information and knowledge workers of all kinds in businesses, and annual personal computer sales total 2.1 million units, about one million workstations are in use with annual sales of about 150,000 units per year. Sales of professional workstations are actually growing at a faster rate than sales of general-purpose personal computers as businesses recognize the importance of increasing the productivity of their knowledge workers. Figure 14.4 provides some examples of knowledge work occupations that are finding professional workstations useful.

The specific features of knowledge work systems depend on the profession supported. Designers will want machines with powerful graphics displays, whereas lawyers may be more interested in huge database storage abilities provided by optical disks. Financial analysts will typically desire a 300-megabyte optical disk, refreshed each week, with a complete listing of financial data for all 4,000 public corporations.

FOCUS ON *Technology*

IBM Introduces Line of Workstations

After years of embarrassing failures in the workstation market, International Business Machines Corporation has finally unveiled a line of products that should make it a significant player.

Although the machines' impressive performance specifications were disclosed ahead of time, IBM still managed to impress software developers, securities analysts, and consultants by setting prices lower than expected. The starting price turned out to be $13,000.

Bob Djurdjevic, a consultant with Annex Research, said the price/performance ratio of IBM's machines is several times better than competitors' workstations.

Securities analysts said that if IBM meets its goals, it could generate $4 billion to $5 billion of revenue a year from this line in two to three years; by comparison, IBM's total revenue was $64 billion last year.

Market researchers generally put the total technical workstation market at just $4.5 billion for 1989, but the market is the fastest-growing part of the computer industry. In addition, IBM is aiming at the broader market for technical computing, which includes other sizes of machines and covers applications beyond the simulation and modeling work traditionally done on workstations. IBM says this broader market is several times the size of the workstation market.

IBM still faces plenty of obstacles. Technology has been moving fast in the workstation market, with performance doubling every 15 months, so IBM is going to have to show that it can continue to develop its technology rapidly. Competitors are expected to bring out machines as early as this summer that will boost their performance significantly by putting multiple processors into a single machine.

In addition, IBM must convince software developers to provide loads of applications to run on IBM's system as soon as possible. IBM has had problems with its operating system, which delayed some of that work, but it has gone to great lengths to hurry things along. It has even paid many companies to move their software to the IBM hardware. IBM said that it should have more than 1,500 major applications available by the end of 1990—many more than was generally expected.

Source: Excerpted from Paul B. Carroll, "IBM Introduces Line of Workstations; Industry Analysts Impressed by Prices," *The Wall Street Journal*, February 16, 1990, p. B8. Excerpted by permission of The Wall Street Journal,

14.3 Leading-Edge Applications: Knowledge Work Systems

Instead of giving a single example of a leading-edge application, we have chosen to highlight two very different applications that serve different professionals. After describing these applications, we will briefly summarize the systems in terms of where information is obtained and how it is processed or transformed.

Figure 14.4

Examples of Knowledge Workers and the Knowledge Workstations that Help Them Do Their Jobs

Specialized workstations involving unique hardware and software have been developed for many knowledge occupations. Architects can now use CAD (computer-aided design) software to design structures and test areas of stress to improve the structure's safety. Other knowledge workstations, as we shall see later in this chapter, help scientists simulate the effects of weakened molecular bonds, or help lawyers eliminate time-consuming legal research.

Architects	CAD (computer-aided design): Design building and floor plans.
Engineers	CAD/CAM (computer-aided design/computer-aided manufacturing): Manage manufacturing operations and control machinery.
Judges, Lawyers	Legal research workstations: Access legal databases, write legal briefs and opinions.
Scientists	Visualization workstations: Perform three-dimensional modeling.
Reporters	Text publishing workstations: Write news stories and translate into newspaper layout.
Actuaries	Modeling workstations: Use complex mathematical models to calculate insurance risks, pension plan funding.
Programmers	Programmer workbench systems: Use CASE tools to produce software programs.
Managers (some)	Management workstations: Access large databases, provide graphic displays, electronic mail, and word processing.

Using Artificial Realities to Design Drugs with Computers at Novo-Nordisk

The fastest growing segment of the professional knowledge workstation market is an area variously referred to as visualization, rendering, or "artificial reality." This area has no single definition, but it involves computer-driven, interactive graphics software that can so precisely simulate the three-dimensional world in which we live that human end-users believe or "feel" they are actually participating in the simulation. The resulting confusion between reality and simulation is somewhat akin to a Woody Allen movie in which the film story stops to permit the director and actors to make direct comments to the audience.

Progress in science has always depended on instruments that permit scientists to "see" what heretofore was invisible. The microscope, telescope, electron microscope, radio telescope, and scientific instrumentation of all kinds have played a powerful role in discovery. Observation often precedes theory. Artificial reality begins with very high quality interactive graphics. These professional knowledge worker tools typically require specialized software and special graphics workstations, although increasingly these capabilities are being built into less expensive workstations. These tools are especially important for the design of new chemicals and drugs, whose intricate submicroscopic behavior has kept scientists from fully understanding them.

For 50 years, Novo-Nordisk A/S, a research company based in Copenhagen, Denmark, has produced enzymes and insulin for industrial purposes. Recently, Novo designed a new form of insulin that acts faster than natural human insulin in the body. For the first time, Novo's genetic engineers used visualization technology based on a Silicon Graphics (Mountain View, California) workstation and a new visualization software package called Charmm. The hardware can perform 10 million instructions per second (about ten times as fast as a personal computer), has 8 million bytes of RAM, and has a hard disk with 1.5 gigabytes of space (1.5 trillion bytes of information!) that holds a vast amount of molecular data. The data for the insulin molecule are based on Novo's own research and that of other researchers in genetic engineering. In the background is another computer, a DEC Vax 785, which stores thousands of protein combinations and supplies data to the more sophisticated visualization tools.

According to Dr. Steffen Peterson, Novo's manager of protein engineering, the thrust of Novo's work is to modify naturally occurring enzymes and proteins to fit particular market needs: "Nature may not be able to produce an enzyme that is stable at high temperature, or to survive acidic conditions. So we have to compose it ourselves by mutating enzymes."[1]

Novo's director of research got the idea that an insulin could be produced that would more readily be used by the human body. Novo scientists believed that if a hydrogen bond in the naturally occurring protein was weakened, insulin would dissolve faster. To demonstrate and prove this, they simulated the behavior of insulin as a function of time.

The visualization techniques allowed Novo scientists to examine 100 pica-seconds (1 pica-second is equal to one-billionth of a second) in the life of a new version of insulin. First, the research team established how the natural insulin molecules arranged themselves. This permitted them to visualize how the hydrogen bonds held the molecule together. Second, they experimented on the screen with various ways and locations for weakening the hydrogen bonds. They discovered many locations in the molecule where the hydrogen bond could be weakened. As a last step, they played visual "what if" and in the process created more than 50 different model insulin molecules with weakened hydrogen bonds. The simulations were so realistic that scientists could develop a sixth sense of where the hydrogen bonds might be weakened. Genetic engineers then formulated these simulated molecules in the lab. These different insulin compounds are now undergoing human trials.

CLARA: Expert Advice for the Legal Experts

Lawyers—like everyone else—cannot remember everything, especially in areas of law in which they have not practiced for many years. Apprentice lawyers just starting out often need the aid of an experienced professional with many years of experience in specialized areas of law just to know what the issues are. CLARA (Computerized Legal Research Aid) is a new software program designed to solve these and related problems.

CLARA is an expert system (described in the discussion of artificial intelligence in Chapter 8) used by corporate and private lawyers as a mentor and research aid. Lawyers begin by selecting the area of law in which they are interested from a menu of 12 possibilities. Next, following a complex logic tree, CLARA asks a series of questions about the circumstances of the legal case. It then reports all possible causes of actions and appropriate case citations.

CLARA explains all of its reasoning and lists citations, research monographs, and related reports. In tests against law professors, CLARA has been found to be very effective and at times superior in discovering little-known facets of the law and obscure citations.

CLARA is not yet fully functional. Completing CLARA will take a long time because all state and local laws have to be fed into the system's memory before it can be fully effective. The resulting data must be stored on a compact disk optical memory with a total capacity of 550 megabytes (millions of bytes of information). Nevertheless, the system can be operated easily on a personal computer.[2]

One state, Arizona, has completed a translation of state law and an index called LIBRA (Legal Integrated Brief Research Assistant). When LIBRA is tied to CLARA, CLARA can be instructed to search Arizona law by name, date, sentence, phrase, paragraph, and other logical criteria. CLARA's developers claim it can complete one hour's research in five minutes. This gives small firms the ability to compete with much larger firms whose market advantage is often research staff, not brilliance.

Now let's review the questions we typically ask of information systems:

- **Where does a knowledge workstation obtain its information?** Both of the systems described above obtained a great deal of information (and expertise) from external scientific, engineering, and legal databases. This information often must be internalized, or stored on local disks. Of course, much of the information is generated as a result of local knowledge workers' experiments and writing.
- **What does a knowledge workstation do to the information?** Despite their very different origins and uses, both of these knowledge workstations appear to do a great deal more processing of information and data than typical transaction or management systems would do. Generally, this occurs because knowledge work often requires the application of sophisticated mathematical routines and procedures in order to function.

  In the case of graphics systems, engineering CAD/CAM systems (CAD/CAM stands for computer-aided design/computer-aided manufacturing and is described in greater detail in later chapters), and design workstations, the amount of processing speed and power exceeds that of personal computers and usually requires specialized workstations. Yet as personal computers become more powerful, they will be capable of performing more and more knowledge work.

- **What problems does a knowledge workstation solve?** How can business organizations interested in making a profit make use of basic science? This is the overall problem that knowledge work systems address. Obviously, businesses must first hire knowledge workers. But then business must support these knowledge workers for them to be effective.

  Since World War II, science and business have moved much closer together. Knowledge work systems appear to be providing a critical link between science and business. Knowledge work systems speed up the dissemination of scientific findings to business and make possible the realization of business goals (like product development) in a speedy fashion (see Focus on Organizations).

  Not only have scientific methods contributed to more rational organizations, but science also provides new products and services for business. Our first example of Novo-Nordisk shows how basic science can be converted after many years of technological development into a business product—in this case, insulin. Our second example illustrates how knowledge work systems can help rationalize organizations by providing new methods of legal research.

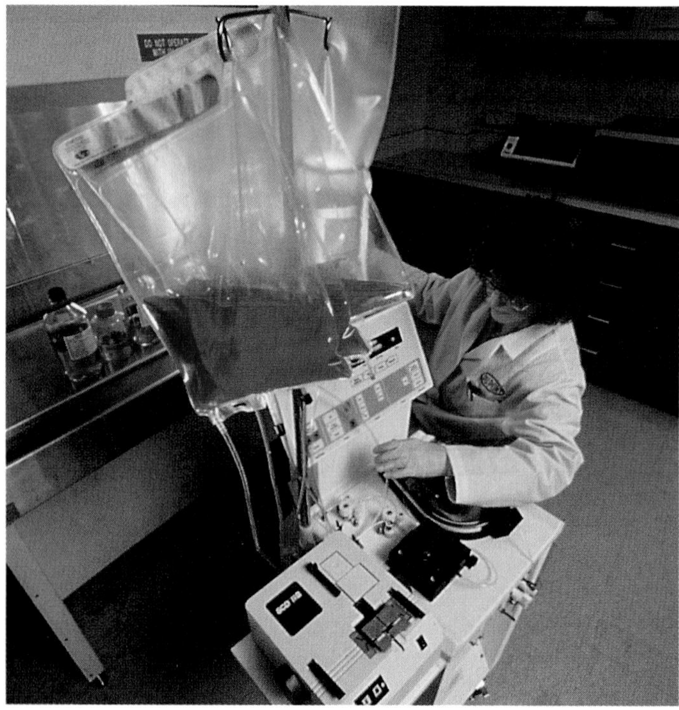

The field of medicine, like other enterprises, has become much more information intense. Years of research on how the body fights disease led to this DuPont instrument, which assists the body in activating white blood cells that destroy cancer cells.

Source: Courtesy of DuPont Company.

FOCUS ON *Organizations*

Merging Art and Engineering

Organizations that design and produce goods are finding that knowledge workstations improve the efficiency of industrial design. Industrial design is a fragile realm where a new product starts out as a creative concept in the head of a designer, who is part artist and part engineer. The functional aspects of a product's design must be balanced with aesthetic and ergonomic concerns. For example, a hand-held appliance must not only be attractive, it must fit the hand well. Furthermore, the design must be easily translated into a finished product.

An advantage of using computers for industrial design is that dead ends don't lead back to a blank sheet of paper. A computer model can be tweaked to satisfy clients' wishes. And if it resides in a three-dimensional database, the design can be transferred to a standard computer-aided design (CAD) system as the basis for subsequent engineering work. Firms can take advantage of the consistency between design, engineering, manufacturing, and marketing, streamlining the entire process of product definition.

For example, a Norwalk, Connecticut, consulting firm called Design Core performs industrial design tasks using design and modeling software from Alias Research Corporation. In the process of designing, it creates a database that can drive the whole engineering process. According to Design Core, the computer-rendered version of a design is so convincing and high-quality that it replaces the physical model. Since the company avoids creating a model, approval comes sooner, and a product can be accurately visualized well before it is actually manufactured.

Jay Crawford, supervisor of design at Colgate-Palmolive corporate headquarters in New York City, encourages his staff to perform the bulk of their design work on the computer. This puts the design group in closer communication with other groups down the line. And because the system encourages them to supply more precise specifications, the designers are doing work that used to be sent to the engineers.

Source: Tom McMillan, "Industrial Design," *Computer Graphics World,* June 1989.

14.4 Challenges of Building Knowledge and Information Work Systems

Knowledge work systems are in many respects on the leading edge of information technology and system development. Although the rewards are potentially great, the costs can be high and the challenges steep. Here we describe the challenges and leave the discovery of solutions for class discussion.

Technology Challenges

Many of the technologies involved in information and knowledge work are uncertain and change rapidly. Often before machinery can be paid for, new

FOCUS ON *People*

Architects Resist Computer-Aided Rendering

On the whole, the architectural world has warmly embraced computer-aided design (CAD) systems for drafting and design work. These systems automate a laborious process that had been done manually for centuries. In particular, three-dimensional CAD systems are appealing because when architects visualize and describe their ideas, they do so in terms of three dimensions.

New software also automates architectural rendering, which is the process of drawing a picture to show a client what a building will look like before detailed plans are completed. Rendering software allows architects to input images for texture mapping to create, for example, remarkably real-looking brick, plaster, and marble surfaces or windows that cast believable reflections. Thus, whereas the traditional hand-rendered architectural drawings had limited ability to show true lighting, reflection, texture, color, and shading variations, the computerized rendering systems remarkably simulate reality.

Some architects have resisted these systems out of a fear computerized renderings would destroy the individuality of their work. Some artistry and imagination in traditional hand-drawn renderings is lost when computerized renderings account for every brick and stone. Renderings are supposed to convey a feel for a building and how striking it will be; they are deliberately meant to be sketchy so that the viewer can fill in some blanks. Architects are concerned that computerized renderings will take away their personal style.

Even Paul Yarmolich, business development manager of Renderman, a leading vendor of rendering software, concedes that the creative element in rendering is still the architect. Computer programs can't capture the nuances of hand renderings. Architects can do renderings better than any computer because they give personality to the picture.

Source: Laura Lang, "Architectural Renderings," *Computer Graphics World,* May 1989.

technologies are available, and sometimes they cost less than existing equipment. Although office automation equipment—like personal computers and printers—appears at first glance to have been reasonably stable over the last five years, a closer look reveals a great difference between the first personal computers of the early 1980s and the models available today. Rapid change and rapid obsolescence make investment in knowledge work systems risky.

People Challenges

With technologies and techniques changing so rapidly, employees are under a great deal of pressure to continue learning and training once they are on the job. Moreover, because techniques can change within a few years, people need to accept the possibility that they will have to learn several new and different jobs in a short time. Since employers often do not provide training, cautious employees may have to obtain training in community colleges and elsewhere just to keep their skills current and valuable. On balance, as jobs require more skills and knowledge, individuals are under increased pressure to raise their levels of skill in order to remain employed.[3]

Focus on People illustrates another people challenge—resistance to knowledge work systems, which might diminish personal style and imagination in the creative process.

Organizational Challenges

Organizations face several challenges in building solid information and knowledge work environments. It is difficult to integrate information and knowledge workers into a traditional, hierarchical organization. Changes in the authority structure and work arrangements need to be made in order to accommodate the goals and ambitions of contemporary workers. Second, organizations have to be much more careful about hiring: organizations must identify and recruit workers who have the capability and desire to learn. Third, organizations must devote more resources to training. When retraining does not work, organizations often have to retire experienced older workers much earlier than in the past. This raises costs as well as significant social issues (discussed in Chapter 16).

Summary

- Knowledge workers are those employees who create new information and knowledge.
- Knowledge work systems are applications of information technology expressly designed to enhance the productivity of knowledge workers.
- Knowledge work is distinguished from other work by its reliance on a corpus of knowledge, its place in a university curriculum, its certification by the state, and the presence of professional societies with regulatory power.
- Knowledge worker roles include interpreting the corpus of knowledge to business managers and leaders, acting as internal consultants, and playing the role of change agents.
- In general, knowledge workers require a unique work setting to accomplish their work.
- Knowledge work systems require a more powerful hardware and software platform than office systems.
- Building effective information and knowledge work systems is challenging because of the pace of technological change, the need for continual training and change on the part of employees, and the requirements for organizational learning.

Key Terms

Knowledge work

Knowledge workers' roles in business

External knowledge base

Review Questions

1. What is the difference between data work and knowledge work?
2. What are the four distinguishing features of knowledge work?
3. Why are knowledge workers treated differently than other kinds of workers?
4. What are the generic elements of a knowledge work system?
5. Describe five ways in which a professional knowledge work system differs from an office personal computer.
6. What is an "artificial reality"?
7. Why will it take a long time to make CLARA fully operational?
8. What are the three kinds of challenges involved in building knowledge and information work systems? Give an example of each kind of problem or find an example in a business magazine.

Discussion Questions

1. Why are knowledge work systems playing an increasingly important role in American corporations? Do you expect that this trend will continue or reach a plateau?

2. Choose a professional occupation such as engineer, doctor, lawyer, or scientist, and describe a professional workstation for that occupation.

3. Devise some policies to help a manufacturer of home care products like Toro Company (described in the opening case study) attract and retain more knowledge workers. What kinds of people, technology, and organizational policies would be effective?

Problem-Solving Exercises

1. Visit a local engineering consulting firm, and write a brief description of the kinds of knowledge workstations you observe.

2. University students are knowledge workers in training. As such, they have unique workstation requirements. Write a description of what you think would be an ideal "student workstation."

Notes

1. John Webster, "Modeling Molecules," *Computer Graphics World,* July 1989.
2. David Gancher, "Computer Mentor," *Computerland Magazine,* March/April 1988.
3. For evidence on the overall aggregate rise in skill levels (despite earlier expert predictions that computers would "de-skill" the labor force), see David R. Howell and Edward N. Wolff, "Changes in the Skill Requirements of the U.S. Labor Force, 1960–1985," C. V. Starr Center for Applied Economics, New York University, August 1988.

Problem-Solving Case

Walking through a Factory before It Is Built

Imagine walking through your new $14 million factory designed especially for your company's new plastics processing technology. In Bay 14 you reach out and throw the lever of a globe valve only to discover that you cannot rotate the lever because a concrete wall is in the way! An immediate correction is needed to bring the factory to life next week. Estimated cost of repiping or moving the wall: somewhere between $14,000 and $25,000. In general, in large-scale industrial construction projects in chemicals, oil refining, and pulp paper mills, about 10 percent of the total cost involves reworking. These costs are significant in large projects.

In the past, plant designers would create intricate plastic models costing anywhere from $25,000 to $1 million in order to perform space management and process design checks. But recently, computer-aided design (CAD) software, which was first used to design products, has been extended to plant design. The idea is to build a computer model of the proposed factory and then go "inside" the factory and walk around. Combustion Engineering, Inc. (C-E) and Bechtel Software, Inc., along with several other engineering firms, use and sell plant design software.

The cost of the new systems can be expensive. Sophisticated packages cost about $50,000 for the software alone, plus another $20,000 for hardware. However, due to the cost of reworking factories once they are built and the cost of wasted time of expensive knowledge workers like engineers and designers, this investment pays off within the first year.

One vendor reports that its software has been used in over $10 billion worth of construction and that retrofits and errors in design have been reduced to less than 1 percent of total project cost.

Plant design software has a number of advanced features. It allows users to move around interactively inside a factory design. This new software also permits users to interactively select an object—like a valve—and display a text panel on the features of the valve that are stored in a database. Other features of this software include the ability to obtain accurate measurements directly from the screen so that clearances can be checked and planned properly.

As the cost of workstations declines, more and more uses will be found for plant design software. Bechtel—a construction firm—is extending its system to support construction planning so that users who build plants can simulate construction. Machines can be moved on and off the factory floor to check for clearances; construction cranes can be added to see how construction should be sequenced. Forces can be studied: if a machine "bounces" when a force is applied, construction details can be altered by bolting the machine to the floor.

Another area of future expansion is facilities management and maintenance. Aker Engineering, a Norwegian marine construction company that designs offshore platforms for the North Sea, delivers a workstation with software along with its designs to its customers. Clients use the walk-through software models for maintenance planning. "Our customers want to work

smarter," notes an engineer from Aker. "They want smart buildings that result from intelligent design, and they want maintainable buildings and structures. The software is now a part of the building, so to speak."

Source: Based on Laura Lang, "Walking with Confidence," *Computer Graphics World,* October 1989.

Case Study Questions

1. What are the major features of plant design software?
2. What are some of the advantages of using plant design software rather than hand-drawn architectural plans of a building?
3. What is the meaning of "smart buildings" in the context of this case?
4. In what ways does this software enhance the productivity of knowledge workers?

C H A P T E R · F I F T E E N

Management Support Systems

Chapter Outline

15.1 Introduction: Management Support Systems

15.2 What Managers Do
- Traditional Views
- The Behavioral View: Multiple Roles
- Managers and Information
- The Realistic Setting: Culture, Politics, and Bureaucracy
- Managers and Information Technology

15.3 Management Information Systems
- Leading-Edge Application: Mrs. Fields Cookies

15.4 Decision Support Systems
- Leading-Edge Application: Juniper Lumber, Ltd.

15.5 Executive Support Systems
- Leading-Edge Application: Lockheed Corporation's MIDS System

15.6 The Challenge of Building Management Support Systems
- People Challenges
- Organizational Challenges
- Technology Challenges

Learning Objectives

After reading and studying this chapter, you will:

1. Be aware of what managers do in a business and how they use information.
2. Understand the characteristics of management support systems.
3. Be familiar with management information systems and how they work.
4. Be able to describe decision support systems and how they work.
5. Know what executive support systems are and how they work.
6. Understand the significant challenges of building management support systems.

How Lockheed-Georgia Keeps Flying

Lockheed-Georgia's executives used to float on a sea of paper churned out by the company's information systems. Lockheed is an aerospace firm with 19,000 employees who perform highly technical work for the Air Force. With sophisticated aerospace projects and a large number of information and knowledge workers, Lockheed produces tons of paper reports each week. To keep up with the paperwork, executives often had to move around the country with suitcases of computer printouts.

This is no longer the case. Beginning in the mid-1980s, Lockheed decided to fly over the sea of paper by building an executive support system called MIDS (Management Information Decision Support). Lockheed's president, Robert Ormsby, wanted to be able to look at specific information immediately on screen. He wanted current, up-to-date reports instead of computer printouts that were days, and sometimes weeks, old.

The resulting MIDS system combines graphics and data to display over 800 screens to senior executives in all areas of the company, from manufacturing to personnel and finance. For instance, a manufacturing executive can check on the production status of the C5-B by calling up a display that shows the plane's location in production, assembly status, and production schedule. A human resources executive can find out how contributions are going to the

United Way. A finance executive can find out whether cash flow for the entire company is meeting the corporation plan.

The information produced by the MIDS system is not the usual mainframe computer printout. Instead, the MIDS system presents information in instantly understandable graphic and text formats. A hard copy can be obtained from one of many local printers, and the information can be displayed on overhead projectors in a conference room. A 15-minute tutorial session is all that it takes to become a MIDS system user. Because of this ease of use and the power of the information, utilization has grown from 12 daily users with 69 screens to 70 users with 800 screens.

Six people sift information from Lockheed's existing information systems and, based on management's requests and their own common sense, determine what information goes into the MIDS system. Each day, 150 to 170 of the 800 screens are refreshed with current data.

Because the MIDS system gives senior executives an overview of the big picture at Lockheed, they call it their "executive life support system."

Source: Susan S. Hoffman, "Lockheed Execs Fly MIDS," *Information Week*, September 7, 1987.

Keeping track of thousands of employees, controlling business finances, and planning for the future are just some of the tasks of modern managers. What should we do if cash flow falls below expectations? How far behind in the production schedule are we? Why are so many employees leaving after four or five years? What products are showing the fastest sales growth? Why are our net revenues declining while our sales are growing? These are typical of the questions that managers face every day.

Such questions usually do not have simple answers, and they require managers to use a great deal of judgment. Information systems can play a powerful role in helping managers find answers and develop solutions. In this chapter, we will describe what managers do and explain how information technology is used to support the management of business firms.

15.1 Introduction: Management Support Systems

In a previous chapter, we described how information technology directly supports the transactions of a business—the functions in which the product is actually made and sold. In this chapter, we will be concerned with how information technology supports the management of a business. We will describe the three generic kinds of management support systems: management information systems, decision support systems, and executive support (or information) systems (as in the Lockheed case study above). Each type of system will be illustrated by a real-world example.

Figure 15.1 shows the characteristics of the various management support systems and where they fit into the hierarchy of the firm. **Management information systems (MIS)** provide routine summary reports about the firm's performance; such systems are used to monitor and control the business and predict future performance. **Decision support systems (DSS)** are interactive systems under user control that provide data and models for solving semistructured problems. A **semistructured problem** is one in which only parts of the problem have a clear-cut answer provided by a well-accepted methodology.

Both MIS and DSS are generally concerned with daily operations and with problems that are structured or semistructured. (**Structured problems,** such as those described in Chapter 12, are repetitive and routine and have a specified procedure for handling them; in contrast, unstructured problems are novel and nonroutine, with no agreed-upon procedure for solving them. Semistructured problems combine elements of both types.) Most of the

Management information systems (MIS)
Management support systems that provide routine summary reports on the firm's performance; used to monitor and control the business and predict future performance.

Decision support systems (DSS)
Interactive systems under user control that are used in solving semistructured problems.

Semistructured problem
A problem in which only parts have a clear-cut answer provided by a well-accepted methodology.

Structured problem
A routine, repetitive problem for which there is an accepted methodology for arriving at an answer.

Figure 15.1

The Three Types of Management Support Systems

An executive support system (ESS) serves the senior or executive management level in an organization. It supports the strategic, long-term planning that is required of this level. Executives often must use data from outside the firm, such as information about legal regulations, market conditions, and competing firms' activities. Many of the decisions they must make are unstructured—that is, the questions are open-ended and the decisions involve unpredictable factors. Management information systems (MIS) and decision support systems (DSS) serve middle and low-level managers, who must deal with short-term, daily operational issues. Much of the information required for these systems is internal, and the systems help managers make structured or semistructured decisions that often involve routine procedures.

Management Support Systems

Executive Information Systems
- Strategic planning
- Long-term time frame
- External information
- Unstructured decisions

↕

Management Information Systems and Decision Support Systems
- Daily/monthly/yearly planning
- Short-term time frame
- Internal information
- Structured or semi-structured decisions

information for these kinds of decisions comes from within the business, and the time frame is relatively short term (e.g., this week, this month, or this year).

Executive support systems (ESS)
Graphic-oriented systems designed for senior management that provide generalized computing and telecommunications facilities and combine internal and external information; used for long-term planning.

Executive support systems (ESS) generally support the strategic planning function in a business, for which the time frame is relatively long term. Such activities involve largely unstructured, open-ended questions and decisions pertaining to unpredictable future events; they also tend to require a great deal of information from a business's external environment. Senior executives, for example, need information on government activities and regulations, new laws, the actions of competitors, market conditions, and so forth. ESS also tend to be more graphics oriented than other management support systems.

Although all of these management systems are different, they often exchange information with one another and are related to one another through this information flow. These various systems can be seen as layers in a business organizational cake.

But before we examine each of these systems in detail, we must take a look at what managers do when they manage a business. That will give us a good idea of the kinds of problems managers face and why they build information systems to help solve those problems.

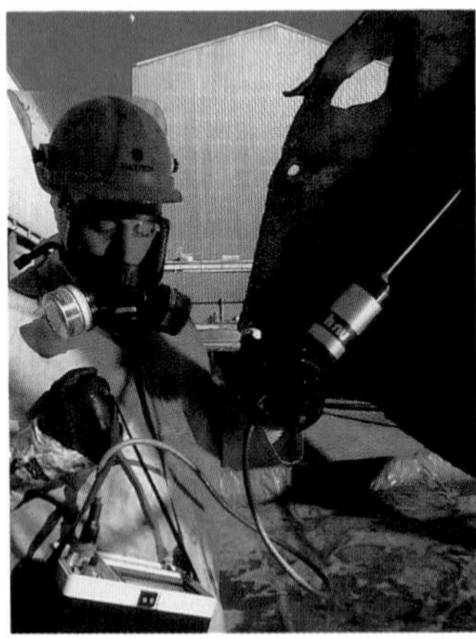

An S&ME employee cleans an underground petroleum tank. Westinghouse Electric Corporation acquired S&ME, Inc. to complement and enhance its capabilities in the cleanup of hazardous wastes. Decision support systems can greatly assist with many kinds of business functions, including acquisitions.

Source: Courtesy of Westinghouse Electric Corporation.

15.2 What Managers Do

There are many descriptions of what managers do, including "getting things done through other people,"[1] "leading an orchestra,"[2] and using business resources to accomplish goals. Each of these descriptions has some validity. Since ancient times, management has been associated with great accomplishments and achievements, such as the irrigation works of the Sumerians (6500 B.C.), the pyramids of Egypt (4000 B.C.), the Great Wall of China (1000 B.C.), and the like. Managers have traditionally been concerned with criteria for measuring progress toward some goal. Management also involves the coordination of many (sometimes thousands) of workers.

Managers clearly are not the people who actually do "the work"; instead they are responsible for determining what work will be done, where it will be done, and for what purpose. And because any business is composed of specialists, managers are in a sense like symphony orchestra conductors trying to get individuals to work together so that "music" results.

Traditional theories of management
Views of management that see its primary functions as being planning, organizing, leading, and controlling.

Managing
The process of using business resources to accomplish goals, coordinate the work of many workers, and establish criteria for measuring progress toward the established goals.

Traditional Views

Classical writers on management, like the French industrialist Henri Fayol (1841–1925), who rose to become the director of a major French mining company, described management as involving five activities: planning, organizing, commanding, coordinating, and controlling. Contemporary writers on management have reduced these features to four management functions: planning, organizing, leading, and controlling (see Figure 15.2).[3] Thus, according to **traditional theories of management, managing** can be defined as the effort to accomplish business goals through planning, organizing, leading, and controlling.

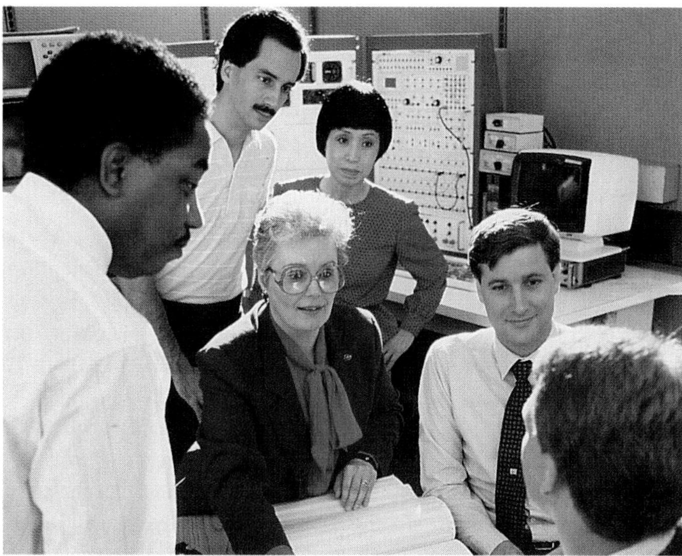

Honeywell Inc. manager Kathryn Ybarra won a technical achievement award for leading a 30-person engineering team that contributed to the success of Honeywell's Traffic Alert and Collision Avoidance System. Managers must juggle planning, organizing, leading, and controlling functions to accomplish business goals.

Source: Courtesy of Honeywell Inc.

Figure 15.2

The Four Major Functions of Management: Planning, Organizing, Leading, and Controlling

The classical view defines management as the effort to meet business goals through these four activities. By planning, the manager establishes the goals of the firm and sets up tasks by which employees will work to achieve these goals. Organizing involves assigning staff and resources to accomplish these tasks. Effective managers lead their employees by motivating them to do their work well, and they control employees in the sense of monitoring business activities and making corrections where necessary.

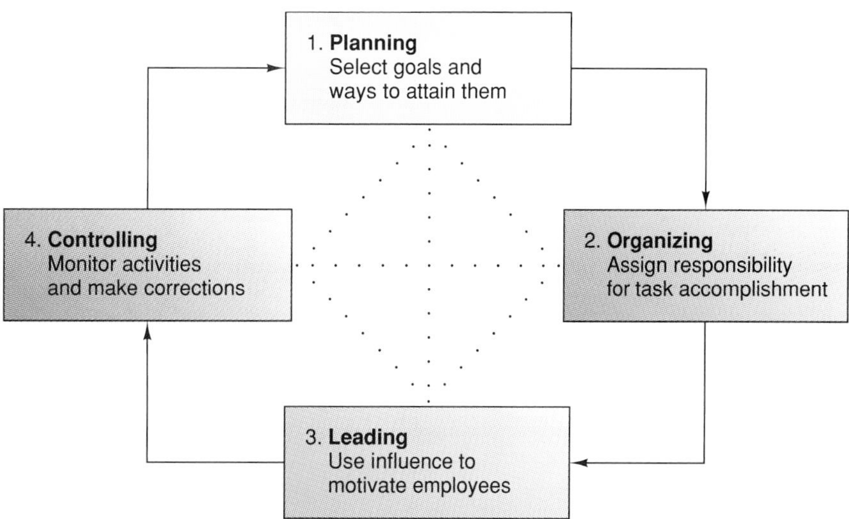

Source: Exhibit 1.1, "The Four Functions of Management," from *Management* by Richard L. Daft, p. 6, copyright © 1988 by The Dryden Press, a division of Holt, Rinehart and Winston, Inc. Reprinted by permission of the publisher.

FOCUS ON People

How Two PC Managers Traveled the Decade of Change

If personal computers (PCs) grew up in the 1980s, so did their managers. By the mid-1980s, some far-sighted companies were realizing that the PC would become a part of the corporate computing structure. But standards had to be imposed even as users were becoming more sophisticated and sure of themselves. Meanwhile, cost-conscious managers were beginning to ask what the company was getting for its PC dollar—and how to share the information in one machine with other corporate databases. Here two managers explain how they are coping with these changes.

Laurent Levy, LAN Supervisor, Rochester Telephone Corporation

"When the 1980s began," remembers Laurent Levy, "I was nowhere near a computer. I didn't know a monitor from a disk." Today, he's a local area network (LAN) supervisor at the Rochester Telephone Corporation, and his servers share space with the mainframes in the corporate data center, which used to be the realm solely of mainframes and minicomputers.

So many critical applications run on the telephone company's 1,000 networked PCs that "life stops when the LAN stops," he explained.

Levy took over LAN support at Rochester Telephone in the summer of 1987, just as the number of connected workstations was rocketing from 100 to more than 1,000.

"In the early days, if the LAN went down, it was at worst an inconvenience," he said. "Secretaries still had their typewriters, executives would still dictate memos to their secretaries." Now, every executive has a PC. While very large, mission-critical applications are still on mainframes, executives do their own word processing, and without the LAN, "everything would come to a halt," Levy said.

Levy is wrestling with creating standards to govern the

Source: Robert L. Scheier, "How Four PC Managers Traveled the Decade of Change," adapted from *PC Week*, December 25, 1989/January 1, 1990, pp. 54-55.

Planning refers to defining the goals of the business and describing how it will fulfill these goals. Organizing involves assigning responsibility for accomplishing the necessary tasks and assigning appropriate resources. Leading means motivating employees to achieve organizational goals. Controlling involves monitoring the activities of the business and making corrections where necessary. The Focus on People describes how two managers are meeting the challenges presented by the rapid growth in the use of personal computers.

The Behavioral View: Multiple Roles

The traditional view is perfectly adequate for describing the basic functions of management, but it does not tell us how managers do what they do. How do managers actually go about planning, organizing, leading, and controlling? For this we must turn to contemporary behavioral scientists who have studied managers in daily action. The results are surprising. A typical manager's morning might look like this:[4]

development of applications on the LAN. "We don't want to become bogged down in bureaucracy and procedures and rules," he said, "but on the other hand, the LAN has grown so large so fast [that these issues] have to be addressed."

Levy predicts there will be a strong demand for support personnel in the 1990s, as the rising power of PCs increases their importance to corporate America. "What I also see is 30 or 40 years down the line, PC people could wind up in the same position as MIS people are now," he said. "You have to continually stay on top of the technology, not rest on your laurels."

Virginia Johnson, Manager of Computer Services, Hughes Aircraft Company

Once you've got the PCs on the desktops, how do you get the most out of them? That's the classic question that Virginia Johnson is trying to answer.

While she does, the growth phase for PCs has slowed down a bit in the human resources department of Hughes Aircraft Company in Los Angeles, where Johnson is manager of computer services. "There are so many PCs out there not being utilized," she said. "We want to spend more money training people, getting more utilization out of the existing hardware, before we invest more capital in PCs."

At first, most of her PC support time was taken up teaching users how to use common tools such as word processing and graphics—"how to automate a lot of the manual things they were doing." Today, with users more sophisticated, less time is spent teaching such basic skills. Instead, the support staff carries the torch for such causes as proper data backup and the need for companywide guidelines for applications development.

"How can we control what we give the users so we can ensure that they don't destroy themselves?" Johnson said. "The role is more advisory versus technical support. We don't necessarily need to provide [users] with information, but to help them understand how to use it."

The group also hopes to settle on guidelines for choosing off-the-shelf applications, both to save money and to make supporting them easier.

- **7:35 A.M.:** Wendy Henshaw arrives at her office, unpacks her briefcase, gets some coffee, and looks over a "to do" list.
- **7:40:** Wendy and her immediate subordinate, Frank Williams, discuss their weekend activities. Wendy shows Frank some recent pictures.
- **8:00:** Wendy and Frank discuss a meeting for next week with production managers.
- **8:20:** Another subordinate, Janet Watson, drops in and joins the conversation about next week's meeting. Janet will start preparing slides for the presentation next week and wants some guidance on appropriate slide colors.
- **9:00:** Wendy attends a meeting of marketing specialists planning for a new product release. She is upset that her department has not been informed even though it is responsible for the marketing effort.
- **11:00:** Wendy's boss, Harrison White, drops by for a short unplanned meeting. He wants a report as soon as possible on last

week's production shortfall. Wendy promises to get it out this afternoon.

- **11:20:** Wendy's secretary comes in with an office get-well card for another secretary who is hospitalized. Her secretary reminds her that tomorrow is the staff luncheon to celebrate the birth of a co-worker's child.
- **11:40:** A staff person stops by with the figures on last week's production shortfall. Wendy has to show the staffer how to reformat them for her boss.
- **11:45:** Wendy takes a call from a friend.
- **12:00:** Wendy goes to lunch with a human relations recruiter to discuss corporate recruitment policies.

Wendy spends the afternoon in one brief meeting after another interrupted by several phone calls and appointment requests; she also devotes one hour to returning calls. This is what a typical manager does in order to fulfill the functions of planning, organizing, leading, and controlling.

This realistic world of the manager has six characteristics. (1) Managers perform high-volume, high-speed work, involving a large number of very different topics. (2) The pace is unrelenting, and the phone rarely stops ringing. (3) The work is characterized by variety, fragmentation, and brevity. There is very little time to "think about things." (4) Managers tend to be issue oriented because they spend attention on the things that need attention immediately. If something is not an issue, it often is not attended to. (5) Managers also have a complex web of personal contacts and interactions, which range from working with clerical workers to sympathizing and working with other managers. (6) Managers have a strong preference for verbal communications.[5]

Behavioral theories of management
Views of management that stress three roles—interpersonal, informational, and decisional.

According to **behavioral theories of management,** the traditional notion of management as planning, organizing, leading, and controlling is a little simplistic. All of these functions are performed, but not in any rational, sequential manner. Moreover, behavioral theorists perceive the manager's roles a bit differently than traditional theorists do.

When John T. Kotter observed real-world managers, he found that they engage in three basic activities:[6]

- **Establishing agendas:** Managers set long-term (three to five years) goals.
- **Building a network:** Managers develop a network of business and community contacts at all levels.
- **Executing agendas:** Managers use their personal networks to accomplish their goals.

A contemporary researcher, Henry Mintzberg, studied the characteristics of management work and found that managers perform ten roles, which fall into three major categories (see Table 15.1). A role is a set of expectations for a person who occupies a specific status. In other words, occupants of the manager position are expected to perform three types of roles:

Table 15.1

Management Roles

Category	Role	Activity
Interpersonal	Figurehead	Perform ceremonial and symbolic duties such as greeting visitors or signing legal documents.
	Leader	Direct and motivate subordinates; train, counsel, and communicate with subordinates.
	Liaison	Maintain information links both inside and outside the organization; use mail, phone calls, and meetings.
Informational	Monitor	Seek and receive information, scan periodicals and reports, and maintain personal contacts.
	Disseminator	Forward information to other organization members; send memos and reports, and make phone calls.
	Spokesperson	Transmit information to outsiders through speeches, reports, and memos.
Decisional	Entrepreneur	Initiate improvement projects; identify new ideas and delegate idea responsibility to others.
	Disturbance handler	Take corrective action during disputes or crises; resolve conflicts among subordinates; adapt to environmental crises.
	Resource allocator	Decide who gets resources; scheduling, budgeting, and setting priorities.
	Negotiator	Represent department during negotiation of union contracts, sales, purchases, and budgets; represent departmental interests.

Source: Adapted from Henry Mintzberg, "Managerial Work: Analysis from Observation," *Management Science* 18 (1971), pp. B97–B110.

- **Interpersonal roles:** Here managers are expected to act like human beings with a full set of emotions. They are expected to perform symbolic duties like attending birthday parties and giving out employee awards; they are expected to motivate, counsel, and support employees, and they are expected to act as liaisons to the larger firm and outside world on behalf of employees. In the traditional view, these roles were all considered "leadership."
- **Informational roles:** Managers are expected to monitor the activities of the business, disseminate information through reports and memos, and act as a spokesperson for the business. In the traditional theories, these informational roles were poorly understood and subsumed under all categories.
- **Decisional roles:** Managers are, of course, supposed to make decisions. They are expected to make decisions about new products,

Interpersonal roles
The activities of managers that involve performing symbolic duties; motivating, counseling, and supporting workers; and acting as liaisons to the larger firm and the outside world on behalf of employees.

Informational roles
The activities of managers that involve monitoring the activities of the business, disseminating information through reports and memos, and acting as spokespersons for the business.

Decisional roles
The activities of managers that involve making decisions about new products, handling disturbances in the business, allocating resources, and negotiating among persons with different points of view.

which involves acting like entrepreneurs; to handle disturbances in the business; and to allocate resources by budgeting, scheduling, and setting priorities. Additionally, managers are expected to be able to negotiate among individuals with different points of view.

The behavioral perspective gives us a much more realistic and complex view of what managers do. The managerial role clearly involves much more than simply planning, organizing, leading, and controlling. Managers are also expected to nurture, care, inform, motivate, and decide.

Managers and Information

Actual studies of managers have found that they spend most of their time talking with other people—not analyzing statements, calculating results, or reading formal reports (see Figure 15.3). More than half of a manager's time is spent in meetings—in some businesses, this occupies 75 percent of a manager's time.[7]

What this means is that the vast majority of information that an executive takes in comes through the grapevine in the form of comments, opinions, gossip, and short stories. Only a very small part of a manager's total information comes through formal information systems or message systems.

Figure 15.3

Managers and Information

Research on how managers obtain information shows that for the most part they get it from other people. A hefty 75 percent of a manager's time is spent in meetings—50 percent planned but 25 percent unplanned. Another 10 percent of the day is spent either making or receiving telephone calls, and 5 percent passes in clerical work. This leaves a scant 10 percent of a manager's time devoted to analysis: reading reports and research, making calculations, analyzing statements.

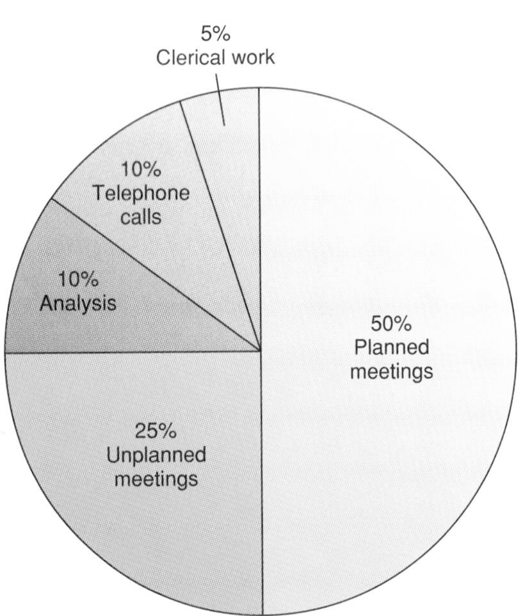

Figure 15.4

A Realistic View of a Manager's Environment

Managers do not operate in a vacuum. They must deal with, and sometimes surmount, three factors within a firm. One is the company's culture, the framework of assumptions and acceptable behaviors that are expected of employees in general and managers in particular. Another is the company's politics, often arising from competition with other managers for valuable resources. A third factor is bureaucracy: the day-to-day rules and procedures governing the firm's operations. Any of these factors can affect a manager's ability to do the job.

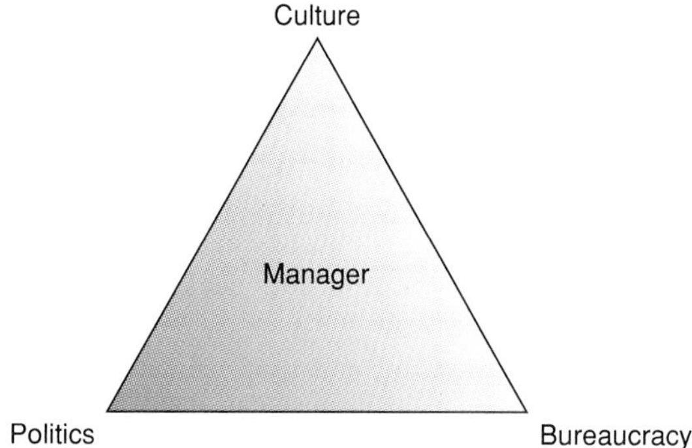

To some extent, this situation is changing. Prior to the advent of business information systems, there were only manual systems of information collection and distribution. With the advent of computers, formal information systems, telecommunications systems such as electronic mail and subscriber databases like CompuServe, and presentation systems like electronic blackboards, information technology is playing a much larger role than in the past and will play a still larger role in the future.

The Realistic Setting: Culture, Politics, and Bureaucracy

Complicating the behavioral picture described above, but making it even more realistic, are the features of business discussed in Chapter 2. To a large extent, managers are not free agents (see Figure 15.4). They have to work within a given culture (certain basic business assumptions) and within a political environment where other managers are competing for resources. Furthermore, they must thoroughly understand the rules, regulations, and day-to-day procedures of how the business works (the bureaucracy) before they can accomplish their agendas. The following story gives some idea of the situation:

> *Ten years ago last summer, I resigned as an editor at* Fortune *magazine and went to work for Ford Motor Company in Detroit. My new job was to communicate company positions on regulatory issues.*
>
> *At the time I felt I was on a wonderful adventure of learning and personal fulfillment. In retrospect it was a shattering experience. At first I loved working at Ford because as a kid I was insecure and I wanted jobs that made me feel and appear important. At Ford I felt I was in the big time of world capitalism—I finally hit the jackpot. I*

FOCUS ON *Organizations*

Hustle and Vision as the Plan

Many people who write about management say you have to have a detailed strategic plan that outlines some big strategic move that your competitors cannot follow. But running a successful company involves a lot more than a strategic plan. Most of these writers and managers totally ignore hustle.

A large number of successful companies do not have a long-term strategic plan and do not pay that much attention to their rivals. Instead, they focus on doing things well and getting it right the first time. If anything, they are fanatic about high-quality products and services. These successful firms concentrate on moving fast, elaborating on existing products and services, and just plain hustle. Hustle is their style and their strategy.

The very finest financial organizations have more than a plan and more than a well-designed set of controls. They have leaders with vision—a deep shared understanding of what their firm is about and where it is headed. Goldman Sachs and Morgan Guaranty, two New York–based investment banking firms that are very successful, make a religion out of teamwork and making the customer happy.

A vision does not require exhaustive analysis or a computer. The only way to make the vision real is through superior execution. The key is hustle that outlasts product cycles and wins despite unremitting competition.

Source: Amar Bhide, "Hustle as Strategy," *Harvard Business Review*, September-October 1986.

loved the view from my office, the panelling in the office, and the elegant Ford logo with its huge curving engraving.

I liked the people with whom I worked, but ultimately I could not take the politics of the office, the politics of the corporation. The corporation often took public positions not because it believed them but because they improved relationships with customers, suppliers, or competitors.

Inside the company there was a constant battle for turf control among the key players and their staffs. There was a tremendous amount of time spent advocating this position or that simply because it served some special group in the company. People often did not want to take responsibility for decisions. One person I know would reject papers from his staff that were too clear cut and forced him to make a decision. This executive actually wanted to remain fuzzy on the issues rather than come to a decision.[8]

The behavioral view reminds us that managers ultimately are people. The Focus on Organizations suggests that the most important strategic resource of the firm is the employees who work there.

Table 15.2

How Information Systems Help Managers

Information technology can assist business managers in many, but not all, of the roles that Mintzberg defined. Management information systems (MIS) are helpful in the informational role, as managers assess a firm's performance and attempt to predict its future. An MIS can also help a manager handle conflicts or problems. A decision support system (DSS) can help clarify decisions regarding resource allocations. However, we do not yet have information technologies that directly assist other key managerial roles such as "figurehead," "leader," "entrepreneur," and "negotiator."

Role	Management Support Systems
Interpersonal roles	
Figurehead	None exist
Leader	None exist
Liaison	Electronic communication systems
Informational roles	
Nerve center	MIS
Disseminator	Mail office systems
Spokesperson	Office and professional systems Workstations
Decisional roles	
Entrepreneur	None exist
Disturbance handler	MIS helpful
Resource allocator	DSS
Negotiator	None exist

Source: Adapted from Henry Mintzberg, "Managerial Work: Analysis from Observation," *Management Science* 18 (1971).

Managers and Information Technology

We can use the behavioral view of managers to get a good idea of how information technology might actually help managers. Table 15.2 relates the ten managerial roles to the actual use of information systems. As you can see, information technology is currently not very helpful in many managerial roles. For instance, there really are no information systems that directly assist a manager's figurehead or leader roles. Moreover, systems do not directly assist the manager as entrepreneur or negotiator (although certain decision support systems are helpful, as we describe later).

Nevertheless, in many areas information technology can be of direct assistance in the solution of management problems. Management information systems (described in the next section) directly help the manager monitor and control the business. This is a very powerful role. Decision support systems are central to a manager's decision-making roles and are especially helpful in allocating resources, as we will see in Section 15.4. In addition, recent DSS are being developed to handle crisis situations and to assist negotiators in selected situations. Executive support systems are beginning to have an impact on how leaders actually perform their leadership roles and are being used to support the spokesperson function as well, as we will see in Section 15.5.

15.3 Management Information Systems

Management information systems (MIS) provide managers with reports on the firm's performance, both past and present. They serve the managers' informational role by helping to monitor actual business performance and predict future performance, thus permitting managers to intervene when things are not going well; hence, they assist in controlling the business.

MIS are generally dependent on underlying transaction processing systems for their data. In other words, MIS summarize and report on the basic operations of the company. The system compresses the basic transaction data by summarization and presents the information in long reports, which are usually produced on a regularly scheduled basis and answer structured, routine questions. Figure 15.5 shows how a typical MIS transforms raw data from transaction processing systems in order inventory, production, and

Figure 15.5

An MIS Helps Managers Access Transaction-Level Data

A management information system (MIS) provides routine summary reports on the firm's performance. Generally, an MIS obtains its data from the company's transaction processing systems, the systems that perform the firm's basic business procedures. As this diagram shows, raw transaction-level data from three functional areas—order inventory, production, and accounting—are funneled through each department's transaction processing system to be collected as data in MIS files. Managers can use the MIS software to access these data.

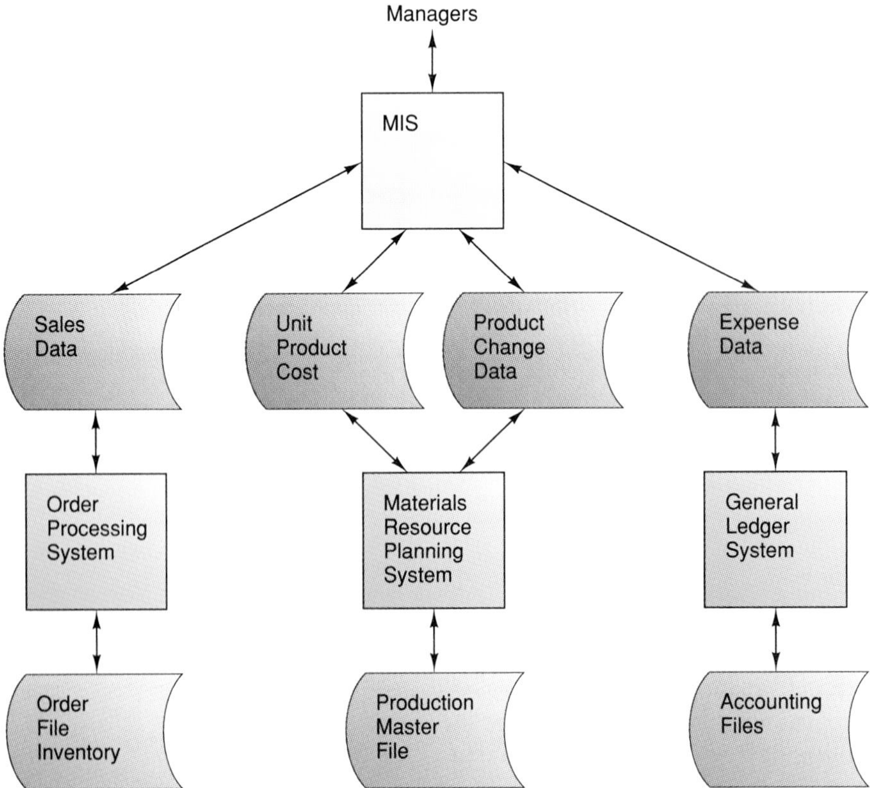

accounting into MIS files. Managers can access the MIS files using the MIS software.

Perhaps the best way to see how an MIS works is to look at a real-world, or in this case, a cookie world, MIS. As you read the following case study, ask yourself these questions: Where does an MIS obtain its data? What does it actually do with the data? What management and business problems does this system solve? What difference does the MIS make for the firm?

Through in-store information management, La Ruche Picarde, operators of Mammouth hypermarkets in France, ensures that perishables like fish are always fresh. Using NCR hardware, store and department managers have sales and inventory data available in any format that is needed to monitor business performance and predict future performance.

Source: Courtesy of NCR Corporation.

Leading-Edge Application: Mrs. Fields Cookies

Who would pay 75 cents for a cookie? Several million Americans, Europeans, and Japanese, that's who. When Debbie Fields started Mrs. Fields Cookies in 1984, no one expected her to make much money. Bankers turned her down, and she built the corporation one store at a time. By 1989, Mrs. Fields Cookies had gross revenues of $170 million.[9]

Each night after business closes, the managers of Mrs. Fields 500 cookie stores, 120 La Petite Boulangerie bakery-cafes, and 15 combination shops, turn on their Tandy 1000 personal computers, which automatically dial the company's headquarters in Park City, Utah, via an 800 number. The local managers have already loaded into a fixed corporate report form that records the day's transactions, including the following information:

- How many of each kind of cookie were sold.
- How many of each type were sold in each hour of the business day.
- How many workers were employed.
- How much inventory of what type is on hand.
- Time cards of employees who worked.
- New employee applications.
- How much money was deposited in the bank.
- Any other free text messages to Debbie Fields or her manager husband, Randy Fields, who developed the system.

The information is rapidly uploaded via a local modem to headquarters, where it is stored on a minicomputer IBM System 38.

In the early morning at headquarters in Park City, a corporate manager called a store controller uses a personal computer to call up the information from the 50 to 75 stores he or she monitors. The store controllers look for things like the following:

- Expected versus actual sales (exceptions from plan).
- Expected versus actual production.
- Expected versus actual labor costs per unit.
- Excess or insufficient inventory.
- Unexpected deviations from typical bank deposits.

The store controllers then intervene based on their analysis of sales and other data.

The local store managers can request the central system to provide a production schedule, a labor force schedule (who should work when), skills testing of potential employees, inventory control (when to order new inventory and supplies), production tool parts and problem diagnosis, and even payroll. Each local store manager can decide which of these central services are desirable. The local managers retain control over hiring and firing and the mix of products to sell. Still, many managers prefer to have the central system take as much of the administrative burden as possible.

The philosophy upon which Randy Fields built the system was that financial accounting does not make the company any money—it just tells you how much money you made. What makes money is getting information from the field as fast as possible and changing to meet market demands. Fields also wanted to do away with as much paper as possible by putting all corporate forms on the computer. "Each paper form costs us 2 cents just to file at headquarters," notes Fields. Eliminating forms from the system has added up to a saving of $700,000 each year.

The Fields realize now that they bet the future of their company on the MIS they call a Retail Operations Intelligence (ROI) System. In 1986 the Fields' operation almost collapsed; they had 135 stores and only 20 people at headquarters. The old sales tracking system required local store managers to keypunch in the daily sales data using Touch Tone phones. When Mrs. Fields Cookies expanded by adding 70 new stores in the Northeast, the new system was designed simply because the old one no longer worked.

The development of the MIS has permitted the company to monitor a much larger number of stores with a reduced corporate staff. As Mrs. Fields Cookies expands into other retail food operations, the ROI system will be the backbone of the company. ROI has been so successful that Randy Fields has established a subsidiary, "Fields Software Group," to market the ROI system to other food retailers. Fields Software Group is expecting sales of $30 to $40 million in five years.

This case study is a leading-edge example of how personal computers, minicomputers, and telecommunications can be used in a contemporary fashion to create a very powerful management information system. Let's go back and examine our list of questions, which should reveal a little more clearly just what an MIS actually does:

- **Where does an MIS obtain its data?** Like Mrs. Fields' ROI, most MIS obtain the raw data from transaction processing systems (TPS) like those described in Chapter 12. In the case of Mrs. Fields' MIS, the cash register captures sales data on time and type of product sold and summarizes this for inclusion into the local store's personal computer.
- **What does an MIS actually do with the data?** Most MIS perform simple, repetitive summaries of transaction data and report exceptions or deviations from a plan. For instance, Mrs. Fields' MIS summarizes daily sales, labor input, and inventory utilization. In addition, the central headquarters has a plan that describes expected average output, cost, and inventory for each store. When a local store deviates

from this corporate plan, central headquarters managers are alerted that something may be wrong. Thus, this exception or deviation report signals management that efforts may be needed to change local store procedures.

But Mrs. Fields' ROI system is a leading-edge system, and it provides a good deal more than simple summary and exception reports. In many respects, it functions like a decision support system (described in Section 15.4) because it provides recommendations for production schedules, labor schedules, and the like.

- **What management and business problems does this system solve?** In general, MIS are good at handling routine, repetitive kinds of problems that are well structured—that is, those for which there is an accepted methodology for arriving at an answer. For instance, in answer to the question, "How many people should I employ?" the Mrs. Fields' MIS can make a good estimate based on the amount of predicted sales and the long historical experience that is captured in the system.

  The system would not handle less-structured problems, such as "Given that there has been a snow storm, that it is Christmas time with increased traffic indoors, and that there has been a large sales campaign for Mrs. Fields Cookies, what is an optimal hourly labor force for a specific store?" Answering these less-structured questions is more the province of sophisticated decision support systems, which are described in the next section.

  In general, from a management perspective, MIS are critical to the operational control of the business. Because such systems report and summarize the basic transactions and compare them to a plan, they are vital in providing managers with the right information in a timely fashion. In the case of Mrs. Fields, the ROI system provides headquarters and central management with a bird's-eye view of how the company performs each day.

  From a business perspective, MIS help solve the problem of size by reducing coordination costs. As businesses grow and increase the scale of their operations, it is critical to achieve economies of scale. Ideally, as businesses grow, they should be able to make products more cheaply because they buy and sell in volume and have larger production runs. On the other hand, as Mrs. Fields found out with its old sales order system, coordination costs grow as the firm expands, and potentially they can prevent a business from reaping the benefits of large scale. MIS help reduce the costs of growth and make it possible for businesses to operate on a large scale with only minimal increases in coordination and management costs.

- **What difference does this MIS make for the firm?** Mrs. Fields' MIS really had strategic consequences for the firm because it permitted the company to expand from 160 stores to over 500 stores. Because the competition probably did not have such a powerful MIS, you could say that the MIS provided a temporary but important strategic competitive advantage. Furthermore, the MIS experience gained in building the ROI system has become a salable product and is being sold to other firms. In this sense, Mrs. Fields' MIS had a strategic consequence because it led to new products.

As we have seen, MIS are good at handling structured, repetitive problems; when a more interactive and flexible approach is desired, decision support systems, described in the next section, can be used.

15.4 Decision Support Systems

Sales of the Perkin-Elmer Cetus DNA Amplification System exceeded projections in 1988. A decision support system could be used to predict sales performance.

Source: Courtesy of Perkin-Elmer Corporation.

Although just about any computer that delivers information might be called a "decision support system," DSS are conceptually very different from MIS or TPS. Decision support systems (DSS) generally take less time and money to develop than MIS, are interactive in the sense that the user interacts with the data directly, and are useful for solving semistructured problems. As we noted earlier, a semistructured problem is one in which only parts of the problem have a clear-cut answer provided by a well-accepted methodology. Figure 15.6 summarizes major differences between an MIS and a DSS. Based on these characteristics, we can arrive at a working definition of a DSS: it is an interactive system under user control that provides data and models to support the discussion and solution of semistructured problems.

The generic DSS has three components. Figure 15.7 illustrates a DSS serving the same three business functional areas shown in Figure 15.5. The database of a DSS is a collection of information often taken from the firm's own internal transaction systems. Generally, this transaction information is summarized and transmitted to the DSS so that its database, unlike an MIS, contains data from inventory, production, and accounting.

Figure 15.6

Differences between an MIS and a DSS

Although these two concepts can overlap (see the example of Mrs. Fields Cookies), there are several basic differences. An MIS usually reports summaries of basic business transactions and notes exceptions from expected performance; its output is usually routine reports. It uses relatively simple analytical tools such as averages and summations to solve structured problems. A DSS, on the other hand, uses more sophisticated analytical and data modeling tools to solve semistructured problems. It provides data to support management decision making on issues that are less routine than those handled by an MIS.

MIS	DSS
• Reports summaries of basic transactions and exceptions from plan • Uses simple analytical tools • Solves structured, repetitive problems • Produces routine reports	• Provides data and models for decision making • Uses sophisticated analysis and modeling tools • Solves semi-structured problems • Provides interactive answers to nonroutine questions

Figure 15.7

Three Components of a DSS: Database, Model Base, and Easy-to-Use Software System

Here we see a DSS that serves the same three functional areas shown in Figure 15.5: order processing, production, and accounting/finance. Like an MIS, the DSS draws its data from the firm's transaction processing systems. However, the DSS model base contains much more sophisticated analytical and modeling tools than would be found in an MIS. The DSS software systems allows users with little computer experience to access these data, often on-line.

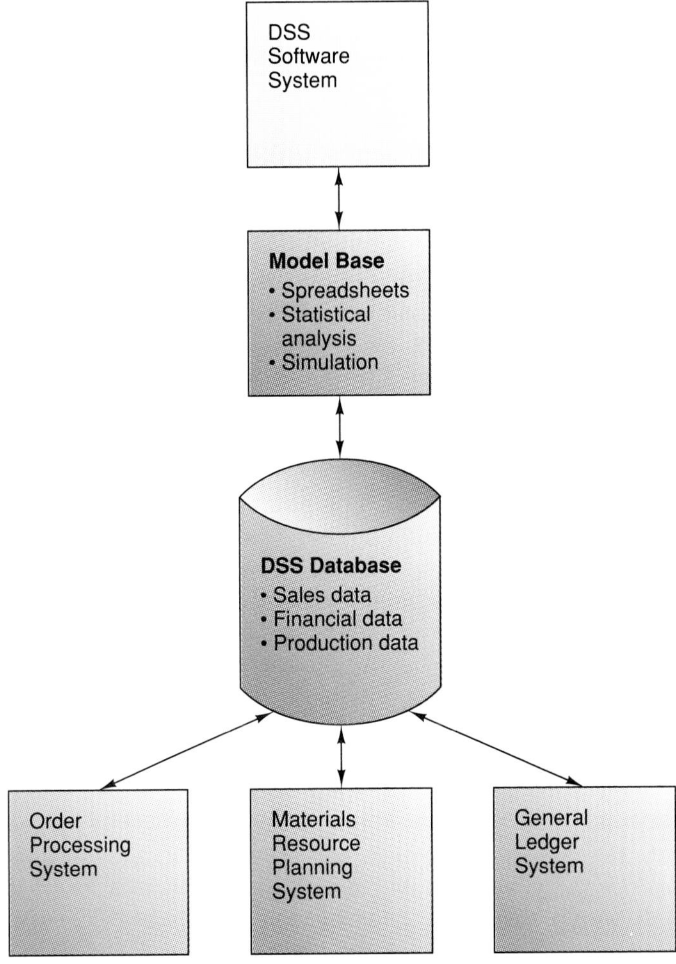

A second element of a DSS is a **model base,** or the analytical tools the system utilizes. Perhaps this is the critical difference between an MIS and a DSS. As we noted in the preceding section, MIS generally have very simple analytical tools—averages, summations, deviations from plan, and the like. DSS, however, usually have very sophisticated analytical and modeling tools, such as built-in spreadsheets, statistical analysis, and simulation.

Model base
The analytical tools used by an information system; in a decision support system, it will include very sophisticated tools such as built-in spreadsheets, statistical analysis, and simulation.

The third element of a DSS is a software system that permits easy interaction between users of the system (who often have no computer expertise) and the database and model base.

Distinguishing between an MIS and a DSS is not always easy, as the following case study illustrates. Generally, MIS produce routine reports on a batch basis with a regular schedule—every day, week, or month. DSS produce such reports, but they also permit the user to ask new and unanticipated questions and to intervene directly on-line to change the manner in which the data are presented. Once again, as you read the case study, keep the following questions in mind: Where does the DSS obtain its data? What does the DSS actually do with the data? What management and business problems does this system solve? What difference does the DSS make for the firm?

Leading-Edge Application: Juniper Lumber, Ltd.

Juniper Lumber Company, Ltd., is a New Brunswick, Canada, forest products company that produces 50 million board feet of lumber annually, with revenues of $19 million. Juniper employs 160 people in addition to several scores of contractors who cut much of the raw wood and deliver it to company mills.

When the company's president, J.B. O'Keefe, moved to Juniper, company production and sales records were totally manual; they were orderly but often out of date and behind schedule. O'Keefe wanted production reports by 4:00 P.M. every day so he could discover where bottlenecks were occurring, but instead he had to wait until 11:00 A.M. the next morning to find out what was going on.

Frustrated by the existing manual system, O'Keefe set about building a DSS that could both deliver routine reports and permit users in the company to find answers to specific questions that might arise. Figure 15.8 illustrates the system, which accepts input from customer, contractor, and product location records. Data are stored in transaction processing files, funneled to a database, and accessed through the DSS.

One unique feature of the system was that it relied on a microcomputer. O'Keefe wanted a system that could be operated in a remote environment that often suffered power failures. The company plant is located 50 miles from the nearest small town, and programmers are few and far between. Hence the system would have to work without a lot of technical support. It would have to be understandable to clerks, accountants, and managers in place. Finally, a microcomputer was suitable in part because the processing volumes were quite low and the file sizes were small. There were only 100 customer records, 350 contractor records, and about 500 product/location records (a product and its storage locations).

The Juniper Lumber Information System (JLIS) gives users a choice of prewritten reports or direct access to data. Figure 15.9 shows both kinds of output. In addition, the data can be loaded directly into a Lotus 1-2-3 spreadsheet, and from there further analysis can be performed.

When the designers of the system returned to Juniper Lumber several years after installing the system, they found that the system's spreadsheet capabilities for analyzing and projecting future sales and incomes were being

Figure 15.8

Juniper Lumber's DSS

Juniper Lumber Company, Ltd., is a Canadian logging firm whose plant is located 50 miles from the nearest town. In this remote setting, power failures are frequent and technical staff are hard to find. Thus, reliability and ease of use were crucial issues for the company's DSS, which was designed to operate on a microcomputer for those reasons. The DSS takes its input from internal transaction processing systems—customer information and accounts receivable, and product inventory orders and sales. The DSS allows managers to assess production bottlenecks more quickly and has reduced waste by 36 percent.

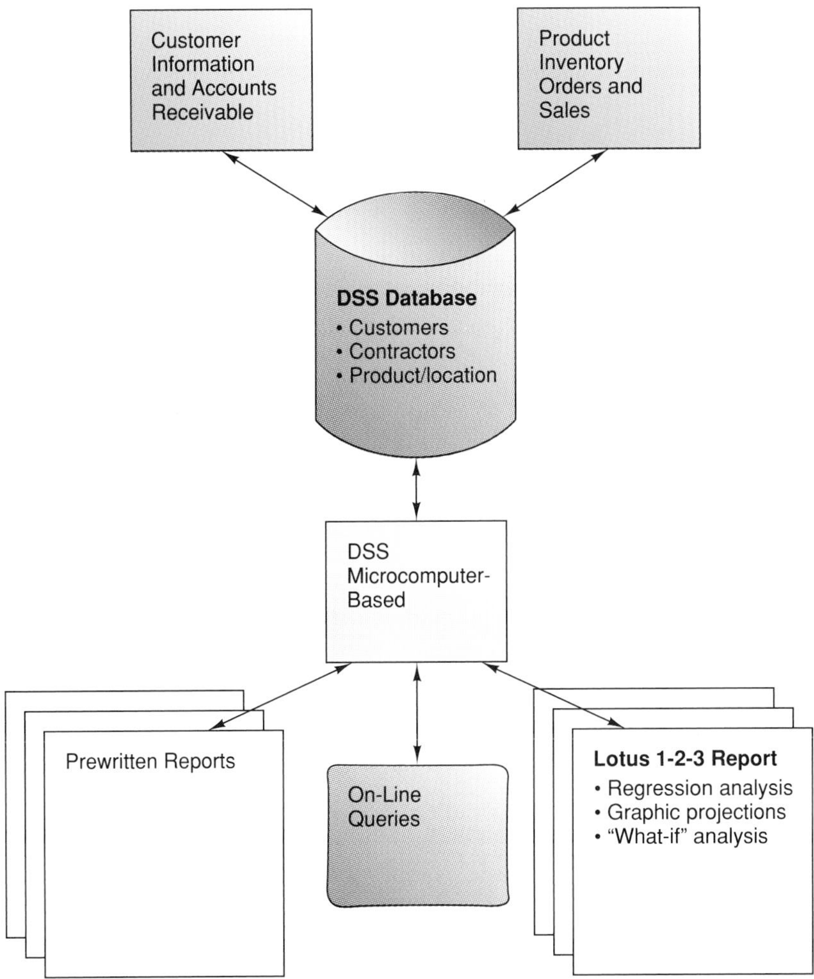

used much more than had been expected. This meant the system was being used more and more as a decision support device, working interactively with management, rather than merely as a "report generator."

One example of how the JLIS is being used as a DSS is the interactive monitoring of saw-log quality and production. Each saw log is supposed to yield, on average, 38 board feet of dressed (cut and finished) lumber. For a variety of reasons, the quality of saw logs varies: some are too short, some

Figure 15.9

The Juniper Lumber DSS Provides a Variety of Outputs

Here we see samples of output from the Juniper Lumber Company DSS illustrated in Figure 15.8. Panel a is a listing of available prewritten reports. Panel b is a list of on-line queries managers can make. In addition to these reports, the system can also provide data for Lotus 1-2-3 spreadsheet software, allowing managers to do further statistical analyses.

(a) Pre-Written Reports

```
                    Juniper Lumber Company
 >> DIRECTORY OF FILES -- LUMBER <<

 ••  1. Customer File by Product      •• 15. Movement Slips
 ••  2. Order Header File             •• 16. Resequenced Movement Slip
 ••  3. Cash Receipts                 •• 17. Sawlog Receipts -- FBM Scale
 ••  4. Resequenced Sawlog Receipts   •• 18. Transaction Descriptors
 ••  5. Invoices Received             •• 19. Downtime History File
 ••  6. Checks Issued                 •• 20. Production History File
 ••  7. Order Line Items              •• 21. Order Headers -- Posted
 ••  8. Product File                  •• 22. Operator Security File
 ••  9. Cutting Tally File            •• 23. Resequenced Tally Cards
 •• 10. Volume Tables                 •• 24. Movement Slips -- Posted
 •• 11. Location Master File          •• 25. Resequenced Order Lines
 •• 12. Contractor History by Prod.   •• 26. Tally Cards -- Posted
 •• 13. Contractors and Suppliers     •• 27. Sawlog Receipts -- Posted
 •• 14. Order Lines -- Posted         •• 28. Woodyard Report File


      •••  1. For INPUT.           ••  3. For DISPLAY.
      •••  2. For EDIT.            ••  4. For DELETE.
    Please enter your Selection; or ^ to Return to Executive Menu
      ENTER FUNCTION  -/           SELECT FILE     --/
```

(b) On-Line Query Reports

```
                    Juniper Lumber Company
 MMMMMMMMMMMMMMMMMMMMMMMM> XRT Quick-Query Writer <MMMMMMMMMMMMMMMMMMMMMMMM

 ••  1. Vol. Calc. -- Cutting         •• 17. Inv. Update -- Pur. Wood
 ••  2. Inv. Update -- Cutting        •• 18. Order Lines -- Purge File 7
 ••  3. Scale Report -- Cutting       •• 19. Trucking/Slashing Schedule
 ••  4. Open Orders by Date Prom.     •• 20. Loading Schedule
 ••  5. Inv. Update (2) -- Mov.       •• 21. By-Product Sales Report
 ••  6. Inv. Update -- Mov. Slip      •• 22. Mov. Slips -- Create File 24
 ••  7. Inventory Update -- Shipping  •• 23. Mov. Slips -- Purge File 15
 ••  8. Total Open Order              •• 24. Sawlog Rec. -- Create File
 ••  9. Production Update             •• 25. Sawlog Rec. -- Purge File 17
 •• 10. Tally Cards -- Create File    •• 26. Order Headers -- Create File
 •• 11. Tally Cards -- Purge File 9   •• 27. Order Headers -- Purge File
 •• 12. Downtime Report               •• 28. Detailed Inventory Listing
 •• 13. Crown Report                  •• 29. Zero fields 17,19 for File
 •• 14. Order Lines -- Create File    •• 30. DAILY SALES LISTING
 •• 15. Vol. Calc. -- Pur/Cut Wood    •• 31. Monthly Sales/Production
 •• 16. Scale Report -- Pur. Wood

 MMMMMMMMMMMMMMMMMMMMMMMMMMMMMMMMMMMMMMMMMMMMMMMMMMMMMMMMMMMMMMMMMMMMMMMMMM


 Enter Report # you wish to Process; ^ to Abort --/
```

are filled with knots and twists. The mill saw operator is supposed to correct for these variations by choosing a variety of saw logs to maintain average productivity targets. In the past, mill saw operators were often inattentive to this problem, and productivity gyrated wildly.

The JLIS permits the mill superintendent to monitor productivity at the end of each day. Based on the 4:00 P.M. report, the superintendent can direct the mill operator to rebalance the selection of logs to achieve desirable productivity targets.

As for President O'Keefe, two years after the system was installed, he called it "the best investment I ever made." The accountant and controller left the company for other jobs, and they were not replaced. The office clerical staff was reduced from ten to six persons. The overall waste from log operations was reduced 36 percent.[10] O'Keefe noted, "The system was one of the most influential factors in the survival of the company in the lumber business in the face of events occurring in the past two years. The system permitted us to make rapid decisions, and to remain lean and responsive to the market."

Now let's return to the questions we raised at the beginning of the case study:

- **Where does the DSS obtain its data?** In this case, virtually all of the data was taken from the Juniper Lumber Company's internal transaction files. Although much of the data for DSS in general is internally generated, some DSS require data from external sources such as government reports and projections or market firm research.
- **What does the DSS actually do with the data?** Simple reporting tools dominate this particular DSS, but the availability of spreadsheet programs, and the possibility of easily transferring data to Lotus 1-2-3 (a spreadsheet package), led to the use of more sophisticated modeling techniques such as regression analysis, simple graphic projections of performance, and "what if" analysis. Managers were asking and answering questions like, "If log qualities continue as in the past, how many board feet of finished lumber can we expect?"
- **What management and business problems does this system solve?** A central management problem involves monitoring and controlling a production process—what we described above as the informational role of the manager. JLIS solved this problem by providing information and giving managers enough time to control production.

  From a business view, a critical problem is adjusting business behavior to external environmental conditions—price changes, marketing changes, and competition. Although this particular DSS was not primarily oriented toward external data and events, the president nevertheless felt that the new system permitted him to meet external competitive challenges. A second business problem—typical perhaps of many extractive industries—involves the challenges presented by a hostile physical environment. One of Juniper's problems was how to bring sophisticated computing facilities to a site far removed from programmers and computer experts. How could a relatively untrained staff take advantage of the potential of information systems? JLIS excelled in solving this problem.

- **What difference does the DSS make for the firm?** Because this system permitted key management officials access to on-line information and rapid access to plant conditions, the president believes this DSS directly contributed to the firm's survival in a very competitive environment. Obviously, one direct benefit was the lowering of costs while productivity increased. A less tangible benefit provided by the system was the ability to respond to problems that could not readily be predicted in advance.

It is only a short step to the next kind of management support system. As we have seen, MIS and DSS are primarily internally oriented—they track, monitor, control, and simulate internal environments. Executive support systems, which are described in the next section, are designed to track both internal and external processes and to serve the very top levels of management.

15.5 Executive Support Systems

Development engineers examine coated paper produced at Dow Chemical Company's new latex coating and finishing facility, which was built to test new latex products. An executive information support system can help determine where and when to build a new plant or which new products to launch.

Source: Courtesy of The Dow Chemical Company.

Executive support systems, or ESS (sometimes called executive information systems, or EIS), differ from MIS and DSS in several ways. Characteristically, ESS[11]

- Are designed explicitly for the purposes of senior management.
- Are used by senior management without technical intermediaries.
- Require a greater proportion of information from outside the business.
- Contain both structured and unstructured data.
- Use state-of-the-art integrated graphics, text, and communications technology.

ESS are the most recent addition to managerial support systems, and they are still evolving. Many ESS do not yet have all of the characteristics outlined above. Nevertheless, all ESS are uniquely designed for the senior management of companies. One can think of them as generalized computing, telecommunications, and graphics systems that, like a zoom lens, can be focused quickly on detailed problems or retracted for a broad view of the company.

The ESS that have emerged so far in the early 1990s usually fall into one of three types. Some ESS focus on executive communications and office work. These systems begin by building powerful electronic mail networks and then expand outward to include new officelike functions, such as document processing, scheduling of executives' time, and so forth. A second type of ESS simply provides a more convenient interface to corporate data. Such systems deliver more business performance data faster than a typical MIS can and usually present the data in a graphic mode. A third type of ESS focuses on developing elaborate scenarios, applying sophisticated statistical models to company forecasts, and utilizing other tools that are designed to

Figure 15.10

An ESS Accesses Data from Both Internal and External Sources

An ESS (executive support system) is an information system geared to the needs of senior management. Since senior-level executives must plan long-term business strategies, they need to consider not only information from internal sources but data from external sources as well. Here we illustrate a generic ESS that includes a database and a model base. Its data come both from internal transaction processing systems and from outside databases (Dow Jones News or Dialog, perhaps). The ESS software uses integrated graphics, communications, and text to provide an easy-to-use interface for senior managers, who often have little experience with computers.

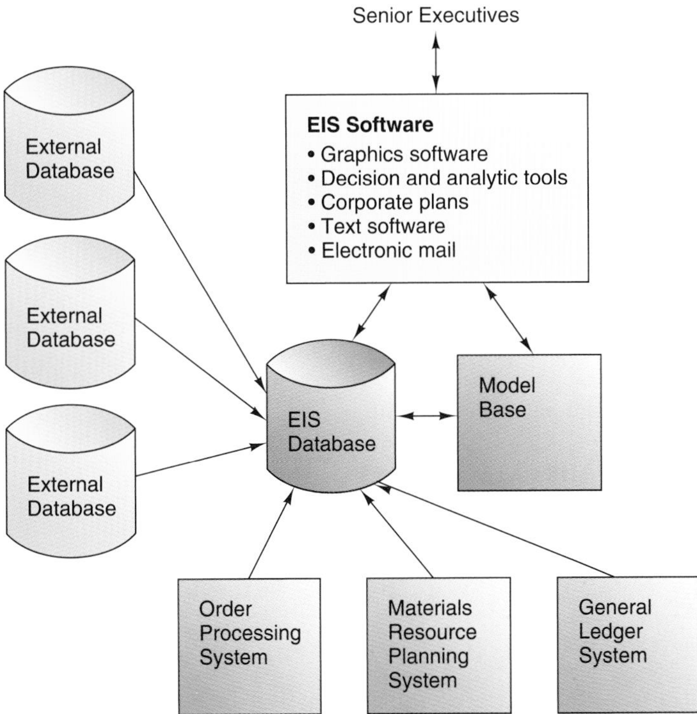

expand a senior manager's ability to plan for the future.[12] Figure 15.10 shows a generic model for an ESS, which supplies data from the order processing, materials resource planning, and general ledger systems (transaction processing systems). In addition to these internal sources, data enter from external databases, are manipulated in the ESS database and model base, and are accessed through ESS software.

You might ask, "Haven't senior managers been using computers all along? Who are using all the MIS and DSS, not to mention the personal computers?" The answer to the first question is "no." Until very recently, senior managers generally did not believe it was appropriate for them to operate a keyboard, a skill they identified with clerical work. Senior managers generally left it to assistants and clerical workers to find and present the data. Virtually all MIS and DSS are designed for corporate professional staff, both professional knowledge workers and middle managers (see the

FOCUS ON *Problem Solving*

The Shape of Things to Come

Educating senior management about information technology is the number one priority for 1990 among MIS managers in the automotive/heavy equipment, banking/financial services, chemicals, and computers/electronics industries, according to "Critical Issues of Information Systems Management for 1990," a survey of 243 North American companies by the Index Group. Overall, educating upper management about MIS ranked second, up from third in last year's Index survey, in the top 20 priorities for that year.

For the most part, the survey respondents indicated that their efforts to educate upper management had made a difference, with 46 percent reporting success. But more than one-third, 36 percent, said their efforts had made little impact on the organization.

Those who reported their efforts had been successful cited a collaboration between business executives and technologists in the learning process, nontechnical and relevant discussions, and new management blood.

Those MIS executives who said their educational efforts had not had an impact on the company blamed a lack of interest on the part of senior management, old notions, unconvincing arguments, and a preoccupation with immediate concerns.

Across all of the respondents' companies, two factors were clear: the education of management regarding MIS must be made relevant to the manager's department, and discussions must be conducted in business terms.

Senior executives who are interested in boning up on information technology have various sources, including in-house and vendor-sponsored seminars and management development programs, trade and business publications, in-house discussion groups, reading materials, the MIS department, the MIS steering committee, knowledgeable computer users, executive peers, and ad hoc conversations.

Source: "The Shape of Things," *MIS Week,* March 5, 1990, p. 38.

Focus on Problem Solving for a discussion of the need to educate senior management in the uses of MIS). ESS are the only systems explicitly designed for senior executives.

In 1989 *Computerworld Magazine,* a trade journal, conducted a survey of top executives and CEOs (chief executive officers) of *Fortune 1000* companies. A hundred CEOs responded. Although the majority agreed that information systems were playing a strategic role in the survival of their companies, and that they paid much more attention to information systems than in the past, the majority also said they do not use a personal computer or terminal at home or work on a regular basis.[13]

In the next section, we present an example of a real-world ESS by continuing the story of Lockheed-Georgia's MIDS system, which we introduced in the chapter-opening case study. There we described Lockheed as a corporation of 19,000 employees working on complex defense projects, all of which produce a voluminous output of corporate reports. Imagine how difficult it must be for a senior manager to keep track of important information!

As you read the case study, keep in mind our now-familiar questions: Where does the ESS obtain its data? What does the ESS actually do with the data? What management and business problems does this system solve? What difference does the system make for the firm?

Leading-Edge Application: Lockheed Corporation's MIDS System

Lockheed's president Roger Ormsby had no lack of data. Each week he received literally hundreds of reports from the MIS Department and a host of other departments. Ormsby and other senior managers found that it was difficult to locate any specific piece of information in this sea of reports. Worse, the existing reports were weeks out of date by the time people read them. And because the reports had different authors, they did not even use similar language or time periods. For instance, Human Relations reports might be using a calendar-year reporting unit, while Finance might use a fiscal-year unit.

Ormsby directed the development of the MIDS (Management Information and Decision Support) system to correct these deficiencies. The overall goal was a rapid inquiry system that non-computer-literate senior executives could use to get a bird's-eye view of overall corporate activities without the intervention of professional staff.

A key development decision at the beginning of the project was to evolve the system slowly over time rather than try to build it all at once. The MIDS system began with 30 screens, which executives said they wanted, and has since expanded to 800 screens. The premier consideration from the beginning was ease of use: developers wanted a system that senior executives could learn to use in 15 minutes! Moreover, the information had to be presented in a form that managers really wanted to see without requiring the user to possess spreadsheeting or database skills.[14]

Ormsby and the system developers wanted data not only about Lockheed but about the rest of the world as well. Internal sources included transaction processing systems, financial systems, and human resources. External databases included news services, customers, other Lockheed companies, and the Washington, D.C., office. Both hard and soft data are found in the system. For instance, the MIDS system can display free text notes from other executives explaining a change in company policy.

An important software design feature mandated by the ease-of-use goal was the development of screen standards. All displays of information have a screen number, title, and the date when last updated, as well as the source of the information and the person to call if more detail is required. Executives can stop a screen at any time to flip forward or backward to other screens. Color is used in a standard way: green means ahead of target, yellow means on schedule or budget, and red means behind schedule or over budget. All of the MIDS system software was designed in-house. Indeed, when the MIDS system was built in the early 1980s, no executive support software was available.

The MIDS system did not require a large investment in hardware. Currently, executives gain access to the system through IBM XT computers on their desktops. The XTs are connected by a network to a Digital Equipment Corporation minicomputer (VAX 780), which stores all the information centrally. Executives do not have printers in their offices, and they have tried to eliminate as much paper as possible anyway. All printed output is queued to four printers in the central MIDS system office.

Generally, the MIDS system is used by senior executives in all functional areas nearly every day just to keep tabs on company performance. Many unanticipated uses have sprung up as well. One unanticipated use of the system is to aid sales. It is common for a prospective buyer of Lockheed planes to call senior executives to discuss a deal. On receiving such a call, an executive can call up on a terminal a display of the aircraft model, quantity on hand, dollar value of the offer, availability for delivery, previous purchases by the prospect, and sales representative's name and location for the week.

Now let's return to the questions we posed at the beginning of this case study:

- **Where does the ESS obtain its data?** Most of the data for the MIDS system come from internal TPS, MIS, and DSS operated by various units of Lockheed-Georgia. However, unlike these other systems, a considerable part of the MIDS system's information is drawn from external news services (e.g., Dow Jones News, Associated Press News, and so forth), external databases (described in previous chapters), and other companies (customers, suppliers, and competitors).

  ESS are typically much more externally oriented than MIS or DSS because senior executives are responsible for taking environmental factors into account when planning for the company. (See the Focus on Technology for an example.)
- **What does the ESS actually do with the data?** The MIDS system compresses or summarizes detailed data streams and reports them in a graphic format. In general, it provides little or no complex statistical analysis but instead presents the data in simple bar, pie, and line charts.
- **What management and business problems does this system solve?** The MIDS system appears to function primarily as a sophisticated monitoring and control tool for senior executives (the second type of ESS described above). By giving senior executives very timely data on company performance, without the intervention of others, the ability of executives to run the company (as opposed to being run by the company) is expanded. Second, the MIDS system performs some officelike functions (the first type of ESS) insofar as it permits free-form text, reports, and graphs to be printed and displayed.

  Finally, the MIDS system appears helpful but not critical for planning. The system lacks sophisticated projection and simulation abilities, but it can assist planning and thinking about the future by powerfully summarizing the current state of affairs in a timely fashion.

  From a business perspective, the MIDS system significantly enhances Lockheed's ability to cope with rapidly changing environments. Changes in production schedules, cost of supplies, and sales orders immediately become apparent on MIDS system screens. Sec-

FOCUS ON *Technology*

American Cyanamid Uses an ESS to Track Competitors

American Cyanamid uses an ESS to provide competitive intelligence information. Mark Albala, manager of executive support at the Wayne, New Jersey–based chemical firm, says that the Dow Jones News/Retrieval Service plays an important part in the company's executive support system.

The ESS is fed news daily from a newspaper clipping service provided by Dow Jones. News about competitors is screened out and routed to a special file, which is reviewed by senior managers daily. A committee of senior managers has defined who the competitors are, and by tracking them closely, the managers believe they have an edge. The ESS enables them to know exactly what other companies are doing on a timely basis.

Source: Information Week, May 23, 1988.

ond, the business cost of coordinating such a large business is very likely reduced with a system like MIDS. Consider that the 800 screens maintained on the MIDS system require only six persons to refresh each day. Without the MIDS system, an entire corporate staff of perhaps 20 persons would be required to produce a similar amount of information.

- **What difference does the system make for the firm?** Senior managers at Lockheed have stated in several publications that they could not run the company at the current level of responsiveness without the MIDS system. They believe the system provides a critical advantage when selling planes in the marketplace.

15.6 The Challenge of Building Management Support Systems

As this chapter suggests, building information systems that adequately support what managers do is a complex matter. To illustrate this complexity, it might be useful to contrast building a management support system with building a bridge across a river—a typical civil engineering project. In the case of the bridge, landmasses evolve slowly over centuries and essentially can be counted on not to change much. The materials and technology of building generally do not change within a decade or so. Utilization and demand for the bridge's services are more difficult to predict, but in the short term of, say, five years, demand can be predicted with some accuracy.

None of these features obtain for MSS. What managers want in terms of information can change radically in a few months. The technology can easily change within two years. Actual demand for service can mushroom or plummet in a short span, depending on the utility of the system and environmental demands.

Rather than thinking of MSS as civil engineering projects, it may be more useful to think in terms of organic analogies, like ecosystems or gardens. The problem is how to build an information system that, like a garden, will be adaptable to changing weather patterns, productive, and easy to work with.[15] Here we briefly describe some of the people, organizational, and technology challenges that firms face in building robust, adaptable MSS.

People Challenges

One challenge in building an MSS is finding out exactly what kinds of information managers really want and need. You might think that managers could easily identify the information they need, but this has proved not to be so. In different situations, different information is needed. Some information is constant, but as situations change, the information needs also change. To some extent, this challenge can be solved by developing systems in an evolutionary manner over long periods of time.

A second people challenge is presented by the many different levels of computer skills in the business, which make it difficult for system builders to know what kinds of skills users have. As more and more management students learn computer skills in college, MSS can become more sophisticated. In the future, system builders will be able to assume that users are computer literate.

Organizational Challenges

We have said little in this chapter about costs. A system like Lockheed's MIDS, however, can easily cost a million dollars over its lifetime of, say, five years. It is even difficult to determine the lifetimes of systems because they change so much over time. Managers did not cost justify the MIDS system—they simply built it because they felt they needed it. But not all business organizations could afford this attitude. In any event, the question arises, "Are these expenditures worth it?" Answers are difficult to find because the benefits of these systems are intangible; that is, they cannot be given a precise monetary value. For instance, it is hard to place a dollar value on "more rapid decision making." Nor can "faster response to customers" be quantified.

A second organizational challenge presented by MSS is that a significant amount of organizational change may be required before a firm can build and install an MSS. It may be necessary to redesign the business before the computer databases can be integrated into a system like MIDS. As the MIDS system case study showed, various departments may use different definitions of the fiscal year, may have different measures of success, and may not want to share their data with other organizational units.

Technology Challenges

Perhaps the most difficult technological challenge in building an MSS is establishing compatibility with existing systems in the business. In the case of the MIDS system, some of the data drawn from incompatible internal Lockheed systems had to be rekeyed into the MIDS system. When you want to build a new capability like the MIDS system, you always have the problem of establishing compatibility with existing systems. In the case of Mrs. Fields' MIS, this was not a problem because the entire transaction reporting system was redesigned. In larger companies, this is not possible.

A second technology challenge concerns obsolescence. In the few years that the concept of executive support systems has existed, specialized software and hardware companies have sprung up to provide answers. Many software firms are now offering executive support and MIS software products to help solve these problems. For example, Commander EIS, a new software package, will incorporate internal and external databases; it also allows the information to be tailored to each executive's needs and offers powerful graphics tools along with touch-screen reporting (for executives who are reluctant to use a keyboard). Essentially, such products promise to do much of the work for you: they will help you determine what information executives need to see, how to train them, and how to operate the systems in diverse machine environments.

One problem facing businesses is whether to be a leader or a follower. If you are a leader, as Lockheed has been, you will have the capability first but will suffer the disadvantage of having to develop it yourself at great cost. Moreover, whatever you build will be rapidly outdated. If you are a follower, you can adopt commercial off-the-shelf solutions at a lower cost. As a follower, however, you will have the capability last and perhaps not find all that you want on the shelf.

Summary

- The three major types of management support systems found in business firms are MIS, DSS, and ESS. These systems serve different groups and interests in the firm. In order to understand how these systems work, you need to know something about what managers do.
- In the traditional view, managers plan, organize, lead, and control.
- In the contemporary behavioral view, managers perform three major types of roles: interpersonal, informational, and decisional.
- Managers receive most of their information from group and interpersonal, informal communications. But the information they receive from formal systems can be decisive.
- Information systems can be of most help in decisional and informational roles.
- MIS (management information systems) are routine reporting systems used to monitor and control businesses.
- DSS (decision support systems) are interactive systems under user control that are used in solving semistructured problems.

• ESS (executive support systems) are graphic-oriented systems designed for senior management that provide generalized computing and telecommunication facilities for monitoring and controlling a business.

• Builders of MSS have discovered that determining exactly what information managers want in MSS is not always easy and that the skills of managers are changing rapidly.

• Businesses may have to reorganize themselves before they can build powerful MSS. Moreover, the benefits of MSS are difficult to quantify.

• It is difficult for businesses to develop new MSS that are compatible with existing systems. Early innovators in MSS find their systems can become obsolete unless substantial investments are made in technology.

Key Terms

Management information systems (MIS)
Decision support systems (DSS)
Semistructured problem
Structured problem
Executive support systems (ESS)
Traditional theories of management
Managing
Behavioral theories of management
Interpersonal roles
Informational roles
Decisional roles
Model base

Review Questions

1. What is the traditional view of management? What are the major functions of management?
2. How do behavioral descriptions of management differ from traditional views?
3. What are the behavioral characteristics of modern management?
4. What are the three categories of management roles discovered by behavioral scientists?
5. In which of these roles can information technology make an important contribution? In which role is the contribution of information technology not large?
6. What can managers do to change corporate culture, politics, and bureaucracy?
7. What is a management information system? Where does it get its information, what does it do to that information, and what difference does it make for the firm?
8. What is a decision support system? How does it differ from an MIS?
9. What is an executive support system? How does it differ from an MIS and a DSS?
10. List and briefly describe three challenges to building management support systems.

Discussion Questions

1. Your boss has asked you to come up with some alternative ideas about how computers can be used to support the decision-making needs of top management. What kinds of systems would you recommend? Which would you recommend first?

2. What will be the impact on the systems in a business firm of hiring a large number of computer-literate, recent college graduates?

3. In what ways could a management support system of any kind help a manager perform his or her leadership roles?

Problem-Solving Exercises

1. Interview a manager at a local business or corporation. Write an analysis of his or her daily activities and the information required for these activities. What information systems does the manager currently use? What additional information systems would you suggest to help the manager with his or her work?

2. Find a description of a senior manager of a corporation in *Business Week, Forbes, Fortune,* or other business magazines. Write a description of the kinds of decisions the manager has to make and suggest an executive support system or a decision support system that might be useful for this executive.

Notes

1. James A. Stoner and Charles Wankel, *Management,* 3d ed. (Englewood Cliffs, N.J.: Prentice-Hall, 1986).
2. Peter F. Drucker, *Management: Tasks, Responsibilities, Practices* (New York: Harper & Row, 1974).
3. For an excellent contemporary introduction to management, see Richard L. Daft, *Management,* 2d ed. (Hinsdale, Ill.: Dryden Press, 1991).
4. John T. Kotter, "What Effective General Managers Really Do," *Harvard Business Review* (November-December 1982).
5. Henry Mintzberg, "Managerial Work: Analysis from Observation," *Management Science* 18 (October 1971). See also Kotter, "What Managers Do."
6. Kotter, "What Managers Do."
7. Margrethe Olson, "Manager or Technician? The Nature of the Information Systems Manager's Job," *MIS Quarterly* (December 1981).
8. Paul Weaver, "Life among Motown's Machiavellis," *The New York Times,* October 2, 1988. See also Paul Weaver, *The Suicidal Corporation.*
9. "MIS Holds Together a Crumbling Cookie," *Information Week,* March 13, 1989.
10. J.B. O'Keefe and P.F. Wade, "A Powerful MIS/DSS Developed for a Remote Sawmill Operation," *MIS Quarterly* (September 1987).
11. George Houdeshel and Hugh J. Watson, "The Management Information and Decision Support (MIDS) System at Lockheed-Georgia," *MIS Quarterly* (March 1987).
12. John F. Rockart, "Executive Support Systems and the Nature of Executive Work," working paper, Management in the 1990s Project, CISR WP #135 (MIT Sloan School, April 1986).
13. *Computerworld,* April 17, 1989.
14. Houdeshel and Watson, "MIDS System at Lockheed-Georgia."

15. Kenneth C. Laudon and Jane P. Laudon, "How You Can Manage Very Large Scale System Projects," National Science Foundation working paper (New York University Center for Research on Information Systems, April 1989). See also Omar A. El Sawy and Burt Nanus, "Toward the Design of Robust Information Systems, unpublished paper (University of Southern California Graduate School of Business Administration, July 1987).

Problem-Solving Case

Day in the Life of Tomorrow's Manager

6:10 A.M. The year is 2010 and another Monday morning has begun for Peter Smith. The marketing vice-president for a home-appliance division of a major U.S. manufacturer is awakened by his computer alarm. He saunters to his terminal to check the weather outlook in Madrid, where he will fly late tonight, and to send an electronic-voice message to a supplier in Thailand.

Meet the manager of the future. A different breed from his contemporary counterpart, our fictitious Peter Smith inhabits an international business world shaped by competition, collaboration, and corporate diversity. (For one thing, he's just as likely to be a woman as a man and—with the profound demographic changes ahead—will probably manage a work force made up mostly of women and minorities.)

Comfortable with technology, he's been logging on to computers since he was seven years old. A literature honors student with a joint M.B.A./advanced-communications degree, the 38-year-old joined his current employer four years ago after stints at two other corporations—one abroad—and a marketing consulting firm. Now he oversees offices in a score of countries on four continents.

Tomorrow's manager "will have to know how to operate in an any-time, any-place universe," says Stanley Davis, a management consultant and author of *Future Perfect*, a look at the 21st-century business world. Adds James Maxmin, chief executive of London-based Thorn EMI PLC's home-electronics division: "We've all come to accept that organizations and managers who aren't cost-conscious and productive won't survive. But in the future, we'll also have to be more flexible, responsive, and smarter. Managers will have to be nurturers and teachers, instead of policemen and watchdogs."

7:20 A.M. Mr. Smith and his wife, who heads her own architecture firm, organize the home front before darting to the supertrain. They leave instructions for their personal computer to call the home-cleaning service as well as a gourmet-carryout service that will prepare dinner for eight guests Saturday. And they quickly go over the day's schedules for their three- and six-year-old daughters with their nanny.

On the train during a speedy 20-minute commute from the suburbs to Manhattan, Mr. Smith checks his electronic mailbox and also reads his favorite trade magazine via his laptop computer.

The jury is still out on how dual-career couples will juggle high-pressure work and personal lives. Some consultants and executives predict that the frenetic pace will only quicken. "I joke to managers now that we come in on London time and leave on Tokyo time," says Anthony Terracciano, president

of Mellon Bank Corporation in Pittsburgh. He foresees an even more difficult work schedule ahead.

But others believe that more creative uses of flexible schedules as well as technological advances in communications and travel will allow more balance. "In the past, nobody cared if your staff had heart attacks, but in tomorrow's knowledge-based economy we'll be judged more on how well we take care of people," contends Robert Kelley, a professor at Carnegie Mellon University's business school.

8:15 A.M. In his high-tech office that doubles as a conference room, Mr. Smith reviews the day's schedule with his executive assistant (traditional secretaries vanished a decade earlier). Then he heads to his first meeting: a conference via video screen between his division's chief production manager in Cincinnati and a supplier near Munich.

The supplier tells them she can deliver a critical component for a new appliance at a 10 percent cost saving if they grab it within a week. Mr. Smith and the production manager quickly concur that it is a good deal. Although they will have to change production schedules immediately, they will be able to snare a new customer who has been balking about price.

Whereas today's managers spend most of their time conferring with bosses and subordinates within their own companies, tomorrow's managers will be "intimately hooked to suppliers and customers" and well versed in competitors' strategies, says Mr. Davis, the management consultant.

The marketplace will demand customized products and immediate delivery. This will force managers to make swift product-design and marketing decisions that now often take months and reams of reports. "Instant performance will be expected of them, and it's going to be harder to hide incompetence," says Ann Barry, vice-president of research at Handy Associates Inc., a New York consultant.

10:30 A.M. At a staff meeting, Mr. Smith finds himself refereeing between two subordinates who disagree vehemently on how to promote a new appliance. One, an Asian manager, suggests that a fresh campaign begin much sooner than initially envisioned. The other, a European, wants to hold off until results of a test market are received later that week.

Mr. Smith quickly realizes this is a cultural, not strategic, clash pitting a let's-do-it-now, analyze-it-later approach against a more cautious style. He makes them aware they're not really far apart, and the European manager agrees to move swiftly.

By 2010, managers will have to handle greater cultural diversity with subtle human-relations skills. Managers will have to understand that employees don't think alike about such basics as "handling confrontation or even what it means to do a good day's work," says Jeffrey Sonnenfeld, a Harvard Business School professor.

12:30 P.M. Lunch is in Mr. Smith's office today, giving him time to take a video lesson in conversational Chinese. He already speaks Spanish fluently, learned during a work stint in Argentina, and wants to master at least two more languages. After 20 minutes, though, he decides to go to his computer to check his company's latest political-risk assessment on Spain, where recent student unrest has erupted into riots. The report tells him that the disturbances are not anti-American, but he decides to have a bodyguard meet him at the Madrid airport anyway.

Technology will provide managers with easy access to more data than they can possibly use. The challenge will be to "synthesize data to make effective decisions," says Mellon's Terracciano.

2:20 P.M. Two of Mr. Smith's top lieutenants complain that they and others on his staff feel a recent bonus payment for a successful project was not divided equitably. Bluntly, they note that while Mr. Smith received a hefty $20,000 bonus, his 15-member staff had to split $5,000, and they threaten to defect. He quickly calls his boss, who says he will think about increasing the bonus for staff members.

With skilled technical and professional employees likely to be in short supply, tomorrow's managers will have to share more authority with subordinates and, in some cases, pay them as much as or more than the managers themselves earn.

While yielding more to their employees, managers in their 30s in 2010 may find their own climb up the corporate ladder stalled by superiors. After advancing rapidly in their 20s, this generation "will be locked in a heated fight with older baby boomers who won't want to retire," says Harvard's Sonnenfeld.

4:00 P.M. Mr. Smith learns from the field that a large retail customer has been approached by a foreign competitor promising to quickly supply him with a best-selling appliance. After conferring with his division's production managers, he phones the customer and suggests that his company could supply the same product but with three slightly different custom designs. They arrange a meeting later in the week.

Despite the globalization of companies and speed of overall change, some things will stay the same. Managers intent on rising to the top will still be judged largely on how well they articulate ideas and work with others.

In addition, different corporate cultures will still encourage and reward divergent qualities. Companies banking on new products, for example, will reward risk takers, while slow-growth industries will stress predictability and caution in their ranks.

6:00 P.M. Before heading to the airport, Mr. Smith uses his video phone to give his daughters a good-night kiss and to talk about the next day's schedule with his wife. Learning that she must take an unexpected trip herself the next evening, he promises to catch the SuperConcorde home in time to put the kids to sleep himself.

Source: Carol Hymowitz, "Day in the Life of Tomorrow's Manager: He, or She, Faces a More Diverse, Quicker Market," *The Wall Street Journal,* March 20, 1989. Reprinted by permission of The Wall Street Journal,

Case Study Questions

1. Examine the text again to discover one feature of contemporary executives' lives that the article assumes will not change by the year 2010. How might technology change this aspect of future corporate life?
2. What kinds of personal information systems might be very handy for the future executive? You might think of both new hardware and software.
3. The case argues that business will increasingly become global, yet it must remain personal and customized. What impact will these business trends have on the development of management support systems?
4. Would you like to live like this future management couple? Why or why not?

CHAPTER · SIXTEEN

Social and Organizational Impacts *of* Computers

Chapter Outline

16.1 Introduction: The Social and Organizational Impacts of Computers
- Concepts of Responsibility and Liability
- Categorizing Social and Organizational Impacts

16.2 General Social Impacts of Computers
- Political Issues
- Social Issues

16.3 Organizational Impacts
- Work Issues
- Organizational Issues

16.4 Computer Crime and Other Threats
- The Vulnerability of Information Systems
- The Major Threats to Computerized Information Systems
- Security and Computer Crime
- Other Security Problems: Hackers and Computer Viruses

16.5 Safeguarding Information Systems: Approaches and Techniques
- General Controls
- Data Security
- Documentation
- Disaster Recovery Planning
- Application Controls
- Problem Solving with Controls
- Safeguarding Microcomputers

16.6 Leading-Edge Application: Digital Envelopes for Networks

Learning Objectives

After reading and studying this chapter, you will:

1. Be aware of the major social and organizational impacts that computer-based systems have had on advanced societies.
2. Understand how advanced, democratic societies can protect themselves from the potential negative outcomes of computer systems.
3. Be aware of the major threats to computer-based information systems.
4. Be familiar with the meaning, impact, and causes of computer crime, computer viruses, and other security problems.
5. Know why controls over specific applications and the firm's overall computing environment are essential.
6. Be able to describe the most important kinds of general and application controls.
7. Understand the special considerations governing microcomputer controls and disaster planning.

AT&T Rings Off: Chaos Results from Software Error

On Monday, January 15, 1990, the AT&T long-distance network collapsed, taking much of the nation's business with it. The problem originated with a software upgrade to AT&T's Signaling System 7 (SS7), an out-of-band signaling and control mechanism used by AT&T, MCI, and Sprint Communications Company. A software bug not discovered during routine testing had unfortunately been installed throughout AT&T's entire national long-distance network in the previous month. A simple error in the logic of a single program statement caused AT&T's computers to become confused and shut down. The software was installed on all 114 of AT&T's switching computers throughout the country. When the bug first manifested itself in the New York area computer, other computers in the network became confused and could not set up calls. It took AT&T engineers nine hours to determine how the bug operated and to fix it.

About half of all 800 line service was lost in the country. Fortunately, it was a holiday—Martin Luther King's birthday—and overall call demand was moderate. Some of the hardest hit were American Express, MasterCard, Visa, and credit authorization firms that rely on the network to verify credit. Millions of customers found out it was better to carry cash this day and leave the American Express card at home.

About 148 million calls were attempted during the outage, about 75 million of which were not completed. Significant economic disruptions and temporary loss of orders resulted, although the total costs will probably never be known. AT&T probably suffered the most: its advertising slogan has been "make the right choice." Many firms took the outage in stride, noting that this was the first time in 33 years that AT&T long-distance had gone down. Still, many firms are now considering spreading their 800 service among several companies just as a precaution.

Source: "AT&T Rings Off," *Information Week*, January 22, 1990.

This story is just one example of the way computers have affected our society, businesses, and work lives. Even our personal health and safety are increasingly put into the hands of computer hardware and software. Furthermore, our legal and political systems are not well equipped to deal with emerging computer health and work impacts.

The consequences of the software bug for AT&T's long-distance network shows how vulnerable computerized systems—and the services that depend on them—are to disruption and damage. Valuable data can easily be destroyed, bringing business activities to a complete standstill. This incident, along with many others described in this chapter, illustrates how dependent our society has become on computers and information systems.

16.1 Introduction: The Social and Organizational Impacts of Computers

It is common to find newspaper headlines like "Computers Threaten Factory Jobs" or "Computers Threaten Privacy" or "Computers Flatten Organizational Hierarchy." Behind these headlines is the idea that computers act by themselves to change society, organizations, and people. Computers, in this view, "impact" society in the same way a huge iceberg collides with a ship. Hopefully, in this chapter, you will discover that this is not a helpful way to think about the social consequences of computers even though it is very popular and convenient.

Instead, we want to emphasize that behind all computing equipment (hardware and software) are engineers and designers who made conscious decisions about how the technology would perform in a technical sense. Once the equipment leaves the factory, systems analysts, programmers, and end-users like yourselves determine how the computing equipment will actually perform its tasks. Through their decisions, these same people, sometimes unconsciously or unintentionally, determine how computer-based systems will change jobs, organizations, and people's lives. Finally, programmers, analysts, and end-users work for organizations whose managers generally make the decisions about the ultimate goals or purpose of computer-based information systems. There is a long chain of decisions and decision makers in the journey from a simple "computer" to the "social impacts of computers."

Academic researchers who have closely examined both positive and negative impacts of computers generally find that whatever good or evil comes from computers can usually be traced backward in time to some key design decisions. Computers per se have little or no impact on people, organizations, or societies. Instead, it is the uses of computers by people and organizations that have impacts.[1] Although this seems at first glance to be a subtle difference, it has profound consequences for how we think about computer impacts, and especially for how we develop public policies for dealing with negative computer impacts.

Concepts of Responsibility and Liability

In this chapter we want to emphasize the concepts of ethical responsibility and legal liability. The concept of **responsibility** is based on the idea that individuals, organizations, and societies are free moral agents who act willfully and with intentions, goals, and ideas. Because individuals, organizations, and societies are free moral agents, they can be and are held morally accountable by their fellow citizens and other governments and societies. These "higher authorities" can morally exact a payment for any harm done. Thus, to be responsible means that one is accountable to higher authorities for his or her actions.

Responsibility
The idea that individuals, organizations, and societies are free moral agents who act willfully and with intentions, goals, and ideas; consequently, they can be held accountable for their actions.

Liability extends the idea of responsibility to the area of laws. Liability is the legal obligation of someone who has engaged in proscribed behavior to make a payment to those they have harmed; liability is established by laws that set out legal remedies for proscribed behavior. In societies governed by laws, individuals, organizations, and even governments are legally liable for their actions.

Liability
The idea that people may be obligated by law to compensate those they have injured in some way; liability is established by laws that set out legal remedies for proscribed behavior.

These considerations of responsibility and liability are important for understanding the impacts of computers. Computer impacts do not just "happen" without human intervention. People and organizations who use computers in such a way that harm comes to others are morally responsible and can be held accountable just as the operators of motor vehicles can be held accountable for their actions. In some instances, specific laws govern the use of computers. Because computers are so new, however, the legal framework governing their use is still evolving.

Categorizing Social and Organizational Impacts

Computers and their alleged impacts are so common that cataloging the impacts is difficult at first. One approach to the problem is to consider that the concerns raised about the impacts of computers are not about computers per se but about traditional, long-standing issues of an industrial society. For instance, people are very concerned about the impact of computers on freedom, creativity, and education because these are important, enduring

Figure 16.1

The Social and Organizational Impacts of Computers

No one would deny that computers have exerted a tremendous influence on our lives. This figure summarizes some of the major ways in which computers have affected our society on both the individual and organizational levels. As you can see, technology affects us in many ways, ranging from the individual concerns of freedom and privacy to the organizational issues of company structure and strategy.

The Impacts of Computers

Social Impacts	**Organizational Impacts**
Political Issues:	Work Issues:
• Freedom and privacy	• Quality of work
• Due process	• Productivity
• Freedom of information	• Authority
• Balance of power	• Training
Social Issues:	Organization Issues:
• Crime	• Structure
• Demography	• Efficiency
• Dependence	• Dependence
• Education	• Strategy

human concerns. Computers are important because they potentially affect long-standing social issues like autonomy, creativity, vulnerability, and morality.

We can use this insight to categorize and discuss the impacts of computers. Figure 16.1 divides the impacts of computers into two broad categories: impacts on social issues and impacts on organizational issues. This is not an exhaustive list, and you can certainly add many issues to the list.

When you look at the issues in each category, notice that none of these issues is new and that none has really been "created" by the computer. Freedom, due process, dependence, productivity, and other issues are all long-standing concerns of our society and most other advanced industrial societies. We will discuss these later in the chapter.

Social impacts
The effects of computers on society, including both political issues, such as the effect of computers on freedom and privacy, and social issues, such as their effects on crime, demography, and education.

Organizational impacts
The effects of computers on organizations, including both work issues, such as the effect of computers on quality of work, authority, productivity, and training; and organizational issues, such as computers' effects on organizational structure, efficiency, and strategy.

The **social impacts** of computers can be divided further into two smaller groupings: political issues and social issues. Outstanding political issues affected by computers are freedom and privacy, due process, freedom of information, and the balance of political power. Leading social issues are crime, demography (the distribution of people and jobs), dependence, and education.

The **organizational impacts** of computers can also be divided into two smaller groupings: work issues and organizational issues. The leading work issues involve questions of how computers impact quality of work, productivity, authority, and training. The outstanding organizational issues are organizational structure, efficiency, dependence, and strategy.

16.2 General Social Impacts of Computers

According to several national surveys, the majority of Americans believe that computers are reducing our basic freedom by invading our privacy. In addition, large percentages of Americans believe that computers are causing social change to occur too rapidly. They cite computer crime, relocations of factories and workers, and excessive dependence on machines as some of the problems brought about by computers.

Political Issues

In 1947 George Orwell published a novel entitled *1984*, in which a centralized, machine-based surveillance system, referred to as "Big Brother," controlled the society through close surveillance of personal lives, fear, and punishment. Big Brother kept track of the minute details of what people said, what they purchased, whom they spoke with, and what materials they read. Perhaps no single image of the modern computer-based information system has had such a large impact. Orwell's best-selling novel raised many questions central to the modern computer-based age: How much should government snoop on its citizens? What rights do citizens have to be free from government snooping? Do citizens also have a right to keep personal information from private industries such as privately owned banks, credit bureaus, and retailers? Should schools, other citizens, and even foreign governments be given access to any or all of a person's personal files and records, purchase patterns, medical records, and telephone records?

Americans are concerned that computer-based information systems will reduce their **freedom** (the ability to act and think without restraint) and invade their **privacy** (the right of individuals and organizations to be left alone and to be secure in their personal papers) in several ways. On the one hand, they are concerned about the **freedom of information;** this refers to the right of citizens to have access to government in order to be informed participants in the political process and to protect themselves against government abuse. Storing information in large government computers may make it more difficult for citizens and reporters to find out what the government is doing. On the other hand, Americans are concerned that computer-based systems in the hands of large organizations—both government and business—will enable the organizations to invade their privacy. Furthermore, they fear that these huge and powerful organizations may treat people without regard for the rules of **due process;** due process refers to the right to be treated fairly and in accordance with the established legal procedures (such as the right to appeal or have an attorney).

Freedom
The ability to act and think without constraint.

Privacy
The right of individuals and organizations to be left alone and to be secure in their personal papers.

Freedom of information
The right of citizens to have access to information stored by government and private organizations in order to be informed participants in the political process and to protect themselves from government abuse.

Due process
The right to be treated fairly in accordance with established legal procedures, including such things as the right to appeal and the right to an attorney.

Why are computers involved in this controversy? Didn't these problems exist before computers? Indeed, some of the world's most notorious dictatorships existed long before computers. But with computer-based information systems, huge private and government databases that contain detailed personal information on citizens can be created inexpensively and efficiently.

What information is available on you and where does it come from? The following information about you is available to just about any business (or individuals in business) and government in the United States:

- Credit records.
- Income.
- Debts and payment history.
- Personal data (e.g., Social Security number, age, birth date, family history, ethnicity).
- Reading materials like magazines and book clubs.
- Listening materials like record clubs.
- Motor vehicle information.
- Driver license information, including infractions.
- Federal and state loans.
- Telephone calls.
- Medical records.
- Insurance records.
- School records.
- Employment history.
- Legal judgments, hearings, and so on.
- Marital history.

Most of this information originates with you through the process of borrowing money, participating in a government program, or purchasing goods. Consumers and borrowers—that's all of us—routinely give information voluntarily to retailers and creditors so we can purchase goods on credit. At least once a month, millions of banks, retailers, credit card companies, mail-order houses, and others send computer tapes or other electronic files detailing their customers' purchases and payment activities to credit bureaus. These files contain detailed personal information on bank balances, credit history, income, family makeup, employment, driving record, and the like for nearly every consumer in the United States and many foreign countries as well. The three largest national credit bureaus (see Table 16.1) resell this information either as ordinary credit reports or as lists of names to marketing companies who want to know about you. In addition to these national bureaus, there are more than two hundred "superbureaus" that serve small businesses in local and state regions. Superbureaus obtain their information from the three companies in Table 16.1 and other sources. Credit reports cost about $10 to $50, depending on the detail requested. A list of names and addresses showing, for instance, all of the college students in the San Francisco metropolitan area who purchased computer software in 1989 would cost about 10 to 20 cents a name. TRW Credit Data has a new product: it will sell you your own credit record for $10!

The federal, state, and local governments are a second major source of personal information about you. Citizens routinely and voluntarily give up a large amount of personal information to obtain college loans, small business loans, or other government benefits.

Table 16.1

The Largest Credit Bureaus

	1988 Revenues (Millions of Dollars)	Number of Records (Millions)
TRW	$335	155
Trans Union	300	155
Credit Bureaus/Equifax	259	100

Why does the existence of huge, computerized, national information systems threaten freedom, privacy, and due process? First, consider that both government and private industry have used information in such files to intimidate their political opponents of the moment. As a result, these institutions have had what the courts call a "chilling effect" on political debate and have interfered with the exercise of political freedoms. For instance, if you take a public position against a corporation or a state agency, damaging information may be found about you in national data files and released to the press in order to destroy your credibility. Have you ever visited a mental health professional? Have you ever had a medical condition that you would not like to be made public? Have you ever committed an infraction of a law, statute, or regulation? Does your record include frank and critical comments by teachers or others? If you fall into any of these categories—and most of us have something negative on our many records—then you can be potentially embarrassed or even neutralized politically. You may not have done anything illegal, but chances are you have done something embarrassing that shows up on a national record system somewhere.

Second, consider whether the information is accurate or not. Have you inspected the information held about you in national files? What if it is used to make decisions about you but is not really accurate or true, or is no longer true? (See the Focus on Organizations for examples of inaccurate information on credit reports.) This raises the issue of due process—treating people fairly.

What can you and society do about these issues of privacy, freedom, access to information, and due process? When confronted with modern technologies that have some negative consequences but many positive benefits, the United States has typically passed laws to blunt the impact of the negative consequences while permitting society to benefit from the technology. In the case of computer-based information systems, the U.S. Congress has passed several significant laws that attempt to govern record keeping in this society (European countries and Canada have even stronger legislation[2]):

- **Freedom of Information Act (1966):** This statute gives citizens and all organizations the right to access federal government records with few exceptions. This legislation has been the single most powerful information legislation in American history, giving individuals, writers, reporters, and even private corporations unprecedented access to unclassified government records.

FOCUS ON *Organizations*

Problems in Your Credit Record?

Every now and then, someone with a good job, someone who pays his or her bills regularly, is denied a loan. The reason may be spelled out on the person's credit report.

A credit report lists the various debts a person has assumed and shows the person's history of repaying what he or she owes. A typical report lists the person's payment history with banks, department stores, and credit card companies. Information about payments to utilities is less likely to be listed unless the payments are consistently late. This information is stored in electronic databases, usually owned by one of three companies: TRW, Trans Union, or Credit Bureaus/Equifax. For a fee, these credit bureaus allow lenders to tap into their information.

Sometimes an applicant is denied a loan because of an error in his or her credit report. According to TRW, its reports are challenged by about one-quarter of the 1.3 million consumers who ask to see them each year. However, the trade association for credit bureaus says that actual errors occur in only 0.3 percent of the 500 million reports issued each year.

Errors may occur if a credit bureau mixes data on two people with similar names. For example, one man learned that his credit report contained his mother's mortgage—possible because they had first names with similar spellings. People whose names include Jr., Sr., or III may be especially vulnerable to such errors.

Errors in Social Security numbers are another source of problems. If an applicant or credit bureau transposes two digits in the applicant's Social Security number, the agency could go on collecting credit information for the person with that number.

How can you know if your credit report contains errors? First, before you apply for an important loan or after you have been denied credit, request a copy of your report. The credit bureau will sell you a copy, or, if you have been denied credit, the lender is required by law to let you look for free. Check whether the name and Social Security number on the report are accurate. If you detect an error, contact the credit bureau to identify it. The bureau must investigate your request and delete data that it cannot verify.

If a credit bureau insists that there is no mistake, you are entitled to submit a memo of up to 100 words explaining the problem. Whenever the bureau releases your report, it attaches a copy of your memo. Thus, you can at least tell your side of your credit story.

Source: Don Dunn, "When You Don't Get Credit Where Credit Is Due," *Business Week*, October 2, 1989, pp. 116–117.

- **Fair Credit Reporting Act (1970):** Under this statute, credit agencies cannot share credit information with anyone but authorized customers; the act also gives citizens the right to inspect their records and be notified of their use for employment or credit. The law is easily circumvented because access is given to anyone with "a reasonable business need."
- **Privacy Act (1974):** This law defines citizens' rights and management's responsibilities for federal government records. The law has had little effect because the Office of Management and Budget (the president's budget agency) does not enforce the law vigorously, and the language is too vague.

- **Right to Financial Privacy Act (1978):** This statute attempts to limit federal government searches of your bank records. State and local governments are not covered, and increasingly the FBI, IRS, and other federal agencies use loopholes to gain access.
- **Video Privacy Protection Act (1988):** Under this act, video rental records cannot be sold or released without a court order or consent of the person renting the video.
- **Computer Matching and Privacy Act (1988):** This statute regulates computer matching of computer files in different agencies to verify eligibility for federal programs and to identify delinquent debtors. The law does nothing about law enforcement and tax-matching programs, and it has many other loopholes.

Despite a number of laws seeking to protect privacy, the pressure of commercial interests to obtain access to personal information, coupled with powerful new technologies, has served to weaken existing laws. Indeed, some argue that we are headed toward a dossier society in which virtually all important decisions made about us will be guided by large-scale national information systems operating with few controls.[3] Nevertheless, the principles laid out by Congress in its preamble to the **Privacy Act of 1974** (see below) can be useful in extending legislation to cope with the age of electronic networks, personal computers, and huge, easily accessed private databases. (Note: Material in brackets is the authors'.)

Privacy Act of 1974
A federal statute that defines citizens' rights in regard to and management's responsibilities for federal government records; sets out some of the principles for regulating computer technology in order to protect people's privacy.

The Privacy Act of 1974
Public Law 93–579

Be it enacted by the Senate and House of Representatives of the United States of America in Congress assembled, That this Act may be cited as the "Privacy Act of 1974."

Sec. 2.

(a) The Congress finds that—

(1) the privacy of an individual is directly affected by the collection, maintenance, use, and dissemination of personal information by Federal agencies;

(2) the increasing use of computers and sophisticated information technology, while essential to the efficient operations of the Government, has greatly magnified the harm to individual privacy that can occur from any collection, maintenance, use, or dissemination of personal information;

(3) the opportunities for an individual to secure employment, insurance, and credit and his right to due process, and other legal protections are endangered by the misuse of certain information systems;

(4) the right to privacy is a personal and fundamental right protected by the Constitution of the United States; and

(5) in order to protect the privacy of individuals identified in information systems maintained by Federal agencies, it is necessary and proper for the Congress to regulate the collection, maintenance, use, and dissemination of information by such agencies.

The Privacy Act of 1974
Public Law 93–579 (*continued*)

(b) The purpose of this Act is to provide certain safeguards for an individual against an invasion of personal privacy by requiring Federal agencies, except as otherwise provided by law, to—

(1) permit an individual to determine what records pertaining to him are collected, maintained, used, or disseminated by such agencies;
[No secret records or record systems]

(2) permit an individual to prevent records pertaining to him obtained by such agencies for a particular purpose from being used or made available for another purpose without his consent;
[Informed consent]

(3) permit an individual to gain access to information pertaining to him in Federal agency records, to have a copy made of all or any portion thereof, and to correct or amend such records;
[Right of inspection]

(4) collect, maintain, use, or disseminate any record of identifiable personal information in a manner that assures that such action is for a necessary and lawful purpose, that the information is current and accurate for its intended use, and that adequate safeguards are provided to prevent misuse of such information;
[No record systems without statutory authority and the principle of management responsibility]

(5) permit exemptions from the requirements with respect to records provided in this Act only in those cases where there is an important public policy need for such exemption as has been determined by specific statutory authority; and
[Exemptions only by law]

(6) be subject to civil suit **for any damages which occur as a result** of willful **or intentional action which violates any individual's** rights under this Act. [Emphasis added.]
[Civil liability for damages]

[Sections 3 and 4 of the Act define the key terms of the above preamble and the mechanisms for enforcing and administering the Act].

Note that Congress did not claim computers were the cause of privacy problems. Rather it is the use of computers by the federal government and private organizations that constitutes the threat.

Social Issues

Aside from concerns of privacy and freedom of information, computers are associated with a number of other broad social impacts. Computers—like other technologies such as automobiles—can be used for the commission of crime. Indeed, entirely new kinds of crime become possible with computers: theft of computer data and services, disruptions of business, and spreading of computer viruses. Section 16.4 is devoted to computer crime.

A second broad area of social concern is how computers affect demography, the distribution of workers, jobs, and businesses. One concern is the emergence of "distributed work." In the 1970s, some people predicted that **telecommuting** would be the trend of the future: vast numbers of workers would stay at home working on computers tied into corporate networks and computer databases. This was supposed to have several benefits: fuel consumption would decline dramatically as commuters abandoned the highways for home offices; working women (and men) would be able to spend more time with their families; and efficiency would increase as workers no longer struggled just to get to work each day. Several negative effects were also predicted: urban areas would be abandoned for suburbs and exurbs (communities even farther from central cities than suburbs); poor people who needed jobs would live in cities with declining employment; and the isolated workers at home would tend to be women and minorities who would miss out on promotion opportunities at central headquarters.

Telecommuting
Working at home on a computer tied into corporate networks and databases.

Computer dependence
The state of relying on computers to provide vital services; in a computer-dependent society, the malfunctioning of computers may cause extensive damage to lives and/or property.

Few of these impacts actually happened, but the trends are suggestive of significant changes in the distribution of work (see Table 16.2). The biggest change has come in the area of supplemental work at home, especially with computers. Between 17 and 24 million households in the United States have personal computers, and about half of these households use the computers for supplemental work. Studies of managers in particular find them doing extra night and weekend work with their computers. The percentage of the labor force who work full-time at home for others has increased far less. In general, employees have found it is better to get out of the house and go to work despite long commutes.

A third broad area of social concern involves **computer dependence**—the fact that we as a society have become very dependent on computers to provide vital services. If computer hardware or software malfunctions, people are not just inconvenienced, as they would have been a few years ago; instead their lives are put in jeopardy. If the telephone system's computerized switches break down for a few minutes, as described in the vignette "AT&T Rings Off" at the beginning of this chapter, entire industries (from mail-order retailing to data communications) can lose revenues amounting to hundreds of millions of dollars.

When a serious fire at a major telephone switching center disrupted service for 35,000 customers, Illinois Bell employees installed a new switch within one month—a job that normally takes one year. Because of the vital role telephones and telecommunications traffic play in business, telephone companies make herculean efforts to restore service when it is disrupted.

Source: Courtesy of Ameritech.

Table 16.2

Who Works at Home

	(Percentage of the Labor Force in 1988)	Change*
Full-time, self-employed	7.3%	+ 1%
Part-time, work for others	12.3	+20
Full-time, work for others	5	+10
Percentage of supplemental work with computers	6	+50

* Indicates change over surveys done in the previous year (1987).

Source: Nicholas P. Vitalari and Alladi Venkatesh, "An Emerging Distributed Work Arrangement: A Theoretical and Empirical Examination of Supplemental Work at Home," NSF IST-8313470 (University of California at Irvine Graduate School of Management, 1989).

FOCUS ON *Technology*

Death by Software: Malfunction Error Code 54

On the morning of March 21, 1986, Voyne Ray Cox lay face down on a table beneath a linear accelerator radiation machine at the East Texas Cancer Center in Tyler, Texas. Mr. Cox was in the last phases of radiation treatment following surgery on a tumor in his shoulder. Cox felt at ease with the machine. It was much like an X-ray machine, painless, and virtually silent.

The technicians left the room after setting the machine. Then Cox heard a frying sound and felt a sharp pain like an electric shock in his shoulder. After a second burst from the machine, he rolled across the table in pain. After a third shock, Cox jumped from the table and called for help.

The radiation oncologist, asked about a potential overdose of radiation, told Cox he had not even received the recommended dose. The accelerator had turned itself off and registered on its screen "Malfunction 54," an error code indicating discrepancy but not overdose.

Within days Cox showed signs of injury; he was vomiting blood and experiencing pain throughout his body. By June he was paralyzed. In September he died in a Dallas hospital. Cox's wife is suing the radiation therapist, the oncologist, the treatment center, and the manufacturer of the machine called a Therac 25.

As the Cox case became public knowledge, other cases surfaced in the press and the courts. A year earlier, in 1985, Caty Yarbrough, a patient at Kennestone Regional Oncology Center in Marietta, Georgia, had received a painful overdose that resulted in complete removal of her breast. In Yakima, Washington, a patient had received 11,000 rads of radiation from a Therac 25; 1,000 rads can be fatal.

Atomic Energy of Canada Limited (AECL), the manufacturer of the Therac, began working with the treatment center in Tyler, Texas, to find the problem. It turns out that if the up-arrow key is used to edit treatment parameters on the screen, software controlling the radiation levels will malfunction, permitting very high doses of radiation to strike the patient. In one test of this problem, over 25,000 rads were produced in a second—enough to kill most humans. AECL recommended a temporary fix: users should pry off the up-arrow key and put tape over the key stub to prevent its use.

Lawyers for many plaintiffs have filed suits according to the shotgun approach: sue everyone involved and find out in court who is really liable. The cases hinge on whether the courts find software is a service or a product (like a lawn mower). Legally, there is a big difference. If software is found to be a service, the plaintiffs will have to prove the manufacturer was actually negligent. Plaintiffs will have to scrutinize the history of the software production and show that the manufacturer failed to supervise the programmers properly. The programmers could also be sued and found liable. If software is found to be a product, then "strict liability" obtains. Under this rule, plaintiffs do not have to show negligence in product liability suits. The mere fact of injury usually establishes liability.

Palo Alto attorney Susan Nycum, an expert on computer software law, argues that "It's a horrible tragedy, but I don't think very many computer experts are really surprised. After all, software's written by people and people make mistakes."

AECL withdrew from the linear accelerator business in 1985 because of competitive pressures and not, so it says, because of software liability problems. The Food and Drug Administration (FDA), which approved the use of the Therac in the United States and must approve any software upgrades, says that it will not withdraw or ban the machine. "A complete ban would require an extensive study of risk assessment," the agency explained. The FDA notes that most of the medical centers using the Therac 25 are multimillion-dollar facilities actually built around the machine. It would not be easy for these medical centers to abandon the machine.

Source: Ed Joyce, "Software Bugs: A Matter of Life and Liability," *Datamation*, May 15, 1987.

If your business lost a day's worth of orders because of a telephone system failure, whom would you blame? Would it be your fault for depending on the phone system and for failing to prepare for this emergency by having an alternative company to provide backup service? Is it the phone company's fault for failing to provide a product or service? What blame belongs to the federal government regulators who are supposed to help develop telephone systems that serve the public interest?

We have not yet developed solid answers to these questions, and even the courts are confused. In cases of personal injury, there is no clear law of software liability or even agreement about whether software is a product or a service. If computer software has a glitch, the powerful tools controlled by that software can kill and maim people, as the Focus on Technology illustrates.

As we come to depend on computer hardware and software, we become vulnerable. In general, the technology is advancing much faster than our ability to develop moral principles and legal doctrines. This does not mean, however, that society—you and I—is not responsible for the impacts of computers, or that society cannot choose the computer impacts it wants or is willing to live with. Industrial societies have a long history of regulating technologies to assure that they serve the public interest. The choices are not easy. In the Focus on Technology case, for instance, there are many benefits to the continued use of the Therac 25; when properly used, it has saved many lives.

16.3 Organizational Impacts

Although the use of computers raises significant issues at the societal level, it is in the workplace, where computers are directly used, that impacts first become apparent. These organizational impacts affect two areas: the nature of work and the structure and purpose of organizations.

Work Issues

Next to "Big Brother," the most common and long-standing fear of computer-based information systems is that they will degrade the quality of work by removing skill and craftsmanship, increase the authority of superiors by tightening surveillance, and reduce the training of workers as machines take on more and more sophisticated work. Other concerns center around the impact of computers on the **quality of work life**—the degree to which jobs are interesting, satisfying, and physically safe and comfortable. The following outline summarizes the major dimensions of work potentially affected by computerization:

Quality of work life
The degree to which jobs are interesting, satisfying, and physically safe and comfortable.

1. Nature of work
   - Productivity
   - Frequency of tasks
   - Ease of tasks

- Quality of training
- Quality of service and product

2. Quality of employment
   - Job satisfaction
   - Job quality
     - Variety
     - Satisfaction with work group
     - Autonomy
     - Challenge
     - Ability to see results of work
   - Pressure
   - Mental health
   - Quality of management

Some have predicted that the mental and physical health of workers will decline as they are exposed to high-pressure jobs paced by a computer that requires them to use small muscle groups in the hands, arms, and eyes, leading to strain and fatigue. Research has found that in some instances, computer-based systems do indeed have powerful negative impacts on the quality of working life. At the same time, many other instances have been documented in which systems had very positive effects on work: in these cases, work was upgraded and made more interesting and self-paced. Systems can boost workers' productivity as well. Much depends on the kinds of jobs examined, the kinds of management involved, and the history and culture of the company. Researchers now believe that the impacts "produced" by computers result from management decision making and the designs of systems developers.

For instance, in the largest and most sophisticated study to date of the impact of computerization on clerical work, researchers closely observed 485 service representatives for a large utility who worked in ten offices and six different cities.[4] The utility was changing from a microfiche- and paper-based customer record system to a computer-based system. The office layout and architecture were changed as well by replacing the open-floor offices of the past with cubicles for workers to work undisturbed. The major goal of the changes was to reduce the costs of responding to customer complaints.

The research found that simple models of computer impacts do not work (see Figure 16.2). The technology made doing simple things easier, but also made it harder to perform complicated tasks. Job pressure declined, happiness increased, and mental health improved. On the down side, skills were lost because jobs were less complex, interesting, and challenging; previous training was made irrelevant; and there was decreased involvement with other workers. The authors also found the impacts of the technology depended on the quality of management. In offices with better management, the negative consequences were lessened.

It is important to remember that this study looked only at office clerical workers and did not look at sales personnel or office knowledge

Figure 16.2

How Computerization Affected Clerical Employees at One Company

The chart illustrates that automation does not always affect people's jobs in a totally negative way. It became easier for workers to perform common tasks, for instance, and employees' mental health improved. Computerization exerted some negative effects as well: the variety and challenge of tasks declined. The mixed results indicate that simple models of "computer impacts" are often unrealistic.

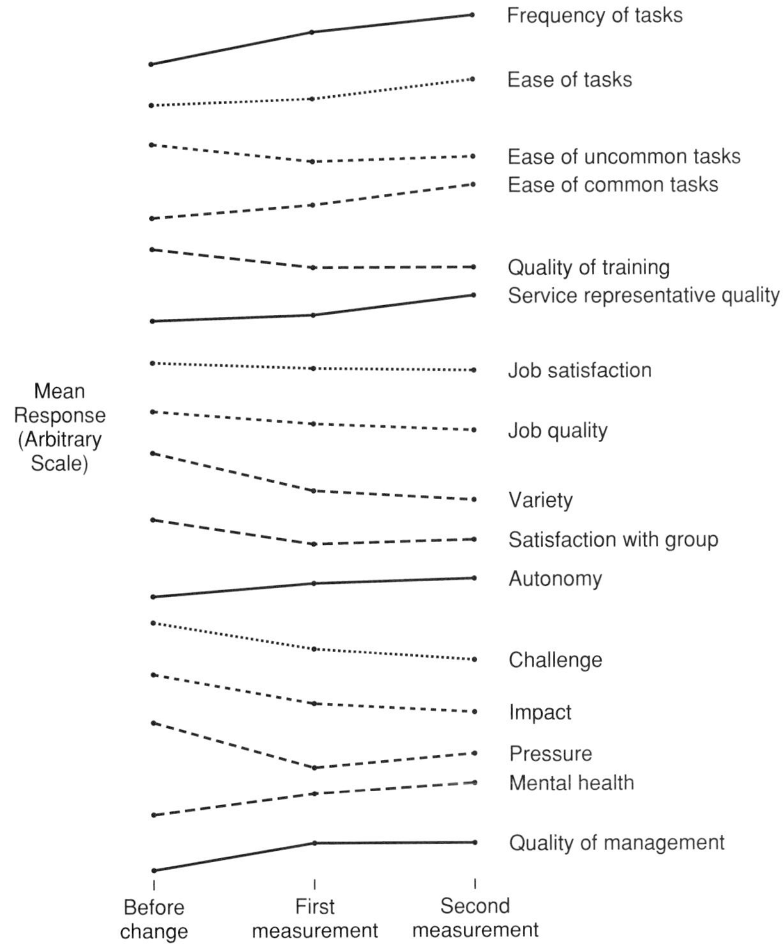

Source: Robert Kraut, Susan Dumais, and Susan Koch, "Computerization, Productivity and Quality of Work Life," *Communications of the ACM* 32 (no. 2, February 1989), p. 226.

workers. Computers have tended to have far more positive effects on professional and knowledge workers: their skills are amplified by computing equipment, and they tend to have more control over their work. Computers have also tended to enhance most qualities of work in factories.

General Electric (GE), for example, has managed to computerize one of its factories and increase worker satisfaction at the same time by upgrading the responsibilities of its workers. GE's electrical distribution equipment factory in Salisbury, North Carolina, is a model of worker-driven automa-

Dr. Richard Hutchings, a chemist and section manager for new products at the Drackett division of Bristol-Myers Squibb, creates new products. Computers aid the work of knowledge and professional workers, increasing productivity.

Source: Courtesy of Bristol-Myers Squibb Company.

tion. In the past, workers were not allowed to correct automation glitches, nor did they know how. Foremen were called first, then maintenance workers, then field engineers. Finally, new parts would be ordered and installed by the maintenance crew. Fixing a problem could take days or even weeks.

In the new factory organization, GE cut through the bureaucratic bottlenecks of the old system by allowing workers to talk directly with field engineers or even call in the manufacturers of the equipment. Bob Hedenskog, automation equipment operator in the new plant, recently ordered $40,000 worth of parts on his own initiative. Bob also serves on the hiring committee that determines who will be hired and what machines they will be trained for. First-level managers—foremen—have been eliminated. The number of worker hours to produce an electrical panel has dropped two-thirds; delivery time has been cut by a factor of ten.

These kinds of changes and efficiencies in the manufacturing sector will be more common in the future. The Bureau of Labor Statistics reports that by the year 2000, factory jobs will decline from 19 million to 18.2 million workers. At the same time, the kinds of jobs available in factories are expected to change radically. There will be several hundred thousand new jobs for engineers, technicians, managers, and computer scientists, but there will be hundreds of thousands fewer jobs for assemblers, laborers, and machine setters—the traditional blue-collar jobs.[5]

Organizational Issues

While work and supervision are affected almost immediately when new computer systems are installed, over longer periods of time the structure of organizations can change as well. By organizational structure, we mean the number of different levels in an organization, the type of work and workers involved, and the distribution of incomes. It is argued that computers are affecting organizational structures in two ways: First, many believe that contemporary information systems are making organizations flatter by reducing the number of middle managers, making organizations more efficient and productive. Second, some have pointed out that because organizations now have extensive telecommunications facilities, they no longer need employees. Instead, the organizations can rely on external contractors in an electronic marketplace to do the work, supervising them electronically and accepting or rejecting their work on a contract basis.

Computers have generally been seen as a major potential source of long-term unemployment in advanced economies. Since commercial computers first began to be widely used in the late 1950s, there has been a persistent fear that computers would reduce the need for all kinds of workers and lead to much higher levels of unemployment. The number of secretaries would decline radically, so it was thought, because computers would reduce paperwork. The number of blue-collar factory workers would decline because robots would take over their jobs.

The evidence to support these beliefs about computers' impact on organizational structure is slim. While computers have proved very useful for producing letters, quickly calculating spreadsheets, and printing lists of customers, this has not led to any wholesale decrease in white-collar jobs. Contrary to the negative predictions, jobs for secretaries, middle managers, and accountants have been the fastest growing occupations in the entire labor force since 1960!

Why? In general, employers have taken advantage of the higher efficiencies created by computers in selected tasks to assign other work to secretaries, accountants, and managers. Instead of firing accountants who used to manually calculate a few spreadsheets a week, employers have retrained accountants to use computers to produce hundreds of spreadsheets a week, analyze many different scenarios using the new software, supervise expenditures more closely, and achieve higher-quality work. The same thing has occurred with secretaries. Instead of firing large numbers of secretaries, employers have tended to retain or even hire more secretaries to put out more letters to achieve more sales and greater market penetration. In the case of managers, employers have found it much more productive to hire more middle managers than ever—especially young college graduates—rather than shrink the middle management group. Middle managers are expected to use the new technology to increase sales, contact more customers, prepare more precise estimates of business conditions, and make more complete future plans.

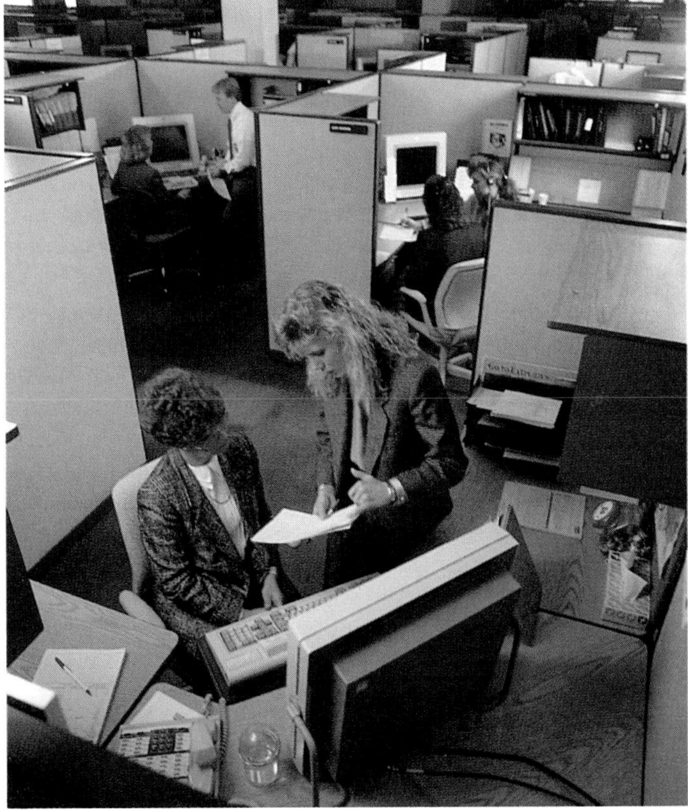

Customer service representatives in sales operations at Dow Corning take steps to solve shipping problems. White-collar occupations continue to be a rapidly expanding part of the U.S. labor force as employees use new technologies to achieve higher quality work.

Source: Courtesy of Dow Corning Corporation.

In fact, computers have tended to increase—not decrease—the amount of paperwork in advanced economies. Predictions that we would soon have a paperless office, an inkless society, and a checkless banking system have proven totally false. Instead, as the number of computers has increased, so has the number of computer-driven printers and computer-controlled copying machines. As a result, paper production has risen dramatically.

From 1959 to 1986—a period in which the United States underwent the most intense computerization of any society on earth—printing and writing paper production increased from 6.83 million to 21.99 million tons, or 320 percent, while the real gross national product increased only 280 percent. From 1981 to 1984, one consulting firm estimated that U.S. business use of paper went from 850 billion to 1.4 trillion pages. Between 1986 and 1990, printed material went from 2.5 trillion pages to 4 trillion pages.

Mail has been one area of stellar growth: from 1936 to 1990, U.S. mail increased from 80 billion to 170 billion pieces. The direct-mail industry has revolutionized retailing by offering low-cost goods through the mail at bargain prices. In urban areas, mail increases 10 percent annually.[6] Checks are also thriving: in 1988 banks cleared 60 billion checks, roughly 70 times the number of electronic fund transfers. Even credit cards use paper—each credit card purchase produces three paper copies.

The predictions about the decline of paper were wrong for several reasons. One mistake was to think that information was a fixed quantity—the more on computers, the less on paper. Actually, the reverse has been true—the bigger the computer, the bigger the printer, and the more paper that is needed to display the information. Second, people like paper. Reading paper is about 30 percent faster than reading a computer screen. Third, paper is reliable and portable. A computer needs a power supply, but paper gets along fine without batteries or cords. Finally, as we saw in previous chapters, the economy has undergone a transformation in which the number of information and knowledge workers—whose jobs involve paper—has increased, and the number of production workers has declined.

This brings us back to the question of whether computers have actually caused a decline in employment. Of course, in an economic downturn it is customary for both blue- and white-collar workers to be let go. To some extent, this has been happening for several years. The number of factory workers in the United States has declined through much of the 1980s, and many Fortune 500 corporations have closed down expensive corporate headquarters, adopted a more decentralized structure, and moved to less expensive locations like the Southwest and the Southeast. In the process, several thousand middle and upper-middle managers were let go (usually to management jobs in smaller, rapidly expanding companies). But there is no evidence that computers have had anything to do with these normal business-cycle adjustments. Indeed, virtually all formal studies of the labor force have concluded that employment levels and employment for various occupations depend on several factors, only one of which is the introduction of new technology.

If computers have not been flattening organizational structures by decreasing the employment of expensive middle managers and clerical workers, what does this mean for productivity and efficiency? Has the investment in computers had any positive impacts in this area? The answer is starting to become clear.

Computers have indeed had a powerful positive role to play in changing the strategy of businesses. Computer-based systems have revolutionized business procedures in some industries—notably retailing, financial services, and manufacturing. Computers have helped to create entirely new products, and they have contributed to—not caused—the transformation of the American economy into an information and knowledge economy. None of these developments has invariably resulted in vast gains in efficiency or productivity, however. Many business organizations have failed to turn the technological benefits into economic gains in productivity. Growth in productivity in the white-collar, or "information," sector and the service sector of the American economy has been abysmal—about 2 percent a year for the last decade (see Chapter 1). But productivity in factories has been superb over the same period—nearly 6 percent annual increases in productivity, which is on a par with the Japanese and Germans. The challenge facing us all is to look more closely at investments in computer systems in the information sector of the economy—the white-collar, information, and knowledge jobs where most of us now work—with an eye to capturing economic benefits for the bottom line of the business.

16.4 Computer Crime and Other Threats

In addition to the social and organizational impacts that we have just examined, our growing dependence on computers is affecting our lives in other ways. In this section, we will examine some of the threats to information systems that organizations must guard against.

The Vulnerability of Information Systems

Although computer-based information systems can help solve a firm's problems, they are vulnerable to many more kinds of threats than manual systems. Events such as a fire or electrical power failure can have a massive impact because so much of a firm's information resources are concentrated in one place. Valuable data can be destroyed if computer hardware malfunctions or if individuals tamper with computerized files.

According to a nationwide study conducted by the Center for Research on Information Systems at the University of Texas at Arlington, the longer computer services are disrupted, the more difficult it is to perform basic business functions. As Figure 16.3 illustrates, almost half of the businesses surveyed predicted they would experience a total or critical loss of business functions if they suffered an outage lasting approximately one week. Such losses might occur in a matter of hours for banks or other financial institutions, where information systems themselves are the major sources of activity and revenue for the firm.

The Major Threats to Computerized Information Systems

The major threats to computerized information systems are disasters, such as fire or electrical failure; user errors; hardware malfunctions or software

Computers assist with the manufacturing of computers in this Compaq Computer Corporation facility. Careful investment in technological tools can increase efficiency and productivity.

Source: Courtesy of Compaq Computer Corporation.

errors; and computer crime. These threats and their impacts are summarized in Table 16.3.

On-line information systems and those based on telecommunications networks are especially vulnerable because they link information systems in many different locations. As a result, unauthorized access or abuse can occur at a multitude of access points. Figure 16.4 illustrates the vulnerabilities of a generic telecommunications network.

Security

All of the policies, procedures, and technical tools used to safeguard information systems from unauthorized access, alteration, theft, and physical damage.

Computer crime

The deliberate theft or criminal destruction of computerized data or services; the use of computer hardware, software, or data for illegal activities; or the illegal use of computers.

Security and Computer Crime

Of special concern to builders and users of information systems are the issues of security and computer crime. **Security** refers to all of the policies, procedures, and technical tools used for safeguarding information systems from unauthorized access, alteration, theft, and physical damage. Although the greatest threats to computer systems come from accidents and human error, a major objective of computer security is to prevent **computer crime** (which includes the deliberate theft or criminal destruction of computerized data or services, the use of computer hardware or software to illegally alter or destroy data, and the application of computer technology to perpetrate a crime) and to prevent legal but unauthorized access to computer systems.

Figure 16.3

When Computers Fail, Companies Suffer

Although computer-based systems have many advantages, they also have a distinct disadvantage: they are much more vulnerable than manual systems. Moreover, firms that have computerized their business transactions tend to become very dependent on the computers to perform these crucial functions. Thus, when computers "go down" for whatever reason, firms experience a definite loss of business function. This chart shows that the longer the period of outage, or time when computer services are disrupted, the more serious the consequences become for that firm. In fact, for some firms, doing without computers for several days leads to total loss of business function.

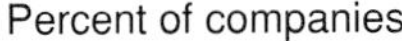

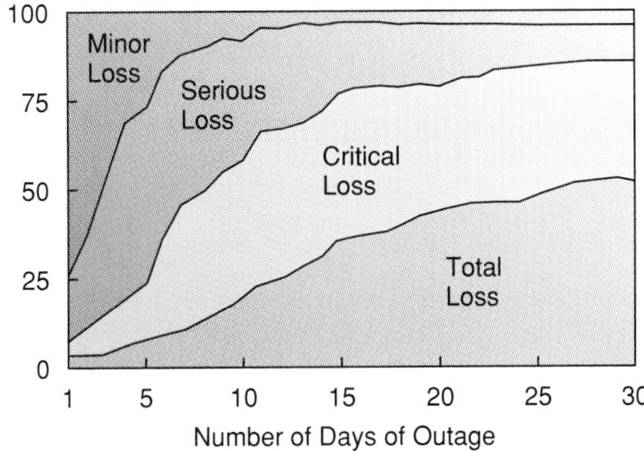

Source: Center for Research on Information Systems, The University of Texas at Arlington. As reprinted in Steven R. Christensen and Lawrence L. Schkade, "Surveying the Aftermath," *Computerworld,* March 13, 1989. Reprinted with permission.

Sources and Types of Computer Crime · Computer crime can range from a teenage prank to international espionage. Although monetary theft is the most common form of computer crime, it can also involve theft of services, information, or computer programs; alteration of data; damage to software; and trespassing (see Figure 16.5).

Losses from computer crime are difficult to quantify because many computer crimes go undetected and corporations are reluctant to publicize such problems. It is clear, however, that the concentration of assets in computer form makes computer crime a high-loss, high-risk proposition for a business firm. Even if the crime does not involve major theft, it can severely damage a business's operations or record keeping. For example, as the Focus on People describes, USPA, Inc. and IRA, Inc., an insurance and brokerage firm based in Fort Worth, Texas, could not pay 550 employees for several weeks when a former programmer wiped out 168,000 payroll records.

Studies by the General Accounting Office and the Orkand Corporation, a consulting firm, have estimated that computer crime causes annual losses of $15.4 million to $1.5 billion for the computerized banking network in the United States. The Bank Administration Institute estimated

Table 16.3

Major Threats to Computerized Information Systems

Threat	Impact
Fire	Computer hardware, files, and manual records may be destroyed.
Electrical power failure	All computer processing is halted; hardware may be damaged, and "disk crashes" or telecommunications disruptions may occur.
Hardware malfunction	Data are not processed accurately or completely.
Software errors	Computer programs do not process data accurately, completely, or according to user requirements.
User errors	Errors inadvertently introduced by users during transmission, input, validation, processing, distribution, and other points of the information processing cycle destroy data, disrupt processing, or produce flawed output.
Computer crime	Illegal use of computer hardware, software, or data results in monetary theft or destruction of valuable data or services.
Computer abuse	Computer systems are used for unethical purposes.

that U.S. banks lost over $1 billion in 1986 because of information systems abuse.

Contrary to popular impression, the vast majority of these crimes were committed by authorized insiders. The National Center for Computer Crime Data in Los Angeles estimated that 70 percent of reported computer crimes were perpetrated by people inside the organization. For example, employees from the magnetic peripherals arm of the Control Data Corporation were arrested for diverting as much as $20 million in company goods and cash using Control Data's automated purchasing and inventory records.[7]

Other Security Problems: Hackers and Computer Viruses

Hacker
A person who gains unauthorized access to a computer network for profit, criminal mischief, or personal reasons.

Nevertheless, loss and damage from **hackers** attempting to penetrate information systems from the outside cannot be dismissed. The press has reported numerous incidents of inventive teenagers who invade computer networks for profit, criminal mischief, or personal thrills.

One of the most notorious of these hackers was the "Shadow Hawk." Anton Valukas, the U.S. attorney in Chicago, has alleged that 18-year-old Herbert M. Zinn of Chicago, under the *nom de guerre* "Shadow Hawk," stole $1.2 million of AT&T proprietary software by penetrating the Bell Laboratories national network. Between July and September 1987, the Shadow Hawk copied 52 AT&T proprietary programs by penetrating a Bell Labs network linking sites in Naperville, Illinois, Warren, New Jersey, and Burlington, North Carolina, as well as a computer at Robbins Air Force

Figure 16.4

A Telecommunications Network Is Vulnerable at a Number of Points

Potential security problems—unauthorized access or abuse of the system—can occur at many points in a telecommunications network. Unauthorized access and illegal connections can occur at the input stage. It is also possible to "tap" communications lines and illegally intercept data. Within the CPU itself, either the hardware or software can fail, and stored files can be accessed illegally, copied, or stolen. Telecommunications systems linked by satellite are even more vulnerable because transmissions can be intercepted without using a physically attached device.

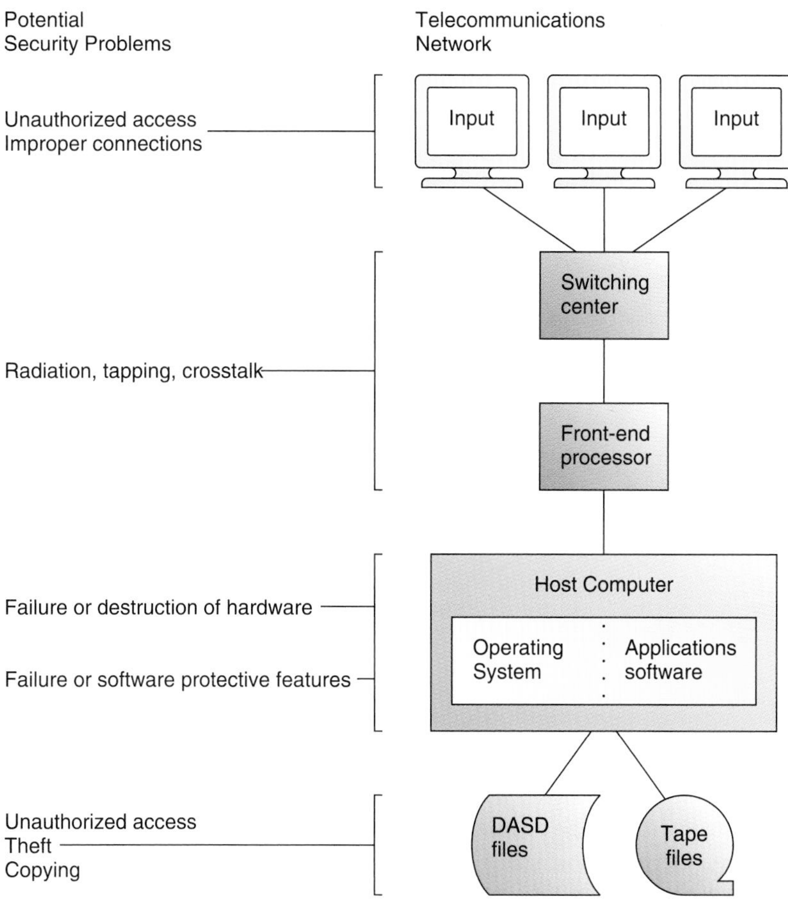

Base in Georgia. The criminal juvenile charges filed against Zinn contended that Zinn then published the passwords for breaking into the network on electronic bulletin boards in Chicago and Texas. Federal agents located Zinn through telephone numbers stored on files in the AT&T computers that were invaded. If convicted, Zinn could face three years in a federal prison for juvenile offenders.[8]

Sophisticated personal computer users are also becoming increasingly adept at connecting their personal computers to the nation's telephone network to eavesdrop, charge calls to another person's bill, destroy data, dis-

Figure 16.5

The Major Types of Computer Crime

Computer crime is a large and growing problem for businesses. The term "computer crime" covers a wide range of activities; the common denominator is that it involves using computer hardware or software to perform a criminal act. The most common computer crime is stealing money from an organization; next most common is stealing information or programs. Definite statistics regarding the amount of computer crime can be difficult to come by; many firms, fearing negative publicity, don't report security abuses.

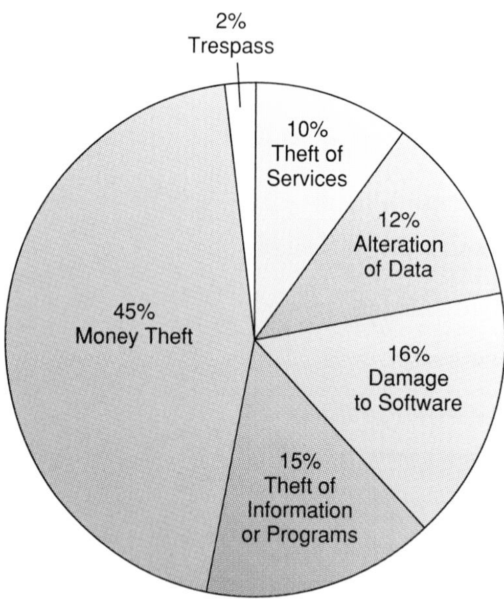

Source: InformationWEEK, February 22, 1988. Reprinted by permission of InformationWEEK Magazine, a CMP Publication, Manhasset, NY.

rupt telephone switching services, or penetrate computer systems linked via telecommunications.

Most recently, alarm has risen over hackers propagating **computer viruses,** rogue software programs that spread rampantly like viruses from system to system. Information systems become congested and malfunction as the viruses endlessly replicate themselves. Depending on the intent of the creator, the virus might flash a harmless message such as "Merry Christmas!" on computer terminals, or it might systematically destroy all of the data in the computer's memory.

Computer virus
A rogue software program that spreads rampantly through computer systems, destroying data or causing the systems to become congested and malfunction.

The most notorious computer virus epidemic occurred in November 1988, when a brilliant computer science student introduced a program that spread uncontrollably throughout a nationwide Department of Defense data network. Created by Robert Tappan Morris, the son of one of the U.S. government's most respected computer security experts, the virus program rapidly reproduced itself throughout Arpanet, the Advanced Research Projects Agency Network, which links research centers, universities, and military bases.[9]

FOCUS ON *People*

Computer Felon Plants a Time Bomb

At 3:00 A.M. on a Saturday morning, Donald Gene Burleson broke into the offices of USPA, Inc. and IRA, Inc. in Fort Worth, Texas, and sat down at his terminal. Until he had been fired three days earlier, Burleson had been the firm's computer security officer. The former programmer used a three-day-old security password to sign onto the firm's IBM System 38 minicomputer and erased 168,000 payroll records. He also built a program into the system to erase records on a monthly basis. Burleson tied the program to erase files to legitimate files and put it on a time switch.

Burleson thought his actions would go undetected. In fact, the firm did make a cursory check of its systems after Burleson was fired but failed to turn up anything. The damage and "time bomb" were discovered by a fellow programmer who came to the office one weekend to figure out how a new bonus system would affect the company's payroll. Every time the programmer ran tests, the payroll came up with zeros. The company then shut down the computer for two days and found Burleson's programs.

Burleson was convicted of harmful access to a computer, a third-degree felony. The prosecution only proved $12,000 in damages for actual downtime of the system and the cost to fix the payroll accounts. But 550 employees did not get checks for several weeks. If the time bomb had not been discovered so soon, it would have created havoc.

Source: J. A. Savage, "Computer Time Bomb Defused: Felon Nailed," *Computerworld*, September 26, 1988, p. 24.

Morris introduced the program through a Cornell University terminal by signing onto a computer at the artificial intelligence laboratory at the Massachusetts Institute of Technology. The virus rapidly raged through computers using a particular version of the UNIX operating system, moving from computer to computer as a piece of electronic mail through the Arpanet Sendmail program. Once inside Sendmail, however, the virus program used a "backdoor" feature to bypass Sendmail's electronic mailboxes, or files for storing personal messages, and entered the host computer's control programs. From there the virus moved on to other computers and spread rapidly throughout the Arpanet network. Morris intended his program to reside quietly on Arpanet computers, but it was quickly detected as it echoed back and forth throughout the network in minutes, copying and recopying itself thousands of times.

Computer security experts concluded that this virus contained no harmful hidden features and left data files unharmed, but it did clog the Arpanet computers and eventually caused the network to shut down. More than 6,000 computers were infected. The Defense Department asserted that it was impossible for classified military networks that manage nuclear weapons systems and store vital secrets to be penetrated in this manner.

Incidents such as this continue to occur on a smaller scale because personal computers are so plentiful and their networking software and equipment are relatively easy to use. A working group of computer network

TRW's computer center houses one of the largest single databases in the nation. Security is multilayered to protect such important systems.

Source: Courtesy of TRW Inc.

manufacturers has recommended the following preventive measures for combating software viruses, which will lessen but never eliminate the problem:[10]

1. Make backup copies as soon as you open a new software package and store the copies off-site.
2. Quarantine each new piece of software on an isolated computer and review it carefully before installing it on a network.
3. Restrict access to programs and data on a "need-to-use" basis.
4. Check all programs regularly for changes in size, which could be a sign of tampering or virus infiltration.
5. Be especially cautious with "shareware" and "freeware" programs, which have been a prime entry point for viruses.
6. Institute a plan for immediate removal of all copies of suspicious programs and backup of related data.
7. Make sure all purchased software is in its original shrink wrapping or sealed-disk containers.

16.5 Safeguarding Information Systems: Approaches and Techniques

Safeguarding and securing computer information systems can no longer be treated as an afterthought but must be integral to the problem-solving process. Effective problem analysis and solution design include considerations of how the information system can be protected and controlled.

The specific technology, policies, and manual procedures for protecting assets, accuracy, and reliability of information systems are called **controls.** There are two types of controls: **general controls,** which can be applied to the overall business and computing environment of a firm, and specific **application controls,** which govern individual information system applications.

Controls
The specific technology, policies, and manual procedures used to protect the assets, accuracy, and reliability of information systems.

General Controls

General controls are all of the organization-wide controls, both manual and automated, that affect the overall activities of computerized information systems. In other words, they provide an umbrella for all information systems in the firm. General controls ensure the following:

- The security and reliability of computer hardware.
- The security and reliability of software.
- The security of data files.
- Consistent and correct computer operations.
- Proper management of systems development.

They also include **management controls,** which provide appropriate management supervision and accountability for information systems. Table 16.4 presents examples of general controls in each area.

General controls
Organization-wide controls, both manual and automated, that affect overall activities of computerized information systems.

Application controls
Manual and automated procedures to ensure that the data processed by a particular application remain accurate, complete, and valid throughout the processing cycle.

Management controls
A type of general control that provides appropriate management supervision and accountability for information systems (e.g., establishing formal written policies and procedures and segregating job functions to minimize error and fraud).

Data Security

Data security entails both preventing unauthorized use of data and ensuring that data are not accidentally altered or destroyed. Data security must be

Data security
A control aimed at preventing the unauthorized use of data and ensuring that data are not accidentally altered or destroyed.

Table 16.4

General Controls for Information Systems

Control	Example
Hardware	Restricting access to machines/terminals; checking for equipment malfunction.
Software	Requiring logs of operating system activities; restricting unauthorized access to software programs.
Data security	Using passwords; restricting access to terminals to limit access to data files.
Operations	Establishing procedures for running computer jobs correctly; establishing backup and recovery procedures for abnormal or disrupted processing.
Systems development	Requiring management review and audit of each new information system project for conformity with budget, solution requirements, and quality standards; requiring appropriate technical and business documentation for each system.
Management	Establishing formal written policies and procedures; segregating job functions to minimize error and fraud; providing supervision and accountability.

provided for both data storage and data usage in both on-line and batch systems. A fundamental data security policy is to restrict access on a "need-to-know" basis—in other words, allowing individuals only the kind of data they need to do their jobs. Especially sensitive kinds of data, such as salaries or medical histories, may need to be restricted even further.

Data security must be especially tight for on-line information systems, since they can be accessed more easily than batch systems by nontechnical specialists. One of the principal data security techniques is the use of passwords, or secret words or codes giving individuals authority to access specific portions of an information system or systems. A password may be required to log on to a system, to access data and files, to change data in the system, and to view sensitive data fields.

Data security is often multilayered, with passwords for logging on tied to overall operating system software and additional passwords and security restrictions established by data security features of specific applications. For example, Figure 16.6 illustrates the multilevel data security system for a mortgage loan system. User identification and authorization are checked first at the system software level when staff first log on. A former employee whose password has been deleted would be unable to access the system at all. The banking specialist and loan officer must then provide a password to access customer mortgage account files; a clerk would be unable to access these files. At the individual data field level, only the loan officer would be allowed access to annual income data. The banking specialist would not be allowed to view this sensitive information.

One problem with passwords is that they are not used carefully enough. Unauthorized individuals can easily discover another person's password if he or she writes it down on a piece of paper and carelessly leaves it by a desk or terminal. Yet individuals cannot be expected to memorize all of their passwords, especially if they need numerous passwords for many different applications, or if the passwords are periodically changed.

An additional data security safeguard is to use encryption to scramble data into a coded form before transmission on a telecommunications network and to decode the data upon arrival. An authorized user enters a unique, secret key that is not stored anywhere on the system, which triggers the encoding process. The U.S. Bureau of Standards adopted the Data Encryption Standard (DES) in 1977 for encrypting commercial data such as that used by banks, government agencies, and other organizations.

Documentation

Documentation
A control that involves establishing and maintaining a clear-cut explanation of how an information system works from both a business and a technical standpoint; includes system, user, and operational documentation.

Documentation is a critical, but often overlooked, element of information system control. It is critical because information systems will not work properly unless clear-cut explanations of how they work from both business and technical standpoints are available. Each information system solution requires three levels of documentation: system documentation, user documentation, and operational documentation.

System documentation describes the design, structure, and software features of an information system solution. User documentation is essentially business documentation, detailing manual procedures and how an

Figure 16.6

A Data Security System

Data security is a vital consideration for all firms. It involves protecting sensitive data by preventing unauthorized access and making sure that the data cannot be changed or erased. This figure illustrates a multi-level data security approach for a mortgage loan system that requires all employees to provide an authorized password when logging on. Staff must supply an additional password to access customer mortgage account files. A former employee whose password has been deleted would be unable to access the system at all; a clerk would be able to access the system but not the mortgage account files. A banking specialist could access mortgage account data but would be restricted from viewing the Annual Income field. A loan officer, however, would be able to view all the data.

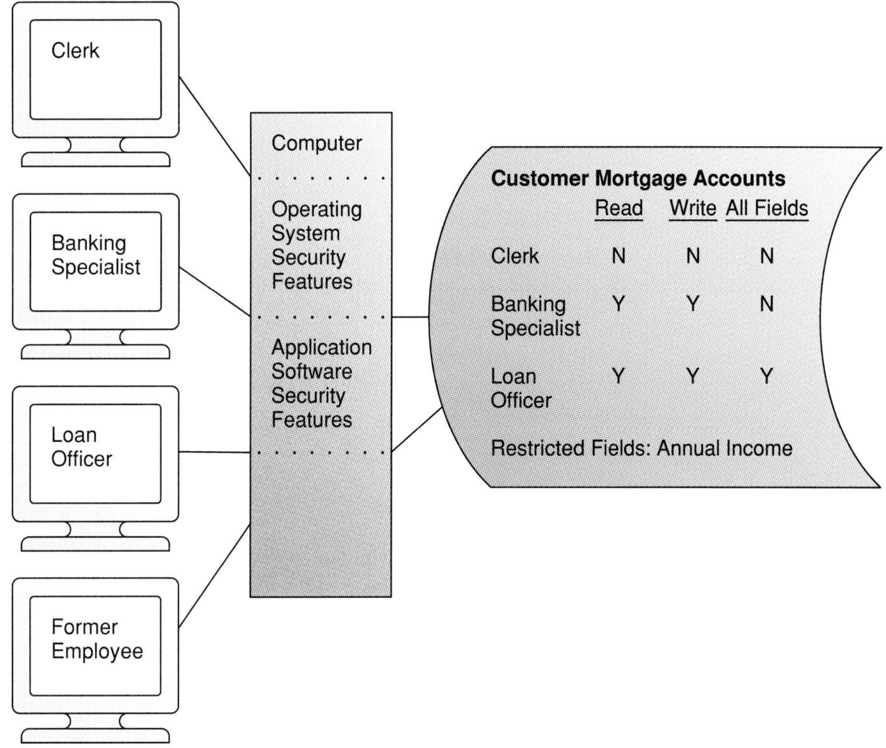

information system solution is used from a business standpoint. Operational documentation describes the steps for running and operating a system, or for backup and recovery, that would be used in a corporate data center. Table 16.5 provides examples of all three kinds of documentation.

Disaster Recovery Planning

A wise step for firms that are highly dependent on computerized information systems is to develop a **disaster recovery plan.** Such a plan enables firms to bounce back quickly from any physical disasters, such as fires, floods, power disruptions, or sabotage, that have disrupted their computer processing. A disaster recovery plan typically provides for immediate access to alternative computer hardware and restoration of software programs,

Disaster recovery plan
A plan that enables a firm to recover from an emergency in which all or part of its information system is destroyed; provides for immediate access to alternative computer hardware and the restoration of software programs, data, and telecommunications facilities.

Table 16.5

Examples of Information System Documentation

System documentation
System flowcharts
Structure charts
File and record layouts
Program listings
User documentation
Functional or business description of system
Data input instructions
Transaction authorizations
Sample data input forms or on-line input screens
Report distribution lists
Output report samples
Error correction procedures
Business controls
Operational documentation
Computer job setups
Run control procedures
Backup and recovery procedures
Hardware and operating system requirements
Disaster recovery plan

data, and telecommunications facilities. The following are key elements of a disaster recovery plan:

- Identifying the most critical business functions and their vulnerabilities.
- Knowing what hardware, software, files, and human resources are required to resume processing of critical applications.
- Training personnel to follow the recovery plan correctly.
- A step-by-step course of action for implementing the plan.

A key component of disaster recovery is backing up and restoring data for critical applications (see the Focus on Problem Solving for an example of a backup system). Disaster recovery plans must also be sensitive to how much of these data flows through personal computers and telecommunications links as well as residing in mainframes. Firms utilize either internal or external disaster recovery sites.

For example, the Beneficial Data Processing Corporation, the data processing subsidiary of Beneficial Corporation in Peapack, New Jersey, relies on its own distributed processing facilities for disaster recovery. It has distributed processing to local branches so that the branches can operate for several days if the main computer center is lost. Figure 16.7 illustrates another option—the use of multiple computer centers. The Elkay Corporation split its applications between two mainframe computers, one in Oak Brook,

FOCUS ON *Problem Solving*

Forbes Fire Destroyed PCs but Not Data

When a fire broke out on the sixth floor of the Forbes building in New York City, the publishing firm's main computer hub was just a floor below. Although the IBM 4381 mainframe was not affected, about 26 personal computers (PCs), mostly IBMs used in the advertising department, were destroyed.

"Things got a little hairy there for a while, but we didn't lose any data," said Joseph Demarte, director of data processing. "Although there was six inches of water in the computer room, the IBM mainframe was unaffected, and we were able to recover the hard drives from the PCs and transfer the data onto other PCs—so nothing was lost," he said.

Even if the fire had damaged the mainframe, Demarte said that the firm makes backup tapes nightly and ships them to a facility in New Jersey. "The most we could have lost would have been a day's worth of work," he said. "We are a standard DOS shop, so if our computers were completely unusable, we could have retrieved our backup tapes and set up at a temporary site until we were able to return to the building."

Source: "Forbes Fire Destroyed PCs but Not Data," *MIS Week*, March 5, 1990, p. 26.

Illinois, and the other in Broadview, Illinois. The mainframes are connected to each other and to remote sites via dedicated data lines. Each mainframe can back up the other. In fact, when operations at the Oak Brook site were disrupted by a fire at an Illinois Bell switching station in 1988, Elkay transferred data tapes and personnel to its Broadview data center and continued functioning.

Sungard Disaster Recovery Services and Comdisco Disaster Recovery Services are specialized external disaster recovery services. They provide fully operational data processing and telecommunications backup facilities to subscribers on less than 24-hours notice. These include computer hardware and software for a firm to run its applications on request, plus technical assistance in disaster planning testing and use of recovery centers.

Application Controls

So far we have looked at general controls that monitor the firm's overall computing environment. In addition to these broad general controls, there are specific controls, called application controls, that govern individual in-

Figure 16.7

Using Multiple Computer Centers to Protect a Firm against Disasters

The Elkay Corporation in Illinois protected itself against possible disasters by splitting its operations between two mainframe computers. Its Oak Brook mainframe handles corporate applications, while the Broadview site controls manufacturing applications and order entry. However, the two computer centers are connected using telecommunications lines, both to each other and to remote sites, and each can take over the other's functions in less than a day. The plan paid off when a fire at an Illinois Bell switching station disrupted phone service to the Oak Brook center. Elkay transferred data tapes and personnel to the Broadview center and continued operating from there.

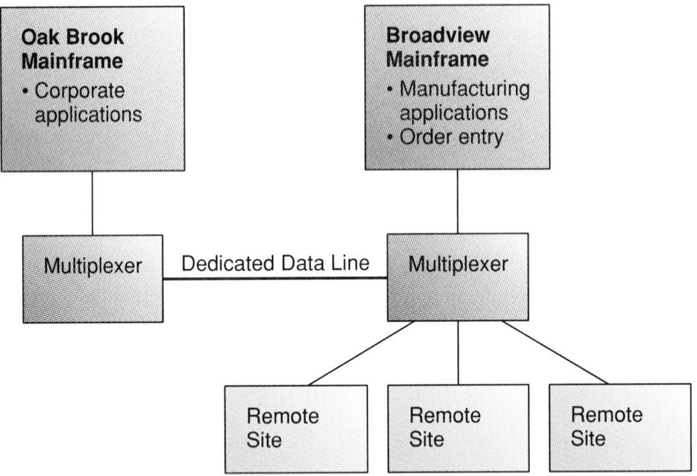

formation system applications. Application controls consist of both manual and automated procedures to ensure that the data processed by a particular application remain accurate, complete, and valid throughout the processing cycle. There are three types of application controls: (1) input controls, (2) processing controls, and (3) output controls (see Figure 16.8).

Input controls
Application controls that ensure the accuracy and completeness of data entering the information system.

Processing controls
Application controls that ensure the accuracy and completeness of data during updating.

Output controls
Application controls that ensure that the results of computer processing are accurate, complete, and properly distributed.

Input controls ensure the accuracy and completeness of data when the data enter an information system. **Processing controls** ensure the accuracy and completeness of data during updating, and **output controls** ensure that the results of computer processing are accurate, complete, and properly distributed. Some of the most important application control techniques are procedures for authorizing and validating input and output, programmed edit checks, and control totals.

A firm can establish formal procedures that allow only selected individuals to authorize input of transactions into a system or to review system output to make sure that it is complete and accurate. These are known as authorization and validation procedures. For example, the signature of the head of the Payroll Department might be required to authorize corrections to employee time cards before such transactions are entered into the payroll system. The Payroll Department head might likewise be required to "sign off" on the results of each payroll processing run, indicating that he or she has reviewed the results and that they are complete and processed properly.

Figure 16.8

Application Controls and General Controls Work Together to Promote System Security and Accuracy

General controls govern the security and accuracy of the overall computing environment. They include such safeguards as data security measures, routine error checks in hardware, restriction of access to programs, and standards for system development. Application controls govern individual system applications. There are three types of application controls, corresponding to the three basic steps in computing: input, processing, and output. At each step there are specific types of application controls that check for errors, incomplete data, and inappropriate data. Note that the same control techniques, such as control totals and authorization checks, can be used at different points in the processing cycle.

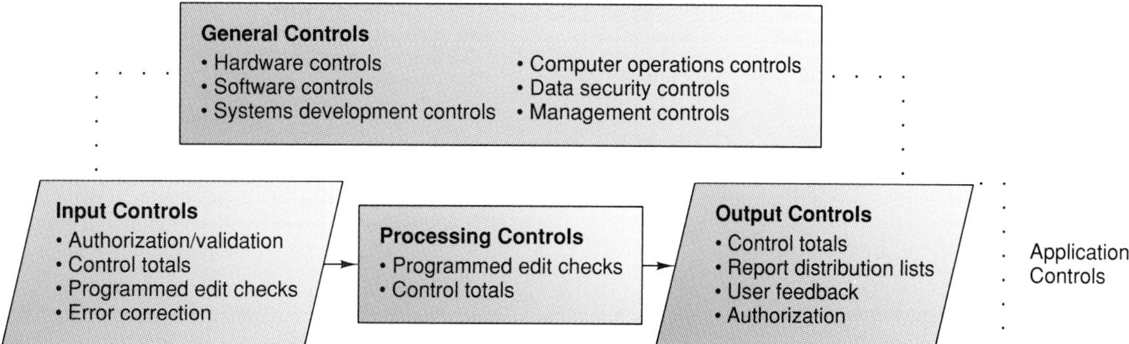

Programmed edit checks are a common technique for checking input data for errors before the data are processed. Transactions that fail to meet the criteria established in computerized edit routines will be rejected. For example, an order processing system might check the product codes on the order transaction to make sure they are valid by matching them against the product codes on an inventory master file. If the product code does not conform to any existing product codes, the order transaction will be rejected. Sometimes preprogrammed edit checks are used as a processing control as well. Figure 16.9 describes some of the most important techniques for programmed edit checks.

Programmed edit check
An application control technique for checking input data for errors before the data are processed; it uses a computerized checking procedure.

Control totals are used at all points in the processing cycle to ensure completeness and some level of accuracy. An information system can make a manual or automated count of the number of transactions processed during input, processing, or output or of total critical quantities, such as order amounts. These totals can then be compared manually or by computer, with discrepancies signaling potential errors. Table 16.6 summarizes the major types of control totals—record counts, quantitative totals, hash totals, and run-to-run control totals.

Control totals
A manual or automated count of the number of transactions processed during input, processing, or output, or of critical quantities, such as order amounts; this count is then compared manually or by computer to a second count; discrepancies in the counts signal errors.

Problem Solving with Controls

An integral part of solution design is making sure an information system has the proper controls. It is essential that vulnerabilities be identified during problem analysis and that solution alternatives consider different options for controls. We can apply our people, technology, and organizational framework to control issues.

Figure 16.9

Programmed Edit Checks Are a Valuable Application Control Technique

Programmed edit checks can be used in both the input and processing phases to ensure data accuracy. Special edit check programs read input transactions and scan their data fields for accuracy. The most common types of edit techniques are the format check, the existence check, the reasonableness check, and the check digit. Transactions that do not meet the criteria of these checks are rejected and reported. The transactions must be corrected to pass the edit criteria before they can become part of the updated files.

Programmed Edit Checks

Technique	Description
1. Format check	The system checks the contents, size, and sign of individual data fields. Example: A telephone long distance code should be a 3-position numeric field.
2. Existence check	The system checks for valid codes by comparing input data fields to tables or master files. Example: State code should be one of the valid state codes on a state code table.
3. Reasonableness check	The system checks to see if selected fields fall within specified limits. Example: An employee's gross pay can't exceed six figures.
4. Check digit	The check digit is an extra reference number added to an identification code bearing a mathematical relationship to the other digits. The check digit is input with the other data, recomputed by the computer, and compared with the one input. Example: The check digit for vendor code 29743 is 9. The vendor code with appended check digit would be 297439.

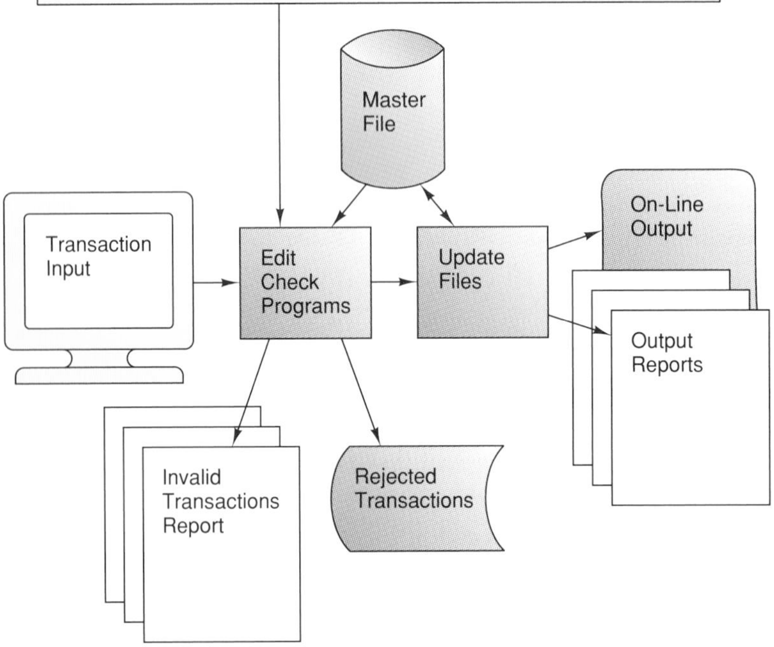

Table 16.6

Major Types of Control Totals

Control	Description	Example
Record counts	Counts the total source input documents and compares this total to the number of records at other stages of input preparation.	Number of order forms should match the total number of order input transactions for a batch order entry system.
Quantitative totals	Totals a quantitative field such as total sales or total orders for a batch of transactions and compares this number to a manual total established for this group of transactions.	Total order amount should match the order total for a batch of order transactions in a batch order entry system.
Hash totals	Totals nonquantitative data fields for control purposes and compares them to a total manually established for group transactions.	Total product code numbers should match a total established manually for a batch order entry system.
Run-to-run controls	Totals can be generated during processing to compare the number of input transactions to the number of transactions that have updated a file, or to output totals. The totals can represent total transactions processed or totals for critical quantities.	Total number of time cards input should equal the total number of employees updated on the payroll master file during processing and the total number of employees with paychecks generated.

Technology	Organization	People
Hardware malfunction	Management supervision	Insider crime
Software errors	Segregation of functions	Training
Program security	External pressure (privacy laws, need to distribute systems and data)	Ease of use of controls
Telecommunications security		User errors
Database security		

The logical and physical design of an information system solution should establish the criteria for ensuring completeness and accuracy of input, processing, and output. Figure 16.10 illustrates how analysis and design of controls fit into the problem-solving process. At each step in the problem-solving process, there are specific control issues that must be addressed.

Not all information systems use application controls to the same degree, nor do they need to do so. Much depends on the nature of the application and the criticality of its data. We can expect major banking and financial systems to use more controls than other systems because so much money and credibility is at stake.

Safeguarding information systems can be a very costly and complicated process. Moreover, a system that has too many controls—that is "overcon-

Figure 16.10

Control Issues Must Be Considered at Each Step of the Systems Development Process

Earlier in the book we examined the problem-solving steps involved in developing a new system. This diagram illustrates that at each step in the problem-solving process, there are crucial control issues to be considered. From the very beginning of the system development process, criteria should be established for both general and application controls.

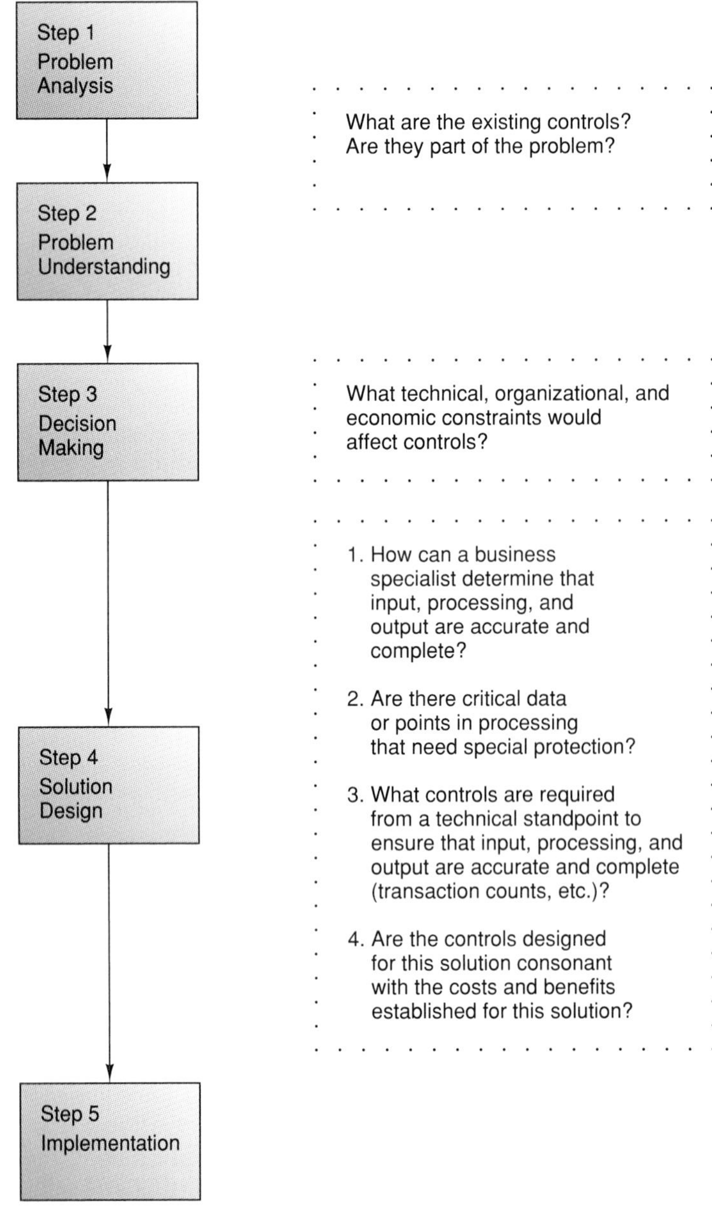

Table 16.7

A Microcomputer Security Checklist

1. Is personal computer equipment stored in a locked room or attached firmly to work areas?
2. Are disks locked in drawers or filing cabinets? Are disks with critical data stored in a fireproof place?
3. Are data on hard disks backed up regularly?
4. Have individuals authorized to use each machine and application been formally identified?
5. Does each microcomputer application have input, processing, and output controls?
6. Have a procedure and individual been authorized for verifying the data in each application?
7. Are there standards, passwords, and other precautions for downloading and uploading data between microcomputers and mainframes or minicomputers?
8. Are individuals using microcomputers held accountable for security?
9. Have training and formal documentation for microcomputer security been instituted?

Source: William E. Perry, "What You Need to Know about Computer and Data Security," *Computers in Accounting,* December 1987.

trolled"—can be so unwieldy and difficult to use that business professionals may be discouraged from using it at all. The problem-solving process must weigh the benefits of each control or safeguard against financial costs and ease of use to determine the right mix for each application.

Safeguarding Microcomputers

Stand-alone microcomputer systems tend to have less formal and stringent controls than those that are mainframe or minicomputer based. This pattern will change as microcomputers become networked or linked to mainframes for cooperative processing. Likewise, as applications formerly relegated to mainframes are downsized to microcomputers, they will require serious controls if they entail critical data. Table 16.7 lists some considerations for **microcomputer security.**

Microcomputer security
The policies, procedures, and technical tools used to safeguard microcomputers from unauthorized access; usually less formal than the controls for mainframes and minicomputers.

16.6 Leading-Edge Application: Digital Envelopes for Networks

Scientists and engineers rely on their computer networks for exchanging research results and carrying on conversations that could not take place by telephone. They too are concerned about breaches of privacy and security since messages can be easily intercepted and read by intruders. To deal with this problem, Internet, the computer network linking hundreds of academic, government, and corporate networks, has instituted a new method for transmitting messages with an unbreakable code.

Under the new system, not only will messages be encrypted, but concealed information will be embedded in the message that will clearly show the recipient that the person who says he or she sent the message was the actual sender. The system will also inform the recipient with certainty that the message has not been altered.

In other words, Internet will have "digital envelopes," which can only be opened by the addressee, containing messages with "digital signatures" that cannot be forged. This means of encryption will be offered to the four hundred computer networks that are linked to Internet.

The encryption technique, called PKE, will be based on a technique devised by RSA Data Security, Inc. of Redwood City, California. It uses "public key encryption techniques" developed in the late 1970s at the Massachusetts Institute of Technology. PKE assigns each user two "keys," one public and one secret. The public key is published in a directory. The sender uses the recipient's public key to send a message, and the recipient uses his or her secret key to decode it.[11]

The Digital Equipment Corporation has engaged RSA to provide the same encryption technology proposed for Internet. Recognizing that security is an essential ingredient of distributed computing, Digital plans to integrate this technology into a broad range of software and hardware products. Digital's use of encryption technology could give it a competitive edge in the network computing market.

Summary

- Computers do not "impact" society directly, but the decisions made about how to use computers do have impacts.
- People and organizations are responsible, and in some cases liable, for the consequences of their use of computers.
- The social impacts of computers include the political issues of freedom and privacy, due process, freedom of information, and the balance of political power, as well as the social issues of crime, distribution of people and jobs, computer dependence, and education.
- The organizational impacts of computers include the work issues of quality of work, productivity, authority, and training, as well as the organizational issues of organizational structure, efficiency, dependence, and strategy.
- In general, many of the predicted social impacts of computers have not occurred. Advanced societies have been able to regulate computer technology when necessary in order to minimize the negative impacts of computers while still enjoying the benefits of the technology.
- Computer information systems are more vulnerable to destruction, error, abuse, and crime than manual systems because data are concentrated in electronic form, in which they can be more easily accessed, altered, or destroyed.

- The major threats to computerized information systems are disasters, such as fire or electrical failure; user errors; hardware malfunction and software errors; and computer crime.
- Computer crime involves using software and hardware to alter or destroy data or merely applying computer technology to perpetrate a crime. The major types of computer crime are monetary theft; theft of services, information, or computer programs; alteration of data; damage to software; and trespassing. The vast majority of computer crimes are committed by insiders.
- Hackers and computer viruses are growing security risks, largely because of the upsurge in networked computing.
- Controls refer to the specific technology, policies, and manual procedures for protecting the assets, accuracy, and reliability of information systems. General controls govern the overall business and computing environment of a firm, and specific application controls govern individual information system applications.
- General controls consist of hardware controls, software controls, data security controls, systems development controls, computer operations controls, and management controls.
- Data security, which involves restricting access to data in computer information systems, is essential, especially in on-line information systems. Two important techniques for promoting data security are the use of passwords and encryption.
- Complete user, system, and operational documentation and disaster recovery planning are other critical components of information system control.
- Application controls consist of input, processing, and output controls. Principal application control techniques include control totals, programmed edit checks, and procedures for authorizing and validating input and output.
- Analysis and design of information system controls must be included at various stages of the problem-solving process. A solution design must consider the costs and benefits of each control as well as ease of use.
- Special requirements of microcomputer systems must be addressed by a security plan.

Key Terms

Responsibility
Liability
Societal impacts
Organizational impacts
Freedom
Privacy
Freedom of information
Due process
Privacy Act of 1974
Telecommuting
Computer dependence
Quality of work life
Security
Computer crime
Hacker
Computer virus

Controls
General controls
Application controls
Management controls
Data security
Documentation
Disaster recovery plan
Input controls
Processing controls
Output controls
Programmed edit check
Control totals
Microcomputer security

Review Questions

1. What do responsibility and liability mean?
2. Do computers have impacts, or is it the uses to which computers are put that have impacts?
3. List some of the major societal and organizational impacts of computers.
4. Explain the meaning of the following terms: privacy, due process, freedom of information, and freedom.
5. Compare the predictions of how computers would impact organizations with the reality.
6. How have computers affected clerical, professional, and managerial work?
7. Why are computer information systems more vulnerable than manual systems? What kinds of computer information systems are the most vulnerable?
8. List the major threats to computer information systems.
9. What is computer crime? Name various types of computer crime.
10. What is security? What is its relationship to computer crime? To hackers?
11. What is a computer virus? How can computer virus attacks be prevented?
12. What are controls? Distinguish between general controls and application controls.
13. List and describe each of the general controls required for computer information systems.
14. What kinds of techniques can be utilized for promoting data security?
15. Why is documentation so important for safeguarding and controlling information systems?
16. What is a disaster recovery plan? What are some of the key elements of such a plan?
17. What are the three types of application controls? Describe the techniques that are used for each.
18. Describe special safeguards required to protect microcomputer-based information systems.

Discussion Questions

1. People should not be held responsible for what their computers do. Discuss.

2. There is no such thing as a totally secure system. Discuss.

3. If you were designing an information system, how would you determine what controls to use?

Problem-Solving Exercises

1. Devise a new Privacy Act that would protect citizens from potential invasions of privacy by large organizations. Can you think of any new principles of privacy protection? (See the description of the Privacy Act of 1974.)

2. Write an analysis of what might happen if each of the general controls for computer information systems were not in place.

3. The solution design for the North Lake Bank mortgage payment system in Section 11.6 in Chapter 11 notes that the controls for this application remain the same as before. Based on the information supplied in this text, write a description of what those controls might be.

Notes

1. See, for instance, Alan F. Westin, *Privacy and Freedom* (New York: Atheneum Press, 1978). See also Kenneth C. Laudon, "A General Model for Understanding the Relationship between Information Systems and Organizations" (National Science Foundation and Center for Research on Information Systems Working Paper. New York University, 1989); John King and Kenneth Kraemer, *Change and Control in Computing: Managing the Information Systems Function in Organizations* (Los Angeles: Jossey-Bass, 1989); and their excellent article on models for thinking about the impact of computers in John King and Kenneth Kraemer, "The Dynamics of Change in Computing Use: A Theoretical Framework," *Computer Environment Urban Systems,* November 1, 1986.
2. David Flaherty, *Privacy and Government Databanks—An International Perspective* (London: Mansell Publishing, 1979).
3. See Kenneth C. Laudon, *Dossier Society: Value Choices in the Design of National Information Systems* (New York: Columbia University Press, 1986).
4. Robert Kraut, Susan Dumais, and Susan Koch, "Computerization, Productivity and Quality of Work-Life," *Communications of the ACM* 32, no. 2 (February 1989), p. 226.
5. Doron P. Levin, "Smart Machines, Smart Workers," *The New York Times,* October 17, 1988.
6. Edward Tenner, "Bad News for Trees," *Computerworld,* May 30, 1988.
7. Larry Stevens, "Security Systems: Getting Management to Shell Out," *Computerworld,* December 14, 1987.
8. "Bell Tolls for Shadow Hawk," *Computerworld,* August 15, 1988.
9. "Computer 'Virus' Injected in Military Computers," *The New York Times,* November 4, 1988, pp. A1, A21.
10. Patricia Keefe, "Checkpoints against Viruses," *Computerworld,* September 19, 1988.
11. Vin McLellan, "Data Networks to Use Code to Insure Privacy," *The New York Times,* March 21, 1989.

Problem-Solving Case

Electronic Vaults for Banks

Comdisco Disaster Recovery Services, Inc. and Sungard Recovery Services, Inc. are offering 24-hour, seven-day-a-week vaulting services. Through "electronic vaulting," backup data for an executing application can be backed up and transmitted electronically to a secure site.

Traditional disaster recovery services require that a firm physically transport backup tapes of its data from its data center to a remote facility, which is usually hours away, and then to a recovery center. Electronic vaulting, in contrast, transmits the data to be backed up electronically to the recovery site. Thus up-to-date data are maintained at both the electronic vaulting firm and the client's own information systems. If the client's data center shuts down, data can be accessed immediately from the electronic vault.

According to Jim Bigham, a vice-president at Prudential-Bache Securities, Inc., electronic vaulting eliminates the need to prepare a number of backup tape pickups each day. Once a particular application (system) finishes running, a firm can transmit the data to the off-site "vault." A firm whose data center has experienced a fire or electrical crash can restore its information processing much faster.

Such services are especially appealing to banks and other financial institutions that process large volumes of on-line transactions each day. In the event of a data center disaster, they could not survive for more than a few hours without functioning information systems. Some critical applications are worth up to $20,000 a minute. The ability to rebound immediately from system failure can represent a competitive advantage.

The Comdisco vaulting arrangement is very software intensive, relying on direct communication between a client's mainframe and a dedicated host computer at the Comdisco hot site in Carlstadt, New Jersey. Data can be transmitted at speeds ranging from 9.6 kilobits per second on T1 lines to 6 megabits per second over T3 fiber-optic lines and will be stored on IBM 3480 cartridge tapes.

Client firms will have the option of transmitting data either in batch or interactive modes or by designated times of the day using Network Datamover, bulk-transfer software from System Center, Inc. Comdisco will also offer remote transaction-logging software from E-Net Corporation and is remarketing the 3800 communications processor from NTX Communications Corporation to furnish channel speed communications. The price of Comdisco vaulting services ranges from $2,500 to $20,000 per month. This covers one shift of use and all of the required technical support for storing backup data on tape.

A similar vaulting service from Sungard, called Sunvalt, is based on a channel-extensions approach using high-speed data switches from the Data Switch Corporation at both the client's data center and the Sungard hot site

in Philadelphia. Each customer will receive a dedicated vault within the hot site that can store up to 15,000 IBM 3480 cartridge tapes. To maintain high security, each vault is walled off and accessible only by card keys. The cost of the Sungard service will range from $3,500 to $15,000 per month.

Source: Alan Alper, "Curing Backup Blues," *Computerworld,* June 6, 1988; and Tari Schreider, "If You Can't Afford to Wait . . . ," *Computerworld,* July 11, 1988.

Case Study Questions

1. What problems could be solved through electronic vaulting?
2. What problems might be encountered if a firm used electronic vaulting?
3. How would a firm determine whether to use electronic vaulting? Describe the factors for making this decision.

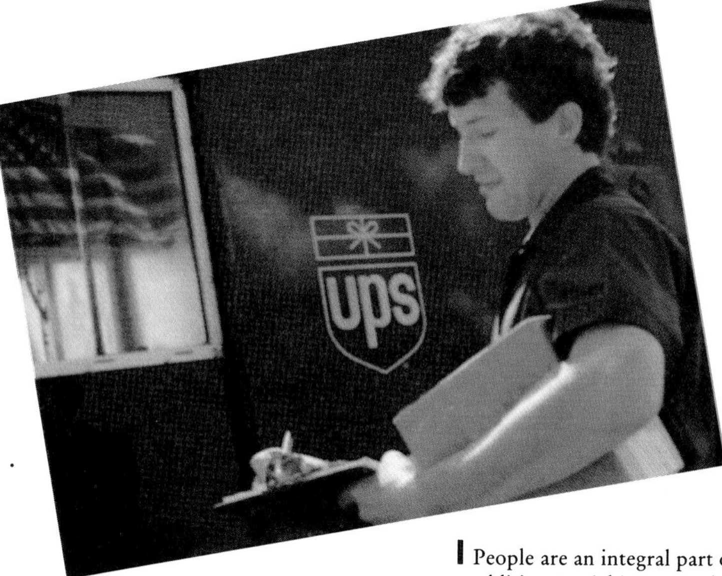

UPS Delivers with Personal Computers

People are an integral part of UPS. In addition to picking up and delivering packages, they collect much of the data required by UPS's information systems.

Source: Courtesy of United Parcel Service.

United Parcel Service (UPS) is the largest and most successful package delivery company in the world: It delivered 2.8 billion packages last year in the United States and 180 other countries. It is many times larger than Federal Express and has recently moved aggressively into the business of overnight package delivery.

With this huge volume of business, it might seem that keeping track of deliveries would require several mainframe computers. Until recently, that was true. In its Paramus, New Jersey, computer center, UPS still operates three large IBM mainframes. Linked to these centralized mainframes are thousands of terminals across the country. At each terminal, UPS employees enter information, which the mainframes process to be able to track each package and establish schedules for local delivery.

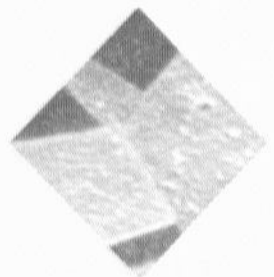

But that is the past at UPS, according to John Byrne, the company's personal computer support manager. "Over the last couple of years," said Byrne, "we made the strategic decision that the PC price/performance curve was going to be better than the minicomputer or mainframe curve." In other words, the company has determined that the smaller personal computers will increasingly be able to deliver more performance for the money than larger computer models.

UPS uses PCs for 50 major corporatewide applications. For its U.S. field operations alone, the company has about 20,000 PCs linked in 254 local area networks. Recently, UPS signed an agreement with AT&T to purchase 4,000 new PCs for $29 million. These machines will be used in UPS's worldwide network of package distribution centers and for its central information-processing applications.

Many factors are driving the company's move away from mainframes and toward PCs. First, the business is expanding, and UPS would like to offer better service to customers, taking advantage of its newly instituted applications in teleservicing and telemarketing. Also, the total volume of packages and documents is expanding, quickly exceeding the capacity of the mainframes and mainframe networks already installed.

In the past, UPS developed all its new software on the mainframe. But internal studies have found that in terms of time and money, software development on the PC is about 36 percent more productive than mainframe development. According to Byrne, this information led the company to have its developers work at PC workstations.

The new PC workstations are being slotted first for deployment in UPS customer service telephone centers. These centers take calls from customers who are requesting that a package be picked up or that UPS trace a package. Some of the information needed to handle these requests is stored on the mainframe; other information is on minicomputers. The PCs store local information. Depending on where the package was sent and what the customer wants, the UPS employee will use one of these types of computers. In many instances, the information concerns a local package, and the local area network contains all the needed information. In other instances, the information is stored on a mainframe that the PC can access.

UPS customer service telephone center representatives can track packages worldwide in seconds with their personal computers.

Source: Courtesy of United Parcel Service.

The Packaging Tracking System enables UPS employees to scan packages at the origin and destination locations with a bar-code device. The information is then transmitted to the central mainframe computer.

Source: Courtesy of United Parcel Service.

Another new PC application is the Advanced Label Imaging System. In this system, package tracking stubs are fed into a PC-driven scanning device that reads about 7,000 tags an hour. This image information goes to a mainframe, which stores it for use on PCs that employees use for calling into the mainframe when they trace packages or route them. The information is never typed in by hand. When a customer calls, a UPS employee can bring up the image of the airbill on a screen in seconds.

While these are relatively small applications, UPS will soon be converting its entire Package Management Information System over to PC hardware from one of its IBM mainframes. The system's purpose is to process the driver time cards and delivery and pickup information from UPS's North American centers.

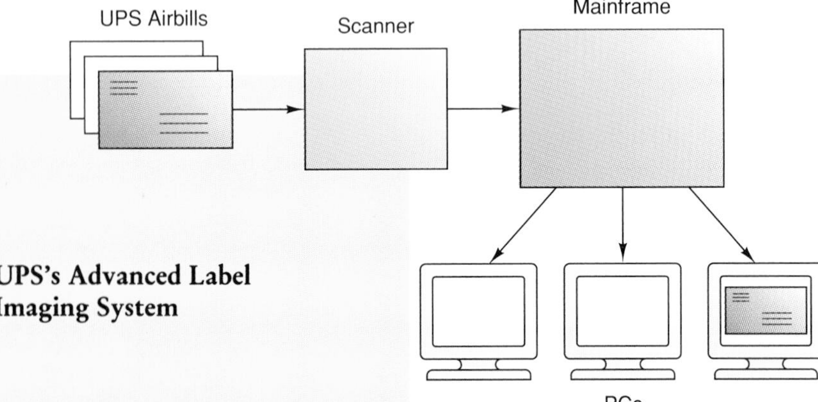

UPS's Advanced Label Imaging System

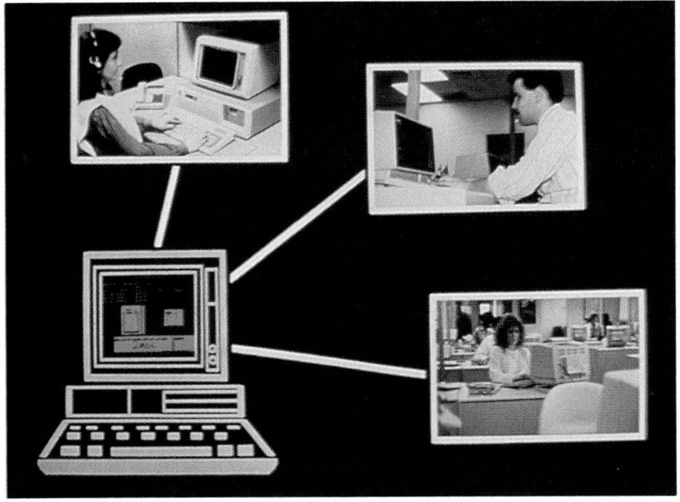

The Advanced Label Imaging System is an online image retrieval service that captures data and images from air labels.

Source: Courtesy of United Parcel Service.

About the general move away from mainframes, Byrne said, "PC interfaces can be more friendly and much easier to maintain for the user. Response time is much better when you're not dealing with communication lines or a huge mainframe network." Currently, UPS is considering replacing its minicomputers with more local area networks, but this will depend on how well the networks can handle the volume of transactions. In some cases, they seem to be competitive with minicomputers.

Although UPS is shifting many existing applications to the PCs, the company still uses mainframes, and it still maintains centralized control of its computing resources, including purchasing, development, and repair work for hardware and software. All requests from field offices to purchase computing equipment must be approved centrally to assure that the new equipment is compatible with existing systems and the future direction of the company.

Source: Based on George Briggs, "UPS Prefers PC LANs over Mainframes," *MIS Week,* March 5, 1990, pp. 18–22.

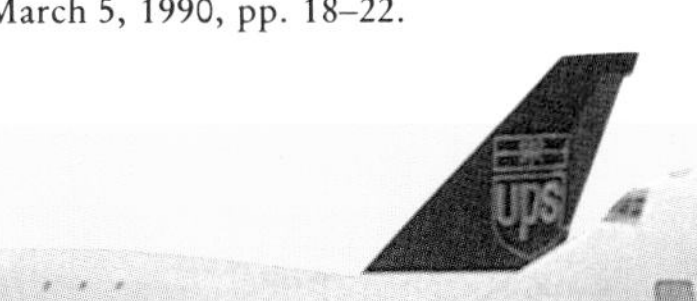

Aircraft schedules and routes are determined from the output of UPS's information systems.

Source: Courtesy of United Parcel Service.

Glossary

Accounts payable systems Accounting systems that keep track of amounts owed by a firm to its creditors.

Accounts receivable systems Accounting systems that keep track of amounts owed to the firm.

Ada A programming language developed for the Department of Defense to be portable across diverse brands of hardware; it also has nonmilitary applications and can be used for business problems.

Address The particular location in primary storage where data or program instructions are stored.

Analog signal A continuous sine wave form over a certain frequency range, with a positive voltage representing a 1 and a negative charge representing a 0; used for voice transmissions.

Applicant tracking systems Human resources systems that maintain data about applicants for jobs at a firm and provide reports to satisfy federal, state, and local employment regulations.

Application controls Manual and automated procedures to ensure that the data processed by a particular application remain accurate, complete, and valid throughout the processing cycle.

Application generator Software that can generate entire information system applications without customized programming; the end-user specifies what needs to be done, and the generator creates the appropriate program code.

Application software Programs designed to handle the processing for a particular computer application.

Applications software package A prewritten, precoded, commercially available program that handles the processing for a particular computer application (e.g., spreadsheet or database software for a personal computer).

Application solution The use of an information system to solve a problem.

Arithmetic-logic unit (ALU) The component of the main processor that performs arithmetic and logical operations on data.

Artificial intelligence (AI) The study and creation of machines that exhibit humanlike qualities, including the ability to reason.

Artificial intelligence shell The programming environment of an artificial intelligence system.

ASCII A seven- or eight-bit binary coding scheme used in data transmission, microcomputers, and some larger computers; stands for American Standard Code for Information Interchange.

Assembler A program that translates assembly language into machine code so it can be used by the computer.

Assembly language A programming language used for second-generation software; it consists of natural language–like acronyms and words such as add, sub(tract), and load and is considered a symbolic language.

Asynchronous transmission A method of transmitting one character or byte at a time when data are communicated between computers with each string of bits comprising a character framed by control bits.

Attribute A characteristic or quality of a particular entity.

Backward reasoning A strategy for searching the rules in a knowledge base in which the inference engine begins with a hypothesis and proceeds by asking the user questions about selected facts until the hypothesis is either confirmed or disproved.

Bandwidth The range of frequencies that can be accommodated on a particular telecommunications medium.

Bar code Specially designed bar characters that can be read by OCR scanning devices; used primarily on price tags and supermarket items.

BASIC A programming language frequently used for teaching programming and for microcomputers; although it is easy to learn, it does not easily support sound programming practices.

Basic business system A system that serves the most elementary day-to-day activities of an organization; it supports the operational level of the business and also supplies data for higher-level management decisions.

Batch input and processing An approach to input and processing in which data are grouped together as source documents before being input; once the data are input, they are stored as a transaction file before processing, which occurs some time later.

Baud A change in voltage from positive to negative and vice versa. The baud rate at lower speeds corresponds to a telecommunications transmission rate of bits per second. At higher speeds the baud rate is less than the bit rate because more than one bit at a time can be transmitted by a single signal change.

Behavioral theories of management Views of management that stress three roles—interpersonal, informational, and decisional.

Benefits systems Human resources systems that maintain data about employees' life insurance, health insurance, pensions, and other benefits, including changes in beneficiaries and benefits coverage.

Bit A binary digit that can have only one of two states, represented by zero or one.

Bit mapping A technology often used for displaying graphics on a video display terminal; it allows each pixel on the screen to be addressed and manipulated by the computer.

Bottom-up approach An approach to intelligent machines that concentrates on trying to build a physical analog to the human brain.

Business environment The aggregate conditions in which a business organization operates; the general environment includes government regulations, economic and political conditions, and technological developments, while the task environment includes persons or entities with which the firm is more directly involved, such as customers, suppliers, and competitors.

Business functions The various tasks performed in a business organization—for example, manufacturing and production, sales and marketing, finance and accounting, and human resources activities.

Business interface The parts of an information system that business specialists must interact with (e.g., on-line data entry screens or reports).

Business organization A complex, formal organization established for the purpose of producing products or services for a profit.

Bus network A network in which a number of computers are linked by a single loop circuit made of twisted wire, cable, or optical fiber; all messages are transmitted to the entire network and can flow in either direction, with special software identifying which component receives each message.

Byte A single character of data made up of a combination of bits that a computer processes or stores as a unit; the unit in which computer storage capacity is measured.

C A programming language with tight control and efficiency of execution like assembly language; it is portable across different microprocessors and is easier to learn than assembly language.

Cash management systems Financial systems that keep track of the receipt and disbursement of cash by a firm; they may also forecast the firm's cash flow.

CD-ROM An optical disk system used with microcomputers; it is a form of read-only storage in that data can only be read from it, not written to it; stands for Compact Disk/Read-Only Memory.

Central processing unit (CPU) A hardware component of a computer system, consisting of primary storage and a main processor; it processes raw data and controls other parts of the computer system.

Channel A link by which voices or data are transmitted in a communications network.

Character printer A printer that prints one character at a time; such printers are very slow, outputting 40 to 200 characters per second.

Coaxial cable A transmission medium consisting of thickly insulated copper wire; it can transmit a larger volume of data than twisted wire and is faster and more interference-free; cannot be used for analog phone conversations.

COBOL A programming language with English-like statements designed for processing large data files with alphanumeric characters; the predominant programming language for business applications; stands for COmmon Business Oriented Language.

Combinatorial explosion The difficulty that arises when a problem requires a computer to test a very large number of rules to reach a solution; even a very fast computer cannot search through all the possibilities in a reasonable amount of time.

Communications software Software used in transmitting data via telecommunications links between computer systems and computer terminals.

Compiler A language translator program that translates an entire higher-level language program into machine language.

Computer Physical device that takes data as input, transforms these data by executing a stored program, and outputs information to a number of devices.

Computer crime The deliberate theft or criminal destruction of computerized data or services; the use of computer hardware, software, or data for illegal activities; or the illegal use of computers.

Computer dependence The state of relying on computers to provide vital services; in a computer-dependent society, the malfunctioning of computers may cause extensive damage to lives and/or property.

Computer hardware The physical equipment used for the input, processing, and output work in an information system.

Computer literacy Knowledge about the use of information technology equipment; it involves knowing about hardware, software, telecommunications, and information storage techniques.

Computer mouse A hand-held device that can be moved on a desk top to control the position of the cursor on a video display screen.

Computer software Preprogrammed instructions that coordinate the work of computer hardware components and perform the business processes required by each business information system.

Computer virus A rogue software program that spreads rampantly through computer systems, destroying data or causing the systems to become congested and malfunction.

Concentrator A device that collects and temporarily stores messages from terminals in a buffer or temporary storage area and sends bursts of signals to the host computer.

Controller A device that supervises communications traffic between the CPU and peripheral devices such as terminals and printers.

Controls The specific technology, policies, and manual procedures used to protect the assets, accuracy, and reliability of information systems.

Control totals A manual or automated count of the number of transactions processed during input, processing, or output or critical quantities, such as order amounts; this count is then compared manually or by computer to a second count; discrepancies in the counts signal errors.

Control unit The component of the main processor that controls and coordinates the other components of the computer.

Conversion strategies Plans and methods for changing from an old system to a new system; include parallel conversion, direct cutover, pilot study, and phased approach.

Cooperative processing The division of processing work for transaction-based applications among mainframes and personal computers.

Cost-effectiveness Being economical in terms of providing benefits that exceed costs; measured by cost-benefit analysis.

Critical thinking The sustained suspension of judgment with an awareness of multiple perspectives and alternatives.

CRT An electronic tube that shoots a beam of electrons that illuminate pixels, or tiny dots, on a video display screen; stands for cathode ray tube.

Customization The modification of a software package to meet a firm's unique requirements.

Cylinder Represents circular tracks on the same vertical line within a disk pack.

Data Raw facts that can be shaped and formed to create information.

Database A group of related files; more specifically, a collection of data organized so they can be accessed and utilized by many different applications.

Database management system (DBMS) Software that serves as an interface between a common database and various application programs; it permits data to be stored in one place yet be made available to different applications.

Data definition language The part of a database management system that defines each data element as it appears in the database before it is translated into the form required by various application programs.

Data dictionary The component in a database management system that stores definitions and other characteristics of data elements; it identifies what data reside in the database, their structure and format, and their business usage.

Data flow The movement of data within an information system; a data flow can consist of a single data element or multiple data elements grouped together and can be manual or automated.

Data flow diagram A graphic diagram that shows both how data flow to, from, and within an information system and the various processes that transform the data; used for documenting the logical design of an information system.

Data management software Software that is used for such applications as creating and manipulating lists, creating files and databases to store data, and combining information.

Data manipulation language A special tool in a database management system that manipulates the data in the database.

Data redundancy The presence of duplicate data in multiple data files.

Data security A control aimed at preventing the unauthorized use of data and ensuring that data are not accidentally altered or destroyed.

Data word The number of bits or bytes that a computer can manipulate or store as a unit.

Data work Work that primarily involves the processing, use, or dissemination of information.

Decisional roles The activities of managers that involve making decisions about new products, handling disturbances in the business, allocating resources, and negotiating among persons with different points of view.

Decision making The process of debating objectives and feasible solutions and choosing the best option; the third step of problem solving.

Decision support systems (DSS) Interactive systems under user control that are used in solving semistructured problems.

Demodulation The process of converting analog signals into digital form.

Desktop publishing Applications for producing documents that combine high-quality type and graphics with a variety of layout options, allowing users to produce professional-quality reports and documents.

Digital signal A discrete flow in which data are coded as 0-bits and 1-bits and transmitted as a series of on-and-off electrical pulses; used for communication between computers and by some telephone systems.

Direct-access storage device (DASD) Magnetic disks, including both hard and floppy disks; called *direct access* because in this technology the computer can proceed immediately to a specific record without having to read all the preceding records.

Direct cutover A conversion strategy in which the old system is replaced entirely with the new system on an appointed day; no system is available if the new system fails.

Disaster recovery plan A plan that enables a firm to recover from an emergency in which all or part of its information system is destroyed; provides for immediate access to alternative computer hardware and the restoration of software program, data, and telecommunications facilities.

Disk access time The speed at which data can be located on magnetic disks and loaded into primary storage or written onto a disk device.

Distributed database A complete database or portions of a database that are maintained in more than one location.

Distributed processing The distribution of processing among multiple computers linked by a communications network.

Documentation A control that involves establishing and maintaining a clear-cut explanation of how an information system works from both a business and a technical standpoint; includes system, user, and operational documentation.

Document management technology Information technology that is used for producing and managing the flow of documents in an organization; includes word processing, desktop publishing, and optical disk storage.

DOS An operating system for 16-bit microcomputers; PC-DOS is used with the IBM Personal Computer; MS-DOS is used with other 16-bit microcomputers that function like the IBM PC.

Dot-matrix printer An impact printer that uses a print head composed of many small hammers or pins that strike an inked ribbon as the print mechanism moves from side to side; such printers are usually faster than letter-quality printers but produce lower-quality output.

Double-sided disk A floppy disk on which data can be stored on both sides.

Downloading The process of extracting data from mainframes, reformatting these data, and placing them in a microcomputer.

Downsizing The process of moving problem-solving applications from large computers, such as mainframes or minicomputers, to smaller computers, such as microcomputers.

Due process The right to be treated fairly in accordance with established legal procedures, including such things as the right to appeal and the right to an attorney.

EBCDIC An 8-bit binary coding scheme used in IBM and other mainframe computers; stands for Extended Binary Coded Decimal Interchange Code.

Electronic data interchange (EDI) The direct computer-to-computer exchange of standard business transaction documents, such as invoices, bills of lading, and purchase orders, between two separate organizations.

Electronic mail The computer-to-computer exchange of messages.

Entity A person, place, or thing on which information is maintained.

EPROM A memory device in which the memory chips can be erased and reprogrammed with new instructions; stands for erasable programmable read-only memory.

Execution cycle The portion of a machine cycle in which the required data are located, the instruction is executed, and the results are stored.

Executive support systems (ESS) Graphic-oriented systems designed for senior management that provide generalized computing and telecommunications facilities and combine internal and external information; used for long-term planning.

Expert systems Software applications that seek to capture expertise in limited domains of knowledge and experience and apply this expertise to solving problems.

External knowledge base A knowledge base that is outside the organization, such as libraries of articles, collections of scientific or legal findings, and links to other professionals in universities or other businesses.

Fault-tolerant computer systems Systems with extra hardware, software, and power as backups against system failure.

Fax (facsimile) machine A machine that can transmit documents containing both text and graphics over telephone lines; the sending machine digitizes and transmits the image, which is reproduced as a facsimile (fax) by the receiving machine.

Feasibility The quality of being suitable, given a firm's internal and external constraints, including financial resources.

Feedback Output that is returned to appropriate members of the organization to help them refine or correct the input phase.

Fiber optics A transmission medium consisting of strands of clear glass fiber bound into cables through which data are transformed into beams of light and transmitted by a laser device; it is faster, lighter, and more durable than wire media but also more expensive and harder to install.

Field A grouping of characters into a word, a group of words, or a complete number.

File A group of related records.

File server A computer with a large hard disk whose function is to allow other devices to share files and programs.

Finance and accounting function The division of a business organization that manages the firm's financial assets (finance) and maintains the firm's financial records (accounting).

Flat panel display A technology that uses charged chemicals or gases sandwiched between panes of glass to display output on a screen; used in lightweight, portable computers.

Floppy disks Flexible, inexpensive disks used as a secondary storage medium; primarily used with microcomputers.

Formal systems Information systems that rely on mutually accepted and relatively fixed definitions of data and procedures for collecting, storing, processing, and disseminating information.

FORTRAN A programming language developed in 1954 for scientific, mathematical, and engineering applications; stands for FORmula TRANslator.

Forward reasoning A strategy for searching the rules in a knowledge base in which the inference engine begins with information entered by the user and searches the rule base to arrive at a conclusion.

Fourth-generation development The construction of information systems with little or no formal assistance from technical specialists, useful for smaller, informal systems and personal computer applications.

Fourth-generation language Programming languages that are less procedural than conventional languages (i.e., they need only specify what is to be done rather than provide the details of how to do it) and contain more English language–like commands; they are easier for nonspecialists to learn and use than conventional languages.

Frames A way of organizing knowledge based on shared characteristics; an object is defined by its characteristics and can be related to any other object in the database that shares those characteristics.

Freedom The ability to act and think without constraint.

Freedom of information The right of citizens to have access to information stored by government and private organizations in order to be informed participants in the political process and to protect themselves from government abuse.

Front-end processor A computer that manages communications for a host computer to which it is attached; the front-end processor is largely responsible for collecting and processing input and output data to and from terminals and performing such tasks as formatting, editing, and routing for the host computer.

Full-duplex transmission A form of transmission over communication lines in which data can be sent in both directions simultaneously.

General controls Organization-wide controls, both manual and automated, that affect overall activities of computerized information systems.

General Problem Solver A model of human problem solving that attempted to avoid the combinatorial explosion by reducing the number of rules through which a computer would have to search; useful for restricted areas, such as chess, but not for general problem solving.

Geographic information systems Software used in producing maps or performing geographic modeling; such systems may be two dimensional or three dimensional.

Gigabyte A measure of computer storage capacity; equals 1,073,741,824 bytes.

Graphical user interface The feature of a microcomputer operating system that uses graphical symbols, or icons; rather than typing in commands, the user moves the cursor to the appropriate icon by rolling a mouse on a desk top.

Graphics language A fourth-generation language for displaying computerized data in graphical form.

Groupware Software that attempts to expedite all the functions of a typical work group (e.g., tracking the calendars of all or related individuals in an office, scheduling meetings, and sharing ideas and documents).

Hacker A person who gains unauthorized access to a computer network for profit, criminal mischief, or personal reasons.

Hierarchical database model The organization of data in a database in a top-down, treelike manner; each record is broken down into multilevel segments, with one root segment linked to several subordinate segments in a one-to-many, parent-child relationship.

Half-duplex transmission A form of transmission over communication lines in which data can move in both directions, but not simultaneously.

Hard disk A thin steel platter about the size of a phonograph record with an iron oxide coating; generally several are mounted together on a vertical shaft.

Hierarchy The arrangement of persons in a business organization according to rank and authority. Persons at the bottom of the hierarchy report to those on the next level who have more authority; these persons, in turn, report to the next level and so on, up to senior management.

High-level language A programming language that consists of statements that, to some degree, resemble natural languages, such as English.

Host computer The main computer in a network.

Human resources function The division of a business organization that concentrates on attracting and maintaining a stable work force for the firm; it identifies potential employees, maintains records on existing employees, and creates training programs.

Hypertext A way of delivering information that transcends the limitations of traditional methods by branching instantly to related facts rather than following a predetermined organization scheme.

Impact printer A printer that forms characters by pressing a typeface device, such as a print wheel or cylinder, against paper and inked ribbon.

Implementation The process of putting the solution of a problem into effect and evaluating the results and performance in order to make improvements; the fifth, and last, step of problem solving.

Index A list, for a file or database, of the key field of each record and its associated storage location.

Indexed sequential-access method (ISAM) A way of storing records sequentially on a direct-access storage device that also allows individual records to be accessed in any desired order using an index of key fields.

Inference engine The process of searching through the rule base in an expert system; either a forward reasoning strategy or a backward reasoning strategy is used.

Informal structure A network of personal relationships within a formal business organization.

Information Data that have been shaped or formed by humans into a meaningful and useful form.

Informational roles The activities of managers that involve monitoring the activities of the business, disseminating information through reports and memos, and acting as spokespersons for the business.

Information and knowledge economy An economy in which the majority of new wealth (gross national product) is produced by creating or processing information.

Information center A facility that provides training, tools, standards, and expert support for solution design by end-users.

Information system A set of interrelated components working together to collect, retrieve, process, store, and disseminate information for the purpose of facilitating planning, control, coordination, and decision making in businesses and other organizations.

Information systems literacy Knowledge and hands-on facility with information technologies, together with a broadly based understanding of business organizations and individuals from a behavioral perspective and a similar understanding of how to analyze and solve business problems.

Information work Work that primarily involves the creation or processing of information.

Ink-jet printer A printer that produces an image by spraying electrically charged ink particles against paper through holes in the printhead.

Input The capture or collection of raw data resources from within a business or from its external environment.

Input controls Application controls that ensure the accuracy and completeness of data entering the information system.

Input/output bus width The number of bits that can be moved at one time between the CPU and the other devices of a computer.

Instruction cycle The portion of a machine cycle in which an instruction is retrieved from primary storage and decoded.

Integrated Services Digital Network (ISDN) An emerging international standard for extending common carrier digital service (sharing voice messages, digital information, and video pictures) to homes and offices from central telephone company centers.

Integrated software package A software package that provides two or more applications, such as spreadsheets and word processing, allowing for easy transfer of data between them.

Intelligent database search machine A "master" machine that can direct a search of a very large database by giving the target pattern to many machines that search simultaneously; when a machine finds a possible match, it sends it to the controller machine, which makes the final assessment.

Intelligent machines Physical devices or computers that mimic the way people think.

Interpersonal roles The activities of managers that involve performing symbolic duties; motivating, counseling, and supporting workers; and acting as liaisons to the larger firms and the outside world on behalf of employees.

Interpreter A language translator program that translates a higher-level language program into machine code by translating one statement at a time and executing it.

Key field A field in a record that uniquely identifies that record so that it can be retrieved, updated, or sorted.

Keypunch An early form of inputting data in which data were coded onto 80-column cards, with each location on the card representing a character.

Key-to-disk A form of inputting in which data are keyed directly onto magnetic disks.

Key-to-tape A form of inputting in which data are keyed directly onto magnetic tape.

Kilobyte The usual measure of microcomputer storage capacity; equals 1,024 bytes.

Knowledge The stock of conceptual tools and categories used by humans to create, collect, store, and share information.

Knowledge and data workers The employees in a business organization who create and/or disseminate knowledge (e.g., engineers) or data (e.g., clerical workers) to solve business problems.

Knowledge- and information-intensive products Products that require a great deal of learning and knowledge to create and often require information technologies to deliver in a timely fashion.

Knowledge base A model of human knowledge used by artificial intelligence systems; consists of rules, semantic nets, or frames.

Knowledge engineer Specialist trained in eliciting information and expertise from other professionals in order to translate the knowledge into a set of production rules, frames, or semantic nets.

Knowledge systems Information systems used by knowledge workers in business organizations to solve questions requiring knowledge and technical expertise.

Knowledge work Work that (1) is based on a codified body of findings and results; (2) can be taught in a school as principles, procedures, and methods; (3) is certified by the state or a university; and (4) is regulated by a professional body that sets standards.

Knowledge workers' roles in business Business positions that involve interpreting the firm's external knowledge base; playing an active role as advisers and internal business consultants; and initiating, promoting, and evaluating new projects that incorporate new developments and changes into the firm.

Laser printer A printer that produces an image by scanning a laser beam across a light-sensitive drum; the toner that adheres to the charged portions of the drum is then pulled off onto the paper.

Letter-quality printer An impact printer that produces a high-quality image by pressing the image of a fully formed character against inked ribbon.

Liability The idea that people may be obligated by law to compensate those they have injured in some way; liability is established by laws that set out legal remedies for proscribed behavior.

Light pen An input device with light-sensitive photoelectric cells in its tip that is used to input data by "writing" on a video display device; usually used for graphics.

Line printer A printer that prints an entire line at a time; can reach speeds of 3,000 lines per minute.

Local area network (LAN) A transmission network encompassing a limited area, such as a single building or several buildings in close proximity; widely used to link personal computers so that they can share information and peripheral devices.

Logical design The part of a solution design that provides a description of the general level of resources, the operational process, and the nature of outputs that the solution should require; it describes what the solution will do, not how it will work physically.

Logical Theorist Software developed by Herbert Simon and Alan Newell that mimicked deductive logic; that is, it selected correct rules and postulates in order to create a coherent logical chain from premises to conclusion.

Logical view The presentation of data as they would be perceived by end-users or business specialists.

Machine cycle The series of operations involved in executing a single instruction.

Machine language The programming language used in the first generation of computer software; consists of strings of binary digits (0 and 1).

Magnetic disk The most popular secondary storage medium; data are stored by means of magnetized spots on hard or floppy disks.

Magnetic ink character recognition (MICR) A form of source data automation in which an MICR reader identifies characters written in magnetic ink; used primarily for check processing.

Magnetic tape A secondary storage medium in which data are stored by means of magnetized and nonmagnetized spots on tape; it is inexpensive and relatively stable but also is relatively slow and can store information only sequentially.

Mainframe A large computer, generally having 50 to 500 or more megabytes of RAM.

Management controls A type of general control that provides appropriate management supervision and accountability for information systems (e.g., establishing formal written policies and procedures and segregating job functions to minimize error and fraud).

Management information systems (MIS) Management support systems that provide routine summary reports on the firm's performance; used to monitor and control the business and predict future performance.

Managing The process of using business resources to accomplish goals, coordinate the work of many workers, and establish criteria for measuring progress toward the established goals.

Manual system An information system that uses only paper and pencil technology and does not rely on computers.

Manufacturing and production function The division of a business organization that produces the firm's goods or services.

Megabyte A measure of computer storage capacity; equals 1,048,576 bytes.

Megahertz A measure of clock speed, or the pacing of events in a computer; equals one million cycles per second.

Microcomputer A small, desktop or portable computer, generally having 256 kilobytes to 16 megabytes of RAM.

Microfilm and microfiche Media that record output as microscopic filmed images that can be stored compactly.

Microprocessor A silicon chip containing an entire CPU; used in microcomputers.

Microsecond A measure of machine cycle time; equals one one-millionth of a second.

Microwave A transmission medium in which high-frequency radio signals are sent through the atmosphere; used for high-volume, long-distance, point-to-point communication.

Middle management The persons in the middle of the hierarchy in a business organization; they carry out the programs and plans of senior management by supervising employees.

Millisecond A measure of machine cycle time; equals one one-thousandth of a second.

Microcomputer security The policies, procedures, and technical tools used to safeguard microcomputers from unauthorized access; usually less formal than the controls for mainframes and minicomputers.

Minicomputer A medium-sized computer, generally having 1 to 100 megabytes of RAM.

Model base The analytical tools used by an information system; in a decision support system, it will include very sophisticated tools, such as built-in spreadsheets, statistical analysis, and simulation.

Modem A device used to translate digital signals into analog signals and vice versa, a necessity when computers communicate through analog lines; stands for MOdulation and DEModulation.

Modulation The process of converting digital signals into analog form.

Module A logical way of partitioning or subdividing a program so that each component (i.e., module) performs a limited number of related tasks.

Multiplexer A device that enables a single communications channel to carry data transmission from multiple sources simultaneously.

Multiprocessing The simultaneous use of two or more CPUs under common control to execute different instructions for the same program or multiple programs.

Multiprogramming The concurrent use of a computer by several programs; one program uses the CPU while the others use other components, such as input and output devices.

Multitasking The multiprogramming capability of single-user operating systems, such as those for microcomputers; it enables the user to run two or more programs at once on a single computer.

Nanosecond A measure of machine cycle time; equals one one-billionth of a second.

Natural languages Languages, including idioms, which are used by humans (examples: English, Russian, French).

Network database model The organization of data in a database so that each data element or record can be related to several other data elements or records in a many-to-many relationship.

Network gateway The network software that links a local area network to another network, such as the public telephone system or another corporate network.

Network topology The shape or configuration of a network; the most common topologies are the star, bus, and ring.

Neural network Hardware or software that emulates the physiology of animal or human brains.

Nonimpact printer A printer, such as a laser, ink-jet, or thermal-transfer printer, that does not form characters by pressing a typeface device against ribbon and paper.

Nonvolatile Property of memory that means that its contents will not be lost if electric power is disrupted or the computer is turned off.

Object code The machine-language version of source code after it has been translated into a form usable by the computer.

Objectives The goals of an organization.

Office activities The activities performed by an office in an organization, consisting of (1) managing documents, (2) scheduling individuals and groups, (3) communicating with individuals and groups, (4) managing data on individuals and groups, and (5) managing projects.

Office data management technology Information technology that centers around desktop databases for client or customer tracking, project tracking, calendar information, and other information required for office jobs.

Office roles The functions played by an office in an organization, consisting of (1) coordinating and managing people and work, (2) linking diverse organizational units and projects, and (3) coupling the organization to the external environment.

Office scheduling technology Information technology used to coordinate individual and group calendars, such as electronic calendars.

On-line database A service that supplies information external to the firm, such as stock market quotations, general news and information, or specific legal and business information.

On-line input An input approach in which data are input into the computer as they become available rather than being grouped as source documents.

On-line real-time processing A type of processing in which data are processed as soon as they are input into the system rather than being stored for later processing.

On-line transaction processing (OLTP) A transaction processing mode in which transactions entered on-line are immediately processed by the CPU.

Operating system The systems software that manages and controls the activities of the computer.

Operational systems Information systems used in monitoring the day-to-day activities of a business organization.

Optical character recognition (OCR) A form of source data automation in which optical scanning devices read specially designed data off source documents and translate the data into digital form for the computer; bar codes are an example of OCR technology.

Optical disk A disk on which data are recorded by laser beams rather than by magnetic means; such disks can store data at densities much greater than magnetic disks.

Order processing systems Sales and marketing systems that record and process sales orders, track the status of orders, produce invoices, and often produce data for sales analysis and inventory control.

Organizational impacts The effects of computers on organizations, including both work issues (such as the effect of computers on quality of work, authority, productivity, and training) and organizational issues (such as computers' effects on organizational structure, efficiency, and strategy).

Organization perspective A way of viewing a problem in which emphasis is placed on the firm's formal rules and procedures, production process, management, politics, bureaucracy, and culture as sources of its problems and the way in which they can contribute to a solution.

OS/2 An operating system that supports multitasking and is used with 32-bit IBM Personal System/2 microcomputers.

Output The transfer of processed information to the people or business activities that will use it.

Output controls Application controls that ensure that the results of computer processing are accurate, complete, and properly distributed.

Packet switching The breaking up of a block of text into packets of data approximately 128 bytes long; a value-added network gathers data from its subscribers, divides the data into packets, and sends the packets on any available communications channel.

Page printer A printer that can print an entire page at a time; can reach speeds of more than 20,000 lines per minute.

Parallel conversion A conversion strategy in which the old system and the new system run in tandem until it is clear that the new system is working correctly.

Parallel processing A type of processing in which more than one instruction is processed at a time; used in supercomputers.

Parallel sensor systems A system in which each node continually receives information from lower-level sensors, evaluates the information, requests more if needed, and reports to higher-level machines.

Partitioned database A database that is subdivided so that each location has only the portion of the database that serves its local needs.

Pascal A programming language that consists of smaller subprograms, each of which is a structured program in itself; it is used on microcomputers and for teaching programming but is not well suited for business applications.

People challenge The problems posed by the interrelationship of technology and humans; refers both to the problems rapid changes in technology present for individuals and businesses and to the need to design systems individuals can control and understand.

People perspective A way of viewing a problem in which emphasis is placed on the firm's employees as individuals and their interrelationships as sources of its problems and the way in which they can contribute to a solution.

Perceptive systems Sensing devices used in robots that can recognize patterns in streams of data.

Perceptron A machine devised by Frank Rosenblatt that could perceive letters or shapes and could be taught, or corrected, when it made mistakes; an example of the bottom-up approach to artificial intelligence.

Phased approach A conversion strategy in which a new system is introduced in steps.

Physical design The part of a solutions design that translates the abstract logical system model into specifications for equipment, hardware, software, and other physical resources.

Physical view The presentation of data as they are actually organized and structured on physical storage media.

Picosecond A measure of machine cycle time; equals one one-trillionth of a second.

Pilot study A conversion strategy in which a new system is introduced to only a limited part of an organization; if the system is effective there, it is installed throughout the rest of the organization.

PL/1 A programming language developed in 1964 by IBM for business and scientific applications; not as widely used as COBOL or FORTRAN.

Plotter A device that is used for outputting high-quality graphics; pen plotters move in various directions to produce straight lines, whereas electrostatic plotters use electrostatic charges to produce images from tiny dots on treated paper.

Point-of-sale systems Sales and marketing systems that capture sales data at the actual point of sale through the cash register or hand-held laser scanners.

Positions systems Human resources systems that maintain information about positions (slots in a firm's organization chart); they maintain data about filled and unfilled positions and track changes in positions and job assignments.

Postimplementation The use and evaluation of a new system after it is installed; the last stage of the traditional systems life cycle.

Primary storage The component of the CPU that temporarily stores program instructions and the data being used by these instructions.

Privacy The right of individuals and organizations to be left alone and to be secure in their personal papers.

Privacy Act of 1974 A federal statute that defines citizens' rights in regard to, and management's responsibilities for, federal government records; sets out some of the principles for regulating computer technology in order to protect people's privacy.

Private branch exchange (PBX) A central private switchboard that handles a firm's voice and digital communications needs.

Problem analysis The consideration of the dimensions of a problem to determine what kind of problem it is and what general kinds of solutions may be appropriate; the first step in problem solving.

Problem understanding The investigation—fact gathering and analysis—of a problem, leading to better understanding; the second step of problem solving.

Process control systems Manufacturing and production systems that use computers to monitor the ongoing physical production processes.

Processing The conversion of raw input into a more appropriate and useful form.

Processing controls Application controls that ensure the accuracy and completeness of data during updating.

Process specifications The logical steps for performing a process; they appear in documents accompanying lower-level data flow diagrams to show the various steps by which data are transformed.

Production workers The employees in a business organization who actually produce or create the firm's products.

Productivity challenge The need to increase U.S. productivity and bring it into line with the growth in computing power.

Program A series of statements or instructions to the computer.

Program/data dependency The close relationship between data stored in files and the specific software programs required to update and maintain those files, whereby any change in data format or structure requires a change in all the programs that access the data.

Programmed edit check An application control technique for checking input data for errors before the data are processed; it uses a computerized checking procedure.

Project definition The process of investigating a perceived problem to determine whether a problem actually exists and, if so, whether it requires further analysis and research; the first stage of the traditional systems life cycle.

Project management technology Software that helps managers track and plan projects.

PROM A memory device in which the memory chips can be programmed only once and are used to store instructions entered by the purchaser; stands for programmable read-only memory.

Protocol The set of rules governing transmission between two components in a telecommunications network.

Prototyping Building an experimental, or preliminary, system or part of a system for business specialists to try out and evaluate.

Pseudocode A method of documenting the logic followed by program instructions in which English-like statements are used to describe processing steps and logic.

Quality control systems Manufacturing and production systems that monitor the production process to identify variances from established standards so that defects can be corrected.

Quality of work life The degree to which jobs are interesting, satisfying, and physically safe and comfortable.

Query language A higher-level, easy-to-use, fourth-generation language for accessing data stored in databases or files.

RAM A memory device used for the short-term storage of data or program instructions; stands for random-access memory.

Random file organization A way of storing data records so that they can be accessed in any sequence, regardless of their physical order; used with magnetic disk technology.

Read/write head An electromagnetic device that reads or writes the data stored on magnetic disks.

Record A grouping of related data fields, such as a person's name, age, and address

Recording density The number of bits per inch that can be written on the surface of a floppy disk.

Register A storage location in the ALU or control unit; it may be an instruction register, an address register, or a storage register, depending on what is stored in it.

Relational database model The organization of data in a database in two-dimensional tables called relations; a data element in any one table can be related to any piece of data in another table as long as both tables share a common data element.

Removable-pack disk system Hard disks stacked into an indivisible unit called a pack that can be mounted and removed as a unit.

Repetition construct A series of statements that repeats an instruction as long as the results of a conditional test are true; one of three basic control constructs in structured programming.

Replicated database A central database that is duplicated at all other locations.

Report generator A software tool that extracts data from files or databases to create customized reports that are not routinely produced by existing applications.

Request for Proposal (RFP) A detailed list of questions for software vendors to answer as part of the process of evaluating a software package; the questions are designed to determine the extent to which the software package meets the requirements specified during the solution design process.

Responsibility The idea that individuals, organizations, and societies are free moral agents who act willfully and with intentions, goals, and ideas; consequently, they can be held accountable for their actions.

Ring network A network in which a number of computers are linked by a loop of wire, cable, or optical fiber in a manner that allows data to be passed along the loop in a single direction from computer to computer.

Robotics The study of physical systems that can perform work normally done by humans, especially in hazardous or lethal environments.

ROM A memory device used for the permanent storage of program instructions; stands for read-only memory.

Sales and marketing function The division of a business organization that sells the firm's product or service.

Scanner An electronic device that reads text or graphics and inputs the information into a computer automatically without human typing.

Schema The logical description of an entire database; it lists all the data items and the relationships among them.

Secondary storage The relatively long-term storage of data outside the CPU.

Sector method for storing data A method of storing data on floppy disks in which the disk is divided into pie-shaped pieces, or sectors; each sector has a unique number that becomes part of the address.

Security All of the policies, procedures, and technical tools used to safeguard information systems from unauthorized access, alteration, theft, and physical damage.

Selection construct A series of statements that tests a condition; depending on whether the results of the test are true or false, one of two alternative instructions will be executed; one of three basic control constructs in structured programming.

Semantic nets A way of representing knowledge when the knowledge is composed of easily identified objects with interrelated characteristics; objects are classified according to the principle of inheritance so that the objects in lower levels of the net "inherit" all the general characteristics of the objects above them.

Semiconductor chip A silicon chip upon which hundreds of thousands of circuit elements can be etched.

Semistructured problem A problem in which only parts have a clear-cut answer provided by a well-accepted methodology.

Senior management The persons at the top of the hierarchy in a business organization; they have the most authority and make long-range decisions for the organization.

Sequence construct A series of statements that are executed in the order in which they appear, with control passing unconditionally from one statement to the next; one of three basic control constructs in structured programming.

Sequential file organization A way of storing data records so that they must be retrieved in the physical order in which they are stored; the only file organization method that can be used with magnetic tape.

Simplex transmission A form of transmission over communications lines in which data can travel in only one direction at all times.

Single-sided disk A floppy disk on which data can be stored on only one side.

Social impacts The effects of computers on society, including both political issues, such as the effect of computers on freedom and privacy, and social issues, such as their effect on crime, demography, and education.

Sociotechnical perspective An approach to information systems that involves the coordination of technology, organizations, and people; in this approach, information technology, organizations, and individuals go through a process of mutual adjustment and discovery as systems are developed.

Solution design The development of a solution to a problem, including both logical and physical design; the fourth step of problem solving.

Source code The higher-level language translated by operating system software into machine language so that the higher-level programs can be executed by the computer.

Source data automation Advanced forms of data input technology that generate machine-readable data at their point of origin; includes optical character recognition, magnetic ink character recognition, digitizers, and voice input.

Specialization The division of work in a business organization so that each employee focuses on a specific task.

Spreadsheet software Software that provides the user with financial modeling tools; data are displayed on a grid and numerical data can easily be recalculated to permit the evaluation of several alternatives.

Star network A network in which a central host computer is connected to several smaller computers and/or terminals; all communications between the smaller computers or terminals must pass through the host computer.

Storage technology Physical media for storing data (e.g., magnetic disks or tapes) and the software governing the organization of data on these media.

Stored-program concept The concept that a program cannot be executed unless it is stored in the computer's primary storage along with the required data.

Strategic business challenge The need for businesses to develop the ability to change quickly in response to changes in the external environment, technology, or markets.

Strategic impact systems Information systems that focus on solving problems related to the firm's long-term prosperity and survival; in particular, they are used to help a firm maintain its competitive advantage.

Strategic-level systems Information systems used in solving a business organization's long-range, or strategic, problems.

Structured design A software design principle according to which a program is supposed to be designed from the top down as a hierarchical series of modules, with each module performing a limited number of functions.

Structured problem A routine, repetitive problem for which there is an accepted methodology for arriving at an answer.

Structured program flowchart A method of documenting the logic followed by program instructions; uses graphic symbols to depict the steps that processing must take in a specific program, using the three control structures of structured programming.

Structured programming A way of writing program code that simplifies control paths so that programs can be easily understood and modified by others; it relies on three basic control constructs—the sequence construct, the selection construct, and the repetition construct.

Structured Query Language (SQL) A data manipulation language for relational database management systems that is an emerging business standard.

Subschema The specific set of data from a database that each application program requires.

Supercomputer A very sophisticated and powerful computer that can perform complex computations very rapidly.

Synchronous transmission The transmission of characters in blocks framed by header and trailer bytes called flags; allows large volumes of data to be transmitted at high speeds between computers because groups of characters can be transmitted as blocks, with no start and stop bits between characters as in asynchronous transmission.

System flowchart A diagram that documents the sequence of processing steps that take place in an entire system; most useful for physical design in which such diagrams show the sequence of processing events and the files used by each processing step.

Systems analysis The study and analysis of problems of existing information systems; it includes the identification of both the organization's objectives and its requirements for the solution of the problems.

Systems design A model or blueprint for an information system solution to a problem; it shows in detail how the technical, organizational, and people components of the system will fit together.

Systems software Generalized software that manages computer resources such as the CPU, printers, terminals, communications links, and peripheral equipment.

Systems study The process of describing and analyzing problems of existing systems, specifying solution objectives, describing potential solutions, and evaluating various solution alternatives; the second stage of the traditional systems life cycle.

Tactical systems Information systems used in solving a business organization's short-term, or tactical, problems, such as how to achieve goals and how to evaluate the process of achieving goals.

Technology challenge The gap that has developed between the rapid advances in computer hardware and our ability to write useful software for it; also, the gap between the changes in both hardware and software and businesses' ability to understand and apply them.

Technology perspective A way of viewing a problem in which emphasis is placed on information technology hardware, software, telecommunications, and database as sources of business problems and how they can contribute to a solution.

Telecommunications technology Physical media and software that support communication by electronic means, usually over some distance.

Telecommuting Working at home on a computer tied into corporate networks and databases.

Teleconferencing The use of telecommunications technology to enable people to meet electronically; can be accomplished via telephone or electronic mail.

Telemarketing systems Sales and marketing systems that track the use of the telephone for contacting customers, offering products, and following up sales.

Thermal-transfer printer A printer that produces high-quality images by transferring ink from a wax-based ribbon onto chemically treated paper.

Time-sharing A technique in which many users share computer resources simultaneously (e.g., one CPU with many terminals); the computer spends a fixed amount of time on each program before proceeding to the next.

Top-down approach An approach to intelligent machines that concentrates on trying to develop a logical analog to the human brain.

Top-down design A principle of software design according to which the design should first consider the program's main functions, subdivide these functions into component modules, and then subdivide each component module until the lowest level of detail has been reached.

Touch screen A sensitized video display screen that allows data to be input by touching the screen surface with a finger or pointer.

Track A concentric circle on a hard disk on which data are stored as magnetized spots; each track can store thousands of bytes.

Traditional file environment The storage of data so that each application has its own separate data file or files and software programs.

Traditional systems life cycle The oldest methodology for building an information system; consists of six stages (project definition, systems study, design, programming, installation, and postimplementation) that must be completed sequentially.

Traditional theories of management Views of management that see its primary functions as being planning, organizing, leading, and controlling.

Training and skills systems Human resources systems that maintain records of employees' training and work experience so that employees with appropriate skills for special assignments or job requirements can be identified.

Transaction A record of an event to which a business must respond.

Transaction processing system A basic business system that keeps track of the transactions necessary to conduct a business and uses these transactions to update the firm's records. Another name for basic business systems.

Transformation of the American economy The shift in the American economy from the production of manufactured goods toward the production of information and knowledge products and services.

Turing test A test devised by Alan Turing to determine if a machine is intelligent. A computer and a human are placed in separate rooms connected by a communications link; if the human is not aware that he or she is communicating with a machine, the machine is intelligent.

Twisted wire The oldest transmission medium, consisting of strands of wire twisted in pairs; it forms the basis for the analog phone system.

Universal Product Code A coding scheme in which bars and the width of space between them represent data that can be read by OCR scanning devices; frequently used in bar codes.

UNIX A machine-independent operating system for microcomputers, minicomputers, and mainframes; it is interactive and supports multiuser processing, multitasking, and networking.

Value-added network (VAN) A multimedia, multipath network managed by a private firm that sets up the network and charges other firms a fee to use it.

Vector processing A technique in which supercomputer software breaks a complex problem down into vectors, or groups of similar operations, and assigns each operation to a specially designed processor that can operate in tandem with others, enabling it to process the calculations hundreds of times faster than an ordinary computer chip.

Very-high-level programming language A programming language that produces program code with far fewer instructions than conventional languages; used primarily by professional programmers.

Video display terminal A screen on which output can be displayed; varieties include monochrome or color, and text or text/graphics.

Virtual storage The division of programs into small fixed- or variable-length portions; only a small portion is stored in primary memory at one time so that programs can be used more efficiently by the computer.

Voice mail A telecommunications system in which the spoken message of the sender is digitized, transmitted over a telecommunications network, and stored on disk until the recipient is ready to listen; at this time the message is reconverted to audio form.

Voice output Output that emerges as spoken words rather than as a visual display.

Volatile Property of memory that means that its contents will be lost if electric power is disrupted or the computer is turned off.

Wide area network (WAN) A telecommunications network covering a large geographical distance; provided by common carriers that are licensed by the government.

Winchester disk system A hermetically sealed unit of hard disks that cannot be removed from the disk drive.

Word processing software Software that handles such applications as electronic editing, formatting, and printing of documents; may include advanced features to correct spelling errors, check grammar, and offer a thesaurus for synonyms and antonyms.

Workstation A desktop computer with powerful graphics and mathematical processing capabilities as well as the ability to perform several tasks at once.

WORM An optical disk system in which data can be recorded only once on the disk by users and cannot be erased; stands for Write Once, Read Many.

Name Index

Ada (Countess of Lovelace), 158
Alavi, Maryam, 413
Albala, Mark, 541
Alper, Alan, 235, 250, 593
Alsop, Stewart, 172
Anderson, Andy, 69
Andres, Clay, 170
Andretti, Mario, 306
Armstrong, W. Evan, 456

Babbage, Charles, 259
Bain, Jim, 33, 34
Baker, Sharon, 180
Barry, Ann, 547
Baumol, William J., 459, 460, 461, 462
Beasley, John, 397
Bender, Donald H., 331
Bender, Eric, 284
Berliner, Hans, 262
Betts, Mitch, 74, 353
Bhide, Amar, 524
Bigham, Jim, 592
Bikson, Tora K., 486
Blahnik, Glen, 487
Blithes, Eve M., 170
Bluestone, Mimi, 175
Bochenski, Barbara, 427
Booker, Ellis, 104
Brandt, Richard, 103
Brown, Michael, 151
Bucken, Mike, 397
Burgard, Michael J., 415
Burleson, Donald Gene, 575
Burns, M. Anthony, 293, 294
Burstein, Jerome S., 154, 155, 157, 160, 161

Canning, Richard, 413
Carlucci, Frank, 25
Carroll, Paul B., 500
Cash, Joseph L., 202
Chao, Matthew, 129
Chen, Ken, 42
Christensen, Steven R., 571
Clark, Evert, 175
Coffee, Peter C., 322
Cohen, Michael D., 331
Collicott, George, 456
Collins, Edward, 284
Cortese, Amy, 193, 284
Cox, Voyne Ray, 562
Crawford, Jay, 505
Crouse, Roger L., 407
Crowe, William J., Jr., 25
Culnan, Mary J., 450
Currid, Cheryl, 309
Cushman, John H., Jr., 48

Daft, Richard L., 517, 545
Dalton, Richard, 91
Daly, Chris, 439
Daly, James, 235, 250, 331
Darrow, Barbara, 208
David, Martin, 179, 180
Davis, Dwight B., 254, 284, 285
Davis, Stanley, 546
Dear, Brian, 11
Del Otero, Thomas, 245
Demarte, Joseph, 581
Denker, Arnold, 262
Derry, Steve, 103, 104
Desposito, Joe, 473
Dhar, Vasant, 284
Djurdjevic, Bob, 500
Donnelly, A. Duane, 175
Double, Mike, 42
Dreyfus, Hubert L., 284
Dreyfus, Stuart E., 284
Dreyfuss, Joel, 326
Drucker, Peter F., 545
Dumais, Susan, 565, 591
Dunn, Don, 558
Dunn, William L., 295, 296
Dyson, Esther, 26, 360

El Sawy, Omar A., 546
Engardio, Pete, 294
Ernst, Martin L., 486
Evans, Elizabeth, 69
Eveland, J. D., 486

Fayol, Henri, 516
Feder, Barnaby J., 69
Feigenbaum, Edward A., 284
Feuche, Mike, 376
Fields, Debbie, 527
Fields, Randy, 528
Flaherty, David, 591
Fletcher, Philip B., 75
Fong, Diana, 130
Forsythe, Jason, 64

Freedman, David H., 164
Fuerst, Irene, 176

Gancher, David, 508
Gates, William, 11, 326
Gelernter, David, 278, 284
Gemmell, Patricia, 11
Getts, Judy, 151
Ghosh, Sushmito, 284
Giuliano, Vincent E., 458, 486
Gogan, Harlene, 180
Green, Jesse, 175
Grochow, Jerrold M., 376
Gutek, Barbara A., 486
Gutenberg, Johannes, 464

Habeck, Milton C., 142
Haley, Clifton E., 4
Hamilton, Rosemary, 134
Hammonds, Keith H., 486
Hansen, Augie, 162
Hardesty, Julie, 64
Harp, Charles, 451
Harper, Charles M. (Mike), 75
Hartog, Curt, 413
Haug, Gary, 487
Helms, Glenn L., 331
Herger, Wally, 391
Hoerr, John, 331
Hof, Robert D., 103
Hoffman, Susan S., 514
Houdeshel, George, 545
Howell, David R., 508
Hughes, Glenn, 159
Hutchings, Richard, 566
Hymowitz, Carol, 548

Iles, Doug, 134

Jacobs, Sue, 297
Javaruski, John J., 202
Jobs, Steve, 26, 129, 333, 373
Johnson, Samuel Curtis, 142
Johnson, Virginia, 519
Jones, Ed, 204
Joni, Sajnicole, 269
Joyce, Ed, 562

Kay, Alan, 326
Kay, Sheryl, 447
Keefe, Patricia, 591
Kelley, Robert, 547
King, John, 591
Kirkpatrick, David, 128
Klepper, Robert, 413
Knight, Robert, 142
Koch, Susan, 565, 591
Kotter, John T., 520, 545
Kraemer, Kenneth, 591
Kraut, Robert, 565, 591

Lalonde, Daniel, 175
Landau, Ralph, 30
Lang, Laura, 175, 506, 510
Laube, Sheldon, 360
Laudon, Jane P., 331, 546
Laudon, Kenneth C., 38, 63, 331, 546, 591
Lego, Paul E., 3
Leone, Dave, 231
Leong, Kathy Chin, 216, 450
Levick, Diane, 202
Levin, Doron P., 591
Levy, Laurent, 518, 519
Lewis, Geoff, 4
Lewis, Peter H., 100, 124
Lockwood, Russ, 245
Lonn, Dana, 491, 492
Lucky, Robert, 11

Mace, Scott, 391
Mahnke, John, 439
Marbach, William D., 281
March, James G., 331
Margolis, Nell, 34
Markoff, John, 11, 246, 250
Martin, Edward G., 154, 155, 157, 161, 169
Maxmin, James, 546
McCorduck, Pamela, 284
McCulloch, Warren, 261
McKernan, John R., Jr., 170
McLaughlin, Michael J., 34
McLellan, Vin, 591
McMillan, Tom, 505
NcNealy, Scott, 331, 332, 333
McPartlin, John P., 108, 128
Mednis, Edmar, 262
Micossi, Anita, 488
Miles, J. B., 231
Miller, Duane R., 95
Minsky, Marvin, 261
Mintzberg, Henry, 520, 521,525, 545
Montoya, Al, 176
Moore, Gordon, 100
Moran, Robert, 250
Morgan, Hank, 277
Morris, Robert Tappan, 574, 575
Murrell, Leonard, 103, 104

Nanus, Burt, 546
Newell, Alan, 261
Norris, Floyd, 450
Noyce, Robert, 100
Nycum, Susan, 562
O'Keefe, J. B., 532, 535, 545
Olsen, Johan P., 331
Olson, Margrethe, 545
Oppenheim, Jeffry, 175
Ormsby, Robert, 513, 539
Orwell, George, 555
Otte, Ruth, 3

Papert, Seymour, 261
Pascal, Blaise, 158
Pascal, Zachary G., 120
Pelton, Charles, 103, 470
Perry, William E., 587
Peterson, Steffen, 502
Petramala, Teresa L., 452
Pike, Helen, 23, 31
Pitta, Julie, 274, 373
Pitts, Walter, 261
Plato, 14
Pollack, Andrew, 134, 257
Port, Otis, 103, 140
Porter, Michael, 63
Puttre, Michael, 8, 175

Quinn, Michael, 89

Radding, Alan, 103, 211, 250
Rhodes, Wayne L., Jr., 413
Rickard, John, 476
Risley, Ron, 126
Roach, Stephen S., 30
Robbin, Alice, 179, 180
Robertson, Ken, 385, 386
Rockart, John F., 545
Rosenblatt, Frank, 261
Rothfeder, Jeffery, 320
Russell, Bertrand, 261

Saffo, Paul, 480
Sanders, Pat, 63, 64
Savage, J. A., 74, 575
Scheier, Robert L., 518
Schine, Eric, 294
Schkade, Lawrence L., 571
Schlusselberg, Dan, 498
Schneider, Jerry, 391
Schonberg, Harold C., 262
Schrieder, Tari, 593
Schroeder, Roger G., 63
Schwan, Charles, 451
Scofield, Christopher, 284
Sculley, John, 333
Seltzer, William, 118
Shakespeare, William, 132
Shapira, Zur, 331
Sharrott, Lawrence, 450
Shroeder, Roger G., 486
Simon, Herbert, 261

Sims, Calvin, 226, 331
Singer, Penny, 331
Skrinde, Richard, 211
Smith, Adam, 5
Sonnenfeld, Jeffrey, 547, 548
Spirig, John E., 413
Starbuck, William H., 38, 486
Starr, C. V., 508
Steinberg, Mike, 15
Stevens, Lawrence, 250, 591
Stoner, James A., 545
Stout, Larry, 208
Strauss, Howard Jay, 120
Sumner, Mary, 403

Teagan, Mark, 413
Tenner, Edward, 591
Terracciano, Anthony, 546, 548
Thomas, Carol, 377
Tolly, Kevin, 486
Tomczak, Margaret A., 376
Triplett, Sam, 429
Turing, Alan, 256
Turner, Jon A., 38, 63, 284

Vaislopoulos, Audrey, 492, 498
Valukas, Anton, 572
Venkatech, Alladi, 561
Vitalari, Nicholas P., 561
Von Neuman, John, 98

Wade, P. F., 545
Wakely, David, 65
Wallace, Robert G., 75
Wankel, Charles, 545
Watson, Hugh J., 545
Weaver, Paul, 545
Webster, John, 508
Weick, Karl E., 331
Weis, Allan, 89
Weiss, Ira, 331
Westin, Alan F., 331, 591
Whitehead, Alfred North, 261
Whitney, Morgan M., 285
Wiener, Norbert, 260, 261
Williamson, Mickey, 75, 476
Wilson, Wolly, 447
Wirth, Niklaus, 158
Wolff, Edward N., 459, 460, 461, 462, 508
Worth, Brian, 212
Wurts, John S., 274

Yarbrough, Caty, 562
Yarmolich, Paul, 506
Ybarra, Kathryn, 517
Young, Liz, 413

Zaks, Jeffrey M., 181
Zinn, Herbert M. ("Shadow Hawk"), 572, 573

Organization Index

Adapso, 391
Advanced Research Project Agency Network (Arpanet), 574
Aesculys Research Corp., 498
Aetna Life & Casualty Co., 202
Aker Engineering, 509, 510
Alias Research Corp., 505
Amdahl Corp., 476
American Airlines, 146, 425–426, 427, 447
American Cyanamid, 541
American Express, 274, 447
American Federation of State, County, and Municipal Employees (AFSCME), 488
American Management Systems, Inc., 376
American National Standards Institute (ANSI), 204
American President Cos., Ltd., 373
American Stock Exchange, 428, 440
American Telephone & Telegraph (AT&T). *See* AT&T
Ameritech, Mobile Access Data Service of, 90
Ameritrust, 217
Amoco, 67
Annex Research, 500
Annson Systems Division, 59
Apollo Computer, 332
Apple Computer Corp., 26, 97, 129, 206, 233, 326, 333
Arco Oil and Gas Corp., 110
Arizona, University of, 480
Arpanet, 574
Artificial Intelligence Laboratory (MIT), 274
ASEA Corp., 285
Ashton-Tate, 195, 204
Association of PC User Groups, 391
AT&T (American Telephone & Telegraph Co.), 23, 24, 216, 217, 231, 234, 235, 241, 296, 488, 496, 551–552
  Bell Laboratories, 11, 160, 281, 572
Atlantic Bancorp., 250
Atlantic Casualty & Insurance Co., 305, 306
Atmospheric Environment Service (Environment Canada), 455
Atomic Energy of Canada Limited (AECL), 562
Avon Corp., 58

Bank Administration Institute, 571
Bank of America, 140
Baxter Healthcare Corp., 59
Bechtel Group, Inc., 389
Bechtel Software, Inc., 509
Bell Laboratories, 11, 160, 281, 396, 488, 572
BellSouth Corp., 121, 363
Beneficial Data Processing Corp., 580
Benetton, 50, 107, 108
Bergen Brunswig, 392
Block, H & R, 295
Blue Cross/Blue Shield of Massachusetts, 136
BMW, 479, 481–483
Borg Warner Corp., 103, 104
Borland International, Inc., 195, 204
Bristol-Myers Research Institute (Tokyo), 494
Bristol-Myers Squibb, 566
British Telecom, 241
Brodart Company, 437, 439
Budd Co., 59
Budget Rent A Car Corp., 4
Burlington Industries, 144

Caere Corp., 124
Calgary, University of, 476
California Department of Motor Vehicles, 117
California Occupational Safety and Health Administration, 128
Carnegie-Mellon University, 262, 547
Cash n' Carry stores, 429
CBS Records, 244, 245
Center for Research on Information Systems (University of Texas), 569
Central Point Software, 151
Chase Manhattan Bank, 451
Chevron, 67
Chicago Mercantile Exchange, 440–442
Chrysler, 59, 116
Circuit City Stores, Inc., 435–437
Citibank, 67
Citizens and Southern Bank (Atlanta), 452
Claiborne, Liz, 238
Cleveland Public Library, 15
Client Support Center (Exxon Corporate Headquarters, N.Y.), 406

Colgate-Palmolive, 505
Combustion Engineering, Inc. (C-E), 509
Comdisco Disaster Recovery Services, Inc., 581, 592
Communications Workers of America (CWA), 488
Compagnie de Location d'Equipement Cle Ltée., 287
Compaq Computer Corp., 570
Comprehensive Loss Underwriting Exchange, 202
Compression Labs, Inc., 241
CompuServe, 206, 236
Computer Associates, Inc., 165
Computervision, 491
Conagra, Inc., 75
Conservation and Protection Service (Environment Canada), 455
Control Data Corp., 89, 572
Coopers and Lybrand, 269
Covia, 244
Cray Research, 89
Credit Bureaus/Equifax, 557, 558
Cummins Engine Co., 117, 118

Dartmouth College, 158
Data General Corp., 306
Datapoint, 233
Data Switch Corp., 592
Design Core, 505
Digital Equipment Corp. (DEC), 97, 180, 231, 233, 331, 588
Discovery Channel, The, 3, 4
Domino's Pizza, 215, 216
Domtar Canada, 24
Donnelley, R. R., & Sons, 253, 254
Dow Chemical Company, 530
Dow Corning, 297, 567
Dow Jones & Co., 116, 295, 296, 310
Dow Jones News/Retrieval Service, 305, 541
Dun & Bradstreet Corp., 16, 116
Du Pont, 451

Eastman Kodak Company, 376
East Texas Cancer Center, 562
Echlin, Inc., 93
Elco Industries, 431–433
Elkay Corp., 580, 582
Embassy Suite, 227
E-Net Corp., 592
Environment Canada, 455–456, 457
Equifax, Inc., 202
Equitable Life Assurance Society, 487
Exxon, 406

Fannie Mae. *See* Federal National Mortgage Association
Federal Aviation Administration (FAA), 73, 74
Federal Bureau of Investigation (FBI), 353, 464
Federal Express, 151, 171
Federal National Mortgage Association, 58, 59
Federal Savings and Loan Insurance Corp. (FSLIC), 359
First Bankers Corporation of Florida, 250
First Bank System (Minneapolis), 452
First Florida Bank (Tampa), 428, 429
First Railroad and Banking Company of Georgia, 250
First Union Bank of Charlotte, North Carolina, 250, 251
Florida Commercial Banks, Inc., 250
Food and Drug Administration (FDA), 562
Food Emporium, 380
Ford Motor Co., 87, 284, 285
Ford Motor Credit Co., 438
Fox Software, Inc., 175
France Telecom, 241
Future Technology Surveys, 130

Gap, The, 50
General Accounting Office, 571
General Electric (GE), 241, 451, 565, 566
General Electric Information Services, 452
General Motors Corp., 171, 451
Genetech, 165
Geophysical Systems Corp., 320
GM, 116
GM Hughes Electronics, 258
Gold Hill Computers, 269
Goldman Sachs, 524
Grand Union Supermarket, 379–380
GTE, 141
GTE Spacenet, 251

Hampton Inn, 227
Handy Associates, Inc., 547
Hanes, 7
Harbinger Computer Services, 452
Harrah's Hotel, 243
Harris Corp., 159
  Information Systems Department of, 397
Harvard Business School, 547, 548
Heath and Sons, L. S., 23
Henry Ford Hospital, 123
Hewlett-Packard, 263, 287, 288, 331, 332
  ChemStation, 499
Hilton Hotels, 6, 8, 12, 67
Hitachi America Telecommunications, 231
Holiday Corp., 225, 227
Honda/Acura, 116
Honeywell, Inc., 24, 517
Houston Lighting & Power, 274
Hughes Aircraft Co., 519

IBM, 11, 89, 96, 97, 98, 104, 157, 197, 204, 217, 223, 233, 331, 373, 427, 447, 496, 500
  Color Graphics Center of, 407
  Information Systems Productivity Center of, 406, 407
Illinois Bell, 561, 581, 582
Index Group, 539
Indianapolis Water Co., 208
Institute for Research on Poverty, 179
Intel Corp., 100, 233, 277
Interactive Data Corp., 206
Internal Revenue Service, 464
International Business Machines Corp. *See* IBM
International Data Corp., 93
International Resources, 23
International Standards Organization, 223
IRA, Inc., 571
ITT, 493
ITT Hartford Insurance Group, 202

Johnson, S. C., & Son Corp., 142
Jones, Edward D., & Co., 206
Juniper Lumber Company, Ltd., 532–536

Kaiser Electronics, 175, 176
Kennestone Regional Oncology Center, 562
Kenworth, 434
Klopman Fabrics, 401
K mart Corporation, 242
Knight-Ridder, Inc., 295
Kodak, 286
Kurzweil Computer Products, Inc., 123

La Petite Boulangerie, 527
La Ruche Picarde, 527
L'eggs Brands, Inc., 60
LGS Group, Inc., 385
Library of Congress, 280
Little Company of Mary Hospital (LCM), Evergreen Park, IL, 59
Lockheed Corp., 80, 539–541
Lockheed-Georgia, 513–514, 540
Loma Linda University, 95
Lotus Development Corp., 204, 296

Maimonides Medical Center, 335–336, 340–343

Maine Department of Education, 169
Mammouth hypermarkets, 527
Management Sciences of America, Inc., 402
Manpower, Inc., 236, 237
Manufacturers Hanover, 274
Marathon Oil, 44
Marine Midland Bank, 452
Martin Marietta Corp., 201
Massachusetts Institute of Technology (MIT), 260, 261, 575, 588
  Artificial Intelligence Laboratory of, 274
MasterCard, 237, 424, 425, 551
McCord Winn, 40
McCormack & Dodge, 400
McDonnell Douglas, 470
  Information Services, 452
MCI, 231, 234, 235, 551
McKain, 90
Mead Data Central, 205, 257, 295
Mellon Bank Corporation, 547, 548
Mercer, William M., Inc., 389
Merrill Lynch, 409
Metaphor Computer Systems, 373
Microsoft Corp., 11, 204, 326
Milton Roy, analytical products division of, 319
Mitel, 231
Mobil Oil, 462
Moody's Investor Services, 16
Morgan Guaranty, 524
Motorola, 277
Mrs. Fields Cookies, 527–530

National Center for Computer Crime Data, 572
National Parks Service (Environment Canada), 455
National Science Foundation, 130
Nester, Inc., 277
Neuron Data Corp., 269
New Jersey Division of Motor Vehicles, 405
New Mexico Department of Human Services, 487
Newspaper Guild, 487
New York Life, 33, 34
New York Mercantile Exchange, 441
New York State Department of Motor Vehicles, 301, 302, 305, 311
New York Stock Exchange, 440
New York Telephone Co., 225
New York Transit Authority, 397
NeXT, Inc., 131
Nielsen, A. C., 16
North Carolina, University of, 121
Northrop Corp., 46, 48, 470
Northwest Digital Research, 171
Northwestern Financial Corp., 250
Novo-Nordisk AIS, 501–502, 504
NTX Communications Corp., 592

Office & Professional Employees International Union (OPEI), 487
O'Hare International Airport, 244, 245
Ohio Bell, 186, 224
Ontario Hydro Power System, 211, 212
Oracle Corp., 195
Orkand Corp., 571
Overland Park, 377

Panhandle Eastern Corp., 220
Penney, J. C., 234, 235
Pepperidge Farm Corp., 423–424, 425
Pepsi Cola, 306, 333
Peterbilt, 434
Philadelphia National Bank, 67
Phillips Petroleum Co., 66, 75
Pitney Bowes Credit Corp., 347
Price, Waterhouse, 360
Princeton University, 120
Prudential-Bache Securities, Inc., 592
Putnam Fund, 206

Quaker Oats, 41
Quotron, 116, 206

Relay and Telecommunications Division (Westinghouse Electric Corp.), 271
Research Triangle Institute, 180
Reuters Holdings P.S.C., 440, 441
Reynolds and Reynolds Company, The, 116
RJR Nabisco, 451
Robbins Air Force Base, 572–573
Robotics and Automation Consulting Center, 285
Rockwell International, 10, 127
Rohm Corp., 473
RSA Data Security, Inc., 588
Ryder Systems, Inc., 293, 294, 305

S&ME, Inc., 516
Seagram Company, Ltd., 63, 64
Sears, Roebuck & Company, 451
Second Skin Swimwear, Inc., 30, 31
Securities Industry Automation Corp., 428
Security Pacific National Bank, 194
Seismograph Service Corp., 320
Selectronic Services of Chicago, 253, 254
Services Employees International Union, 487
Shell Oil, 67
Shoprite, 380
Singapore Futures Exchanges, 441
Smith, A. O., Automotive Products Company, 299, 300, 305, 310, 311, 316
Social Security Administration, 109
Software Publishers Association, 391
Software 2000 Inc., 439
Sogi Informatique Ltée., 287
Southern Bancorporation, Inc., 250
Spring, 231, 551
Stanford Resources, Inc., 120
Strategic Air Command, 327
Sungard Disaster Recovery Services, 581, 592
Sun Microsystems, 95, 305, 331, 332
Sybase Corp., 131
Symbolics, Inc., 274
System Center, Inc., 592

Tandem Computers, Inc., 409, 410
Telephone and Data Systems, Inc., 302
Texas Commerce Bank, 472
Texas Instruments, 144, 233, 277, 285
Texas, University of, 569
Textron, Inc., 40
Thorn EMI PLC, 546
Toro Company, 491
TrackData Corp., 225
Trans Union, 557, 558
Travelers Corp., The, 35, 426
TRW, 289, 305, 324, 327, 556, 557, 558, 576

Union Pacific Railroad, 240
Unisys Corp., 189, 401
United Airlines, 244, 245, 246, 427
United Data Services, 377
United Illuminating, 232
United Parcel Service (UPS), 594, 595, 596, 597
United Refrigerated Services, Inc., 242
United States government. *See also* individual listings
  Air Force, 130, 327
  Census Bureau, 179, 208, 460, 492, 494
  Coast Guard, 413, 414
  Defense Department, 139, 140, 158, 305, 322
  General Accounting Office (GAO), 73
  Geological Survey, 208
  House Armed Services Committee, 139
  House of Representatives, 391
  Interior Department, 455
  Internal Revenue Service, 464
  Justice Department, 216, 352, 353
  Labor Department, 128, 460
  Labor Statistics Bureau, 457, 492, 494
  Navy, 470
  Treasury Department, 451

United Telecom, 377
United Way, 514
Universities. *See* university by state name
US Air, 315
USPA, Inc., 571

Vancouver Stock Exchange, 135
Verity Corp., 257
Visa, 551
Vons Companies, 22, 23

Wells Fargo, 65, 66, 67, 68, 69
Westinghouse Electric Corporation, 3, 4, 273, 516
Wetterau Incorporated, 198
Weyerhaeuser, 30
Windows/Presentation Manager Association, 391
World Data Center of California, 425

Xerox Corporation, 127, 136, 233
Xerox PARC (Palo Alto Research Center), 373

Yale, 278

Subject Index

Access control software, 223
Accounting and financial systems, 437–442
Accounts payable system, 437
Accounts receivable system, 52–54, **437**
Ada, 158–159, 166
Address, 78
ADRS/Business Graphics, 407
ADS-Online, 165
Advanced-warning radar system, 139
AEGIS system, 25
AI. *See* Artificial intelligence
Airline Control Program/Transaction Processing Facility (ACP/TPF), 447
Airline industry, 459
Airline reservations system, 146, 424–427
Air traffic control, and computer overloads, 73–74
Aldus Pagemaker, 170
Algorithm, 185
Allocation of resources, by command language translator, 145
Amdahl Corporation products, Project/2, 476
American economy, transformation of, 457–459
American National Standards Institute (ANSI), 83
Analog signal, 218
Andersen Consulting products, 417–418, 419
ANSI, 83
Answer*Net reservations system, 6, 8, 12
APL, 165
Apollo Reservation System, 244–246, 427
Apollo workstation, 132
Apple products. *See also* Macintosh
  Appletalk, 233
  LaserWriter, 127
  Macintosh, 97, 115, 465
Appletalk, 233
Applicant tracking systems, 443
Application controls, 577
  and data security, 581–583, 584
  and electronic vaults, 592–593
Application generator, 164, 404
Application solution, 337
Applications software, 141, 143
Applications software package, 165–169
  microcomputer, 167–169
Architects, and CAD, 506
Arcnet, 233
Arithmetic-logic unit (ALU), 77, **78**
Arpanet Sendmail program, 575
Art, and CAD, 505
Artificial intelligence (AI), 255
  in business, 253–285
  fields of study in, 256
Artificial intelligence shell, 269
  and Ford Motor Co., 285
Artificial reality, 496–497
  and drug design, 501–502
ASCII (American Standard Code for Information Interchange), **83,** 84, 483
Assembler, 143
Assembly language, 142, 153–154
Asynchronous transmission, 219, 220
AT&T Mail, 238
AT&T products
  Signaling System 7 (SS7), 551–552
  6300, 382
  3B1, 175
  3B2/400, 175–176
ATM, 266–267. *See also* Automated teller machine
Attribute, 183
Audio Distribution System, 481
Audit, of traditional system, 389
Autographix graphics workstations, 95
Automated ordering service, 215–216
Automated teller machine (ATM), 429
Automation
  of information work, 464–479
  office, 455–488
  and Seagram's sales force, 63–64
Automobile companies, 59
Automobile insurance, databases and, 202
Automobile makers, and Smith, A. O., problem solving, 299–300

Backup tapes, 469
Backward reasoning, 270–271
Bandwidth, 227
Bank card, in supermarkets, 23

A boldface entry and page number indicates a key term and the page number on which its definition can be found.

Banking, 440
  and electronic bill paying, 451–452
  electronic vaults for, 592–593
  mainframe applications in, 358–364
  VSAT network in, 250–251
  and WEBS system, 65–67, 68
Banks, telecommunications systems in, 217
Bar code, 123
  in retailing, 107–108
Baseband products, 233
BASIC (Beginner's All-purpose Symbolic Instruction Code), 143, **158,** 160, 166
Basic business systems, 424–425
  building, 446–447
  examples of, 429–446
  features of, 425–429
Batch input and processing, 118, 119
Baud, 226
Baxter Healthcare Management Services Division, 59
Behavior theories of management, 518–522, **520**
Bellcore, 275–277
Benefits systems, 443
Billing system, patient, 349–352
Bill-of-materials system, 45–49
Binary system, 81–83
Bit, 81, 110, 182, 219
Bit mapping, 129
Bits per second (BPS), 226
Blue collar occupations, 458
Bottom-up approach, 259, 260
  neural networks and, 275
Bpi (bytes per inch), 109
BPS Graphics, 163
Brain, neural networks and, 275, 276
Brokerage industry, 409–410
B-2 bomber, 48
Buffer, 127
Bugs, and software industry, 391
Bulletin board system, 244
Bureaucracy
  and manager's environment, 523–524
  and problem solving, 311
Burroughs Corporation products, Model 3955 mainframe, 342
Business
  components of, 34–40
  major functions of, 36, 37
  office roles in, 465–468
  organization levels in, 37–38
  organizing new, 38
Business environment, 38–40
Business functions, 36
Business/information systems. *See also* Information systems
  basic, 423–452
  and competitive advantage, 55–61
  components of, 8–12
  examples of, 44–45
  functional, 42–44
  uses of, 32–64
Business interface, 394
Business organization, 34–35
Business problem analysis, 293–333
Bus network, 228–230
Byte, 78, 182

C, 160, 162, 166
CAD (computer-aided design), 205, 501
  and plastics processing factory, 509–510
  at Weyerhaeuser, 30
CAD/CAM (computer-aided design/computer-aided manufacturing) workstation, 501
Caere Corporation products, Parallel Page Reader, 125
Calculators, 464
Canada, office automation in Environment Canada, 455–456
Capacity planning, 305–308
Careers
  educational requirements for, 60–61
  in information systems, 18, 19
  skills for, 19, 20
Cartographic data, 208
CASE, 376–377, 416–419
Cash management systems, 439–440
Caucus, 479
CD-ROM (Compact Disk/Read-Only Memory), 116, 117–118, 470
Cellular telephone, 4
  and laptop computer, 90
Central processing unit (CPU), 76–77
  components of, 77–80
Centrex system, 217
C5-B, 513
Change agents, knowledge workers as, 495–496
Channel, 220–221
Character printer, 125
Charitable contribution deduction system, 443–446
Checkless society, 286
Checks
  and electronic bill paying, 451–452
  and MICR, 122
Chemical vapor deposition (CVD), 86
ChemStation, 499
Chess, Hitech machine and, 262
Chips, 77
  microprocessor, 94
  superchips, 99
CLARA (Computerized Legal Research Aid), 502
Clearing system, 442
Clerical employees, computerization and, 565
Client tracking, 360
Clothing industry, Benetton system in, 107–108
Coaxial cable, 224
COBOL (COmmon Business-Oriented Language), 143, **155**–**157,** 166
Codes, 149
  machine and assembly language, 154
Coding schemes, 83
Combinatorial explosion, 262–263
Command language translator, 145
Communication, letters and, 3
Communications network, 470
Communications satellites, 225, 226
Communications technologies, office, 472–474
Compact disk, 116
COMPAQ products
  Deskpro personal computers, 306
  personal computers, 472
  Portable III, 181
Competitive strategies
  basic, 57
  and business information systems, 55–61
Compiler, 149, 150
Complex industries, 312
CompuServe, 236
CompuServe Forums, 309
Computed tomography (CT), 498
Computer-aided design. *See* CAD
Computer-aided software engineering (CASE), 376–377, 416–419
Computer-based information systems (CBIS), 7
Computer conferences, 11
Computer crime, 560, 569–576, **570**
  major types of, 574
  security and, 570–572
Computer dependence, 561
Computer failure, 571, 572
Computer hardware, 11, 74–104
  generations of, 83–86
Computer-integrated manufacturing (CIM) systems, 431
Computer Integrated Telephony (CIT) project, 231
Computer literacy, 13
Computer Matching and Privacy Act (1988), 559
Computer mouse, 121
Computers, 76
  classification of, 87–89
  concepts and components of, 76–89
  and intimate computing, 326
  and language translation, 130
  in offices, 465
  storage capacity of, 81–82

time, size, and processing power of, 80–81
value of, 26
Computer software, 11–12
Computer systems
choosing suppliers of, 320
conversion strategy for new, 328
downsizing of, 103–104
hardware components of, 76
vs. information systems, 12–13
malfunction of, 551–552, 562
overloaded, 73–74
social and organizational impact of, 550–593
Computer systems application
at Maimonides Medical Center, 335–336, 340–342, 343
to patient billing system, 349–352
Computer track ball, 121
Computer virus, 574–576
combating, 576
Computer Virus Act (1989), 391
Computerworld Magazine, 538
Concentrator, 222
Connection Machines, 295
Consumer credit, 556
Context diagram, of patient billing system, 366
Continuous-feed paper, 135
Control constructs, of structured programming, 372
Controls, 577, 583–587. *See also* Data security
application, 581–583
design of, 323, 325
Control system, at Pepperidge Farm, 423–424
Control bits, 219
Controller, 222
Control totals, 583, 585
Control unit, 78
Conversion strategy, 328
Cooperative processing, 93
Coordinator, The, 478–479
CORA (Customer Order Relaying Assistant), 271–273
Cost-benefit analysis, 320
Cost-effectiveness, 319–321
Covia Open Systems Manager software, 244–246
CPM (Critical Path Method), 151, 152, 476
CPU, 108
memory capacity of, 149
Cray supercomputers, 99
Credit bureaus, and information privacy, 556–557
Credit information systems, 435
Credit report, errors in, 558
Credit verification, disruption in, 551–552
Critical thinking, 293–333, **299**
CRT (cathode ray tube), **128**
Culture
and manager's environment, 523–524
and problem solving, 310–311
Currency Management: Millenium, 400
Customer credit information systems, 435
Customer service representatives, 567
Customization, 400–401, 402
Cycles, machine, 79
Cylinder, 112

Data, 14
nuclear accelerator theory of, 16
organizational terms and concepts, 181–183
in traditional file environment, 183
Data automation. *See* Source data automation
Database, 182, 257. *See also* Database management system
and auto insurance, 202
design of, 323, 324
distributed, 203
in DSS, 530, 531
for electric utilities, 212
financial, 116
and intelligent search machine, 280–281
partitioned, 203–205
problem-solving matrix for, 201
problems with, 308–309
replicated, 203
Database approach, 188–197
and problem solving, 197–201
Database design, 198–200
Database management system (DBMS), 189–192
models of, 192–197
Database software, 180
Database system, at Department of Justice, 353
Data definition language, 190
Data dictionary, 191–192, 368–369
Data dumps, 204
Data Encryption Standard (DES), 578
Data entry, traditional, 118–120
Data entry screens, and prototyping, 395
Data flow, 365
Data flow diagram, 364–368
symbols, 365
zero-level and first-level, 367
Data General products, MV 4000, 306
Data hierarchy, 182
Data management software, 168
Data management technology, 474
Data manipulation tool, 190
Data redundancy, 187
Data security, 577–578
application controls and, 581–583
and multiple computer centers, 582
Data storage. *See* Storage
Data transmission, 217–220
Dataword length, 93
Data worker, 460–461
dBase III, 444
dBase III Plus, 200, 342, 351, 352, 397
dBase IV, 169, 195, 200, 351, 352, 474
DB2, 204
Decimal system, 82
Decisional rules, 521
Decision making, 297, 317–321
Decision support system (DSS), 515, 525, 530–536
at Juniper Lumber, Ltd., 532–536
DEC. *See* Digital Equipment Corporation products
Dedicated lines, 234
Demodulation, 218
Design
fast-tracking approach to, 385–386
structured, 371–372
DESIGN/1, 417
Designs
logical, 322–324
physical, 324–325
Desktop publishing, 170, **471**–472
Dialcom, 238
Dictionary, data, 368–369
Digital envelopes, 588–589
Digital Equipment Corporation (DEC) products
PDP 11/44 minicomputer, 107–108
Vax 780, 540
Vax 785, 502
Vaxcluster, 201
Vax minicomputers, 97
Digital revolution, 464
Digital signal, 218
Digital signal processors, 493
Digital transmission modes, 218–220
Digitized images, 124–125
Direct-access storage device (DASD), 111, 113
Direct cutover, 328
Direct file organization, 183–184, 185, 186
Disaster recovery plan, 579–581
Discovery Channel, 3
Disk
floppy, 113–115, 116
hard, 111–112
magnetic, 111–115
optical, 116
systems, 112
Disk access time, 112

Disk-stored document, 469
DISOSS (Distributed Office Support System), 465, 481
Display Write, 237, 481
Distilled spirits industry, 63–64
Distributed database, 203
Distributed processing, 91–92
  linking computer network, 92
Distributed work, 561
Distribution system, prototype of, 392
Documentation, 578
  process specifications as, 367, 368
  and security, 578–579, 580
  and system solution, 327–328
Document management technology, 469
DOS, 151
Dot-matrix printer, 125
Double-sided disk, 115
Dow Jones newspaper clipping service, 541
Downloading, 92
Downsizing, 92, 103–104
Drugs, design of, 501–502, 504
Dunn & Bradstreet Credit Report, 16
Due process, 555

EasyLink, 238
EBCDIC (Extended Binary Coded Decimal Interchange Code), **83,** 84, 109, 110, 483
Economy, transformation of American, 457–459
Electric utilities, database system for, 212
"Electronic army," 309
Electronic bill payment, 451–452
Electronic bulletin board, 11, 244
Electronic calendars, 482
Electronic communities, 11
Electronic data interchange (EDI), 67, **241**–243
Electronic mail (E-mail), 3, 11, 69, **238**–240
  at BMW, 482
  software for, 360
Electronic reservation system, 425–427
Electronic spreadsheet software, 168
Electronic trading, on Chicago Mercantile Exchange, 440–442
Electronic vaults, 592–593
Electrostatic plotter, 127
E-mail. *See* Electronic mail
Employee involvement program, 300
Employees. *See also* Human resources
  involvement of, 313, 315–316
  training of, 313, 315, 347, 377
Enable, 169
Encryption, 578, 588
Engineering, and CAD, 505
Engineering workstation, at Toro Company, 491–492
Entity, 182, 183
Entrepreneurs, 38
Environment, 9–10, 38–40
  and problem solving, 310–312
EPROM (erasable programmable read-only memory), **80**
Epson products, FX-286, 382
Equal Employment Opportunity (EEO), 443
Ergonomics, 9–10, 313–314
Error control software, 223
ESS, American Cyanamid use of, 541
Ethernet, 228–230, 233
European Community, Quaker Oats and, 41
Execution cycle (E-cycle), **78,** 79
Executive information system (EIS), 536
Executive support systems (ESS), 515, **516,** 536–541
Expert systems, 259, 263–273
  building, 271, 272–274
  components of, 264–271
  limitations of, 273
  production rules in, 266
  role of, 271
External constraints, 318–319
External knowledge base, 495
External news services, 540

Facilities management and maintenance, with CAD, 509–510
Facsimile (FAX) machine, 4, **240,** 469
Factory design, with CAD, 509–510
Fair Credit Reporting Act (1970), 558
Fannie May Loan Stratification Service, 58–59
Farm Credit Program, 91
Farm Journal, 193
Fast-tracking approach, to solution design, 385–386
Fault-tolerant computer systems, 428
Feasibility, of problem-solving solutions, 318–319, 320
Feedback, 5–6, 260–261
Fiber optics, 224
Field, 182
Fields Software Group, 528
Fifth generation computers, 98–99
File, 182
File organization, 181, 183–185
File server, 232
File Talk, 414
Finance and accounting function, 36, **50–53**
  information systems, 52
Financial databases, 116
Financial futures trading, 441–442
Financial Manager™, The, 474, 475
Financial systems, 437–442
Finite element analysis (FEA), 491–492
Firm, functional areas of, 466–467
First generation computers (1951–1958), 83–85
First generation software, 142
First-level data flow diagram, 367
Flat organizations, 37–38
Flat panel display, 129
Floppy disk, 113–115, 116
  sector method on, 115
  storage capabilities of, 116
Flowchart
  program, 374, 375
  system, 369–370
Focalpoint, 246
FOCUS Table Talk, 414
Food products, Pepperidge Farm, 423–424
Forbes building, fire in, 581
ForComment, 478
Formal systems, 7
FORTRAN (FORmula TRANslator), 143, **154**–155, 166
Fortune 1000 companies, 538
Forward reasoning, 269
FOUNDATION, 417
  Data Modeller, 417
  INSTALL/1, 418
  METHOD/2, 418, 419
Fourth-generation development, 390
Fourth-generation language, 162–165, 166
Fourth-generation software, 143–144
Fourth-generation systems development, 401–409
  examples of, 403
  software tools, 403–404
Fourth-generation technology (1979–present), 86
Foxbase, 168, 474
Foxbase +, 195
Frames, 267, 268
Framework, 169
Freedom, 555
Freedom of Information Act (1966), 557
Freestyle system, 288
Front-end processor, 221–222
Full-duplex transmission, 219, 221
Full Impact presentation graphics software, 170
Functional business systems, 42–44
Future Perfect, 546

Gantt chart, 419
Gatorade, 41
General Accounting Office, 25
General controls, 577
General detail information system (GDIS), 414

General Ledger: Millenium, 400
General ledger systems, 437
Genetic engineering, 501–502
Geographical Information Systems (GIS), 208
Geographic information systems, 169–171
Gigabyte, 81
Globex financial system, 441–442
Goods industries, 459
Goods work, 461
Government agencies, and software package solutions, 397
Graphical user interface, 152
Graphics Forum, 309
Graphics language, 163, 404
GraphPlan, 163
GRiDPAD, 287
Groupware, 474, 477–479
  at University of Arizona, 480

Hacker, 572
Half-duplex transmission, 219, 221
Hard copy, 45, 47
Hard disk, 111–112
  systems, 112
Hardware. *See also* Computer hardware
  computer, 11
  design of, 325
  systems software, application software, 143
  and system solution, 327
Harris Corporation products
  8300 Integrated Newspaper System, 289
  Night Hawk computer system, 159
Harvard Graphics, 163
Hashing algorithm, 185
Heuristics, 263
Hewlett-Packard products
  ChemStation, 499
  HP 3000 minicomputers, 435
  Laserjet Plus, 127
  modeling software, 171
  New Wave environment, 287, 288
Hierarchical database model, 192–194
Hierarchy, 36
Higgins, 478
High-level language, 142
Hilton Answer*Net reservations system, 6, 8, 12
Hitech, 262
Hospitals
  Maimonides Medical Center records management problem, 335–336
  University Hospital's Charitable Contribution Deduction System, 443–446
Host computer, 221–222

Human resources, 35, 36
  and problem solving, 313–317
  strategic issues in, 313–317
Human resources function, 54–55
Human resources systems, 442–446
  payroll systems as, 439
  and prototyping, 395
HyperCard, 206–209, 267
HyperTalk, 207
Hypertext, 206

IBM products
  AS/400 system, 439
  AT, 465
  at BMW, 481–482
  Cross System Product, 386
  DB2, 195
  DISOSS, 465
  and DOS, 151, 152
  4341 mainframe, 103
  4381 mainframe, 439
  43XX series, 400
  IMS (Information Management System), 193–194
  IMS Fast path, 194
  and Information Systems Productivity center, 407
  laser printers, 135
  9370 computer, 117
  and OS/2, 151, 152
  Personal Computer, 96
  Personal Computer AT, 414
  Personal System 2/Model 70 microcomputer, 94
  Personal System/2 series, 96
  Professional Office System, 75, 234
  PROFS, 465
  Series/1, 234
  701, 83
  SNA, 465
  Systems Network Architecture (SNA), 223, 234
  System/38, 103, 424, 527
  3480 tape storage, 593
  3090 mainframe, 94
  30XX series, 400
  Token Ring Network, 230, 233
  in tracking system, 444
  workstations, 500
  XT computers, 465, 539
Icons, 152–153
Image processing, 124–125
Impact printer, 125, 135
Implementation, 297
IMS (Information Management System), 193–194
Income and tax liability, spreadsheet software and, 353–358
Index, 185

Indexed sequential-access method (ISAM), 184
Inference engine, 269, 270
Infonet, 238
Informal structure, 36
Information, 14
  organizing, 178–212
  privacy of personal, 556–561
Informational roles, 521
Information and knowledge economy, 457
Information and knowledge workers, 459–464
Information centers, 406–409
Information clearinghouse, 67
Information Express, 67
Information industries, 459
Information services, Dow Jones on-line database as, 295
Information storage technology, 108–118
  magnetic disk, 111–115
  magnetic tape, 109–111
  optical disk technology, 116–118
Information system (IS), **4**–**5**
  activities of, 6
  alternatives to, 384–415
  approaches to studying, 12–16
  in business, 5–8
  business placement of, 40–44
  business uses of, 32–64
  components of, 8–12
  computerized, 6–7
  designing solutions for, 335–383
  formal, 7
  informal, 7
  as management aid, 525
  purpose of studying, 16–19
  purposes of, 40–41
  role of in firm, 43
  safeguarding, 576–587
  skills for, 18–19
  sociotechnical view of, 17
  software for, 139–176
  threats to computerized, 569–570, 572
  vulnerability of, 569
Information systems literacy, 13, 14
Information technologies, 74–75
  senior management and, 538
  trends in, 97
Information work, 457. *See also* Knowledge and information work
Information workers, distribution of, 461–462, 463
Ingres database, 212
  software, 180
Ink-jet printer, 126
Input, 5, 6
  designing, 323, 325

Input and output devices, 76, 108–136
Input controls, 582
Input/output (IO) bus width, 93
Input technology, 118–125
Installation stage, of systems life cycle, 389
INSTALL/1, 418
Instruction cycle (I-cycle), **78,** 79
Instruction execution constructs, 372
Insulin, 504
Insurance companies, information systems in, 33–34
Integrated business system, 75
Integrated circuit technology, 85, 464
Integrated Services Digital Network (ISDN), 223, **243**–244
Integrated software package, 169
Intellect, 163, 164
Intelligent database search machine, 280–281
Intelligent devices, 221
Intelligent machines, 259
Intel products
  8088 microprocessor, 93–94
  80286 chip, 94
  80386 microprocessor, 94, 281
  80486 chip, 94
  i860 microprocessor™, 99
  Micro 2000 chip, 100
  N-10 microprocessor, 99
Interactive PC Link, 400
Interest rates, and mainframe computer applications, 359–364
Interface, graphical user, 152
International marketing, 41
Internet, 587
Interpersonal roles, 521
Interpreter, 149
Interviews, 302
ITT products, digital signal processors, 493

Japan
  and employee involvement, 315
  productivity in, 22
"Johnsonizing," 142
Jot program, 131
Juniper Lumber Information System (JLIS), 532–538

Key field, 183
Keypunch, 118–120
Key-to-disk machine, 120
Key-to-tape machine, 120
Kilobyte, 81
Knowledge, 14
Knowledge and data workers, 37
Knowledge- and information-intense products, 458–459
Knowledge and information systems, building challenges, 505–507
Knowledge and information work
  office automation and, 454–488
  professional work systems and, 490–510
Knowledge base, 264–266
Knowledge engineer, 265, **267**–269
Knowledge-level sales and marketing organizations, 49–50
Knowledge systems, 43, 46, 49, 50, 52, 55
Knowledge work, 460, 461, 463
  characteristics of, 494
  workers' roles, 495
Knowledge workers, list of, 501
Knowledge workers' roles in business, 495
Knowledge workstations, 498–499
Knowledge work systems, 496–499
  general requirements of, 497
Kodak products, KIMS, 286

Labor force. *See also* Workers
  changes in, 458–459, 460
  information and knowledge workers in, 459–464
  office workers in, 461–462
Labor unions, and office automation, 486–488
Languages
  computer, 142–144
  natural, 256–257
  programming, 153–165
Language translation, 130, 149, 150
LANs. *See* Local area network
Laptop computer, 75, 90, 91
Laser optical disk, 116
Laser printer, 125–**126,** 473
Law
  CLARA system for, 502–503
  LIBRA system for, 503
Law firm, spreadsheet application at, 353–358
LCD printers, 473
LED printers, 473
Legal and regulatory compliance, and human resources, 313, 316–317
Legal research service, 205
Legal research workstations, 501
Legislation
  and information privacy, 557–560
  and software industry, 391
Letter-quality printer, 125
Letters, 3
LEXIS, 205, 257
Liability, 553
LIBRA (Legal Integrated Brief Research Assistant), 503
Life cycle, traditional systems, 386–391
Light-emitting diode (LED) printer, 125, 473
Light pen, 121
Line printer, 125
Liquid crystal shutter (LCD) printer, 125–126, 473
Lisp (List Processing language), 269, 273, 274
Local area networks (LANs), 204, **232**–233, 244, 287, 472–474, 518–519
Logical design, 303, 322–324
  at Maimonides Medical Center, 341
  scope of, 338
Logical view, 188
Logical theorist, 261–262
Lotus Development Corporation products
  Lotus Notes, 360
  One Source, 296
  1-2-3®, 168, 397, 405

Machine control systems, 430
Machine cycle, 78, 79
Machine language, 142
Machine language code, 154
Macintosh, 465
  Appletalk network for, 233
  HyperCard, 206–209
  operating system of, 151, 152
Magnetic disk, 111–115
Magnetic ink character recognition (MICR), 122
Magnetic tape, 109
  data storage on, 110
Mailbox, 78
Mainframe, 87
  future of, 98
  graphics language for, 163
  office systems based on, 465
Main memory, 77
Maintenance Control Management System, 198
Management
  behavioral theory of, 518–522
  educating, 538
  functions of, 517
  improved, 60
  levels of, 37–38
  and problem solving, 311
Management controls, 577
Management information systems (MIS), 515, 525, 527–530
  at Mrs. Field's Cookies, 527–530
Management plan, 524
Management support systems, 43, 513–548
  challenges to building, 541–543
  types of, 515

Management workstations, 501
Managers
environment of, 523–524
functions of, 516–525
in future, 546–548
and information, 522–523
and information technology, 525
roles of, 520–522
Managing, 516
Manual system, 10
Manufacturing and production function, 44–49
information system for, 46
Manufacturing and production systems, 429–433
Manufacturing resource planning (MRP-II) systems, 431
Maps. *See* Geographical information systems
Marketing
international, 41
and sales, 49–50
Marketing and selling, as business function, 367
Marketing strategies, 58
Marketing systems, 434–437
MASTIR (Mortgage-backed Accounting and Securities Trading Information Retrieval), 409
McCormack & Dodge products, customizable software of, 400
MCI Mail, 238
Medical resonance imaging (MRI), 498
Medicine, computers in, 498, 562
Megabyte, 81
Megahertz (MHz), 93
Memory, 79–80
main, 77
and virtual storage, 149
Metaphor software, 373
METHOD/1, 418, 419
Microcomputer, 87–88, 89–97
application packages, 167–169
choosing operating system for, 150–153
in DSS, 532
Microcomputer security, 587
Microfilm and microfiche, 129
Microprocessor, 86
generations of, 94
Microprocessor technology, 93–94
Microsecond, 81
Microsoft products, Bookshelf, 116
Microsoft Word, 167
Microsoft WORKS, 169
Microwave systems, **225**
Middle management, 37
MIDS (Management Information Decision Support), 513
at Lockheed-Georgia, 539–541
Military
and Ada, 158–159
Coast Guard personnel tracking, 413–415
and perceptive systems, 258–259
and Stealth bomber development, 48
and technology, 24–25
Millisecond, 81
Minicomputer, 87
MIPS, 85
Model base, 531
Modeling, workstations, 501
Modem, 218, 219
Modular programming, 373
Modulation, 218
Module, 371
Monitoring software, 146
Moody's Investor Services, 16
More/2, 253–254
Mortgages, and mainframe computer applications, 359–364
Mortgage underwriting, neural network, 277–278
Motorola products, 68000, 68020, 68030, 68040 chips, 94
Mouse, computer, 121
MS-DOS, 151, 152
MultiFinder, 152
MultiMate, 167
Multiplan, 168
Multiple Neural Network Decision System, 278
Multiple output technology, 127
Multiplexer, 222
Multiprocessing, 148
Multiprogramming, 146–147
Multitasking, 147

Nanosecond, 81
Nantucket Corporation products, Clipper as, 342
Natural language, 256–257
NCR products, 141, 527
9300, 9400, 9500, 215
Nestor products
mortgage underwriting neural network, 277–278
Multiple Neural Network Decision System, 278
NetWire, 309
Network
communications, 470
digital envelopes for, 587–588
neural, 259
telecommunications, 227–237
Network control software, 223
Network database model, 194–195
Network gateway, 232
Network technology, 286–287
Network topology, 227–230
Neural network, 259, 275–277
News services, 540
Newswire coverage, 360
New York State Motor Vehicles Office, 301–303
NEXIS, 257
Nexpert Object, 269
NEXRAD system, 189
NeXT Computer, 117, 129–132, 373
1984, 555
NLQ products, printer, 382
Nomad2, 163, 164, 165
Nonfinancial institutions, 452
Nonimpact printer, 125, 135–136
NonStop SQL, 409, 410
Nonswitched lines, 234
Nonvolatile memory, **80**
Nuclear accelerator theory of data, 16
Numerical control systems, 430

Object code, 149, 150
Object-oriented programming software (OOPS), 373
Occupations, blue- and white-collar, 458
Off-campus housing, design project for, 380–381
Office activities, 468–477, **469**
Office automation
at BMW, 479–483
at Environment Canada, 455–456
of information work, 464–479
systems, 455–488
union role in, 486–488
Office data management technology, 474
Office roles, 465–468
Offices
communications technology in, 472–474
functions of, 468
systems in, 468–477
Office scheduling technology, 474
Office workers, as information workers, 461–462
Olympics, project management for, 476
One Source, 296
On-line database, 205, 295
services, 206
On-line input, 118, 119
On-line real-time processing, 118, 119
On-line transaction processing (OLTP), 427
OOPS (object-oriented programming software), 373
Open Systems Interconnection (OSI), 223
Operating system, 144–148
microcomputer, 150–153

Operational systems, 43–44, 46, 50, 52, 55
Operations, improved, 60
Operations Management courses, 48–49
OPTI-III™ automated optical inspection system, 258
Optical character recognition (OCR), 122, 123, 124
Optical disk, 116, 342, 343
storage, at Maimonides Medical Center, 340–342, 343
storage technology, 336
Optical scanners, 342
Oracle, 180, 195, 201
Order processing program, structure chart for, 371
Order processing systems, 435
Order system, at Pepperidge Farm, 423–424
Organizational impacts, 554
work issues, 563–569
Organizational problem-solving perspectives, 305, 309–312
Organizational pyramid, 37
Organizational structure, computers and, 566–569
Organization perspective, 299
Organizations, and information systems, 8–9
OS/2® (Operating System/2), 151, 152
Output, 5, 6
designing, 322, 325
Output controls, 582
Output devices, 76–77
Output technology, 125–129

Packet switching, 236
Page printer, 125
Paper glut, 335–336
"Paperless" age, 286–289
Paperwork, and computers, 568
Paradox, 169, 195, 474
Parallel conversion, 328
Parallel processing, 88
Parallel sensor systems, 278–280
Parity bit, 110, 219
Parity check, 85
Parity track, 110
Partitioned database, 203–205
PartsVision electronic parts cataloging system, 116
Pascal, 158, 160, 166
Passwords, 578
Patient billing system, 349–352
context diagram of, 366
data dictionary entries for, 368–369
system flowchart for, 370
Payroll operations, at Consolidated Chemical Corporation, 344–348
Payroll systems, 439, 442–443
PBX, 230–232
PC-DOS, 151, 152
Penney's wide area network, 234, 235
Pen plotter, 127
People. *See also* Human resources
and basic business systems, 446–447
and information systems, 9–10
and knowledge and information work systems, 506–507
and MSS, 542
People challenge, 23
People perspective, 299
and problem solving, 305, 313–317
Perceptive systems, 258–259
Perceptron, 261
Personal computer, 89, 465. *See also* Microcomputer
evolution of uses, 518–519
in fourth-generation systems, 403–404
Personal Consultant, 285
Personal information management software, 475
Personal information managers (PIMs), 475
Personal System/2, 373
Personnel, Coast Guard tracking of, 413–415
Personnel management information system (PMIS), 413
Personnel record-keeping system, 56, 448
Personnel system, at Consolidated Chemical Corporation, 344–348
PERT (Program Evaluation and Review Technique), 476
Phased approach, 328
Physical database design, 200
Physical design, 303, 324–325
at Maimonides Medical Center, 342, 343
of patient billing system, 352
specifications, 339
of spreadsheet software application, 358–359
Physical view, 188
Physicians, 498
Picosecond, 81
Pilot study, 328
Pitney Bowes products, facsimile machines as, 240
Pixel (picture element), 128
"Pizza box," 332
Planning, 517–518
PL/1 (Programming Language 1), **157**–158, 166
Plotter, 127
selecting, 134
Point-of-sale system, 353, **435**
Political issues, and computers, 555–560
Politics, and manager's environment, 523–524
Positions system, 443
Postimplementation stage, **389**
Postscript (TM Adobe Systems), **471**
Primary storage, 77
Principia Mathematica, 261
Printers, 125–127, 473
paper feed in, 135
selecting, 134–136
Privacy, 555
Privacy Act of 1974, 558, **559**–560
Privacy of information, 556–561
Private branch exchange (PBX), 230–232
Problem analysis, 297
Problem solving, 293–333
with controls, 583–587
database application, 349–352
and database concepts, 197–201
decision-making, 317–321
designing solutions, 321–325
five-step model of, 301–303
implementing solutions, 325–328
life cycle stages and, 387–389
mainframe application, 358–364
management and procedures, 343–348
and new technology, 339–342
organizational perspectives on, 309–312
spreadsheet application, 353–358
in systems analysis and design, 336–339
Problem-solving matrix, for database model, 201
Problem-solving perspectives, 305–317
Problem-solving process, steps in, 298
Problem understanding, 297
Procedures, design of, 323, 325
Process control systems, 430
Processing, 5, 6
batch input and, 118
design of, 323
image, 124–125
Processing controls, 582
Process specifications, 367, **368**
Producing, as business function, 36
Product design, 30–31
Production function, and manufacturing function, 44–49
Production Management courses, 48–49
Production process, 44–45
Production (service) **workers, 37**
Productivity, of information workers, 463–464
Productivity challenge, 22
Productivity tools, 407
Products, creation of, 58–59
Professional Office Systems (PROFS), 237, 407, 465

Professional work systems, 491–510
PROFS. *See* Professional Office Systems
Program, 140
Program/data dependence, 188
Program flowcharts, 374, 375
Programmed edit check, 583, 584
Programmer workbench systems (workstations), 501
Programming, structured, 372
Programming languages, 153–165
Programming stage, of systems life cycle, 389
Project definition, 387
Project management technology, 475–477, **476**
Project Steer, 34
Project/2, 476
PROLOG, 269
PROM (programmable read-only memory), **80**
Protocol, 223
Prototyping, 390
  as system solution alternative, 392–396
Pseudocode, 375
Publishing, 289
  desktop, 170, 471
Purchasing systems, 429

Quality control systems, 430
Quality of work life, 563–569
Quattro, 168
Query language, 163, 164
  in fourth-generation systems, 404, 405

RAM (random-access memory), **79,** 470
Random file access methods, 185–186
Random (direct) **file organization, 183**–184, 186
RBase, 169
RDMS, 212
Read/write head, 111, 112
Real estate development, design system for, 381–383
Receiving systems, 429–430
Record, 182
Recording density, 115
Record-keeping system personnel, 56, 443
Records management, at Maimonides Medical Center, 335–336
Reduced instruction set computing (RISC), 99–100, 331, 332
Register, 78
Relational database management system (RDBMS), 212
Relational database model, 195–197
  for purchasing system, 199
Removable-pack disk system, 112, 113
Rendering, 501
  software for, 506
Renderman, 506
Repetition construct, 372
Repetitive strain injury (RSI), 128
Replicated databases, 203
Report generator, 163–164, 404
Request for Proposal (RFP), 399
Responsibility, 553
Retail Operations Intelligence (ROI) System, 528–530
RFP, 399
Right to Financial Privacy Act (1978), 559
Ring network, 229, **230**
RISC. *See* Reduced Instruction Set Computing
RISC chips, 99–100
Robotics, 257–258, **430**–431
Robots, 80, 281
  at Ford Motor Company, 284–285
ROM (read-only memory), **79**–80
RPG III, 164

SABRE (Semi-Automated Business Research Environment) system, 424–425, 427
Sales and marketing function, 49–50
  information systems for, 50, 51
Sales and marketing systems, 434–437
Sales information system, at Seagram, 63–64
Sales system, of Circuit City Stores, Inc., 435–437
Sam (computer), 281
SAS, 407
Satellites, 225, 226
Scanmaster document scanners, 481
Scanners, 23, 123, 469
Scheduling, 145
Schema, 188–189
Science, drug design and, 501–502, 504
Secondary storage, 109
Second generation computers (1959–1963), 85
Second generation software, 142–143
Sector method for storing data, 115
Securities trading systems, 440–442
Security, 570. *See also* Data security
  checklist for, 587
  computer crime, 570–572
  hackers and, 572–574
Security control software, 223
Selection construct, 372
Semantic nets, 265, 266
Semiconductor chip, 77
Semistructured problem, 515
Sendmail program, 575
Senior management, 37
Sequence construct, 372
Sequential file organization, 183, 184
Service industries, 459
Service occupations, 460
Services, creation of, 58–59
Service work, 461
Service workers, 37
Sharp products, PC-1500A, 432
Signaling System 7 (SS7), 551–552
Signals, 218
Silicon chip, 77, 86
Simplex transmission, 19, 221
Simulations, 496–497
Single-sheet paper, 135
Single-sided disk, 115
SIPP Access, 179–180
Smalltalk, 373
"Smart" missiles, 259
Smart System, 169
SNA (Systems Network Architecture), 465
  at BMW, 481, 482
Social impacts, 554
  political issues, 555–560
  social issues, 560–563
Social Security numbers, errors in, 558
Sociotechnical perspective, 15–16
Sociotechnical skills, 19
Sociotechnical view, 17
Software
  applications, 141, 165–169
  CAD, 509
  computer, 11–12
  customized, 400–401, 402
  database, 180
  data management, 168
  design of, 324–325
  and desktop publishing, 170
  fourth-generation, 163–165, 403–404
  generations of, 141–148
  and industry safeguards, 391
  integrated package, 169
  intelligent, 259
  at Johnson, S. C., & Son, 142
  as life cycle alternative, 390
  malfunctions of, 562
  of McCormack & Dodge, 400
  personal information management, 475
  for problem solving, 139–176, 306–308
  rendering, 506
  spreadsheet, 168
  systems, 141
  and system solution, 326, 327
  telecommunication, 222–223
  voice recognition, 144
  word processing, 167
Software application vendors, 400

Software packages
 application, 404
 pre-written, 398
 as system solution, 396–401
Software system, in DDS, 532
Software 2000 Inc. products, 439
Solutions design, 297
Source code, 149, 150
Source data automation, 121–125
SPARC station, 1, 95, 332
Specialization, 36
Spreadsheet application, at Haskell, Simpson, and Porter, 353–358
Spreadsheet software, 168
 Lotus Notes, 360
SQL (Structured Query Language), **191,** 197, 204, 405, 407, 409
Stanfins-R (Standard Finance System Redesign) project, 158
Star network, 228, 229
Statistical Analysis Software (SAS), 163
Statistical progress control system, of Elco Industries, 431–432, 433
Stealth bomber, 48
Storage
 secondary, 109
 technology, 12, 108–118
 virtual, 148, 149
Storage technology, 12, 108–118
"Store and forward" device, 222
Stored-program concept, 140
Storing images, 289
Strategic business challenge, 22
Strategic impact systems, 57–60
Strategic-level systems, 42–44, 46, 50, 51–52, 55
Strategic plan, 524
Structured design, 371–372
Structured problem, 515
Structured program flowchart, 374, **375**
Structured programming, 372
Structured Query Language (SQL), 191, 197
Subschema, 189
"Sun Survival Kit," 332
Sunvalt, 592
Sun workstation, 132
SuperCalc, 168
Superchips, 99
Supercomputer, 88, 89
Supermarket business
 design project for, 379–380
 technology in, 23
Suppliers, choosing, 320
Supply Requisition System (SRS), 69
Survey of Income and Program Participation (SIPP), 179
Surveys, 302
Sweden, and employee involvement, 316
Switched lines, 234
Symphony, 169
Synchronous transmission, 219, 220
System development process, control issues and, 586
System flowchart, 369–370
 for patient billing system, 370
 symbols, 369
Systems analysis, 301, **336**–339
 steps in, 337
Systems-building tools and methodologies, 364–377
Systems design, 301, **336**–339
 steps in, 337
Systems Network Architecture, 223
Systems software, 141, 144–153
 hardware application software and, 143
Systems solution, 325–328
 fourth-generation, 401–409
 at Merrill Lynch, 409–410
 prototype as, 392–396
 software packages for, 396–401
Systems study, 387

Tactical systems, 43, 46, 49, 50, 52, 55
Tandem products, 66
 NonStop SQL computer, 410
 TXP-class computers, 235
Tandy products, 1000 personal computer, 527
Task Force on Felon Identification in Firearm Sales, 353
Technology, 10
 and basic business systems, 447
 and humans, 23–26
 information storage, 108–118
 input, 118–125
 and knowledge and information work systems, 505–506
 managers and, 525
 manual system and, 10
 and MSS, 542
 NeXT Computer, 129–132
 for 1990s, 326
 office communications, 472–474
 office data management, 474
 office scheduling, 474
 output, 125–129
 problem solving and, 339–342
 project management, 474–477
 storage, 12
 and supermarket business, 23
 telecommunications, 12, 220–227
 and USS *Vincennes* error, 24–25
Technology challenge, 20–22
Technology perspective, 299, 305–309
Telecommunications, 215–251, 308
 applications of, 237–244
 common uses of, 217
 digital transmission modes, 218–220
 networks, 227–237
 signals in, 218
 software, 222–223
 system components, 220–222
 technology, 220–227
 vulnerability of, 573
Telecommunications media, transmission capacity of, 228
Telecommunications technology, 12
Telecommuting, 561
Teleconferencing, 240–241
Telemail, 238
Telemarketing systems, 435
Telephone bill, 363
Terminals, video display, 127–129
Text publishing workstations, 501
Thermal-transfer printer, 126
Third-generation software, 143
Third-party networks, 452
Time measurement, 80–81
Time-sharing, 148, 351
Token Ring network, 233, 342
T-1 link, 241
Top-down approach, 259, 260
Top-down design, 371
Topographical models, 171
Toshiba computers, 90
Total On-us Processing and Services (TOPAS) system, 194
Touch screen, 120
Track, 111
Track ball, 121
Tracking systems, 443–446
Traditional file environment, 183–188
Traditional systems life cycle, 386–390
 alternatives to, 390
Traditional theories of management, 516
Training, employee, 313, 315. *See also* Employees
Training and skills systems, 443
Transaction, 424
Transaction data, MIS and, 526
Transaction processing, 443
 and bill paying, 451–452
 need for skilled workers in, 447
Transaction processing system, 424–425, 428, 432
Transform algorithm, 185
Transformation of the American economy, 457–459
Transistors, 85, 464
Transmission control software, 223
Transmission media, 223–225, 226
Transmission rates, measuring, 228

Transmission Utilization Department Outage System (TUDOS), 212
Trellis machine, 278–280
Turbulence, 312
Turing test, 256, 281
Twisted wire, 224
Tymnet VAN, 236
Typewriters, 464

Ungerman-Bass product, token ring network, 342
Unisys Corporation products, 401
  mainframe, 212, 245
  NEXRAD system, 189
United States
  economy of, 457–459
  labor force in, 458–459, 460
  productivity in, 22
U.S. armed forces. *See* Military
U.S. government agencies and departments. *See* Organization Index
Universal Product Code, 123
UNIX (XENIX)
  C language and, 160, 162
  at Kaiser Electronics, 175–176
  workstations, 132, 331
User interface, 10, 314
USS *Vincennes,* 24–25
Utility programs, 149–150

Vacuum tube technology, 83–85
Value-added networks (VANs), 235–237
Vaporware epidemic, 171, 172
Variable rate mortgages, and mainframe computer applications, 359–364
VAX computer, 180
  8650 machine, 212
VDTs (video display terminals)
  safety of, 487
  screen radiation, 314
Vector processing, 98–99
Very-high-level programming language, 164–165
Very-large-scale integrated circuit technology (VLSIC), 86
Videocarts, 23
Video display terminal (VDT), 127–129
Video Privacy Protection Act (1988), 559
Video-Save mail-order cassettes, design system for, 381
Video teleconferencing, 241
Virtual storage, 148, 149
Visualization, 501–502
VLSIC. *See* Very-large-scale integrated circuit technology
Voice Boards, 144
Voice input devices, 124–125
Voice mail, 238–240
Voice output devices, **129**
Voice recognition software, 144
Volatile memory, **79**
Von Neuman computer model, 259
VP Graphix, 163
VP-Planner Plus, 168
VSAT (very small aperture terminal) satellite communication system, 225, 226
  Holiday Inn network, 225, 227

Wang products
  Freestyle System, 287–288
  Integrated Image System, 323
  VS, 414
Warehouse, automated, 392
Wealth of Nations, The, 5
Weather data analysis, 189
Welfare data, 179–180
Wells Electronic Banking System (WEBS), 65–67, 68
White-collar occupations, 458, 460, 567
Wholesale Integrated Banking (WIN), 68–69
Wide area network (WAN), 233–234, 235
Winchester disk system, 112
WordPerfect, 167, 309
Word processing, 469–471
Word processing software, 167
WordStar, 167
Work, computer impact on quality of, 563–569
Workers. *See also* Labor force
  at home, 561
  information and knowledge, 459–464
  occupations of, 461
Workstation computing, 95
Workstations, 94–96, 127, 498–499
  CAD, 205
  of Hewlett Packard-Apollo Computer, 332
  IBM line of, 500
  knowledge, 499
  at Maimonides Medical Center, 342
  and NeXT Computer, 132
  Sun Microsystems, Inc., and, 331–333
  types of, 501
WORM (Write Once, Read Many), 116–117
Write Now program, 131

Zenith Z-181 laptop computers, 91
Zero-level data flow diagram, 367